The New Local Government Series
No. 8

TOWN AND COUNTRY PLANNING IN BRITAIN

The New Local Government Series
Series Editor: Professor Peter G. Richards

TOWN AND COUNTRY PLANNING IN BRITAIN

J. B. CULLINGWORTH

Ninth Edition

London
GEORGE ALLEN & UNWIN
Boston   Sydney

George Allen & Unwin (Publishers) Ltd,
40 Museum Street, London WC1A 1LU, UK

George Allen & Unwin (Publishers) Ltd,
Park Lane, Hemel Hempstead, Herts HP2 4TE, UK

Allen & Unwin, Inc.,
Fifty Cross Street, Winchester, Mass. 01890, USA

Allen & Unwin Australia Pty Ltd,
8 Napier Street, North Sydney, NSW 2060, Australia

First published in 1964. Second edition 1967. Second impression 1969. Third edition 1970. Fourth edition 1972. Fifth edition 1974. Sixth edition 1976. Second impression 1977. Seventh edition 1979. Eighth edition 1982. Ninth edition 1985. Second impression 1986.

British Library Cataloguing in Publication Data

Cullingworth, J. B.
 Town and country planning in Britain—9th ed.
—(The New local government series; no. 8)
1. City planning—Great Britain   2. Regional
planning—Great Britain
I. Title   II. Series
711'.0941   HT169.G7
ISBN 0−04−711013−9

Library of Congress Cataloging in Publication Data

Cullingworth, J. B.
 Town and country planning in Britain.
(The New local government series ; no. 8)
Bibliography: p.
Includes index.
1. City planning—Great Britain.   2. Regional
planning—Great Britain.   I. Title.   II. Series.
HT169.G7C8   1985   307.7'6'0941   84−28262
ISBN 0−04−711013−9 (pbk.: alk. paper)

Set in 10 on 11 point Times by Typesetters (Birmingham) Ltd,
and printed in Great Britain
by Biddles Limited, Guildford, Surrey

Town and Country Planning in Britain

By the same author:

CONTENTS

Planning Appeals
'Third Party' Interests
The Changing Nature of Public Inquiries
Dissatisfaction with Road Inquiries
Planning Inquiry Commissions
Statutory Provision for Public Participation
The Skeffington Report
Planning Aid
Environmental Education
In Conclusion

Joint Venture Schemes
Land Authority for Wales
The Countryside
New Towns
Urban Renewal: The Inner City
Enterprise Zones
Other Inner-City Programmes
Old Housing
Regional Planning
The M25
The 1983 White Paper
Planning and the Public
The Planning Inspectorate

PREFACE TO NINTH EDITION

It is now over twenty years since the first draft of this book was prepared. At that time 'town and country planning' seemed a fairly straightforward activity of local and central government (together with a number of specialised agencies). True, there were signs of stress which increased during the 1960s as development plans became outdated, as car ownership and use grew, and as the spectre loomed up of a population increase of some 20 million by the end of the century.

The Planning Advisory Group Report, *The Future of Development Plans*, and its legislative outcomes, gave promise of new machinery which could react more sensitively and speedily to the forces of change. The promise was not fulfilled, partly because of a veritable orgy of institutional reorganisation, but also because so many other things changed. Above all, public opinion has changed – or, to be more precise, a wide range of attitudes are now being expressed by a multiplicity of different 'publics'. Things have changed mightily since the PAG Report could blandly suggest that their proposed new planning system 'should provide a real stimulus to public interest in the work of planning authorities, and provide those authorities with a new opportunity for winning public support for their proposals'.

In addition, major fields of debate and policy initiatives have blossomed since the end of the 1970s: North Sea Oil, energy and a wide range of concerns for the environment. The Wildlife and Countryside Bill attracted an unprecedented (and, to the government, quite unexpected) degree of public interest. Other issues have waned: the steam has gone out of devolution, while 'organic change' in local government has come and gone at a remarkable speed – though issues of central–local relationships remain and, indeed, have acquired a higher stridency with the Local Government, Planning and Land Act of 1980 and even more so with the proposed abolition of the Greater London Council and the metropolitan county councils.

Again, issues such as regional planning continue to be in a virtually constant state of flux, and to describe current policies (even to the extent that such may be thought to exist) is akin to trying to nail jelly to a wall. Increasing concern over the relevance of policies for regional problems defined in traditional terms (namely, the relative degree of unemployment) became complicated first by unemployment in the inner city (where the complex of interrelated problems seems particularly baffling), and later by such widespread economic degeneration that their relevance has come into question. At the time of writing, the Thatcher government has decided that the regional problem is essentially a *social* problem, and policies to deal with it are in the pipeline.

The eighth edition of this book was a substantial revision. The object was to move the focus to the appropriate issues of the 1980s, but there is no way in which a comprehensive statement could be encompassed within the confines of a modest book. Indeed, it is no longer clear how 'town and country planning' should be defined or where its limits are. The very term seems dated and inadequate.

In this new edition a complete revision has been rejected in favour of a lengthy appendix dealing with planning in the period from 1980 to mid-1984. The hope is that some of the confusions and dilemmas of the mid-eighties will be resolved by the time a further new edition is called for. Unfortunately, there are no grounds for believing that this will be the case.

J. BARRY CULLINGWORTH
Unidel Professor
College of Urban Affairs and Public Policy
University of Delaware
Newark, Delaware, USA 19716
June 1984

Chapter 1

THE EVOLUTION OF TOWN AND COUNTRY PLANNING

THE PUBLIC HEALTH ORIGINS

Town and country planning as a task of government has developed from public health and housing policies. The nineteenth-century increase in population and, even more significant, the growth of towns led to public health problems which demanded a new role for government. Together with the growth of medical knowledge, the realisation that overcrowded insanitary urban areas resulted in an economic cost (which had to be borne at least in part by the local ratepayers) and the fear of social unrest, this new urban growth eventually resulted in an appreciation of the necessity for interfering with market forces and private property rights in the interest of social well-being. The nineteenth-century public health legislation was directed at the creation of adequate sanitary conditions. Among the measures taken to achieve these were powers for local authorities to make and enforce building by-laws for controlling street widths, and the height, structure and layout of buildings. Limited and defective though these powers proved to be, they represented a marked advance in social control and paved the way for more imaginative measures. The physical impact of by-law control on British towns is depressingly still very much in evidence; and it did not escape the attention of contemporary social reformers. In the words of Unwin:

much good work has been done. In the ample supply of pure water, in the drainage and removal of waste matter, in the paving, lighting and cleansing of streets, and in many other such ways, probably our towns are as well served as, or even better than, those elsewhere. Moreover, by means of our much abused building bye-laws, the worst excesses of overcrowding have been restrained; a certain minimum standard of air-space, light and ventilation has been secured; while in the more modern parts of towns, a fairly high degree of sanitation, of immunity from fire, and general stability of construction have been maintained, the importance of which can hardly be exaggerated. We have, indeed, in all these matters laid a good foundation and have secured many of the necessary elements for a healthy condition of life; and yet the remarkable fact remains that there are growing up around our big towns vast districts, under these very bye-laws, which for dreariness and sheer ugliness it is difficult to match anywhere, and compared with which many of the old unhealthy slums are, from the point of view of picturesqueness and beauty, infinitely more attractive.[1]

It was on this point that public health and architecture met. The enlightened experiments at Saltaire (1853), Bournville (1878), Port Sunlight (1887) and elsewhere had provided object lessons. Ebenezer Howard and the Garden City Movement were now exerting considerable influence on contemporary thought. The National Housing Reform Council (later the National Housing and Town Planning Council) were campaigning for the introduction of town planning. Even more significant was a similar demand from local government and professional associations such as the Association of Municipal Corporations, the Royal Institute of British Architects, the Surveyors' Institute and the Association of Municipal and County Engineers. As Ashworth has pointed out, 'the support of many of these bodies was particularly important because it showed that the demand for town planning was arising not simply out of theoretical preoccupations but out of the everyday practical experience of local administration. The demand was coming in part from those who would be responsible for the execution of town planning if it were introduced.'[2]

THE FIRST PLANNING ACT

The movement for the extension of sanitary policy into town planning was uniting diverse interests. These were nicely summarised by John Burns, President of the Local Government Board, when he introduced the first legislation bearing the term 'town planning' – the Housing, Town Planning, Etc. Act 1909:

The object of the Bill is to provide a domestic condition for the people in which their physical health, their morals, their character and their whole social condition can be improved by what we hope to secure in this Bill. The Bill aims in broad outline at, and hopes to secure, the home healthy, the house beautiful, the town pleasant, the city dignified and the suburb salubrious.[3]

The new powers provided by the Act were for the preparation of 'schemes' by local authorities for controlling the development of new housing areas. Though novel, these powers were logically a simple extension of existing ones. It is significant that this first legislative acceptance of town planning came in an Act dealing with health and housing. And, as Ashworth has pointed out, the gradual development and the accumulated experience of public health and housing measures facilitated a general acceptance of the principle of town planning. 'Housing reform had gradually been conceived in terms of larger and larger units. Torrens' Act (Artizans and Labourers Dwellings Act, 1868) had made a beginning with individual houses; Cross's Act (Artizans and Labourers Dwellings Improvement Act, 1875) had introduced an element of town planning by concerning itself with the reconstruction of insanitary areas; the framing of bye-laws in accordance with the Public Health Act of 1875 had accustomed local authorities to the imposition of at least a minimum of regulation on new building, and such a measure as the London Building Act of 1894 brought into the scope of public control the formation and widening of streets, the lines of buildings frontage, the extent of open space around buildings, and the height of buildings. Town planning was therefore not altogether a leap in the dark, but could be represented as a logical extension, in accordance with changing aims and conditions, of earlier legislation concerned with housing and public health.'[4] The 'changing conditions' were predominantly the rapid growth of suburban development – a factor which increased in importance in the following decades.

> In fifteen years 500,000 acres of land have been abstracted from the agricultural domain for houses, factories, workshops and railways . . . If we go on in the next fifteen years abstracting another half a million from the agricultural domain, and we go on rearing in green fields slums, in many respects, considering their situation, more squalid than those which are found in Liverpool, London and Glasgow, posterity will blame us for not taking this matter in hand in a scientific spirit. Every two and a half years there is a County of London converted into urban life from rural conditions and agricultural land. It represents an enormous amount of building land which we have no right to allow to go unregulated.[5]

The emphasis was entirely on raising the standards of *new* development. The Act permitted local authorities (after obtaining the permission of the Local Government Board) to prepare town planning schemes with the general object of 'securing proper sanitary conditions, amenity and convenience', but only for land which was being developed or appeared likely to be developed.

Strangely it was not at all clear what town planning involved. Aldridge, writing in 1915, noted that it certainly did not include 'the remodelling of the existing town, the replanning of badly planned areas, the driving of new roads through old parts of a town – all these are beyond the scope of the new planning powers'.[6] The Act itself provided no definition: indeed, it merely listed nineteen 'matters to be dealt with by General Provisions Prescribed by the Local Government Board'. The restricted and vague nature of this first legislation was associated in part with the lack of experience of the problems involved: Nettleford even went so far as to suggest that 'when this Act was passed, it was recognized as only a trial trip for the purpose of finding out the weak spots in local government with regard to town and estate development so that effective remedies might be later on devised'.[7]

Nevertheless, the cumbersome administrative procedure devised by the Local Government Board – in order to give all interested parties 'full opportunity of considering the proposals at all stages'[8] – might well have been intended to deter all but the most ardent of local authorities. The land taxes threatened by the 1910 Finance Act, and then the First World War, added to the difficulties. It can be the occasion of no surprise that very few schemes were actually completed under the 1909 Act.

INTERWAR LEGISLATION

The first revision of town planning legislation which took place after the First World War (the Housing and Town Planning Act of 1919) did little in practice to broaden the basis of town planning. The preparation of schemes was made obligatory on all borough and urban districts having a population of 20,000 or more, but the time limit (1 January 1926) was first extended (by the Housing Act 1923) and finally abolished (by the Town and Country Planning Act 1932). Some of the procedural difficulties were removed, but no change in concept appeared. Despite lip-service to the idea of town planning, the major advances made at this time were in the field of housing rather than planning. It was the 1919 Act which began what Marion Bowley has called 'the series of experiments in State intervention to increase the supply of working-class houses'.[9] The 1919 Act accepted the principle of state subsidies for housing and thus began the nationwide growth of council house estates.[10] Equally significant was the entirely new standard of working-class housing provided: the three-bedroom house with kitchen, bath and garden, built at the density recommended by the Tudor Walters Report[11] of not more than twelve houses to the acre. At these new standards, development could generally take place only on virgin land on the periphery of towns, and municipal estates grew alongside the private suburbs – 'the basic social products of the twentieth century', as Asa Briggs has termed them.[12]

This suburbanisation was greatly accelerated by rapid developments in transportation – developments with which the young planning machine could not keep pace. The ideas of Howard and the Garden City Movement, of Geddes and of those who like Warren and Davidge, saw town planning not just as a technique for controlling the layout and design of residential areas, but as part of a policy of national economic and social planning, were receiving increasing attention,[13] but in practice town planning often meant little more than an extension of the old public health and housing controls.

Various attempts were made to deal with the increasing difficulties. Of particular significance were the Town and Country Planning Act of 1932, which extended planning powers to almost any type of land, whether built-up or undeveloped, and the Restriction of Ribbon Development Act 1935, which, as its name suggests, was designed to control the spread of development along major roads.[14] But these and similar measures were inadequate. For instance, under the 1932 Act planning schemes took about three years to prepare and pass through all their stages. Final approval had to be given by Parliament, and schemes then had the force of law – as a result of which variations or amendments were not possible except by a repetition of the whole procedure. 'Interim development control' operated during the time between the passing of a resolution to prepare a scheme and its date of operation (as approved by Parliament). This enabled – but did not require – developers to apply for planning permission. If they did not obtain planning permission, and the development was not in conformity with the scheme when approved, the planning authority could require the owner (without compensation) to remove or alter the development.

All too often, however, developers preferred to take a chance that no scheme would ever come into force, or that if it did no local authority would face pulling down existing buildings. The damage was therefore done before the planning authorities had a chance to intervene.[15] Once a planning scheme was approved, on the other hand, the local authority ceased to have any planning control over individual developments. The scheme was in fact a zoning plan: land was zoned for particular uses – residential, industrial, and so on – though provision could be made for limiting the number of buildings, the space around them, etc. In fact, so long as the developer did not try to introduce a non-conforming use he was fairly safe. Furthermore, most schemes in fact did little more than accept and ratify existing trends of development, since any attempt at a more radical solution would have involved the planning authority in compensation they could not afford to pay. In most cases the zones were so widely drawn as to place hardly more restriction on the developer than if there had been no scheme at all. Indeed, in the half of the country covered by draft planning schemes in 1937 there was sufficient land zoned for housing to accommodate 300 million people.[16]

ADMINISTRATIVE SHORTCOMINGS

A major weakness was, of course, the administrative structure itself. At the local level the administrative unit outside the county boroughs was the district council. Such authorities were generally small and weak. This was implicitly recognised as early as 1919, for the Act of that year permitted the establishment of joint planning committees. The 1929 Local Government Act went further, by empowering county councils to take part in planning, either by becoming constituent members of joint planning committees or by undertaking powers relinquished by district councils. A number of regional advisory plans were prepared, but these were generally ineffective and, in fact, were conceived as little more than a series of suggestions for controlling future development, together with proposals for new main roads.

The noteworthy characteristic of a planning scheme was its regulatory nature. It did not secure that development would take place: it merely secured that if it did take place in any particular part of the area covered by the scheme it would be controlled in certain ways. Furthermore, as the Uthwatt Report stressed, the system was 'essentially one of local planning based on the initiative and financial resources of local bodies (whether individual local authorities or combinations of such authorities) responsible to local electorates . . . The local authorities naturally consider questions of planning and development largely with a view to the effect they will have on the authorities' own finances and trade of the district. Proposals by landowners involving the further development of an existing urban area are not likely in practice to be refused by a local authority if the only reason against the development taking place is that from the national standpoint its proper location is elsewhere, particularly when it is remembered that the prevention of any such development might not only involve the authority in liability to pay heavy compensation but would, in addition, deprive them of substantial increases in rate income.'[17]

The central authority – the Ministry of Health – had no effective powers of initiation and no power to grant financial assistance to local authorities. Indeed, their powers were essentially regulatory and seemed to be designed to cast them in the role of a quasi-judicial body to be chiefly concerned with ensuring that local authorities did not treat property owners unfairly.

The difficulties were not, however, solely administrative. Even the most progressive authorities were greatly handicapped by the inadequacies of the law relating to compensation. The compensation paid either for planning restrictions or for compulsory acquisition had to be determined in relation to the most profitable use of the land, even if it was unlikely that the land would be so developed, and without regard to the fact that the prohibition of development on one site usually resulted in the development value (which had been purchased at high cost) shifting to another site.[18] Consequently, in the words of the Uthwatt Committee, 'an examination of the Town Planning maps of some of our most important built-up areas reveals that in many cases they are little more than photographs of existing users and existing lay-outs, which, to avoid the necessity of paying compensation, become perpetuated by incorporation in a statutory scheme irrespective of their suitability or desirability'.[19]

These problems increased as the housing boom of the 1930s developed; 2,700,000 houses were built in England and Wales between 1930 and 1940. At the outbreak of war one-third of all the houses in England and Wales had been built since 1918. The implications for urbanisation were obvious, particularly in the London area. Between 1919 and 1939 the population of Greater London rose by about three-quarters of a million on account of natural increase but by over one and a quarter million by migration.[20] This growth of the metropolis was a force which existing powers were incapable of halting, despite the large body of opinion favouring some degree of control.

THE DEPRESSED AREAS

The crux of the matter was that the problem of London was closely allied to that of the declining areas of the North and of South Wales – and both were part of the much wider problem of industrial location. In the South-East the insured employed population rose by 44 per cent between 1923 and 1934, but in the North-East it fell by 5·5 per cent and in Wales by 26 per cent. In 1934 8·6 per cent of insured workers in Greater London were unemployed, but in Workington the proportion was 36·3 per cent, in Gateshead 44·2 per cent and in Jarrow 67·8 per cent. In the early stages of political action these two problems were divorced. For London, various advisory committees were set up and a series of reports issued – the Royal Commission on the Local Government of Greater London (1921-3); the London and Home Counties Traffic Advisory Committee (1924); the Greater London Regional Planning Committee (1927); the Standing Conference on London Regional Planning (1937); as well as *ad hoc* committees and inquiries, for example, on Greater London Drainage (1935) and a Highway Development Plan (the Bressey Report, 1938).

For the depressed areas, attention was first concentrated on encouraging migration, on training schemes and on schemes for establishing the unemployed in smallholdings. Increasing unemployment accompanied by rising public concern (especially after hunger marches on the one hand and articles in *The Times*[21] on the other) necessitated further action. Government 'investigators' were appointed and, following their reports,[22] the Depressed Areas Bill was introduced in November 1934 – to pass (after the Lords had amended the title) as the Special Areas Act.[23]

Under the Act a Special Commissioner for England and Wales, and one for Scotland, were appointed, with very wide powers for 'the initiation, organisation, prosecution and assistance of measures to facilitate the economic development and social improvement' of the

Special Areas. The areas were defined in the Act and included the North-East coast, West Cumberland, industrial South Wales – and, in Scotland, the industrial area around Glasgow. By September 1938 the Commissioners had spent, or approved the spending of, nearly £21 million, of which £15 million was for the improvement of public and social services, £3 million for smallholdings and allotment schemes, and £½ million on amenity schemes such as the clearance of derelict sites.[24] Physical and social amelioration, however, was intended to be complementary to the Commissioners' main task: the attraction of new industry. Appeals to industrialists proved inadequate; in his second report, Sir Malcolm Stewart, the Commissioner for England and Wales, concluded that 'there is little prospect of the Special Areas being assisted by the spontaneous action of industrialists now located outside these Areas'. On the other hand, the attempt actively to attract new industry by the development of trading estates achieved considerable success, which at least warranted the comment of the Scottish Commissioner that there had been 'sufficient progress to dispel the fallacy that the Areas are incapable of expanding their light industries'.

Nevertheless, there were still 300,000 unemployed in the Special Areas at the end of 1938, and although 123 factories had been opened between 1937 and 1938 in the Special Areas, 372 had been opened in the London area. Sir Malcolm Stewart concluded, in his third annual report, that 'the further expansion of industry should be controlled to secure a more evenly distributed production'. Such thinking might have been in harmony with the current increasing recognition of the need for national planning, but it called for political action of a character which would have been sensational. Furthermore, as Neville Chamberlain (then Chancellor of the Exchequer) pointed out, even if new factories were excluded from London it did not follow that they would forthwith spring up in South Wales or West Cumberland. The immediate answer of the government was to appoint the Barlow Commission.

THE BARLOW REPORT

The Barlow Report is of significance not merely because it is an important historical landmark, but also because, for a period of at least a quarter of a century, some of its major recommendations were accepted as a basis for planning policy.

The terms of reference of the Commission were 'to inquire into the causes which have influenced the present geographical distribution of the industrial population of Great Britain and the probable direction of any change in the distribution in the future; to consider what social, economic or strategic disadvantages arise from the concentration of industries or of the industrial population in large towns or in particular areas of the country; and to report what remedial measures if any should be taken in the national interest'.

These very wide terms of reference[25] represented, as the Commission pointed out, 'an important step forward' in contemporary thinking. Reviewing the history of town planning they noted that:

> Legislation has not yet proceeded so far as to deal with the problem of planning from a *national* standpoint; there is no duty imposed on any authority or Government Department to view the country as a whole and to consider the problems of industrial, commercial and urban growth in the light of the needs of the entire population. The appointment, therefore, of the present Commission marks an important step forward. The evils attendant on haphazard and ill-regulated town growth were first brought under observation; then similar dangers when prevalent over wider areas or regions; now the investigation is extended to Great Britain as a whole. The Causes, Probable Direction of Change and Disadvantages mentioned in the Terms of Reference are clearly not concerned with separate localities or local authorities, but with England, Scotland and Wales collectively: and the Remedial Measures to be considered are expressly required to be in the national interest.

After reviewing the evidence, the Commission concluded that 'the disadvantages in many, if not most of the great industrial concentrations, alike on the strategical, the social and the economic side, do constitute serious handicaps and even in some respects dangers to the nation's life and development, and we are of opinion that definite action should be taken by the Government towards remedying them'. The advantages of concentration were clear – proximity to market, reduction of transport costs and availability of a supply of suitable labour. But these, in the Commission's view, were accompanied by serious disadvantages such as heavy charges on account mainly of high site values, loss of time through street traffic congestion and the risk of adverse effects on efficiency due to long and fatiguing journeys to work. The Commission maintained that the development of garden cities, satellite towns and trading estates could make a useful contribution towards the solution of these problems of urban congestion.

The London area, of course, presented the largest problem, not simply because of its huge size, but also because 'the trend of migration to London and the Home Counties is on so large a scale and of so serious a character that it can hardly fail to increase in the future the disadvantages already shown to exist'. The problems of London were thus in part related to the problems of the depressed areas:

> It is not in the national interest, economically, socially or

strategically, that a quarter, or even a larger, proportion of the population of Great Britain should be concentrated within 20 to 30 miles or so of Central London. On the other hand, a policy:

(i) of balanced distribution of industry and the industrial population so far as possible throughout the different areas or regions in Great Britain;

(ii) of appropriate diversification of industries in those areas or regions;

would tend to make the best national use of the resources of the country, and at the same time would go far to secure for each region or area, through diversification of industry, and variety of employment, some safeguard against severe and persistent depression, such as attacks an area dependent mainly on one industry when that industry is struck by bad times.

Such policies could not be carried out by the existing administrative machinery: it was no part of statutory planning to check or to encourage a local or regional growth of population. Planning was essentially on a local basis; it did not, and was not intended to, influence the geographical distribution of the population as between one locality and another. The Commission unanimously agreed that the problems were national in character and required a central authority to deal with them. They argued that the activities of this authority ought to be distinct from and extend beyond those of any existing government department. It should be responsible for formulating a plan for dispersal from congested urban areas – determining in which areas dispersal was desirable; whether and where dispersal could be effected by developing garden cities or garden suburbs, satellite towns, trading estates, or the expansion of existing small towns or regional centres. It should be given the right to inspect town planning schemes and 'to consider, where necessary, in co-operation with the Government Departments concerned, the modification or correlation of existing or future plans in the national interest'. It should study the location of industry throughout the country with a view to anticipating cases where depression might probably occur in the future and encouraging industrial or public development before a depression actually occurred.

But though the Commission were agreed on the 'objectives of national action' and on the necessity for a central authority, they were not agreed on the powers to be given to this authority. The majority recommended that it should be a National Industrial Board consisting of a chairman and three other members appointed by the President of the Board of Trade after consultation with the Ministers of Health, Labour and Transport, and the Secretary of State for Scotland. This Board should have research, advisory and publicity functions, but also (in view of the necessity for immediate action in the London area) executive powers to regulate additional industrial building in London and the Home Counties. These 'negative powers' should be extendable by Order in Council to other areas. Finally the Board should be required to decide what additional powers they needed to carry out their functions.

Three members of the Commission (Professor J. H. Jones, Mr George W. Thomson and Sir William E. Whyte), though signing the majority report, prepared a 'note of reservations'. They argued that the control of industrial development in the London area was an indequate measure to achieve the 'objectives of national action'. Such controls needed to be operated over the whole country. Furthermore, they believed that it was even more important for the government 'to create more favourable conditions of life and work in other parts of the country and thereby weaken the inducement to seek work in or near London'. In their view the powers of the Commissioners for the Special Areas should be largely transferred to the new board which should be given powers to enable them to offer such inducements as they thought necessary to make effective the policy of securing a better balance and a greater diversification of industry throughout the country. Regional administration was essential, and a series of divisional boards should be set up as an integral part of the new authority.[26]

A minority of the Commission (Professor Patrick Abercrombie, Mr H. H. Elvin and Mrs H. Hichens) felt unable to put their signatures to the main recommendations. They went even further in their criticisms of the inadequacy of these than the three members who signed the 'note of reservations'. In their view the problems were of immediate urgency, particularly since an unprecedented amount of new factory building was under way in connection with the rearmament programme. They felt that the majority report seemed to imply that there was ample time for preparation and research, whereas in fact the problem was an immediate one. The urgency of the situation demanded the setting up of a powerful body with executive powers. The Board proposed by the majority was not strong enough: what was required was a new ministry exercising full executive powers. This ministry would 'need to be fitted into the scheme of central and local government if it is to function properly'. It would obviously have to take over the planning functions of the Ministry of Health (and possibly some of their housing functions), as well as some of the planning powers of the Ministry of Transport. The work of the Commissioners for the Special Areas should be transferred to it – and at the same time extended to the whole country.

The differences between the three sets of recommendations were less striking than their unanimous condemnation of the existing situation and the inadequacy of both policy and machinery for dealing with it. All were agreed that a far more positive role for government was required, that control should be exercised over new factory building at least in London and the Home Counties, that dispersal from the larger urban concentrations was desirable, and that measures should be taken to anticipate regional economic depression. The differences centred largely on how such policies should be translated into terms of administrative machinery.

THE IMPACT OF WAR

The Barlow Report was published in January 1940 – some four months after the start of the Second World War. The problem which precipitated the decision to set up the Barlow Commission – that of the depressed areas – rapidly disappeared. The unemployed of the depressed areas now became a powerful national asset. A considerable share of the new factories built to provide munitions or to replace bombed factories were located in these areas.[27] By the end of 1940 'an extraordinary scramble for factory space had developed'; and out of all this 'grew a war-time, an extempore, location of industry policy covering the country as a whole'. This emergency wartime policy – paralleled in other fields, such as hospitals – not only provided some 13 million square feet of munitions factory space in the depressed areas which could be adapted for civilian industry after the end of the war; it also provided experience in dispersing industry and in controlling industrial location which showed the practicability (under wartime conditions at least) of such policies. The Board of Trade became a central clearing-house of information on industrial sites. During the debates on the 1945 Distribution of Industry Bill, their spokesman stressed:

> We have collected a great deal of information regarding the relative advantage of different sites in different parts of the country, and of the facilities available there with regard to local supply, housing accommodation, transport facilities, electricity, gas, water, drainage and so on . . . We are now able to offer to industrialists a service of information regarding location which has never been available before.[28]

Hence, though the Barlow Report (to use a phrase of Dame Alix Meynell) 'lay inanimate in the iron lung of war', it seemed that the conditions for the acceptance of its views on the control of industrial location were becoming very propitious: there is nothing better than successful experience for demonstrating the practicability of a policy.

The war thus provided a great stimulus to the extension of town and country planning into the sphere of industrial location. And this was not the only stimulus it provided. The destruction wrought by bombing transformed 'the rebuilding of Britain' from a socially desirable but somewhat visionary and vague ideal into a matter of practical and defined necessity. Nor was this all: the very fact that rebuilding was clearly going to take place on a large scale provided an unprecedented opportunity for comprehensive planning of the bombed areas and a stimulus to overall town planning. In the Exeter Plan, Thomas Sharp urged that 'to rebuild the city in the old lines . . . would be a dreadful mistake. It would be an exact repetition of what happened in the rebuilding of London after the Fire – and the results, in regret at lost opportunity, will be the same. While, therefore, the arrangements for rebuilding to the new plan should proceed with all possible speed, some patience and discipline will be necessary if the new-built city is to be a city that is really renewed.'[29] In Hull, Lutyens and Abercrombie argued that 'there is now both the opportunity and the necessity for an overhaul of the urban structure before undertaking this second refounding of the great Port on the Humber. Due consideration, however urgent the desire to get back to working conditions, must be given to every aspect of town existence.'[30] The note was one of optimism of being able to tackle problems which were of long standing. In the metropolis (to quote from the *County of London Plan*) 'London was ripe for reconstruction before the war; obsolescence, bad and unsuitable housing, inchoate communities, uncorrelated road systems, industrial congestion, a low level of urban design, inequality in the distribution of open spaces, increasing congestion of dismal journeys to work – all these and more clamoured for improvement before the enemy's efforts to smash us by air attack stiffened our resistance and intensified our zeal for reconstruction.'[31]

This was the social climate of the war and early postwar years. There was an enthusiasm and a determination to undertake social reconstruction on a scale hitherto considered utopian. The catalyst was, of course, the war itself. At one and the same time war occasions a mass support for the way of life which is being fought for and a critical appraisal of the inadequacies of that way of life. Modern total warfare demands the unification of national effort and a breaking down of social barriers and differences. As Titmuss noted, it 'presupposes and imposes a great increase in social discipline; moreover, this discipline is tolerable if – and only if – social inequalities are not intolerable'.[32] On no occasion was this more true than in the Second World War. A new and better Britain was to be built. The feeling was one of intense optimism and confidence. Not only would the war be won: it would be followed by a similar campaign against the forces of want. That there was much that was inadequate, even intolerable, in prewar Britain had been generally accepted. What was new was the belief that the problems could be tackled in the same way as a military operation.[33] What supreme confidence was evidenced by the setting up in 1941 of committees to consider postwar reconstruction problems – the Uthwatt Committee on Compensation and Betterment, the Scott Committee on Land Utilisation in Rural Areas and the Beveridge Committee on Social Insurance and Allied Services. Perhaps it was Beveridge who most clearly summed up the spirit of the time – and the philosophy which was to underlie postwar social policy:

> The Plan for Social Security is put forward as part of a general programme of social policy. It is one part only of an attack upon five great evils: upon the physical Want with which it is directly concerned, upon Disease which often causes Want and brings many other troubles in its train, upon Ignorance which no democracy can afford among its citizens, upon Squalor which arises mainly through haphazard distribution of industry and population, and upon Idleness which destroys wealth and corrupts men, whether they are well fed or not, when they are idle. In seeking security not merely against physical want, but against all these evils in all their forms, and in showing that security can be combined with freedom and enterprise and responsibility of the individual for his own life, the British community and those who in other lands have inherited the British tradition, have a vital service to render to human progress.[34]

It was within this framework of a newly acquired confidence to tackle long-standing social and economic problems that postwar town and country planning policy was conceived. No longer was this to be restricted to town planning 'schemes' or regulatory measures. There was now to be the same breadth in official thinking as had permeated the Barlow Report. The attack on Squalor was conceived as part of a comprehensive series of plans for social amelioration. To quote the 1944 White Paper *The Control of Land Use*:

> Provision for the right use of land, in accordance with a considered policy, is an essential requirement of the Government's programme of post-war reconstruction. New houses, whether of permanent or emergency construction; the new layout of areas devastated by enemy action or blighted by reason of age or bad living conditions; the new schools which will be required under the Education Bill now before Parliament; the balanced distribution of industry which the Government's recently published proposals for maintaining employment envisage; the requirements of sound nutrition and of a healthy and well-balanced agriculture; the preservation of land for national parks and forests, and the assurance to the people of enjoyment of the sea and countryside in times of leisure; a new and safer highway system better adapted to modern industrial and other needs; the proper provision of airfields – all these related parts of a single reconstruction programme involve the use of land, and it is essential that their various claims on land should be so harmonized

as to ensure for the people of this country the greatest possible measure of individual well-being and national prosperity.[35]

THE NEW PLANNING SYSTEM

The pre-war system of planning was defective in several ways. It was optional on local authorities; planning powers were essentially regulatory and restrictive; such planning as was achieved was purely local in character; the central government had no effective powers of initiative, or of co-ordinating local plans; and the 'compensation bogey' – with which local authorities had to cope without any Exchequer assistance – bedevilled the efforts of all who attempted to make the cumbersome planning machinery work.

By 1942 73 per cent of the land in England and 36 per cent of the land in Wales had become subject to 'interim development control', but only 5 per cent of England and 1 per cent of Wales was actually subject to operative schemes;[36] and there were several important towns and cities as well as some large country districts for which not even the preliminary stages of a planning scheme had been carried out. Administration was highly fragmented and was essentially a matter for the lower-tier authorities: in 1944 there were over 1,400 planning authorities. Some attempt to solve the problems to which this gave rise was made by the (voluntary) grouping of planning authorities in joint committees for formulating schemes over wide areas, but, though an improvement, this was not sufficiently effective.

The new conception of town and country planning underlined the inadequacies. It was generally (and perhaps uncritically) accepted that the growth of the large cities should be restricted. Regional plans for London, Lancashire, the Clyde Valley and South Wales all stressed the necessity of large-scale overspill to new and expanded towns. Government pronouncements echoed the enthusiasm which permeated these plans. Large cities were no longer to be allowed to continue their unchecked sprawl over the countryside. The explosive forces generated by the desire for better living and working conditions would no longer run riot. Suburban dormitories were a thing of the past. Overspill would be steered into new and expanded towns which could provide the conditions people wanted – without the disadvantages inherent in satellite suburban development. When the problems of reconstructing blitzed areas, redeveloping blighted areas, securing a 'proper distribution' of industry, developing national parks, and so on, are added to the list, there was a clear need for a new and more positive role for the central government, a transfer of powers from the smaller to the larger authorities, a considerable extension of these powers and – most difficult of all – a solution to the compensation-betterment problem.

The necessary machinery was provided in the main by the Town and

Country Planning Acts, the Distribution of Industry Acts, the National Parks and Access to the Countryside Act, the New Towns Act and the Town Development Act.

The 1947 Town and Country Planning Act brought almost all development under control by making it subject to planning permission. But planning was to be no longer merely a regulative function. Development plans were to be prepared for every area in the country. These were to outline the way in which each area was to be developed or, where desirable, preserved. In accordance with the wider concepts of planning, powers were transferred from district councils to county councils. The smallest planning units thereby became the counties and the county boroughs. Co-ordination of local plans was to be effected by the new Ministry of Town and Country Planning. Development rights in land and the associated development values were nationalised. All owners were thus placed in the position of owning only the existing (1947) use rights and values in their land. Compensation for development rights was to be paid 'once and for all' out of a national fund, and developers were to pay a 'development charge' amounting to 100 per cent of the increase in the value of land resulting from the development. The 'compensation bogey' was thus at last to be completely abolished: henceforth development would take place according to 'good planning principles'.

Responsibility for securing a 'proper distribution of industry' was given to the Board of Trade. New industrial projects (above a minimum size) would require the board's certification that the development would be consistent with the proper distribution of industry. More positively, the board were given powers to attract industries to development areas by loans and grants, and by the erection of factories.

New towns were to be developed by *ad hoc* development corporations financed by the Treasury. Somewhat later (in 1952) new powers were provided for the planned expansion of towns by local authorities. The designation of national parks and 'areas of outstanding natural beauty' was entrusted to a new National Parks Commission, and local authorities were given wider powers for securing public access to the countryside. A Nature Conservancy was set up to provide scientific advice on the conservation and control of natural flora and fauna, and to establish and manage nature reserves. New powers were granted for preserving amenity, trees, historic buildings and ancient monuments. Later controls were introduced over river and air pollution, litter and noise. Indeed, the flow of legislation has been unceasing, partly because of increased experience, partly because of changing political perspectives, but perhaps above all because of the changing social and economic climate within which town and country planning operates.

THE CENTRAL PLANNING AUTHORITY

The new conception of town and country planning raised the difficult problem as to how the extended responsibilities were to be fitted into the organisation of central government. Was the Ministry of Health – the department responsible for housing and other local government matters – to retain its existing executive powers in relation to town and country planning and, at the same time, expand its activities into the broad policy fields of regional and national planning? Should there be a separate Ministry of Town and Country Planning and, if so, should it be responsible both for the framing of policies and for their implementation? Would it be preferable to leave the latter with the Ministry of Health and set up a separate National Planning Authority which could also have certain responsibilities in the field of industrial location and transport? Should Scotland be dealt with in the same way as England and Wales?

Such questions were not quickly answered. Indeed, the problems they pose are still with us, and it is doubtful whether any ideal solution exists. Town and country planning in its wider sense embraces a large part of the activities of government. A separate all-embracing ministry is a contradiction in terms. An all-powerful 'grand co-ordinating' ministry does not square with the facts of administrative and political life. There must be some division of responsibilities and, at the same time, some means of co-ordination which is acceptable to the individual ministries. The *modus operandi* devised at any one point of time will reflect not only the particular urgencies of the existing situation, but also the views and personalities of the politicians and administrators whose task it is to interpret them. The importance of these factors is highlighted by the story of the setting up of the Ministry of Town and Country Planning.[37]

The new town and country planning was born in the ancient Office of Works – a department which had become increasingly active with government building since the rearmament programme started. In September 1940 this office became the Ministry of Works and Buildings – responsible for 'the proper co-ordination of building work, the carrying out of government building programmes, the control of building materials, and research into building and conservation of materials'. At the invitation of Ernest Bevin, then Minister of Labour, Sir John (later Lord) Reith became the first minister of this department – an appointment which exercised considerable influence on later developments in the organisation of planning.

Reith was not only enthusiastic about the new post; as he records in his autobiography *Into the Wind*, he was already 'looking beyond the war to the problems of planning and reconstruction', and was hoping that however much responsibility the Ministry of Works and Buildings might initially be given, 'it would acquire still more – by doing things that had not been thought of and for which no one else had staked claims'. Indeed, almost immediately he proposed that his ministry 'should be ready to take up responsibility for . . . planning and reconstruction arising out of the war and post-war period'. This met with objection from the Ministry of Health (the department then responsible for town and country planning). This dispute was settled only after the Lord Privy Seal (Mr Attlee) had acted as arbiter.

The outcome was that the Ministry of Health retained their normal town and country planning functions while Lord Reith was to plan for the future. This he did by means of a Reconstruction Group in his department, as well as by setting up two committees – the Uthwatt Committee on Compensation and Betterment and the Scott Committee on Land Utilisation in Rural Areas. The reports of these committees together with that of the Barlow Commission constituted the famous trilogy which had a great influence on postwar planning.

Relationships between Lord Reith and Mr Arthur Greenwood (who had been appointed Minister without Portfolio with special responsibility for all postwar reconstruction problems) and the Ministry of Health were not easy. The boundaries between town and country planning on the one hand and general social and economic planning were not always clear. Lord Reith, however, was authorised to proceed on three assumptions which he announced in the House of Lords in February 1941:

(1)   That the principle of planning will be accepted as national policy and that some central planning authority will be required;
(2)   that this authority will proceed on a positive policy for such matters as agriculture, industrial development and transport;
(3)   that some services will require treatment on a national basis, some regionally and some locally.[38]

For a while Lord Reith retained his personal responsibility for long-term planning while the Minister of Health retained his statutory planning functions. Following an interim report of the Uthwatt Committee,[39] and 'to ensure that the administration of the Town and Country Planning Act and any legislation implementing the recommendations made in the first report of the Uthwatt Committee shall proceed in conformity with long-term planning policy as it is progressively developed', a Committee of the Privy Council was appointed: Lord Reith (as chairman), the Minister of Health and the Secretary of State for Scotland.

The next development was the fusion of Lord Reith's Reconstruction Group and the Town and Country Planning Division of the Ministry of Health. This created some misgivings, particularly on the part of the Minister without Portfolio. A proposal to create both a new department for town and country planning and a new executive council for policy and development was rejected by the Cabinet: instead all the town and country planning functions of the Ministry of Health were transferred to a reorganised Ministry of Works and Planning. Lord Reith's apparent victory proved to be a hollow one: within a fortnight of the Cabinet decision he was asked to resign.[40]

With the exit of Lord Reith (and his replacement by Lord Portal who, according to Reith, 'disliked planning') the sands shifted. Furthermore, the Ministry of Health was now overburdened. The alternatives were now to create a new department or a non-departmental body. The latter proposal – on which a four-man committee set up under Lord Samuel's chairmanship could not agree – was rejected by the Cabinet on the ground that planning policy was essentially political and could not be removed from parliamentary control. Furthermore, experience which had been gained with the Ministry of Works and Planning showed that the subject required 'the whole-time services of a front-rank minister'[41] and also that this minister 'should not only be, but should also appear to be, entirely impartial in his judgment as to the right use of any particular piece of land: if he can be regarded as a minister already predisposed by reason of his other ministerial duties to lean to a particular type of land use he will for that very reason be less able to exercise his influence'.[42]

In short, the decision was taken to set up a separate Ministry of Town and Country Planning.

The decision was not unanimously applauded, especially since the legislation merely dealt with machinery: 'the way in which it will be used will depend on the powers which the House confers on the minister hereafter'. Greenwood was particularly concerned about what he considered to be the implicit assumption that town and country planning could neatly be made the responsibility of a single department. In the debates on the Minister of Town and Country Planning Bill, he said:

I cannot overemphasize what I think Government inquiries and enlightened public opinion . . . have undoubtedly proved, namely the complexities of the issues involved and the paramount importance of collective responsibility for policy by the ministers whose departments will have to take a hand in carrying the plans into effect. You cannot make a super-department which will take the life blood of the Ministry of Agriculture, the Board of Trade and the Ministry of Health and so on.

But the general discussion was inconclusive – as it had to be, since the legislation did little more than establish the new department, with a minister charged with the duty of 'securing consistency and continuity in the framing and execution of a national policy with respect to the use and development of land throughout England and Wales'.

The new ministry had responsibilities only for England and Wales. In Scotland central responsibility remained with the Department of Health for Scotland. Neither of these two departments was responsible for the location of industry. The 'Barlow policy' for industrial location was accepted, as was the Beveridge principle of full employment, but, to quote from the 1944 White Paper on *Employment Policy*:

> no single department could undertake the responsibility for formulating and administering the policy for the distribution of industry . . . This is essentially a policy of the Government as a whole, and its application in practice will involve action by a number of different departments, each of which will adapt its administration to conform with the general government policy. The main responsibility will rest with the Board of Trade, the Ministry of Labour and National Service, the Ministry of Town and Country Planning and the Scottish Office. Standing arrangements will be made for supervising and controlling, under the Cabinet and as part of the central government machinery, the development and execution of the policy as a whole . . . It is necessary, however, that there should be a single channel through which government policy on the distribution of industry can be expressed . . . [This] shall be the Board of Trade.[43]

In short, the Ministry of Town and Country Planning was to be responsible for town and country planning, the Ministry of Health for housing, and the Board of Trade for industrial location, but there would be 'standing arrangements' for co-ordination where necessary.

LOCAL PLANNING AUTHORITIES

The shaping of a local government structure to meet new needs raises problems of an acute nature. There are inherent problems of devising units which are viable in terms of size and financial resources for the administration of different services. But of even greater practical importance is the problem of securing political agreement for change – at the level of both national and local politics. The need for reform at any one point of time may be clear to the reformers, but to demonstrate and prove the beneficial effects (which are often of a long-term nature) is quite a different matter. Usually local government reform is a matter of real interest only to academics, politicians and local government officers. Since these cannot agree (even on the necessity for change) the result is commonly a deadlock. Local government may then be bypassed, and services transferred to government departments, or *ad hoc* authorities – as has happened, for example, with the licensing of passenger road services, trunk roads, hospitals, public assistance, valuation for rating and the major public utilities of gas and electricity.

Early postwar attempts to reorganise local government were abortive but (as described in the following chapter) major changes were made for London in 1963, for England and Wales in 1972, and for Scotland in 1973. The 1947 Town and Country Planning Act, however, transferred responsibility for planning to the major authorities – the counties and county boroughs. This reduced the number of planning authorities from 1,441 to 145 – a reduction of 90 per cent. This obviously greatly enlarged the areas of local planning authorities, but two further steps were required.

First, as the Scott Committee pointed out:

the local planning authority should be the same authority or combination of authorities as executes the principal local government functions involving the use of land. Within this framework the extremely important functions will devolve on the smaller authorities of affording the county planning authorities the benefit of their local knowledge in the formulation of plans, and the county authorities must consult the district councils accordingly; whilst in due course the responsibility for the execution of works within the approved scheme may fall on the district councils.[44]

Accordingly, the 1947 Act required county councils to consult with district authorities in the preparation of their plans and enabled them to delegate powers of controlling development to district councils (or to decentralise these powers to subcommittees charged with responsibility for certain areas).

Secondly, although the Act enlarged the areas over which planning powers were to be exercised by single authorities, the need still existed in some parts of the country (particularly in the case of conurbations) for larger planning areas. The Act therefore gave the minister power to set up joint planning boards for combined areas. This could be done either with the agreement of the local authorities concerned or, following a local inquiry, by the minister. In fact this power was never used. A similar power to establish joint advisory committees, on the other hand, was used.

REGIONAL ADMINISTRATION

Within the new structure there was no formal place for regional authorities. The need for wider planning areas was recognised in the provision made for joint planning boards and joint advisory committees, but these constituted a typical English compromise which excited little enthusiasm. Bevan, when Minister of Health, echoed the general feeling: a joint board, he said, 'has no biological content; it has no mother and it has no progeny; it is a piece of paper work'.[45] In the absence of a formal creation of executive, financially responsible, organs of regional government, it was left to the ministry themselves to undertake such regional planning as was to be effected – by co-ordinating the efforts of the separate planning authorities and reconciling and amending the plans prepared by them and submitted to the ministry for approval. This, indeed, was one of the functions implied by the duty with which the ministry were charged of 'securing consistency and continuity in the framing and execution of a national policy with respect to the use and development of land throughout England and Wales'.

What might at first sight have been regarded as a clear advance towards regionalism was the wartime establishment of civil defence regions and the appointment of regional commissioners. These were set up to deal with the conditions which might have arisen had communications been disrupted. This organisation – into eleven regions – was retained after the war, but the regions were (and still are) 'no more than civil service creations, established for the dispatch of business; they are not, in any sense, "organic" units'.[46] The Ministry of Town and Country Planning appointed regional planning officers as early as 1943. As the scope and complexity of planning legislation grew, the regional machinery was expanded. By 1948 there was an office in each region under the control of a regional controller. The initial object of the regional offices was to give advice to local authorities, but the establishment of regional controllers marked a new step towards solving the increasing number of conflicting claims over land use from government departments. The regional controllers presided over regional planning committees composed of representatives from the various other government departments in the region. But this was simply an administrative device to cope with the interdepartmental frictions.

In view of the absence of regional machinery in the final outcome, it is interesting to note Reith's original proposals (submitted to Churchill in 1940) for

a central authority to frame and be responsible for the execution of a national plan covering the basic objectives; to lay down the general principals of planning; to supervise planning, design, finance, execution; regional machinery to apply the national plan and to co-ordinate and control the work of local authorities; Exchequer assistance to supplement local funds in approved development.[47]

Since there was now no middle tier, it followed that the central authority would be greatly concerned with the day-to-day work of local authorities (and the time-consuming business of appeals against local authorities), and thus face the danger of paying insufficient attention to wider issues which needed to be dealt with at central government level.

REFERENCES AND FURTHER READING: CHAPTER 1

1 R. Unwin, *Town Planning in Practice: An Introduction to the Art of Designing Cities and Suburbs* (T. Fisher Unwin, 1909), pp. 3-4.
2 W. Ashworth, *The Genesis of Modern British Town Planning* (Routledge & Kegan Paul, 1954), p. 180.
3 *Parliamentary Debates*, Vol. 188, col. 949, 12 May 1908.
4 W. Ashworth, op. cit., p. 181.
5 John Burns, the President of the Local Government Board, in the Second Reading Debates on the Housing, Town Planning, Etc. Bill 1908, *Parliamentary Debates*, Vol. 188, col. 958, 12 May 1908.
6 H. R. Aldridge, *The Case for Town Planning* (National Housing and Town Planning Council, 1915), p. 459.
7 J. S. Nettleford, *Practical Town Planning* (St Catherine Press, London, 1914), p. 179.
8 'This necessity . . . involves considerable delay; the careful consideration of a case in all its aspects and the arrangements for holding of the necessary local inquiries must necessarily take a substantial amount of time.' Local Government Board, Circular, 3 May 1910, Order No. 55373 (reprinted in J. S. Nettleford, op. cit., pp. 392-6).
9 M. Bowley, *Housing and the State 1919-1944*, (Allen & Unwin, 1945), p. 15.
10 Some authorities - notably London, Liverpool and Manchester - had built houses under earlier legislation, but these were statistically insignificant. Generally the building of houses by local authorities was regarded as a step to be taken only in the last resort.
11 *Report of the Committee on Questions of Building Construction in Connection with the Provision of Dwellings for the Working Classes*, Cd 9191 (HMSO, 1918).
12 A. Briggs, *History of Birmingham* (Oxford University Press, 1952), Vol. 2, p. 228.
13 See, for example, E. Howard (ed. F. J. Osborn), *Garden Cities of Tomorrow* (Faber, 1946); P. Geddes, *Cities in Evolution* (Benn, 1915); H. Warren and W. R. Davidge (eds), *Decentralization of Population and Industry: A New Principle in Town Planning* (King, 1930).
14 See J. B. Cullingworth, *Environmental Planning, Vol. I, Reconstruction and Land Use Planning 1939-1947* (HMSO, 1975), ch. VII, 'Restriction of ribbon development'.
15 See W. Wood, *Planning and the Law* (Marshall, 1949), p. 45, on which this account is based.
16 *Report of the Royal Commission on the Distribution of the Industrial Population* (Barlow Report), Cmd 6153 (HMSO, 1940), p. 113, para. 241.
17 *Final Report of the Expert Committee on Compensation and Betterment* (Uthwatt Report), Cmd 6386 (HMSO, 1941), pp. 8-9, paras 13-14.
18 These problems (of 'floating value' and 'shifting value') are discussed in Chapter 7.
19 Uthwatt Report, op. cit., pp. 17-18, para. 30.
20 P. Abercrombie, *Greater London Plan 1944* (HMSO, 1945), pp. 27 and 190. The area referred to is that of the Greater London Plan.
21 'Places without a future' (County Durham), *The Times*, 20, 21, 22 March 1934.

22   *Reports of Investigations into the Industrial Conditions in Certain Depressed Areas*, Cmd 4728 (HMSO, 1934). The investigators were J. C. C. Davidson, Euan Wallace, Sir William Portal and Sir Arthur Rose.

23   The full title was Special Areas (Development and Improvement) Act 1934.

24   This account is based on *Reports of the Commissioner for the Special Areas (England and Wales)* (1935-8); *Reports of the Commissioner for the Special Areas in Scotland* (1935-8); and A. Meynell, 'Location of industry', *Public Administration*, vol. XXXVII (Spring 1959), pp. 9ff. See also R. C. Davison, *British Unemployment Policy: The Modern Phase since 1930* (Longman, 1938); and PEP, *Location of Industry*, 1939.

25   A summary of the type relevant in the present context cannot do justice to the wealth of material to be found in the report and the twenty-six volumes of evidence. Only the main issues and recommendations are outlined here; further discussion is contained in later chapters. (Except where otherwise indicated quotations are from the Barlow Report.)

26   The majority report recommended that 'for the purpose of securing the advice and assistance of persons having local knowledge and experience in matters affecting the functions of the Board, the Board to have power to establish divisional or regional bodies to study problems of industrial location throughout the country'. The three members signing the Note of Reservations saw these divisional bodies as having much greater scope and forming an integral advisory and executive part of the new machinery.

27   A. Meynell, op. cit., p. 13, from which the subsequent quotations are taken.

28   *HC Debates*, Vol. 409, 21 March 1945; the Minister of Production (Mr Oliver Lyttelton) on the Second Reading of the Distribution of Industry Bill.

29   T. Sharp, *Exeter Phoenix* (Architectural Press, 1947), p. 10.

30   E. Lutyens and P. Abercrombie, *A Plan for Kingston upon Hull* (Brown, 1945), p. 1.

31   J. H. Forshaw and P. Abercrombie, *County of London Plan* (Macmillan, 1943), p. 20.

32   R. M. Titmuss, 'War and social policy', in *Essays on 'The Welfare State'* (Allen & Unwin, 1958), p. 85. See also the same author's *Problems of Social Policy* (HMSO and Longman, 1950).

33   cf. the statement by Mr Tomlinson on the introduction of the first postwar Housing Bill: 'Housing should be tackled as a military operation.' *HC Debates*, Vol. 416, col. 901, 26 November 1945.

34   *Social Insurance and Allied Services*, Report by Sir William Beveridge, Cmd 6404 (HMSO, 1942), p. 170.

35   *The Control of Land Use*, Cmd 6537 (HMSO, 1944), p. 3, para. 1.

36   Statistics are given in the Uthwatt Report, p. 9, footnote.

37   This account leans heavily on D. N. Chester and F. M. G. Willson, *The Organization of British Central Government 1914-1956* (Allen & Unwin, 1957), particularly pp. 162-8 and 176-80. See also references given by Chester and Willson, especially Lord Reith's autobiography, *Into the Wind* (Hodder & Stoughton, 1949). A fuller detailed account of the establishment of 'the central planning authority' is now to be found in J. B. Cullingworth, *Environmental Planning, Vol. I, Reconstruction and Land Use Planning 1939-1947* (HMSO, 1975).

38   *HL Debates*, Vol. 118, cols 479-80, 26 February 1941.

39   *Interim Report of the Expert Committee on Compensation and Betterment*, Cmd 6291 (HMSO, 1941).

40   According to Reith's autobiography, Churchill had apparently been told 'that the Conservatives demanded my expulsion and that I can be replaced by a good Tory. Moving too fast, too much planning all round; even fear of land nationalization perhaps. And this was at the time when Churchill was "yielding to public pressure".' *Into the Wind*, op. cit., pp. 445-6.

41 The quotations are from *HC Debates*, Vol. 386, cols 417-18, Second Reading Debates on the Minister of Town and Country Planning Bill, 26 January 1943.

42 'For instance if a question were to arise as to whether a particular piece of land should be utilized for building or utilized for agriculture the fact that the Minister of Planning is also Minister of Works might make it appear that he would lean rather to a building use than to an agricultural use.' (loc. cit.)

43 White Paper, *Employment Policy*, Cmd 6527 (HMSO, 1944), p. 13.

44 *Report of the Committee on Land Utilization in Rural Areas*, Cmd 6378 (HMSO, 1942), p. 82, para. 223.

45 Quoted in W. A. Robson, *The Development of Local Government* (Allen & Unwin, 2nd edn, 1948), p. 58.

46 J. W. Grove, *Regional Administration* (Fabian Society, 1951), p. 41. cf. Institute of Public Administration, 'The position of regional and local authorities in relation to the central authority', *Public Administration*, vol. XXV (Autumn 1947), p. 190: 'The war organization has not produced regionalism: it was a purely decentralization scheme.'

47 *Into the Wind*, op. cit., p. 422.

Chapter 2

CENTRAL AND LOCAL GOVERNMENT

CENTRAL GOVERNMENT ORGANISATION

In *Beyond the Stable State*, Donald Schon argues that 'if government is to learn to solve new public problems, it must also learn to create the system for doing so and to discard the structure and mechanisms grown up around old problems. The need is not merely to cope with a particular set of new problems, or to discard the organisational vestiges of a particular form of governmental activity which happen at present to be particularly cumbersome. It is to design and bring into being the institutional processes through which new problems can continually be confronted and old structures continually discarded.'[1]

How far recent years have seen the development of really new and relevant 'institutional processes' is a big question which cannot be examined adequately here, but certainly there have been a remarkable number of organisational changes. In this chapter, attention is focused first on changes in the structure of central government, though the reader is warned that these take place at a rate which defeats the chronicler who attempts to provide an up-to-date picture.

Throughout the 1950s town and country planning was the responsibility of the Ministry of Housing and Local Government – the central department also responsible (as the name suggests) for housing and a range of local government services. These included water and sewerage, refuse collection and disposal, burial grounds and crematoria, clean air and river pollution, together with the general structure (including reorganisation) and finance of local government. In April 1965 certain functions (for example, in relation to water resources, national parks and responsibility for the Land Commission and Leasehold Enfranchisement Bills) were transferred to a new Ministry of Land and Natural Resources. This ministry was, however, short-lived: its functions were returned to the Ministry of Housing and Local Government in February 1967. Of rather longer life was the Department of Economic Affairs (October 1964 to October 1969) which was responsible for the regional economic planning system.

In October 1969 the Labour government created an 'overlord' for local government and regional planning with major responsibilities for local government reorganisation and 'environmental pollution in all its forms'. The overlord – the Secretary of State for Local Government and Regional Planning – had federal powers in relation to the

Ministry of Housing and Local Government and the Ministry of Transport, together with direct responsibility for the regional planning councils and boards which were transferred from the Department of Economic Affairs. At the same time, the Board of Trade's responsibilities in the field of regional economic development went to another super-ministry: the Ministry of Technology.* This had responsibility for industrial development certificates (but not office development permits, which were transferred to the Ministry of Housing and Local Government), industrial estates in development areas, building grants and loans. The rationale here was that the ministry which was responsible for dealing with the greater part of private and public industry should also be responsible for executive decisions concerning the location of industry.

THE DEPARTMENT OF THE ENVIRONMENT

This organisation of central government functions had a life of only one year before the Conservative government (elected in June 1970) carried the process one stage further.[2] Housing, construction, transport, planning, local government and a number of other environmental functions were centralised in a huge Department of the Environment under a Secretary of State for the Environment.[3] Except in Scotland and Wales, where the Scottish and Welsh Offices (together with their own secretaries of state) have major responsibilities, the DoE became responsible for 'the whole range of functions which affect people's living environment'.

The White Paper described the new department's function as follows:

It will cover the planning of the land – where people live, work, move and enjoy themselves. It will be responsible for the construction industries, including the housing programme and for the transport industries, including public programmes of support and development for the means of transport. There is a need to associate with these functions responsibility for other major environmental matters: the preservation of amenity, the protection of the coast and countryside, the preservation of historic towns and monuments, and the control of air, water and noise pollution: all of which must be pursued locally, regionally, nationally and in some cases internationally. And it will have the leading responsibility for regional policy: certain economic aspects, including industrial developments in the regions, will remain with the Department of Trade and Industry, but the Department of the Environment will

*The ministry was, however, split in 1974 into the Department of Trade and the Department of Industry.

have important executive powers for the development of regional infrastructure and the maintenance of regional services. It will also have the particular responsibility of ensuring that people's rights are adequately protected wherever they are affected by the proposals of their neighbours or of public authorities. Local authorities are profoundly involved in these fields and the new Department will, therefore, carry responsibility at the centre for the structure and functioning of local government as well as for regional affairs.[4]

The secretary of state has final responsibility for all the functions of the department (including all statutory powers). He is, however, concerned primarily with strategic issues of policy and priority, including public expenditure, which determine the operations of the department as a whole.

Originally the DoE was divided into three main parts, each under a separate minister - housing and construction; transport industries; and local government and development. Several changes have taken place since 1970 and currently transport is again a separate department with its own minister.

SCOTLAND AND WALES

In Scotland, somewhat similar changes were made as long ago as 1962, when town and country planning and environmental services were transferred from the Department of Health to the Scottish Development Department which at the same time took over all the local government, electricity, roads and industry functions of the Scottish Home Department.[5]

In 1973 a major change was made with the establishment of the Scottish Economic Planning Department. This is concerned with industrial and economic development in Scotland, including the Scottish aspects of regional policies both in a UK and EEC context. It has a major concern with North Sea Oil and has also taken over responsibility (from the Department of Industry) for direct support to industry, factory building and industrial estates. Its responsibilities also extend to new towns (because of their essential function in Scotland of facilitating economic development) and the new Scottish Development Agency.

In Wales, increasing responsibilities over a wide field have been transferred to the Welsh Office. It now has broadly the same range of executive responsibilities as the Departments of the Environment and Transport have in England. These include town and country planning, housing, local government, environmental services, new towns, roads, national parks, ancient monuments and historic buildings. It also includes agriculture and responsibility for selective financial assistance to industry in Wales, as well as general responsibility for economic development.[6]

In the following account the term 'secretary of state' is used for the sake of simplicity, but it should be interpreted to refer to the Secretaries of State for the Environment, for Scotland and for Wales. Similarly, references to the Department of the Environment should be read as applying, *mutatis mutandis*, to the Scottish Office and the Welsh Office.

CENTRAL–LOCAL RELATIONSHIPS

The secretary of state is charged with the duty of 'securing consistency and continuity in the framing of a national policy with respect to the use and development of land'. The powers are very wide and, in effect, give the department the final say in all policy matters (subject, of course, to parliamentary control).[7] The extent of these powers is too wide to permit an adequate summary: they are discussed in detail at appropriate points in other chapters. For many matters the secretary of state is required or empowered to make regulations; this delegated legislation covers a wide field. For example, one Order (the Use Classes Order) classifies industrial and commercial uses and permits 'changes of use' within each of the categories without the need for planning permission. Similarly, the advertisement regulations specify certain types of advertisement for which permission is 'deemed' to be given, and the General Development Order provides a detailed list of types of development which do not require planning permission. One function of the department is thus (within the limits laid down by Parliament) to make legislation.

In a wide range of matters, approval is necessary for proposals made by a local authority. A development plan, for example, does not become operative until it has been approved by the secretary of state. This approval can stipulate modifications in the plan; the secretary of state has great discretionary powers here, since he is acting administratively and quasi-judicially. If a local planning authority fail to produce a plan (or a plan 'satisfactory to the Secretary of State'), he can act in default. Decisions of a local planning authority on applications for planning permission can, on appeal, be modified or revoked – even if the development proposed is contrary to the development plan. Proposals which the secretary of state regards as being sufficiently important can be 'called in' for his decision.

In spite of all these powers, it is not the function of the secretary of state to decide detailed planning policies. This is the business of local planning authorities. The secretary of state's function is to co-ordinate the work of individual local authorities and to ensure that their development plans and development control procedures are in harmony with broad planning policies. That this often involves rather closer relationships than might *prima facie* be supposed follows from the nature of the governmental and administrative processes. The line dividing policy from day-to-day administration is a fine one. Policy has to be translated into decisions on specific issues, and a series of decisions can amount to a change in policy. This is particularly important in the British planning system, where a large measure of administrative discretion is given to central and local government bodies. This is a distinctive feature of the planning system. There is virtually no provision for external judicial review of local planning decisions: instead, there is the system of appeals to the secretary of state. A foreign observer (Daniel Mandelker) sees the position clearly:

> The absence of a written constitution makes the statute controlling in England. External review of the merits of local planning decisions is afforded by the Minister of Housing and Local Government. His Ministry is a national agency exercising a supervisory power over local government and having no exact counterpart in the United States. Appeals are taken to the Minister from local refusals of planning permission and from permissions with onerous conditions. English courts can review Ministerial decisions, but their role in the determination of planning policy is peripheral.
>
> The area of discretion in English planning administration is enlarged further by the lack of separation of functions which is traditional to American government. In America, the zoning ordinance is enacted by the local legislative body but is usually administered by the executive department and by nonelective boards created for this purpose. In England the local elected council which adopts the development plan also administers it. The failure to separate function in English planning has the healthy effect of forcing attention to the relationship between the individual decision and the general objectives to which, in a small way, it contributes. But this institutional framework blurs the distinction between policy making and policy applying and so enlarges the role of the administrator who has to decide a specific case.[8]

It is this broad area of discretion which brings the department in close contact with local planning authorities (though, as is explained later, it is not the only factor). The department in effect operate both in a quasi-judicial capacity and as developers of policy.

The department's quasi-judicial role stems in part from the vagueness of planning policies. Even if these policies are precisely worded, their application can raise problems. Since a local authority have such a wide area of discretion, and since the courts have only very limited powers of action, the department have to act as arbiter over what is fair and reasonable. This is not, however, simply a judicial process. A decision is not taken on the basis of legal rules as in a court of law: it involves the exercise of a wide discretion in the balance of public and private interest within the framework of planning policies. The procedure basically consists of the lodging of objections either to proposals in a draft development plan or to the decision of a local authority on a planning application. Such objections (or appeals, as the latter are called) are made to the secretary of state, who then holds an inquiry in public. These inquiries are carried out by inspectors of the department but the final decision is the formal responsibility of the secretary of state. There is no appeal against his decision except on a question of law.

The department's role in policy formulation is not easy to summarise. Policies are usually couched in very general terms – preservation of amenity, restraining urban sprawl, and so on – which give local authorities considerable leeway. Formal guidance (circulars, memoranda, bulletins, and so on) often does not provide a clear indication of the action which should be followed in any particular case. Proposals have to be considered 'on their merits' within the broad framework of a set of principles. These principles can – and do – change, at least in emphasis. Usually the change is gradual, perhaps even coming without a conscious step. And the motivating power may well be the local authorities themselves rather than the department. All this makes it very difficult to present a clear-cut picture of central-local relationships. The truth is that the position is not clear-cut. What is clear is that there is little approaching a situation in which the central department determine policy while local governments carry the policy into effect as agents. As Miller has nicely put it, the larger authorities 'have built up local administrations that can properly be regarded as citadels of local power'. Though central government may lay down national policies, 'it is in the twists and emphases which councils give to central policies, and the degree of co-operation or unwillingness which they show, that their own power lies. They do not have the paper guarantees of local sovereignty which states in a federal system possess, but they have some of the reality of power which comes from being on the spot, knowing the special qualities and demands of the local people, and being costly and difficult to replace if the central government finds them unsatisfactory.'[9]

It is common to talk of central-local government relationships as constituting a 'partnership', and, though any such single term must oversimplify the situation, the description is apposite. Nevertheless, the extent of the central government's responsibilities, its 'power of the purse' (particularly under the 1980 Local Government, Planning and Land Act), has 'inevitable inherent contradictions' and 'produces a situation where the role of the department in relation to planning, land conversion and development is essentially an ambiguous one. Policy choices and conflicts arise over, for instance, whether to adopt a responsive or interventionist role in relation to development pressures and the balance to be struck between concern for the development industry and sponsorship of local authorities whose interests may well conflict with those of the private sector'.[10]

The intervention can take a particularly dramatic form when functions are transferred to *ad hoc* agencies appointed by central government. This was the case with the new town development corporations[11] and even more so with the urban development corporations for the inner city areas (initially restricted to Merseyside and the London Docklands).* A major political push for municipalisation or for the sale of council houses also can override normal central–local relationships.[12]

It must be repeated, however, that local planning authorities are not agents of the department. Though the departments can – and do – exercise many direct controls, they prefer (in accordance with British traditions) to wield their power in a gentlemanly fashion by way of exhortation, advice and informal contacts. This is particularly important at officer level. The chief planning officers of local authorities are not strangers to the department's officials: on the contrary, relationships between them are close. And they are members of a small (but active) profession in which policy issues are constantly being discussed.

Further reference must also be made to the circulars, bulletins and handbooks published by the department, and the studies on which some of them are based. Quite apart from straightforward statements of broad policies, these contain a great deal of technical guidance. It needs to be stressed that planning policies often raise technical issues which are beyond the competence of local authority staffs, or at least need a wider background of experience than is always to be found in a planning authority.

Nevertheless, central–local relationships are in a constant state of flux and the role of the secretary of state is frequently an ambiguous one. This is perhaps most apparent in relation to planning appeals where he is not only making a judgement as between a prospective developer and a local authority, but making that judgement in the context of his own policy. It is worth examining this quasi-judicial role in more detail.

PLANNING APPEALS

An unsuccessful planning applicant can appeal to the secretary of state and a large number in fact do so.[13] Appeals decided during 1978–9 numbered 9,570 of which 28 per cent were allowed (Table 2.1).

Here the secretary of state has very wide powers. He may reverse the local authority's decision or subject it to conditions. He may quash or modify conditions which they have imposed. He may make those conditions more onerous, or he may even go to the extent of refusing

*See Chapter 10 below.

planning permission altogether if he decides that the local authority should not have granted it even with the conditions imposed.

Though each planning appeal is considered and determined on its merits, the cumulative effect is an emergence of the department's views on a wide range of planning matters. These have been made more explicit in a somewhat erratic series of 'statements of policy'. Up to 1959 (1963 in Scotland) there were *Bulletins of Selected Appeal Decisions*. In 1969 DoE started issuing *Development Control Policy Notes*: these continued up to 1975. In 1974 a single volume of *Selected Enforcement and Allied Appeals* was published.[14]

Table 2.1   *Planning Appeals in England and Wales 1967–1978/9*[15]

	Net total received	Total decided	Allowed Number	%	% of total decided by written representation
1967	7,831	8,495	1,974	23·2	44·7
1968	7,274	7,081	1,778	25·1	53·6
1969	5,752	6,557	1,901	29·0	49·6
1970	6,173	5,786	1,578	27·3	48·0
1971	7,389	5,828	1,311	22·5	46·9
1972	11,822	6,216	1,539	24·8	64·8
1973	15,499	11,409	2,503	21·9	76·2
1974/5	7,588	13,159	2,962	22·5	73·6
1975/6	8,344	11,739	3,133	26·7	71·9
1976/7	9,292	9,238	2,737	29·6	69·5
1977/8	8,322	8,970	2,610	29·1	74·2
1978/9: sec. 36	10,125	9,570	2,657	27·8	73·7
: sec. 53	41	28	10	35·7	17·9

The figures relate to appeals under section 36, Town and Country Planning Act 1971 (and corresponding earlier legislation) to the Secretary of State for the Environment or to the Secretary of State for Wales, against decisions of local planning authorities or their failure to give decisions within the statutory period on applications made to them for planning permission for development, or for determination under section 53 of the Act as to whether an application for planning permission is required.

The effect of these on the policy of individual authorities may be difficult to assess, but clearly they are likely to have a very real influence. Local planning authorities are unlikely to refuse planning consents for a particular type of development if they are convinced that the department would uphold an appeal.

It is not, of course, every planning appeal that raises an issue of policy. Yet until 1969 all had to be dealt with by the department's inspectorate. Nearly three-quarters are now settled by correspondence after an informal visit to the site and without a local inquiry. (This is termed 'the written representations procedure'.) The Franks Committee on Administrative Tribunals and Inquiries argued that it was

not satisfactory 'that a government department should be occupied
with appeal work of this volume, particularly as many of the appeals
relate to minor and purely local matters, in which little or no departmental policy entered'.[16] An analysis of the subject matter of appeals
undertaken by the department (and reported in the 1967 White Paper
Town and Country Planning) confirmed this. About 60 per cent concerned small-scale development; many of these raised issues of purely
local significance. They included such matters as minor residential
development, small groups of shops, small caravan sites, betting
shops, garages and minor changes of use. Rather more than a quarter
related to single houses. Another relevent point was that, of all
appeals made during the five years 1962 to 1967, 97·5 per cent were
decided as the inspector recommended.

In view of the delay which was inevitable in this appeals system and
the huge administrative burden it placed on the department, considerable thought has been given to possible alternatives. The solution
adopted by the 1968 Planning Act is for the determination of certain
classes of appeals by inspectors. The classes are determined by the
regulation and can thus be amended in the light of experience.[17] The
trend has been to increase the range until the proportion reached 85 per
cent in 1980. A consultation paper[18] issued in 1980 suggested that the
great majority of appeals should now be transferred. It was argued that
this would significantly speed up the system without creating difficulties
for either appellants or local authorities. In support of this it was
pointed out that the secretary of state normally (that is, in 98 per cent
of cases) follows an inspector's recommendations. Moreover, the pro-

Table 2.2   *Planning Appeals in England,*
Quarterly Statistics 1979–80[19]

Number of appeals:	Quarter ended:		
	31.12.79	*31.3.80*	*30.6.80*
In hand at start of quarter	8,056	8,589	9,163
Received during quarter	3,290	4,350	3,660
Withdrawn during quarter	686	665	658
Decided during quarter	2,071	3,111	2,578
In hand at end of quarter	8,589	9,163	9,587
Analysis of appeals decided:			
Secretary of state inquiry	225	220	203
Secretary of state written representation	160	137	159
Transferred inquiry	486	487	485
Transferred written representation	1,200	2,267	1,731
Appeals allowed:			
As percentage of total decisions	31%	29%	32%

portion of appeals allowed was roughly the same for secretary of state decisions (28·4 per cent) as for inspectors' decisions (26·5 per cent).

The consultation paper added that 'many cases which are now the subject of a local inquiry, could perfectly well be settled by the less cumbersome and time consuming procedure of written representations'.

The proposals (together with those for an increase in the size limits of development permitted by the General Development Order, which are discussed in the following chapter) have been criticised by the Royal Town Planning Institute[20] because it concentrates only on the roles of DoE, the inspectors, local planning authorities and appellants. 'What about the direct involvement of the public?' This is a wide issue which is considered in a more appropriate context in the last chapter.

In March 1981 it was announced that the government had decided 'to divest itself of responsibility for adjudicating on all but a small number of planning appeals'. Only matters of major importance would be retained for decision by the secretary of state – 'where there is a possibility of interdepartmental conflict or where the sites or issues in dispute are considered to be of more than local interest'. Examples suggested were the applications by the British Airports Authority to develop Stansted, by the National Coal Board to mine in the Vale of Belvoir and by the Atomic Energy Authority to make test drillings for the possible disposal of nuclear waste. (The list is a perverse one since, as argued in the final chapter, these are precisely the types of issue which are unsuited for any normal form of planning inquiry.) In addition, there are 'large road schemes which are the joint responsibility of the Departments of the Environment and Transport, and projects involving "sensitive" sites such as the banks of the Thames in London, or where changes are proposed to outstanding buildings or landscapes'.[21]

'CALL-IN' OF PLANNING APPLICATIONS

The power to 'call in' a planning application for decision by the secretary of state is quite separate from that of determining an appeal against an adverse decision of a local planning authority. This power is not circumscribed: the secretary of state may call in any application, and his decision is final. Though there is no general statement of policy as to which applications will normally be called in, there are several categories which are particularly liable. In the first place, all applications for development involving a substantial departure from the provisions of a development plan which the local planning authority intend to grant must be sent to the secretary of state, together with a statement of the reasons why they wish to grant the permission. This procedure enables the secretary of state to decide whether the development is sufficiently important to warrant its being called in for his own determination. Secondly, mineral workings often raise problems of more than local importance and the national need for particular minerals has to be balanced against planning issues. Such matters cannot be adequately considered by local planning authorities and, in any case, involve technical considerations requiring expert opinion of a character more easily available to the department. For these reasons, large numbers of applications for permission to work minerals have been called in. Furthermore, there is a general direction calling in all applications for the winning and working of ironstone in certain counties where there are large-scale ironstone workings. Thirdly, the power of call-in is generally used when the matter at stake is (as in the case of minerals) of more than local importance or interest.

Little information is readily available on the use of this procedure but Dobry's review of development control[22] noted that 'in recent years' (that is, recent to 1973) the call-in procedure had tended to be used only for the following kinds of applications:

(a) cases raising issues of national, regional, or otherwise more than local importance;

(b) cases which arouse more than local opposition, for example, the redevelopment of the Monico site in Shaftesbury Avenue;

(c) cases which, for any reason, it might be unreasonable to ask the local planning authority to decide, for example, involving development proposed by foreign governments (the decision on which could be diplomatically sensitive), or development raising unfamiliar problems on which adequate technical advice was not available to the local planning authority, for example, the first application for a processing plant for North Sea Gas;

(d) cases associated with a different issue which can be decided only by the secretary of state, for example, applications for town centre redevelopment associated with a compulsory purchase order.

In 1973 160 planning applications were called in – out of a total of two-thirds of a million.[23]

When an application is called in, the secretary of state must, if either the applicant or the local planning authority so desire, hold a hearing or public inquiry. The public inquiry is more usual, particularly in important cases.

Since 1968 the secretary of state has had power to refer development proposals of a far-reaching or novel character to an *ad hoc* Planning Inquiry Commission. This power has not yet been used: the Roskill Commission on the third London airport was set up under non-statutory powers, while the Greater London Development Plan Inquiry was established under the *general* powers to hold local inquiries provided by the Town and Country Planning Act (now section 282 of the 1971 Act). For major inquiries such as Windscale, Belvoir and Stansted, this special form of inquiry might have been considered particularly apt: that it was not so considered gave rise to much debate (which is dealt with in the final chapter).

INDUSTRIAL LOCATION CONTROL

Though the Department of the Environment (together with the Scottish and Welsh Offices) is the main department dealing with environmental issues, many other departments have responsibilities which bear upon these issues. Indeed, 'town and country planning' is highly interrelated with a wide range of other matters, some of which may well be of crucial importance in determining planning problems and policies. Such matters include transport, the distribution of industry, the location of offices and employment. The first of these is the subject of a separate chapter, while the other three are to some extent covered in the chapter on regional planning. However, there are several organisational aspects and mechanisms of control which can be conveniently discussed here in a chapter focused on institutional matters.

Policies relating to industrial location control can be divided into two categories. First, there are the negative controls operated via the Industrial Development Certificate (IDC) scheme, under which any industrial building or extension above a certain size requires the certification by central government that it is consistent with the 'proper distribution of industry'. Secondly, there are the more positive powers to attract industries to areas of high unemployment.

Until October 1969 the central department responsible for industrial location was the Board of Trade. At that date these responsibilities were transferred to a new Ministry of Technology together with those of the Department of Economic Affairs in relation to regional economic development. This left the Board of Trade with functions relating to external commercial policy and such matters as civil aviation, shipping, tourism, hotels and insurance. In October 1970 the Ministry of Technology and the Board of Trade were merged in a large Department of Trade and Industry (DTI), but further reorganisation in 1974 brought matters full circle, and it is now the Department of Industry which is responsible for industrial location and industrial aspects of regional policy.

The control of industrial location is entirely a central government responsibility. Though certain local authorities have appointed industrial development officers and many act in concert through industrial development associations, they have no statutory responsibility for industrial location policy. This may appear to be an overstatement, since an important part of a local authority's development plan will be concerned with the land use implications of employment change. Indeed there has been increasing emphasis on the economic base of planning. The Labour government explicitly associated local authorities with its 'industrial strategy'[24] of 1975. This 'emphasised the primary importance for national economic recovery of improving industrial performance and increasing productive potential', and sought 'the fullest possible co-operation of all authorities' by way of encouraging new firms, operating planning and building regulations approvals expeditiously, making council housing available for key workers and, indeed, 'seeking to ensure that industry is given a higher priority across the whole range of its policies'.[25]

Nevertheless, local authority powers in this field are limited and, in practice, are much more concerned with siting than with general issues of location. The distinction is important. Though local authorities can erect factories in an attempt to encourage industrial growth, their real power lies in approving or rejecting planning applications for industrial development on particular sites. The question as to whether this industrial development should take place at all in the area is a matter for the Department of Industry. In short, the department are responsible for the *location* of industry, whereas local authorities are responsible for the *siting* of industrial developments. It follows that the Department of Industry have an extremely important role to play: they are an executive as well as a policy-making body.

The general policy of the Department of Industry is to encourage industrial expansion in areas of high unemployment and to restrict it in congested areas. This has been the interpretation of 'the proper distribution of industry' – a phrase which is nowhere defined in the legislation, though the department are required (when considering whether an IDC should be granted) to have 'particular regard to the need for providing appropriate employment in development districts'.

Until 1972 no application for planning permission for the erection of an industrial building exceeding a certain floor area could be made unless it was accompanied by an IDC. Following the 1972 White Paper *Industrial and Regional Develoment*,[26] IDCs were dispensed with in Development Areas. At the same time the exemption limit was fixed at 15,000 square feet except in the South East Economic Planning Region where the limit became 10,000 square feet. In 1979 IDCs were no longer required in intermediate areas (thus making *all* assisted areas exempt from control). The exemption limit below which IDCs are not now required was raised to 50,000 square feet. In short, IDC control has been very considerably reduced as a policy instrument.

An IDC is generally made valid for the area of a local authority. The department do not inquire whether the proposed site – if one has been chosen – is suitable. This is an issue of land use which falls within the scope of the local planning authority's functions. It thus follows that the granting of a certificate by the department does not guarantee that the authorised development will – or can – take place.

During the 1960s legislation was directed towards a tightening up of the controls. Thus, the Control of Office and Industrial Development Act 1965 extended the meaning of 'related development' to effect greater control over the creation of a substantial area of floor space by the accumulation of individual pieces of development, each of which is below the exemption limit. Similarly, the Industrial Development Act 1966 extended the meaning of 'industrial building', thereby bringing under IDC control all buildings used or designed for use for scientific research. ('Scientific research' is defined as 'any activity in the fields of natural or applied science for the extension of knowledge'.) This Act also provided powers which ensure that planning permission is needed before space approved for 'ancillary purposes' such as storage can be converted to production use.

During the 1970s, however, economic performance was so poor that a major change in policy began to emerge. While special incentives were still maintained (and increased) in the areas of high unemployment, wider measures were needed to stimulate growth nationally. The 1972 White Paper[27] set out a range of proposals, and the 1972 Industry Act followed.

Preferential assistance is given to three types of 'assisted area': Special Development Areas where the need for new employment is most acute (for example, Clydeside and Tyneside); Development Areas (including the whole of Scotland, Wales and the North, most of the North-West, Yorkshire & Humberside and parts of the South-West and East Midlands regions); and Intermediate Areas (covering the remaining parts of the North-West and Yorkshire & Humberside regions, and the Nottinghamshire-Derbyshire coalfield area). The Conservative government which took office in 1979 announced a considerable reduction in these areas in the framework of the outcome of a review of regional industrial policy.[28]

General incentives (for example, depreciation allowances for investment in machinery and tax allowances for new industry building) are supplemented in the assisted areas by regional development grants, selective financial assistance and the provision of advance factories.[29]

With the growth of 'inner city' policies and increased emphasis (within a context of widespread high unemployment) on the encouragement of small businesses, local authorities are again being pressed to take a more active role in the promotion of industrial development. The Inner Urban Areas Act of 1978[30] provides new powers for designated authorities to make loans or grants and to declare (Business) Improvement Areas (which are discussed further in Chapter 11). Changes in development controls (which are discussed in Chapter 4) have also been introduced.

OFFICE DEVELOPMENT PERMITS

Pressures for the control of office development were resisted throughout the late 1950s and early 1960s on the ground that it would be
impracticable. A 1963 White Paper, issued by a Conservative government, argued the case well:

> The machinery for controlling the issue of industrial development
> certificates depends on knowledge of the firm which occupies the
> factory and on an assessment of the need for that firm to carry on its
> manufacture in a particular area. Many new factories are purpose-
> built and have heavy machinery installed; occupiers do not change
> often. New office blocks, on the other hand, are more often than
> not built for letting; this is, indeed, often the only way in which
> modern accommodation can be provided in units of a suitable size
> for small and medium-sized firms. Consequently, when the
> developer seeks planning permission he may not know how many
> tenants he will have or who his tenants will be; and these tenants
> may change at frequent intervals. A Government Department trying
> to administer a control of this sort would, therefore, be without the
> basic information needed for the purpose. Even when a tenant was
> known it would be extremely difficult to judge the case put forward
> in support of an office in the central area by a commercial or pro-
> fessional firm. The Government do not believe that it would be
> practicable to administer a system of control of office occupation
> either effectively or equitably.[31]

Action along three lines was proposed and carried into effect. First,
planning controls over new office building were tightened. The issue
here was a complicated legal one. In brief, the existing legislation
allowed a 10 per cent increase in cubic capacity to owners rebuilding
their premises. Since new buildings have lower ceilings and less
circulation space, a 10 per cent increase in cubic capacity could involve
as much as 40 per cent increase in floor space. Attempts by local
planning authorities to restrict this involved the risk of paying heavy
compensation. The Town and Country Planning Act 1963 removed
any compensation liabilities which might arise when permission is
refused for an increase in *floor space* of more than 10 per cent.[32]

Secondly, an attempt was made to disperse more government
offices. It had been government policy for many years to disperse
headquarters departments and self-contained branches which could
function away from London without loss of administrative efficiency.
In 1962, of the total headquarters staff of 125,000, some 25,000
already worked outside London, and there were plans for moving a
further 7,000. It was felt, however, that it was time for a thorough re-
examination of the situation. A review was undertaken by Sir Gilbert

Flemming. His (unpublished) report recommended the transfer of some 18,000 jobs from central London.[33]

Thirdly, a Location of Offices Bureau was set up to encourage the decentralisation of office employment from central London. Its main function at this time was to provide an information and publicity service.

The return of the Labour government in 1964 was followed by the introduction of direct controls over office building through Office Development Permits. The legislation (Control of Office and Industrial Development Act 1965 – now consolidated in the 1971 Town and Country Planning Act) applied the control only in the metropolitan region, but provided for its extension by Order to any other part of Great Britain. In August 1965 it was extended to the Birmingham conurbation and in July 1966 to major parts of southern England and the East and West Midlands. It was subsequently restricted to the South East Economic Planning Region.[34]

In 1976 the DoE published an interdepartmental review of national policy in relation to office location.[35] This concluded that central London firms were now under such pressure from rising costs and staffing difficulties that special government measures to promote decentralisation were no longer necessary. Specific measures to encourage the movement of office jobs to assisted areas, however, were still needed.

Though controls were relaxed, they were extended in time. (They were due to expire in August 1977, but by the Control of Office Development Act 1977 they were extended to August 1982.) In the South-East the policy in the late 1970s was, to quote the White Paper on *Policy for the Inner Cities*, 'to steer to inner areas outside central London those firms which can demonstrate that a move to an assisted area is not practicable'. However, some speculative office development would be permitted in the inner areas 'where there is a shortage of office space, reasonable transport facilities, and the development is judged to be of maximum benefit in a declining area'.

In August 1977 the Location of Offices Bureau was given a new remit. Instead of being concerned with the decentralisation of office employment, it was charged 'to attract international concerns so that they locate office employment in this country' and 'to give particular attention to the promotion of office employment in inner urban areas'. (In the case of London this excluded the City and West End.)

The wheel had come full circle! The story ends with the abolition of both Office Development Permits in 1979 and the Bureau in 1981.

EMPLOYMENT POLICIES

Employment is, of course, one of the principal economic considerations in town and country planning, and its importance has become increasingly recognised as the general state of the economy has worsened. It cannot be said that employment policies are, as yet, very successfully integrated with physical planning policies. At least in part, this is due to organisational separatism and the fact that local authorities have little responsibility for employment policies: they are essentially a function of central government.

Until 1974 employment policies were the direct responsibility of the Department of Employment. In that year the Employment and Training Act of 1973 came into operation, and the Manpower Services Commission was set up to manage the government's employment and training services.[36] The main purpose of this change was to transfer direct control from central government to representatives of employers, employees, local government and educational interests (who form the Commission). The Secretary of State for Employment retains responsibility for such matters as general manpower policy, manpower aspects of regional policy and regional economic planning, and the department's unit for manpower studies. The Commission has three operating divisions: the Employment Service Division (ESD), the Training Services Division (TSD) and the Special Programmes Division (SPD). The ESD runs the national network of employment offices (which are being replaced by Jobcentres) and also the various schemes of financial assistance to facilitate the mobility of labour. There are now two major schemes – the Employment Transfer Scheme and the Job Search Scheme. These provide grants and allowances to help with travel and subsistence expenses in finding a new job, and in moving house to take up a job.

The TSD are responsible for managing and developing training programmes. There are twenty-three industrial training boards which are financed in part by levies on employers' payrolls. An independent Industrial Training Service (ITS) – sponsored by the Commission – helps firms, employers' associations and industrial training boards to identify training needs and to formulate training policy. A Government Training Opportunities Scheme (TOPS) promotes training in Colleges of Further Education, in industry and in some fifty 'skill-centres'.

The Commission, through its Special Programmes Division, also administers the Youth Opportunities Programme and various initiatives designed to create jobs or work experience for young people. The latest of these (1981) is a £332 million 'Community Enterprise Programme'. Among the provisions of this programme, young people who have been unemployed for six months or more will have temporary jobs in clearing derelict sites or improving 'community landscapes'. Among the schemes listed as examples are 'drainage, construction of footpaths and removal of debris in country parks; clearing canals and footpaths, stabilising sand dunes; tree planting to replace dead elms; and creating conservation areas for rare animals and birds'.[37]

Thus by a curious route a new environmental improvement policy has developed.

LOCAL GOVERNMENT IN LONDON

The map of local government areas in Britain has been radically redrawn in recent years. London government was reorganised by an Act of 1963, English and Welsh local government by an Act of 1972, and Scottish local government by an Act of 1973.

The London Government Act 1963 came into operation in 1965. In brief, the Act established a Greater London Council covering an area of about 1,600 square kilometres and a population of nearly 8 million (now less than 7 million); and thirty-two new London boroughs, plus the unmolested ancient City of London. These replaced the London County Council, twenty-eight metropolitan boroughs, the county council of Middlesex and the county boroughs of Croydon, East Ham and West Ham. Considerable parts of Essex, Hertfordshire, Kent and Surrey were transferred to the new Greater London area.

In this area the London boroughs are the main local authorities, but the Greater London Council has important functions in relation to strategic planning and services which need to be planned and administered over a wide area – overall planning, main highways, traffic control, overspill housing and the fire and ambulance services.

The GLC have the responsibility of preparing the strategic development plan (now technically a 'structure plan') for the whole of the Greater London area. (This was published in 1969.) It lays down the policies relating to population, housing, employment, transport and, indeed, all major issues which come within the compass of strategic planning. Within this 'strategic framework', the London borough councils each produce their own local development plans. Originally it was intended that these would also be structure plans, but this was changed in 1972. The change was necessitated by the length of time required to process the Greater London Development Plan. As the Minister for Local Government and Development stated in the House of Commons:[38] 'the processing thereafter of a further 33 Borough structure plans will be so time-consuming that there is every prospect that the strategic plan itself will have required further modification in the light of changing circumstances before the last structure plan has been approved and local plans adopted'. The boroughs will therefore be required only to prepare local plans within the framework of the GLC structure plan.

The position in London is unique. The relationship between the GLC and the London borough councils is not the same as that between a county and a county district. The boroughs are large authorities with major responsibilities in their areas: indeed, they are *the* local authorities for their areas. The GLC are the local planning authority for Greater London _as a whole_: the boroughs are the planning authorities for their areas – though there is a complex web of interrelationships. In certain areas, such as Covent Garden, and in relation to certain types of development of strategic importance such as transport terminals, university development, major places of public assembly, the GLC themselves are the local planning authority. Planning applications for other developments of 'strategic significance' have to be referred by the borough councils concerned to the GLC, and there is a wide range of provisions for consultations.

A convenient summary of the situation in relation to the development plan and the 'partnership' of the GLC and the boroughs is to be found in the _Statement_ of the Greater London Development Plan.[39] This underlines the fact that the GLDP is intended to form the 'context' for the borough plans which will follow it; but in practice a hard and fast division of functions is neither possible nor desirable. Indeed, it is possible (to say the least) that, as the borough plans are prepared within the 'context', issues will emerge that require a revision of the context. The GLDP is therefore essentially a conceptual plan at this stage. It states a set of principles for the future development of Greater London which will have to undergo a 'process of validation' over a number of years.

The _Statement_ couches the issues very much in technical terms, but in reality the crucial problems are policy and political ones. The policies and politics of the individual boroughs are not necessarily consonant with those of the GLC. It is not without good reason that the Redcliffe-Maud Commission[40] (majority) stressed the advantages of the all-purpose authority – 'local government in its simplest, most understandable and potentially most effective form'. But in some areas (a few, according to the majority report; everywhere, according to Senior's 'memorandum of dissent')[41] there are overriding benefits to be obtained from a two-tier structure. Nowhere is this clearer than in London and, indeed, the GLC are currently rethinking their position following the report of an inquiry they commissioned from Sir Frank Marshall.[42] The main conclusion was that the GLC should be a strategic authority setting broad metropolitan objectives and policies, and achieving them through the overall control of resources. This implies a significant change in the 'partnership' of the GLC and the boroughs, or what the GLC inelegantly refer to as an 'iterative process'. Whatever it is called, however, it does not make life easy; on the contrary, it underlines the fact that planning has far more to do with politics than with technical issues.

ENGLISH LOCAL GOVERNMENT

Prior to reorganisation, English local government was divided first into county boroughs and administrative counties. Administrative counties were further divided into three types of county districts – municipal (or 'non-county') boroughs, urban districts and rural districts. Only county boroughs (of which there were seventy-nine) and administrative counties (of which there were forty-five) were planning authorities, though there were varying degrees of delegation to county districts.

The Redcliffe-Maud Commission recommended fifty-eight all-purpose authorities for the whole of England outside four conurbations. One of these, Greater London, had already been reorganised on a two-tier system in the mid-1960s. For the other three (centred on Birmingham, Manchester and Liverpool) the Commission recommended a two-tier system of metropolitan and metropolitan district authorities.

The Conservative government rejected the unitary system, and the Local Government Act of 1972 established a two-tier system of counties and districts throughout the country. In six areas there are metropolitan counties (Greater Manchester, Merseyside, South Yorkshire, Tyne & Wear, West Midlands and West Yorkshire) with a total of thirty-six metropolitan districts. Outside these metropolitan areas are thirty-nine counties and 296 districts (Table 2.3).

Most of the new counties bear the same name as those which they supersede (though the boundaries are not always the same). There are, however, four new names: Avon (centred on Bath and Bristol, and incorporating parts of the former counties of Gloucestershire and Somerset); Cleveland (centred on Hartlepool and Teesside, and incorporating parts of the former counties of Durham and the North Riding of Yorkshire); Cumbria (encompassing the former county boroughs of Barrow-in-Furness and Carlisle, the whole of Cumberland and Westmorland and parts of Lancashire and the West Riding of Yorkshire); and Humberside (incorporating Grimsby, Kingston upon Hull and parts of the counties of the East and West Riding of Yorkshire and of Lincolnshire).

Basically, therefore, there is an entirely new structure of local government in the metropolitan areas while elsewhere reorganisation has been based largely on the old shires. The metropolitan counties bear only a slight resemblance, however, to the concept put forward by the Redcliffe-Maud Commission for the local government of the West Midlands, Merseyside and Greater Manchester conurbations. Instead of having boundaries extending well beyond the built-up areas (to a further distance of some 30–50 km), they are much more tightly circumscribed. Indeed, their areas extend little beyond the built-up conurbations. Yet the rationale for metropolitan counties (which was accepted and applied also to West Yorkshire, South Yorkshire and Tyne & Wear) was the need for a local government unit of a large size capable of working out 'effective policies for dealing with their massive housing and transportation problems' and planning and

Table 2.3 The New English Local Authorities

Metropolitan counties

Name	Mid-1979 population[43] (thousands)	Number of metropolitan districts
Greater Manchester	2,648	10
Merseyside	1,532	5
South Yorkshire	1,301	4
Tyne & Wear	1,156	5
West Midlands	2,696	7
West Yorkshire	2,064	5

Non-metropolitan counties

Name	Mid-1979 population (thousands)	Number of districts
Avon	924	6
Bedfordshire	499	4
Berkshire	682	6
Buckinghamshire	536	5
Cambridgeshire	579	6
Cheshire	927	8
Cleveland	569	4
Cornwall	419	7
Cumbria	470	6
Derbyshire	898	9
Devon	952	10
Dorset	591	8
Durham	603	8
East Sussex	655	7
Essex	1,447	14
Gloucestershire	497	6
Hampshire	1,460	13
Hereford and Worcester	618	9
Hertfordshire	952	10
Humberside	850	9
Isle of Wight	115	2
Kent	1,456	14
Lancashire	1,370	14
Leicestershire	836	9
Lincolnshire	534	7
Norfolk	686	7
North Yorkshire	663	8
Northamptonshire	523	7
Northumberland	290	6
Nottinghamshire	974	8
Oxfordshire	542	5
Salop	370	6
Somerset	416	5
Staffordshire	1,000	9
Suffolk	598	7
Surrey	994	11
Warwickshire	469	5
West Sussex	644	7
Wiltshire	516	5

undertaking 'redevelopment, with its widespread consequences, on the scale required where so much of the urban fabric is obsolete'.

So far as planning is concerned, there is no difference between the powers of metropolitan and non-metropolitan counties. They are responsible for structure planning, for agreeing with the district councils a framework for local plan preparation, for consultation on matters of common concern and for the determination of major development control issues. This is discussed in more detail in the following chapter.

In other fields, the metropolitan districts have a much wider range of functions than the non-metropolitan districts: they are, for instance, the local authority for education, social services and libraries (which elsewhere are the responsibility of the counties).

The overall picture, however, is by no means as neat as this summary suggests. Some services (such as parks, museums and swimming baths) can be provided by either the county (metropolitan and non-metropolitan) or the district. Highway maintenance is divided between counties and districts. Housing is a district function, but counties have reserve powers. Moreover, the legislation provides for the discharge of any local authority function 'by any other authority' (except for police, education and social services): this was mainly to allow districts which were formerly county boroughs to continue to operate, on an agency basis, services which were transferred to the counties. The final result is confusing and, with some services, the division of responsibilities is blurred. Nowhere is this more so than is the case with planning (though hopefully matters will be improved by the Local Government, Planning and Land Act 1980).

Reference also needs to be made to parish councils and meetings (of which there are over 10,000 in England). These were not abolished by the 1972 Act: on the contrary, their powers were extended. Of particular importance is the right of parish councils to be consulted on planning applications affecting their areas. A number of non-statutory 'neighbourhood councils' have also been established in the larger urban areas.[44] Unlike the situation in Scotland and Wales, there is no statutory provision for such bodies at the present time.

WELSH LOCAL GOVERNMENT

Local government reorganisation in Wales reduced the number of local authorities from 181 to forty-five. In place of thirteen counties, 164 districts and four county boroughs, there is a complete two-tier system of eight counties and thirty-seven districts (Table 2.4). Three of the counties have been formed by dividing up the former county of Glamorgan. Monmouthshire has remained largely unchanged but is now called Gwent. The other four new counties spread over large areas of the sparsely populated North, Central and West Wales.

Table 2.4   *The New Welsh Local Authorities*

Counties	Mid-1979 population (thousands)	Number of districts
Clwyd	385	6
Dyfed	326	6
Gwent	436	5
Gwynedd	226	5
Mid Glamorgan	538	6
Powys	107	3
South Glamorgan	391	2
West Glamorgan	367	4

There are no metropolitan counties, and the division of functions between counties and districts is very similar to that between non-metropolitan counties and districts in England. One difference is that the Welsh districts are responsible for refuse disposal as well as refuse collection (which is divided between the English counties and districts).

The Welsh reorganisation abolished parish councils, and provides for statutory community councils which, like the English parish councils, have the right to be consulted on planning applications affecting their areas.

SCOTTISH LOCAL GOVERNMENT

The Wheatley Commission[45] recommended that the four Counties of Cities, twenty-one large burghs, 176 small burghs, thirty-three counties and 196 districts of Scotland should be replaced by a two-tier structure of seven regional and thirty-seven district authorities. With some modifications, this general structure was accepted by the government. Following amendments made by Parliament (particularly the addition of Fife as a separate region and the exclusion of several districts around Glasgow from the Glasgow District), the Local Government (Scotland) Act 1973 provides for a two-tier system except in the three island areas of Orkney, Shetland and the Western Islands (which become 'most-purpose' authorities).

There are nine regional and fifty-three district councils. Together with the three island authorities there are thus sixty-five local authorities of which forty-nine have planning powers.

The fact that, unlike the situation in England, not all local authorities have planning powers is a result of the difficulties of devising a local government structure for those parts of the country which cover a large area but contain few people. By allocating planning powers in these areas of scattered population to the regional authority it was possible to increase the number of districts (and thereby also reduce their enormous geographical size).

There are thus three different types of area:

(i) in the Central, Fife, Grampian, Lothian, Tayside and Strath-clyde regions planning is divided between regional and district authorities;

(ii) in the Borders, Dumfries & Galloway and Highland regions planning is allocated to the regions: the districts have no planning functions. these three regions are termed 'general planning authorities';

(iii) in the three island areas of Orkney, Shetland and the Western Islands there are no districts: there is thus only one local authority who undertake the functions of both a regional planning authority and a district planning authority. These authorities are termed 'island areas' (not regions) and are designated as 'general planning authorities'.

In effect, therefore, there is a two-tier planning system in six regions, and a 'general' planning authority system elsewhere. The former include nine-tenths of the population of Scotland.

The regions vary greatly in size – Strathclyde (with a population of 2½ million) has nearly half the country's population. Districts range in population from around 10,000 in Skye & Lochalsh and Badenoch & Strathspey, to nearly half a million in Edinburgh and nearly 800,000 in Glasgow (Table 2.5).

Table 2.5   *The New Scottish Local Authorities*

Regions	*Mid-1979 population*	*Number of districts*
Borders	99,938	4
Central	271,177	3
Dumfries & Galloway	142,547	4
Fife	340,170	3
Grampian	469,168	5
Highland	190,507	8
Lothian	750,728	4
Strathclyde	2,431,101	19
Tayside	401,661	3
Islands authorities		
Orkney	18,134	
Shetland	22,111	
Western Isles	29,758	

There is a clearer distinction, at least in concept, between the functions of the regions and the districts than is the case south of the Border. The regions were conceived as strategic authorities and are responsible for 'regional planning functions', all highways, public transport, education, social work and water (which in England and Wales has been allocated to *ad hoc* authorities). The districts are responsible for local planning, housing, refuse collection and disposal and a range of other local services. As is explained in the following chapter, the division of planning functions was, from the start, made on a much better basis than in England and Wales. Nevertheless there remains some blurring, particularly in relation to industrial development, tourism, countryside planning, recreation, museums and community centres where the functions are exercised concurrently by regional and district authorities.[46]

The Scottish Act provides for the establishment of community councils, where there is a demand for them, under schemes prepared by district (or islands) authorities. Their purpose is 'to ascertain, co-ordinate and express to the regional, district and islands councils, and other public bodies, the views of the community' and 'to take such action in the interests of the community as appears to its members to be desirable and practicable'. Some 'alternatives for community council schemes' have been prepared by the Scottish Development Department.[47]

FUNCTIONS REMOVED FROM LOCAL GOVERNMENT

To complete this rapid sketch of the reorganised local government system, it is necessary to point to several services which have been removed from local government. One of the major reasons for the reorganisation was to make local government better able to carry out its functions: it was even hoped that some functions which had been transferred earlier to *ad hoc* bodies could be brought back into local government. With one significant exception, this was not to be; indeed, personal health services and (except in Scotland) water and sewage disposal functions have been removed from local government. This is mainly because these services need areas far larger than those of the new counties. In Scotland, with the establishment of large regional authorities, regional water boards (set up in 1967) were abolished and their functions transferred to the regions.[48] Nevertheless, as in England and Wales, personal health services were moved to a reorganised health services organisation. This is now responsible for a unified health service which also encompasses the hospitals and the general practitioner services (doctors, dentists, opticians and pharmacists). But though 'unified' in this sense, this adhocery has resulted in a split between personal health services and social work services.

Water supply (together with water conservation, sewerage and sewage disposal) was transferred to nine English water authorities and a Welsh National Water Authority. These took the place of sixty-one local water authorities, 101 joint boards, thirty-three statutory undertakers, 1,300 local sewage disposal authorities and twenty-nine river authorities.[49]

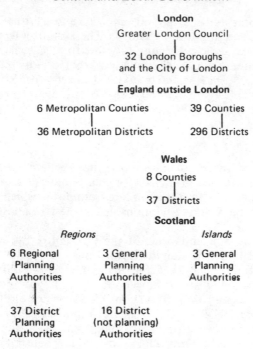

London

Greater London Council

32 London Boroughs
and the City of London

England outside London

6 Metropolitan Counties	39 Counties
36 Metropolitan Districts	296 Districts

Wales

8 Counties

37 Districts

Scotland

Regions   *Islands*

6 Regional Planning Authorities	3 General Planning Authorities	3 General Planning Authorities
37 District Planning Authorities	16 District (not planning) Authorities	

Figure 2.1   *The new local government structure*

ORGANIC CHANGE IN LOCAL GOVERNMENT

Dissatisfaction with the local reorganisation outlined in the previous pages has been widespread.[50] For a while it became intertwined with the debate on devolution – to Scotland, Wales and the English regions.[51] But there was constant criticism of the stresses of the two-tier system, not only in London[52] but also in the former large county boroughs which were 'demoted' on reorganisation. The upshot was a proposal for 'organic' change.[53] This concept is one of limited change enabling 'improvements to be made in a pragmatic way in the distribution of functions between county and district authorities'. A White Paper published in January 1979[54] set out a range of proposals, of which those relating to planning were uniquely different from the remainder in that they were to apply to all local authorities (in England). Essentially the proposal was that responsibility for development control should lie almost entirely with districts: counties should retain responsibiiity for only a limited number of special categories such as applications concerning mineral working and applications straddling the boundaries of national parks.

Though conceived as limited in character, the proposals as a whole

were seen by some as not going far enough[55] and by others as constituting a radical and important change.[56] The Labour government did
not stay in power sufficiently long to come to any decision, but the
proposals for changes in development control (for which there was a
wide agreement)[57] were enacted in the Conservative government's
Local Government, Planning and Land Act of 1980. (They are discussed in Chapter 4.)

FURTHER SCOTTISH PROPOSALS

Though the local government minister has declared that 'organic
change' is dead,[58] further proposals for change have emerged north of
the Border. These are from the Stodart Committee which was established to review the working relationships in the reorganised Scottish
system.[59]

Most of the recommendations of the Committee are designed to
allocate responsibility for individual functions specifically to one tier.
Thus it is recommended that regional councils should have sole
responsibility for industrial development and promotion, while
district councils should alone be responsible for leisure and recreation,
tourism, countryside and nature conservation. For planning, however, the division between the tiers should remain. This *prima facie*
surprising recommendation is related to the more sensible division of
planning functions effected in the Scottish reorganisation – an issue to
which we return in the following chapters.

REFERENCES AND FURTHER READING: CHAPTER 2

1   D. A. Schon, *Beyond the Stable State* (Temple Smith, 1971; Penguin, 1973).
2   White Paper, *The Reorganisation of Central Government*, Cmnd 4506 (HMSO,
    1970).
3   See P. Draper, *Creation of the DoE: A Study of the Merger of Three Departments
    to form the Department of the Environment*, Civil Service Studies 4 (HMSO,
    1977).
4   *The Reorganisation of Central Government*, op. cit.
5   Unlike the Department of the Environment, the Scottish Development Department
    publishes an annual report: see, for example, *Scottish Development Department:
    Report for 1979*, Cmnd 7924 (HMSO, 1980).
6   Central Office of Information, *Environmental Planning in Britain*, Reference
    Pamphlet 9 (HMSO, 1979), pp. 4–5. The Welsh Office publishes an annual report:
    Cymru: Wales (HMSO).
7   See Central Policy Review Staff, *Relations Between Central Government and Local
    Authorities* (HMSO, 1977); R. Buxton, *Local Government* (Penguin, 2nd edn,
    1973) (particularly ch. 3); and J. A. G. Griffith, *Central Departments and Local
    Authorities* (Allen & Unwin, 1966) (particularly ch. 5).
8   D. R. Mandelker, *Green Belts and Urban Growth* (University of Wisconsin Press,
    1962), pp. 4–5.
9   B. Miller, 'Citadels of local power', *The Twentieth Century*, vol. 162 (October
    1957). This short and now elderly essay nicely conveys the quintessence of local
    government in a way which many larger works fail to do.

10 S. Barrett, M. Stewart and J. Underwood, *The Land Market and Development Process: A Review of Research and Policy*, University of Bristol, School for Advanced Urban Studies, Occasional Paper 2 (University of Bristol, 1978), pp. 4–5.

11 A discussion of relationships between the Department of the Environment and the new town development corporations is to be found in J. B. Cullingworth, *Essays on Housing Policy* (Allen & Unwin, 1979), pp. 14–20. A highly detailed account is provided in the author's *Environmental Planning, Vol. III, New Towns Policy* (HMSO, 1979).

12 The 1980 Act is a neat illustration of the continual conflict between 'freeing' and 'controlling' local government. The financial provisions and the restrictions placed on direct labour organisations may be contrasted with the 'relaxations of controls' over clean air, pollution, etc., etc. On the latter see Department of the Environment, *Central Government Control over Local Authorities*, Cmnd 7634 (HMSO, 1979). A useful discussion of several aspects of this legislation is to be found in *The Local Government Planning and Land Bill: A Series of Short Essays*, University of Birmingham, Institute of Local Government Studies, (University of Birmingham, 1980).

13 This discussion relates particularly to appeals under section 36 of the Town and Country Planning Act 1971. It does not deal specifically with advertisement appeals, appeals against enforcement notices, appeals to determine whether in doubtful cases planning permission is required, or appeals in respect of a local authority's failure to give a planning decision within prescribed time-limits – though the principles discussed are generally the same. Section 36 of the 1971 Act covers appeals against a decision of a local planning authority to refuse planning permission, or against conditions imposed on a grant of permission.

14 The publisher in all cases was HMSO. A list of the titles of the *Development Control Policy Notes* is given in the Bibliography to this volume. All the publications, together with a digest of planning decisions (H. J. J. Brown, 'Planning law and practice from the decisions'), are to be found in D. Heap, *Encyclopedia of the Law of Town and Country Planning*. Important current decisions are reported in the *Journal of Planning and Environment Law* and in the *Estates Gazette*.

15 Department of the Environment, *Development Control Statistics 1978–79* (DoE, 1980), Tables 26 and 27.

16 *Report of the Committee on Administrative Tribunals and Enquiries*, Cmnd 218 (HMSO, 1957), pp. 85–6, para. 388.

17 See SI 1972 No. 1652; SI 1974 No. 420; SI 1977 No. 477; and SI 1977 No. 1939.

18 Department of the Environment, *Consultation Paper on the Planning Appeal System* (DoE, 1980).

19 The figures are from the new series of quarterly statistics on planning applications which started for the quarter ended 31 December 1979. They are issued directly by the Department of the Environment but are reproduced in the *Journal of Planning and Environment Law*.

20 Royal Town Planning Institute, *Memorandum of Observations on the Consultation Paper on Planning Appeals* (1981).

21 *The Times*, 17 March 1981.

22 Department of the Environment, *Review of the Development Control System: Final Report by George Dobry QC* (HMSO, 1975), p. 51.

23 loc. cit.

24 White Paper, *An Approach to Industrial Strategy*, Cmnd 6315 (HMSO, 1975). For a brief account of this see G. E. Cameron, 'The national industrial strategy and regional policy', in D. Maclennan and J. B. Parr, *Regional Policy: Past Experience and New Directions* (Martin Robertson, 1979), ch. 14.

25 DoE Circular 71/77, *Local Government and the Industrial Strategy* (HMSO, 1977). (This circular was cancelled by Circular 22/80, *Development Control – Policy and Practice*, HMSO, 1980, *q.v.*)

26 White Paper, *Industrial and Regional Development*, Cmnd 4942 (HMSO, 1972).

27 op. cit.
28 *HC Debates*, cols 1302–21, 17 July 1979. See also *Industry Act 1972: Annual Report for the Year Ended 31 March 1980*, HC Paper (1979–80) 772 (HMSO, 1980).
29 See the Annual Reports on the Industry Act 1972, for example, the Report for 1979–80 referred to in the previous note.
30 See DoE Circular 68/78, *Inner Urban Areas Act 1978* (HMSO, 1978).
31 White Paper, *London: Employment, Housing, Land*, Cmnd 1952 (HMSO, 1963).
32 For a full discussion see the author's *Environmental Planning, Vol. IV, Land Values, Compensation and Betterment* (HMSO, 1981), ch. 7.
33 A further examination of this issue was announced in the 1970 White Paper on *The Reorganization of Central Government* (Cmnd 4506): this one was published in 1973 under the title *The Dispersal of Government Work from London* (Cmnd 5322), though it is better known as the Hardman Report.
34 See the *Annual Reports* on Control of Office Development, published as House of Commons Papers. The last report (for the year ended 31 March 1979) was HC Paper (1978–9) 158 (HMSO, 1979).
35 Department of the Environment, *The Office Location Review* (DoE, 1976).
36 See Manpower Services Commission, *Annual Reports; Towards A Comprehensive Manpower Policy* (1976) and *MSC – Review and Plan* (1977).
37 Manpower Services Commission, Press Release, 12 February 1981. For a succinct review of job creation programmes, see *Direct Job Creation in the Public Sector* (Organisation for Economic Co-operation and Development, 1980).
38 *HC Debates*, 10 November 1970.
39 Greater London Council, *Greater London Development Plan: Statement*; see also *Report of Studies* and *Tomorrow's London* (all GLC, 1969).
40 *Royal Commission on Local Government in England, Vol. 1: Report* (Redcliffe-Maud Report), Cmnd 4040 (HMSO, 1969).
41 *Royal Commission on Local Government in England, Vol. 2: Memorandum of Dissent by Mr D. Senior*, Cmnd 4040-1 (HMSO, 1969).
42 F. Marshall, *The Marshall Inquiry on Greater London: Report to the Greater London Council* (GLC, July 1978). See also *Report from County Hall 1977–79* (GLC, 1979).
43 Office of Population Censuses and Surveys, *Mid-1979 Population Estimates*, OPCS Monitor, 24 June 1980.
44 See the Consultation Paper *Neighbourhood Councils in England* issued by the Department of the Environment in July 1974, and Advisory Group on Neighbourhood Councils, *A Voice for Your Neighbourhood: The Neighbourhood Council* (HMSO, 1977).
45 *Report of the Royal Commission on Local Government in Scotland* (Wheatley Report), Cmnd 4150 (HMSO, 1969).
46 Generally, see E. Young, *The Law of Planning in Scotland* (Hodge, Glasgow, 1978).
47 Scottish Development Department, *Community Councils: Some Alternatives for Community Council Schemes in Scotland* (HMSO, 1974).
48 See Scottish Development Department, *Water in Scotland: A Review* (HMSO, 1980).
49 See B. J. Payne, *Water Authorities and Planning Authorities: A Study of Developing Relationships*, University of Manchester, Department of Town and Country Planning, Occasional Paper 1 (University of Manchester, 1978).
50 For a recent critical analysis see two papers by L. J. Sharpe: 'Reforming the grass roots: an alternative analysis', in D. Butler and A. H. Halsey (eds), *Politics and Policy* (Macmillan, 1978), and 'The failure of local government modernization in Britain: a critique of functionalism', *Canadian Public Administration*, vol. 24 (Spring 1981), pp. 92–115. Sharpe argues that the reorganisation laid far too much emphasis on functional criteria at the cost of a loss in democratic quality.

51 Amongst the library of reports are: Royal Commission on the Constitution, *Vol. I: Report*, Cmnd 5460; *Vol. II: Memorandum of Dissent by Lord Crowther-Hunt and Professor A. J. Peacock*, Cmnd 5460-1 (HMSO, 1973); White Paper, *Devolution to Scotland and Wales: Supplementary Statement*, Cmnd 6585 (HMSO, 1976); Office of the Lord President of the Council, *Devolution: The English Dimension - A Consultative Document* (HMSO, 1976); White Paper, *Devolution: Financing the Devolved Services*, Cmnd 6890 (HMSO, 1977); Scotland Act 1978; and Wales Act 1978. See also E. Craven (ed), *Regional Devolution and Social Policy* (Macmillan, 1975).

52 See F. Marshall, *The Marshall Inquiry on Greater London: Report to the Greater London Council* (GLC, 1978); G. Rhodes, *The New Government of London: The First Five Years* (Weidenfeld & Nicolson, 1972); and D. L. Foley, *Governing the London Region: Reorganisation and Planning in the 1960s* (University of California Press, 1972).

53 White Paper, *Organic Change in Local Government*, Cmnd 7457 (HMSO, 1979).

54 op. cit.

55 For example by the National Executive of the Labour Party: see *Local Government Reform in England*, October 1978.

56 See J. D. Stewart, S. Leach and C. K. Skelcher, *Organic Change: A Report on Constitutional, Management and Financial Problems* (Association of County Councils, November 1978).

57 See, for example, Expenditure Committee, Eighth Report, Session 1976-7, *Planning Procedures*, HC (1976-7) 395 (HMSO, 1977)

58 Mr Tom King as reported in *Local Government Chronicle*, 20 July 1979.

59 *Report of the Committee of Inquiry into Local Government in Scotland*, Cmnd 8115 (HMSO, 1981).

Chapter 3

THE LEGISLATIVE FRAMEWORK

Under the prewar system of planning, an operative planning scheme was in effect a zoning plan. A developer could visit a local town hall and ask to see the planning scheme: he would be shown a written document and a series of coloured maps, each colour representing some particular use. From the published scheme, the developer would find that particular pieces of land were zoned for industry, for open space, for residential development at not more than eight houses to the acre, and so on. The great advantage of this system to the developer was that there were no doubts as to what development would be permitted: it was all written down and had the force of law. But therein lay one of its gravest shortcomings: certainty for the developer meant inflexibility for the local authority. One way of circumventing this was for planning authorities to take advantage of the time-consuming and cumbersome procedure for preparing and obtaining approval to their schemes by remaining at the draft stage for as long as possible. Yet this had the opposite danger: the flexibility thereby attained could easily become mere expediency.

The 1947 system attempted to achieve a balance between these two extremes by the introduction of the flexible development plan which was essentially a statement of development proposals. This was intended to show, for example, 'which towns and villages are suitable for expansion and which can best be kept to their present size; the direction in which a city will expand; the area to be preserved as an agricultural green belt and the area to be allocated to industry and to housing'.[1]

The 1947 Act defined a development plan as 'a plan indicating the manner in which a local planning authority propose that land in their area should be used, whether by the carrying out thereon of development or otherwise, and the stages by which any such development should be carried out'. Furthermore, it was required that the development plan should 'define the sites of proposed roads, public and other building and works, airfields, parks, pleasure grounds, nature reserves and other open spaces, or allocate areas of land for use for agricultural, residential, industrial or other purposes'.

Unlike the prewar 'operative scheme', the development plan did not of itself imply that permission would be granted for particular developments even if it appeared that they were clearly in harmony with the plan. Development control was achieved by a system of planning permissions. The development plan merely set out the intentions of the local planning authority. Though a developer was able to find out from the plan where particular uses would be likely to be permitted, his specific proposals still needed to be considered by the local planning authority. When considering applications, the authority were expressly directed to 'have regard to the provisions of the development plan', but the plan was not binding in any way, and, indeed, authorities were instructed to have regard not only to the development plan but also to 'any other material considerations'. Furthermore, in granting permission to develop, the authority could impose 'such conditions as they think fit'.[2]

However, though local planning authorities had considerable latitude in deciding whether to approve applications, they had to be clear on the planning objectives for their areas; otherwise they had no adequate basis on which they could judge the merits and shortcomings of particular applications. This was the essential purpose of the development plan.

The development plan consisted of a series of documents. The *Report of Survey* provided the background to, and the basis of, the plan, but had no statutory effect. The statutory documents were a 'written statement' and a series of maps. The written statement was a short formal (indeed excessively short and formal) summary of the main proposals of the plan. It did not contain any argument substantiating the proposals or any of the factual material on which these were based. The maps were of several types. In counties they included a 'county map' and a related 'programme map' (at a scale of one inch to the mile) covering the whole of the administrative county. For areas requiring more detailed planning there were 'town maps' together with programme maps at the larger scale of six inches to the mile. In the case of a county borough there was, of course, no county map: the principal maps were the town map and its related programme map.

The county and town maps indicated the developments which were expected in the twenty-year period of the plan (and possibly some important developments which were expected somewhat later) and the pattern of land use proposed at the end of the period. (In areas for which no notation was given – which could be extensive in counties – it was intended that the main existing uses should remain undisturbed.) A programme map showed the stages by which the proposed development was to be achieved.

A formidable amount of work was involved in the preparation of development plans. The 1947 Act required local planning authorities to submit plans to the minister for approval within three years (by 1 July 1951), 'or within such extended period as the minister may in any particular case allow' but, not surprisingly, most authorities could not meet the deadline. (Only twenty-two did, in fact, do so.)

The task of the central department was to assess the general provisions of the plan, to weigh all objections to it, to hold a public local inquiry, to consider the report of the inspector on the inquiry and finally to approve the plan (usually with modification). About half the plans had been approved by 1955 and the bulk had been approved by 1959; but three were not approved until the early 1960s: Denbighshire, part of Glamorgan and Manchester.

Development plans, unlike the old 'operative schemes', were not intended to be final statements – even of broad intentions. Local planning authorities were obliged to review them at least every five years, and additionally could propose amendments at any time. The impossibility of coping with the preparation and approval of plans on the original time-scale greatly delayed the review procedure, and many local authorities were still engaged on their first review in the mid-1960s. This was one of the major reasons for changing the system and introducing structure plans.

The reviews followed the same process as the initial plan: survey, draft written statement and maps, submission to the department, local public inquiry, and approval with or without modification. Alterations or additions to development plans could be made at any time. Often these 'amendments' amounted to more detailed plans for particular areas. In counties, the town maps for the districts were commonly submitted in this way. Another type of detailed planning often submitted as a formal amendment was a 'comprehensive development area' plan (now replaced by the 'action area' procedure discussed later).

THE PLANNING ADVISORY GROUP REPORT

The system of development plans and development control set up under the Town and Country Planning Act of 1947 operated for two decades without significant change. During this time the system proved its value, but it would be surprising if what was appropriate for the mid-1940s was equally relevant to the 1970s. Furthermore, not only had the tempo of social and economic change increased but also the system tended to develop its own rigidities. This was particularly the case with development plans. Unlike the 1932 Act 'schemes', they were intended to show only broad land-use allocations. But the definition of 'development plan' in the 1947 Act was a plan 'indicating the manner in which the local planning authority propose that land in their area should be used'. This, together with the way in which plans were mapped, led inexorably towards greater detail and precision. 'The plans have thus acquired the appearance of certainty and stability which is misleading since the primary use zonings may themselves permit a wide variety of use within a particular allocation, and it is impossible to forecast every land requirement over many years ahead.'[3] Above all:

it has proved extremely difficult to keep these plans not only up to date but forward looking and responsive to the demands of change. The result has been that they have tended to become out of date – in terms of technique in that they deal inadequately with transport and the interrelationship of traffic and land use; in factual terms in that they fail to take account quickly enough of changes in population forecasts, traffic growth and other economic and social trends; and in terms of policy in that they do not reflect more recent developments in the field of regional and urban planning. Over the years the plans have become more and more out of touch with emergent planning problems and policies, and have in many cases become no more than local land-use maps.[4]

In short, the system became out of tune with contemporary needs and forward thinking, and it was being bogged down in details and cumbersome procedures. The quality of planning suffered, and delays were beginning to bring the system into disrepute. As a result, public acceptability, which is the basic foundation of any planning system, was beginning to crumble.

It was within this context of thinking that the Planning Advisory Group was set up in May 1964 to review the broad structure of the planning system and, in particular, development plans. Their report, *The Future of Development Plans*, published in 1965, proposed a basic change which would distinguish between policy or strategic issues and detailed tactical issues. Only the former would be submitted for ministerial approval: the latter would be for local decisions within the framework of the approved policy.

For urban areas with populations over 50,000 a new type of 'urban plan' was proposed which concentrated on the broad pattern of future development and redevelopment, and dealt with the land use/ transport relationships in an integrated way, but which excluded the detailed land use allocations of the current town maps. Similarly for the counties, a new form of 'county map' was proposed which dealt with the distribution of population and employment, the major communications network, the main policies for recreation and conservation, green belts, and the general development policy for towns and villages.

These were to provide a coherent framework of planning policy and would be submitted for ministerial approval. Each would identify 'action areas' which would require comprehensive planning and on which action would be concentrated over a period of some ten years.

Local planning authorities would have power to prepare 'local plans', which would not be submitted for approval, but would conform with the policies laid down in the urban plan or county plan. These would serve as a guide to development control and a basis for the more positive aspects of environmental planning. The most significant of local plans would be those for the action areas. Ministerial approval of the action areas would be limited to the policy proposed, and the local planning authorities would prepare 'action area plans', which would provide the detailed basis for implementation.

These types of plans could not be produced by planning authorities acting in isolation: they needed to form part of a regional strategy and also of what was termed a sub-regional pattern. Here – assuming a continuation of the existing structure of local government – the regional context would be provided by the economic planning councils and boards:

> These are likely to be primarily concerned with creating the conditions for economic growth in some regions and controlling the pace of growth in others, within the framework of national economic planning. As a part of this process, they will have to be concerned with physical planning issues which are of regional significance, with the overall distribution of population and employment, green belt policy and any other limitations on growth in the conurbations. They must also encompass other physical factors of regional significance such as communications, water resources and major industrial projects; the economic implications of major development projects (motorways, docks, airports); and the impact of economic decisions on physical planning. It will consequently be necessary to associate local planning authorities with the regional planning process and to ensure that their development plans give effect to the intentions of the regional plan.[5]

THE NEW PLANNING SYSTEM

Following a White Paper published in 1967,[6] legislative effect to the proposals of the Planning Advisory Group was given by the Town and Country Acts of 1968 (for England and Wales) and 1969 (for Scotland). It is essential for an understanding of this legislation – and the difficulties which have arisen in its local implementation – that the assumptions upon which it was based be appreciated: it was predicated on the reorganisation of local government into unitary authorities, at least in so far as planning was concerned. In essence the concept was one of a single authority responsible for preparing a broad strategic structure plan, within the framework of which detailed local plans would be elaborated, and development control would be administered. We shall return to this after describing the provisions of the 1968 and 1969 Acts (which have now been consolidated in the Act of 1971 for England and Wales, and the Act of 1972 for Scotland).

STRUCTURE PLANS

Structure plans, which are prepared by county planning authorities in

The Legislative Framework

The Legislative Framework

England and Wales and by regional or general planning authorities in Scotland, have to be submitted for approval by the appropriate secretary of state. They consist of a written statement accompanied by 'diagrammatic illustrations' setting out and justifying broad land use policies (but not detailed land allocations) for the area, policies for the management of traffic and measures for the improvement of the physical environment. The legislation provides that the written statement *must*:

(a) formulate the local planning authority's policy and general proposals in respect of the development and other use of land in that area (including measures for the improvement of the physical environment and the management of traffic);
(b) state the relationship of those proposals to general proposals for the development and the other use of land in neighbouring areas which may be expected to affect that area; and
(c) contain such other matters as may be prescribed or as the secretary of state may in any particular case direct.

The term 'plan' is perhaps misleading, since it might be expected to involve a map; but there is to be no map. Unlike the previous development plans (which required county and town maps, with related programme maps), the structure plan has to be accompanied only by 'diagrams, illustrations, and descriptive matter'. This is a change of no small significance: on the contrary it represents a major break from the traditional physical design character of British planning.[7]

The plan has to 'have regard to current policies with respect to the economic planning and development of the region as a whole' and 'to the resources likely to be available' for its implementation. High ideals must therefore be tempered by the facts of life.

Of particular note is the character of the survey which is to precede the plan. Differences in the content and scope of the surveys required under the earlier and the new legislation highlight the major change in planning philosophy. The 1947 legislation was largely concerned with land use: 'a development plan means a plan indicating the manner in which a local planning authority propose that land in their area should be used'. The 'survey' required as a preliminary to this dealt predominantly with physical matters. Under the current legislation, emphasis is laid on major economic and social forces and on broad policies or 'strategies' for large areas. The 'survey' becomes a major part of the planning process. Unlike the earlier legislation, the Acts spell out the coverage of the survey. In the forefront are 'the principal physical and economic characteristics' of the area and, to the extent that they are relevant, of neighbouring areas as well. In formulating the structure plan, particular attention has to be paid 'to current policies with respect to the economic planning and development of the region as a whole' and to likely availability of resources. It is within this strategic framework that 'local plans' are to be drawn up. The structure plan is essentially a statement of general policy designed to channel major forces in socially and economically desirable directions.[8]

Another major change follows from this. Under the '1947 philosophy', a development plan had to be reviewed 'at least once every five years' and, for this purpose, fresh surveys had to be carried out. This proved totally impracticable for reasons already outlined. Under the new system, the 'survey' is a continuing operation. Though some authorities had already adopted this approach, the 1947 concept implied an assembly and interpretation of 'survey material' which was reviewed quinquennially and which led to an amendment of the development plan. The new concept sheds a mass of detail and focuses attention on the major trends: the continual review is designed to ensure that the strategy remains appropriate and adequate. The review relates essentially to the survey; when the continuing review indicates that the structure plan is in need of alteration, the local planning authority will take the initiative of drawing up a new plan. Alternatively, the secretary of state can direct an authority to submit proposals for an alteration to their structure plan if he regards it as necessary in view of, for instance, major proposals in another area which will have an impact in the authority's area.

There is another significant difference in the wording of the requirement for a survey in the new Act. Whereas the earlier Acts required a local authority to 'carry out' a survey, the new legislation refers to the duty to *institute* a survey. This change was deliberately designed to facilitate the employment of consultants, particularly by local planning authorities who were short of the necessary skilled staff.

Increasingly the central department has stressed the importance for county planning authorities 'to concentrate on issues of key structural importance and their inter-relationships'.[9] At the same time 'unnecessary elaboration' has to be avoided:

> It is, in particular, no part of the responsibility placed upon authorities to prepare material solely to equip them to deal with all arguments which may possibly be advanced at the examination in public.[10]

With the experience that has been gained with structure plans, the DoE has been able to spell out with greater clarity the functions which a structure plan must serve. Circular 4/79 lists these as follows:

(*a*)   to state and justify the county planning authority's policies and general proposals for the development and other use of land in the area concerned (including measures for the improvement of the physical environment and the management of traffic). It should therefore provide guidance for development and development control on matters of structural importance. Structural matters:

(i) either (a) affect the whole or a substantial part of the structure plan area; or (b) influence the development of the area in a significant way; and

(ii) are proposals of the county planning authority which are subject to statutory approval by the Secretary of State;

(b) to interpret national and regional policies in terms of physical and environmental planning for the area concerned. National and regional policies tend to be primarily economic and social. The structure plan is the stage in the planning system when these policies are integrated with the economic, social and environmental policies of the area and expressed in terms of the effect on land use, the environment and the transport system; and

(c) to provide the framework for local plans, which then in turn provide more definitive guidance for development and development control.[11]

Hopefully, this advice is stemming the tendency for structure plans to be replete with generalities of a motherhood nature and vague aims which (to quote Layfield, as Inspector on the Greater London Development Plan Inquiry) 'do not mean anything because they can mean anything to anyone'.[12]

ACTION AREAS

Structure plans 'indicate' action areas where major change, by development, redevelopment or improvement, may be expected. This, ideally, involves more than simply picking out areas where the local authority thinks that action is needed. The intention is that the survey will identify and outline problems which require action; the written statement of the structure plan will discuss these problems, determine priorities and indicate areas where action is required not only on a comprehensive basis, but also at an early date. It will also discuss the nature of the required action, its extent and its feasibility in financial terms.

Action areas, it should be noted, are *indicated*, not *defined*. This deliberate wording was chosen for two reasons. First, if the boundaries of an action area were to be defined precisely and be subject (as part of the structure plan) to ministerial approval, this would involve the very thing which the new system is designed to avoid: detailed consideration by the department and the embodiment of inflexible proposals in a statutory document. Secondly, it was thought likely that it would intensify the problems of planning blight. If boundaries were drawn on a map they would most probably have to be redrawn when more detailed plans were prepared. Thus, some people who thought they would be affected would find that they had been misled, and others who thought they would not be affected would find that they were in fact within an action area. Objections would be made to a structure plan on the basis of individual interests rather than on the basis of the general nature of the proposals.

In short, the definition of an action area would be foreign to the essential concept underlying the structure plan – that it deals with general issues in broad terms; it is a policy document, not a physical design plan. Fundamentally it is a matter of words and diagrams, not of maps.

Once 'adequate publicity' has been given to a structure plan (a matter which is dealt with in Chapter 12) it is submitted to the secretary of state (who may approve it in whole or in part and with or without modifications and reservations; or reject it). Objections can be made, as with the old development plans, but instead of a local public inquiry, there is an 'examination in public'. This is concerned, not with the hearing of objections from property owners and others whose interests are affected by the structure plan, but much more broadly with the major policies which are enshrined in the plan. (This is discussed further below.)

.

LOCAL PLANS

Local plans were conceived as detailed elaborations of the broad policies incorporated in a structure plan and approved by the secretary of state. They consist of a written statement, a map on an ordnance survey base, together with 'diagrams, illustrations and descriptive matter'. Local plans have four main functions:

(*a*)   to develop the policy and general proposals of the structure plan and to relate them to precise areas of land;
(*b*)   to provide a detailed basis for development control;
(*c*)   to provide a detailed basis for co-ordinating the development and other use of land; and
(*d*)   to bring local and detailed planning issues before the public.[13]

There are three types of local plan: district plans, action area plans and subject plans. A district plan is concerned with the detailed planning of an area of substantial size 'where the factors in local planning need to be studied and set out in a comprehensive way'. They typically relate to the whole of a small town or a major sector of a larger one.

An action area plan deals with an area subject to 'intensive change by development, redevelopment or improvement by public authorities or private enterprise, or a combination of these methods and agencies'. Action areas replace the comprehensive development areas (CDAs) of the 1947 legislation.

A subject plan, as its name suggests, deals with specific aspects of planning such as conservation, housing, or landscaping. They are called by the name of the 'subject' to which they relate.

The most radical feature of a local plan is that at no time does it require to be approved by the secretary of state (though he has the power to direct that a local plan 'shall not have effect' unless he approves it: this is a reserve power intended to be used only in the exceptional case). The rationale for this (originally) was that a local plan would be prepared within the framework of a structure plan; and since structure plans would be approved by the secretary of state, local authorities could safely be left to the detailed elaboration of local plans. This went to the very kernel of the philosophy underlying the new legislation – that the department should be concerned only with strategic issues, and that local responsibility in local matters should become a reality.[14]

There were (and remain) two additional safeguards. First, the local authority are required to give 'adequate publicity' to their proposals *before* they are included in a local plan, and to give 'adequate opportunity' for the making of representations on their proposals. In these and similar ways public participation is actually written into the legislation. Second (with one important difference), the normal statutory procedure applies for the deposit of plans, the making of objections and the holding of a hearing or inquiry by an independent inspector and the publication of the inspector's report. The important difference from the traditional procedure is that the inspector reports to the local authority, not to the secretary of state. This follows, of course, from the principle that the local plan is a local authority, not a central authority, matter. It is clear that public participation is more than a desirable adjunct to the new system – it is an essential feature. If public participation fails, so will the system. (This issue is discussed, within a wider context, in the final chapter of this book.)

These two 'safeguards' remain intact following significant amendments made necessary by the particular character of local government reorganisation – which was very different from that envisaged when the new planning system was introduced. Indeed, as a result of these amendments they have become of greater importance. It is, however, now possible for a local plan to be adopted in advance of the approval of a structure plan.

EXPEDITED PROCEDURE FOR LOCAL PLANS

Unlike the English Act, the Town and Country Planning (Scotland) Act 1977 enables a Scottish planning authority to adopt (that is, to approve) a local plan where there is not yet an approved structure plan. Previously they were required to *prepare* a local plan, but could not *adopt* it unless it conformed generally with an approved structure plan. It followed that if there was no approved structure plan there could be no adoption of a local plan. This was particularly inhibiting in areas where action on urgent local planning problems could not await completion of the structure plan process, for example, in areas of 'oil-related expansion' and in the decaying inner cities.[15]

A similar provision was made for England and Wales in the Inner Urban Areas Act 1978 but this was specifically concerned with designated inner areas. The 1980 Local Government, Planning and Land Act, however, extends the provision generally under what is termed 'expedited procedure'. This change points to a basic problem of the structure and local planning system (and the two-tier system of local government which is operating it). It seems clear that the complexity of structure plans, the separation of structure and local plan-making and the time involved in both are leading to precisely the same difficulties as beset the former development plan system.

There are differences between the position in England and Wales and that in Scotland, and thus Scotland is more easily discussed separately.

LOCAL GOVERNMENT REORGANISATION AND THE NEW PLANNING SYSTEM IN ENGLAND AND WALES

As already noted, the new planning system[16] was devised in advance of local government reorganisation, and was based on the assumption that a single authority would be responsible for both structure planning and local planning. The 1972 Local Government Act, however, established two main types of local authority and divided these functions between them. Thus, while counties are responsible for broad planning strategy (structure planning), districts are independently responsible for local planning (and most matters of planning control). This division has necessitated a series of complex statutory provisions for redefining the respective roles of the two types of authority, particularly since the government's intention was that 'the reorganised system should everywhere be based on two forms of operational authorities: [the government] do not see the relationship between the two as implying that some authorities are answerable to others'.[17] In short, a system which was originally conceived as a unitary one had to be divided into two parts which would be as clearly differentiated from each other as possible. Before outlining how this has been done, it is relevant to describe more fully the original conception.

Under the 1968 Act, the new-style development plans were conceived as a two-part process: the purpose of a structure plan was to provide a broad strategic framework for the preparation of local plans; and local plans had to 'conform generally' to an approved structure plan. Since the same authority was to be responsible for both plans, there was no need to make legislative provision to ensure that a local plan did in fact 'conform generally', or even to spell out what this meant. Moreover, since this was the case, the secretary of state, having approved the structure plan, could safely leave the detailed elaboration of its policies at the local level to the (same) local authority *without the necessity of further approval.*

Clearly, once the responsibility for local plans is allocated to a different authority, this concept breaks down, since the districts may have very different ideas from the counties on the way in which the general policies in a structure plan are to be elaborated in their areas. The scope for conflict is very great, particularly since district authorities are independent political entities who are not subservient to the county. Furthermore, to the extent that districts are responsible for local plans, there is an inevitable temptation for counties to formulate their 'policy and general proposals' in greater detail than would be the case if there were no division of functions. In this way they can keep a tighter rein on the districts. But, of course, this is quite foreign to the original concept and, as already pointed out, the DoE are increasingly stressing that counties should concentrate on those issues which are of key structural importance to the area concerned, and their interrelationships.

Whether because of this good advice or because of the heavy load of work, the situation does appear to be changing. Barras and Broadbent note:

> During the 10 years since the initial legislation two changes have particularly affected methods of plan preparation. Firstly, whereas the scope of Structure Plans was initially interpreted by local authorities as very broad and all-embracing, the sheer volume of work required to produce such a plan has forced authorities to become increasingly selective. Thus while the original Development Plan Manual defined the scope of the plan as '. . . the social, economic and physical systems of an area, so far as they are subject to planning control or influence . . .', the subsequent Circular 98/74 stresses a selective concentration on the 'core' issues of employment, housing and transport, plus '. . . those (other) issues which are of key structural importance to the area concerned . . .'. This advice has been further refined in Circular 55/77, emphasising issues which 'may involve the study of several topics'. Secondly, whereas the early plans tended to focus on economic and population growth, and the spatial allocation of this growth, recent plans have been much more concerned with problems such as economic decline, unemployment, poor housing and the regeneration of inner city

areas. This is partly because of the current economic crisis and partly because some of the later plans have been produced by the larger conurbation metropolitan counties.[18]

DEVELOPMENT PLAN SCHEMES

The problem has been further compounded by the delays in the preparation of structure plans (itself due in part to the departure from the original concept of 'broad strategies'): these delays – and the necessity of consultations with the districts – have resulted in a complex and difficult web of political relationships. Shortages of staff (for a system which has multiplied the number of planning authorities) have added to the difficulties. Certainly, planning cannot be neatly divided between 'county strategy' and 'district tactics'. Statutory provisions requiring counties to consult districts on structure plans, or to certify that a local plan conforms to an approved structure plan, and such like, are legalistic devices which are of far less importance than the working relationships which are established between counties and districts. These working relationships, by their very nature, must be a matter for local authorities to devise. Nevertheless, the Local Government Act provides for a specific procedure 'designed to promote effective co-operation in the planning field and to minimise delay, dispute and duplication'. This is the requirement for the preparation of a 'development plan scheme'. Following consultations between the county and its constituent districts, a document must be prepared (and submitted to the secretary of state) setting out the allocation of responsibility and the programme for the preparation of local plans.

This has been a matter of considerable controversy. Theoretically, it provides a legal opportunity for a county council to seize the power to undertake responsibility for local plans (though the district could appeal to the secretary of state). But the objective is precisely the opposite: to secure a constructive and sensible relationship in plan-making between counties and districts which is appropriate to individual circumstances.

It might have been expected that, since local plans are now to be prepared by an authority different from that which is responsible for the structure plan, tighter provisions would have been introduced to ensure that local plans 'conform' with the policies set out in a structure plan. Not so: indeed, the opposite has happened. The original legislative provisions sensibly allowed a local planning authority (envisaged, it must be stressed, as a unitary authority) to prepare a local plan at the same time as a structure plan was being undertaken. But, with the binary system, since it was inconceivable that districts should do no plan preparation until the county structure plans had been approved, this provision has been carried over to allow districts to prepare local plans while the county is preparing its structure plan.

This has now been taken much further by the 'expedited procedure' for the *adoption* of local plans in advance of the approval of a structure plan.

The formal requirements of a development control scheme are that it must:

(*a*)   designate the authority by whom each local plan is to be prepared;

(*b*)   specify the title, nature and scope of each local plan;

(*c*)   specify the area to which each plan is to apply;

(*d*)   set out a programme for the preparation of local plans;

(*e*)   where appropriate, indicate the relationship between the local plans; and

(*f*)   specify any local plan to be prepared concurrently with the structure plan.[19]

The arrangements, however, are flexible and can be changed to accommodate changing circumstances.

CONTENT OF PLANS

Some account has already been given of the intended content of plans – and, in the case of structure plans, of their changing character. Given the enormous variety in plans it is difficult to generalise. Some are highly technical, others are legalistic, and some read like jolly public relations documents. Barras and Broadbent noted that some authorities, such as Merseyside and West Yorkshire, 'are using their structure plans as an advocacy statement of general social and economic development policies' and as a case for more Exchequer funds.[20] However, 'in direct contrast, DoE is requiring authorities to strike out all policies that are not land use policies'.[21] Barras and Broadbent comment that 'the future evolution of the system will depend on which of these opposing views prevails, with the issues of most concern being the role of resources, the relation of the structure plan to shorter-term capital programmes, and plan implementation and review'.

A study of Welsh structure plans, by Ian Bracken and David Hume, came to a dismal conclusion:

The present development plans system is now twelve years old. Structure Plans have taken much longer to prepare than was originally envisaged, and many commentators are now concerned that the present system has inherited many of the problems and disadvantages which characterised the old planning system. Indeed it may give rise to new problems. The optimism and faith evident in the late sixties for this novel system of flexible strategic planning appears now to have largely evaporated, and the main concern among Structure Planners is now more a pragmatic one, namely the satisfactory completion and approval of their Plans. The concept of planning as an on-going, monitored and adaptive process has now fallen second to the more immediate desire of winning approval from the Secretary of State. In this sense, 'end-state' planning is still alive and well in Britain.[22]

Less study has been made of local plans, though note should be taken of Patsy Healey's wide review. It is interesting to note her comment that the official role of local plans is under challenge from several directions:

> Many local authorities and the planners who work for them are seeking to relate local plans to integrated local authority approaches to policy making and implementation. Planners are also often critical of the relevance of the local plan, with its many procedural complications, to local land use and development problems. In effect, they are often asking for a local plan with stronger powers and with more local discretion in using them. Developers, on the other hand, have been calling for clarity, consistency and quick decisions from the planning system, given that they have to put up with it in the first place. The public, meanwhile, if interested in local plans at all, often seem to me to see them as a general vehicle for solving local problems and/or for keeping out unwanted development.[23]

THE NEW SYSTEM IN SCOTLAND

The new system in Scotland[24] differs in several significant ways from that south of the Border. Some may be attributed to the much more thorough-going nature of the Scottish local government reorganisation; others may legitimately be attributed to a canny move to avoid some of the difficulties of the English system.

The three major changes in planning legislation are the introduction of 'regional reports', an amendment of the mandatory provisions relating to structure plans and a provision under which local plans are required to be prepared 'as soon as practicable'.

REGIONAL REPORTS

Some of the Scottish regions are far larger than is appropriate for a structure plan. Nevertheless, there is a need for a policy plan to cover the whole of the area. This need is met by the innovation of the 'regional report'. But the opportunity has been taken to make this a flexible feature of the new planning system. Though it may indeed relate to the whole of a region, the legislation enables it to be used to serve a variety of purposes. It may be used to provide a basis of discussion between the secretary of state and a region about general development policy; it may provide a basis of guidance for the preparation or review of structure plans; and, in the absence of a structure plan, it may serve as a guide to district planning authorities and developers on planning policies. A regional report may cover the whole or part of a region. Moreover, it may be restricted in its scope to particular issues.

In striking contrast to structure plans, there is no formal procedure for the preparation, submission, or approval of a regional report. The only requirements are that a regional report shall be based on a survey, that affected local authorities shall be consulted, that it shall be submitted to the secretary of state (who shall 'make observations' on it) and that it shall be published (together with the secretary of state's observations).

Though the secretary of state does not formally approve or amend a regional report, planning authorities are required, in their planning practice, to 'take account' of both the report and the secretary of state's 'observations'.

The secretary of state can also direct a regional or planning authority to submit a regional report and, in default, prepare a regional report himself.

STRUCTURE PLANS FOR PARTS OF AN AREA

As originally envisaged, structure plans were to be single plans covering the whole area of the authority responsible for their preparation Though there was provision for a structure plan to be submitted by instalments, the assumption was that these would eventually build up to a single plan which would then be kept up to date as a whole. This concept was radically changed by provisions introduced in the 1973 Local Government (Scotland) Act, which enabled regional and general planning authorities to prepare structure plans for different parts of their areas. The intention is that the regions should be divided into areas which, by virtue of their geography and cohesion in terms of socio-economic structure and the pattern of communications, form natural structure plan units. Moreover, it is no longer necessary for all parts of a region to be covered by structure plans.

The significance of this change is more striking when it is appreciated that, with the introduction of regional reports, there are three (not two) levels of planning: regional, structure and local. It is unlikely that all three will be necessary in all areas. It is much more likely that regional reports and structure plans will be seen as alternatives. At the least, there will be the possibility of a flexible approach which the English system denies.

Given this loosening up of the procedures for large-scale planning it is not surprising that changes have also been made in relation to local plans.

Local plans were conceived as detailed elaborations of proposals sketched out as matters of broad policy in a structure plan. This concept was abandoned in the 1973 Act: 'every general and district planning authority shall, as soon as practicable, prepare local plans for all parts of their district'. Thus local plans are now mandatory and are to be prepared as soon as possible and thus (probably typically) in advance of a structure plan.[25]

The only qualification to this is in cases where a structure plan (or a regional report) is under way and would have a significant impact on the area to be covered by a proposed local plan. Effect is given to this by requiring a district planning authority to obtain the consent of the regional planning authority to the preparation of a local plan. This consent is not to be unreasonably withheld, and the district will have the right of appeal to the secretary of state. (In line with the current emphasis on avoidance of formal proceedings, there would not be a public inquiry: the secretary of state would decide the matter as simply as possible and his decision would be final.) This procedure, of course, does not apply to general planning authorities since they are responsible for regional, structure and local plans.

Local plans remain the responsibility of the districts (except in the areas of general planning authorities) and therefore are subject to 'approval' only by the authorities who prepare them – unless they are 'called in'. This may be done either by the secretary of state or by the regional planning authority. Again there is machinery for appeal but no public inquiry.

The 'call-in' power of regional authorities is a new one. The circumstances in which this can be used are set out in the 1973 Act and are:

(i)   when a local plan is urgently required to implement the provisions of an approved structure plan, and the district planning authority concerned have failed to adopt an appropriate local plan; *or*

(ii)   when the district or more than one district planning authority is likely to be affected by the local plan in question; *or*

(iii) when the local plan does not conform to a structure plan approved by the Secretary of State; *or*

(iv) when the implementation of the local plan will render unlikely the implementation of any other local plan relating to their district.

THE EXAMINATION IN PUBLIC

As already noted, structure plans are subject, not to a public inquiry, but to an 'examination in public'.[26] The distinction is that, whereas a public inquiry is concerned with the hearing of objections, the examination in public is an investigation of selected matters affecting the secretary of state's consideration of a structure plan. Though the rights of individuals to object to a structure plan (and the duty of the secretary of state to consider all objections) are maintained, there is no longer any right for objectors to present their case at an inquiry. The examination deals with only those matters which the secretary of state considers need examination in public. Moreover, he determines who shall participate in the examination (whether or not they have made objections or representations).

This is a major departure from traditional practice. Its rationale is far more than the negative one of avoiding lengthy, time-consuming and quasi-judicial public inquiries. It is related essentially to the basic purpose and character of a structure plan. A structure plan does not set out detailed proposals and, therefore, does not show how individual properties will be affected. It deals with broad policy issues: the examination in public focuses on these, and on alternatives to those set out in the plan. These include such matters as the future level and distribution of population and employment; transportation policies; and availability of resources for major proposals of the plan.

But the examination does not deal with all the key policy issues. Only those on which the secretary of state needs to be more fully informed by means of discussion at an examination are selected. In short, the examination is intended to assist the secretary of state in determining his views on the plan and in arriving at his decision.

The matters needing examination are most likely to arise from clashes between the proposals of a plan and those of a neighbouring area or wider regional and national policies. Additionally, major inconsistencies within the plan or issues on which there is unsettled controversy may be the subject of examination.

Circular 4/79 lists the following 'questions in which the Secretary of State is interested':

1. *National Policies and General Considerations*
Does the plan correctly interpret national policies (as evidenced by White Papers, department circulars, etc)?

Are the demands on financial resources controlled by Government departments in scale with what available advice indicates is likely to be forthcoming? Are the demands on other resources realistic?

Does the plan adequately fulfill its function in the development plan system, e.g. is the plan likely to be useful as a framework for local plans and for relevant aspects of development control?

Is the plan in a form likely to facilitate monitoring and review?

2 *Regional Policies and Considerations*

Is the plan compatible with the guidelines of accepted regional strategies and policies?

3 *Policies of Neighbouring Planning Authorities*

Is the plan compatible with the structure plans for adjoining areas?

4 *Conflicts Within and Between the Policies and General Proposals of the Plan*

Does the plan contain adequate reasoned justification for the policies and general proposals put forward?

Are the policies and proposals put forward in the plan consistent with each other and related to the issues identified by the authority?

5 *Controversy*

How well does the plan deal with points which have aroused substantial controversy?

The issues selected are published in advance (together with a list of those selected to participate). There is an opportunity for written comments on these to be sent to the department but, although the secretary of state has power to add to the list of issues or participants, major changes are not envisaged since the selection will have been made on the basis of the contribution which the examination of the selected matters can make to his decision on the plan.

The examination is carried out typically by a panel with an independent chairman. The chairman has the discretion (both before and during an examination) to invite additional participants.

This new procedure clearly gives rise to difficulties, particularly since there is likely to be considerable criticism from any objectors who are excluded from participation in the examination. In this connection it is important to stress that the examination is envisaged as only one part of the process by which the secretary of state considers the plan, while the plan itself is only part of the total process. Of crucial importance in this process is the extent to which effective citizen participation has taken place in the preparation of the plan. This is a statutory requirement and, in submitting a structure plan to the secretary of state, a local planning authority must include a statement on publicity, public participation and consultations. The selection of matters for examination will be closely linked to the effectiveness of the public participation which has been achieved. The hope is that public participation will highlight some of the crucial issues on which alternative policies need to be examined.

A detailed study by the Birmingham Institute of Judicial Administration has recommended against the prior selection of issues and for having the examination in public earlier in the structure plan process (at the early draft plan stage). The important conclusion, however, is that 'the examination in public occupies a central position within the structure planning process, providing a forum for the expression of a wide variety of opinion on strategic planning issues. The provisions for public participation and consultation during the preparation of structure plans cannot be regarded as an adequate substitute for this type of formal, public hearing.'[27]

REFERENCES AND FURTHER READING: CHAPTER 3

1 *Town and Country Planning Bill 1947: Explanatory Memorandum*, Cmd 7006 (HMSO, 1947), p. 5.
2 See DoE Circular 96/75, *The Town and Country Planning (Development Plans) Direction 1975* (HMSO, 1975).
3 Planning Advisory Group, *The Future of Development Plans* (HMSO, 1965), p. 5. This is the 'traditional' planning explanation in line with 'the heavy design bias in British town planning'. (J. Jowell, 'The limits of urban planning', *Current Legal Problems 1977*, p. 66.) Jowell quotes Foley's comment on British planners: 'They viewed the metropolitan community as having a special physical form that could be grasped and reduced to *maplike* graphic presentation.' (D. Foley, *Controlling London's Growth: Planning the Great Wen 1940–1960*, University of California Press, 1963, p. 53.) By contrast, Jowell continues: 'A jurisprudential analysis . . . would stress the factors militating towards certainty, predictability and accountability . . . The 1947 Act resulted in a rule-model, occasioned by many factors, all of them perfectly understandable in terms of human behaviour and organisational behaviour. Developers preferred to know exactly where they stood; they could plan thus with greater certainty. The public preferred to know "the rules of the game" so that deals could not be struck in disregard of the public interest, and so that "like" cases would be treated alike. And the bureaucracy, perhaps spurred on by a "design bias", were, as all bureaucracy, content to take refuge behind the "rule" which shielded them from public pressure, and allowed routine handling of applications for planning permission.'
4 Planning Advisory Group, op. cit., p. 6.
5 Planning Advisory Group, op. cit., pp. 10–11.
6 White Paper, *Town and Country Planning*, Cmnd 3333 (HMSO, 1967).
7 See J. Jowell, op. cit., who comments (p. 68): 'From a legal perspective, we can identify two main features of the change in the planning structure. First, a move away from plans as a set of interlocking rules to plans as statements of general policies. (No maps, nothing too specific, is required.) Plans as laws thus become less specific, more general as guides to human behaviour. Secondly, a broadening of the scope of policies which may be contained in plans. Land uses alone were appropriate before. Now, in the realisation that land uses cannot be controlled in isolation, other matters are listed in the Act and Regulations. These include the distribution of population and employment, housing, education, and any other relevant matters.'
8 Jowell and Noble have commented that 'the first crop of structure plans seems to fall short of their initial expectations. A firm ministerial hand has insisted that non land-use criteria be excluded as policies and concrete proposals.' J. Jowell and D. Noble, 'Planning as social engineering: notes on the first English structure plans', *Urban Law and Policy*, vol. 3 (1980), p. 311.
9 DoE Circular 4/79, *Memorandum on Structure and Local Plans* (HMSO, 1979), p. 1, para. 2. (Circular 4/79 replaced Circular 55/77.)
10 op. cit., p. 13, para. 2.8.
11 op. cit., p. 12, para. 2.1.
12 *Greater London Development Plan: Report of the Panel of Inquiry* (HMSO, 1973), p. 27. Quoted by J. Jowell, op. cit., p. 68. cf. the 'Primary Aim' of the Dudley County Borough Structure Plan: 'To provide the maximum opportunity for individuals to choose their own conception of the "better life"', or the 'Primary Objective' of the Teeside Structure Plan: 'To promote the physical and mental well-

being of each individual in the community.' (Quoted by J. Jowell and D. Noble), op. cit., p. 297.

13 DoE Circular 4/79, *Memorandum on Structure and Local Plans*, p. 29, para. 3.1.

14 Inquiries into local plans are subject to a code of practice issued by the Department of the Environment in 1977: *Local Plans: Public Local Inquiries – A Guide to Procedure*. (Like the code of practice for structure plan examinations in public, this is 'freely available', but is published by the Department of the Environment and is not available through HMSO.)

Of particular significance is the fact that the secretary of state has ruled that, 'for the time being', he will appoint all inspectors for local plan inquiries. The inspector continues to report to the local authority, however, not to the secretary of state.

For Scotland, the SDD have issued Circular 28/1976, *Development Plans*, Planning Advice Notes, 14: *The Approach to Development Planning*, 15: *Structure Plans – Form and Content*, and 16: *Local Plans – Form and Content* (all November 1976); Circular 19/1977, *National Planning Guidelines*; and 30/1977, *Development Planning and Development Control*.

15 SDD Circular 16/1977, *Town and Country Planning (Scotland) Act 1977* (Scottish Development Department, 1977).

16 See generally, R. Buxton, 'Planning in the new local government world', *Journal of Planning and Environment Law*, 1974, pp. 60–72.

17 White Paper, *Local Government in England: Government Proposals for Reorganisation*, Cmnd 4584 (HMSO, 1971).

18 R. Barras and T. A. Broadbent, 'The analysis in English structure plans', *Urban Studies*, vol. 16 (1979), p. 2. See also D. L. Smith, 'The progress and style of structure planning in England: some observations', *Local Government Studies*, October 1974, pp. 21–34; J. B. McLoughlin and J. Thornley, *Some Problems in Structure Planning: A Literature Review* (Centre for Environmental Studies, 1972); and M. Drake *et al.*, *Aspects of Structure Planning in Britain* (Centre for Environmental Studies, 1975).

19 See DoE Circular 4/79, op. cit., p. 31, para. 3.16.

20 R. Barras and T. A. Broadbent, op. cit., pp. 2–4. See also R. Barras, 'A resource allocation framework for strategic planning', *Town Planning Review*, vol. 49 (1978), pp. 296–305; and R. Barras, *Current Issues in Structure Planning* (Centre for Environmental Studies, 1978).

21 On this point see J. Jowell and D. Noble, op. cit., pp. 293–317. As an illustration, the following policies were deleted from the Dudley Structure Plan:

As appropriate, either allow owners of unfit houses to demolish them or make them fit: or purchase unfit houses and then improve or demolish them.
Carry out regular inspections of the housing stock in order to ascertain its condition.
Make full use of the procedures for enforcing repairs and give financial assistance for carrying them out.
Declare and implement General Improvement Areas where appropriate.
Establish and adopt a programme for the improvement of Council Housing.
Enter into agreements with occupiers not wishing to improve such that occupiers are rehoused and their dwellings are purchased, improved and sold or let after improvement.

22 I. Bracken and D. Hume, *An Analysis of Welsh Structure Plans*, University of Wales Institute of Science and Technology, Department of Town Planning, Papers in Planning Research 5 (University of Wales, 1980), p. 96. For a Scottish view on 'The future for development planning', see the article with that title by Urlan Wannop, *The Planner*, vol. 67 (1981), pp. 14–18.

23 P. Healey, *Statutory Local Plans: Their Evolution in Legislation and Administrative Interpretation*, Oxford Polytechnic, Department of Town Planning, Working Paper 36 (Oxford Polytechnic, 1979). This study also contains a most useful bibliography. (See also her later paper, *The Implementation of Selective Restraint*

Policy: Approaches to Land Release for Local Needs in the South East, Oxford Polytechnic, Department of Town Planning, Working Paper 45, Oxford Polytechnic, 1980.)

24 Generally see E. Young, *The Law of Planning in Scotland* (Hodge, Glasgow, 1978). See also M. Wilkinson and B. Howat, *Regional Reports and Structure Plans in Scotland* (The Planning Exchange, Glasgow, 1977); and *Scottish Planning Law and Practice*, published three times a year by the Planning Exchange (186 Bath Street, Glasgow G2 4HG).

25 Technically, a plan could not be 'adopted' before approval of the structure plan. This requirement was abolished in 1977. See SDD Circular 16/1977, *Town and Country Planning (Scotland) Act 1977* (Scottish Development Department, 1977).

Though the legislation requires all parts of a district to be covered by local plans, 'the areas with greatest need for new plans must be tackled first. Other areas can wait: in areas of low priority "as soon as practicable" could mean several years.' SDD Circular 28/1976, *Development Plans* (Scottish Development Department, 1976), para. 4.1.

26 See Department of the Environment booklet, *Structure Plans: The Examination in Public* (DoE, 1973) (amended by Circular 39/78, DoE, 1978); and Scottish Development Department, *Code of Practice for the Examination in Public of Structure Plans* (Scottish Development Department, 1977).

27 'Structure planning and the examination in public', evidence to the Environment Sub-Committee of the Expenditure Committee, *Eighth Report from the Expenditure Committee, Session 1976-77, Planning Procedures* (HMSO, 1977), Vol. 2, p. 596. See also L. Bridges and C. Vielba, *Structure Plan Examinations in Public: A Descriptive Analysis*; and C. A. Vielba, *A Survey of Those Taking Part in Two Structure Plan Examinations in Public* (University of Birmingham, Institute of Judicial Administration, 1976); L. T. Bridges, 'The approval of structure plans - the Staffordshire case', *Journal of Planning and Environment Law*, 1978, pp. 599-609; J. Dunlop, 'The examination in public of structure plans: an emerging procedure', *Journal of Planning and Environment Law*, 1976, pp. 8-17; and A. Samuels, 'Structure plan examination in public', *Journal of Planning and Environment Law*, 1975, pp. 125-38.

Chapter 4

THE CONTROL OF DEVELOPMENT

THE SCOPE OF CONTROL

With certain exceptions, all development requires the prior approval of the local planning authority. The authority have considerable discretion in this matter. Though they must 'have regard to the provisions of the development plan' they may take 'any other material considerations' into account.[1] Indeed they can approve a proposal which 'does not accord with the provisions of the plan'.[2]

The planning decisions of the authority can be one of three kinds: unconditional permission, permission 'subject to such conditions as they think fit', or refusal. The practical scope of these powers is discussed in a later section. Here it is necessary merely to stress that there is a right of appeal to the secretary of state against conditional permissions and refusals. If the action of the authority is thought to be *ultra vires* there is also a right of appeal to the courts. Furthermore, planning applications which raise issues which are of major importance, or are of a particular technical nature, can be 'called in' for ministerial decision.

Development control necessarily involves some procedure for enforcement. This is provided by 'enforcement notices' under which an owner who carries out development without permission or in breach of conditions can be compelled to 'undo' the development – even if this involves the demolition of a new building. A 'stop notice' can also be used in conjunction with an enforcement notice to put a rapid stop to the carrying out or continuation of development which is in breach of planning control.

These are very strong powers, and clearly it is important to establish the meaning of 'development', particularly since the term has a legal meaning far wider than in ordinary language.

THE DEFINITION OF DEVELOPMENT

In brief, development is 'the carrying out of building, engineering, mining or other operations in, on, over or under land, or the making of any material change in the use of any buildings or other land'.[3] There are some legal niceties attendant upon this definition with which it is fortunately not necessary to deal in the present outline. Some account of the breadth of the definition is, nevertheless, needed. 'Building operations', for instance, include rebuilding operations, structural alterations of or additions to buildings and – somewhat curiously – 'other operations normally undertaken by a person carrying on business as a builder'; but maintenance and improvement works which affect only the interior of the building or which do not materially affect the external appearance of the building are specifically excluded. The demolition of a building does not *of itself* constitute development, though, of course, it may form part of a building operation, or lead to the making of a material change in the use of the land upon which it stood. Moreover, as is discussed later, there is special protection for historic buildings.

The second half of the definition introduces quite a different concept: development here means not a physical operation, but a change in the *use* of a piece of land or a structure. The change has to be 'material', that is, substantial – a concept which it is clearly difficult to define; and which, indeed, is not defined in the Act. A change in *kind* (for example from a house to a shop) is material, but a change in *degree* is material only if the change is very substantial. For instance, the fact that lodgers are taken privately in a family dwelling-house does not of itself constitute a material change so long as the main use of the house remains that of a private residence. On the other hand, the change from a private residence with lodgers to a declared guest-house, boarding house or private hotel would be material. Difficulties arise with changes of use involving part of a building with secondary uses and with the distinction between a material change of use and a mere interruption.

Two changes of use are specifically declared in the legislation to be material. First, if a building previously used as a single dwelling-house is used as two or more dwelling-houses (thereby making decisions under the Rent Restriction Acts on what constitutes a 'separate dwelling' relevant to planning decisions).[4] Second, the deposit of refuse or waste material on land 'notwithstanding that the land is comprised in a site already used for that purpose, if either the superficial area of the deposit is thereby extended, or the height of the deposit is thereby extended and exceeds the level of the land adjoining the site'; in other words, the deposit of refuse or waste material always constitutes development unless the deposit is made in a hole – and the shape of the hole is important because though a hole can be filled to the level of the adjoining land the superficial area must not be increased.

This is by no means the end of the matter, but enough has been recorded to show the breadth of the definition of development and the technical complexities to which it can give rise. Reference must, nevertheless, be made to one further issue. Experience has shown that complicated definitions are necessary if adequate development control is to be achieved, but the same tortuous technique can be used to exclude matters over which control is not necessary. Apart from certain matters which are specifically declared not to constitute development (for example, internal alterations to buildings, works of road maintenance, or improvement carried out by a local highway authority within the boundaries of a road), and others which though possibly constituting development are declared not to require planning permission, there is provision for the secretary of state to make a Development Order specifying classes of 'permitted' development, and a Use Classes Order specifying groups of uses within which interchange is permissible.

The distinction between the Use Classes Order and the General Development Order is that the former lists changes of use which do not constitute development, while the latter lists activities which, though constituting development, do not require *ad hoc* permission. The distinction was of importance during the time when development charges were imposed, since if there was no 'development' then no development charge was payable, whereas development was, by definition, eligible for a charge. (In fact, however, exemption from development charge was specifically made for many of these permitted developments.) Those complexities are now mainly of historical interest and are not discussed further in this book.

THE USE CLASSES ORDER

To deal first with the latter: the Use Classes Order[5] prescribes classes of use within which change can take place without constituting development. Thus Class X is 'use as a wholesale warehouse or repository for any purpose', and Class XII is 'use as a residential or boarding school or residential college'. For some classes, particular uses which would otherwise fall into a category are specifically excluded: for example, Class I is 'use as a shop for any purpose except (i) a shop for the sale of hot food; (ii) a tripe shop; (iii) a shop for the sale of pet animals or birds; (iv) a cat's-meat shop; (v) a shop for the sale of motor vehicles'. As a result, to change a sweet shop into a book shop does not constitute development, but to change a shoe shop into a 'noxious trade' such as a tripe shop does. These categories, it should be stressed, refer only to changes of use – not to any building work. Furthermore, the Order gives no freedom to change from one class to another; whether such a change constitutes development depends on whether the change is 'material'. It should also be noted that in granting permission for a particular use a local planning authority may impose conditions restricting that use and thus prevent the changes in use allowed by the Order. For instance, a local planning authority may decide that an office of a special character might be allowed in a residential area but at the same time may not wish the premises to be available for any type of office use. Conditions could be imposed on the planning permission which would overrule the general permission given for such a change in use by the Use Classes Order (Class II is 'use as an office for any purpose').

THE GENERAL DEVELOPMENT ORDER

The General Development Order[6] gives the developer a little more freedom by listing classes of 'permitted development'. If a proposed development falls within these classes then no application for planning permission is necessary – the General Development Order itself constitutes the permission. The Order includes certain developments by public authorities and nationalised industries, the erection of agricultural buildings (other than dwelling-houses), and permits the change of use from a shop for the sale of hot food, a tripe shop, and so on (as listed in Class I of the Use Classes Order), to any other type of shop – but not, of course, the other way round.

Permissions given under this Order are not unqualified. Apart from a general limitation relating to development which 'requires or involves the formation, laying out or material widening of a means of access to an existing highway which is a trunk or classified road or creates an obstruction to the view of persons using any highway by vehicular traffic at or near any bend, corner, junction or intersection so as to be likely to cause danger to such persons', particular conditions are laid down for each of the different classes of development listed. Thus, under Class I, the enlargement or other alteration of a dwelling-house is permitted (including the building of a garage) subject to limitations of size and elevation.

This by no means complete account of 'development' is sufficient for present purposes. The cynic may perhaps be forgiven for commenting that the 'freedom' given by the Use Classes Order and the General Development Order is so hedged by restrictions, and frequently so difficult to comprehend (though he may note with relief that painting is not subject to control – unless it is 'for purpose of advertisement, announcement or direction') that it would be safer to assume that any operation constitutes 'development' and requires planning permission. The framers of the legislation have here been helpful. Application can be made to the local planning authority (either as part of an application for planning permission or as a separate application) for a 'determination' as to whether a proposed operation constitutes 'development' and if so, as to whether planning permission is required. Should the local planning authority determine that the proposals do constitute or involve development, they have to inform the applicant of grounds on which they have reached this decision and also his rights of appeal. Most planning decisions are administrative acts against which appeal lies only to the secretary of state, but in the case of a determination of whether planning permission is required, the question is a mixed one of fact and law: thus not only is there the normal right of appeal against the local authority's decision to the secretary of state, there is also a right of appeal against his decision to the High Court.

CONDITIONAL PERMISSIONS

A local planning authority can grant a planning permission subject to conditions.[7] This can be a very useful way of permitting development which would otherwise be undesirable. Thus residential development in an area liable to subsidence can be permitted subject to the condition that the foundations are suitably reinforced, or a garage may be approved in a residential area on condition that 'no panel beating or paint spraying is carried out, and the hours of business are kept within reasonable limits'. The local planning authority's power to impose conditions is a very wide one. The legislation allows them to grant permission subject to 'such conditions as they think fit' – but this does not mean 'as they please'. The conditions must be appropriate from a planning point of view: 'the planning authority are not at liberty to use their powers for an ulterior object, however desirable that object may seem to them to be in the public interest. If they mistake or misuse their powers, however *bona fide*, the court can interfere by declaration and injunction.'[8] Three types of condition are specifically referred to in the legislation:

(1) Conditions can be imposed for regulating the development or use of *any* land under the control of the applicant, whether or not it is the land to which the application relates, so long as there is a definite relationship between the object of the condition and the development permitted.
(2) A 'time condition' can be imposed on a permission. This is referred to in the legislation as 'permission granted for a limited period only'. Such a condition is particularly appropriate where the proposed development is undesirable on a long-term view, but there is no reason why a temporary permission should not be granted. This would occur where a local authority have definite plans for redevelopment in the near future.
(3) A condition can be imposed requiring operations to commence within a specified time. It should be borne in mind that planning permissions normally run with the land. This particular condition can be imposed where the planning proposals for the area will require substantial revision, but the degree of risk that the proposed development will conflict with these proposals is not sufficient to justify outright refusal.

Until the passing of the 1968 Act, there was no general time-limit within which development had to take place: unless a specific condition was imposed, planning permission development could take place at any time. The 1968 Act, however, made all planning permissions subject to a condition that development is begun within five years. If the work is not begun within this time-limit, the permission lapses. The secretary of state or the local planning authority can vary the period, and there is no bar to the renewal of permission after that period has elapsed (whether it be five years or more or less).

The purpose of this provision is to prevent the accumulation of unused permissions and to discourage the speculative landhoarder. (For this reason it applies to pre-1968 Act permissions as well as later ones.) Accumulated unused permissions could constitute a difficult problem for some local authorities: they create uncertainty and could make an authority reluctant to grant further permissions, which might result in, for example, too great a strain on public services. The provision is directed towards the bringing forward of development for which permission has been granted, and thus to enable new allocations of land for development to be made against a reasonably certain background of pending development.

The provision relates, however, only to the beginning of development and this apparently includes 'digging a trench or putting a peg in the ground'. But (if permission is not a pre-1968 Act one) the trench-digger may be brought up against a further provision: he may be served with a 'completion notice'. Such a notice states that the planning permission lapses after the expiration of a specified period (of not less than one year). Any work carried out after then becomes liable to enforcement procedures.

PLANNING AGREEMENTS, BARGAINING AND PLANNING GAIN

Under section 52 of the 1971 Town and Country Planning Act, local planning authorities have power to make 'agreements'. These 'Section 52 Agreements' have become the object of increasing contention, with local authorities seeing them as a means of 'bargaining' for 'planning gain', while developers, at the extreme, regard them as 'blackmail'.[9] A classic (or, more accurately, notorious) example was the Centre Point agreement under which a large increase in density was allowed in exchange for the planning gain of land for road purposes.[10]

Section 52 provides that:

A local planning authority may enter into an agreement with any person interested in land in their area for the purpose of restricting or regulating the development or use of the land, either permanently or during such period as may be prescribed by the agreement; and any such agreement may contain such incidental and consequential provisions (including provisions of a financial character) as appear to the local planning authority to be necessary or expedient for the purposes of the agreement.

Local authorities have had similar powers for many years (the origin was the 1932 Planning Act),[11] but it was not until the property boom of the early 1970s that they have become widely used.[12] Indeed, a number of authorities have taken 'the opportunity offered by the current preparation of the new statutory local plans to institutionalise negotiated planning control . . . the draft Westminster District Plan, for example, indicates unequivocally the council's intention to pursue certain planning goals through agreements, in addition to establishing certain minimum gains to be included in planning applications or to be secured through negotiated amendments to submitted applications'.[13] An action area plan for Fareham, Hampshire, similarly states that 'planning permission for development in the proposed areas will not be granted until . . . negotiations between developers and the local authority for financial contributions have been concluded'.[14]

The property boom was certainly a factor in the increase of bargaining: developers were pressing for planning permissions while local authorities were experiencing financial difficulties in providing the necessary infrastructure. Indeed, a 1973 White Paper,[15] after noting that 'the prospect of heavy expenditure on ancillary services often makes local authorities reluctant to give planning permission for housing on land which is otherwise ripe for development', proposed an extension of planning agreements and a compulsory infrastructure charge:

> The Government believes that we should now apply more widely the principle which underlies such agreements and that the developer should be required to pay for those publicly provided services which make the development feasible. The Government is therefore consulting the local authority associations and the housebuilding industry about provisions, to be included in early legislation, which will require developers to contribute towards the cost of services provided by public authorities in connection with the development of land with planning permission.[16]

This particular proposal was not carried further, but the ensuing legislation did strengthen the powers for making agreements.[17]

Agreements, however, extended far beyond the most generous definition of infrastructure. Moreover, some agreements have enabled local authorities to obtain 'gains' which could not legally be achieved through a condition.[18]

The crux of the matter is that attitudes on the character and scope of planning have changed. Social and economic factors now loom large and can, indeed, be seen as being of greater importance than purely land use matters – though the courts would not necessarily accept such a line of reasoning (as, for instance, when Lord Widgery held that the London Borough of Hillingdon could not impose a condition that the occupants of a private housing development should be people on the council's waiting list).[19] Additionally, 'the move from development plans to structure plans itself intends a move to flexible and broad criteria for decision, which in turn allows the decision-maker wide discretion and hence room for manoeuvre when resolving applications for planning permission'.[20]

The extent to which authorities can achieve gains depends, of course, on their bargaining power which in turn may be related to current (and local) economic conditions. The situation in London in 1974 was very different from that one year later in a northern authority who commented that 'getting a developer to build anything is, in our eyes, a planning gain'.[21]

The growth of planning agreements gives rise to a number of concerns. The ethics of bargaining are debatable; there is scope for unjustifiable coercion; and equal treatment as between applicants can be abandoned in favour of charging what the market will bear at any particular time. Additionally, bargaining is a closed, private activity which sits uneasily astride the current emphasis on open government and public participation.

The central government has paid surprisingly little attention to the issues involved. In Grant's words:

> There is a general awareness that the Department of the Environment has from time to time frowned upon the more extreme examples of bartering which have caught its attention, usually only through planning appeals, but has winked benevolently at many of the more sophisticated procedures now employed by planning authorities. Moreover, concepts of legality and ethics have tended in official statements to become confused, and somewhat vague utterances as to the types of transactions likely to be thought 'proper' by the Department have left authorities considerable leeway to make their own ethical judgements.[22]

Indeed, there is little by way of departmental guidance except in appeal decisions.[23] A very recent decision appears to reflect Mr Michael Heseltine's characteristically strong views: 'Refusal merely on the basis of wanting social infrastructure is not to be tolerated in a free society.'[24] A fuller and more analytical statement would be useful.[25]

CHARGING FOR PLANNING APPLICATIONS

> The Secretary of State may by regulations make such provision as he thinks fit for the payment of a fee of the prescribed amount to a local planning authority . . . in respect of an application made to them under the planning enactments for any permission, consent, approval, determination or certificate.

Thus does section 87 of the Local Government, Planning and Land Act 1980 make provision for charges for planning applications. This represents a marked break with planning traditions which have held (at least implicitly) that development control is of general communal benefit and directly analogous to other forms of public control for which no charges are made on individuals. In the words of the strongly worded policy statement of the Town and Country Planning Association:

Development control as an essential part of the planning system has no other purpose than to secure the right type of development in the right place in the interest of the community as a whole. It is the community as a whole, through legislation, that has decided that this regulatory activity is required and therefore, in our view, it should be the community as a whole that pays for this service and not individual applicants for planning permission.[26]

The Thatcher administration, on the other hand, 'do not believe that the community as a whole should continue to pay for all the sorts of things that it has paid for in the past . . . In the general review that has taken place to see where we can reduce spending from the public purse . . . we came to the conclusion that the cost of development control was an area where some part of the cost should be recovered.'[27]

The cost to local authorities of development control and enforcement was estimated (in 1980) at about £50 million a year: it is envisaged that the fees will recoup about £30 million.

The Bill provided additionally for fees for appeals but this was dropped in the face of widespread objections from both sides of the House.

Apart from issues of principle, perhaps the major practical objection put forward against charges is that it would lead to an increase in evasion: the incentive to undertake development without applying for planning permission would rise in line with the rate of charge (particularly for 'householder' types of development). Fears on this score were heightened by the stance being taken by the DoE on enforcement of planning controls: Circular 22/80 advised that 'this permissive power' should be used 'only where planning reasons clearly warrant such action, and there is no alternative to enforcement proceedings'.[28]

No doubt the fee structure will change over time, and a detailed schedule is therefore not appropriate. In brief, however, the initial scheme (taking effect from 1 April 1981) includes £40 per dwelling, £40 for every 75 square metres of floor space for commercial and industrial buildings, £40 for each tenth of a hectare for the erection of plant and machinery (all subject to a maximum of £2,000). For house extensions, shopfronts and such like, there is a flat fee of £20, and for changes of use and advertisement hoardings £40.[29] Disabled people applying for permission to improve access to, or the facilities of their homes, are exempt.[30]

ENFORCEMENT OF PLANNING CONTROL

If the machinery of planning control is to be effective, some means of enforcement is essential.[31] Under the prewar system of interim development control there were no such effective means. A developer could go ahead without applying for planning permission, or could even ignore a refusal of permission. He took the risk of being compelled to 'undo' his development (for example, demolish a newly built house) when – and if – the planning scheme was approved, but this was a risk which was often worth taking. And if the development was inexpensive and lucrative (for example, a petrol station or a grey-hound racing track) the risk was virtually no deterrent at all. This flaw in the prewar system was remedied by the strengthening of enforcement provisions.

Development undertaken without permission is not an offence in itself; but ignoring an enforcement notice is – there is a maximum fine following conviction of £1,000 and a penalty of £50 for each day during which the requirements of the notice remain unfulfilled.

These are very drastic powers; but there are a number of safeguards. In the first place, a local authority can serve an enforcement notice only 'if they consider it expedient to do so having regard to the provisions of the development plan and to any other material considerations'; in short, they must be satisfied that enforcement is necessary in the interests of good planning. Secondly, in the case of building or other operations (but not of material changes of use) the notice must be served within four years of the development being carried out. Thirdly – and this meets the case of development carried out in good faith, or ignorance – application can be made for retrospective permission. It is hardly likely that a local authority would grant permission for a development against which they had served an enforcement notice, but they could, of course, attach conditions; and for the owner there is the usual right of appeal. Fourthly, there is a right of appeal against an enforcement notice to the secretary of state and to the courts. Appeals can be made on several grounds, for example, that permission ought to be granted, that permission has been granted and that no permission is required.

A further enforcement device was introduced by the 1968 Act: the 'stop notice'.[32] This is an attempt to prevent delays in the other enforcement procedures (and advantage being taken of these delays) resulting in the local authority being faced with a *fait accompli*. Previously, when an appeal was lodged against an enforcement notice, there was nothing to stop development continuing while the appeal was being 'determined'. The appeal could take several months, particularly in cases where a local inquiry was held. No liability was involved, since, until the enforcement order was made (if it was), no offence was being committed. The stop notice prohibits the continuation of development which is alleged (in the enforcement notice) to be in breach of planning control. Development carried out in contravention of a stop notice constitutes an offence. Local authorities must, however, use this power with circumspection, since if the enforcement notice is quashed on appeal they are liable to pay compensation for loss due to the stop notice.

The stop notice provisions were strengthened in 1977,[33] but local authorities were warned that their discretionary power to issue notices should be used only where speed is essential. The DoE advise:

> Authorities should first be reasonably satisfied in their own judgment that there is a breach of planning control, that it should be enforced against, and that the enforcement can be effective. Secondly, the question whether it is expedient to require the activity to cease by the use of the speedy stop notice procedure will usually depend primarily upon the character of the activity and its effect on the locality, but regard should be had to the interests of all affected persons whether as neighbours or as persons carrying on the activity. Particular care should be exercised where the service of a stop notice would cause the early cessation of a business providing a person's livelihood or which would adversely affect industrial production or affect a considerable number of jobs. It should be borne in mind that stopping a particular activity could have effects extending far beyond that activity, e.g. by causing a factory to close down because there was nowhere for its products to be stored temporarily.[34]

Thus good planning must have due regard for economic realities. The emphasis on this was greatly increased in 1980. Before discussing this, however, it is appropriate to deal with other powers related to enforcement.

REVOCATION, MODIFICATION AND DISCONTINUANCE

The powers of development control possessed by local authorities go considerably further than the granting or withholding of planning permission. They can interfere with existing uses and revoke a permission already given, even if the development has actually been carried out.

A revocation or modification order is made when the development has not been undertaken (or before a change of use has taken place). The local authority must 'have regard to the development plan and to any other material considerations', and an order has to be confirmed by the secretary of state. Compensation is payable on two grounds: first, for any expenditure or liabilities incurred after the permission has been granted (for example, expenditure on the preparation of plans); and second (following the 1954 Act), for the loss in the development value of the land. The logic in the latter is based on the curious situation caused by the abolition of development charges. The granting of planning permission increases the value of the land in question but, since no development charge is now levied, the development value is thus given to the owner along with the planning permission. The revocation of that permission deprives the owner of a value which has been specifically given to him; hence compensation is payable. (Before the 1954 Act, logic demanded otherwise. The fact that revocation thereby deprived the owner of potential development value did not in itself warrant compensation, since if permission had been given the development value would be transferred to the state through the development charge.)

A revocation or modification order is not very often made. One case which attracted some attention was that of the Eton Fish and Chip Restaurant.[35] This concerned an application for planning permission to use premises in Eton High Street as a fish and chip restaurant. The Eton Urban District Council granted permission (under delegated powers), but after a petition, mainly from local shopkeepers, decided to seek a revocation order on the ground that 'the existence of a fish and chip restaurant in the High Street would be detrimental to the amenities, would cause nuisance, offence and annoyance to occupiers of properties in the vicinity and to users of the public highway, and would adversely affect the general appearance of the High Street'. The order was confirmed by the minister. In this particular case it would seem that planning permission had been given after inadequate consideration of publicity. The revocation was therefore a rectification of a 'mistake'.

Quite distinct from these powers is the much wider power to make a discontinuance order. This power is expressed in extremely wide language: an order can be made 'if it appears to a local planning authority that it is expedient in the interests of the proper planning of their area (including the interests of amenity)'. Again ministerial confirmation is required and compensation is payable – for depreciation, disturbance and expenses incurred in carrying out works in compliance with the order. Under this power, action can be taken against any development (or use) whether it was specifically permitted under the postwar planning Acts or established prior to the Acts. It would appear that an order will be confirmed only if the case is a strong one. In rejecting a discontinuance order on a scrap metal business in an 'attractive residential area', for instance, the minister said: 'the fact that such a business is out of place in an attractive residential area must be weighed in the light of an important distinction between the withdrawal of existing use rights, as sought in the discontinuance order, and the refusal of new rights'. In this particular case, the minister did 'not feel justified in overriding the proper interests of the objector as long as his business is maintained on an inoffensive scale'.[36] Other cases have established the principle that a stronger case is needed to justify action to bring about the discontinuance of a use than would be needed to warrant a refusal of permission in the first instance.

It needs to be stressed that British planning legislation does not assume that existing non-conforming uses must disappear if planning policy is to be made effective. This may often be the avowed policy, but the Planning Acts explicitly permit the continuance of existing uses.

This problem of non-conforming uses is an extremely difficult one. As the Uthwatt Committee pointed out:

> The question whether the right to maintain, replace, extend and use an existing building is to subsist in perpetuity, notwithstanding that the building does not conform to the provisions of the scheme is fundamental in relation to the replanning of built-up areas. On the one hand, it would not be equitable, without compensation, at any time and for any reason to remove, or to prohibit the maintenance, replacement, extension or use of an existing building. On the other hand, an unqualified right, unless compensation is paid, to replace non-conforming buildings and to maintain existing uses permanently is inconsistent with the present conception of planning. The problem is one of finding a proper balance between the two considerations.[37]

The Committee proposed that a 'life' should be placed on nonconforming uses and that at the expiration of that life the use should be brought to an end without compensation. This recommendation was not accepted, and thus local planning authorities can extinguish a non-conforming use only by paying compensation: this can be a very expensive business.

PROTECTING SMALL BUSINESSES

The changing nature of 'town and country planning' is nowhere more apparent than in the area of what Circular 22/80 calls *Planning and Business Activity*.[38] Relevant previous circulars are cancelled, and local authorities 'are now asked to pick out for priority handling those applications which in their judgement will contribute most to national and local economic activity'.

Particular emphasis is laid on small businesses which 'the Government are particularly keen to encourage'.[39] Indeed, in striking contrast to earlier ideas about the separation of industry and housing, 'the characteristics of industry and commerce . . . have changed . . . There are many businesses that can be carried on in rural and residential areas without causing unacceptable disturbance . . . The rigid application of "zoning" policies (where indeed it continues) can have a very damaging effect.'

Moreover, far from 'planning out' non-conforming industry (which was a worthy planning aim in earlier years) such industry 'substantially eases the problems of starting and maintaining small-scale businesses if permission can be given for such uses to be established in redundant buildings such as disused agricultural buildings, industrial, warehouse, or commercial premises, on derelict sites, or in unsuitable housing'.

There are many generations of qualified town planners who would have failed their examinations had they suggested such a thing. Yet the circular as published is a considerably 'softened version' of one which was circulated among local authority associations in July 1980. This came under heavy fire for implying that small firms set up without planning permission should only have enforcement orders issued against them if alternative premises were available.[40] A shadow of this remains in a section on *Enforcement and Discontinuance*.

ENFORCEMENT AND DISCONTINUANCE: 1980 STYLE

While stressing that nothing in the Circular (22/80) should be taken as condoning a wilful breach of planning law, there is a highly significant 'however':

> However, the power to issue an enforcement notice alleging that there has been a breach of planning control is discretionary and is only to be used if the authority 'consider it expedient to do so having regard to the provisions of the development plan and to any other material considerations'. This permissive power should be used, in regard to either operational development or material changes of use, only where planning reasons clearly warrant such action, and there is no alternative to enforcement proceedings. Where the activity involved is one which would not give rise to insuperable planning objections if it were carried out somewhere else, then the planning authority should do all it can to help in finding suitable alternative premises before initiating enforcement action.

Similarly, 'but with even more force', discontinuance orders are appropriate 'only if there appears to be an overriding justification on planning grounds'.

CONTROL OF DEVELOPMENT UNDERTAKEN BY GOVERNMENT
DEPARTMENTS

Development by government departments does not require planning
permission, but there have been special arrangements for 'consultations' since 1950.[41] Increased public and professional concern about
the inadequacy of these led to new (but still non-statutory) arrangements during the 1970s, culminating in DoE Circular 7/77.[42] This
asserts clearly that, before proceeding with development, government
departments will consult the local planning authorities when the
proposed development is one for which specific planning permission
would, in normal circumstances, be required.

Further, 'even when consultation would not be required' on this
basis:

> Departments have agreed to notify the local planning authority of
> development proposals which are likely to be of special concern to
> the authority or to the public – for example where there could be a
> very substantial effect on the character of a conservation area, or
> where there could be a significant planning impact beyond the
> Department's own site, whether visually or otherwise (e.g. in the
> generation of traffic). In any notification case of this kind the local
> planning authority will be given an opportunity to decide whether,
> in their view, the proposal should be advertised so as to give the
> public a chance to comment and for discussion with the Department
> about ways in which the proposal might be amended to overcome
> any objections to the proposed development.

These provisions apply to all bodies entitled to Crown exemption
from planning control, including health authorities and the industrial
estates corporations. The Crown Estate Commissioners and the
Duchies of Cornwall and Lancaster have agreed to consult local
authorities about their proposals in the same way.

The formal procedure is for the government department to send to
the local authority a 'notice of proposed development'. The local
authority can then make 'representations' to the department concerned and, if any differences of view cannot be resolved, the matter is
referred to the DoE. The next steps 'depend upon the circumstances',
and range from an informal meeting to a non-statutory public inquiry.

The spirit of the procedures, however, is indicated by the undertakings on publicity: 'Although development proposals of departments are not subject to statutory publicity it is intended that they
should be given just as much publicity as if the notice of proposed
development were an application for planning permission.'

CONTROL OF DEVELOPMENT UNDERTAKEN BY LOCAL
AUTHORITIES AND STATUTORY UNDERTAKERS

Development undertaken by local authorities and statutory undertakers is also subject to special planning procedures. ('Statutory
undertakers' are defined as 'persons authorized by any enactment to
carry on any railway, light railway, road transport, water transport,
canal, inland navigation, dock, harbour, pier or lighthouse undertaking, or any undertaking for the supply of electricity, gas, hydraulic
power or water'.) Where a development requires the authorisation of a
government department (as do developments involving compulsory
purchase orders, work requiring loan sanction and developments such
as local authority housing on which government grants are paid) the
authorisation is usually accompanied by 'deemed planning
permission'. Much of the normal development of local authorities and
statutory undertakers (for example, road works, laying of underground mains and cables) is 'permitted development' under the
General Development Order. Local planning authorities are also
'deemed' to have permission for any development in their area which
accords with the provisions of the development plan. The secretary of
state has power, however, to require them to apply for his permission
in any particular case. Other local authorities are normally required to
obtain planning permission from the local planning authority. If a
local planning authority wish to develop in the area of another
planning authority they must apply to that authority for planning
permission in the same way as would a private developer.

Statutory undertakers wishing to carry out development which is
neither 'permitted development' nor authorised by a government
department have to apply for planning permission to the local planning authority in the normal way, but in the case of 'operational land'
appeals are considered jointly by the secretary of state and the
'appropriate minister'. ('Operational land' is land which, in respect of
its nature and situation, is not 'comparable with land in general'. This
is a rather imprecise definition, but land used for railway sidings or a
gas works is operational land whereas land used for showrooms or
offices is not.) Until recently, statutory undertakers could be 'controlled' only on the payment of compensation by the local planning
authority.

The privileged position of statutory undertakers has not escaped
criticism, and two highly controversial developments proposed in 1967
created a public outcry. The first was the proposal by the Southern
Gas Board to erect a 39-metre-high gasholder in the historic centre of
Abingdon. The second was the proposal by the Gas Council for a
terminal at Bacton in East Anglia to process North Sea Gas.

In the former case the minister withdrew the Gas Board's right of
'permitted development', and planning permission for the gasholder
was refused. Compensation of £250,000 was involved, and this was

met on a fifty-fifty basis between the local authorities concerned and the Gas Board.

In the Bacton case, permission for development was given after two exhaustive public inquiries, but subject to rigorous conditions.

These cases brought matters to a head. The original justification for the special position of statutory undertakers was that they are under an obligation to provide services to the public and cannot, like a private firm in planning difficulties, go elsewhere. If a planning authority wished to restrict their activities, it was held that it was only right for the extra costs to be reimbursed.

In the debates on the 1968 Town and Country Planning Bill, the minister said that the climate of opinion had now changed. It was still necessary for planning to pay sensible attention to the need to provide essential public services economically. But modern industrial undertakings had to be prepared to conduct their businesses in a way which minimised ugliness and to accept any reasonable cost involved in making their buildings, plant and operations acceptable to public opinion.

A working party of officials of statutory undertakers and government departments was set up to consider the planning implications of developments by statutory undertakers and to review the relevant planning legislation. The first fruit of their work was legislation which provided that no land which was not already operational could become so unless certain planning requirements were met. The most important of these is that there shall be a specific planning permission for development for operational purposes. Moreover, a long-standing compensation principle was breached: compensation for refusal of planning permission was abolished in certain types of case.

The privileged position of statutory undertakers was further reduced in 1973 when a 'code of practice' was agreed between departments and 'commended' by the appropriate ministers to statutory undertakers.[43] Essentially this 'asks' statutory undertakers 'to ensure that both planning authorities and the public know of proposals for permitted development that are likely to affect them significantly before the proposals are finalised'. Though there is 'difficulty of defining classes of development and sensitive areas in general terms', this in itself 'makes it the more important that there should be local consultation between statutory undertakers and planning authorities'.

CARAVANS

In view of the controversy (and extensive litigation) on caravan sites which occurred in the 1950s, caravan sites were made subject to special control in 1960 (by Part I of the Caravan Sites and Control of Development Act 1960).[44] This legislation has remained as a separate code and is not consolidated in the Town and Country Planning Act of 1971. (The Caravan Sites Act, which deals mainly with the protection from eviction of caravan dwellers and gypsies, is similarly separate: this is touched on later in this section.)

Sir Arton Wilson's report, *Caravans as Homes*, highlighted the problems of residential caravanning.[45] In 1959 about 60,000 caravans in England and Wales were being used as homes by some 150,000 people – mainly young married couples, often with small children. About 80 per cent of caravan dwellers hoped to move into normal dwellings. To quote the report, they live in caravans 'because they could not get other dwellings in the right places or on the right terms; or because caravans meet their needs for cheapness, convenience or mobility'. Some simply like caravan life.

The report estimated that about 38,000 of the 60,000 caravans were on sites for which permission, usually conditional or temporary, had been given; about 12,000 had 'existing use' rights; and about 10,000 were on sites which appeared to contravene planning control. With some notable exceptions, local authorities tended to regard caravans as a sub-standard form of accommodation and (less debatably) difficult to control. (It was the publicity given to a case in Egham which led to the setting up of the Arton Wilson Committee.) The caravan interests, on the other hand, argued the case for recognition of caravanning as an acceptable way of life and pressed for more positive approaches by the local authorities.

The 1960 Act gave local authorities new powers to control caravan sites, including a requirement that all caravan sites had to be licensed before they could start operating (thus closing loopholes in the planning and public health legislation). These controls over caravan sites operate in addition to the normal planning system: thus both planning permission and a licence have to be obtained. Most of the Act dealt with control, but local authorities were given wider powers to provide caravan sites. The *Policy Note* on caravans states:

> Planning policy recognizes the demand for sites. The main objectives of policy are, first, to enable the demand to be met in the right places, while preventing sites from springing up in the wrong places; and, second, to allow caravan sites, where permitted, to be established on a permanent or long-term basis, in order to facilitate the provision of proper services and equipment and to allow the occupants reasonable security of tenure.[46]

In fact, in 1973, of the 6,930 residential caravan planning applications decided in England and Wales, nearly a third were refused and over three-fifths were granted for a limited period only. Only 619 were granted without a time-limit.[47] In 1975/6 there were 5,524 applications: 1,622 were refused, 3,355 were granted for a limited time only and 547 were granted without a time-limit. Local authorities face strong pressure from their ratepayers 'to preserve local amenities and property values', to which caravans are seen as a threat. The DoE may be clear as to what 'planning policy recognizes', but the reality differs considerably from the official statement.[48]

Holiday caravans are subject to the same planning and licensing controls as residential caravans. To ensure that a site is used only for holidays (and not for 'residential purposes'), planning permission can include a condition limiting the use of a site to the holiday season. Conditions may also be imposed to require the caravans to be removed at the end of each season or to require a number of pitches on a site to be reserved for touring caravans.

The DoE *Policy Note* states that it is the aim 'to steer holiday caravan development to a limited number of areas, usually those in which caravans are already established, rather than allow them to be scattered more widely'.[49]

In 1975/6, of the 1,763 planning applications for holiday caravan sites, 892 were refused, 586 granted for a limited period and 285 granted without a time-limit.

A review of caravanning and camping has been in hand since 1978 and it has been announced that legislation is to be introduced for a unified system of control over sites for touring caravans and tents.[50]

One group of caravanners is particularly unpopular: gypsies, or, to give them their less romantic description, 'persons of nomadic life, whatever their race or origin' (but excluding 'members of an organized group of travelling showmen, or persons engaged in travelling circuses, travelling together as such'). The appalling conditions in which the majority of the 15,000 gypsies live in England and Wales were portrayed in the 1967 report of the DoE's Sociological Research Section, *Gypsies and Other Travellers*.[51] As was stated in the foreword to this report, the basic problem is that no one wants gypsies around: 'all too often the settled community is concerned chiefly to persuade, or even force, the gypsy families to move on'. Under Part II of the Caravan Sites Act 1968 local authorities in England and Wales (but not Scotland) have a duty to provide adequate sites for gypsies 'residing in or resorting to' their areas.[52]

A report on the operation of the Act prepared by Sir John Cripps[53] (stimulated by sporadic violence on gypsy encampments) underlined the lack of progress. Between 1970 and 1976 only 105 additional local authority sites had been provided by local authorities in England and Wales. The total number of sites (including those in existence in 1970) was 133, accommodating about 2,000 families. Cripps pointed to the legislative enactments which, together with social (and anti-social) pressures, have dogged gypsies:

> Over centuries gypsies have been persecuted in varying degrees; but now they are as much the victims of general trends and events

taking place without regard to or for them. The growing complexity of laws and regulations, with a concomitant increase in form-filling, is an aspect with which I am not directly concerned. A series of Town and Country Planning, Public Health, Local Government, Caravan and Private Acts, and the byelaws they permit, have steadily eroded their choice of habitation. In particular, the number of stopping places available to them has been drastically reduced over a period of three or four decades during which the travelling population has been on the increase, although I have not been able to discover the measure of it.[54]

Cripps's message was clear: the living conditions of many gypsies was scandalous, and no improvement in the slow rate of progress could be expected without a high level of commitment by central government. A major element in this was a proposed 100 per cent grant to local authorities on the capital cost of providing gypsy caravan sites. This was accepted and such grants have been available since 1979.[55]

Progress, however, has continued to be slow, and in the two years 1979–80 additional sites were provided for only 112 gypsy families.[56]

PURCHASE NOTICES

A planning refusal does not of itself confer any right to compensation. On the other hand, revocations of planning permission or interference with existing uses do rank for compensation, since they involve a taking away of an existing right. There are other circumstances in which planning controls so affect the value of the land to the owner that some means of reducing the hardship is clearly desirable. For example, the allocation of land in a development plan for a school will probably reduce the value of houses on this land or even make them completely unsaleable. In such cases the affected owner can serve a notice on the local authority requiring them to purchase the property at an 'unblighted' price. Broadly, such a purchase notice can be served if, as a result of a planning action, land becomes 'incapable of reasonably beneficial use'. In all cases ministerial confirmation is required. The cases in which a purchase notice can be served include:

(i)   refusal or conditional grant of planning permission;
(ii) revocation or modification of planning permission;
(iii) discontinuance of use;
(iv) 'planning blight'.

Normally, if an owner is refused permission to develop his land (or if onerous conditions are laid down) there is nothing he can do about it - except, of course, appeal to the secretary of state. But, if the refusal or the conditions prevent him from obtaining 'reasonably beneficial use' of the land, he can serve a purchase notice. 'The question to be considered in every case is whether the land in its existing state and with its existing permissions (including operations and uses for which planning permission is not required) is incapable of reasonably beneficial use. In considering what capacity for use the land has, relevant factors are the physical state of the land, its size, shape and surroundings, and the general pattern of use in the area. A use of relatively low value may be reasonably beneficial, if such a use is common for similar land in the neighbourhood.'[57]

A purchase notice is not intended to apply in a case in which an owner is simply prevented from realising the full potential value of his land. This would imply the acceptance in principle of paying compensation for virtually all refusals and conditional permissions. It is only if the existing and permitted uses of the land are so seriously affected as to render the land incapable of reasonably beneficial use that the owner can take advantage of the purchase notice procedure.

BLIGHT NOTICES

Redress by way of a purchase notice provided for owners affected by planning blight was introduced in 1959. It was extended in 1968 (since when it has been termed a 'blight notice') and further extended in 1973. The object is to deal with the problem presented to certain classes of owners by the fact that a development is planned to take place on their land at some future (probably uncertain) date. A development plan may, for instance, show the line of a proposed road, though not necessarily the year in which it is to be constructed. In the meantime, an owner who wishes to move and sell his property has to wrestle with the problem of 'blight'. These purchase notice provisions are restricted to owner-occupiers of houses and small businesses who can show that they have made reasonable attempts to sell their property but have found it impossible to do so except at a substantially depreciated price because of certain defined planning actions. These include land designated for compulsory purchase, or allocated or defined by a development plan for any functions of a government department, local authority, statutory undertaker, or the National Coal Board; and land on which the secretary of state has given written notice of his intention to provide a trunk road or a 'special road' (that is, a motorway).

The introduction of the new type of development plan under the 1968 Act involved revised provisions in relation to planning blight. Briefly, the effect of these is that in those areas where a structure plan comes into force, blight caused by either the structure plan or the previous development plan is covered by the planning blight provisions until a local plan allocating land succeeds the old development plan. That local plan then becomes the relevant plan for the blight provisions. Since local plans provide a much more precise indication of the possibility of public acquisition of any land, the structure plan is then no longer relevant.

Structure plans, however, lack this precise indication. Whether they will give rise to more or to less planning blight than the old development plan system remains to be seen. The Planning Advisory Group thought it unlikely that there would be any more, and 'in so far as they show less detail (e.g. town map primary school and minor open space allocations) it may be less'.[58] On the other hand, in the debates on the Bill it was officially stated that:

> When we are dealing with the structure plan for which there is no local plan in force, we have a new problem which is that, owing to the diagrammatic nature of the plans, no one will be able to say with certainty that this does or does not affect the claimant's property, but that nevertheless, because of that very uncertainty, a wider number of properties may be affected.

After parliamentary pressure,[59] the secretary of state advised a wider range of circumstances in which local authorities were urged to use their discretionary powers.[60] In 1973 the Land Compensation Act gave statutory effect to these, and made other significant changes to the planning blight provisions. It also extended them to cover land affected by new town designation orders, slum clearance orders and new street orders.

THE LAND COMPENSATION ACT 1973

The 1973 Act extends beyond planning blight and takes us into the much broader field of the law relating to compensation. This is an extremely complex field, and only an indication of some of the major features can be attempted here.[61]

The provisions of the Act can be rapidly summarised under five headings which relate to the five main parts of the Act.

(1) *Compensation for Depreciation Caused by Use of Public Works*

This creates a statutory right to compensation for a fall in the value of property arising from the use of highways, aerodromes and other public works which have immunity from actions for 'nuisance'. The depreciation has to be caused by physical factors such as noise, fumes, dust and vibration and the compensation is payable by the authority responsible for the works. The use of new roads or runways is thought to be the most likely to give rise to such depreciation.

(2)   *Mitigation of Injurious Effect of Public Works*
There is a range of powers under this heading, for example, in relation
to sound insulation; the purchase of owner-occupied property which is
severely affected by construction work or by the use of a new or
improved highway; the erection of physical barriers (such as walls,
screens, or mounds of earth) on or alongside roads to reduce the
effects of traffic noise on people living nearby; the planting of trees
and the grassing of areas; and the development or redevelopment of
land for the specific purpose of improving the surroundings of a highway 'in a manner desirable by reason of its construction, improvement, existence or use'.

(3)   *Provision for Benefit of Persons Displaced from Land*
Of particular significance here is the provision for Home Loss Payments as a mark of recognition of the special hardship created by
compulsory dispossession of one's home. Since these payments are for
this purpose they are quite separate from, and are not dependent
upon, any right to compensation or the Disturbance Payment which is
described below. Logically they apply to tenants as well as to owner-
occupiers and are given for all displacements whether by compulsory
purchase, redevelopment, or any action under the Housing Acts.

Additionally, there is a general entitlement to a Disturbance
Payment for persons who are not entitled to compensation, and local
authorities are given a duty 'to secure the provision of suitable
alternative accommodation where this is not otherwise available on
reasonable terms, for any person displaced from residential accommodation' by acquisition, redevelopment, demolition, closing orders, and
so on. This provision goes a long way towards implementing the
recommendation on rehousing obligations of the Central Housing
Advisory Committee.[62]

(4)   *Compulsory Purchase*
A number of changes are made in the law relating to the assessment of
compensation. These are aimed at improving the provisions and meeting some particular problems. A right is also given to the advance
payment of compensation.

(5)   *Planning Blight*
Important changes are made to the planning blight provisions. In
particular the classes of land in respect of which blight notices may be
served are extended, for example, to land affected by proposals in
structure plans or local plans submitted to the secretary of state, to
new town areas covered by a draft or substantive New Town Designation Order, and to dwellings and other buildings within areas declared
to be a Clearance Area (in Scotland, a Housing Action Area).

DEVELOPMENT CONTROL POLICIES

The subheading for this section looks like a play on words, but it is intended to point up the fact that, while development control is one of the instruments by which planning policies are implemented, there are also policies relating to the actual operation of the control. For example, it could be the policy that each application should be dealt with very thoroughly and carefully, irrespective of the time and cost involved. Needless to say that is not the policy. Indeed, there has been a succession of attempts to 'streamline the planning process' and to make it more 'efficient'.

The reasons for these have differed. Currently (1981), the concern is with the economic costs of control, with cutting public expenditure and with 'freeing' private initiative from unnecessary governmental controls. In the early 1970s, the concern was with the enormous increase in planning applications and planning appeals. This, of course, stemmed from the property boom of the period. The resultant delay created a political situation which was dealt with in traditional style by setting up an inquiry: this produced the three Dobry Reports.[63]

These are now part of 'planning history', but it is live history: the issues are still very much with us in the early 1980s, and there is no guarantee that the current resolution of them will prove sufficiently resilient to withstand the unpredictable changes in the context within which they operate. It is therefore useful to set out in some detail the position as it was prior to the 1980 Local Government, Planning and Land Act.

DEVELOPMENT CONTROL IN ENGLAND AND WALES 1972-80

Before reorganisation, development control in England and Wales was the responsibility of county boroughs and counties, though in the counties there was a wide measure of delegation to districts. The amount of delegation depended on the size and staffing of the districts, but there was a clear trend to greater delegation during the 1960s. There was, however, much criticism (except on the part of the district councils) of the efficiency of *any* system of delegation. In their evidence to the Redcliffe-Maud Commission, the Ministry of Housing and Local Government (as it then was) argued that it led neither to an improved speed nor to a better quality of development control: the advantages which flowed from delegating some of the work load to district councils was offset by the shortage of qualified planning staff in most district offices, by the limited range of problems which arose within any one area, by the difficulties caused by the natural inclination of district councils to take a 'narrow view', and by the extra administrative complications that limited delegation usually entailed.

The ministry thought that decentralisation of planning control to area committees of the planning authority produced better results than delegation to another elected body. This view was supported by the report of the *Management Study on Development Control*.[64] The management consultants who undertook this study concluded that, within the context of the two-tier system in administrative counties, area committees provided the best method of reconciling the rights of individuals with speed of decision, low cost and the interests of the wider community.

Delegation was essentially a means of attempting to adjust planning machinery to an out-dated local government system. It was the primary purpose of reorganisation to recast local government in a way which would make such palliatives unnecessary. But this was not to be, and the new structure made district–county relationships even more crucial to the smooth working of the planning system. As with development plans, counties were responsible for strategic issues while districts were responsible for local issues. But since the districts were not subservient to the counties, the concept of 'delegation' was inappropriate, and thus it became essential for there to be clear guide-lines to distinguish county issues from district issues.

This was done in detail in the Local Government Act of 1972. Though all planning applications were made, in the first instance, to the district, those which fell within the category of 'county matters' were determined by the county council. These included applications:

(*a*)   that related to the working of minerals;
(*b*)   that 'would conflict with, or prejudice the implementation of, fundamental provisions of the structure plan';
(*c*)   that 'would be inconsistent with a local plan prepared by the *county council*';
(*d*)   that 'would be inconsistent in any respect with any statement of planning policy adopted by the county planning authority or with any proposals of theirs for development which in either case have been notified by them to the district planning authority'.

This system (unlike that north of the Border) was cumbersome in the extreme. Though it worked with reasonable smoothness in some cases, this was a result of good county–district relationships which were able to overcome the inherent difficulties of the division of responsibilities as set out in (virtually incomprehensible) detail in Schedule 16 of the 1972 Act.

DEVELOPMENT CONTROL IN SCOTLAND

In Scotland, development control is a district or general planning authority function but, as in England, certain powers are allocated to the upper-tier authority. The powers of the region were never as far-reaching (or set out in such detail) as was the case in the English counties prior to the 1980 Act. Moreover, there is no reference to 'county matters'. The Scottish provisions simply supplement the powers previously exercised solely by the secretary of state by a power of regional planning authorities to call in applications where:

(i) the proposed development does not conform to a structure plan approved by the secretary of state; *or*

(ii) the proposed development raises a new planning issue of general significance to the district of the regional planning authority.[65]

This power is exercisable only in cases where the application is not called in by the secretary of state himself.

Planning appeals continue to be lodged with the secretary of state, but regional planning authorities are notified of all appeals and have the right to take part in the appeal proceedings. Regional planning authorities are also informed of proposals for revocation, modification and discontinuance of use orders, and can make representations or objections on them to the secretary of state. Finally, they have default powers to make such orders themselves if they think that an order is necessary to prevent 'material prejudice' to an approved structure plan.

These powers of a regional planning authority in relation to development control are essentially rights of intervention to give effect to regional planning policies. They are defined in straightforward terms (avoiding the complexities of the English legislation). In all cases there are simple rights of appeal to the secretary of state to enable him to resolve any disputes between a district and a region.

STREAMLINING THE PLANNING MACHINE:
THE DOBRY REPORTS

The background to the Dobry Reports has already been indicated: in arithmetical terms, between 1968 and 1972 the number of planning decisions by local authorities in England and Wales increased from 425,000 to 615,000 (Table 4.1), while the number of appeals rose even more dramatically. At the end of November 1973 16,354 were outstanding, and the average period from receipt to decisions ranged up to sixty-five weeks (for cases decided by the secretary of state after a local inquiry).

This unforseen situation developed at the very time when local authorities were also facing the problems of reorganisation and of the introduction of structure planning. Pressure therefore mounted for 'streamlining the planning machine'. The DoE issued advice[66] (in a circular bearing this title) on a wide range of administrative matters related to planning applications, increased their inspectorate to deal with appeals, and appointed Mr G. Dobry, QC, to undertake a rapid review of the development control system.

Table 4.1   *Planning Decisions of Local Authorities, England and Wales 1962–78/9*[67]

	Total decisions	Permissions granted	
		Number	%
1962	397,301	333,495	84
1963	411,563	345,651	84
1964	461,715	378,695	82
1965	443,387	364,935	82
1966	415,052	345,799	83
1967	422,553	358,338	85
1968	426,286	359,449	84
1969	402,714	342,889	85
1970	414,301	351,624	85
1971	463,301	385,989	83
1972	614,862	493,097	80
1973	622,652	491,174	79
1974/5	414,900	330,800	80
1975/6	454,206	379,821	84
1976/7	446,142	378,447	85
1977/8	441,612	378,998	86
1978/9	500,901	432,570	86

Dobry issued three reports: an interim and a final report on *The Development Control System*, and a report on *The Control of Demolition*.[68]

The two reports on development control are lengthy, detailed and very difficult to summarise (partly because of the almost staccato style in which the main analysis and recommendations are presented). Dobry's detailed recommendations (which total 161) are aimed, in his words, at giving greater freedom to harmless development but also at guarding against harmful development by retaining the current scope of planning control; at separating from the main stream of applications all those which might cause harm, and disposing of 'main stream applications' by rapid and routine procedures; and applying the same approach to appeals. Among the more important features of the proposed system are:

(i)   a single standard application form;
(ii)   a leaflet explaining how to fill it in;
(iii) information centres and (later) advice centres to help applicants and interested parties;

(iv)   full publicity, to nationally laid down standards, for all planning applications.
 (v)   the division of the planning applications into two classes:
       (A) minor and uncontroversial and
       (B) major and/or controversial;
(vi)   a simpler and speedier treatment for Class A applications, and a realistic but strict timetable for Class B applications;
(vii) a firm timetable for the principal steps for processing applications (which is set out in the Dobry Report);
(viii) separate public consultation codes for each of these classes;
(ix)   the device of deemed permission for Class A applications, so that in default of a decision they are automatically approved;
 (x)   a clearer, stricter definition of responsibility for handling planning applications as between district and county councils;
(xi)   complete revision of the General Development Order to make it clearer and more comprehensible to the public.

The most important issue here is clearly that of dividing applications into two classes. Dobry's argument on this is worth setting out in full:

> It is tempting to assume that minor developments are automatically simple, and that planning authorities, therefore, always need less information and less time to reach sound decisions on them. That is clearly not so. As amenity societies and professional bodies were quick to point out, in commenting on the tentative distinction made in my Interim Report between house-holder applications and others, some quite 'small' proposals raise major questions of principle. It should not be necessary for a small and relatively simple proposal, unlikely to arouse much objection, to run the gamut of the same stringent procedures as a major or controversial proposal. Nor ought it to wait as long for a decision. Some cases, however, including otherwise minor ones which give rise to issues of principle or could arouse controversy, will always demand a lengthier, more stringent appraisal. And so long as we have only one procedure applying to all applications, there is little hope of achieving simplicity and speed for the majority of applications. They will tend to move at the pace of the complex or the controversial few.

Dobry concludes that, therefore, the solution is to have two categories of applications: those that are minor and uncontroversial (Class A), and those that are major or controversial or both (Class B). Applications should be streamed accordingly.

Any attempt to lay down rigid rules for classifying applications 'is doomed to failure', but guidance should be given in a 'national code of practice'. This would ensure that at least the following are treated as Class A:

(i)   all simple cases;

(ii)   all applications conforming with an approved development plan (this may have to be subject to specified limits for an experimental period);

(iii)   development which only just exceeds that permitted by the General Development Order, including Class I (development within the curtilage of a dwelling-house), Class VI (agricultural) and Class VIII (industrial) developments;

(iv)   the approval of reserved matters relating to cases classed as 'A' when outline permission was sought.

Standard consultation procedures are proposed together with strict compliance with time-limits (twenty-one days for Class A, and forty-two days for Class B). Class B applications require more extensive publicity than Class A, but both classes should be subject to both compulsory and discretionary publicity:

Compulsory and Discretionary Publicity

Compulsory		Discretionary
Class A	(1) Site notices or neighbour notification	(1) Notification to local societies
	(2) Notification of parish council	(2) Other compulsory items under Class B
Class B	(1) Site notice *or* neighbour notification	(1) Notification to local societies
	(2) Notification of parish council	(2) Advertisements for individual applications in local newspapers or on notice boards (perhaps specially allocated for that purpose)
	(3) Publication of lists of applications in local newspapers *or* on public notice boards (perhaps specially allocated for that purpose) and to registered local societies	

A notable innovation is the proposal that Class A applications should be deemed granted if not decided upon in forty-two days. No similar proposal is made in relation to Class B applications, but it is recommended that there should be a three-month time-limit which should be strictly adhered to. However, in cases of specially significant development, local authorities should be able to require an 'impact study', and in these cases the time-limit should be six months.

An impact study would describe the proposed development in detail and explain its likely effect on the surroundings. It would comprise a written report and such plans, maps, photographs, diagrams, and so on, as would be needed to assist understanding. In particular, it should deal with the proposed development's effect on traffic, roads and public transport; foul and surface water drainage; publicly provided services, such as schools; the appearance of the neighbourhood; employment; and noise and air pollution. Other aspects to be considered in the statement might include whether the development or its location constitute a hazard (for example, fire risk); whether it is likely to trigger off other development; and investigation of alternative sites.

Dobry lays great emphasis on consultations and meetings between applicants and the local planning authority, particularly in relation to Class B applications. There are a number of recommendations on this, for example, that the planning committee should interview applicants 'in suitable cases' (undefined), particularly where there is a difference of view within the committee.

Other recommendations include the introduction of a stamp duty or similar standard charge for planning applications; the retention of detailed design control ('in spite of its subjective nature'); the use of 'design guides' for 'homogeneous areas' and of 'design briefs' for particular sites; greater delegation to officers; speedy production of structure and local plans (in accordance with a national timetable); stronger control procedures in 'special environmental areas' (for example, national parks, conservation areas and other areas identified in development plans or policies); the establishment of local authority information centres and independent planning advice centres (on which details of current pioneering examples are given in an Appendix to the report).

DOBRY IN PERSPECTIVE

The starting-point for the Dobry inquiry was the lengthening delay in the processing of planning applications, but Dobry was quick to point out that 'not all delay is unacceptable: it is the price we must pay for the democratic planning of the environment'. Moreover, his review took account of factors which were very different from those relevant to 'streamlining the planning machine': the increasing pressure for public consultation and participation in the planning process; and the 'dissatisfaction on the part of applicants because they often do not understand why particular decisions have been made, or why it is necessary for what may seem small matters to be the concern of the planning machinery at all'. Additionally, he noted that 'many people feel that the system has not done enough to protect what is good in an environment or to ensure that new development is of a sufficiently high quality'.

Dobry therefore had a difficult task of reconciling apparently irreconcilable objectives: to expedite planning procedures while at the same time facilitating greater public participation and devising a system which would produce better environmental results. His solutions attempt to provide more speed for developers, more participation for the public *and* better quality development and conservation.

This is effected by the division of applications into 'minor' and 'major'. Despite the inherent difficulties of determining this in advance (at least to the satisfaction of the public and the local amenity societies) it is nevertheless a fact that some 80 per cent of all applications are granted, and that many of these *are* 'simple and straightforward'. Dobry's proposal, in essence, is that the 'simple' should be distinguished and treated expeditiously – though with the opportunity for some participation and with a safety channel to allow them to be transferred to the 'major' category if this should prove appropriate. These Class A applications would be dealt with by officials acting under powers delegated to them by planning committees (or, if this is unacceptable, by small sub-committees of two or three members). Publicity would be restricted in time to twenty-one days and decisions would be reached within forty-two days – failing which an application would be deemed to be approved.

This would, so Dobry believes, relieve the overloaded planning machine to deal more thoroughly with the major and/or controversial applications (which he suggests would constitute less than a half and, hopefully, only a third of the total). These would receive greater scrutiny than hitherto, and the period for decision would be increased from the present statutory (but – when applied to all applications – impracticable) two months to three months. They would receive greater public advertisement, and more important applications would need to be accompanied by an 'impact study'.

Dobry's scheme is an heroic attempt to improve the planning control system to everybody's satisfaction. It must thus inevitably disappoint everybody. For example, though he makes a number of proposals to increase public participation, his overriding concern for expediting procedures forces him to compress these into an impracticable time-scale. This is particularly so with his Class A applications, where twenty-one days is far too short a period for effective publicity, let alone considered public reaction. Moreover, it is open to question whether the Class A procedure would relieve planning administration or, in fact, overload it still further. In practice, the result might well be either a collapse of the new procedure or a perfunctory and rapid processing which would deny the public participation which Dobry wishes to increase.

In his Interim Report, Dobry explored some possibilities of reducing controls over aesthetic aspects of design (as distinct from 'massing or bulk') and over 'householder applications' ('applications by residential occupiers for their own better use of the property, in accordance with local authority plans or policies and giving rise to no substantial public interest'). Here the rationale was that 'the degree of control must depend upon what is practicable':

However ideal a control system may be in theory, it will not succeed unless there are the resources (and this really means the people) to operate it. In practice it may be vital to exercise priorities, perhaps involving some lessening of control in certain respects or over certain kinds of development, in order to ensure that control is successfully achieved where it matters most. The danger, otherwise, is that work may have to be skimped so that the environment is not adequately protected anywhere, or unacceptable delays may build up. Such consequences are as unacceptable, in economic or social terms, as the environmental ills which control aims to prevent.

He was, however, led away from this line of thought (which warrants much wider examination than Dobry gave it), and the main gist of his final conclusions is in favour of tightening control – including the control of demolition.

But the biggest shortcoming of the Dobry Report is that he never really comes to grips with the major weakness of the development control system: its general isolation from the remainder of the planning process. In Eddison's words:

Although Dobry's terms of reference specifically refer to the 'new system of structure and local plans', the essential relationships are barely mentioned, and certainly not explored, in the Review. Yet these relationships (or lack of them) are really at the heart of the weakness of the development control system . . . Development control is not, in practice, an integral part of policy making and implementation.[69]

Similarly Jowell has commented that 'the major omission of the report is its failure to see development control's place in a planning system whose scope has expanded radically since 1968 . . . somehow development control has not kept pace with this change'.[70] Nevertheless, Dobry has started a debate which may well prove to be of much wider, and of greater long-term significance, than was envisaged when he was commissioned to assist in 'streamlining the planning machine'.

THE CONTROL OF DEMOLITION

It has been generally accepted that demolition of itself does not constitute 'development' and, though there is some legal uncertainty on the matter, local authorities have typically assumed that demolition is outside the ambit of development control. Nevertheless, there are extensive powers (outlined in Chapter 5) to prevent the demolition of buildings of historic or architectural quality – of which the most recent is the Town and Country Amenities Act of 1974 which brings the demolition of all buildings in conservation areas under control.

Nevertheless, there has been increasing disquiet in recent years about the lack of clear and 'blanket' control of demolition, particularly on the part of amenity societies, but also on the part of local authorities who have been concerned at some of the effects of commercial enterprise. Following the resulting parliamentary pressure, Dobry was asked to report specifically on this issue. This he did in a terse report, published in 1974.[71]

He concluded that there were several 'persuasive' arguments in favour of subjecting demolition to control. These were, first, that 'there is a good deal of concern that the planning system should permit town centre and residential development that is sometimes strikingly out of scale or sympathy with the area affected'. Secondly, there is some uncertainty as to the law. Thirdly, there is some 'inconsistency': here the argument, curiously, is that though there are powers for the control over the demolition of certain buildings, there is no 'overall system'. Fourthly, 'and most importantly', there are four practical reasons for the general extension of control over demolition:

(1) *The aftermath of demolition.* Barren sites, inadequately fenced, often become a dumping ground causing general deterioration of the neighbourhood. This is bad everywhere, but I am told is at its worst in twilight and other poorer areas of our cities. Vacant sites are despoiled with random deposits of furniture, broken bottles, dumped cars and other paraphernalia of vandalism and disorder.

(2) *Demolition as a 'fait accompli'* can be used by developers to force the grant of planning permission.

(3) *Premature demolition of houses.* Premature demolition and vacancy of residential accomodation in anticipation of development causes public disquiet.

(4) *Need to preserve commercial and community use.* Premature demolition of shops in a redevelopment area is clearly harmful. Many think that to prevent the demolition of useful residential buildings, theatres and cinemas is equally important.

GOVERNMENT REJECTION OF THE DOBRY REPORTS

The Dobry inquiry was instigated by a Conservative government at a time when the property market was booming. On its completion the boom had collapsed and a Labour government had published their outline proposals for the community land legislation. In short, the planning scene had changed fundamentally. In purely administrative terms, 'authorities concerned with distinguishing between applications for exempt development, excepted development, designated relevant development and non-designated relevant development could not also be expected to distinguish between Class A and Class B applications, and between outline, illustrative, detailed and guideline applications'.[72]

The government's decisions on the Dobry Reports were set out in detail in a 1975 circular.[73] All Dobry's major recommendations for changes in the system were rejected, though it was stressed that their objectives could typically be achieved if local authorities adopted 'the most efficient working methods'. Dobry's view that 'it is not so much the system which is wrong but the way in which it is used' was endorsed, and his *Final Report* was commended 'to students of our planning system as an invaluable compendium of information about the working of the existing development control process, and to local authorities and developers as a source of advice on the best way to operate within it'.

THE EXPENDITURE COMMITTEE REPORTS

Probably the largest collection of material on the operation of the British planning system is to be found in the evidence presented to the Expenditure Committee in the 1976–7 inquiry on *Planning Procedures*.[74] The 1,224 pages are a veritable goldmine of fact and opinion, while the fourteen recommendations which conclude the Committee's 45-page report, together with the government's response to them,[75] provide much for discussion. Some of the matters are dealt with in other chapters: here we are concerned with 'the problem of delay'.

Dobry gave some forthright evidence to the Committee, and was highly critical of the DoE, which he described as being 'lethargic', 'unco-operative' and 'not constructive'. Moreover, officials have 'not got the faintest idea what is going on in the country'.[76] More pointedly he stressed that the only significant DoE response to his report was to exhort local authorities 'to mend their ways', yet there had been repeated exhortations of this nature by previous secretaries of state, to little good effect: 'what reason have we to believe that, this time, it will somehow be miraculously different?'[77]

Dobry argued for radical change with the 'four basic messages' of his report which 'never really got through'. '*First*, the role of the planning control machine must be constructive, not obstructive . . . *Second*, though the planning control machine exists to intervene, it must do so only selectively . . . *Third*, improving the system does not mean simply speeding decision-making and relaxing controls: it requires a judicious mixture of loosening[78] and tightening . . . Lack of control over demolition is perhaps the most notable gap . . . *Fourth*, planning control must take account of economic reality.'[79]

The Committee gave pride of place to the question of delay, and were clearly impressed by Dobry's arguments for 'a more positive, creative attitude towards development on the part of planning officers, and "sanctions" – whether costs, deemed consent, public obloquy or whatever – both to castigate the most scandalously laggard or obstructive, and to reassure the public generally that Parliament's requirement setting time limits to planning decisions is not meaningless'.[80]

Dobry, however, was only one witness, and there were many who took differing lines. Somewhat plaintively, the Committee noted:

> We have received a considerable amount of conflicting evidence on the connected questions of delay and the resulting resource costs. Developers have told us that planning procedures lead to intolerable delays which increase the resource costs of development. Spokesmen for local communities and for several of the amenity societies, who are concerned to have an opportunity of putting forward their views, think that the period for decision is often too short and the process too secretive. The local authorities consider that it is more important to spend time and trouble arriving at a good decision in planning terms than to seek a quick decision for its own sake.[81]

Despite the differing views, the Committee were clear that there really was 'a problem of delay', and they directed their attention to ways in which efficient operation could be improved. In their view, 'not all authorities are operating as efficiently as they might' and (quoting the DoE circular on the Dobry Report) 'the greatest scope for improvement lies in assisting all authorities to reach the standard now set by the best'.[82]

The Committee's first recommendation clearly endorses this: 'a small number of Planning Assessors should be appointed to give help and advice to local planning authorities and to monitor their performance by continual and informal contact'. The department agreed to consider this in consultation with the local authority associations.

Other proposals included: 'that inefficiency should be penalised by being made an additional reason for the award of costs against the local planning authority on appeal' (rejected by DoE); that 'the Secretary of State should consider awarding costs when he reverses on appeal a planning decision which blatantly contradicts national policy as expressed in a circular' (DoE responded that the essence of this recommendation was already established policy); that 'the Department should as a matter of urgency hold discussions with the local authority associations with a view to clarifying the roles of county and district, and taking the necessary action' (DoE responded that this was under discussion with the local authority associations: it is now, of course, implemented by the 1980 Local Government, Planning and Land Act); and that 'a review should be undertaken of the system of plans currently in use' (rejected by DoE).

The Expenditure Committee returned to this field in 1978, and reiterated their recommendations for the appointment of planning assessors and for a review of the planning system.

Though there was no formal (or at least published) 'review' of the planning system, the 1980 Act passed by the subsequent Conservative government certainly effected some major changes in it.

DEVELOPMENT CONTROL: 1980 STYLE

The new government lost no time in preparing a revised development control policy. A draft circular was sent out for comment in mid-1980. It created alarm among the planning profession, partly because of its substantive proposals but also partly because of its abrasive style. 'The Most Savage Attack Yet' expostulated *Municipal Engineering*, while *Planner News* remonstrated that 'Results of D C Circular could be Disastrous'.[83]

An example of the 'objectionable' content of the draft was the call for relaxation of controls over private sector housing: 'Local authorities should not lay down requirements on the mix of house types, provision of garages, internal standards, sizes of private gardens, location of houses on plots and in relation to each other, provision of private open space.'

The circular also said that planning authorities should not attempt to compel developers to adopt designs which were unpopular with customers or clients 'and they shouldn't attempt to control such details as shapes of windows or doors or the colour of bricks'.

On density, the circular played down its importance and commented that 'for many of the redevelopment and infill sites now to be brought into use, densities do not provide reliable performance indicators'.

The revised circular,[84] as published, was written with a lighter touch, but much of the message was very much the same. The passages substituted for those from which the above quotations are taken are illustrative. On design:

Local planning authorities may need to control aspects of the design of housing estates where these have an impact on neighbouring development or agricultural land, for example access or over-shadowing. But functional requirements within a development are for the most part a matter for the developers and their customers. Such matters would include provision of garages, internal space standards (whether Parker Morris or other) and sizes of private gardens. In making provision for open space and in considering the location of houses on plots and their relationship to each other local planning authorities should not attempt to prescribe rigid formulae. They should only regulate the mix of house types when there are specific planning reasons for such control, and in so doing they should take particular account of marketing considerations.[85]

On residential densities:

The Government's general policy is to encourage more intensive development in appropriate locations in order to preserve the countryside and protect better quality agricultural land. Detailed policies on densities are, however, normally considered in structure plans. Developers are usually anxious to build at the highest density acceptable to their potential customers, though what this is may vary from time to time according to the dictates of the market. When considering a planning application for a particular site the character of the site and its surroundings, together with the design and layout of the proposed development and the marketing possibilities, need to be taken into account as well as any density policies for the area as a whole. The Secretaries of State attach particular importance to the provision of low cost starter homes which may only be able to be built at higher than conventional densities. For many of the small redevelopment and infill sites now to be brought into use general density requirements cannot be a reliable guide.[86]

There is much in similar vein. More generally, the emphasis is on securing a 'speeding up of the system' and 'to ensure that development is only prevented or restricted when this serves a clear planning purpose and the economic effects have been taken into account'.

LESS DIVIDED DEVELOPMENT CONTROL

'Jaw not war' is the clarion call of the new division of planning control functions between counties and districts in England and Wales.[87] The 1980 Local Government, Planning and Land Act[88] changes the allocation between county and district planning authorities of development control functions (outside national parks). From 13 January 1981 'district planning authorities will be responsible for determining all planning applications which were formerly classified as county matters' under the Local Government Act 1972.[89]

Broadly, county matters are now confined to applications for mineral and related development, for cement works, and for development that straddles the boundary of a national park. The Town and Country Planning (Prescription of County Matters) Regulations 1980 make applications for waste disposal in England also a county matter.[90]

The 'county matters' are now clearly matters for which county responsibility is self-evidently necessary.[91] They are all exceptions to the general rule of district responsibility. Nevertheless, the 1980 Act makes it abundantly clear that, though districts are the development control authorities, they must direct their decisions to the implementation of the structure plan for their area.[92]

The arrangements for development control schemes are now superseded by new consultation machinery.[93] A Code of Practice has been agreed by a working party of representatives of the local authority associations and DoE: this is set out in full as an appendix to DoE Circular 2/81.

AMENDING THE GENERAL DEVELOPMENT ORDER

A further, and very significant change, made in early 1981, relates to the General Development Order. The background to this is spelled out in clear political terms in a DoE Consultation Paper of February 1980:

> Two of the Government's most important objectives are to reduce the proportion of the nation's wealth consumed by the public sector and to reduce the extent to which individuals are held back by the public sector . . .
>
> A high priority is given to speeding up the planning process by streamlining the system. We must cut out what is unnecessary and concentrate only on what matters. The General Development Order is important in this respect because it defines the boundaries of planning control. It is part of the balance between an individual's freedom to develop his property and the need to protect public amenity.
>
> An overwhelming proportion of planning applications relate solely to small householder developments. These consist mainly of extensions, alterations and garages. In some areas over 50 per cent of planning applications fall into these categories. The vast majority of them are completely uncontroversial. Even where an application does arouse some opposition, issues of public amenity rarely arise. In practice, the planning system is being used to settle disputes between neighbours in a way which was never intended and for which it was not designed. At a time when the need to reduce the size of the public sector is paramount, we do not believe that this is a justifiable way to spend the money of taxpayers and ratepayers.[94]

This political rhetoric would lead one to suppose that the subsequent proposals would be of an equally clear political substance. Yet the amendments are essentially the same as those put by the previous Labour administration in 1977 – but withdrawn in the face of widespread opposition.[95]

The relaxation of planning controls over 'minor developments' involves three changes. First, householders are allowed to extend their houses by up to 15 per cent, or 70 cubic metres if greater, without the need for planning permission. (The previous limits were 10 per cent and 50 cubic metres.) This relaxation does not apply to terraced properties. Secondly, private garages only count as part of the limit on house extensions if they are within 5 metres of the house; otherwise they are treated in the same way as other outbuildings. Thirdly, the limit for permitted extensions to industrial buildings is raised from 10 per cent to 20 per cent, subject to a maximum increase in floor area of 750 square metres (instead of the previous 500 square metres). There is no relaxation of planning controls in national parks, areas of outstanding natural beauty and existing conservation areas. There are also relaxations in relation to small industrial premises.[96]

SEX SHOPS

At the end of a long chapter dealing with a wide range of complex issues, it seems appropriate to strike a lighter note. This is provided, somewhat unexpectedly, by an amendment to the Local Government (Miscellaneous Provisions) (Scotland) Bill 1981 moved by the Scottish Nationalist Member for Dundee East (Mr Gordon Wilson).[97] This proposed a new clause for the planning regulation of sex shops. Anyone operating or seeking to operate premises as a sex shop or a shop dealing in sex magazines and sex aids would need to get planning permission for the specific use. Local authorities considering such applications would have to have regard to the interests of amenity and the proximity of the premises to schools, churches and other shops. Under the present planning law permission is not needed to change the use of an existing shop into a sex shop.

The proposal aroused some moral fervour but was rejected on the grounds that planning law 'might not be related to the sort of moral considerations that arose'. The possibility of some alternative form of licensing was floated. It is thus apparent that while the planning control system can cope with the problems of fish and chip shops,[98] it cannot do so with those arising from sex shops.

REFERENCES AND FURTHER READING: CHAPTER 4

1 'As with the American system, the identification of land in a development plan as suitable for a particular use is a guide rather than a guarantee that a permit will be issued to allow an owner to use it for that new purpose. Unlike the American system, there is no later adoption of a zoning ordinance which translates the guide into a guarantee.' V. Moore, 'The public control of land use: an anglophile's view', *The Urban Lawyer*, vol. 10 (1977), p. 132. Moore points to the proposal of the Expenditure Committee that a review of the planning system should be undertaken including 'the adoption of a wholly different system such as zoning plans bestowing a legal right to develop within the limits specified in zoning ordinances applied to

precisely defined areas'. (*Eighth Report from the Expenditure Committee, Session 1976–77, Planning Procedures, Vol. 1: Report*, HC Paper 395-I, HMSO, 1977, para. 86. The recommendation was rejected by the government: *Planning Procedures: The Government's Response*, Cmnd 7056, HMSO, 1978.)

2   See DoE Circular 96/75, *The Town and Country Planning (Development Plans) Direction 1975* (HMSO, 1975); and M. Purdue, 'The scope of planning authorities' discretion – or what's material?', *Journal of Planning and Environment Law*, 1977, pp. 490–7. Following the Local Government, Planning and Land Act 1980, the 1975 Direction has been cancelled and replaced by the *Town and Country Planning (Development Plans) (England) Direction 1981* which is published in DoE Circular 2/81, *Town and Country Planning: Development Control Functions* (HMSO, 1981).

3   Town and Country Planning Act 1971, section 22(1). Generally, see J. Alder *Development Control* (Sweet & Maxwell, 1979), ch. 2.

4   Any reader who wishes to follow up the technicalities of this is referred to M. Purdue, *Cases and Materials on Planning Law* (Sweet & Maxwell, 1977), pp. 123–6.

5   See DoE Circular 97/72, *The Town and Country Planning (Use Classes) Order 1972* (HMSO, 1972). The Order itself is SI 1972 No. 1385.

6   *Town and Country Planning General Development Order 1977*, SI 1977 No. 289. At the time of writing an amendment to this Order is anticipated. For further discussion see the final section of this chapter.

7   Town and Country Planning Act 1971, section 30. See MHLG Circular 5/68, *The Use of Conditions in Planning Permissions* (HMSO, 1968).

8   *Pyx Granite Co. Ltd* v. *Ministry of Housing and Local Government* [1958] 1 QB 554, 572. This famous case is widely reported in legal texts.

9   A short but useful piece on this is 'Planning gain – bargaining or blackmail?', *Planner News*, December 1980, p. 12. Much more substantial fare is to be found in M. Grant, 'Planning by agreement', *Journal of Planning and Environment Law*, 1975, pp. 501–8; M. Grant, 'The Community Land Act: an overview', *Journal of Planning and Environment Law*, 1977, pp. 614–26, 675–90 and 732–48; M. Grant, 'Developers' contributions and planning gains: ethics and legalities', *Journal of Planning and Environment Law*, 1978, pp. 8–15; J. Jowell, 'The limits of law in urban planning', *Current Legal Problems 1977*, pp. 63–83; J. Jowell, 'Bargaining in development control', *Journal of Planning and Environment Law*, 1977, pp. 414–33; and J. N. Hawke, 'Planning agreements in practice', *Journal of Planning and Environment Law*, 1981, pp. 5–14 and 86–97.

10 The case is documented in detail in S. L. Elkin, *Politics and Land Use Planning: The London Experience* (Cambridge University Press, 1974). See also O. Marriott, *The Property Boom* (Hamilton, 1967; Pan Books, 1969).

11 Town and Country Planning Act 1932, section 34.

12 It was not until 1974 that local authorities generally were empowered (by section 126 of the Housing Act of that year) to enter into positive covenants binding on successors in title, though an increasing number were obtaining local Act powers for this purpose.

13 M. Grant, 'Developers' contributions and planning gains: ethics and legalities', op. cit., p. 8.

14 op. cit., footnote 4 on p. 8.

15 White Paper, *Widening the Choice: The Next Steps in Housing*, Cmnd 5280 (HMSO, 1973).

16 op. cit., para. 24.

17 See Housing Act 1974, section 126.

18 J. Jowell, 'Bargaining in development control', *Journal of Planning and Environment Law*, 1977, pp. 420–1.

19 *R.* v. *London Borough of Hillingdon ex. p. Royco Homes Ltd* [1974] QB 720.

20 J. Jowell, op. cit., p. 428.

21 op. cit., p. 419.

22 M. Grant, 'Developers' contributions and planning gains: ethics and legalities', op. cit., pp. 8-9.

23 An exception is a 1968 circular: 'It is a general principle that no payment of money or other consideration can be required when granting a statutory permission, except where there is specific authority. Conditions requiring, for instance, the cession of land for road improvements or for open space, or requiring the developer to contribute money towards the provision of public car parking facilities, should not, therefore, be attached to planning permissions. Similarly, permission should not be granted subject to a condition that the applicant shall enter into an agreement under section 52 of the Act.' MHLG Circular 5/68, *The Use of Conditions in Planning Permissions* (HMSO, 1968), para. 34.

24 Quoted in 'Planning gain – bargaining or blackmail?', *Planner News*, December 1980, p. 12.

25 DoE Circular 22/80, which *inter alia* is concerned with the adequacy of land supply for private housebuilding, refers to planning agreements in relation to infrastructure: 'In preference to a refusal on the grounds that infrastructure is lacking it is better to consider whether the problem can be solved by an agreement with the developer under section 52 of the Town and Country Planning Act 1971. Even if it is a compelling objection that provision of the necessary infrastructure would be too costly, the possibility that the developer would offer a section 52 agreement which adequately met the objections should be explored before a refusal is issued.'

26 Town and Country Planning Association, 'Policy statement: charges for planning applications', *Town and Country Planning*, vol. 49 (October 1980), p. 307.

27 Speech by the Under-Secretary of State for the Environment (Mr Marcus Fox), *Standing Committee Debates on the Local Government, Planning and Land (No. 2) Bill*, col. 245, 22 April 1980. By contrast, the secretary of state in the previous government held that 'I do not think a scheme can be devised which is at the same time administratively simple, fair to all types of applicant and productive of worthwhile revenue.' (Quoted in op. cit., col. 225.)

28 DoE Circular 22/80, *Development Control – Policy and Practice* (HMSO, 1980), para. 15.

29 Details taken from *The Times*, 18 February 1981.

30 During the debates, a strong case was made for exemptions in amenity areas, for historic buildings and so forth, particularly where the designation required owners to obtain planning permission for operations which would not otherwise have been necessary. This was rejected on the grounds that the list of exemptions would rapidly grow and thus complicate a scheme which was intended to be essentially simple to comprehend and administer. See *Standing Committee Debates*, op. cit., cols. 2208-12, 17 April 1980.

31 For a general discussion of 'Enforcement problems', see the article of that title by A. Samuels in *Journal of Planning and Environment Law*, 1977, pp. 771-80; and J. Davies, 'Enforcement', in *Development Control: Thirty Years On*, Journal of Planning and Environment Law, Occasional Paper (Sweet & Maxwell, 1979), pp. 47-69. See also Department of the Environment, *Memorandum on Enforcement of Planning Control and Allied Matters*, DoE Circular 109/77 (HMSO, 1977); and Department of the Environment, *Selected Enforcement and Allied Appeals* (HMSO, 1974) which deals with points of law and technicalities which have arisen on appeals.

32 Originally, stop notices applied only to 'operations'. The 1977 Town and Country Planning (Amendment) Act (and its Scottish counterpart) extended them to material change in use. This Act also strengthened the provisions in various detailed ways. See DoE Circular 82/77, *Town and Country Planning (Amendment) Act 1977* (HMSO, 1977), and SDD Circular 16/1977, *Town and Country Planning (Scotland) Act 1977* (Scottish Development Department, 1977).

33 See previous note.
34 DoE Circular 82/77, op. cit., para. 3.
35 *Journal of Planning Law*, 1957, pp. 783-5, and *Journal of Planning Law*, 1958, pp. 334-7 and 384-5.
36 *Journal of Planning and Property Law*, 1962, pp. 753-4.
37 *Final Report of the Expert Committee on Compensation and Betterment*, Cmd 6386 (HMSO, 1942), p. 98, para. 241.
38 DoE Circular 22/80, *Development Control - Policy and Practice* (HMSO, 1980), para. 11.
39 op. cit., paras 12-14.
40 *Municipal Journal*, 5 December 1980.
41 Ministry of Town and Country Planning, Circular 100, 1950, *Development by Government Departments*.
42 DoE Circular 7/77, *Development by Government Departments* (HMSO, 1977). Previous circulars were 80/71, 71/72 and 67/74. The 1977 circular is amended by Circular 2/81, to take account of the reallocation of development control functions under the Local Government, Planning and Land Act 1980. For Scotland, see SDD Circular 49/1977, *Development by Government Departments* (Scottish Development Department, 1977).
43 DoE Circular 12/73, *Town and Country Planning General Development Order 1973* (HMSO, 1973), Appendix C: 'Development by statutory undertakers: consultation and publicity'. For Scotland, see SDD Circular 25/1973, *Post Office Operational Land* (Scottish Development Department, 1973); and SDD Circular 52/75, *Town and Country Planning (Development by Planning Authorities) (Scotland) Regulations 1975* (Scottish Development Department, 1975).
44 See DoE Circular 42/60, *Caravan Sites and Control of Development Act 1960* (HMSO, 1960).
45 *Caravans as Homes* (Arton Wilson Report), Cmnd 872 (HMSO, 1959).
46 MHLG Development Control Policy Notes No. 8, *Caravan Sites* (HMSO, 1969; rev. edn, 1974).
47 Department of the Environment, *Development Control Statistics 1975/76* (DoE, 1977), Table 1. (Statistics for this class of development are no longer separately published.)
48 The issues raised by mobile homes are similar. See Department of the Environment, *Report of the Mobile Homes Review* (HMSO, 1977).
49 DoE, *Caravan Sites*, op. cit.
50 *HC Debates*, col. 610, 5 November 1980.
51 See also the Scottish report, *Scotland's Travelling People* (HMSO, 1971); and B. Adams *et al.*, *Gypsies and Government Policy in England* (Heinemann, 1976).
52 DoE Circular 49/68, *Caravan Sites Act 1968* (HMSO, 1968).
53 *Accommodation for Gypsies: A Report on the Working of the Caravan Sites Act 1968*, by John Cripps (HMSO, 1977).
54 op. cit., para. 2.5.
55 DoE Circular 57/78, *Accommodation for Gypsies: Report by Sir John Cripps* (HMSO, 1978); and DoE Circular 11/79, *Accommodation for Gypsies: Grant Towards the Capital Cost of Providing Gypsy Caravan Sites* (HMSO, 1979).
56 F. Pearce, 'Gloomy prospect for gypsies', *Municipal Engineering*, 26 August 1980.
57 MHLG Circular 26/69, *Purchase Notices* (HMSO, 1969), Appendix I, para. 4.
58 Planning Advisory Group, *The Future of Development Plans* (HMSO, 1965), p. 51, para. 7.33.
59 See the debate on the Private Member's *Planning Blight and Worsenment Bill*, *HC Debates*, 27 February 1970. (The Bill, introduced by Mr Walter Clegg, failed to get a second reading.)
60 DoE Circular 46/70, *Town and Country Planning Acts 1962 to 1968: Planning Blight* (HMSO, 1970).
61 Further detail is to be found in DoE Circular 73/73, *Land Compensation Act 1973*

(HMSO, 1973); DoE Roads Circular 44/73, *Land Compensation Act 1973: A New Approach to the Planning and Design of Roads* (DoE, 1973); and, for Scotland, SDD Circular 84/1973, *Land Compensation (Scotland) Act 1973* (Scottish Development Department, 1973).

62   See Central Housing Advisory Committee, *Council Housing: Purposes, Procedures and Priorities* (HMSO, 1969), ch. 7.
63   The Dobry Reports were: *Control of Demolition* (1974); *Review of the Development Control System*, Interim Report (1974); and *Review of the Development Control System, Final Report* (1975) (all HMSO).
64   Ministry of Housing and Local Government, *Management Study on Development Control* (HMSO, 1967).
65   Local Government (Scotland) Act 1973, section 179 (1). For a discussion of this regional power see E. Young, 'Call in of planning applications by regional planning authorities', *Journal of Planning and Environment Law*, 1979, pp. 358–70.
66   DoE Circular 142/73, *Streamlining the Planning Machine* (HMSO, 1973).
67   Department of the Environment, *Development Control Statistics 1978–79* (DoE, 1980), Table 1. The figures for 1978–9 are provisional.
68   See note 63 above.
69   T. Eddison, *Town and Country Planning*, April 1975.
70   J. Jowell, 'Development control' (a review article on the Dobry Report), *Political Quarterly*, vol. 46, no. 3 (July–August 1975).
71   *Control of Demolition: Report by George Dobry Q.C.* (HMSO, 1974).
72   *Journal of Planning and Environment Law*, January 1976.
73   DoE Circular 113/75, *Review of the Development Control System* (HMSO, 1975). It should be added that many of Dobry's recommendations for improvements in the working methods of local planning authorities were accepted: see DoE Circular 9/76, *The Dobry Report: Action by Local Planning Authorities* (HMSO, 1976).
74   *Eighth Report from the Expenditure Committee, Session 1976–77, Planning Procedures: Vol. 1, Report; Vol. 2, Evidence; Vol. 3, Appendices*, HC Papers 395-I, 395-II and 395-III (HMSO, May 1977).
75   *Planning Procedures: The Government's Response to the Eighth Report from the Expenditure Committee, Session 1976–77, HC 395*, Cmnd 7056 (HMSO, 1978).
76   *Planning Procedures*, op. cit., Vol. 2, Q. 109, 114, 115, etc.
77   op. cit., Vol. 3, p. 733.
78   Dobry rejected GDO relaxation 'because I became convinced that it was an unnecessarily crude response to the problem. It risks tipping the baby of control out with the bathwater of delay. Or – to change the metaphor – if the development industry is seen as a powerful but potentially dangerous machine, my solution was to modify the design of the protective guard so that the machine could operate more efficiently without too much increase in risk. Extension of the GDO amounts to disconnecting a large part of that protective guard altogether.' op. cit., Vol. 3, p. 735.
79   op. cit., Vol. 3, pp. 733–4.
80   op. cit., Vol. 1, para. 31.
81   op. cit., Vol. 1, para. 32.
82   DoE Circular 9/76, op. cit., para. 1.
83   *Municipal Engineering*, 29 July 1980; and *Planner News*, September 1980.
84   DoE Circular 22/80, *Development Control – Policy and Practice* (HMSO, 1980).
85   op. cit., Annex A, 'Planning permission for private sector house-building', para. 14.
86   loc. cit., para. 12.
87   'Two heads are better than one?: effects of the new Act on development control', *Planner News*, January 1981, pp. 4–5.
88   Section 86 of the Local Government, Planning and Land Act 1980.
89   Paragraph 32 (*d*) of Schedule 16 of the Local Government Act 1972.
90   DoE Circular 2/81, *Local Government, Planning and Land Act 1980; Health Services Act 1980 – Town and Country Planning: Development Control Functions* (HMSO, 1981), para. 2.

91 See the *Standing Committee Debates* on the 1980 Bill, 16 and 17 April 1980.
92 See Local Government, Planning and Land Act 1980, section 86.
93 DoE Circular 74/73 is cancelled. (See Circular 2/81, para. 4.)
94 Department of the Environment, *Planning Controls over Minor Development: Amending the General Development Order 1977* (DoE, 27 February 1980), p. 1.
95 SI 1977 No. 1781. See *Journal of Planning and Environment Law*, 1978, pp. 2-3. The Amendment Order is SI 1981 No. 245.
96 For the background to this, see Department of the Environment, *Consultation Paper: Planning Relaxations for Small Industrial Premises* (DoE, July 1980) and, as an example of the response from the planning profession, the *Memorandum of Observations* on this paper by the Royal Town Planning Institute (September 1980). See also *Development Costs and Delays* (Hillier Parker May and Rowden, February 1977).
97 *HC Debates*, 23 March 1981.
98 See the earlier discussion in this chapter on the Eton High Street fish and chip restaurant. The plot thickens when one inquires into the position of MacDonalds and Burger King, Kentucky Fried Chicken, Pizza Parlours and such like. These fast food establishments have been careful to designate themselves as restaurants rather than shops. See I. Turner, 'Fish and chips, fast food and the Use Classes Order', *Journal of Planning and Environment Law*, 1981, pp. 80-5.

Chapter 5

PLANNING THE ENVIRONMENT

AMENITY

'Amenity' is one of the key concepts in British town and country planning: yet nowhere in the legislation is it defined. The Act legislation merely states that 'if it appears to a local planning authority that it is expedient in the interests of amenity', they may take certain action – in relation, for example, to unsightly neglected waste land[1] or to the preservation of trees. It is also one of the factors that may need to be taken into account in controlling advertisements and in determining whether a discontinuance order should be made. It is a term widely used in planning refusals and appeals: indeed the phrase 'injurious to the interests of amenity' has become part of the stock-in-trade jargon of the planning world. But like the proverbial elephant, amenity is easier to recognise than to define – with the important difference that, though all would be agreed that an elephant is such, there is considerable scope for disagreement on the degree and importance of amenities: which amenities should be preserved, in what way they should be preserved and how much expense (public or private) is justified.

The problem is relatively straightforward in so far as trees are concerned. It is much more acute in connection with electricity pylons – yet the Central Electricity Generating Board is specifically charged not only with maintaining an efficient and co-ordinated supply of electricity but also with the preservation of amenity. Here the question is not merely one of sensitivity but also of the enormous additional cost of preserving amenities by placing cables underground.

Apart from the problems of cost, there is the problem of determining how much control the public will accept. Poor architecture, ill-conceived schemes, 'mock-Tudor' frontages may upset the planning officer, but how much regulation of this type of 'amenity-injury' will be publicly acceptable? And how far can negative controls succeed in raising public standards? Here emphasis has been laid on design bulletins, design awards and such ventures as those of the Civic Trust – a body whose object is 'to promote beauty and fight ugliness in town, village and countryside'. Nevertheless, local authorities have power not only to prevent developments which would clash with amenity (for example, the siting of a repair garage in a residential area) but also to reject badly designed developments which are not intrinsically harmful. Indeed 'outline planning permission' for a proposal is often given on the condition that detailed plans and appearances meet the approval of the authority.

Since the 1950s there has been a marked sharpening of interest in amenity, caused partly by the rapid rate of development, and an awareness of the inadequacy of the planning system automatically to preserve and enhance amenity. The Transport Act of 1968, for instance, enables the use of a road by vehicles to be prohibited on amenity grounds for certain periods of the day. Perhaps the most striking provision is to be found in the Countryside (Scotland) Act 1967 and the Countryside Act 1968 which requires every minister, government department and public body to have regard to the desirability of conserving the natural beauty and amenity of the countryside in all their functions relating to land. Lawyers may rightly point out that this does not constitute, of itself, an effective restriction on any statutory power or discretion, but it is an important statement of policy and one which the statutory and voluntary guardians of amenity will seize upon whenever it is infringed. There is more to planning than law.

The preservation and development of amenity thus form a basic objective of planning policy. From this point of view, amenity can hardly be discussed separately. Nevertheless, there are certain matters where planning controls are specifically, and almost exclusively, concerned with amenity. The control of advertisements is a prime example of this.

CONTROL OF ADVERTISEMENTS

The need to control advertisements has long been accepted. Indeed, the first Advertisements Regulation Act of 1907 antedated by two years the first Town Planning Act. But, even when amended and extended (in 1925 and 1932), the control was quite inadequate. Not only were the powers permissive, they were also limited. For instance, under the 1932 Act, the right of appeal (on the ground that an advertisement did not injure the amenities of the area) was to the magistrates court – hardly an appropriate body for such a purpose. The 1947 Act set out to remedy the deficiencies.[2] There are, however, particular difficulties in establishing a legal code for the control of advertisements. Advertisements may range in size from a small window-notice to a massive hoarding; they vary in purpose from a bus-stop sign to a demand to buy a certain make of detergent; they could be situated alongside a cathedral, in a busy shopping street, or in a particularly beautiful rural setting; they might be pleasant or obnoxious to look at; they might be temporary or permanent; and so on. The task of devising a code which would take all the relevant factors into account and, at the same time, achieve a balance between the conflicting interests of legitimate advertising or notification and 'amenity' presents real problems. Advertisers themselves frequently complain that decisions in apparently similar cases have not been consistent with each other. The official departmental view is that no case is exactly like another, and hard and fast rules cannot be applied: each case has to be considered on its individual merits in the light of the tests of amenity and – the other factor to be taken into account – public safety.

The control of advertisements is exercised by regulations.[3] The secretary of state has very wide powers of making regulations 'for restricting or regulating the display of advertisements so far as appears to the Secretary of State to be expedient in the interests of amenity or public safety'. The question of 'public safety' is rather simpler than that of amenity – though there is ample scope for disagreement: the relevant issue is whether an advertisement is likely to cause danger to road users (and also to 'persons who may use any railway, waterway – including coastal waters – dock, harbour or airfield'). Examples are advertisements which obstruct the line of sight at a corner or bend, or obstruct the view of a traffic sign or signal, and illuminated advertisements which are likely to dazzle or confuse road users or are likely to be mistaken for traffic lights.

The definition of an advertisement is not quite as complicated as that of 'development', but it is very wide: 'advertisement means any word, letter, model, sign, placard, board, notice, device or representation, whether illuminated or not, in the nature of, and employed wholly or partly for the purpose of, advertisement, announcement or direction'. Five classes of advertisement are 'excepted' from all control – those on enclosed land, within a building, on or in a vehicle, incorporated in and forming part of the fabric of a building, and displayed on an article for sale. As one might expect, there are some interesting refinements of these categories, which can be ignored for present purposes (though we might note, in passing, that a vehicle must be kept moving, or to use the more exact legal language, must normally be employed as a moving vehicle on any highway or railway – and the same applies to vessels). With these exceptions, no advertisements may be displayed without 'consent'. However, certain categories of advertisements can be displayed without 'express consent'; so long as the local authority takes no action, they are 'deemed' to have received consent. These include bus-stop signs and timetables, hotel and inn signs, professional or trade plates, 'To Let' signs, election notices, statutory advertisements and traffic signs.[4]

Except in relation to advertisements to which the 'deemed consent' procedure applies, a local authority can serve a discontinuance order when they are satisfied that removal is necessary 'to remedy a substantial injury to the amenity of the locality or a danger to members of the public' (Table 5.1). There is the normal right of appeal to the secretary of state.

Table 5.1 Advertisement Applications, England and Wales 1978/9[6]

Type of authority	Within areas of special control			Outside areas of special control			
	Discontinuance notices served	New proposals		Discontinuance notices served	New proposals		Total decisions
		Consent granted	Consent refused		Consent granted	Consent refused	
Non-metropolitan counties	–	1,129	652	34	11,627	3,678	17,120
Metropolitan counties	–	65	27	18	4,975	1,524	6,609
London boroughs	–	2	6	19	4,254	745	5,026
England	–	1,196	685	71	20,856	5,947	28,755
Wales*	–	319	141	–	863	301	1,624
England and Wales	–	1,515	826	71	21,719	6,248	30,379

*Figures for Radnor DC and Montgomery DC not available.

This is not, however, all there is to advertisement control. In some areas, for example, national parks or near a cathedral, it may be desirable virtually to prohibit all advertisements of the poster type and seriously to restrict other advertisements including those normally displayed by the ordinary trader. Accordingly, local planning authorities have power to define 'areas of special control' where 'special protection on grounds of amenity' is thought desirable. (By 1969 over a third of England and Wales had become subject to this 'special control'.)⁵ Within an area of special control the general rule is that no advertisement may be displayed; such advertisements as are given express consent are considered as exceptions to this general rule.

This has proved a very difficult field in which to obtain unanimity, but the effectiveness of the controls and agreements is very apparent to the European (and, still more, the American) visitor.

CONSERVATION

Britain has a remarkable wealth of historic buildings, but changing economic and social conditions often turn this legacy into a liability. The cost of maintenance, the financial attractions of redevelopment, the need for urban renewal, the roads programme and similar factors often threaten buildings which are of architectural or historic interest.

This is a field in which voluntary organisations have been particularly active – as witness the work of the National Trust, the Ancient Monuments Society, the Society for the Protection of Ancient Buildings, the Victorian Society and others. As is so often the case, voluntary effort preceded state action. The Society for the Protection of Ancient Buildings was founded in 1877. The National Trust (or to use its full name, the National Trust for Places of Historic Interest or Natural Beauty) was founded in 1895. Though the first state action came in 1882 with the Ancient Monuments Act, this was important chiefly because it acknowledged the interest of the state in the preservation of ancient monuments. Such preservation as was achieved under this Act (and under similar Acts passed in the following thirty years) resulted from the goodwill and co-operation of private owners. It was not until 1913 that powers were provided to compulsorily prevent the damage or destruction of monuments.

Strictly speaking, the Ancient Monuments Acts are outside the realm of town and country planning, but their objectives and scope demand that they be considered within the same context.

Provisions relating to ancient monuments have been amended several times, the latest being 1979 when the Ancient Monuments and Archaeological Areas Act was passed.⁷ The term 'ancient monument' is defined very widely in the 1913 Act: it is defined even more so in the Act of 1979. An ancient monument is 'any scheduled monument' and 'any other monument which in the opinion of the Secretary of State is of public interest by reason of the historic, architectural, traditional, artistic or archaeological interest attaching in it'.[8]

This is so broad a definition that it could include almost any building, structure, or site of archaeological interest made or occupied by man at any time. The legislation requires the secretary of state to prepare a 'schedule' of monuments which appear to him to be 'of national importance'. In this he is advised by three Ancient Monuments Boards for England, Scotland and Wales.[9]

There are over 12,000 of these 'scheduled monuments' in Britain (of which 800 are in the charge of the Department of the Environment). These monuments are protected and any works have to be approved by the secretary of state. Such approval is known as 'scheduled monument consent'.[10] Where consent is refused, compensation is payable if the owner thereby suffers loss.

The 1979 Act also empowers the secretary of state to acquire compulsorily any ancient monument 'for the purpose of securing its preservation'. (Note that this power applies to any ancient monument, not solely those which have been scheduled.)

The 'archaeological areas' in the title of the 1979 Act represent a quite new concept. Such areas, designated by the secretary of state, are 'areas of archaeological importance'. No further definition is provided. The objective is to provide facilities for the investigation and recording of archaeological remains prior to development.[11] This is known as 'rescue archaeology', and was the subject of much discussion before the Bill was drafted.[12]

In a designated area, development is subject to detailed control and is allowed only on the approval by the local authority of an 'operations notice'.

Both the secretary of state and any local authority can give financial assistance for archaeological investigation.

Grants are also available under the Historic Buildings and Ancient Monuments Act 1953, for the preservation of 'buildings of outstanding historic or architectural interest' – and of their contents and adjoining land. They can also purchase such buildings or accept them as gifts. Three Historic Buildings Councils (for England, Scotland and Wales) were set up as advisory bodies. The 1953 Act was passed primarily to deal with the problems of preserving houses or buildings which were inhabited or 'capable of occupation' – these were not covered by the earlier legislation. Between 1953 and 1979 some £50 million of grants were allocated by the Historic Buildings Councils.[13]

LISTED BUILDINGS

Under planning legislation, the central departments maintain lists of buildings of 'special architectural or historic interest'.[14] There are two objectives here. First, 'listing' is intended to provide guidance to local planning authorities in carrying out their planning functions. For example, in planning redevelopment, local authorities will take into account listed buildings in the area. Buildings in a slum clearance area may be preserved with the aid not only of grants from the Historic Buildings Council but also with house improvement grants available under the Housing Acts.[15] Secondly, and more directly effective, when a building is listed no demolition or alteration which would materially alter it can be undertaken by the owner without the approval of the local authority. This is technically termed 'listed building consent'.

Applications for listed building consent have to be advertised, and any representation must be taken into account by the local authority before they reach their decision. Where demolition is involved, the local authority have to notify the appropriate local amenity society, and a number of other bodies, namely, the Ancient Monuments Society, the Council for British Archaeology, the Georgian Group, the Society for the Protection of Ancient Buildings, the Victorian Society, as well as the Royal Commission on Historical Monuments. Again, any representations have to be taken into account when the application is being considered.

If, after all this, the local authority are 'disposed to grant consent' for the demolition (and, in certain cases, the alteration) of a listed building, they have to refer the application to the secretary of state so that he can decide whether to 'call in' the proposal and deal with it himself.

All these provisions apply to listed buildings (of which there were, in 1978, some 260,000 in England and Wales alone),[16] but the secretary of state has power to list a building at any time, and local authorities can serve a 'building preservation notice' on an unlisted building; this has the effect of protecting the building for six months, thus giving time for considering whether or not it should be listed.

With a listed building the presumption is in favour of preservation. Indeed 'listing' is in essence a collective preservation order. It is an offence to demolish or to alter a listed building unless listed building consent has been obtained. This is different from the general position in relation to planning permission where an offence arises only after the enforcement procedure has been invoked. Fines for illegal works to listed buildings are related to the financial benefit expected by the offender.

The legislation also provides a deterrent against deliberate neglect of historic buildings. This was one way in which astute owners could circumvent the earlier statutory provisions: a building could be neglected to such an extent that demolition was unavoidable, thus giving the owner the possibility of reaping the development value of the site. In such cases the local authority can now compulsorily acquire the building at a low price, technically known as 'minimum compensation'. If the secretary of state approves, the compensation is assessed on the assumption that neither planning permission nor listed building consent would be given for any works to the building except for those for restoring it to, and maintaining it in, a proper state of repair; in short, all development value is excluded.

The strength of these powers (and others not detailed here) reflect the concern which is felt at the loss of historic buildings. They are not, however, all of this penal nature. Indeed, ministerial guidance has emphasised the need for a positive and comprehensive approach. (Grants are available under the Local Authorities (Historic Buildings) Act 1962, the Historic Buildings and Ancient Monuments Act 1953, the Ancient Monuments and Archaeological Areas Act 1979, the Housing Acts and – the latest newcomer – the National Heritage Act (which is outlined in the following section).[17] Local authorities can also purchase properties by agreement, possibly with Exchequer aid under the 1953 Act. Furthermore, an owner of a building who is refused 'listed building consent' can, in certain circumstances, serve a notice on the local authority requiring them to purchase the property. This is known as a 'listed building purchase notice'. The issue to be decided here is whether the land has become 'incapable of reasonably beneficial use'. It is not sufficient to show that it is of less use to the owner in its present state than if developed.

More important is the emphasis on areas, as distinct from individual buildings, of architectural or historic interest. This was introduced by the Civic Amenities Act 1967 (promoted as a Private Member's Bill by Duncan Sandys, President of the Civic Trust, and passed with government backing). This gave statutory recognition for the first time to the area concept, and made it a duty of local planning authorities 'to determine which parts of their areas are areas of special architectural or historic interest, the character of which it is desirable to preserve or enhance' and to designate such areas as 'conservation areas'. When a conservation area has been designated, the Act requires special attention to be paid in all planning decisions to the preservation or enhancement of its character and appearance.

The 1974 Town and Country Amenities Act extended the powers of local authorities in dealing with conservation areas and the preservation of historic buildings. In particular, it brought the demolition of most buildings in conservation areas under control.

In 1979 there were over 4,000 conservation areas in Great Britain – ranging from the whole of the centres of such historic sites as Chester to small rural villages.[18]

In spite of all this, there is widespread concern about the adequacy of finance for historic buildings and areas, about the 'secrecy' of the DoE listing procedure,[19] about a proposal to transfer some responsibility for deciding on the demolition of listed buildings,[20] and about legal ('pre-listing') and illegal demolitions,[21] and about the inadequate staffing of the DoE.[22]

Nevertheless, there is good news as well. First, following the adoption of wider criteria for assessing interwar buildings, the Environment Secretary (Michael Heseltine) has listed thirty-seven buildings of the 1914–39 period. These include London's Dorchester and Savoy Hotels, Broadcasting House and Waterloo Bridge.[23] Secondly, a new source of funds has emerged with the National Heritage Memorial Fund.

NATIONAL HERITAGE ACT

In 1946 a National Land Fund was established as a memorial to those who lost their lives during the war. Some £50 million of Exchequer funds were allocated to the Fund for use to assist organisations whose purpose was to promote appreciation and enjoyment of the country-side. The money was used for the purchase by the secretary of state of buildings of outstanding architectural or historic interest, together with their contents.[24] The Fund was 'raided' by the Exchequer in 1957[25] and became moribund. 'The folly of this was illustrated by the contro-versial sale of the assets of the Mentmore estate in 1977 which exposed the need for a fund which could exercise similar powers to those of the Secretary of State, with sufficient resources, and without excessive central government control.' This is what the National Heritage Act of 1980 does:

> There shall be a fund known as the National Heritage Memorial Fund, to be a memorial to those who have died for the United Kingdom.

In addition to normal Exchequer payments into the Fund, further payments can be made in relation to property accepted in satisfaction of tax debts.

The Fund is administered by a body of trustees. They can make loans or grants for any property (in the widest sense of the term) which is 'of importance to the national heritage'.[26]

PRESERVATION OF TREES AND WOODLANDS

Trees are clearly – so far as town and country planning is concerned – a matter of amenity.[27] Indeed, the powers which local authorities have with regard to trees can be exercised only if it is 'expedient in the interests of amenity'. Where the local authority are satisfied that it is 'expedient', they can make a tree preservation order – applicable to trees, groups of trees, or woodlands. Such an order can prohibit the cutting down, topping, or lopping of trees except with the consent of the local planning authority.

Mere preservation, however, leads eventually to decay and thus defeats its object. To prevent this, a local authority can make replanting obligatory when they give permission for trees to be felled. The aim is to avoid any clash between good forestry and the claims of amenity. But the timber of woodlands always has a claim to be treated as a commercial crop, and though the making of a tree preservation order does not necessarily involve the owner in any financial loss (isolated trees or groups of trees are usually planted expressly as an amenity), there are occasions when it does.

Yet though woodlands are primarily a timber crop from which the owner is entitled to benefit, two principles have been laid down which qualify this. First, 'the national interest demands that woodlands should be managed in accordance with the principles of good forestry', and secondly, where they are of amenity value, the owner has 'a public duty to act with reasonable regard for amenity aspects'. It follows that a refusal to permit felling or the imposition of conditions on operations which are either contrary to the principles of good forestry or destructive of amenity ought not to carry any compensation rights. But where there is a clash between these two principles compensation is payable.

Thus in a case where the 'principles of good forestry' dictate that felling should take place, but this would result in too great a sacrifice of amenity, the owner can claim compensation for the loss which he suffers. Normally a compromise is reached whereby the felling is deferred or phased. The commercial felling of timber is subject to licence from the Forestry Commission and special arrangements exist for consultation between the Commission, the central department and the local planning authority.

Planning powers go considerably further than simply enabling local authorities to preserve trees. The National Parks and Access to the Countryside Act 1949 enabled planning approvals to be given subject to the condition that trees are planted, and local authorities themselves have power to plant trees on any land in their area. With the increasing vulnerability of trees and woodlands to urban development and the needs of modern farming, wider powers and more Exchequer aid have been provided by successive statutes. Local planning authorities are now *required* to ensure that conditions (preferably reinforced by tree preservation orders) are imposed for the protection of existing trees and for the planting of new ones. This, together with the department's continuous emphasis on the importance of trees, has led to a substantial increase in the number of tree preservation orders being made. In March 1977 nearly 26,000 orders were in force in England.[28]

Co-ordination of voluntary effort in relation to the promotion of tree-planting and the protection of trees is effected through the Tree Council. This is 'a forum for some 25 national voluntary organisations and professional associations with a central aim to promote the conservation, planting and good maintenance of amenity trees and woodlands'.[29]

GOOD DESIGN

Good design is an elusive quality which cannot easily be defined. As Sir William Holford has said,[30] 'design cannot be taught by correspondence; words are inadequate, and being inadequate may then become misleading, or even dangerous. For the competent designer a handbook on design is unnecessary, and for the incompetent it is almost useless as a medium of instruction.' Yet local authorities have to pass judgement on the design merits of thousands of planning proposals each year, and pressure is mounting from governmental, official and professional bodies for higher design standards to be imposed. The principles of good design and their execution lie outside the scope of this book; here reference can be made only to the powers and practices of local authorities, and some of the particular problems which arise. It needs to be stressed, however, that good design is not basically a matter of cost, but of the combined skills and sensitivity of the architect, the client and the builder.

Planning authorities have a clear legal power to grant planning permission subject to conditions relating to design and appearance. Planning permission is frequently given for a proposed development on the basis of an 'outline application', and subject to the condition that the detailed plans meet with their approval: if the detailed plans are unsatisfactory they can be rejected. There is a difficult problem here which basically stems from the fact that it is not the function of the planning authority to provide developers with good designs, and the amendment of a poor design may produce a compromise result almost as unsatisfactory as the original. Furthermore, the impossibility of laying down generally applicable principles (except that of employing a 'good' architect!) makes the task of the local planning authority a difficult one. A well-staffed and organised authority will spend considerable time with developers discussing sketch-plans – but not all authorities are well staffed or organised, and the importance which is placed on this aspect of planning control varies greatly between authorities. Some have prepared notes for the guidance of developers, and there are various publications of the DoE and of voluntary bodies which have the same objective.[31] Major developments are often referred to the Royal Fine Art Commissions for their opinion.[32]

There has been much controversy over this question of aesthetic design. A neat illustration of the arguments is provided by a quotation from the Expenditure Committee's report on *Planning Procedures*:

The Royal Institute of British Architects said that at best aesthetic

control 'has conduced to acceptable mediocrity, and has not prevented much bad building or the destruction of many pleasant
places'; they argued that 'in the interest of cost and effectiveness
detailed control of external appearance should be greatly reduced',
and that the quality of design could best be improved if all applications for planning permission were submitted by qualified architects.
On the other hand, a representative of the Association of District
Councils told the Sub-Committee that 'The architect is trained to
analyse the problems of the client in terms of floor space, then design
from the inside outwards. The last thing he does is the external
exploration of the client's floor requirements. Planners do it the
other way round, the impression of the building seen in the street.'
The Royal Institution of Chartered Surveyors strongly disagreed
with the proposal for an architects' monopoly of applications.[33]

Clearly professional sensitivities are very much to the fore in this
debate! The Expenditure Committee, though having 'some sympathy'
with the RIBA's view, considered that 'complete removal of aesthetic
control would be quite unacceptable to public opinion'. Nevertheless,
they felt that planning authorities needed to 'exercise restraint in this
regard, since it would be most undesirable to stifle creativity and
innovation'. They concluded that planning authorities should reject
applications solely on the grounds of aesthetic detail only in 'sensitive
areas' such as national parks, conservation areas and listed buildings.
They also proposed that recommendations relating to aesthetic
matters should be handled only by 'appropriately qualified officers',
and that the department should issue revised guidance to planning
authorities.
The views of the secretary of state (Mr Michael Heseltine), which
had been expressed at the RTPI Summer School, were reproduced in
DoE Circular 22/80:

Far too many of those involved in the system – whether the planning
officer or the amateur on the planning committee – have tried to
impose their standards quite unnecessarily on what individuals want
to do . . . Democracy as a system of government I will defend
against all comers but as an arbiter of taste or as a judge of aesthetic
or artistic standards it falls short of a far less controlled system of
individual, corporate or institutional patronage and initiative.[34]

Mr Heseltine may have been expressing a strong personal view here
(and he has been a particularly outspoken and personally influential
secretary of state), but the official policy clearly reflects it:

Planning authorities should recognise that aesthetics is an extremely
subjective matter. They should not therefore impose their tastes on

developers simply because they believe them to be superior.
Developers should not be compelled to conform to the fashion of
the moment at the expense of individuality, originality or traditional styles. Nor should they be asked to adopt designs which are
unpopular with their customers or clients.

Nevertheless control of external appearance can be important
especially for instance in environmentally sensitive areas such as
national parks, areas of outstanding natural beauty, conservation
areas and areas where the quality of environment is of a particularly
high standard. Local planning authorities should reject obviously
poor designs which are out of scale or character with their surroundings. They should confine concern to those aspects of design
which are significant for the aesthetic quality of the area. Only
exceptionally should they control design details if the sensitive
character of the area or the particular building justifies it. Even
where such detailed control is exercised it should not be over-
fastidious in such matters as, for example, the precise shade of
colour of bricks. They should be closely guided in such matters by
their professionally qualified advisers. This is especially important
where a building has been designed by an architect for a particular
site. Design guides may have a useful role to play provided they are
used as guidance and not as detailed rules.

Control of external appearance should only be exercised where
there is a fully justified reason for doing so. If local planning
authorities take proper account of this policy there should be fewer
instances of protracted negotiations over the design of projects and
a reduction in the number of appeals to the Secretaries of State on
matters of design. When such appeals are made the Secretaries of
State will be very much guided by the policy advice set out in this
circular in determining them.[35]

THE CONTROL OF POLLUTION

Concern about pollution is not new: it was as early as 1273 that action
in Britain was taken to protect the environment from polluted air: a
royal proclamation of that year prohibited the use of coal in London.
(It was not effective, despite the dire penalties: it is recorded that a
man was sent to the scaffold in 1306 for burning coal instead of
charcoal.)

What is new (apart from the abolition of capital punishment) is,
first, the huge scale of the pollution problem and, secondly, the
increasing determination to tackle it. 1970 – European Conservation
Year – saw the publication of the White Paper on *The Protection of
the Environment*,[36] and the establishment of a Royal Commission on
Environmental Pollution. Previously there had been numerous
inquiries on specific problems of pollution – from the Beaver

Committee on air pollution to the Pippard Committee on 'the effects of heated and other effluents and discharges on the condition of the tidal reaches of the River Thames'; from the Browne Committee on refuse storage and collection to the Wilson Committee on the problem of noise; from the Key Committee on 'the experimental disposal of house refuse in wet and dry pits' to the Jeger Committee on sewage disposal.[37] By contrast the remit of the Royal Commission is boundless: 'to advise on matters, both national and international, concerning the pollution of the environment; on the adequacy of research in this field; and the future possibilities of danger to the environment'.

Also of particular note is the Protection of the Environment Bill, introduced by the Conservative government in 1973, but passed as the Control of Pollution Act 1974 by a Labour government. In its first guise, there was an interesting debate (in the House of Lords) on a proposal to introduce a 'general standard' for environmental protection: this would have required all public bodies to have regard to the impact of any major development (whether public or private) on the environment. This was explicitly based on American legislation (the National Environment Protection Act), with its requirement that any federal project has to be preceded by an 'environmental impact statement'. This proposal made no progress, and the title of the Act is more accurate than that of the initial Bill: it deals with four main issues: the deposit and disposal of waste on land; water pollution; noise, and atmospheric pollution.

It is impossible to deal with all these and other relevant issues within the confines of this chapter; and the selection of issues must be arbitrary. As with 'town and country planning' and 'amenity', 'environmental pollution' admits of no simple delimitation. The issues selected are air pollution, derelict land, minerals and noise.

CLEAN AIR

Those who pollute the air are no longer sent to the gallows, but, though gentler methods are now preferred, it was not until the disastrous London smog of 1952 (resulting in 4,000 deaths) that really effective action was taken – though, as can be seen from Table 5.2, air pollution still ranks highest in the listing of public concerns about pollution.

The Beaver Report of 1954[38] described the effects of air pollution on health and made comprehensive recommendations on the prevention of pollution by smoke from industry and domestic chimneys, grit and dust, sulphur dioxide, motor vehicle exhausts and smoke from railway locomotives. Particularly telling was the Committee's estimate of the economic cost of pollution: £50 million a year through inefficiently burning fuel; £150 million in lost efficiency in agriculture, industry and

Table 5.2 *Concern about Pollution, Great Britain 1976 and 1978*[39]

*'One of the problems concerning
many people today is pollution of the
environment. What types of pollution –
if any – do you personally feel concerned
about?':*

	%	
	1976	*1978*
Air pollution	39	45
Water pollution	40	38
Land pollution	22	20
Noise pollution	11	11
Visual pollution (eyesores, etc.)	12	12
Other types of pollution	4	9
Not concerned	18	11
No answer/don't know	6	6

transport caused by reduced plant growth and hours of daylight and increased illness; and £150 million from corrosion (due largely to sulphur dioxide) – a total of £350 million a year. (These figures are now, of course, much out of date.)

There has been a growing emphasis on reducing air pollution as a part of a more general policy of environmental improvement. The Hunt Committee, for instance, in discussing problems of economic growth, argued that 'tackling air pollution, like clearing derelict land, is a necessary part of the environmental rehabilitation which the older industrial areas need'.[40]

The Clean Air Acts of 1956 and 1968 prohibit the emission of dark smoke, provide for the control of the emission of grit and dust from furnaces and establish a system for the approval by local authorities of chimney heights. However, the principal source of air pollution is domestic smoke and it is here that powers are the most extensive. Local authorities are empowered to establish 'smoke control areas' (subject to approval by the secretary of state) in which the emission of smoke from chimneys constitutes an offence. This involves the conversion of grates to enable smokeless fuels to be burned. Grants are given (normally) equal to seven-tenths of the approved expenditure on the cost of installing smokeless appliances. (Central government reimburse local authorities four-sevenths of their expenditure except where a local authority house is concerned, in which case the proportion is 40 per cent.) The provisions here are flexible. Grant can be made not only on conversion of open grates but also as an alternative an equivalent amount can be given towards the cost of installing central heating or electric space heaters.

A departmental *Memorandum on Smoke Control Areas* stressed the need for detailed surveys of proposed smoke control areas, and the importance of consultation with local fuel producers and distributors, before orders were made defining areas. Caution was urged:

> The establishment of smoke control areas will necessarily be gradual; it will need to be undertaken in stages, over a period of years in the larger towns. Progress will be governed by the supply of smokeless fuels, the rate at which appliances can be converted or replaced, and the rate at which local authorities are able to formulate and carry through their smoke control plans. Above all, progress – and indeed the whole success of the operation – will depend upon public support; upon people's understanding of the problems involved, and their readiness to co-operate in smoke control measures.[41]

So far as industrial emissions to the atmosphere are concerned, there are two systems of control in Britain. Most industrial processes are controlled by local authorities under the Clean Air and Public Health Acts. There are, however, certain processes which, because of their nature or the specialised and complex methods necessary to minimise emissions, are controlled by an expert and centralised inspectorate responsible directly to the Secretary of State for the Environment. This Alkali Inspectorate, as it is termed, originally came into being under the Alkali Act of 1863, now replaced by the Alkali Etc. Works Regulation Act of 1906, and the Alkali Etc. Works Order of 1966. A 1971 Order considerably extends the DoE's control over manufacturing operations which were previously regulated by local authorities. These measures affect grit and dust emissions from mineral industry processes, discharges from processes used in the petro-chemical industry and emissions from the smelting of aluminium.

For several years, because of complaints about dust, the Inspectorate had been called in by local authorities to advise on the control of grit and dust emissions from processes involving the crushing, grinding, drying, heating and handling of metallurgical slags, pulverised fuel ash, limestone, chalk, igneous rocks, gypsum, china clay, ball clay and china stone. These processes have now been 'scheduled' and brought under the direct control of the Alkali Inspectorate.

The 1971 Order also covers petroleum works and the primary smelting of aluminium. Until recently, primary aluminium smelters have operated only in Scotland (and were scheduled under the Scottish Alkali Acts). With the development of smelters in England and Wales, the Alkali Inspectorate have been involved from the outset in specifying the best practicable means of controlling emissions from these.

The 1971 Order also brings under the control of the Inspectorate processes involving the use of di-isocynates and the manufacture and purification of acrylates. (Di-isocynates are used, for example, in the manufacture of expanded plastics; acrylates are used, *inter alia*, for surface coatings for plastic production fibres and textiles.)

As is apparent, this is a highly technical field which involves specialist knowledge not to be expected among local authority staffs: hence the centralisation of responsibility in the Alkali Inspectorate.

More in the public eye is air pollution by motor vehicle exhausts. The United States government are requiring stringent standards – despite strong opposition from manufacturers. The 1970 White Paper *The Protection of the Environment: The Fight against Pollution*,[42] however, states that 'in Europe, due to the differences in climatic conditions, air pollution from petrol-engined vehicles presents a different and less acute problem, and the development of a completely pollution-free car might not be the most sensible use of resources'. The matter is being 'kept under review'; and the Royal Commission on Environmental Pollution, in their first report, have warned against complacency. This is a field in which more research is called for: even though diesel fumes 'can be very offensive . . . there is no firm evidence that the present level of these pollutants is a hazard to health'. But the same can be said of slum housing. It is to be expected that levels of public intolerance will rise, though the cost will have to be borne by a car-owning electorate.[43]

DERELICT LAND

Though there is no statutory definition, derelict land is generally regarded as 'land so damaged by industrial or other development that it is incapable of beneficial use without treatment'.[44] (This is the definition used in connection with the payment of government grants for reclamation.) Derelict land is commonly thought of as a legacy of the Industrial Revolution but this is only part of the picture: of the 43,000 hectares of 'inherited dereliction' in England recorded in 1974 (Table 5.3), some 10,000 hectares represented an *increase* since the end of 1971. Making allowance for land which had been reclaimed, the net increase in derelict land over the period was around 4,000 hectares.[45]

Much derelict land (particularly waste tips and abandoned industrial land) is concentrated in relatively small parts of the older industrial areas of the North, the Midlands and South Wales. It is this 'random incidence' (to use a phrase from the Hunt Committee Report on *Intermediate Areas*) which hinders a more rapid rate of reclamation. Quite small authorities with small resources of money, staff or expertise may find themselves faced with large problems. Even larger authorities may be faced with a formidable problem. The Hunt Committee called for a national programme and the establishment of a derelict land reclamation agency.[46] Both the Scottish and the Welsh

Development Agencies have powers in relation to land reclamation. In England the responsibilities lie with the local authorities.

Great advances in reclamation techniques have been made since the 1930s. Slow and costly 'pick and shovel' methods have now given way to modern earth-moving machines which can move mountains of material at relatively low cost. Techniques of 'making soil' have been refined, and it is now possible to make grass and trees grow in the most uncongenial conditions. Furthermore, rising land values and the need for sites for open space, playing fields and all types of urban development have added an impetus to reclamation in or near urban areas. But local authorities have no statutory duty to reclaim derelict land or to improve its appearance. Their powers are purely permissive and, as is so often the case, much depends on the energy of individual local authorities.

There are various powers available to local authorities quite apart from their normal powers to provide housing, open space and schools under which they can acquire derelict land and reclaim it during the normal course of development. Derelict land can also be acquired under the wider powers provided by the Planning Acts; these enable local authorities to undertake any work for which powers are not already available. Finally, the National Parks and Access to the Countryside Act gives specific powers for the acquisition of derelict land and the restoration and improvement of such land whether or not it is owned by the local authority. There is, thus, no shortage of powers.[47]

Government grants towards the cost of acquisition and reclamation of derelict land are available under several Acts. The detailed provisions and rates of grant change from time to time. Under the Industrial Development Act 1966 the rate was 85 per cent in development areas, provided that the clearance of the land was 'expedient with a view to contributing to the development of industry'. The Local Government Act of the same year provided a 50 per cent grant for other areas. Following the report of the Hunt Committee, the Local Employment Act 1970 provided for 75 per cent grants in intermediate areas and also in 'derelict land clearance areas'. The latter are areas where 'the economic situation in the locality is such' that it is 'particularly appropriate with a view to contributing to the development of industry in the locality' that grants should be paid. The Local Government Act of 1972 raised the rate of grant to 100 per cent in all the assisted areas and in the derelict land clearance areas.

This complicated system is a result of an attempt to give differential assistance according to the local employment needs of different areas. The underlying rationale is (in the words of the Hunt Committee) that an unfavourable environment depresses economic opportunity: dereliction 'deters the modern industry which is needed for the revitalization of these areas and helps to stimulate outward migration'.[48] There is thus a clear ulterior motive. The same is not the case with grants (this time at the rate of 75 per cent) in national parks and areas of outstanding natural beauty.[49] Here the objective is the 'enhancement of natural beauty', or at least the restoration of beauty.

Table 5.3   *Derelict Land, England*[50]

		Hectares
Total derelict land, England, 1974		43,273
of which:		
Spoil heaps 30%		
Excavations and pits 20%		
Military and other service dereliction 9%		
Abandoned British Rail land 21%		
Other forms of dereliction 20%		
Total derelict land 'justifying restoration in 1974'		33,068
Reclamation 1977–8		2,640
of which:		
Spoil heaps	941	
Excavations and pits	604	
Military and other service dereliction	213	
Abandoned British Rail land	269	
Other forms of dereliction	613	

The Inner Urban Areas Act 1978 provides additional powers and loans and grants for dealing with urban dereliction, and the Local Government, Planning and Land Act 1980 extends the powers for grants in aid of the reclamation of land.[51] Significantly, the concept of 'derelict land' is widened to 'land which is derelict, neglected or unsightly land requiring reclamation or improvement'.

These powers should assist in dealing with the varying forms of dereliction.[52] It has to be remembered, however, that dereliction is a continuing process in both urban and rural areas. In some cases operations, such as mineral working, can be subjected to special controls but, as is explained in the following section, safeguarding environmental quality is only one of the several relevant considerations.[53]

CONTROL OF MINERAL WORKING

The reconciliation between economic and amenity interests in mineral working is an obvious matter for planning authorities. It would, however, be misleading to give the impression that the function of planning authorities is simply to fight a continual battle for the preservation of amenity. Planning is concerned with competing pressures on land and with the resolution of conflicting demands. Amenity is only one of the factors to be taken into account. Thus it is a general policy to ensure that mineral working is carried on 'with proper regard for the appearance and other amenities of the area', and that when the working is finished the land should (wherever practicable) not be left derelict but 'restored or otherwise treated with a view of bringing it back to some form of beneficial use'.

At the extreme – where mineral working would involve 'too great injury to the comfort and living conditions of the people in the area or to amenities generally' – mineral working can be limited or even prevented. Here a balance has to be struck between the economic need for minerals and the interests of amenity, and it is relevant (and indeed essential) to consider whether economic needs can be satisfactorily met from other sources with less damage to amenity.

There is, however, the equally important matter of safeguarding mineral deposits. Planning authorities have the positive function of ensuring that mineral deposits are not unnecessarily sterilised by surface development but are kept available for exploitation.

These are the broad policy matters with which planning authorities are concerned. The necessary powers are provided in the Planning Acts. Briefly, these are for the making of the essential survey of resources and potentialities, the allocation of land in development plans, and the control (by means of planning permission) of mineral workings.

The survey required for the development plan is not, of course, simply a geological one. The planning authority have to assess the amount of land required for mineral working, and this requires an assessment of the future demand likely to be made on production in their area.

Mineral undertakers have long-standing powers to obtain rights over land containing mineral deposits. These were extended by regulations made under the Planning Acts (the latest were issued in 1971).[54] With the range of powers available, mineral workings cannot, without good cause, be prevented by private landowners.

Powers to control mineral workings stem from the definition of 'development', which includes 'the carrying out of . . . mining . . . operations in, on, over or under land'. Further, the tipping of waste constitutes development (that is, a material change of use) if, generally speaking, the area or height is extended. Special provisions apply to the National Coal Board's operations, which can be ignored for the moment. Apart from this, all mineral workings, ancillary buildings, depositing of waste and the construction of means of access to sites require planning permission.

Because of the national need for minerals, planning authorities have been strongly advised by the DoE to pay attention to economic considerations: 'a fundamental concern of planning policy must be to ensure a free flow of mineral products at economic cost'. The long-term planning that is required for mineral exploitation means that planning permissions have generally been given for a working with a long life – commonly not less than fifteen years, and on occasion up to sixty years. Before reaching a decision on an application, it is often necessary for the planning authority to consult a number of interested parties, including the Ministry of Agriculture, the Forestry Commission, the regional water authority, and perhaps the Countryside Commission, the Nature Conservancy Council and the Inspector of Ancient Monuments. The representations of these bodies can lead to the making of conditions or the reinforcement of conditions which the planning authority wishes to impose in the interests of amenity. Conditions can be imposed, for example, requiring a phased programme of work in order to minimise the disturbance to agriculture, or a planned programme of working and restoration can be required. Conditions relating to restoration are among the most important. A mineral undertaker cannot, however, be required to put the land to any specific use after extraction has been completed, but *where practicable*, he can be required to leave it in a condition comparable to that in which he found it. Unfortunately, restoration is not always practicable. To quote from *The Control of Mineral Working*:

> The extent to which reclamation is possible will depend first on the physical nature of the quarry. About one-third of the land used for quarrying represents the wet working of gravel; about one-third deep quarries working into hillside or deep holes in the ground or a combination of both; one-sixth shallow quarries; and the remaining sixth, workings in which a thin seam is extracted from beneath thick overburden. Wet gravel pits and other excavations which become waterlogged can be reclaimed only when suitable extraneous material is available at an economic cost; they sometimes have value for fishing, yachting or other recreational purposes, possibly after some landscape treatment has been carried out. Other deep holes can generally be put to use only when filling material is available. Waste material – including any overburden – can sometimes be used to reclaim part of the quarry or to raise the general level sufficiently for use to be made of the whole. (But the cost of such operations can often make this impracticable.) Shallow quarries and some hillside quarries where the floor is not much below the level of the adjoining land can often be brought back to use readily without the necessity of filling. Quarries working thin seams beneath thick overburden can also be readily reclaimed, the most numerous of this class being ironstone quarries.[55]

An exhaustive inquiry into *Planning Control over Mineral Working* was completed by the Stevens Committee in 1976.[56] New legislation was passing through Parliament in 1981.[57]

Of particular interest to the issue of restoration is the Ironstone

Restoration Fund, which was established under the Mineral Workings Act 1951, to assist in the financing of reclamation in the Midlands ironstone field where working was by opencast methods. Generally, ironstone operators and landowners make a contribution to the fund for each ton of ironstone extracted by opencast working. The Exchequer makes a further contribution. Payments are made from the fund for old derelict workings and for new workings where the cost of restoration exceeds a certain sum per acre.

The principle underlying this scheme – that land exploitation carries with it a duty to shoulder at least some part of the costs of restoration – would at first sight seem incapable of extension. A similar principle – that exploitation involves costs to others which should be borne at least in part by the exploiters – is accepted in the Cheshire brine-pumping subsidence scheme. The Brine Pumping (Compensation for Subsidence) Act 1891 provided for payments to certain owners of property damaged by subsidence, from the proceeds of a levy on each ton of white salt produced within the Northwich area. The Cheshire Brine Pumping (Compensation for Subsidence) Act 1952 brought the scheme in line with modern operating conditions and considerably extended the area over which it operated.

The procedure is, thus, basically the same as with ironstone restoration – a levy on all operators related to their production. For a nationalised industry the principle can be extended further, as in the Coal Mining (Subsidence) Acts of 1950 and 1957. These place on the National Coal Board the responsibility for making good any damage caused by subsidence resulting from coal-mining – or the working of coal and other minerals simultaneously. Under the 1950 Act grants were paid by the Treasury to the Board in respect of additional expenditure which the Act imposed on them, but this arrangement was not repeated in the 1957 Act. Thus, the Board carries the whole financial responsibility for subsidence damage.

Restoration can be a difficult and expensive operation. It follows that (as with subsidence) there is a case for 'pooling' in order that, for example, the costs of achieving some socially desirable restoration does not involve prohibitive expense for a particular operator. Some costs can, however, legitimately be placed squarely on individual operators. This is the case with improving the appearance of mineral workings by tree- and shrub-planting. Planning permission for mineral operations can be made conditional on adequate screening being provided.

Planning control over the operations of the National Coal Board is subject to special provisions.[58] Briefly, the continued working of mines begun before 1 July 1948 is 'permitted development', and therefore does not require specific planning approval. The same applies to the continuance of waste-tipping. Furthermore, there is a general permission for any development in connection with coal industry activities (as defined in section 63 of the Coal Industry Nationalisation Act 1946) and carried out in the immediate vicinity of a pithead. However, certain restrictions can be imposed (on the erection of buildings) in the interest of amenity. Mining operations on new sites require planning permission in the ordinary way.

Only 4 per cent of coal output in Britain comes from opencast workings – a very much lower proportion than in other countries. One of the reasons for the low proportion is that, despite its profitability, opencast working arouses considerable opposition – from farmers, local authorities, local inhabitants, amenity organisations and even miners. Clearly the visual impact of opencast working is far greater than that of deep mining, yet the loss of amenity is temporary and full restoration is practicable and usual; indeed, there can be a resultant improvement in amenity.

Opencast coal working began during the war under emergency legislation. It continued under this legislation until 1958 and, though usually constituting 'development', was therefore outside the scope of planning control. The Opencast Coal Act 1958 laid down a special method of control operated by the then Minister of Power (now the Secretary of State for Energy). Notices must be served on the local authorities concerned and, if they raise objections, a public inquiry must be held. The Secretary of State for Energy can direct that planning permission for the operations concerned 'be deemed to be granted'. His direction may include conditions of the sort commonly applied to planning permissions, and must include conditions to secure the restoration of the site. Where the land is in agricultural use, it is normally obligatory for the conditions to provide for the restoration of the land so that it is fit for agricultural use.

Concurrent with the Stevens inquiry on mineral work there was an Advisory Committee on Aggregates under the chairmanship of Sir Ralph Verney.[59] Its report, published in 1976, was the subject of a parliamentary statement in July 1978.[60]

NOISE

'Quiet costs money . . . a machine manufacturer will try to make a quieter product only if he is forced to, either by legislation or because customers want quiet machines and will choose a rival product for a lower noise level.' So stated the Final Report of the Wilson Committee in 1963.[61] This, in one sense, is the crux of the problem of noise. More – and more powerful – cars, aircraft, transistor radios and the like must receive strong public approbium before manufacturers – and users – will be concerned with their noise level. Similarly, legislative measures and their implementation require public support before effective action can be taken.

There is abundant evidence that this is growing: particularly eloquent are the figures collected by the Association of Environmental Health Officers showing that the number of complaints of noise nuisance received by local authorities is increasing rapidly: from 350 per million population in 1971 to 604 in 1975, and 1,003 in 1978.[62]

Transport is a major noise menace. The Transport and Road Research Laboratory have estimated that between 25 and 45 per cent of the urban population live in roads with traffic noise levels likely to be judged undesirable for residential areas; if noise levels were not reduced, the projected increase in vehicles would raise the proportion by 1980 to between one-third and two-thirds. The White Paper on *The Protection of the Environment* maintained that new regulations which came into effect in April 1970 had halted the trend towards increasing noise.[63] It cannot be said that this is apparent: in any case (in the words of the Royal Commission), this will not do much to satisfy the public demand for *less* noise.

Aircraft noise is particularly obnoxious, and a battery of powers has been introduced in legislation such as the Airports Authority Act 1965, and the Civil Aviation Act 1968. This is a field in which international co-operation is particularly important, and the first fruits of the International Conference on Aircraft Noise (convened by the British government) came with the 1970 Air Navigation (Noise Certification) Order. Subsonic jet aircraft are not allowed to land or take off in the United Kingdom unless they have a certificate from the government of the country of registration that they comply with certain defined noise standards. This anticipates an international noise certification scheme in the formulation of which Britain is playing a leading part.

In fact, the evidence is that, despite a predicted growth in air traffic, 'the problem of noise around airports . . . should be substantially improved by 1990, mainly as a consequence of larger, quieter aircraft coming into service'.[64]

This is a field in which legislative provision is very scattered: relevant Acts include those dealing with Road Traffic, Civil Aviation and, most recently, Part III of the Control of Pollution Act (which provides for the introduction of 'noise abatement zones').[65]

OTHER ENVIRONMENTAL POLLUTANTS

Many other pollutants and aspects of pollution would need to be discussed in a comprehensive account, including domestic and industrial waste, pesticides and fertilisers, water resources, litter, car cemeteries, pollution of the sea and radioactive waste disposal. A brief discussion is to be found in the White Paper *The Protection of the Environment*.[66] Further references are given in the Appendix.

THE EEC AND THE ENVIRONMENT

We are in no doubt as to the importance of EEC environment policy. The Common Market is now generating even greater environmental impacts throughout the Community, both at member state level and as a result of the promotion of infrastructure to assist trade in the Community at large.[67]

The European dimension of 'planning the environment' is a relatively new one, and it clearly raises intra-national arguments to a higher inter-national level where the result can easily be deadlock or vacuous agreement. Nevertheless, it is obvious that certain environmental issues can be satisfactorily dealt with only on a European scale. Quite apart from the benefits of 'learning from each other', there are several areas where environmental action makes sense only on a European scale:

Pollution . . . does not stop at national frontiers: the Rhine flows through four European countries; numerous European lakes and water-courses are shared by two or more States; air polluted by sulphur dioxide traverses all of Europe; a country which protects migratory birds is wasting its time if its neighbours massacre them.[68]

It is difficult to keep abreast of the overall EEC scene (though the TCPA's *Planning Bulletin – Europe* helps),[69] partly because of the difficulty of keeping up to date and at the same time, paradoxically being overwhelmed by the sheer amount of 'paper'.[70]

At the time of writing (March 1981) debate appears to be focused on Environmental Impact Analysis. An EEC proposal envisages that all major developments should be mandatorily subject to such an analysis. The House of Lords has welcomed this initiative.[71]

REFERENCES AND FURTHER READING: CHAPTER 5

1   Local planning authorities have power to take action in relation to land which has become unsightly or offensive (section 65 of the Town and Country Planning Act 1971). In the ungainly words of the statute: 'If it appears to a local planning authority that the amenity of any part of their area, or of any adjoining area, is seriously injured by the condition of any garden, vacant site or other open land in their area, the authority may serve on the owner and occupier of the land a notice requiring such steps for abating the injury as may be specified in the notice to be taken within such period as may be so specified.'
2   See, generally, DoE Circular 96/69, *Town and Country Planning (Control of Advertisements) Regulations 1969* (HMSO, 1969). The corresponding Scottish circular is SDD Circular 13/1961, *Town and Country Planning (Control of Advertisements) (Scotland) Regulations 1961* (Scottish Development Department, 1961).
3   *Town and Country Planning (Control of Advertisements) Regulations 1969*, SI 1969 No. 1532 (amended by SI 1972 No. 489, SI 1974 No. 185 and SI 1975 No. 898).

4 'Proposals to amend the Control of Advertisement Regulations by introducing two new "deemed consents" to the six classes of permitted outdoor advertising already specified in Regulation 14 are contained in a consultation paper issued by the Department of the Environment. The two new deemed consents are for

1 Consent for illuminated advertisements on shops and "shop-like' premises, subject to certain specified limits on the number and size of the advertisements and the intensity of the illumination, and

2 Consent for temporary advertisements on hoardings around construction sites on which building operations are taking place, or about to take place, in commercial or industrial areas of towns and cities, subject to certain specified limits on the size of the advertisements and the duration of their display.

The proposals are similar to those made in 1974 but subsequently abandoned. They are not to apply to National Parks, Areas of Outstanding Natural Beauty, Conservation Areas or Areas of Special Control.

The justification for the first proposal is that there already exists a high proportion of "express consents" for such advertising and that to move them into the deemed consent sphere would result in a saving of public expenditure by local planning authorities. The justification for the second proposal is that it too would save public expenditure, and that the presence of hoardings on which properly designed advertisements would be displayed would help to deter the use of the hoarding for the purpose of fly-posting.'

Journal of Planning and Environment Law, 1980, and Department of the Environment, *Proposed New 'Deemed Consents' in Advertisement Control Regulations: A Consultative Paper* (DoE, August 1980). Surprisingly, the proposals emanate, not from the DoE itself, but from the Outdoor Advertising Council, a body which has a strong vested financial interest. (See Royal Town Planning Institute 'comments' dated 13 October 1980, RTPI.)

5 DoE Circular 96/69, op. cit., para. 11; see also the map in the Appendix to this circular.

6 Department of the Environment, *Development Control Statistics 1978/79* (DoE, 1980), p. 20, Table 23.

7 On this generally, see C. M. Brand, *Modern Legislation for the Protection of History: The Ancient Monuments and Archaeological Areas Act 1979*, Scottish Planning Law and Practice, Occasional Papers 2 (The Planning Exchange, 1980).

8 Ancient Monuments and Archaeological Areas Act 1979, section 61 (12). A 'monument' is defined in section 61 (7) as 'any building, structure or work, whether above or below the surface of the land, and any cave or excavation; any site comprising the remains of any such building, structure or work or of any cave or excavation; any site comprising or comprising the remains of, any vehicle, vessel, aircraft or other movable structure or part thereof . . . and any machinery attached to a monument shall be regarded as part of the monument if it could not be detached without being dismantled'.

Brand (op. cit., p. 11) notes that this definition excludes ecclesiastical buildings used for ecclesiastical purposes, and the remains of any vessel protected under the Protection of Wrecks Act 1973.

9 Each of the separate Boards issues an annual report which is published as a House of Commons Paper by HMSO. For 1979, the references are England, HC 623; Scotland, HC 622; and Wales, HC 690 (all HMSO).

10 This procedure, which puts the onus on the person wishing to carry out works on a scheduled monument to obtain consent, was introduced by the 1979 Act. Formerly the onus was on the secretary of state, who had to issue an 'interim preservation notice' (lasting for a maximum period of twenty-one months) or a more permanent 'preservation order' which prohibited any work without his written consent. This brings the arrangements for scheduled monuments in line with those for listed buildings.

11 C. M. Brand, op. cit., pp. 19ff.

12 See, for example, 'Report of the work of the Committee for Rescue Archaeology in 1979', in *Ancient Monuments Board for England: 26th Annual Report 1979* (HMSO, 1980), pp. 22-3; and SDD Circular 68/1978, *Rescue Archaeology in Scotland* (Scottish Development Department, 1978).

13 See the *Annual Reports* of the Historic Buildings Councils for England, Scotland and Wales, all published as HC Papers by HMSO.

14 See generally, DoE Circular 23/77, *Historic Buildings and Conservation Areas - Policy and Procedures* (HMSO, 1977); and, for Scotland, SDD Circular 126/1975, *Town and Country Planning (Listed Buildings and Buildings in Conservation Areas) (Scotland) Regulations 1975* (Scottish Development Department, 1975). The classic report in this area is that by Sir Ernest Gowers, *Report of the Committee on Houses of Outstanding Historic Interest* (HMSO, 1950). There has been a large number of publications since then of which reference might be made to J. Reynolds, *Conservation Planning in Town and Country* (Liverpool University Press, 1976); Journal of Planning and Environment Law Occasional Paper, *A Future for Old Buildings? - Listed Buildings, the Law and the Practice* (Sweet & Maxwell, 1977); and the report of the working party chaired by Lord Montagu, *Britain's Historic Buildings: A Policy for their Future Use* (British Tourist Authority, 1980).

15 On this, see DoE Circular 21/80, *Housing Acts 1974 and 1980 - Improvement of Older Housing* (HMSO, 1980), paras 48 and 74.

16 English Tourist Board, *English Heritage Monitor 1979*. The Table of 'Classified architectural resources' on p. 29 of this *Monitor* records (for England only) 259,870 listed buildings (December 1978); 489 Conservation Areas designated outstanding (February 1979); 11,789 Scheduled Ancient Monuments (December 1977); 1,322 Buildings open to the public (1979); 11,675 listed C of E Churches (January 1979); 60 Cathedrals (1979); and 1,897 Hotels of historic interest.

17 There is also the Architectural Heritage Fund founded in 1976 whose origins lay in the report *Financing the Preservation of Old Buildings* submitted by the Civic Trust to the Department of the Environment in 1971. The report 'looked at the concept of "revolving funds" that buy, restore and resell old buildings, ploughing back the proceeds into further restoration projects. It concluded that many more such funds should be created and that, to assist their cash flow, a national fund should be set up to help with low-interest loans. The establishment of such a fund was adopted as one of the specific aims of the UK Campaign for European Architectural Heritage Year 1975, and in July 1974 the then Secretary of State for the Environment made a commitment to match, from government resources and up to a maximum of £½ million, whatever could be raised from the private sector. This meant that the fund had a potential capital of £1 million, and by the end of Heritage Year the private sector had already contributed more than £400,000 in donations and covenants towards this. The Government's matching contribution is being paid to the Fund on the basis of 50% of loans contracted to be made.' Loans totalling £85,000 were contracted during 1979-80, bringing the total for the period 1976-80 to £434,500 in respect of eighteen loans. *The Architectural Heritage Fund 1976-1979* and *Annual Report 1979-1980*.

18 See Ministry of Housing and Local Government, *Historic Towns: Preservation and Change* (HMSO, 1967); and the four 'Studies in conservation': Bath, Chester, Chichester and York published in separate volumes by HMSO in 1968.

19 See 'Preservation of historic buildings . . . Observations of the Planning Law Committee of the Law Society', *Eighth Report from the Expenditure Committee, Session 1976-77, Planning Procedures* (HMSO, 1977), Vol. 2, pp. 651-2.

20 See *Historic Buildings Council for England Report 1978/79*, HC 529 (HMSO, 1980), pp. 3-4.

21 'The demolition of the Firestone factory before a decision could be made as to whether or not to add the building to a statutory list must focus attention on the achilles heel of the listing process', that is, demolition does not constitute develop-

ment. See 'Firestone and the listing process', *Journal of Planning and Environment Law*, 1980, pp. 712–13. (It was reported in *The Times* of 26 March 1981 that a private prosecution for the allegedly illegal demolition in 1980 of a group of listed seventeenth-century almshouses was being brought by Mr David Pearce, Secretary of the Society for the Protection of Ancient Buildings. This is believed to be the first private prosecution under the 1971 Town and Country Planning Act.)

22 See 'Historic buildings: selective aid', *The Economist*, 14 June 1980, p. 66; and Royal Institution of Chartered Surveyors, *Listed Buildings: A Discussion Paper* (RICS, 1979), para. 2.2. The paper contains a number of proposals relating to planning permission for demolition, finance and procedure.

23 *Building Design*, 23 January 1981.

24 Historic Buildings and Ancient Monuments Act 1953, sections 5 and 7.

25 Finance Act 1957, section 41.

26 See *Third Report from the Expenditure Committee, Session 1977–78, National Land Fund* (HMSO, 1978); White Paper, *A National Heritage Fund*, Cmnd 7428 (HMSO, 1979); and C. M. Brand, 'National Heritage Act 1980', *Scottish Planning Law and Practice*, no. 2 (January 1981), pp. 12–14.

27 See generally, Ministry of Housing and Local Government, *Trees in Town and City* (HMSO, 1958); DoE Circular 36/78, *Trees and Forestry* (HMSO, 1978); and Tony Aldous (ed.), *Trees and Buildings: Complement or Conflict?* (RIBA Publications and The Tree Council, 1979).

28 Central Office of Information, *Environmental Planning in Britain*, Reference Pamphlet 9 (HMSO, 1979), p. 53.

29 *Tree News* (the Tree Council Newsletter). A bibliography on trees and woodlands can be obtained from The Tree Council, 35 Belgrave Square, London SW1X 8QN.

30 W. G. Holford, 'Design in city centres', Part 3 of Ministry of Housing and Local Government, *Design in Town and Village* (HMSO, 1953), p. 71.

31 See, for example, DoE Development Control Policy Note 10, *Design* (HMSO, 1970), and also the report by Sir Robert Matthew and W. P. D. Skillington to the Secretary of State for the Environment, *Promotion of High Standards of Architectural Design* (DoE, April 1974).

32 See the periodic reports of the Royal Fine Art Commission for England and Wales, and the Royal Fine Art Commission for Scotland, published by HMSO.

33 *Eighth Report from the Expenditure Committee, Session 1976–77, Planning Procedures, Vol. 1: Report* (HMSO, 1977), p. xliii, para. 92.

34 Royal Town Planning Institute, *Town and Country Planning Summer School 1979: Report of Proceedings* (RTPI, 1979).

35 DoE Circular 22/80, *Development Control* – Policy and Practice (HMSO, 1980), paras 18–21.

36 White Paper, *The Protection of the Environment: The Fight Against Pollution*, Cmnd 4373 (HMSO, 1970).

37 Beaver Report: Committee on Air Pollution, *Interim Report*, Cmd 9011 (HMSO, 1953), *Report*, Cmd 9322 (HMSO, 1954); Pippard Report: *Pollution of the Tidal Thames* (HMSO, 1961); Browne Report: *Refuse Storage and Collection* (HMSO, 1967); Wilson Report: Committee on the Problem of Noise, *Noise: Final Report*, Cmnd 2056 (HMSO, 1963); Key Report: *Pollution of Waste by Tipped Refuse* (HMSO, 1961); and Jeger Report: Report of the Working Party on Sewage Disposal, *Taken for Granted* (HMSO, 1970).

38 Committee on Air Pollution (Beaver Committee), *Interim Report*, Cmd 9011 (HMSO, 1953); *Report*, Cmd 9322 (HMSO, 1954).

39 Department of the Environment, *Digest of Environmental Pollution Statistics*, No. 1 (HMSO, 1978), p. 91, Table 92; and No. 2, 1979 (HMSO, 1980), p. 109, Table 102.

40 *The Intermediate Areas* (Hunt Report), Cmnd 3998 (HMSO, 1969), p. 141, para. 477.

41 Ministry of Housing and Local Government, *Clean Air Act 1956: Memorandum on Smoke Control Areas* (HMSO, 1956).

42 White Paper, *The Protection of the Environment: The Fight Against Pollution*, Cmnd 4373 (HMSO, 1970).

43 This highly condensed account can be supplemented by a large number of reports by the Royal Commission on Environmental Pollution and by the Department of the Environment series of *Pollution Papers*. These are listed in the Bibliography.

44 'This covers disused or abandoned land requiring restoration work to bring it into use or to improve its appearance. It does not include land which might have a derelict appearance from natural causes, such as marshland, mudflats or sand dunes, neglected woods or farmland, waste land generally or land formerly affected by development but which, with time, has blended into the landscape.' Department of the Environment, *Digest of Environmental Pollution Statistics*, No. 2, 1979 (HMSO, 1980), notes to Table 93 (p. 102).

45 Detailed figures are given in Department of the Environment statistical reports on the *Survey of Derelict and Despoiled Land in England 1974* (DoE, 1975); and in DoE Pollution Paper 16, *The United Kingdom Environment 1979: Progress of Pollution Control* (HMSO, 1979).

46 *The Intermediate Areas*, op. cit., p. 139, para. 467.

47 See DoE Circular 17/77, *Derelict Land* (HMSO, 1977).

48 *The Intermediate Areas*, op. cit., pp. 135-6, para. 457.

49 National Parks and Access to the Countryside Act 1949, section 97 (1).

50 Department of the Environment, *Digest of Environmental Pollution Statistics*, No. 2, 1979 (HMSO, 1980), p. 102, Table 93.

51 Under section 9 of the Local Government Act 1966. The new concept referred to is a lengthy and complex part of the Act: Local Government, Planning and Land Act 1980, section 117.

52 See, for instance, 'Urban wasteland', *Royal Society of Arts Journal*, November 1980, pp. 840-53, and February 1981, pp. 160-73; G. Simpson, 'Making use of derelict land', *Chartered Surveyor*, August 1980, pp. 42-5; Professional Institutions Council for Conservation, *Dereliction of Land* (PICC, 1974) and *The Green Environment in Urban Areas* (PICC, 1979).

53 See also reports by the Civic Trust, *Derelict Land - A Study of Industrial Dereliction and How It May Be Reclaimed* (1964); *Reclamation of Derelict Land: Report of a Civic Trust Conference at Stoke on Trent* (1970); and *Urban Wasteland: A Report on Land Lying Dormant in Cities, Towns and Villages in Britain* (1977).

54 Town and Country Planning (Minerals) Regulations 1971, SI 1971 No. 756.

55 Ministry of Housing and Local Government, *The Control of Mineral Working* (HMSO, rev. ed, 1960).

56 *Planning Control over Mineral Working* (Stevens Report) (HMSO, 1976). See also DoE Circulars 1/78 and 58/78, both of which have the same title, *Report of the Committee on Planning Control over Mineral Working* (both HMSO, 1978). The latter gives the government's response to the Committee's recommendations.

57 The Town and Country Planning (Minerals) Bill 1981. See A. D. Jelley, 'Town and Country Planning (Minerals) Bill', *Journal of Planning and Environment Law*, March 1981, pp. 165-73.

58 See *Scar on the Landscape? A Report on Opencast Coalmining and the Environment* (Council for Environmental Conservation, 1979).

59 *Aggregates: The Way Ahead - Report of the Advisory Committee on Aggregates* (HMSO, 1976).

60 See DoE Circular 50/78, *Report of the Advisory Committee on Aggregates* (HMSO, 1978) which reproduces the parliamentary statement in full.

61 *Committee on the Problem of Noise: Final Report* (Wilson Report), Cmnd 2056 (HMSO, 1963).

62 Department of the Environment, *Digest of Environmental Pollution Statistics*, No. 2, 1979 (HMSO, 1980), p. 76, Table 65. See also DoE, *The United Kingdom Environment 1979: Progress of Pollution Control*, Pollution Paper 16 (HMSO, 1979), ch. 5.

63 White Paper, *The Protection of the Environment*, op. cit., p. 15, para. 48.

64 Department of the Environment, *The United Kingdom Environment 1979: Progress of Pollution Control*, op. cit., p. 24, para. 51.

65 Reference should also be made to the important circular on *Planning and Noise*, issued by the Department of the Environment in 1973 (Circular 10/73).

66 The White Paper *The Protection of the Environment*, op. cit., has sections on pollution by noise and radioactivity and pollution of the air, land, fresh water and the sea and beaches. See also the reports of the Royal Commission on Environmental Pollution and the Department of the Environment series of *Pollution Papers* (all listed in the Bibliography).

67 British Members of the European Environmental Bureau, *The Development of EEC Environmental Policy* (October 1980), p. 1.

68 Commission for the European Communities, *The European Community and Environmental Protection*, 'European File' 2/81 (January 1981), p. 3.

69 The Town and Country Planning Association publishes eight issues a year of its *Planning Bulletin* as a Europe edition. This constitutes a most useful source of information. Additionally there is the 'European Environmental Bureau: British Members' which is fostered by the Council for the Protection of Rural England (at 4 Hobart Place, London SW1W 0HY). Direct from Brussels (Directorate-General for Information, Rue de la Loi 200) is a constant stream of publications. Two specific publications from different sources are M. J. Breakell and S. Hopkins, *Planning in Europe*, published in 1978 by the S. E. Branch of the Royal Town Planning Institute; and C. Wood and N. Lee, *Physical Planning in the Member States of the European Economic Community*, University of Manchester, Department of Town and Country Planning, Occasional Paper 2 (University of Manchester, 1978).

70 Information on the EEC can be obtained in Britain from the Information Office, 20 Kensington Palace Gardens, London W8 4QQ.

71 See European Environmental Bureau (British Members), *Environmental Impact Analysis and the EEC* (September 1980). Reference should also be made to the reports of the Select Committee on European Committees on EEC Environment Policy (for example, 5th Report, Session 1979/80; and 11th Report, 1980/1), published by HMSO.

Chapter 6

PLANNING FOR TRAFFIC

THE CHANGING SCENE

'In past ages, the subject of transport by land was never much debated . . . Today, transport is a matter of passionate public concern.' So wrote Anthony Crosland, as Secretary of State for the Environment, in the introduction to the 1976 consultation document on transport policy.[1] Some of the passion evaporated at the end of the 1970s as its object – the road-building programme – was slashed. How far this was the result of the expressed passion, or, more simply, the opportunity which this expression gave to governments vigorously attempting to cut back on public expenditure, is difficult to say. There seems little doubt, however, that governments (in both the late 1970s and the early 1980s) have found it useful to use appealing and cogent arguments on environmental protection as (at least in part) a justification for major cuts in road programmes. Even the 'environmentally protective' bypasses are proceeding at a slow rate – certainly in comparison with the M1 which was built at an average rate of one mile every eight days. Those days have gone.

The changes which took place in the 1970s (particularly in attitudes) are strikingly illustrated by the changes made to this chapter over the last decade. Only the author is likely to indulge in the comparative textual analysis involved, but the changes are in fact readily apparent. They reflect revised population and car ownership forecasts, the world energy situation and the increased cost of private motoring, a lower rate of economic growth, the need to restrain public expenditure and changing public attitudes to road developments (particularly in urban areas). All these have led to a reduction in planned investment in roads. At the same time they have given added force to the trends towards greater priority for public transport and comprehensive transport planning.

The *Consultation Document* is a good starting point for discussion: this came just at the time when major shifts in the framework of traffic planning were emerging. There were five themes in this document which can be highlighted. First, both the objectives of, and the machinery for, transport planning were in need of review (of clarification if not of dramatic change). Policy had become 'badly blurred'[2] and, despite the planning innovations made by the 1968 Act (outlined below), there was still a lack of 'a proper framework for the co-ordination of transport policy at national and local level . . . pricing and investment decisions for each mode were not taken within the framework of an integrated approach, but in almost total isolation'.[3]

Secondly, 'while no one challenges the inestimable benefits conferred on families and individuals by the growth of car ownership, this trend has serious implications for public transport'. Indeed, 'as car ownership increases (and *should* increase, for personal mobility is what people want, and those who have it should not try to pull the ladder up behind them) the *social* objective of providing mobility for the still large minority without access to a car becomes more and more crucial'.[4] In short, the provision of adequate public transport was growing more difficult – and would continue to do so.

Thirdly and fourthly, there were the concerns for environmental quality and energy conservation (concerns which have increased greatly since the publication of the consultation document).

Finally – and even then (1976) 'overshadowing' everything else – was the current public expenditure situation, which the government was now to deal with.

The cuts followed, but the growth of traffic continued.

THE GROWTH OF TRAFFIC

Between 1950 and 1960 the number of vehicles on the roads of Great Britain more than doubled (from 4,409,000 to 9,383,000). The number doubled again by the end of the 1970s (to 18,625,000) (Table 6.1). In terms of 'traffic' – measured in thousand million vehicle kilometres – the increase over the period 1969 to 1979 was from 198·5 to 275·8,[5] that is, 28 per cent. At the time of writing the latest available

Table 6.1 *Vehicles in Use, Great Britain 1914–79 (in thousands)*[8]

Year*	Cars	Motor cycles	Buses and coaches	Taxis	Goods vehicles	Other† vehicles	Total
1914	132	124	51		82	–	389
1930	1,056	724	53	48	348	44	2,274
1950	2,258	752	78	59	895	368	4,409
1960	5,526	1,861	79	15	1,397	506	9,383
1970	11,515	1,048	78	25	1,618	668	14,950
1975	13,747	1,161	80	32	1,774	706	17,501
1976	14,047	1,220	79	34	1,757	696	17,832
1978	14,069	1,194	73	37	1,703	856	17,932
1979	14,568	1,292	74	37	1,778	876	18,625

*No census was taken in 1977. Figures for 1978 and 1979 are not directly comparable with those for earlier years.
†Other vehicles include agricultural tractors, tricycles, pedestrian controlled vehicles, etc.

forecasts[6] for 1990 (from which an extract is given in Table 6.2) are for
a low of 312·5 and a high of 363·0: these represent increases of 12 and
32 per cent respectively.

Table 6.2   *Road Traffic in Great Britain*[9]

	Thousand million vehicle kilometres	
Actual 1969	198·5	
Actual 1979	275·8	
Forecasts	Low	High
1985	293·8	322·6
1990	312·5	363·0
2000	341·0	432·5
2010	352·0	484·7

The forecasts do not reflect the (popularly anticipated retarding)
impact of the major increase in fuel costs in the early 1980s, but they
are considerably lower than those of even a few years ago.[7] Their
difference from those in the Buchanan Report are dramatic. Buchanan
referred to 'a prospect' of 27 million vehicles by 1980 (the actual figure
for 1979 was 18,625,000) and 'perhaps' 40 million by 2010.[10] These
figures, of course, were based on population projections of the time
which envisaged a population for Great Britain of some 74 million by
the year 2010.[11]

Nevertheless, though the forecasts have been very significantly
reduced, the fact remains that traffic will continue to increase.

INTER-URBAN TRAFFIC

So far as inter-urban traffic was concerned, a long-term policy was
formulated in 1970, following the publication of the 1969 'green
paper' *Roads for the Future: A New Inter-Urban Plan*.[12] The policy
had the following main objectives:

(i) to achieve environmental improvements by diverting long-
distance traffic, and particularly heavy goods vehicles, from a
large number of towns and villages, so as to relieve them of the
noise, dirt and danger which they suffer at present;
(ii) to complete by the early 1980s a comprehensive network of
strategic trunk routes to promote economic growth;
(iii) to link the more remote and less prosperous regions with this
new national network;
(iv) to ensure that every major city and town with a population of
more than 250,000 will be directly connected to the strategic network and that all with a population of more than 80,000 will be
within ten miles of it;

(v)   to design the network so that it serves all major ports and airports; and
(vi)   to relieve as many historic towns as possible of through trunk
road traffic.

TRAFFIC IN TOWNS: THE BUCHANAN REPORT

Traffic between towns gives rise to few problems which cannot be
solved in time by expenditure on road-building and landscaping.
Traffic in towns presents problems of a very different character. It is
these which forcibly demonstrate that the motor car is a 'mixed
blessing' (to borrow the title of an earlier book by Buchanan).[13] As a
highly convenient means of personal transport it cannot (at present)
be bettered. But its mass use restricts its benefits to car users, imposes
severe penalties (in congestion, pollution and reduction of public
transport) on non-motorists, involves huge expenditure on roads and
at worst plays havoc with the urban environment.

A major landmark in the development of thought in this field was
the 1963 Buchanan Report. This masterly survey surmounted the
administrative separatism which until this time prevented the comprehensive co-ordination of the planning and location of buildings on the
one hand, and the planning and management of traffic on the other.
With due acknowledgement to the necessarily crude nature of the
methods and assumptions used, the report proposed, as a basic
principle, the canalisation of larger traffic movements on to properly
designed networks, servicing areas within which environments suitable
for a civilised urban life could be developed. The two main ideas here
were for 'primary road networks' and 'environmental areas'.

There must be areas of good environment – urban rooms – where
people can live, work, shop, look about and move around on foot
in reasonable freedom from the hazards of motor traffic, and there
must be a complementary network of roads – urban corridors – for
effecting the primary distribution of traffic to the environmental
areas.[14]

The simplicity of this concept is in striking contrast to the complexity and huge cost of its application. A striking result of the case
studies included in the report is the scale of the necessary networks
and interchanges. The capital cost of the new primary roads in the
Newbury scheme, for example, was put at about £4½ million. But, as
the accompanying report of the Steering Committee (the Crowther
Report) pointed out: 'This would be once-for-all expenditure. It is
estimated that the motor vehicles registered in the Newbury area will
pay in 1963 about £770,000 in licence duty and fuel duty. By 1983 it is
estimated that the vehicles registered will be paying (assuming

unchanged rates) at the rate of £1,560,000. This admittedly crude calculation serves to show "what a fund of future revenue there is available to finance a programme of urban redevelopment".'

But what of the alternatives? Buchanan stressed that the general lesson was unavoidable: 'If the scale of road works and reconstruction seems frightening, then a lesser scale will suffice *provided there is less traffic.*' Crowther argued that the scope for deliberate limitations on the use of vehicles in towns would be almost impossible to enforce, even if a car-owning electorate were prepared to accept such limitations in principle. Not all would agree and, as traffic has grown, the practical possibilities of the various forms of pricing have assumed an increased significance.[15] Indeed, it is surprising how far opinion on this changed quite soon after the publication of the Buchanan Report. The 1968 White Paper *Transport in London* could say quite blandly (as could not have been said a decade earlier):

> The control of traffic must be regarded as a deliberate part of high-way and transport planning. In many cases regulation is appropriate. But the price mechanism is often more flexible and more sensitive. It may in time prove possible and worthwhile to reflect in charging systems the costs which journeys on overcrowded roads impose on other road users. Meanwhile, parking charges and time-limits can provide effective control. There will have to be control of all street parking in inner London – with preference being given to short-term callers for whom the use of public transport may well be less convenient than for the regular commuter, and to residents. And there will also have to be control over the amount of privately available off-street parking space in new developments which attract a significant number of workers. (In the past, such space has often encouraged additional car commuting.) The GLC has recently announced new policies along these lines. Finally, there is need to control the ways in which publicly available off-street car parks can be used.[16]

To return to Buchanan, the great danger in his view lay in the temptation to seek a middle course between a massive investment in replanning and a curtailing of the use of vehicles 'by trying to cope with a steadily increasing volume of minor alterations resulting in the end in the worst of both worlds – poor traffic access and a grievously eroded environment'.

An improvement of public transport is no answer to these problems, though it must be an essential part of an overall plan; indeed, the case studies show that it is quite impossible to dispense with public transport. The implication is that there must be a planned co-ordination between transport systems, particularly with regard to the work journeys in concentrated centres. On this, the report recommended that 'transportation plans' should be included as part of the statutory development plans. This was accepted and passed into legislation by the 1968 Town and Country Planning Act. But of equal importance is the momentous Transport Act passed in the same year. Many of the provisions of this lie outside the scope of the present book, though they are by no means irrelevant to the issues selected for discussion. Attention here is focused on the machinery for traffic planning, the report of the Urban Motorways Committee and the introduction of Transport Policies and Programmes.

TRAFFIC PLANNING MACHINERY

The 1967 White Paper *Public Transport and Traffic* opened on a lyrical note: 'one of the most precious achievements of modern civilization is mobility. It enriches social life and widens experience.'[17] The implications for planning and transport policy were stressed:

> To build mobility into the urban and rural life of this crowded island without destroying the other elements of good living must be one of the major purposes of transport policy. To achieve this, far-reaching changes in attitudes and administration will be necessary. The provision of transport – whether public or private – can no longer be considered in isolation from other developments. It must be built into the whole planning of our community life so that no factory is sited, no housing estate or 'overspill' developed, no town re-planned without the implications for the movement of people and goods having been studied and incorporated from the outset.

This, of course, was part of the rationale for the structure plans which treated basic transport planning as part of the general planning of the structure of each locality. But the important point is that 'basic transport planning' means far more than 'road planning', particularly since no conceivable road investment programme could support city structures designed on the basis that nearly all journeys were to be made by private car. (And it must not be forgotten that there will always be a significant proportion of households without cars.[18] Even in the United States this is a fifth.) In short, 'our major towns and cities can only be made to work effectively and to provide a decent environment for living by giving a new dynamic role to public transport as well as expanding facilities for private cars'.

Five 'principles of organisation' flow from this:

(1) Since local authorities are responsible for 'planning' they must be the authorities responsible for public transport.
(2) All transport matters for which local authorities are to be responsible – the improvement of the local road network, invest-

ment in public transport, traffic management measures, the balance between public and private transport - must be focused in an integrated transport plan, which in turn is related to the general planning for each area.

(3)   Investment in local public transport must be grant-aided by central government just as investment in the principal road network receives 75 per cent Exchequer grants.

(4)   The main network of public transport must be publicly owned.

(5)   The planning and operation of public transport can only be done intelligently over areas which make sense in transport terms. In some of the major urban areas, the traffic situation is so bad and is deteriorating so rapidly that reorganisation cannot await general legislation on local government.

It was for this last reason that Passenger Transport Authorities were established (under powers provided by the 1968 Transport Act) in South East Lancashire/North East Cheshire (SELNEC - now Greater Manchester), Merseyside, West Midlands, Tyneside and Greater Glasgow. Local government reorganisation made all the English metropolitan county councils Passenger Transport Authorities (thus adding South Yorkshire and West Yorkshire to the list). The Greater Glasgow PTA was transferred to the Strathclyde Regional Council.

It is the duty of a PTA to promote the provision of a co-ordinated and efficient system of public transport in their area. Each PTA appoint a professional management body - the Passenger Transport Executive. The PTEs are responsible for the management and operations of the former municipal passenger transport undertakings and for reaching agreement with the British Railways Board concerning the operation of local rail services.

In non-metropolitan counties, the county council has (under the Local Government Act 1972) a parallel duty to that of a PTA in relation to 'a co-ordinated and efficient system of public transport' in its area. There is corresponding provision in the Scottish Local Government Act for the regional and islands authorities.

In London, the London Transport Executive is the equivalent to the provincial and Scottish PTEs. The Greater London Council is the transport planning authority.

THE URBAN MOTORWAYS COMMITTEE

In July 1972 the report of the Urban Motorways Committee was published.[19] This Committee was established under the chairmanship of Sir James Jones, with the following terms of reference:

(1)   to examine present policies used in fitting major roads into urban areas;

(2) to consider what changes would enable urban roads to be related better to their surroundings, physically, visually and socially;
(3) to examine the consequences of such changes, particularly from the point of view of:
  (*a*) limitations on resources, both public and private;
  (*b*) changes in statutory powers and administrative procedures;
  (*c*) any issue of public policy that the changes would raise;
(4) to recommend what changes, if any, should be made.

The Committee were supported by a full-time team of officials who had the responsibility for a series of research studies and for the preparation of material on problems and procedures. Their report was published separately.[20]

The Committee's main recommendation was that 'the planning of new urban roads should form an integral part of planning the urban area as a whole; and that indirect costs and benefits of building urban roads should be looked at with the same care as the direct cost and movement benefits'.

The first part of this recommendation led (in conjunction with an unpublished review of compensation law) to the White Paper *Development and Compensation – Putting People First*[21] and the Land Compensation Act 1973, which applied to Scotland as well as to England and Wales. (The Scottish provisions were re-enacted in the Land Compensation (Scotland) Act 1973.) The second led to a new system of transport grants and the introduction of Transport Policies and Programmes.

The major emphasis in the first of these changes is on giving a greater priority to the social and human implications of road and other types of public development. As the White Paper put it:

The Government believe the time has come when all concerned with development must aim to achieve a better balance between provision for the community as a whole and the mitigation of harmful effects on the individual citizen. In recent years this balance in too many cases has been tipped against the interests of the individual. A better deal is now required for those who suffer from desirable community developments . . . The answer is not to stop community developments that would make life more comfortable, convenient and pleasant. To do that would simply deprive many people of the opportunity of a better environment. The answer must be to plan new development so as to minimise the disturbance and disruption they can cause and to improve the compensation code to alleviate any remaining distress.[22]

But to talk of 'desirable community developments' begs the issue, and the very pressures which led to the review of road planning procedures and compensation have also led to a more searching attitude to development proposals. Thus the question is no longer how best to develop a road, but whether a road is needed at all, and whether it is not better to allocate the resources to public transport. This was the main theme of the Expenditure Committee's report on *Urban Transport Planning*[23] and arose not only from an appreciation of the physical consequences of major urban highways and their effects on the communities through which they pass, but also from a growing awareness of the wider distributional consequences of current transport policies and the social significance of personal mobility.[24] The Committee went so far as to recommend that policy should be directed towards promoting public transport and discouraging the use of cars for the journey to work in city areas.

TRANSPORT POLICIES AND PROGRAMMES

Transport Policies and Programmes were conceived as comprehensive statements of the objectives and policies which local transport authorities plan to pursue in their areas, together with an expenditure programme. Though initially they were little more than statements of existing commitments, it was expected (in the words of a DoE circular) that they would increasingly be based 'on a proper evaluation of alternative options against explicit objectives within a realistic resource constraint'.[25] The circular continued:

> Eventually, therefore, the TPP will consist of a series of inter-related proposals covering both capital and current expenditure over the whole transport field – public transport, roads, parking, traffic management, pedestrians. It would need to contain some overall assessment of policy county-wide, including the allocation of expenditure between different parts of the county as well as between different types of expenditure. Within this framework the TPP would be broken down as appropriate into sections dealing with each of the major urban areas in the county (which probably pose the most difficult transport problems); with each new town; and with the inter-urban network and the smaller towns. It would identify the most important factors influencing the transport needs of the area in question; the problems arising from them; the council's objectives and its proposals:
> (i)   for investment (in public transport, roads and parking);
> (ii) for pricing and operation of parking and public transport;
> (iii) for the management of the road network (i.e. maintenance, traffic management and environmental and road safety measures).

Unlike development plans, TPPs are not statutory documents; nor are they subject to any formal inquiry procedures. Nevertheless, they must obviously be closely related to structure and local plans. Indeed, once the new system is bedded down, it is envisaged that there will be 'a single process which expresses itself on the one hand in TPPs (for the purpose of grant and resource decisions) and, on the other, in structure and local plans'. It will be the structure and local plans (with their statutory framework for publicity and participation) which will provide the wider context for TPPs.[26]

The multiplicity of transport grants (at different rates, some payable to operators, others to local authorities) was not suited to the comprehensive approach which characterises TPPs. They were therefore replaced by a system under which a unified grant for all transport services is distributed to local authorities on the basis of estimated expenditure. The major support, however, continues to be the Rate Support Grant which provides Exchequer aid towards all local services, including transport. Some specific grants have been absorbed into this: the remainder are now paid through a Transport Supplementary Grant. (In Scotland, with minor exceptions, *all* transport grants are paid through the Rate Support Grant.)[27]

This system represented a major shift in transport policy. Two particularly interesting features are, first, that grant is based not on the actual cost of individual schemes (the traditional procedure), but on county programmes of estimated expenditure backed by a comprehensive statement of transport policies for the area. (This was also expected to allow a reduction in detailed central government controls.) Secondly, financial support for public transport is channelled through local authorities instead of being paid direct to the operators.

It is in this financial context that TPPs assume an important operational status. They are annual statements of policy which will form the basis for grant aid and for loan sanctions. They contain not only financial estimates for the year but also (1) a statement of the county's transport objectives and strategy over a ten to fifteen year period; (2) a five-year rolling programme for the implementation of the strategy; and (3) a statement of past expenditure and physical progress, and the extent to which objectives and policies are being met.[28]

PUBLIC TRANSPORT PLANNING

Both the 1976 Consultation Document and the 1977 White Paper laid heavy emphasis on the development of public transport.[29] The Transport Act 1978 translated this into legislation. Its first purpose was 'to provide for the planning and development of public passenger transport services in the counties of England and Wales'.[30] All non-metropolitan counties were required by the Act 'to develop policies which will promote the provision of a co-ordinated and efficient system of public passenger transport to meet the country's needs . . .

and to prepare and publish a passenger transport plan'. This plan was to have a five-year time-scale and be revised each year.

This statutory requirement for a further plan (that is, in addition to the TPP and the structure plan) may have been more symbolic than substantive. (The Scots have managed without it.)[31] Be that as it may, it was part of a strongly held belief by the Labour government of the time that there were serious deficiencies in transport planning and policy.[32] Part of this, it was felt, could be met by additional statutory plans (and a range of specific provisions relating, for example, to concessionary fares, community bus services and car-sharing). But matters went deeper, and a better basis was needed for co-ordinated pricing and investment decisions.

That there was also public concern on some transport issues was apparent from opposition to specific highway proposals – particularly at Airedale, Winchester and Archway. Though the anti-road lobbies took up an extreme stance[33] there was clearly a broader-based lack of confidence in the system by which highway needs and routes were assessed.

In addition to the new Act, the White Paper promised a more 'effective' and 'flexible' approach to transport planning, with 'more systematic and open' public participation in policy formation, annual White Papers and – in the longer run – policies geared 'to decrease our absolute dependence on transport and the length and number of some of our journeys'. An independent assessment of the government's methods of appraising road schemes and forecasting needs was established and a review of highway inquiry procedures was set up.

THE LEITCH REPORT: TRUNK ROAD ASSESSMENT

The independent assessment (the Leitch Report)[34] was highly critical of the conventional methodologies. These were essentially 'extrapolatory', 'insensitive' to policy changes and partly (though not totally) self-fulfilling. Public concern about road planning was shown to be well founded. There were, however, no easy solutions: indeed the issues were inherently complex. The way forward lay in a more 'balanced' appraisal process, 'ongoing monitoring arrangements' and more openness – with no attempt 'to disguise the uncertainties inherent in the whole process'.

The government's response was positive, and the 1978 White Paper on highway inquiry procedures[35] represented a marked change in approach. National policies are being set out for parliamentary debate each year in a White Paper (of which the first was published in April 1978).[36] These White Papers 'will also serve as an authoritative background against which local issues can be examined at public inquiries into particular road schemes'. Hopefully this will avoid the confusion at local inquiries between national policies and their application in specific areas. This will work, however, only if the methods of assessing national needs (what the Leitch Committee termed 'a highly esoteric evaluation process') are acceptable. Since these cannot properly be examined at local inquiries (or, indeed, by Parliament), they are to be subject to 'rigorous examination' by the independent Standing Advisory Committee on Trunk Road Assessment.[37]

Against this background there has been a major change in highway inquiry procedures. Inspectors are nominated by the Lord Chancellor (not by the secretary of state); information on the reasons for the choice are published in advance, practicable alternative routes are published for consideration and consultants' reports are made available. The aim is to effect 'a closer association between the public consultation and inquiry procedures'. Objectors are provided with 'library facilities'; and pre-inquiry briefing and procedural meetings are held.

It is too soon to establish how this is working out in practice. It will, of course, be impossible to satisfy everyone, particularly when there is objection to a national policy. The 'top priority' for the M25 round London, for instance, was confirmed in the 1978 White Paper, but the 'M25 Co-ordinating Committee' is strongly attacking this, and is calling for an inquiry into motorways as a whole – in place of the 'section by section' inquiries which are in progress.[38]

The new procedures will give greater opportunity for widening the scope of inquiries and thereby for raising issues which cannot be settled by recourse to 'facts'. Of course, it is seldom that 'facts' can settle an issue (cf. the Roskill Inquiry): thus, though the Leitch Committee concluded a survey of 'the effects of trunk road construction on economic growth' with the judgement that these were 'limited', policy remains in favour of the opposite contention.[39] And, despite the breadth of the recent policy reviews of transport policy, much of the case put forward by Friends of the Earth in *Getting Nowhere Fast* remains for debate.[40]

The questions of public participation raised here are discussed further in the final chapter.

POLICY FOR ROADS: ENGLAND 1980

The Thatcher government's 'first comprehensive statement . . . of its policies for the trunk road system in England' was *Policy for Roads: England 1980*, published in June 1980.[41] It opened ominously (and in striking contrast to the 1967 White Paper quoted earlier):

The first priority of the Government is national economic recovery. The road programme has to be judged in that context. We have to strike a balance. New road schemes can bring undoubted economic advantages. Exports can reach their markets more quickly; goods can be distributed more efficiently; traffic can flow more easily and fuel can be saved. At the same time substantial environmental benefits can be gained. Heavy lorries can be taken round cities, towns and villages. People can be freed from the noise, the disturbance and the danger of traffic confined to inadequate roads. But national economic recovery also means reducing public spending.

Against this bleak background, three priorities are set forth. First, 'roads which aid economic recovery and development', of which an 'outstanding example' is the M25 orbital motorway around London.[42] Other port routes of 'clear economic importance' are those to Hull, Immingham, the Haven Ports, Tilbury and Southampton.[43] Another economic objective to be served by the (reduced) road programme is the improvement of communications to areas of economic decline – London's Docklands; the North Devon Link; the Calder Valley; Shotton and Corby.

Secondly, 'roads which bring environmental benefit'. The full list of towns to which this could apply would be a lengthy one, and the appendices to the White Paper list a large number. Particular mention is made of historic towns such as Berwick, Lincoln and Ely; of Stratford-upon-Avon, Ipswich and Chelmsford, which will benefit from the plans for the routes to ports; and of the M25 which will relieve many places on the outskirts of London.

Thirdly, 'preserving the investment already made'. As the motorway and trunk road network expands, increasing amounts are required 'to ensure the proper protection of that investment'. Some motorway repairs are urgent: 'Sections of the M1, M5 and M6 are in particular need of major renovation over the coming years.'[44]

Looking further ahead, 'the balance of the programme is likely to change. The major routes of national importance which remain to be completed will have priority . . . Increasingly, the emphasis will shift to schemes which are required to deal with specific local problems. Many of these will be bypasses of individual towns and villages',[45] a good number of which, within the smaller investment programme, will be started later than envisaged by the previous Labour administration.

In addition to the economic and environmental factors which have weighed so heavily in the elaboration of the new roads policy there is a third factor: 'the way people feel about a scheme. Where there is a real choice, the preferences of those affected will be a major factor in all decisions.' No doubt reflecting on recent experience, the comment is added, 'this does not simply mean paying heed to the most vocal groups, nor does it mean that local interests can always prevail over the needs of the nation as a whole'.[46]

THE HOUSE OF COMMONS TRANSPORT COMMITTEE

The general policies set out in the 1980 White Paper were examined by the House of Commons Transport Committee later in the year. Its report makes fascinating reading (and, incidentally, demonstrates the usefulness of the new system of parliamentary committees).[47]

The Committee apparently intended to take a low-key, analytical and dispassionate approach, but quickly found that they 'had opened something of a Pandora's Box':

> It became apparent that there was considerable disquiet about major issues, such as the way in which the roads programme is formulated and discussed at a national level, the scope and conduct of road inquiries, and the division of responsibility for the execution of the road programme between national and local authorities . . . Despite – or perhaps because of – a plethora of official inquiries, the development of highly sophisticated modelling techniques, and the dissemination of detailed information about the methods used for the assessment of individual road proposals, there is clearly a widespread suspicion that decisions about roads are protected from effective public scrutiny by a bureaucracy which is either happy to have elevated its art into a mystery or which has been overwhelmed by the complexity of the machinery which it has created.[48]

Given the reforms outlined in the previous pages of this chapter, one begins to wonder precisely what would provide a satisfactory system. That question, however, (like many others raised in – or by – the Committee's report) will be ignored here. Instead, attention is focused on the single issue of the 'division of responsibility' for roads: an issue which is of widespread and perpetual importance (*mutatis mutandis*) in many areas of town and country planning.

The point here is that while the Department of Transport (and its Scottish and Welsh counterparts) are responsible for the construction and maintenance of motorways and designated 'trunk' roads, the remainder of the road system is the responsibility of local government. The figures may be surprising: 'The vast majority of the nation's roads are, under this system, the primary responsibility of the county councils, the motorway and trunk road system accounting for only about 6,300 miles of the total network of about 200,000 miles of roads.'[49] (Figures for Great Britain are given in Table 6.3.)

This division of responsibility is largely an 'historical accident' and it gives rise to 'numerous anomalies' of which the classic case is the South Circular Road (the responsibility of the Greater London Council), nicely described by the RAC as 'a collection of signposts'.[51]

The Transport Committee made heavy weather of this issue, partly

Table 6.3   *Kilometres of Roads, Great Britain 1960–79*[50]

Year*	Motor-ways	Other trunk roads	Local authority motor-ways	Other principal roads	Other roads	All roads	Number vehicles per km of road
1960	153	13,424	–	–	298,859	312,436	30
1965	558	13,425	13	–	298,885	312,881	41
1970	1,022	13,441	35	32,549	275,437	322,484	46
1975	1,932	13,471	94	32,831	282,846	331,174	53
1976	2,129	13,489	97	33,133	284,570	333,418	53
1977	2,182	13,161	108	33,529	286,206	335,186	na†
1978	2,307	12,561	108	34,148	287,419	336,455	53
1979	2,366	12,463	119	34,345	288,699	337,992	55
1979 miles	*1,470*	*7,745*	*74*	*21,346*	*179,428*	*210,063*	*89*

*At 1 April.

†No census of vehicles was taken in 1977. Figures for later years are not directly comparable as they are prepared on a different basis.

because (rightly in the author's view) they saw that the role of the Department of Transport would change over the next decade:

> Our own, very provisional view is that the long-term strategy should be focused on the eventual reduction of the Department's functions so that its primary responsibilities should be in the areas of overall strategic road planning, the co-ordination of the road programmes of the individual shire and metropolitan authorities, and the allocation of national resources to assist the authorities in carrying out their programmes.[52]

No doubt this 'very provisional view' will be fleshed out in later reports.[53]

REFERENCES AND FURTHER READING: CHAPTER 6

1   *Transport Policy: A Consultation Document*, 2 vols (HMSO, 1976).
2   op. cit., para. 13.1.
3   op. cit., para. 1.3.
4   op. cit., paras 1.4 and 13.3.
5   British Road Federation, *Basic Road Statistics 1980* (BRF, 1980).
6   Department of Transport, *National Road Traffic Forecasts* (July 1980).
7   Compare J. C. Tanner's forecasts of 1967, 1974 and 1977, *Revised Forecasts of Vehicles and Traffic in Great Britain* (1967); *Forecasts of Vehicles and Traffic in Great Britain, 1974 Revision* (1974); and *Car Ownership Trends and Forecasts* (1977), all published by the Transport and Road Research Laboratory.
8   British Road Federation, *Basic Road Statistics*, annual.

9 British Road Federation, *Basic Road Statistics* 1980 (BRF, 1980), Table 11.
10 Ministry of Transport, *Traffic in Towns*, p. 26, para. 45.
11 This projected huge population increase led to considerable concern about population distribution (as well as to the establishment of several new towns of unprecedented size). See Department of the Environment, *Long Term Population Distribution in Great Britain – A Study*, which was published by DoE in 1971 – after the scare was over. The final chapter of this study is reproduced in J. B. Cullingworth (ed), *Planning for Change*, Vol. 3 of *Problems of an Urban Society* (Allen & Unwin, 1973).
12 Ministry of Transport, *Roads for the Future: A New Inter-Urban Plan* (HMSO, 1969).
13 C. D. Buchanan, *Mixed Blessing: The Motor in Britain* (Leonard Hill, 1958).
14 Ministry of Transport, *Traffic in Towns* (Buchanan Report) (HMSO, 1963), para. 101.
15 This was under discussion at the same time: see, for instance, Ministry of Transport, *Road Pricing: The Economic and Technical Possibilities* (Smeed Report) (HMSO, 1964); and J. M. W. Stewart, *A Pricing System for Roads*, University of Glasgow, Social and Economic Studies, Occasional Paper 4 (Oliver & Boyd, 1965).
16 White Paper, *Transport in London*, Cmnd 3686 (HMSO, 1968).
17 White Paper, *Public Transport and Traffic*, Cmnd 3481 (HMSO, 1967)
18 In 1978 57 per cent of households in Britain had one or more cars (45 per cent one car and 12 per cent two or more cars). The proportion varied, however, from 47 per cent in Scotland to 67 per cent in the South-East outside Greater London. British Road Federation, op. cit., Table 44.
19 Department of the Environment, *New Roads in Towns* (HMSO, 1972).
20 *Report of the Urban Motorways Project Team to the Urban Motorways Committee* (HMSO, 1973).
21 White Paper, *Development and Compensation: Putting People First*, Cmnd 5124, (HMSO, 1972).
22 op. cit., paras. 5–6.
23 *Expenditure Committee, Second Report Session 1972–73, Urban Transport Planning*, 3 vols, HC Paper 57 (HMSO, 1972). See also *Government Observations on the Second Report of the Expenditure Committee*, Cmnd 5366 (HMSO, 1973).
24 See the report, op. cit., paras 25 and 59–61; and the evidence of Meyer Hillman, pp. 235–50; also M. Hillman *et al., Personal Mobility and Transport Policy* (PEP, 1973).
25 DoE Circular 104/73, *Local Transport Grants* (HMSO, 1973).
26 The revised Department of the Environment memorandum on structure planning includes the following:

'The county council's transport policies form an integral part of the overall development policy. The structure plan should formulate policies for the means of movement of people and goods by road, rail or other modes, whether under public or private control. It will provide a framework for local plans and for transport policies and programmes (TPPs) and public transport plans. Transport policies formulated in the structure plan will include policies for the management and development of the road network and for the provision and co-ordination of public transport services. These will need to reflect the policies and financial constraints of the rail and bus operators, which should be referred to as necessary in the reasoned justification. The plan should formulate policies and general proposals for the county council's primary road network, the rail network, and other major transport facilities including airports, ferries, ports, freight interchanges and canals. Where proposals for new freight railheads have been formulated regionally, they should be included in the plan. The county council's primary road network should normally include all existing trunk roads and those proposed trunk roads the lines of which have been statutorily established. The treatment of other trunk road proposals should be the subject of consultation with the Department of Transport or the Welsh Office. Proposals for major improvements to transport facilities should be included, together with broad policy on the priority of minor improvements, for example, on access to the primary road network from other roads. Where appropriate, road traffic restraint policies (including broad car parking policies to be elaborated in the relevant local plans) should be formulated.' DoE Circular 4/79, *Memorandum on Structure and Local Plans* (HMSO, 1979), para. 2.27.

27 See SDD Circular 13/1975, *Regional Roads and Passenger Transport Expenditure: Financial Support* (Scottish Development Department, 1975).

28 For an account of the early operation of this grant system, see P. J. Mackie, 'The new grant system for local transport – the first five years', *Public Administration*, vol. 58 (Summer 1980), pp. 187–206. More generally, see N. P. Hepworth, *The Finance of Local Government* (Allen & Unwin, 4th edn, 1978).

29 *Transport Policy: A Consultative Document*, 2 vols (HMSO, 1976); and White Paper, *Transport Policy*, Cmnd 6836 (HMSO, 1977).

30 The Scots decided that their existing machinery was adequate without the necessity for additional statutory public transport plans. SDD Circular 19/1978 (*The Fourth Transport Policies and Programme*) asked regional and islands councils to place greater emphasis on public transport in their next two annual TPPs. See SDD Circular 56/1978, *Transport Act 1978* (Scottish Development Department, 1978).

31 See previous note.

32 The Consultative Document made several references to 'the authoritative Socialist Commentary report' (*Socialist Commentary*, April 1975).

33 See particularly J. Tyme, *Motorways versus Democracy: Public Inquiries into Road Proposals and Their Political Significance* (Macmillan, 1978).

34 *Report of the Advisory Committee on Trunk Road Assessment* (Leitch Report) (HMSO, 1977). See also A. Samuels, 'New roads: the assessment of need, usefulness and desirability', *Journal of Planning and Environment Law*, 1981, pp. 15–25.

35 White Paper, *Report on the Review of Highway Inquiry Procedures*, Cmnd 7132 (HMSO, 1978).

36 White Paper, *Policy for Roads, England 1978*, Cmnd 7132 (HMSO, 1978). For Wales, the Welsh Office published *Roads in Wales* (1978). The Scottish policy statement was incorporated in the *Report for 1978* of the Scottish Development Department, Cmnd 7556 (1979), ch. V.

37 See Standing Advisory Committee on Trunk Road Assessment (Chairman: Sir George Leitch), *Trunk Road Proposals – A Comprehensive Framework for Appraisal* (HMSO, 1979).

38 M25 Co-ordinating Committee, *M25: The Case for a Public Review* (Friends of the Earth, 1978).

39 See *Report of the Advisory Committee on Trunk Road Assessment*, op. cit., Appendix G, 'The effects of trunk road construction on economic growth'.

40 M. Hamer, *Getting Nowhere Fast* (Friends of the Earth, 1976).

41 White Paper, *Policy for Roads, England 1980*, Cmnd 7908 (HMSO, 1980).

42 For a contrary view, see M25 Co-ordinating Committee, *M25: The Case for a Public Review*, op. cit. In a memorandum to the House of Commons Transport Committee 'Transport 2000' point to the confusion of ends and means here: 'For surely the objectives should read "aiding economic recovery and development", and not "*roads* which aid . . .". Without this change, the roads can be seen as ends in themselves and not as means to an end, and consequently policy makers and administrators can miss other options that are available.' HC Transport Committee, Session 1979–80, *The Roads White Paper: Evidence of Transport 2000*, in HC Paper 673-VI, Session 1979–80 (HMSO, 1980), p. 123. cf. the Leitch Report on the effect of improved road systems on economic growth: p. 92 and Appendix G.

43 This, of course, brings us into the wider field of 'links with Europe', and the EEC transport policy (if such a term can be considered appropriate). On this see House of Commons Transport Committee, *The European Commission's Green Paper on Transport Infrastructure*, HC Paper 466-1-V, Session 1979–80 (HMSO, 1980). The Government's *Observations* are given in HC Paper 35, Session 1980–1 (HMSO, 1980).
44 op. cit., paras. 1–5.
45 op. cit., para. 35.
46 op. cit., para. 9.
47 First Report from the Transport Committee, Session 1980–1, *The Roads Programme*, HC Paper 27, 2 vols (HMSO, 1980).
48 Transport Committee, op. cit., paras 3–4.
49 Transport Committee, op. cit., para. 47. The figures relate to England. It is not clear what the source of these figures is, and the metrication of recently published figures complicates a search. Nevertheless, the general point is clearly valid. This can be seen from Table 6.3 (in miles as distinct from kilometres). Out of a total of 210,063 miles of road in *Great Britain*, 9,215 are trunk motorways or 'other trunk roads'.
50 British Road Federation, *Basic Road Statistics 1980* (BRF, 1980), Table 8.
51 Transport Committee, op. cit., paras 48–9.
52 op. cit., para. 55.
53 There is some wry amusement to be gained from the observation that as public expenditure on roads has fallen, the number of reports dealing with the programme has greatly increased. (Similarly with the length of this chapter: when both public opinion and the availability of public finance supported the road programme, the chapter was modest – if not perfunctory. As conditions change, the chapter lengthens.)

The number of relevant reports which have been omitted from the discussion in this chapter is already of considerable length. The following is a selection: On lorries, a major report is that by Sir Arthur Armitage: *Report of the Inquiry into Lorries, People and the Environment* (HMSO, 1980). (Among other proposals, the report suggests the intriguing prospect of 'Lorry Action Areas'.); Freight Transport Association, *Road Costs: Do Lorries Pay Their Way?* (FTA, 1980). Increased interest in pedestrians and in walking is reflected in M. Hillman and A. Whalley, *Walking IS Transport*, Policy Studies Institute, Broadsheet No. 583 (1979); and J. E. Todd and A. Walker, *People as Pedestrians*, Office of Population Censuses and Surveys, Social Survey Division (HMSO, 1980). See also other studies by M. Hillman and A. Whalley: *The Social Consequences of Rail Closures* (1980); *Fair Play for All: A Study of Access for Sport and Informational Recreation* (1977); and *Transport Realities and Planning Policy* (1976), all available from the Policy Studies Institute.

Among interesting reports from the Transport and Road Research Laboratory are J. M. Hopkin, P. Robson and S. W. Town, *The Mobility of Old People: A Study in Guildford* (1978) and the same authors' *Transport and the Elderly: Requirements, Problems and Possible Solutions* (1978); J. P. Rigby, *Access to Hospitals: A Literature Review* (1978); B. E. Sabey, *Road Safety and Value for Money* (1980); and two studies by S. W. Town, *Non-Transport Influences on Travel Patterns* and *The Social Distribution of Mobility and Travel Patterns* (both 1980).

For a list of more general books, see Planning Bookshop Catalogue, issued periodically by the Town and Country Planning Association, 17 Carlton House Terrace, London SW1Y 5AS.

Chapter 7

PLANNING AND LAND VALUES

THE UTHWATT REPORT

'It is clear that under a system of well-conceived planning the resolution of competing claims and the allocation of land for the various requirements must proceed on the basis of selecting the most suitable land for the particular purpose, irrespective of the existing values which may attach to the individual parcels of land.'[1] It was the task of the Uthwatt Committee, from whose report this quotation is taken, to devise a scheme which would make this possible. Effective planning necessarily controls, limits, or even completely destroys, the market value of particular pieces of land. Is the owner therefore to be compensated for this loss in value? If so, how is the compensation to be calculated? And is any 'balancing' payment to be extracted from owners whose land appreciates in value as a result of planning measures?

This problem of compensation and 'betterment' arises fundamentally 'from the existing legal position with regard to the use of land, which attempts largely to preserve, in a highly developed economy, the purely individualistic approach to land ownership'. This 'individualistic approach', however, has been increasingly modified during the past hundred years. The rights of ownership were restricted in the interests of public health: owners had (by law) to ensure, for example, that their properties were in good sanitary condition, that new buildings conformed to certain building standards, that streets were of a minimum width, and so on. It was accepted that these restrictions were necessary in the interests of the community – *salus populi est suprema lex* – and that private owners should be compelled to comply with them even at cost to themselves.

All these restrictions, whether carrying a right to compensation or not, are imposed in the public interest, and the essence of the compensation problem as regards the imposition of restrictions appears to be this – at what point does the public interest become such that a private individual ought to be called on to comply, at his own cost, with a restriction or requirement designed to secure that public interest? The history of the imposition of obligations without compensation has been to push that point progressively further on and to add to the list of requirements considered to be essential to the well-being of the community.[2]

But clearly there is a point beyond which restrictions cannot reasonably be imposed on the grounds of 'good neighbourliness' without payment of compensation – and 'general consideration of regional or national policy require so great a restriction on the landowner's use of his land as to amount to a taking away from him of a proprietary interest in the land'.

This, however, is not the end of the matter. Planning sets out to achieve a selection of the most suitable pieces of land for particular uses. Some land will therefore be zoned for a use which is profitable for the owner, whereas other land will be zoned for a use having a low – or even nil – private value. It is this difficulty of 'development value' which raises the compensation problem in its most acute form. The development which may legitimately – or hopefully – be expected by owners is in fact spread over a far larger area than is likely to be developed. This *potential* development value is therefore speculative, but until the individual owners are proved to be wrong in their assessments (and how can this be done?) all owners of land having a potential value can make a case for compensation on the assumption that their particular pieces of land would in fact be chosen for development if planning restrictions were not imposed. Yet this 'floating value' might never have settled on their land, and obviously the aggregate of the values claimed by the individual owners is likely to be greatly in excess of a total valuation of all the pieces of land. As Haar has nicely put it,[3] the situation is akin to that of a sweepstake: a single ticket fetches much more than its mathematically calculated value, for the simple reason that the grand prize may fall to any one holder.

Furthermore, the public control of land use necessarily involves the shifting of land values from certain pieces of land to other pieces: the value of some lands is decreased, while that of other land is increased. Planning controls do not destroy land values: in the words of the Uthwatt Committee, 'neither the total demand for development nor its average annual rate is materially affected, if at all, by planning ordinances'. Nevertheless, the owner of the land on which development is prohibited will claim compensation for the full potential development of his land, irrespective of the fact that that value may shift to another site.[4]

In theory, it is logical to balance the compensation paid to aggrieved owners by collecting a betterment charge on owners who benefit from planning controls. But previous experience with the collection of betterment had not been encouraging. The principle had been first established in an Act of 1662 which authorised the levying of a capital sum or an annual rent in respect of the 'melioration' of properties following street widenings in London. There were similar provisions in Acts providing for the rebuilding of London after the Great Fire. The principle was revived and extended in the Planning Acts of 1909 and 1932. These allowed a local authority to claim, first 50 per cent, and then (in the later Act) 75 per cent, of the amount by which any property increased in value as the result of the operation of a planning scheme. In fact, these provisions were largely ineffective since it proved extremely difficult to determine with any certainty which properties had increased in value as a result of a scheme (or of works carried out under a scheme) or, where there was a reasonable degree of certainty, how much of the increase in value was directly attributable to the scheme and how much to other factors. The Uthwatt Committee noted that there were only three cases in which betterment had actually been paid under the Planning Acts, and all these were before the 1932 Act introduced a provision for the deferment of payment until the increased value had actually been realised either by sale or lease or by change of use. In short, it had not proved possible to devise an equitable and workable system.

The Uthwatt Committee concluded that the solution to these problems lay in changing the system of land ownership under which land had a development value dependent upon the prospects of its profitable use. They maintained that no new code for the assessment of compensation or the collection of betterment would be adequate if this individualistic system remained. The system itself had inherent 'contradictions provoking a conflict between private and public interest and hindering the proper operation of the planning machinery'. A new system was needed which would avoid these contradictions and which so unified existing rights in land as to 'enable shifts of value to operate within the same ownership'.

The logic of this line of reasoning led to a consideration of land nationalisation. This the Committee rejected on the grounds that it would arouse keen political controversy, would involve insuperable financial problems and would necessitate the establishment of a complicated national administrative machinery. In their view the solution to the problem lay in the nationalisation, not of the land itself, but of all development rights in undeveloped land.

THE 1947 ACT

Essentially, this is precisely what the 1947 Town and Country Planning Act did. Effectively, development rights and their associated values were nationalised. No development was to take place without permission from the local planning authority. If permission were refused, no compensation would be paid (except in a limited range of special cases). If permission were granted, any resulting increase in land value was to be subject to a development charge. The view was taken that 'owners who lose development value as a result of the passing of the Bill are not on that account entitled to compensation'. This cut through the insoluble problem posed in previous attempts to collect betterment values created by public action. Betterment had been conceived as 'any increase in the value of land (including the buildings thereon) arising from central or local government action, whether positive, for example by the execution of public works or improvements, or negative, for example by the imposition of restrictions on the other land'. The 1947 Act went further: all betterment was created by the community, and it was unreal and undesirable (as well as virtually impossible) to distinguish between values created, for example, by particular planning schemes, and those due to other factors such as the general activities of the community or the general level of prosperity.

If rigorous logic had been followed, no payment at all would have been made for the transfer of development value to the state, but this – as the Uthwatt Committee had pointed out – would have resulted in considerable hardship in individual cases. A £300 million fund was therefore established for making 'payments' to owners who could successfully claim that their land had some development value on the 'appointed day' – the day on which the provisions of the Bill which prevented landowners from realising development values came into force. Considerable discussion took place during the passage of the Bill through Parliament on the sum fixed for compensation and it was strongly opposed on the ground that it was too small. The truth of the matter was that in the absence of relevant reliable information any global sum had to be determined in a somewhat arbitrary way; but in any case it was not intended that everybody should be paid the full value of their claims. Landowners would submit claims to a centralised agency – the Central Land Board – for 'loss of development value', that is, the difference between the 'unrestricted value' (the market value without the restrictions introduced by the Act) and the 'existing use value' (the value subject to these restrictions). When all the claims had been received and examined, the £300 million would be divided between claimants at whatever proportion of their 1948 value that total would allow. (In the event the estimate of £300 million was not as far out as critics feared. The total of all claims eventually amounted to £380 million.)

The original intention was to have a flexible rate of development charge. In some cases 100 per cent would be levied, but in others a lower rate would be more appropriate in order to encourage development 'on account of economic conditions in the country generally, or in particular areas where unemployment is above the average', or where it was important to secure 'a particular piece of development now, instead of in, say, twenty years'.[5] However, when the regulations came to be made, the government maintained that the policy which had been set out during the passage of the Bill through the House was unworkable. The only explanation given for this was that 'the whole conception is that the value of land is divided into two parts – the value restricted to its existing use and the development value. The market value is the sum of the two. If, by the action of the State, the development value is no longer in the possession of the owner of the land, then all he has left is the existing use value. Moreover, the fund of £300 million is being provided for the purposes of compensating the owner of land for this reduced value . . . therefore the owner of land can have no possible claim to any part of the development value and it is logical and right that the State should, where development takes place, make a charge which represents the amount of the development value.'

The whole idea of variable development charges (particularly for the depressed areas) was rejected, and a flat-rate 100 per cent levy introduced.[6]

These provisions – of which only the barest summary has been given here – were very complex, and, together with the inevitable uncertainty as to when compensation would be paid and how much it should be, resulted in a general feeling of uncertainty and discontent which did not augur well for the scheme. The principles, however, were clear. To recapitulate, all development rights and values were vested in the state: no development could take place without permission from the local planning authority and then only on payment of a betterment charge to the Central Land Board. The nationalisation of development rights was effected by the 'promised' payment of compensation. As a result landowners only 'owned' the existing use rights of their land and it thus followed, first, that if permission to develop was refused no compensation was payable, and, secondly, that the price paid by public authorities for the compulsory acquisition of land would be equal to the existing use value, that is, its value excluding any allowance for future development.

THE 1947 SCHEME IN OPERATION

The scheme did not work as smoothly as was expected. In their first annual report the Central Land Board 'noted with concern some weeks after the Act came into operation that despite the liability for development charge land was still being widely offered and, still worse, taken at prices including the full development value'. This remained a problem throughout the lifetime of the scheme – though the magnitude of the problem still remains a matter of some controversy. It is certainly true that conditions were such that developers were prepared to pay more than existing use prices for land; but the conditions were rather extraordinary. As the Board pointed out in their second report:

The evidence available to the Board of prices paid for land for development suggests that sales at or near existing use value are more the exception than the rule. To a large extent this is due to the severe restriction on building. Building licences are difficult to get and the developer who has been fortunate enough to obtain one is often willing to pay a much inflated price for a piece of land upon which to build. In other words, a 'scarcity value' attaches at present to the possession of a licence. The theory that the development charge would leave the developer unwilling or unable to pay more than existing use value for his land is not at present working out in practice, especially since a would-be house-owner who pays building value to the seller of the land, as well as a development charge to the Board, is still paying less in the total cost of his house than he would have to pay for an existing house with vacant possession.

It was to prevent such problems that the Central Land Board had been given powers of compulsory purchase at the 'correct' price. These powers were used – not as a general means of facilitating the supply of land at existing use prices, but selectively, 'as a warning to owners of land in general'.[7] Furthermore, they were used only where an owner had actually offered his land for sale at a price above existing use value. Thus, purchase by the Board would have done nothing to facilitate an increase in the total supply of land for development even if they had been much more numerous. In fact, however, their very rarity served only to make the procedure arbitrary in the extreme and, indeed, may have added to the reluctance of owners to offer land for development at all.

The Conservative government which took office in 1951 were intent on raising the level of construction activity and particularly the rate of private house-building. Though, within the limits of building activity set by the Labour government, it is unlikely that the development charge procedure seriously affected the supply of land, it is probable that the Conservative government's plans for private building would have been jeopardised by it.[8] This was one factor which led the new government to consider repealing development charges. There is no doubt that these charges were unpopular, particularly since they were payable in cash and in full – whereas payment on the claims on the £300 million fund were deferred and uncertain in amount.[9] The position was slightly eased after the announcement that the Central Land Board would accept claims as security for the charge up to 80 per cent of their agreed value. But as a White Paper issued in November 1952[10] explained:

this easement does not by any means apply to all developers and is in any case temporary: setting-off the charge against the claims in this way will not be possible when the fund has been distributed and the money has been spent or locked up in some investment. As time passes and the prospects of development concentrate and mature in particular places, the gap which in many cases already exists between the amount of the claim and the amount of the development charge will grow wider. The theory on which the charge is founded will seem even more elusive, and in practice the collection of development charge will have to be made in the face of increasing public resistance.

The basic difficulty was that purchasers of land were compelled to pay a premium above the existing-use value in order to persuade an owner to sell: a development charge of 100 per cent therefore constituted a permanent addition to the cost of development. Moreover, the basis of the development charge was uncertain:

> Since it is assessed on the difference between the value of the land without permission to develop and its value for the development permitted, the amount of the charge is inevitably a matter of judgement and valuation – and therefore for negotiation, in the same way as the price of land is a matter for negotiation. In some cases quite small adjustments in the two values during the process of such negotiation will have a very large effect on the amount of development charge finally assessed. This is inherent in the nature of the charge, but the effect is to destroy confidence in its validity. Those who view development charge as a tax on development – and they are in the great majority – look for some definite relation between the amount assessed and the cost of the land or of the development; and their failure to find any makes them very critical of the method of assessment.[11]

Further problems began to loom ahead as the final date for payments from the £300 million fund (1 July 1953) drew near. First, the payment of this sum of money over a short period would have a considerable inflationary effect. Secondly, all claimants on the fund would receive payment whether or not they had actually suffered any loss as a result of the 1947 Act. (Some would have already recovered the development value of the land by selling at a high price; others may never have wished to develop their land, and, indeed, might even have bought it for the express purpose of preventing its development.) But the main difficulty was that if compensation were paid out on this 'once for all' basis, 'it would be exceedingly difficult for any future government ever to make radical changes in the financial provisions, however badly they were working. For all the holders of claims on the fund would have to be compensated for loss of development value – those who will be allowed to develop their land as well as those who will not.'

Some amendment of the 1947 Act was clearly desirable, but though there might have been agreement on this, there was no equal agreement on what the amendments should be. There was a real fear that an 'amendment' which satisfied developers would seriously weaken or even wreck the planning machine: the scheme was part of a complex of planning controls which might easily be upset and result in a return to the very problems which the 1947 Act was designed to solve.

Various proposals were canvassed, but the most popular was a reduction in the rate of development charge. The intention was to provide an incentive to owners to sell their land at a price which took account of the developer's liability to pay the (reduced) charge. The government took the view that this was not possible: 'vendors of land, like vendors of any other commodity, will always get the best price that they can, and the development charge, however small, would in effect be passed on, in whole or in part, to the ultimate user of the land'. Furthermore, the government's objective was not merely one of easing the market in land: they were particularly concerned to encourage more private development, and even a low rate of development charge would act as a brake. On the (implicit) assumption that market prices for land would rise, the time would inevitably come when the charge would begin to greatly exceed the corresponding claim on the £300 million fund. Finally, it was felt that once the rate of development charge was reduced there would be no clear principle as to the level at which it should continue to be levied – 'the process of reduction, once begun, would be difficult to stop'. In short, the government held that the financial provisions of the 1947 Act were inherently unsatisfactory and could not be sufficiently improved by a mere modification: what was needed was a complete abolition of development charges.

THE 1954 SCHEME

The abolition of development charges was made on the ground that they had proved 'too unreliable an instrument to act as the lynch-pin of a permanent settlement'. But, at the same time, if the main part of the planning system was to remain, some limit to the liability to compensation for planning restrictions was essential. Otherwise effective planning controls would be prohibitively expensive: the cost of compensation for restrictions, if paid at the market value, would be crippling. The solution arrived at was to compensate only 'for loss of development value which accrued in the past up to the point where the 1947 axe fell – but not for loss of development value accruing in the future'.

There were some clear advantages in this scheme: not only was the state's liability for compensation limited, but it was to be paid only if and when the owner of land suffered from planning restrictions. The compensation would be the 'admitted claim' on the £300 million fund (plus one-seventh for accrued interest on the amount of the claim).

But not all admitted claims were to be met, even where loss of development value was caused by refusal of planning permission or by conditions attached to a permission. The 1932 Act had clearly established the principle that compensation should not be paid for restrictions imposed in the interest of 'good neighbourliness' and this principle was extended. No compensation was payable for refusal to allow a change in the use of a building; or for restrictions regarding density, layout, construction, design, and so on; or for refusal to permit development which would place an undue burden on the community (for example, in the provision of services). Some of these matters clearly fall within the 'good neighbour' concept,[12] while others are based on the principle that compensation is not to be paid merely because maximum exploitation has been prevented so long as development of a reasonably remunerative character is allowed.

The 1954 scheme[13] did not put anything in place of the development charge: the collection of betterment was now left to the blunt instruments of general taxation. Hence the attempt to 'hold the scales evenly between those who were allowed to develop their land and those who were not' was abandoned, but the use of 1947 development values as a 'permanent basis for compensation' safeguarded the public purse. On the other hand this meted out only a very rough justice to owners. The official view – at this date – was that this was not so; to quote the 1952 White Paper:

> It may be suggested that to limit compensation in the way proposed will work unfairly in certain cases. Land which in 1947 had little development value, and therefore no claim or only a small claim on the fund, may at some future date acquire considerable development value. Values will tend to follow the development plans, and land which acquires a high development value will normally be land on which development will be permitted; but there will be exceptions and it may be thought that to limit compensation in these cases will inflict hardship on owners who are refused permission to develop or whose land is bought compulsorily. It is important, however, to remember that all transactions in land since 1947 have taken place in the full knowledge that the 1947 development value was the most that anyone would hope to receive by way of compensation from the £300 million fund. Purchasers in future will be able to safeguard themselves by ensuring that permission to develop is forthcoming before they pay more than current existing-use value or, where a claim on the fund passes with the land, current existing-use value plus 1947 development value.[14]

This, however, ignored the fact that the new scheme established a dual market in land. Compensation both for planning restrictions (in cases where a claim had been admitted) and for compulsory purchase by public authorities was to be paid on the basis of existing use plus any admitted 1947 development value, but private sales would be at current market prices. The difference between these two values might be very substantial, particularly where development of a far more valuable character than had been anticipated in 1947 took place. Furthermore, with the passage of time land values generally would increase, especially if inflation continued. Whatever theoretical justification there might be for a dual market it would appear increasingly unjust.

Moreover, there is a real distinction between the hardships inflicted by a refusal of planning permission (that is, the loss of the development value of land) and that caused by the loss of the land itself (that is, compulsory purchase).[15] In the first case the owner retains the existing use value of his land and is worse off only in comparison with owners who have been fortunate in owning land on which development is permitted and who can therefore realise a capital gain. But in the second case compulsory acquisition at less than market price involves an actual loss since the owner is not only deprived of his property, he is also compensated at a price which might be less than he paid for it and would almost certainly be insufficient to purchase a similar parcel of land in the open market.

Finally, though it must be generally accepted that individuals cannot be protected from foolish actions based on an inadequate knowledge of the law, the situation following the 1954 Act was so complex and – because of the inevitable unpredictability of the necessity for compulsory purchase – so risky that it appeared likely (in retrospect at least) that public opinion would demand a further change. There was an omen of this even while the legislation was passing through Parliament. A certain Mr Pilgrim had bought, in 1950, a vacant plot of land adjoining his house. To pay for this he raised a mortgage of £500 on his house. Some years later the Romford Borough Council compulsorily acquired the land at the existing use value of £65. (No claim had ever been made on the £300 million fund for loss of development value.) Mr Pilgrim committed suicide. Naturally the case attracted a lot of attention and as a result a new provision was introduced in the 1954 Bill to alleviate the position of persons, usually small owners, who suffered loss on compulsory acquisition because there was no established claim on the £300 million fund. This provision permitted the payment of an *ex gratia* supplement in cases of this kind.

One further aspect of the 1954 scheme needs mention here. Compensation for loss of development value was payable in the case of land for which there was an established 1947 development value. This compensation was paid from central government funds, but the decision to refuse planning permission or to impose conditions remained with local authorities. Since this was a clear case of the

Treasury completely underwriting the decisions of local authorities, the latter were exhorted 'to exercise their discretion with due regard to public economy'. Furthermore, an applicant who had been refused planning permission could appeal to the ministry. There was an obvious danger in such a situation – the danger that concern to keep down the compensation bill would affect the ministry's judgement of the planning merits of particular cases. The same applied to the acquisition of land by local authorities: since they had to meet the cost of compensation there was a danger that they would attempt to avoid sites having an admitted claim under the 1947 Act.

To recapitulate, the effect of the complicated network of legislation which was now (1954) in force was basically to create two values for land according to whether it was sold in the open market or acquired by a public authority. In the former case there were no restrictions and thus land changed hands at the full market price. But in the latter case the public authority would pay only the existing (1947) use value plus any agreed claim for loss of 1947 development value.[16] This was a most unsatisfactory outcome. As land prices increased, due partly to planning controls, the gap between existing use and market values widened – particularly in suburban areas near green belt land. The greater the amount of planning control, the greater did the gap become. Thus, owners who were forced to sell their land to public authorities considered themselves to be very badly treated in comparison with those who were able to sell at the enhanced prices resulting in part from planning restrictions on other sites. The inherent uncertainties of future public acquisitions – no plan can be so definite and inflexible as to determine which sites will (or might) be needed in the future for public purposes – made this distinction appear arbitrary and unjust. The abolition of the development charge served to increase the inequity.

The contradictions and anomalies in the 1954 scheme were obvious. It was only a matter of time before public opinion demanded further amending legislation.

THE 1959 ACT: THE RETURN TO MARKET VALUE

Opposition to this state of affairs increased with the growth of private pressures for development following the abolition of building licences. Eventually the government were forced to take action. The resulting legislation (the Town and Country Planning Act 1959) restored 'fair market price' as the basis of compensation for compulsory acquisition. This, in the government's view, was the only practicable way of rectifying the injustices of the dual market for land. An owner now obtained (in theory at least) the same price for his land irrespective of whether he sold it to a private individual or to a public authority.[17]

These provisions thus removed a source of grievance, but they did nothing towards solving the fundamental problems of compensation and betterment, and the result proved extremely costly to public authorities. If this had been a reflection of basic principles of justice there could have been little cause for complaint, but in fact an examination of the position shows clearly that this was not the case.

In the first place, the 1959 Act (like previous legislation) accepted the principle that development rights should be vested in the state. This followed from the fact that no compensation was payable for the loss of development value in cases where planning permission was refused. But if development rights belong to the state, surely so should the associated development values? Consider, for example, the case of two owners of agricultural land on the periphery of a town, both of whom applied for planning permission to develop for housing purposes – the first being given permission and the second refused on the ground that the site in question was to form part of a green belt. The former benefited from the full market value of his site in residential use, whereas the latter could benefit only from its existing value. No question of compensation arose since the development rights already belonged to the state, but the first owner had these given back to him without payment. There was an obvious injustice here which could have eventually led to a demand that the 'penalised' owner should be compensated.

Secondly, as has already been stressed, the comprehensive nature of our present system of planning control has had a marked effect on values. The use for which planning permission has been, or will be, given is a very important factor in the determination of value. Furthermore, the value of a given site is increased not only by the development permitted on that site, but also by the development not permitted on other sites. In the example given above, for instance, the value of the site for which planning permission for housing development was given might be increased by virtue of the fact that it was refused on the second site.

THE LAND COMMISSION 1967–71

Mounting criticism of the inadequacy of the 1959 Act led to a number of proposals for a tax on betterment, by way either of a capital gains tax or of a betterment levy. The Labour government which was returned to power in 1964 introduced both. The 1967 Finance Act introduced a capital gains tax, and the 1967 Land Commission Act introduced a new betterment levy. Broadly, the distinguishing principle was that capital gains tax was charged on increases in the current use value of land only, while betterment levy was charged on increases in development value. The Land Commission was abolished by the Conservative government in 1971, but a summary account of its powers and operations is appropriate.

The rationale underlying the Land Commission Act was set out in a 1965 White Paper:

> In the Government's view it is wrong that planning decisions about land use should so often result in the realizing of unearned increments by the owners of the land to which they apply, and that desirable development should be frustrated by owners withholding their land in the hope of higher prices. The two main objectives of the Government's land policy are, therefore:
> (i) to secure that the right land is available at the right time for the implementation of national, regional and local plans;
> (ii) to secure that a substantial part of the development value created by the community returns to the community and that the burden of the cost of land for essential purposes is reduced.[18]

To enable these two objectives to be achieved a Land Commission was established (with headquarters located at Newcastle upon Tyne – in line with the dispersal of offices policy). The Commission could buy land either by agreement or compulsorily, and they were given very wide powers for this purpose. The second objective was met by the introduction of a betterment levy on development value. This was necessary not only to secure that a substantial part of the development 'returned to the community', but also to prevent a two-price system as existed under the 1954 Act. The levy was deducted from the price paid by the Commission on their own purchases and was paid by owners when they sold land privately. A landowner thus theoretically received the same net amount for his land whether he sold it privately, to the Land Commission, or to another public authority.

Though the Commission could buy by agreement they had to have effective powers of compulsory purchase if they were 'to ensure that the right land is made available at the right time'. There were two reasons for this. First, though the levy was at a rate (initially 40 per cent) thought to be adequate to leave enough of the development value to provide 'a reasonable incentive', some owners of land might still be unwilling to sell. Secondly, though the net price obtained by the owner of land should have been the same irrespective of whether the body to whom he sold it was private or public, some owners might have been unwilling to sell to the Land Commission.

The Act provided two sets of compulsory powers. One was the normal powers available to local authorities, with the usual machinery for appeals and a public inquiry. Under these powers the Commission had to disclose the purpose for which they required the land. These powers could be used for purchasing land scheduled for development in a development plan, or for land permitted for development.

The second set of compulsory powers were not to become operative until the 'second appointed day' and were to be brought into effect only if it appeared 'that it is necessary in the public interest to enable the Commission to obtain authority for the compulsory acquisition of land by a simplified procedure'. They were intended to provide a rapid procedure under which objectors would have no right to state their case at a public inquiry, and the Commission were not required to disclose the purpose for which the land was needed. The purpose here was to deal quickly and effectively with landowners who were holding up development. In fact they did not become operative during the lifetime of the Land Commission.

It was intended that the Commission would often be acquiring land in advance of need. They were, therefore, given wide powers of managing and disposing of land; but they could also develop land themselves. Land could be sold or leased to public or private bodies for any purpose – even if the purpose was different from the one for which the land was purchased. Land which was sold could be made subject to restrictions and future development value could be reserved to the Commission. Such land disposals were known as 'crownhold'.

Normally, the Commission had to dispose of land at the best price they could obtain, but there was one important exception. This was the 'concessionary crownhold disposition' which could be made for land which was to be developed *for housing purposes*. Here the Commission could dispose of land at less than the market price. All such housing land was subject to crownhold restrictions or covenants. In the case of owner-occupiers the Commission had the right of pre-emption on terms which ensured that the amount of the concession (and future increases in development value) accrued to them. Concessionary crownholds were also applicable to 'bodies which can effectively supervise the assignment of such houses', such as housing associations.

The levy differed from the development charge of the 1947 Act in two important ways. First, it did not take all the development value. The Act did not specify what the rate was to be, but it was made clear that the initial rate of 40 per cent would be increased to 45 per cent and then to 50 per cent 'at reasonably short intervals'. (In fact, it never was.)

The second difference from the development charge was that though the levy would normally be paid by the seller, if 'when the land comes to be developed, it still has some development value on which levy has not been taken in previous sales, that residual value will be subject to levy at the time of development'. Thus (ignoring a few complications and qualifications), if a piece of land was worth £500 in its existing use but was sold for £3,500 with planning permission, the levy was applied to the difference, that is, £3,000 – the levy, at the initial rate, was £1,200. If, however, the land were sold (at existing use value plus a 'hope' value that planning permission might be obtained) at £1,000, while the full development value was £3,500, the levy would be paid by both seller and purchaser: £200 by the former and £1,000 by the latter.

Certain bodies were exempt from the levy – for instance, local authorities, new town development corporations, the Housing Corporation and housing societies.

The proceeds of the levy were expected to amount to £80 million in a full year. In fact, however, the amount levied did not approach this figure. In 1968–9 it amounted to £15 million and in 1969–70 £31 million.

The Land Commission's first task was to assess the availability of, and demand for, land for house-building, particularly in the areas of greatest pressure. In their first annual report, they pointed to the difficulties in some areas particularly in the South-East and the West Midlands where the available land was limited to only a few years' supply. Most of this land could not, in fact, be made available for early development. Much of it was in small parcels; some was not suitable for development at all because of physical difficulties; and, of the remainder, a great deal was already in the hands of builders. Thus there was little that could be acquired and developed immediately by those other builders who had an urgent need for land. All this highlighted the need for more land to be allocated by planning authorities for development.

The Land Commission had to work within the framework of the planning system. Though a Crown body, they did not operate as such and thus were subject to the same planning control as private developers. The intention was that the Commission would work harmoniously with local planning authorities and form an important addition to the planning machinery. As the Commission pointed out, despite the sophistication of the British planning system, it was designed to control land use rather than to promote the development of land. The Commission's role was to ensure that land allocated for development was in fact developed – by channelling it to those who would develop it. They could use their powers of compulsory acquisition to amalgamate land which was in separate ownerships and acquire land whose owners could not be traced. They could purchase land from owners who refused to sell for development or from builders who wished to retain it for future development.

In their first report, the Land Commission gently referred to the importance of their role in acting 'as a spur to those local planning authorities whose plans have not kept up with the demand for various kinds of development'. Though they stated their hope that planning authorities would allocate sufficient land, they warned that in some cases they might have to take the initiative and, if local authorities refused planning permission, go to appeal. In their second report their line was much stronger. They pointed out that, in the pressure areas, they had had only modest success in achieving a steady flow of land on to the market. This was largely because these were areas in which planning policies were aimed at containing urban growth and preserving open country.

In 1969–70 the Land Commission purchased 1,000 acres by agreement and a further 240 acres compulsorily. But the use of these compulsory powers was on the increase, and a further 2,500 acres were subject to compulsory purchase at March 1970.

It is not easy to appraise what success the Land Commission achieved. They were only beginning to get into their stride in 1970 when a new government was returned which was pledged to the abolition of the Commission on the grounds that they 'had no place in a free society'. This pledge was fulfilled in 1971 and thus the Land Commission went the same way as their predecessor, the Central Land Board.

THE CONSERVATIVE YEARS 1970–4

Land prices were rising during the late 1960s (with an increase of 55 per cent between 1967 and 1970), but the early 1970s witnessed a veritable price explosion. Using 1967 as a base, prices rose to 287 in 1972 and 458 in 1973 (Table 7.1). Average plot prices rose from £908 in 1970 to £2,676 in 1973 (Table 7.2).

Not surprisingly, considerable pressure was put on the Conservative government to take some action to cope with the problem – though it was neither clear nor agreed what the basic problem was.[19] The favourite 'explanation', however, was 'speculative hoarding',[20] and it was this which became the target for government action (in addition to a series of measures designed to speed up the release and development of land).[21] A White Paper set out proposals for a 'land hoarding charge':

> The Government's measures to secure more planning permissions for housing development will go a long way to remedy the shortage of building land and so remove the occasion for windfall profits based on scarcity values. But they will be frustrated if land speculators can with impunity continue to hoard land with planning permission. Many permissions are not being implemented. In the South East of England (outside London) permissions for new private dwellings substantially exceeded the number started in every quarter since the third quarter of 1970. In the year ending 30 September 1972 planning permissions were given for an estimated 76,000 such dwellings, but only 52,000 were started.
>
> The Government has therefore decided, as the Chancellor of the Exchequer announced in his Budget statement, to promote early legislation to introduce a land hoarding charge. The purpose of this charge is to ensure that land with planning permission for housing is developed promptly, and to penalise the speculative hoarding of such land.[22]

Table 7.1   *Indices of Land Prices 1967–76*[23]

	Index of outrun prices	Index in real terms relative to retail price index
1967	100	100
1968	113	108
1969	141	128
1970	155	132
1971	175	136
1972	287	209
1973	458	305
1974	449	258
1975	318	147
1976	315	125

Table 7.2   *Private Sector Housing Land Prices 1970–79*[24]

	Weighted average price per plot £	Price index per plot or per hectare 1975 = 100
1970	908	49
1971	1,030	56
1972	1,727	94
1973	2,676	146
1974	2,663	145
1975	1,839	100
1976	1,848	100
1977	1,943	106
1978	2,376	129
1979	3,395	183

The charge was to be levied 'for failure to complete development within a specified period from the grant of planning permission'. After this 'completion period' (of four years from the granting of outline planning permission or three years in the case of full planning permission), the charge was to be imposed at an annual rate of 30 per cent of the capital value of the land.

The scheme was clearly a long-term one and, to deal with the urgent problem ('urgent' in political if not in any other terms), a 'development gains tax' and a 'first letting tax' were introduced.

The development gains tax provided for gains from land sales by individuals to be treated, not as capital gains, but as income (and thus subject to high marginal rates). The first letting tax, as its name implies, was a tax levied on the first letting of shops, offices, or industrial premises. In concept it was an equivalent to the capital gains tax which would have been levied had the building been sold.

Both taxes came into operation at the time when the land and property boom turned into a slump. Indeed, it has been suggested that they contributed to it.[25]

THE 1974 LAND WHITE PAPER

The Labour government which was returned to power in March 1974 lost little time in producing its anticipated White Paper on land policy.[26] The objectives of this were:

1 to enable the community to control the development of land in accordance with its needs and priorities; and
2 to restore to the community the increase in value of land arising from its efforts.

The keynote of the White Paper was 'positive planning' – to be achieved by public ownership of development land. The rationale for this was set out at some length:

> Our existing negative planning control provides a valuable check on the market, and would at first sight seem capable of safeguarding our heritage and resolving the conflict between private interests and the public good. But the difficulties inherent in a patchwork quilt of land ownership, and the overwhelming financial problems associated with acquiring land, mean that the best use of land is not always achieved.
>
> This is not to deny that plan-making is a very valuable function of our local authorities; it is rather to point out that the existing powers to implement their plans are restricted by the price that the market puts on some land, and by the fact that the planners' resource is in the hands of private owners rather than at the disposal of the community.
>
> Public ownership of development land puts control of our scarcest resource in the hands of the community, and enables it thereby to take an overall perspective. In addition, by having this land available at the value of its current use, rather than at a value based on speculation as to its possible development, the community will be able to provide, in the places that needs them, the public facilities it needs, but cannot now afford because of the inflated price it has to pay to the private owner.

For England and Scotland, it was decided that the agency for purchasing development land should be local government (thus avoiding the inter-agency conflict situation which arose between local authorities and the Land Commission). For Wales, however, with its smaller local authorities, an *ad hoc* agency was to be created (this became the Land Authority for Wales).

In order 'to restore to the community the increase in value of land arising from its efforts', it was proposed that 'the ultimate basis on which the community will buy all land will be current use value'. Sale of the land to developers, on the other hand, would be at market value. Thus all development value would accrue to the community. Provisionally, however, development values were to be 'recouped' by a 'development land tax'.

THE COMMUNITY LAND SCHEME

The ensuing legislation came in two parts: the 1975 Community Land Act provided wide powers for compulsory land acquisition, while the Development Land Tax Act 1976 provided for the taxation of development values. Thus the twin purposes of 'positive planning' and of 'returning development values to the community' were to be served.

The Community Land Scheme was complex – and became increasingly so as regulations, directions and circulars followed the passing of the two Acts. All that can be attempted here is a short summary.

The scheme was planned to be implemented in three stages. This, it was thought, would 'enable the build-up of authorities' acquisition, management and disposal activities to be matched to available resources, in particular of finance, manpower and expertise'. It would also 'provide the opportunity for authorities and the private sector to develop good working relationships and adapt to their long-term role as partners and co-operators'.[27]

In the first stage, which started on the 'first appointed day' (6 April 1976), authorities had a general duty 'to have regard to the desirability of bringing development land into public ownership'. In doing so, they had 'to pay particular regard to the location and nature of development necessary to meet the planning needs of their areas'. To assist them in carrying out this role, they had new and wider powers to buy land to make it available for development. Following the passing of the Development Land Tax Act of 1976, all land acquisitions by authorities were made at a price *net* of any tax payable by the sellers of development land.

The second phase was to be introduced gradually. As authorities built up resources and expertise, and became able to take on the responsibility for making available all land needed for particular types of development, the secretary of state was to have made orders providing that land for development of the kind designated in the order and in the area specified by the order must have passed through public ownership before development took place. These 'duty orders' were to be brought in to match the varying rates at which authorities became ready to take on such responsibilities.

When duty orders had been made covering the whole of Great Britain, the 'second appointed day' (or SAD Day as critics dubbed it) could be brought in. This would have had the effect of changing the basis of compensation for land publicly acquired from a market value (net of tax) basis to a current use value basis, that is, its value in its existing use, taking no account of any increase in value actually or potentially conferred by the grant of a planning permission for new development.

THE DEMISE OF THE COMMUNITY LAND SCHEME?

The scheme, like its two predecessors, had little chance to prove itself.[28] The economic climate of the first two years of its operation could hardly have been worse, and the consequent public expenditure crisis resulted in a central control which limited it severely.

It is fortunate, however, that a thorough monitoring of the scheme, funded by the Department of the Environment, was undertaken by the School for Advanced Urban Studies at the University of Bristol. The reader is referred to the interim and (forthcoming) final reports of the study.[29]

To speak of the 'demise' of the Community Land Scheme is, however, to exaggerate. The development land tax remains,[30] as does the Land Commission for Wales and certain provisions of the Community Land Act.[31] Moreover, new powers relating to land have been provided: some of these are of a similar hue to those which have been repealed, though others are markedly different.

LAND POLICIES: 1980 STYLE

It is, of course, a major function of planning authorities to ensure that sufficient land is available for forseeable needs within the framework of planning policies. Except where the policy is one of restraint (as may be the case in a national park, for instance), development plans should thus be a form of 'positive planning'. Under the Community Land Scheme local authorities were to take the further step of acquiring appropriate land. Though this is no longer the case, there is a wide range of powers which local authorities can use to make land available for development. In exhorting local authorities to ensure that there is sufficient land for housebuilding (and that adequate consultations are maintained with the industry), emphasis is now being placed on 'five-year supply' periods.[32]

DoE Circular 9/80 deals, *inter alia*, with a 'simplified methodology for future studies' of housing land availability.[33] But of particular interest is the strong wording on the question of shortages:

If an assessment reveals that a 5 year supply of land in line with structure and local plan policies is not available, the authorities concerned should take immediate steps, consistent with those policies, to make up the deficiency. These might include inviting and expediting planning applications, seeking to overcome infra-structure problems quickly, or being prepared to acquire compul-sorily land needed for development which an owner is unwilling to sell. In determining planning appeals for residential development, the Secretary of State will take into account whether, in the context of the advice in this Circular, sufficient housebuilding land has been identified as available for development in the area of the district.

It is also noteworthy that there is a provision in the 1980 Local Government, Planning and Land Act for the secretary of state to *direct* a local authority to 'make an assessment of land which is in its area and which is in its opinion available and suitable for development for residential purposes'.[34] It is not at all clear what circumstances would justify this or (even more problematic) how useful the outcome might be.

VACANT PUBLIC LAND

There has been increasing concern expressed in recent years over the amount of 'unused', 'vacant', 'derelict' or 'dormant' urban land (a variety of terms are used, typically with little precision). With the growing emphasis on inner city renewal, attempts have been made to explore how far such land can be brought into productive use. Concern for this issue stems from a variety of interests, ranging from agricultural production and allotments to aesthetics. Yet the extent and character of 'urban wasteland' (to use a Civic Trust term)[35] is unknown. Indeed, there is even less available information than in the case of derelict land (discussed in Chapter 5).

Several case studies were carried out in the 1970s,[36] of which that of the Liverpool Inner Area Study (1975) is of particular interest.[37] Covering 509 hectares immediately to the east of the city centre, 56 hectares (11 per cent) were found to be vacant (excluding land in temporary use). Only 6 per cent of the vacant land had been land-scaped and maintained. The most striking finding was that more than three-quarters of the vacant land was owned by Liverpool City Council, being reserved chiefly for housing, highways, open spaces and schools. Half the vacant land in the study area had been empty for at least two years and, on the likely level of public and private resources, the consultants predicted that three-quarters would still be vacant in 1980 – five years after their survey.

A national sample survey carried out by local amenity societies for the Civic Trust in 1976 revealed that, of 279 vacant sites, a third were owned by a local authority, and a further tenth by other public bodies.[38]

The 1977 White Paper *Policy for the Inner Cities* dealt with several aspects of vacant land,[39] while the Inner Urban Areas Act 1978 widened the concept of dereliction and provided for grant aid in certain areas. Significantly (in view of the stronger actions of the subsequent Conservative government) public authorities were asked 'to furnish schedules of void sites within the partnership authorities with a view to establishing what could be done to accelerate the development or redevelopment of non-operational sites'.[40] Similarly, a study group of the Association of Municipal Authorities proposed that records of void and underoccupied land and property should be held by all public sector bodies. The information would be formally reported to an appropriate service committee or board, along with a progress report briefly showing land and property brought back into use each year. The public sector would then be required to justify the retention of land held for projects not included in approved programmes and underdeveloped land or property before an independent adjudicator.[41]

REGISTERS OF UNUSED PUBLIC LAND

The 1980 Local Government, Planning and Land Act went further.[42] It provides that the secretary of state may 'compile and maintain a register, of land . . . owned by a public body' which, in his opinion, 'is not being used or not being sufficiently used'. Owners of land so registered can be directed by the secretary of state to dispose of it. These powers are permissive and will certainly be used selectively.[43]

REFERENCES AND FURTHER READING: CHAPTER 7

1 *Report of the Expert Committee on Compensation and Betterment* (Uthwatt Report), Cmd 6386 (HMSO, 1942), p. 13, para. 22.
2 op. cit., p. 20, para. 33. In a footnote there is reference to a dictum of J. Wright ([1927] 1 KB 458): 'A mere negative prohibition, though it involves interference with an owner's enjoyment of property, does not, I think, merely because it is obeyed, carry with it at common law any right to compensation. A subject cannot at common law claim compensation merely because he obeys a lawful order of the State.' However, full acceptance of this common law rule would necessarily result in hardship and inconsistent treatment between individuals (for example, between the owners of land zoned for agriculture and land zoned for building): see op. cit., p. 22.
3 C. M. Haar, *Land Planning in a Free Society* (Harvard University Press, 1951), p. 99.
4 Extraordinarily little analysis has been made of these concepts and still less of their relevance to and logic within the 1947 Act. As Leung has recently noted, 'Few commentators examined the floating value concept critically, although G. L. S. Shackle (*Expectation in Economics*, Cambridge University Press, 1952) introduced the ideas of "focus-gain" and "potential surprise" to explain the likely over-estimation of the compensation payments inherent in the floating value concept and H. P. Parker ("The Financial Aspect of Planning Legislation", *Economic Journal*, Vol. 64, 1954, pp. 72-86) attempted to quantify the likely degree of over-estimation. Neither commentator made it clear, however, whether he was dealing

with the effects of speculation on prices or with the natural tendency to over-estimate in the preparation of compensation claims.

'Many commentators recognised the fallacy of the shifting value argument. They pointed out that when planning permission for development is refused there is no necessary shift of development value and, in Sir Arnold Plant's words, "no law of conservation of value". D. L. Munby ("Development Charge and the Compensation-Betterment Problem", *Economic Journal*, 1954, pp. 87-97) suggested that the original concept of shifting value was an attempt to rebut the argument that town planning would lead to an actual loss of land values. Parker criticised the basic assumptions in the shifting value concept that a particular form of development would give rise to the same development value wherever it occurred, and argued that there was no special relationship between the development value of land and the gross rental value of the building standing on it. Professor Hayek (*Financial Times*, 26 April 1949) pointed out that through planning there would be allocated to land "an entirely fictitious value not having any real basis in nature and not conditioned by the natural selection of choice but artificially attached by the mere virtue of an administrative decision".' H. L. Leung, *Redistribution of Land Values: A Re-examination of the 1947 Scheme*, University of Cambridge, Department of Land Economy (University of Cambridge, 1979), p. 73.

5 *HL Debates*, Vol. 432, col. 983, 29 January 1947. See also *HC Debates*, Vol. 451, cols 294-5, 26 May 1948.

6 The minister (Mr Silkin) made the point that in areas where 'development is desired but is not taking place, the development charge will, by the normal process of valuation, be low. It is bound to be so because the development charge is the difference between the two values, one of which reflects the prospect of development in the area, and it must therefore follow that in an area where the prospects of development are small and development needs to be encouraged, the development charge will be less than in the case where development is not desired to the same extent. Therefore to a considerable degree, the thing will right itself by the normal processes of valuation.' *HC Debates*, Vol. 451, cols 303-4, 26 May 1948.

It is interesting to note that the 1932 Town and Country Planning Act when originally introduced provided for a 100 per cent betterment levy, but this was criticised on the ground that it would take away from owners all incentive to develop their property to the best use. Attempts were made to reduce it to 50 per cent, but the government compromised at 75 per cent.

7 An example given in the 1949-50 report of the Central Land Board was of a plot of land offered for private purchase at £300 and compulsorily acquired by the Board for £10. It was resold, inclusive of development charge for the erection of a house, at £180.

8 The Labour government repeatedly stressed that 'a great deal of land - estimated to be enough for 100,000 houses - has been made available for development without payment of development charge under the "dead-ripe" scheme'. *Town and Country Planning 1943-1951 Progress Report*, Cmd 8204 (HMSO, 1951), p. 13.

9 It was originally expected that claims on the £300 million would be worth very little. Even in January 1951 a claim for £4,193 was sold by auction for £220; other sales took place at 2s 6d (12½ per cent) in the pound. (See R. Turvey, *The Economics of Real Property*, Allen & Unwin. 1957, p. 140.)

10 White Paper, *Town and Country Planning Act 1974: Amendment of Financial Provisions*, Cmd 8699 (HMSO, 1952), p. 4. Unless otherwise indicated the quotations are from this White Paper.

11 Examples of assessment are given in P. Lamb and M. Evans, *The Law and Practice of Town and Country Planning* (Staples, 1951). The following is taken from p. 409:

Assume a residential property with ample grounds, and the owner obtains development permission to erect a small cottage which he proposes to sell or let. Assume that the value of the freehold property is £10,000. The cottage is erected in a position on a part of the land where it would not injuriously affect the house.

The value of the cottage freehold when erected will be £1,500 and the cost of erecting it would be £1,200. The area occupied by the cottage would be approximately half an acre.

The calculation would be on the following lines:

Consent Value

Value of residence		£10,000
Less value of ½ acre of land		£ 50
		£ 9,950
Value of cottage		£ 1,500
		£11,450
Less cost of erecting cottage	£1,200	
Adventurer's profit and risk		
12½% on sale price of house	£ 185	£ 1,385
Net value with development permission		£10,065

Refusal Value

Value of residence		£10,000
Development Charge		£ 65

12   The Act did, however, extend this principle drastically: a matter which evoked some opposition. For a fuller discussion see, for example, F. V. Corfield, *Compensation and the Town and Country Planning Act 1959* (Solicitors' Law Stationery Society, 1959), pp. 53ff.

13   There were two Acts. The Town and Country Planning Act 1953 abolished development charges, while the Town and Country Planning Act 1954 limited compensation for the loss of development values to those sites for which a claim had been approved, and then only under defined circumstances when an application to develop was actually refused.

14   White Paper 1952, op. cit., pp. 7–8.

15   See F. V. Corfield, op. cit., p. 52.

16   Strictly speaking there were therefore three different values for land:
   (i)   Full market price (including development) value in the case of private transactions.
   (ii) Existing (1947) use value in the case of public acquisitions where no admitted claim under the 1947 Act attached to the site.
   (iii) Existing (1947) use value plus that part of an admitted claim which had not yet been paid in all other cases.

17   There were several qualifications, *inter alia*:
   No account was taken of any increase in the value of the site which was brought about by the development scheme for which the land was being acquired.
   If the development scheme increased the value of contiguous land belonging to the same owner, this increase was set off against the compensation payable on the land to be acquired.
   (No account was taken of any decrease in the value of land attributable to the threat of compulsory acquisition.)

18   White Paper, *The Land Commission*, Cmnd 2771 (HMSO, 1965), para. 7.

19   See G. Hallett, *Housing and Land Policies in West Germany and Britain* (Macmillan, 1977), p. 135.

20   The flimsiness of the evidence for the hoarding theory is noted by Hallett, op. cit., p. 136.

21   These were set out in the White Paper *Widening the Choice: The Next Steps in Housing*, Cmnd 5280 (HMSO, 1973).

22 *Widening the Choice*, op. cit., paras 25-6.
23 Department of the Environment, *Housing Policy: A Consultative Document*, Cmnd 6851 (HMSO, 1977), p. 148, Table 11. The index relates to the price per plot of building land for private owners, England and Wales.
24 Department of the Environment, *Housing and Construction Statistics 1969-1979* (HMSO, 1980), p. 4, Table 3. The figures relate to private sector housing land at constant average density in England and Wales. The first column expresses prices in relation to plots: to obtain corresponding weighted average prices per hectare, multiply by 22·868. Weights were revised in 1979. The weighting is explained (op. cit., p. 170) as follows:
    'The weighted average price per plot up to 1978 is an estimate of the average price per plot in a standard collection of parcels of land similar to that developed in the period 1969-1972. From 1979, the standard collection is similar to that developed in the period 1975-1978. The average number of dwellings per hectare in the standard collection is held constant, so that weighted average prices per hectare are a constant multiple of those per plot, and a single index measures the movements of both. Indices from 1979 have been adjusted to be comparable with earlier results, but weighted average prices are not strictly comparable with those given for earlier years. Land prices are very variable, and this leads to difficulties in constructing price indices. The index does provide a guide to trends in prices, but it cannot be taken as being precise. Full details of the methods by which the indices are constructed were published in *Economic Trends No. 244* (February 1974).'
25 'The outcome of the flurry of proposals with which the Conservative Government reacted to the short-lived property boom of 1973 was thus a Development Gains Tax which, at least in the case of personal owners, acted as a major disincentive to bringing forward land for development, and a First Lettings Tax which inhibited commercial and industrial development. Both measures were taken over with relish by the succeeding Labour Government, but the harmful effects of the First Lettings Tax were later realised, and it was abolished in May 1976.' G. Hallett, op. cit., p. 137.
26 White Paper, *Land*, Cmnd 5730 (HMSO, 1974).
27 DoE Circular 121/75, *Community Land - Circular 1: General Introduction and Priorities* (HMSO, 1975), para. 4. On the issue of relationships between the public and private sectors see *Commercial Property Development: First Report of the Advisory Group on Commercial Property Development* (Pilcher Report) (HMSO, 1975).
28 See M. Grant, 'Britain's Community Land Act: a post mortem', *Urban Law and Policy*, vol. 2 (1979), pp. 359-73; and J. E. Emms, 'The Community Land Act: a requiem', *Journal of Planning and Environment Law*, 1980, pp. 78-86.
29 S. Barrett, M. Boddy and M. Stewart, *Implementation of the Community Land Scheme: Interim Report: April 1978*, University of Bristol, School for Advanced Urban Studies, Occasional Paper No. 3 (University of Bristol, 1979).
    Addendum: The School has now announced the publication of *Local Authorities and the Supply of Land to the Private Sector* by S. Barrett and G. Whitting. The announcement states:
    'This Working Paper documents interim research findings and conclusions from a research project entitled *Local Authorities and the Supply of Development Land to the Private Sector* which is funded by the Department of the Environment. The research represents a sequel to an earlier project to monitor *The Implementation of the Community Land Scheme*, which has previously been published as SAUS Occasional Paper No. 3 of the same title.
    During 1978 the Labour administration introduced a number of changes to the operation of the Community Land Scheme (CLS). Section 1 of the report looks at the impact of these changes on local authorities and completes the monitoring of the CLS which the School commenced in January 1977. General conclusions are also drawn relating to the overall impact of the Scheme.

In May 1979, the incoming Conservative administration took immediate steps to curtail any additional expenditure under the CLS pending the repeal of the Scheme. Section II of the Paper seeks to assess the impact of a major policy change on local authorities during the winding-up of the Scheme.

Section III focusses briefly on some of the broader issues of the role of a local authority in the land market and development process: these issues will be developed further in the final stage of the research and will be covered in a further publication.'

30 In the first Conservative Budget Speech, the Chancellor of the Exchequer stated: 'The Development Land Tax . . . has combined with the Community Land Act to prevent much worthwhile development and to increase unemployment in the construction industries. We have already said that we will repeal the Community Land Act. I propose now to deal with the Development Land Tax. In place of the present rates of 66⅔ per cent and 80 per cent, which the previous Government intended should rise to 100 per cent, I propose that Development Land Tax will in future be charged at a single rate of 60 per cent. The amount of development value which can be realised in a financial year without liability to Development Land Tax will be raised from £10,000 to £50,000. Both these changes take effect for disposals made on or after today.

I do not propose to make any further reductions in rate; and the generous increase in the exempt slice should mean that it will not need early revision. Owners of development land will, therefore, have no reason for holding back in the hope of further tax reductions. What I have said today should remove the major uncertainties which have been hanging over the market.'

31 These are set out in Schedule 17 of the Local Government, Planning and Land Act 1980.

32 See DoE Circular 9/80, *Land for Private Housebuilding* (HMSO, 1980). (This may be compared with DoE Circular 102/72, *Land Availability for Housing*, HMSO, 1972.)

33 For a discussion of some wider issues of 'land availability' and a report on Manchester which Circular 9/80 commends to local authorities, see A. Hooper, 'Land availability', *Journal of Planning and Environment Law*, 1979, pp. 752-6, and 'Land for private housebuilding', *Journal of Planning and Environment Law*, 1980, pp. 795-806. (The Manchester report was published by the Department of the Environment in 1979 under the title *Study of the Availability of Private Housebuilding Land in Greater Manchester, 1978-81*.)

34 Local Government, Planning and Land Act 1980, section 116.

35 *Urban Wasteland: A Report on Land Lying Dormant in Cities, Towns and Villages in Britain* (Civic Trust, 1977).

36 See *Urban Wasteland*, op. cit., pp. 11-14.

37 Published by the Department of the Environment: *Vacant Land* (Reference IAS/LI/11) (1976). The summary in the text is reproduced from *Urban Wasteland*, op. cit., p. 14.

38 *Urban Wasteland*, op. cit., p. 16.

39 White Paper, *Policy for the Inner Cities* (HMSO, 1977), paras 12, 28, and Annex, paras 8-16.

40 Association of Municipal Authorities, *Development of Publicly Owned Urban Land* (AMA, 1979), p. 1.

41 op. cit.

42 Local Government, Planning and Land Act 1980, Part X (sections 93-100): 'Land held by public bodies'. The Act does not apply to Scotland. The 'public bodies' are listed in Schedule 16; in addition to local authorities, the list includes new towns, development corporations, urban development corporations, the Housing Corporation, the British Airports Authority, the Civil Aviation Authority, British Shipbuilders, the British Steel Corporation, the National Coal Board, the British Broadcasting Corporation, the Independent Broadcasting Authority, the Post

Office and statutory undertakers (authorities for electricity, gas, water, railways, etc., etc.).

43 An initial list announced by the secretary of state includes: Liverpool, Wirral, Sefton, Manchester, Trafford, Preston, Salford, Stockport, Newcastle upon Tyne, Gateshead, Middlesbrough, Birmingham, Dudley, Stoke, Newcastle under Lyme, Coventry, Leeds, Bradford, Ealing, Wandsworth, Bristol and the area of the Urban Development Corporation for the London Docklands.

The first register to be compiled appears (in March 1981) to be Liverpool. The information contained in it includes:

- the owning body;
- site details including location and grid reference, and approximate areas;
- the interest held and details of tenants;
- current use or previous use if known;
- site characteristics like access and services;
- the authority's reason for retaining the land or the steps it is taking towards its disposal;
- contact name and telephone number for the owning body.

Planning, 27 March 1981 (Planning Bulletin 13/81, 3 April 1981).

Chapter 8

RECREATION AND THE COUNTRYSIDE

Both 'recreation' and 'the countryside' are large subjects which extend far beyond even the most generous definition of 'town and country planning'. The focus of this chapter, however, is on the subject embraced by the two words together. Even so the area remains a large one. It encompasses national parks, access to the countryside, nature reserves, camping, caravanning, rambling and youth hostelling, waterways, parks and many other aspects of recreation. It involves difficult questions of amenity – if only because too many people can easily destroy the amenities they seek. Some of these issues have been discussed in earlier chapters; here we are concerned with some of the major issues not merely of preserving and safeguarding amenities but of catering in a positive way for the increasing demand for leisure.

NATIONAL PARKS AND ACCESS TO THE COUNTRYSIDE

The demand for public access to the countryside has a long history,[1] stretching from the early nineteenth-century fight against enclosures, James Bryce's abortive 1884 Access to Mountains Bill and the attenuated Access to Mountains Act of 1939, to the promise offered by the National Parks and Access to the Countryside Act of 1949 – an Act which, among other things, poetically provides powers for 'preserving and enhancing natural beauty'. Many battles have been fought by voluntary bodies such as the Commons, Open Spaces and Footpaths Preservation Society and the Council for the Protection of Rural England (whose annual reports clearly indicate that their continued activity is still all too necessary), but they worked largely in a legislative vacuum until the Second World War. By the end of the 1920s the campaign for public access to the countryside became concentrated on the need for national parks such as had been established in Europe and North America, but though an official National Park Committee – the Addison Committee – reported (in 1931) in favour of a national policy, no action was taken. The mood engendered by the Second World War augured a better reception for the Scott Committee's emphatic statement that 'the establishment of national parks is long overdue'.[2] The Scott Committee had very wide terms of reference,[3] and for the first time an overall view was taken of questions of public rights of way and rights of access to the open country, and the establishment of national parks and nature reserves within the context of a national policy for the preservation and planning of the countryside. Government acceptance of the necessity for establishing national parks was announced in the series of debates on postwar reconstruction which took place during 1941 and 1943, and the White Paper on *The Control of Land Use*[4] referred to the establishment of national parks as part of a comprehensive programme of postwar reconstruction and land use planning. Not only was the principle accepted but, probably of equal importance, there was now a central government department with clear responsibility for such matters as national parks. There followed a series of reports on national parks, nature conservation, footpaths and access to the countryside.

The Dower Report was a personal report to the Minister of Town and Country Planning by John Dower, published 'for information and as a basis for discussion'.[5] A national park was defined as 'an extensive area of beautiful and relatively wild country, in which, for the nation's benefit and by appropriate national decision and action:

(*a*)   the characteristic landscape beauty is strictly preserved;
(*b*)   access and facilities for public open-air enjoyment are amply provided;
(*c*)   wild life and buildings and places of architectural and historic interest are suitably protected; while
(*d*)   established farming is effectively maintained.'

This conception of a national park was accepted by the Hobhouse Committee which also agreed with Dower's proposal for a special National Parks Commission – 'a body of high standing, expert qualification, substantial independence and permanent constitution, which will uphold, and be regarded by the public as upholding, the landscape, agricultural and recreational values whose dominance is the essential purpose of National Parks'. This Commission would select the areas for national parks and would employ in each park administrative and technical staff, headed by an assistant commissioner. These local executive bodies would act on behalf of the Commission and the local planning authority for each park. Management was to be under the control of an *ad hoc* park committee consisting of a chairman and fourteen members appointed by the Commission, together with fourteen members appointed by the local authorities in whose areas the park was situated. The whole cost of administering the parks was to be borne by the Exchequer.

This administrative organisation was devised in accordance with the conception of *national* parks as envisaged in both the Dower and Hobhouse Reports. Since the legislation departed substantially from these recommendations, it is worth outlining the reasoning to be found in these reports. National parks were to be administered for the benefit of the nation: this apparent tautology had the implication that planning in park areas should not be carried out by the ordinary local government bodies with the Commission acting as an adviser and supplier of grants. Such a system would 'tend to separate and oppose, rather than to unite and fuse, the national and local points of view and requirements; it would multiply delays by inserting an additional rung in the planning ladder; and by dividing responsibility, it would encourage inefficient administration and patchy compromise plans . . . If national parks are provided *for* the nation they should clearly be provided by the nation . . . Their distinct costs should be met from national funds.'

To appreciate the force of this line of reasoning it is necessary to realise that national parks were not envisaged as rural museums. The new administration was viewed not merely as a machine for operating controls, but also as a means for implementing 'a progressive policy of management, designed to develop the latent resources of the national parks for healthy enjoyment and open-air recreation to the advantage of the whole nation'. Among the management functions listed in the two reports were the acquisition of land for specific purposes (the Hobhouse Committee envisaged a tenth of the area of national parks coming into the Commission's hands during the first ten years of these operations); the removal or improvement of disfigurements or 'inappropriate' development (for example, the surface restoration of abandoned mineral workings); the prevention of litter and of damage to crops, walls, trees, and so on, the collection and disposal of rubbish, and the carrying out of repair works; skilled management to foster natural rejuvenation of trees, and a programme of steady and discriminating tree-planting; assisting local highway authorities in the provision of parking places, viewpoints and other subsidiary roadworks needed for the benefit of visitors; the provision (often through voluntary bodies) of holiday accommodation – quiet hostels for elderly people, holiday camps or guest houses for families, camps and hostels for younger people, camping and caravanning sites; the establishment of National Park Centres for field studies; the development of facilities for fishing, riding, small boat sailing; and so on. A capital expenditure of £9,250,000 was proposed over the first ten-year period, with recurrent expenditure rising to £750,000 a year.[6]

THE NATIONAL PARKS AND ACCESS TO THE COUNTRYSIDE ACT 1949

The government, however, took the view that the newly constituted planning authorities (under the 1947 Act) should be given the responsibility for national parks: these authorities were only just beginning to function, and it was considered to be unreasonable at this stage to suggest that they were incapable of meeting this responsibility. A National Parks Commission was to be established but its functions were to be mainly advisory. As might be expected, criticism was centred on this issue, and it was argued that county councils would be concerned primarily with local interests and would not be keen to incur expenditure for the benefit of visitors. One speaker commented that the proposed Commission bore about the same relationship to that recommended by the Dower and Hobhouse Reports as a baby's comforter bore to a real feeding bottle: 'it may by superficial resemblance, attract and soothe the innocent, but it stops short and there is nothing behind it'.[7]

The government were not to be shaken. Probably they felt that they had already take sufficient powers away from local government and that it was politically inadvisable to create another *ad hoc* executive body. Be that as it may, the new functions were laid on the shoulders of local authorities. The National Parks Commission had a predominantly advisory role. (The past tense is used since the National Parks Commission was replaced by the Countryside Commission in 1968.) They had a general duty to advise the minister on matters affecting the natural beauty of the countryside – primarily but not exclusively in national parks and other areas of outstanding natural beauty. Their main executive function was to select, after consultation with the local authorities concerned, the areas where they considered that national parks should be established (Table 8.1). They also had a general responsibility for considering what action was required in the parks in order that these objectives might be fulfilled, but could only make recommendations to planning authorities and 'representations' to the government.

Having decided that executive functions should be the responsibility of local authorities, the problem immediately arose as to what should be done in cases where a park lay in the area of more than one local authority. The Act provided that in such cases a joint planning board was to be the normal organisation, though exceptionally a joint advisory committee might be established as an alternative. In fact, due to the strenuous opposition of local authorities (who were particularly anxious about the financial implications) only two joint boards were set up – for the Peak District and the Lake District parks. Four parks had joint advisory committees as well as separate park planning committees in each of the constituent local authorities. The remaining four parks were wholly within the area of one local authority and were administered by a single local authority committee. (The position following local government reorganisation is outlined later in this chapter.)

Table 8.1   *National Parks at 30 September 1979*

National park	Date designation confirmed	Area in sq. km
Peak District	1951	1,404
Lake District	1951	2,243
Snowdonia	1951	2,171
Dartmoor	1951	945
Pembrokeshire Coast	1952	583
North York Moors	1952	1,432
Yorkshire Dales	1954	1,761
Exmoor	1954	686
Northumberland	1956	1,031
Brecon Beacons	1957	1,344
		13,600*

*9,502 sq. km in England and 4,098 sq. km in Wales; 9 per cent of the total area of England and Wales (151,096 sq. km).

A problem which has particularly exercised the attention of the Commission and the park authorities is that of development by government departments and statutory undertakers. Fears that this would prove a major problem were voiced during the debates on the Bill. Indeed, it was pointed out that 'the demands of these bodies would be more difficult to resist than those of private developers since the Government would in effect be not only the judge but also the defendant'. The catalogue of what Lord Strang, a former chairman of the Commission, has called 'alien intrusions' is a formidable one, and includes defence installations in the North Yorkshire moors and on the Pembrokeshire coast; masts for the GPO, the Air Ministry, the Ministry of Aviation, for defence, or for communications, or for air navigation: masts for the police and other services and for transport undertakings; a nuclear electricity generating station and a pumped storage installation in Snowdonia with the accompanying network of transmission lines on pylons for the supergrid; overhead distribution lines in every part of the country; two oil refineries and an oil terminal on Milford Haven astride the eastern boundary of the Pembrokeshire coast park; recurrent and increasing demands for water in almost every national park, culminating in the great controversy aroused by the claims of the Manchester Corporation upon Ullswater and Bannisdale.[8]

The problem is an intractable one. By their very nature national parks are ideally suitable for military training; they contain valuable mineral deposits; some of them can provide unrivalled water resources; the development programme of the Central Electricity Generating Board involves a wide and high-powered transmission network and thus more and bigger pylons which cannot be hidden in the landscape and which cannot be obviated – except at enormous cost

- by placing cables underground. These are all symptoms of the enormous pressures on land exerted by an affluent society in a densely populated country.

It would, however, be misleading to give the impression that the Commission have had no success. Much more effort is now being expended to make 'inevitable' developments as unharmful as possible. Statutory undertakers such as the Central Electricity Generating Board are now legally required to plan their operations with regard to amenity and to employ landscape architects; and public companies can be obliged or persuaded to do likewise. The nuclear power station in Snowdonia and the development by petroleum companies at Milford Haven can be instanced.

Indeed, in the words of the Sandford Committee:

It is easy to forget, because there is no visible reminder of them, the damaging proposals that would have proceeded but for decisions by park authorities, by Ministers, and in some notable cases by Parliament itself. It would also be ungenerous not to acknowledge in respect of schemes that have been allowed, the immense amount of care and skill, not to mention extra cost, which have been devoted to harmonising them with their surroundings. Notable examples are the abstraction of water from Ullswater and Lake Windermere in the Lake District, and the construction of Llyn Celyn reservoir in Snowdonia.

The Milford Haven Waterway merits special mention. The middle section of the Haven, which was partly developed before designation of the Park, is now dominated by oil refineries and tanks. The oil companies have been persuaded by the park committee to take exceptional pains with the landscaping of these installations. The policy of concentrating industrial development in the middle section of the Haven in order to conserve the outer headlands and the wooded upper Haven and the care taken with the development have been remarkably successful, considering the scale of the installations.[9]

Nevertheless the balance still appears to be weighted very much against the claims of amenity. Or, in the more forceful words of Ethel Haythornthwaite, 'in meeting Mammon so massively accoutred, the national park administration has all the appearance of David before Goliath, but without sling or stone'.[10]

This conflict between utility and beauty arises in a less spectacular but more intense form in connection with the livelihood and living conditions of the people who inhabit the parks. National parks in this country are not vast reserves of the kind found in Africa or America. They are areas of designated land in which ordinary rural life, rural industry and afforestation continue normally. The people living in these areas rightly demand modern amenities such as electricity and telephones, good-quality housing and – obviously – employment. These 'amenities' may clash with those sought by visitors, but the inhabitants cannot be expected to forgo these 'alien intrusions'. Nor should they be expected to shoulder the financial burdens involved in placing cables underground, in using expensive materials in new buildings for the sake of pleasant appearance, or in repairing the damage caused by visitors.[11]

The biggest conflict, however, is that between the twin purposes of the Act: to preserve amenities and to promote the enjoyment of the public. This conflict has increased as the amount and character of recreational demands on the national parks has grown. The implicit assumption in the 1949 Act (which gave equal weight to the twin objectives) that conflicts could be readily resolved has proved to be false.

This crucial issue is discussed further later in this chapter in the context of the Sandford Report and its aftermath.

SCOTTISH POLICIES

Despite obvious expectations to the contrary, there are no national parks in Scotland. Though a Scottish Committee (the Ramsay Committee) recommended, in 1945, the establishment of five Scottish national parks,[12] no action followed. The reasons for this inaction were partly political and partly pragmatic.[13] The essential element of the latter was that (with the exception of the area around Clydeside – and, in particular, Loch Lomond) the pressures which were so apparent south of the Border were absent.

Nevertheless, the secretary of state used the powers of the 1947 Planning Act to issue National Parks Direction Orders. These required the relevant local planning authorities to submit to the secretary of state all planning applications in these areas. (They included Loch Lomond/Trossachs; the Cairngorms; and Ben Nevis/Glen Coe.) In effect therefore (in an almost Gilbertian manner) while Scotland does not have national parks, it has an administrative system which enables controls to be operated as if it did! But of course this approach was inherently negative, and it was not until the Countryside (Scotland) Act of 1967 that positive measures could be taken (apart from the establishment of nature reserves and of national forest parks – both the responsibility of all-Britain authorities).

In the two decades up to 1967 a number of bodies contributed to conservation and recreation in Scotland.[14] The Nature Conservancy established fifty-one national nature reserves (with an area of 89,550 hectares); the Forestry Commission designated five forest parks (covering 104,000 hectares); and there were numerous acquisitions by the National Trust for Scotland of mountain properties for protection and public access – not to mention local authority designated green belts and areas of great landscape value.

The first major institutional innovation, however, was the establishment of the Countryside Commission for Scotland, under the Countryside (Scotland) Act of 1967. This Act also enabled local authorities to establish and maintain country parks. These range from (typically) small intensively used parks of some 10 hectares to large parks of 400 hectares or more. (Exceptional is the 12,000 hectare Strathclyde Regional Park. This is a major land reclamation scheme providing 'a landscape recreation area' lying between Motherwell and Hamilton.[15] It was opened in April 1978.)

Given the range of institutions, policies and initiatives, some mechanism for co-ordination was seen to be required; and this was provided by the Scottish Countryside Commission's *Park System for Scotland*.[16] The strategy embodied in this plan was designed to fit into the two-tier Scottish local government system. It encompasses 'high density recreational areas, visually in or near towns, through a variety of low-density recreational areas, generally remote from urban centres, where recreational use may be secondary to such uses as upland agriculture, forestry or water catchment. A fundamental point has been that the recreational pattern should impose conservation safeguards appropriate to each level or intensity of recreational use. A recreational plan for a region should impose restraints in recreational terms as stringent as those for the conservation of scientific interest or economic land uses such as farming or forestry.'[17]

The park system, as proposed, had four main elements: urban parks; country parks; regional parks; and 'special' parks.

The latter warrants particular comment: these are areas 'already under substantial recreational pressure and having particular attributes of scenic character which give them a national rather than a regional or local significance'. The Countryside Commission for Scotland envisages these as having individual administrative organisations (and presumably finance); but this would require new legislation. In the meantime, the Commission's approach has been 'broadly conceptual'. A major outcome of this has been the report on *Scotland's Scenic Heritage*,[18] published in 1978.

This report identifies forty areas of 'national scenic significance', covering over a million hectares (one-eighth) of the area of Scotland. The report proposes that local authorities should 'incorporate policies in their statutory plans which will protect the overall character of the areas against inappropriate change, and ensure that primary land use activities will continue to be able to thrive'.[19] Legislation will be required. A consultative paper was issued by the Scottish Development Department in late 1979 which dealt with a wide range of amendments to the Countryside (Scotland) Act 1967, for example, on management agreements, regional parks and control of noise and disturbance in sensitive areas of countryside, and changes to the development control system for 'scenic areas'.[20]

AREAS OF OUTSTANDING NATURAL BEAUTY

Both the Dower and Hobhouse Reports proposed that, in addition to national parks, certain areas of outstanding landscape beauty should be subject to special protection. These areas did not (at that time) require the positive management which it was assumed would characterise national parks, but 'their contribution to the wider enjoyment of the countryside is so important that special measures should be taken to preserve their natural beauty and interest'. The Hobhouse Committee proposed that these 'conservation areas' should be the responsibility of local planning authorities, but would receive expert assistance and financial aid from the National Parks Commission. Advisory committees (with a majority of local authority members) would be set up to ensure that they would be comprehensively treated as a single unit. A total of fifty-two conservation areas, covering some 26,000 sq. km was recommended – including, for example, the Breckland and much of central Wales, long stretches of the coast, the Cotswolds, most of the Downland, the Chilterns and Bodmin Moor.

The 1949 Act did not contain any special provisions for the care of conservation areas, the power under the Planning Acts being considered adequate for the purpose. It did, however, give the National Parks Commission power to designate 'areas of outstanding natural beauty' and provided for Exchequer grants on the same basis as for national parks. So far, thirty-three areas have been designated covering 14,493 sq. km (nearly 9·6 per cent of the total area of England and Wales) (Table 8.2).

Areas of outstanding natural beauty are generally smaller than national parks. They are the responsibility of local planning authorities who have powers for the 'preservation and enhancement of natural beauty' similar to those of park planning authorities. In contrast to national parks, however, the emphasis in areas of outstanding natural beauty is on the conservation of landscape beauty. Under the 1949 Act, grant-aid powers in such areas were confined to landscape matters such as tree-planting and clearance of eyesores, together with providing for public access to open country, and setting up warden services.[21] Grant aid is still given only for specific projects, and at a maximum rate of 50 per cent. Lower priority is given to grant aid for recreational purposes. The national parks, on the other hand, receive a 75 per cent block grant on all expenditure, as well as rate support.[22]

There was wide ranging discussion during the 1970s on the question as to whether the designation of areas of outstanding natural beauty served any useful function.[23] Following a review in 1971–3 by the

Table 8.2   *Areas of Outstanding Natural Beauty at 30 September 1979*

Area of outstanding natural beauty	Date designation confirmed	Area in sq. km
Gower	1956	189
Quantock Hills	1957	99
Lleyn	1957	155
Northumberland Coast	1958	129
Surrey Hills	1958	414
Cannock Chase	1958	68
Shropshire Hills	1959	777
Dorset	1959	1,036
Malvern Hills	1959	104
Cornwall	1959	932
North Devon	1960	171
South Devon	1960	332
East Hampshire	1962	391
East Devon	1963	267
Isle of Wight	1963	189
Chichester Harbour	1964	75
Forest of Bowland	1964	803
Solway Coast	1964	107
Chilterns	1965	800
Sussex Downs	1966	981
Cotswolds	1966	1,507
Anglesey	1967	215
South Hampshire Coast	1967	78
Norfolk Coast	1968	450
Kent Downs	1968	845
Suffolk Coast and Heaths	1970	391
Dedham Vale	1970	57
Extension	1978	15
Wye Valley	1971	325
North Wessex Downs	1972	1,738
Mendip Hills	1972	202
Arnside and Silverdale	1972	75
Lincolnshire Wolds	1973	560
Scilly Isles	1976	16
		14,493*

*13,817 sq. km in England and 676 sq. km in Wales; nearly 9·6 per cent of the total area of England and Wales (151,096 sq. km).

Countryside Commission, it was concluded that there was a 'wide endorsement of the concept'. A further review took place in 1978–80 when the Commission submitted that increased pressures on the areas necessitated more positive policies:

When the designation programme began in the 1950s it was the generally held view that a strict policy of development control by local authorities would be sufficient to safeguard landscapes. While strict control is important – particularly to protect AONBs against inappropriate development – landscape and wildlife conservation depend mainly on land management activities such as most farming and forestry activities, which are outside planning control. It is the Commission's view that negative policies of development control are no longer enough. There must be a new emphasis on relating public and private investment and land management practices to landscape conservation goals and social objectives. The recreational and tourist use of these areas needs an active rural economy and diverse social structure.

This review consisted of the preparation and distribution of a discussion paper (from which the above quotation is taken), a major conference[24] and an independent study by K. S. Himsworth on the effects of designation on individual AONBs.[25]

The conclusion again showed a widespread support for the AONB designation, but there was also evidence that 'as a result of a number of factors, including lack of clear planning and management strategies, inadequate resources and in some cases lack of co-ordination between the local authorities jointly responsible for AONBs, the statutory objective of enhancing "natural beauty" has not always been achieved'.

The Commission issued a policy statement which, in essence, elaborated the statement quoted above on the need for more positive planning.

THE COASTLINE

About a third of the coastline of England and Wales is included in national parks and areas of outstanding natural beauty. Additionally, development plans indicate 'areas of high landscape value' and 'areas of scientific interest' – national nature reserves or sites of special scientific interest notified to local planning authorities by the Nature Conservancy. Then there are coastal areas owned or protected by the National Trust. Nevertheless, the pressures on the coastline are proving increasingly difficult to cope with. Growing numbers of people are attracted to the coast for holidays, for recreation and for retirement. Furthermore, there are economic pressures for major industrial development in certain parts, particularly on some estuaries: Milford Haven and Southampton Water are cases in point.

The problem is a difficult one which cannot be satisfactorily met simply by restrictive measures: it requires a positive policy of planning for leisure. An early move in this direction was made in 1963 with a departmental circular, *Coastline Preservation and Development*, to local planning authorities with coastline boundaries.[26] This argued that, because the coast is of exceptional value and subject to heavy pressures for development, it merits special study and control. Authorities with coastal boundaries were, therefore, asked to make a study of their coastal areas in consultation with the National Parks Commission and, for scientific advice, the Nature Conservancy. The circular was followed in 1965 by a letter expressing the deep concern of the planning ministers about the worsening situation and the inadequacy of the measures being taken to prevent the spread of development on the coast. Meanwhile, local planning authorities were exhorted to speed up plans and policies. A 1966 circular asked for clear statements 'of each planning authority's policy for their coastal area in standard cartographic form'.[27] Nine regional conferences on coastal preservation and development were held in 1966 and 1967 and resulted in a series of detailed reports.

These formed the base of a major coastal study on which a number of major reports have been published by the Countryside Commission. Their final reports, *The Planning of the Coastline* and *The Coastal Heritage*, were published in 1970.[28] The former attempted to clarify the problems and to identify the principles which should guide planning action. The latter amplified the arguments for stringent protection of the finest coastal scenery. It proposed that these should be designated as 'heritage coasts', for each of which there would be a delegation of planning and management functions from the local planning authority to a special committee whose members would include nationally supported representatives.

Though rejecting formal designation and special machinery, the government endorsed the underlying objective that special designation and policies should be applied to selected stretches of underdeveloped coastline of high scenic quality.[29] Local authorities were advised to incorporate appropriate policies in their structure and local plans after consultation with the Commission.

At September 1979 thirty-three heritage coasts had been defined, extending laterally over 1,084 km (Table 8.3). (Of these, three have also had their inland boundary defined.)

THE BROADS

During the late 1970s increasing concern arose about the future of the Broads of Norfolk and Suffolk and, at one point, the Countryside Commission considered whether designation as a national park would be desirable. The local reaction was against this, but the Commission's intervention led to the formation of a voluntary consortium of authorities (with powers and financial resources under the provisions of the Local Government Act 1972), now known as the Broads Authority.

Table 8.3   *Heritage Coasts at 30 September 1979*

Completely defined	Date defined	Length in km
Sussex	April 1973	13
North Norfolk	April 1975	63
Suffolk	September 1979	56
Laterally defined		
North Northumberland	February 1973	92
Gower	June 1973	55
Glamorgan	June 1973	22
North Anglesey	July 1973	29
Holyhead Mountain	July 1973	13
Aberffraw Bay	July 1973	8
Great Orme	March 1974	7
Lleyn	March 1974	88
Tennyson	July 1974	33
Hamstead	July 1974	11
South Pembrokeshire	July 1974	66
Marloes and Dale	July 1974	43
St Brides Bay	July 1974	8
St David's Peninsula	July 1974	82
Dinas Head	July 1974	18
St Dogmaels and Moylgrove	July 1974	22
North Yorkshire	October 1974	53
Isles of Scilly	December 1974	64
South Foreland	November 1975	7
Dover–Folkestone	November 1975	7
Hartland (Cornwall)	January 1976	8
Widemouth–Pentire Head	January 1976	50
West Penwith	January 1976	54
Lizard	January 1976	26
Looe–Gribbin Head	January 1976	38
Mevagissey–Amsterdam Point	January 1976	23
Rame Head	January 1976	7
Trevose Head	January 1976	4
St Agnes	January 1976	9
Portreath–Godrevy	January 1976	10
		1,084

The Broads is a unique area, subject to the contrary forces of flooding and (as a result of flood prevention) of conversion of grazing to arable farmland. Discussions are continuing between the large number of interested bodies including the Countryside Commission, the Anglian Water Authority, the Nature Conservancy Council and the Broads Authority.[30]

PUBLIC RIGHTS OF WAY

The origin of a large number of footpaths is obscure. As a result, innumerable disputes have arisen over public rights of way. Before the 1949 Act, these disputes could be settled only by a case-by-case procedure, often with the evidence of 'oldest inhabitants' playing a leading role. The unsatisfactory nature of the situation was underlined by the Scott, Dower and Hobhouse Reports, as well as by the Special Committee on Footpaths and Access to the Countryside.[31] All were agreed that a complete survey of rights of way was essential, together with the introduction of a simple procedure for resolving the legal status of rights of way which were in dispute. The National Parks Act provided for both.

Responsibility for making the survey of paths rests with county councils. Maps are prepared in three stages: draft, provisional and definitive. A 'draft map' shows the paths over which the council, as a result of its survey, decides that there are reasonable grounds for believing that a public right of way exists. When this is published, 'representations' can be made for certain paths to be excluded or new ones added. There is a right of appeal to the secretary of state. This procedure provides an opportunity not only for objections from land-owners, but also for organisations and individuals concerned with the preservation of rights of way to present their case for paths which are not included in the map. After all objections and appeals have been settled, a 'provisional map' is published incorporating all the changes which have been decided. At this stage landowners can contest a path by appealing to Quarter Sessions for a declaration as to the existence or non-existence of rights of way. Subject to certain rights of appeal to the High Court, these declarations are final. When all the disputed cases have been dealt with by Quarter Sessions, a 'definitive map' is published: this provides conclusive evidence of the existence of all rights of way shown on it – though there is provision for revision.

The preparation of this 'Domesday Book' of the 165,750 km of footpaths in England and Wales has proved a laborious and lengthy process. Under the Act, the normal completion date for the prepara-tion of draft maps was to be December 1952; in fact, it was not until June 1960 that all draft maps had been published. By the end of 1971 there still remained eleven counties in England and Wales which had not completed definitive maps.

A Footpaths Committee, under the chairmanship of Sir Arthur Gosling, was appointed in 1967 'to consider how far the present system of footpaths, bridleways and other comparable rights of way in England and Wales and the arrangements for the recording, closure, diversion and maintenance of such routes are suitable for present and potential needs in the countryside and to make recom-mendations'. Their report was published in 1968,[32] and the majority of the recommendations were implemented in the Countryside Act 1968, and the Town and Country Planning Act 1968. These include placing a duty on landowners to maintain stiles and gates, and requiring highway authorities to make a contribution towards the cost, providing for pedal cyclists to use bridleways, and placing a duty on highway authorities to signpost footpaths and bridleways where they leave a metalled road. A special review must be made of roads used as public paths so that public rights over them will be clear.

The Sandford Committee examined problems relating to public rights of way, and concluded that the existing system was not suited to current needs: yet little was being done to improve it.[33] New legislative provisions are included in the Wildlife and Countryside Bill which, at the time of writing, is staggering its way through the House of Lords.

LONG-DISTANCE FOOTPATHS

Though work on the footpaths survey has been disappointingly slow, considerable progress has been made with what are officially termed 'long-distance routes'. These hikers' highways now extend over some 2,528 km and include the 400 km long Pennine Way and the 270 km Offa's Dyke Path (Table 8.4). The designation of these routes has been equally laborious, but they have had the attention and backing of the Commission – who have official responsibility for their establishment. The Commission are the initiating body: they make the proposals, discuss them with the local authorities concerned and present a report to the secretary of state. This shows the route together with existing public rights of way, and may contain proposals for the improvement of paths and the provision of new ones; ferries; and accommodation, meals and refreshments. However, though eligible for Exchequer grant, the implementation of approved proposals rests with district councils. The Commission can negotiate, persuade and offer assistance, but they can go no further. Furthermore, since the completion of the statutory survey of rights of way by local authorities has been slow, the legal status of footpaths is often uncertain. This – and particularly the slow progress made with the creation of new rights of way – has held back the completion of approved long-distance routes.

The first designated long-distance footpath in Scotland was opened in 1980. This is the West Highland Way which runs for 152 km from Milngavie (a suburb of Glasgow) to Fort William at the foot of Ben Nevis.[34] There are, however, other long-distance footpaths at various stages of negotiation, including the 97 km Speyside Way (which uses a length of the former Speyside railway line for about half its length), and the 328 km Southern Upland Way which stretches from Portpatrick on the south-west coast to Cockburnspath on the east coast.[35]

COUNTRY PARKS AND PICNIC SITES

In the early postwar years national recreation policy was largely con-

Table 8.4 Long-Distance Footpaths and Bridleways
at 30 September 1979

	Report approved	Officially opened	Length in km
Pennine Way	July 1951	April 1965	402
Cleveland Way	February 1965	May 1969	150
Pembrokeshire Coast Path	July 1953	May 1970	269
Offa's Dyke Path	October 1955	July 1971	270
South Downs Way	March 1963	July 1972	129
North Downs Way	July 1969	September 1978	227
Ridgeway Path	July 1972	September 1973	137
South-West Peninsula Coast Path:			
North Cornwall	April 1952	May 1973	217
South Cornwall	June 1954	September 1974	214
South Devon	June 1959	September 1974	150
Somerset and North Devon	January 1961	May 1978	132
Dorset	April 1963	September 1974	116
Wolds Way	July 1977	—	115
			2,528

Proposed new routes

Name	Details of route	Stage reached
South Downs Way extension to Winchester	Continuation of South Downs Way from Sussex boundary through Hampshire to Winchester	Route under consideration
Peddars Way and Norfolk Coast Path	Thetford to Hunstanton and Hunstanton to Cromer along the Norfolk Coast	Route under consideration
Cambrian Way	Cardiff to Conway	Route under consideration

cerned with national parks (and their Scottish 'shadow equivalents'), areas of outstanding natural beauty and the coast. Increasingly, however, there has developed a concern for positive policy in relation to metropolitan, regional and country parks.[36] Mention has already been made of the Strathclyde Regional Park which serves Glasgow and its region. In London a similar, but much larger, park is being developed in the Lee Valley under special legislation. The Lee Valley Regional Park Authority was established in January 1967 with members appointed by fifteen local authorities and with powers to precept on the GLC and the county councils of Essex and Hertfordshire. This particular area (amounting to some 4,000 hectares) had been largely derelict for many years. (It is now over a third of a century since Abercrombie's *Greater London Plan* envisaged the valley as 'an opportunity for a great piece of regenerative planning'). It has been graphically described (by the Civic Trust) as 'London's kitchen garden, its well, its privy and its workshop . . . London's back door'. The Lee Valley Regional Park Master Plan proposes a very wide range of facilities for recreation and education including twelve major multi-purpose recreation centres as well as four major centres for youth activity, water sports, motor sports and industrial archaeology. These are to be linked by river, canal, parkland and a park road (with tolls), footpaths and bridleways.

The Lee Valley project is an ambitious scheme. It is an exercise in 'regeneration' as well as in recreational planning. It is perhaps unique. But the concept of a major 'out-of-door' recreational facility has attracted considerable discussion in recent years and is now embodied as part of contemporary wisdom in the 1967 and 1968 Countryside Acts. As the 1966 White Paper *Leisure in the Countryside*[37] explained, 'country parks' can achieve several desirable objectives at one and the same time. Country parks 'would make it easier for town-dwellers to enjoy their leisure in the open, without travelling too far and adding to congestion on the roads; they would ease the pressure on the more remote and solitary places; and they would reduce the risk of damage to the countryside – aesthetic as well as physical – which often comes about when people simply settle down for an hour or a day where it suits them, somewhere "in the country" – to the inconvenience and indeed expense of the countryman who lives and works there'. In 1979 there were 154 recognised country parks in England and Wales.

The Countryside Act also provided powers for local authorities in relation to picnic sites. In the words of the White Paper, these are 'places in the countryside and on the coast where a country park would not be justified, but something better than a lay-by is needed by the family who want to stop for a few hours, perhaps to picnic, perhaps to explore footpaths, or simply to sit and enjoy the view and the fresh air'. Accordingly, local authorities are empowered to provide and manage picnic sites. In 1979 193 picnic sites had been approved.

Statistics and location maps of country parks and picnic sites are to be found in the *Annual Reports* of the Countryside Commission.

WATERWAYS

Leisure in the Countryside[38] promised that the government would seek to evolve, in conjunction with the river authorities, public bodies and others concerned, comprehensive plans for developing the use for recreation of the country's waterways, natural or artificial. A major problem of canals, highlighted in the British Waterways Board's 1966 Report on *The Facts about the Waterways*,[39] is that the minimum cost of keeping non-commercial routes open is at least £600,000 a year. To keep them open for pleasure cruising would add a further £340,000.

Following extensive discussions with the various interested parties and the publication, in 1967, of a White Paper, *British Waterways: Recreation and Amenity*, the 1968 Transport Act provided a 'new charter for the waterways'. The Board's waterways are now classified into three main groups: 'commercial waterways' to be principally available for the commercial carriage of freight; 'cruising waterways' to be principally available for cruising, fishing and other recreational purposes; and 'remainder waterways'.

The effect of the new arrangements is that over 2,250 km of waterways will remain open for pleasure cruising. The Board's annual deficits (on all operations) are borne by the Exchequer. It was originally proposed that the financial position in relation to cruising waterways would be reviewed after five years. However, the government were persuaded that such a formal review would create uncertainty and discourage private commercial investment and development (for example, in the building of marinas or the provision of cruising craft for hire). Instead, an Inland Waterways Amenity Advisory Council was established, one of whose functions is to consider proposals for the closure of individual waterways 'if this becomes necessary in the national interest'. The Council's functions are not, however, narrowly circumscribed; they include the consideration of 'any matter affecting the use or development for amenity or recreational purposes, including fishing, of the Cruising Waterways and any matters with respect to the provision of services and facilities for those purposes on the Cruising Waterways or the Commercial Waterways and, where they think it desirable, to make recommendations on such matters to the Board or to the Secretary of State after consulting the Board'.[40]

THE COUNTRYSIDE COMMISSION

Under the provisions of the Countryside Act 1968, the functions of the National Parks Commission were taken over by the Countryside Commission. Responsibilities in relation to national parks and areas of outstanding natural beauty remain; but to these are added the duty 'to review, encourage, assist, concert or promote the provision and improvement of facilities for the enjoyment of the countryside generally, and to conserve and enhance the natural beauty and amenity of the countryside, and to secure public access for the purpose of open air recreation'.

The Commission have the general duty of advising ministers and public bodies on all matters relating to the countryside: this includes offering advice as they think fit as well as responding when consulted; and they are required to keep under review all aspects of conservation and enjoyment of the countryside. Besides these general duties they have a number of specific duties and powers:

(a) *National Parks:* Subject to ministerial confirmation they are responsible for designating suitable areas as national parks. They are responsible for day-to-day liaison with the parks and have a statutory role in relation to structure plans affecting national parks, national park plans and national parks annual budgets.

(b) *Areas of Outstanding Natural Beauty:* Subject to ministerial confirmation they are responsible for designating suitable areas as AONBs; and they have certain statutory rights as regards advice and consultation.

(c) *Publicity and Information Services:* They have a duty to provide or help with the provision of such services.

(d) *Long Distance Footpaths and Bridleways:* They are charged with the responsibility of making proposals to the secretary of state for such routes.

(e) *Inquiries, Investigations, Research and Experimental Projects* which they may carry out or commission (experimental projects are subject to approval by the secretary of state).

(f) *Grants* which they have power to make to both public and private bodies for countryside purposes.[41]

The Commission publish comprehensive and full annual reports, of which considerable use has been made in this chapter.

Provisions for altering the status of the Commission (whose staff have always been civil servants) are contained in the 1981 Wildlife and Countryside Bill.

NATURE CONSERVATION

The concept of wild life 'sanctuaries' or nature reserves is one of long standing and, indeed, antedates the modern idea of national parks. In other countries some national parks are in fact primarily sanctuaries for the preservation of big game and other wild life, as well as for the protection of outstanding physiological features and areas of outstanding geological interest. British national parks are somewhat different in concept: the emphasis is on the preservation of amenity and providing facilities for public access and enjoyment. The concept of nature conservation, on the other hand, is primarily a scientific one concerned particularly with research on problems underlying the management of natural sites and of vegetation and animal populations.

Nevertheless, as the Huxley Committee pointed out in 1947,[42] there is no fundamental conflict between these two sets of interest: 'Their special requirements may differ, and the case for each may be presented with too limited a vision: but since both have the same fundamental idea of conserving the rich variety of our countryside and sea-coasts and of increasing the general enjoyment and understanding of nature, their ultimate objectives are not divergent, still less antagonistic.' However, to ensure that recreational, economic and scientific interests are all fairly met presents some difficulties. Several reports dealing with the various problems were published shortly after the war.[43] The outcome was the establishment of the Nature Conservancy, constituted by a Royal Charter in March 1949 and given additional powers by the National Parks and Access to the Countryside Act. (It is now the Nature Conservancy Council.)

The Conservancy's main duties are to give scientific advice, to establish and manage nature reserves, and to organise and develop research. It is the question of nature reserves which has particular relevance to the subject of this book (Table 8.5). The Conservancy have powers to acquire land or to enter into agreements with owners in order that nature reserves may be established. In agreement cases the owner remains in full possession and has responsibility for management, but he agrees to manage in accordance with the advice of the Conservancy so as to preserve the scientific interest of the particular area. Local planning authorities can also – in consultation with the Conservancy – set up local nature reserves. The 'declaration' of a reserve does not of itself confer any public right of access whatsoever.

Furthermore, the powers to make access agreements or orders in 'open country' are clearly not applicable to reserves: to make such an order over a nature reserve would be a contradiction in terms. This does not mean, however, that access to reserves is generally prohibited. It is the policy of the Conservancy to allow as much access as is compatible with proper scientific management. About half of the

Table 8.5   *National Nature Reserves 1979*[44]

	Number of reserves	*Area in hectares*
England	81	28,011
Wales	31	9,689
Scotland	52	89,612
Great Britain	164	127,312

land in national nature reserves is generally open to the public without any restriction; the remainder is open only by permit.

The 1968 Countryside Act provided (in section 11) that 'in the exercise of their functions relating to land under any enactment, every minister, government department and public body shall have regard to the desirability of conserving the natural beauty and amenity of the countryside'. In a 1977 Department of the Environment circular, local authorities were reminded that this is defined so as to include the conservation of flora, fauna, and geological and physiographical features:

The Secretaries of State look to local authorities to take full account of national conservation factors both in formulating structure and local plans, and in the consideration of individual planning applications. For example, wildlife and physiographical features in their areas can often be protected by the careful siting and treatment of developments. Local authorities should also consider the impact on nature conservation when undertaking their own developments of various kinds.[45]

The circular deals with national nature reserves (NNRs), sites of special scientific interest (SSSIs) and local nature reserves (LNRs). It also refers to the mammoth *Nature Conservation Review*, published for the Natural Environment Research Council.[46] The first volume of this describes the main habitat types in Britain (coastlands, woodlands, lowland grasslands, heaths and shrubs, peatlands, open water and uplands) and sets out the criteria used in the selection of the 700 sites of national importance described in the second volume.

The circular comments that 'the Review thus provides essential information for national and regional policies for nature conservation in both the wilder countryside and in the selected sites, and it is likely to be a valuable source of reference for all those concerned with rural land use and planning'.

The Ramsar Convention on Wetlands[47] is also briefly discussed. Under this Convention, the UK government has undertaken to conserve wetlands generally and the (thirteen) designated sites in particular.[48] The local authorities concerned have been notified. Further wetlands may be designated.

(Wetlands include 'rivers, lakes, marshes, estuaries . . . forming habitats which are particularly vulnerable to the effects of drainage, alterations to the water-table, water-borne pollution and developments within catchment areas'.)

The circular also refers to the role of the voluntary conservation movement and provides brief guidelines for nature conservation policies (which essentially appear to involve consultations with the Nature Conservancy Council – and its regional officers – and voluntary organisations).

FORESTRY

Forestry is relevant in several ways to the subject matter of this book. In the first place it makes major claims on land: the forest area of Great Britain amounts to over 2 million hectares, or 9 per cent of the land surface. Forestry Commission land totals 1·3 million hectares, of which 884,000 hectares are under plantation.[49] However, an adequate discussion of the land needs for forestry and of forestry policy would take us too far afield.[50] Here attention is briefly focused on the Forestry Commission's recreational policies.

'It is almost a truism that in these small islands it is necessary to reconcile the claims of amenity and economic utilization; if they are kept in watertight compartments there will not be enough land to go round.' So stated the Forestry Commissioners in their 1943 Report on *Post-War Forest Policy*. It is in recognition of this fact that the Forestry Commissioners have evolved a positive policy for providing access facilities in state forests. Indeed, in their special historical review published to mark their sixtieth year of operation, particular pride is expressed in their response to increased demand from the public:

> During the fifties and sixties the public attitude to the countryside became much more positive. Increasing affluence provided more leisure time and greater mobility, from which developed an ever-growing demand for outdoor recreation facilities. The Commission was in a unique position to respond to this demand, and anticipated the statutory requirements of the Countryside Acts of 1967 and 1968 by embarking on a continuing programme of developing forest walks, visitor centres, camping and caravan sites, and later the highly successful forest cabin schemes. By actively encouraging the public to visit its woodlands and by maintaining an open and outward-looking press and public relations policy, the Commission has communicated to millions of people an interest in forestry and an understanding of its place in the nation's economy. We nevertheless recognise that forestry is just one of the many interests in the countryside, and during the past 30 years we have attempted through regular consultation with other countryside agencies to achieve a harmonious balance between competing land uses of optimum benefit to the national interest. The consultation arrangements thus built up for our own operations were extended in 1974 to private forestry grant-aid proposals.[51]

These, of course, are the words of an official annual report (as distinct from an independent assessment), but the statistics of 'public recreational facilities' are impressive. As at 31 March 1980, the Commission had provided 33 camping and caravan sites, 609 picnic places,

648 forest walks and forest nature trails, 29 visitor centres, 23 arboreta, 7 forest drives, and 166 forest cabins and holiday houses.[52]

LANDSCAPE POLICIES

Afforestation is only one (though a very significant one) of the major forces affecting the landscape. It is also the one which probably has given rise to more articulated criticism than the others. The Ramblers Association, for example, in their pamphlet attacking afforestation has argued that 'enough is enough. Too many areas have already been ruined by commercial forestry. There is no strong case for a programme of expansion, and all new plantings should come under planning control.'[53]

Apart from forestry, however, there is the impact of mineral workings, power stations and power lines, motorways, rural depopulation and the revolution in agriculture. Marion Shoard's 'best-seller' (itself a point of significance) *The Theft of the Countryside* emphasises the latter:

A new agricultural revolution is under way. If allowed to proceed unhindered, it will transform the face of England. Already a quarter of our hedgerows, 24 million hedgerow trees, thousands of acres of down and heathland, a third of our woods, and hundred upon hundreds of ponds, streams, marshes and flow-rich meadows have disappeared. They have been systematically eliminated by farmers seeking to profit from a complex web of economic and technological change.[54]

Much has been written on this subject[55] which is both extremely wide in its ramifications and emotive to many who argue about it. Here attention is focused on the role being played by the Countryside Commission.[56]

The Commission published a policy statement in 1977 entitled *New Agricultural Landscapes: Issues, Objectives and Action*.[57] This summarises their 'conclusions and proposals for action' arising out of nearly five years of preparatory work including a consultant's report,[58] a discussion paper[59] and an extensive programme of consultations.

The policy statement calls for 'a major effort on the part of all concerned in the ownership or management of the lowland landscape to take positive action to protect and conserve its unique character'. Six policy objectives are listed:

(i)   to stop unnecessary clearance of features of landscape value;
(ii)   to plant trees and shrubs in greatly increased numbers;
(iii) to ensure that those who need advice and financial help can get it;

(iv)   to ensure that public authorities set a good example on publicly owned land;
(v)   to develop higher standards in the control of development in the countryside;
(vi)   to attract and maintain the interest of the mass media and education authorities in the subject.

Extensive consultations, conferences, demonstration projects and studies have followed.[60] Various bodies have published responses or taken up the issue – for example, the National Farmers' Union, the Country Landowners' Association, the Nature Conservancy and the Advisory Council for Agriculture and Horticulture in England and Wales.[61]

The problems were further discussed in a 1979 paper by the Official Countryside Review Committee entitled *Conservation and the Countryside Heritage*.[62] This Committee proposed a two-tier system for landscape protection.

The objectives here were:

(*a*)   to conserve effectively areas of higher landscape quality on the present scale, but to define more rigorously what is truly outstanding and what is merely good;
(*b*)   to give that which is outstanding a greater degree of protection than in the past, in order to ensure that its character and qualities are preserved, while affording the remaining areas (subject to some marginal adjustments) no less protection than hitherto; and
(*c*)   to provide machinery for the administration of both types of areas which will minimise the friction between national and local interests, and the disparity in Treasury support.

Under the system:

The top tier would consist of small areas of outstanding quality, selected both from within the present National Park and AONB areas and in a few cases from outside. The purpose of such areas would be conservation in the long term of the scenery for its quiet enjoyment, which, of course, would not preclude the continuance of farming. Such areas might cover only a few per cent of the land surface of England and Wales (i.e. a small fraction of the present National Parks and AONBs) and they would, therefore, need to be selected against very high standards. Essential characteristics might be: superlative landscape quality, near absence of population, and capability to regulate access.

The purposes of designation would be:

(*a*)   the conservation of the environment;

(*b*) its quiet enjoyment by the general public, to the extent compatible with (*a*).

There would need to be the strongest possible presumption against any development or other activity in these areas likely to conflict with (*a*) and any such proposed development should be subject to the express approval of Parliament. The land would need to be managed to a very high standard for the purposes set out above, and the special costs of so doing would be met by central Government.

It was proposed that land should be either in public ownership (as much of it already is) or subject to appropriate management agreements. Supervision would be by the Countryside Commission, assisted by local advisory committees.

The second tier would consist basically of the remainder of the present national parks and areas of outstanding natural beauty. 'The characteristics of this further tier would be different from those of the top tier in that the areas concerned would be much larger and more inhabited. They would have important landscape and recreational value in their own right, but would have the additional advantage of providing further protection for the top tier areas which would, in the main, lie outside them.'

The Committee thought that 'the national element' in these second-tier areas should be limited to laying down a broad framework for their management. Administration would be the responsibility of the local authorities concerned 'and should clearly be seen to be so'.

At the time of writing (early 1981) the considered response of the Countryside Commission is awaited.[63] It is, of course, hardly likely that it would favour a scheme which would drastically reduce its responsibilities (what organisation would?). But, as Marion Shoard has pointed out:

> Unfortunately, the approach reflected in the Committee's scheme has little to offer the countryside threatened by agricultural change. The areas it would protect most stringently are almost always areas least in need of protection. If any of our countryside is still completely unthreatened by agricultural change or, for that matter, anything else very much, it is the core areas of our national parks. Yet under the Committee's plan, the second-tier areas would inevitably suffer the consequences of second-class status – indeed the Committee says they would act as 'buffers' for the core first-tier areas.[64]

The scheme bears a resemblance to that suggested by the Sandford Committee (to which there are similar objections). This is discussed in a later section.

It is clear that there is no easy answer to the problems raised here but, as a refreshing change from the cautious deliberations of the multiplicity of bodies which are involved, Shoard's radical proposals can be quoted:

> I believe the only real hope of stemming the tide of destruction lies in the introduction of direct, surgical measures to control the fate of the landscape, coupled with a shift in the distribution of power over the countryside. The tiny group who control the shape of the landscape at present must start to share their power with the nation as a whole. The process that is called for seems to me parallel to the process whereby control over the built environment passed into the hands of the community under the 1947 Town and Country Planning Act. But there will have to be one important difference. The planning of towns is almost entirely a matter for local authorities. But in the country, the local authorities are dominated by the major rural interest groups. If the countryside is to be saved, some voice must be given to the mass of the people who live in towns and cities. I believe that the way to do this is to ensure that certain key decisions are made at regional level, as regional authorities would reflect urban as well as rural interests. So I propose the following arrangements.
>
> 1. The town and country planning system should be extended to cover farmland. Farmers should have to seek the consent of the community for major changes to the countryside, just as industrialists and householders have to seek consent for changes to the built environment.
> 2. Nine regional countryside planning authorities should be set up to cover England and Wales. Their members would be nominated by the county authorities and metropolitan county authorities within their borders. These new regional authorities would draw up plans for the countryside of their regions just as county councils now draw up structure plans, and these plans would set out the priority to be given to agriculture, conservation and recreation in different parts of the region. Local authorities in each region would administer development control in the countryside within the parameters set by the regional countryside plan.
> 3. Organisations and individuals should campaign for better access to and greater understanding of the countryside, in a drive to involve the people of our towns and cities so that they will insist on imposing their view of the shape the landscape should take.
> 4. As an immediate crisis measure, six new national parks should be created immediately in lowland England. These areas, selected for their outstanding quality and the magnitude of the threat they face from agricultural change, would serve as a test-bed for new techniques for reconciling agriculture and conservation. In these

parks, the nation, through the Secretary of State's nominees, would be able to exert a direct influence on the fate of key landscapes.

These four proposals are spelled out in some detail in the final section of Shoard's book (under the general title of 'Stop Thief!').

DEFENCE LANDS

In 1980 defence land holdings in the UK amounted to 220,000 hectares – rather less than 1 per cent of the total area of the country. There has been little change in the decade since 1970 when the holdings totalled 227,000.[65] At first sight this might seem surprising, given the opposition that has been voiced during this period to the military use of land.

In fact nearly half the total of land owned or leased by the Ministry of Defence is used for grazing, other agricultural purposes and other non-military purposes. It is not the amount of the countryside which is at issue, but the location of defence land – of which there are substantial areas in the Dartmoor, Pembrokeshire Coast and Northumberland national parks (as well as smaller areas in several others). Why not, then, simply move military uses to different places?

This question was among those addressed by the Nugent Committee which was set up in 1971 'to review the holding of land in the United Kingdom by the Armed Forces for defence purposes . . . and to make recommendations . . . as to what changes should be made in these holdings and in improved access for the public, having regard to recreation, amenity or other uses which might be made of the land'. The Nugent Committee reported in 1973[66] and quickly underlined the basic difficulty:

> Our review has made us realise that it is virtually impossible to find any new firing ranges in the British Isles where there is not, or would not be, a powerful local objection to such development – not least on grounds of noise . . . Land resources are limited and there is great competition for them. The notion, put forward by some, that there are large areas in this country and particularly in Scotland suitable and available for use for defence purposes has proved, on examination, to be a fallacy. On the other hand, examination has also shown that the amount of land available to the Services to meet their needs, especially for training, is barely adequate. We have been driven reluctantly to the conclusion that, whatever the difficulties may be in retaining existing ranges, they are small compared with those of developing new ones. Thus our appreciation of the national position, between the competing claims of the public for increased amenity and recreation and the Services for adequate training areas, is that there is limited scope for give in our heavily populated islands.[67]

Nowhere are the dilemmas greater than in Dartmoor which was subjected to a special inquiry held by Lady Sharp (former Permanent Secretary of the Ministry of Housing and Local Government).[68] Dartmoor is a relatively small national park, with some unique features. Apart from its exceptionally wild and rugged scenery (the like of which does not exist south of the Peak District, some 400 km away), the park 'carries the most dense collection of visible prehistoric remains in a similar space in north-west Europe'.[69] These specific issues were put before the Sharp inquiry in addition to the more general arguments marshalled by Lady Sayer.[70]

> The value of wild country to the nation – that is its value to human beings present and future – far transcends even its possession of the treasures of our past or the abundance of its wildlife. The greatest value of all lies in what it can still give us of freedom, challenge, and inspiration . . . It is well understood that a proportion of people in this country are unable to feel the inspiration of the untamed hills . . . But there are others, many others, who experience a sense of liberation and renewal whenever they have the chance to set foot on wild land. Millions of quiet people do feel this. They are intelligent and perceptive people of every class and age group . . . They are people who, forced to live a daily life of crowding and stress, find that escape to remote uplands is a very great restorative of mind and body and are willing to make a real physical effort to get out in the wild. National parks are not just a nice but slightly unnecessary and expendable luxury for a fortunate few. They are in fact a vital provision for a very real human need.[71]

The military use of extensive stretches of the Dartmoor National Park clearly conflicts with this. However, it was not without good reason that, during the inquiry, much was made of the meaning of the word 'incompatible'. A spokesman for the Ministry of Defence was pressed by various of the amenity interest groups to admit that military training is incompatible with the purposes of a national park. He agreed that each would be better without the other and that each diminishes the quality of the other; to that extent the word 'incompatible' was appropriate. 'But they have lived together for twenty-five years and can continue to do so.'[72]

Lady Sharp had no doubt that military training was 'exceedingly damaging to the national park' (exacerbated by the low-flying aircraft in the area – Dartmoor is one of the few designated low-flying areas in the UK). Nevertheless:

> 'Incompatible' may mean 'incapable of existing together' and it may mean 'discordant, incongruous, inconsistent'. I accept that military training and a national park are discordant, incongruous and incon-

sistent; but I cannot accept that they are incapable of living together since it is clear that in this country national parks and military training may have to co-exist.[73]

Indeed, at another point, Lady Sharp quotes the National Park Officer as recognising that 'the landscape qualities leading to the designation of the national park are precisely those which have attracted military occupation and use. He thus stated the basic dilemma which has led to the long struggle over the use of Dartmoor.'

On these arguments there is an obvious political choice to be made. However, the issues become more complex when one examines the matter somewhat further. Contrary to expectations, the Nature Conservancy Council submitted that:

> Our unavoidable conclusion is that despite varying levels of use over the past eighty years, use for military training has not significantly damaged the importance of the land from a nature conservation point of view. Our evidence indicates that effects of most activities have been temporary only and that the natural fauna and flora re-establishes itself; nor does any species of plant or animal appear to have materially suffered as a result of these military training uses. Military presence has also had indirect beneficial consequences. It has helped to maintain the traditional grazing regime on Dartmoor which is generally favourable to nature conservation. Recreational use has also been controlled and this may have prevented excessive disturbance or wear and tear in some areas (for example from pony trekking).[74]

Indeed, the Nature Conservancy Council's major concern was to maintain the *status quo* 'and to avoid any intensification of use, whether by the Armed Forces or anyone else'. Similarly, the Ancient Monuments Directorate, though regretting the damage done by the military, also noted that 'if the withdrawal of the Army led to mass public access or commercial reclamation and exploitation, the effects could prove to be even more destructive to the archaeology of the region than the existing use'.[75] But most positive of all was local public opinion: 'it was plain that the great majority of the local people simply do not mind the training; or at any rate think that the advantages outweigh the disadvantages'.[76]

It is interesting to note Lady Sharp's discussion of this (which leads into her conclusions):

> It is a fact that few people, probably very few, are directly interested in getting rid of the training. The objectors certainly include several organisations with large memberships; but the number of those who actively want to walk or ride over the remote moorlands cannot be

large. It was not possible to get any idea of the number; it was said that this is increasing, but there was no real evidence either way. The conclusions to be drawn from this must be a matter of opinion. Lord Foot[77] argued, very eloquently, that national parks might appeal only to a minority, but were not the less important for that. I think this is true; a high value does attach to the solitude and remoteness which Dartmoor could offer if the Armed Forces were not there, even though in the nature of the case few people are physically able to experience it or even want to do so. But this has to be set against the needs of defence whatever they may be; the possible consequences to the military bases in the south-west if deprived of the training facilities – and so to the economy of the region; and perhaps also the possible effects on the very qualities which the opponents of the training are seeking to restore if public access were to become unlimited – or limited only to the extent that the National Park Authority prove able to defend the high moor.

Whether all this adds up to a case for setting a term to the military occupation of part of the national park, it is not for me to say. I accept Lord Foot's argument that there is here a basic conflict of national interests and that to a large extent the resolution of the conflict depends on a value judgment and cannot be made on the basis of the evidence. My opinion is worth no more than anyone else's.[78]

Nevertheless, the purpose of the inquiry was for Lady Sharp to make recommendations. She did: 'I recommend no change in the defence holdings on Dartmoor.' However, she went beyond her terms of reference, and proposed that a decision should be made on the long-term future of Dartmoor. To this the government replied that there were 'no grounds for offering any hope of significant reduction in the demands of military training on Dartmoor in the foreseeable future'.[79]

Both the Nugent Committee and the Sharp Report recommended improvements in 'regular consultative machinery', and this has been acted upon.[80]

This lengthy treatment of the problems of Dartmoor (though very incomplete) serves to illustrate the range of issues which arise in defence lands, the clashes between national park uses and others, and more widely the dilemmas of land use planning in a small relatively crowded island. It can be a matter of no surprise that there is an almost continuous – certainly continual – examination of policies and administrative structures. More often than not, little changes; but the period from 1972 onwards has been particularly productive. First we look briefly at local government reorganisation in relation to national parks.

NATIONAL PARKS AND LOCAL GOVERNMENT REORGANISATION

Under the 1972 Local Government Act, planning functions in a national park are largely allocated to county councils which must establish a national park committee to carry out these functions.[81] There are, however, exceptional provisions for the Lake District and the Peak District: here new planning boards have been set up to replace the previous joint boards. In all cases, however, one-third of the members are appointed by the secretary of state.

The Act provided that, for each national park, a national park officer must be appointed (after consultation with the Countryside Commission); and that a national park plan must be prepared (by April 1977). These plans (all of which are now published)[82] set out the policy for the management of the park and 'the exercise of the functions exercisable' in relation to the park.

A number of functions are, however, to be carried out by district councils concurrently with a park committee or board (for example, tree preservation, treatment of derelict land, public access and the provision of country parks). Moreover, there is provision (subject to the agreement of the Countryside Commission) for arrangements to be made with district councils to carry out any of the functions of a committee or board on an agency basis.[83]

Local government reorganisation has resuscitated debate about the administration of national parks and, in November 1975, it was announced that the Environment Sub-Committee of the Expenditure Committee would be examining this issue in the broad context of an inquiry into 'the operation of the Countryside Act 1968, the National Parks and Access to the Countryside Act 1949 and related legislation, with particular reference to the public expenditure involved, the effect of local government reorganization on the operation of the Acts, and the future development of policy on national parks and public access to the countryside in the light of the Sandford Report'. Before discussing this it is necessary to outline some of the issues raised by the Sandford Report.

THE SANDFORD REPORT 1974

The Sandford Committee were appointed in July 1971 'To review how far the national parks have fulfilled the purpose for which they were established, to consider the implications of the changes that have occurred, and may be expected, in social and economic conditions and to make recommendations as regards future policies.'

The report[84] points to the major changes in farming; the increase in conflict between agricultural and recreational use; the afforestation with conifers which has become 'so extensive as seriously to affect the characteristic beauty of the countryside'; the large amount of physical development 'particularly in the form of mineral extraction, electricity generating stations and transmission lines, reservoirs'; the growth in road traffic and road improvements 'some of them unsightly'; the increase in leisure time and in mobility; the enormous growth in the traditional pursuits of hill walking and climbing (and the associated 'wear and tear of human feet'); increases in camping, caravanning, horse riding . . . and so on.

All these pressures (together with those of the quarter of a million people who live in the national parks) inevitably make questionable the compatibility of the twin purposes of the parks. The Sandford Committee were unequivocal:

> The first purpose of national parks, as stated by Dower and by Parliament – the preservation and enhancement of natural beauty – seems to us to remain entirely valid and appropriate. The second purpose – the promotion of public enjoyment – however, needs to be re-interpreted and qualified because it is now evident that excessive or unsuitable use may destroy the very qualities which attract people to the parks. *We have no doubt that where the conflict between the two purposes, which has always been inherent, becomes acute, the first one must prevail in order that the beauty and ecological qualities of the national parks may be maintained.*[85]

This gives rise to a number of questions, including those of the adequacy of the provisions relating to the protection of the parks, the adequacy of the administrative system and the adequacy of the financial arrangements. These are the three issues in the Sandford Report which are selected for discussion here.[86]

Given the strength of the pressures on the national parks, the question as to whether the statutory powers of protection are adequate clearly arises.

One curiosity is the limited application of the Town and Country Planning (Landscape Areas Special Development) Order 1950.[87] This Order has the effect, where applied, of enabling a planning authority to exercise certain controls over farm buildings (which are generally exempt from planning control under the terms of the General Development Order). The Order applies throughout almost the whole of the Lake District National Park, the northern part of the Peak District and much of Snowdonia National Park.[88] The Committee recommended its extension to the whole of every national park.

Much more difficult to decide upon was whether or not a new and more stringent protection would be useful in connection with 'the areas of the very highest quality of landscape'. The Committee were divided on this issue.[89] Those in favour argued the case for two main reasons:

The first is that past experience and our estimate of future prospects convinces us that the standard of protection against development and the quality of management which we wish to see achieved in these limited but supremely valuable areas would not be attainable throughout the extensive designated areas of the national parks. Our proposal does not imply that lower standards than hitherto should be acceptable in those wider areas; on the contrary existing standards need to be raised, in many areas substantially. But in the wider areas the presumption in favour of amenity cannot, as we have conceded, always prevail. Even with the highest possible standards of control, provision for increasing numbers of visitors, and for the changing needs of residents, inevitably must affect the natural beauty of the more heavily used parts. In the national heritage areas that we propose, the conservation of environmental qualities would be the supreme objective, of national significance and taking precedence over all others.

The second reason is less tangible, but possibly of greater importance. The concept of protected areas such as the national parks, which proved acceptable in the 1940s, reflected a stage in the evolution of the attitudes of British people towards parts of their environment. Now, with a new generation concerned as never before with the effect of man's impact on the environment, we believe that there is a will to determine areas within which society will do all that it can to ensure that their natural beauty remains unimpaired.

The contrary case was based partly on difficulties of definition and selection, and a reluctance 'to complicate an already complex system of classification and control for areas of great landscape beauty or of significance for the conservation of wild life'. It was also felt that 'whatever declarations might be made to the contrary, the introduction of an additional superior category of protected area would inevitably depreciate the status of the remaining areas'.[90]

So far as the administrative system was concerned, the Committee were again divided.[91] Some thought that the new arrangements under the 1968 Countryside Act and the Local Government Act 1972 would prove satisfactory (that is, with the emphasis on the role of positive management under the control of a single authority with a national park officer). Others doubted 'whether a committee of a county council with its limited status and powers will be able to cope as successfully with growing problems as would a board, which, while properly heedful of local interests, would be likely to be more steadfast in achieving the wider public purposes of our parks'. All were agreed, however, that the new arrangements 'must be regarded as on trial', and it was recommended that a review of administration and staffing should be undertaken in 1979.

On finance there was no disagreement: 'we are convinced that much more money needs to be spent upon the national parks'.[92]

GOVERNMENT RESPONSE TO THE SANDFORD REPORT

A lengthy response to the Sandford Report was issued as a Department of the Environment circular in 1976,[93] following the receipt of a large number of comments from interested organisations, debates in the Lords on 2 July 1974 and in the Commons on 17 January 1975, and assistance from the Countryside Commission.

Agreement was expressed on behalf of the secretaries of state concerning the mounting pressures on the parks and the likelihood of more frequent conflict. National Park Authorities could do much, it was stated, 'to reconcile public enjoyment with the preservation of natural beauty by good planning and management . . . But even so, there will be situations where the two purposes are irreconcilable . . . The Secretaries of State accept the Committee's view that, where this happens, priority must be given to the conservation of natural beauty, and they will issue guidance to this effect to the National Park Authorities.'[94]

On the issues selected for discussion above the circular was generally supportive. It was agreed that the scope of the Landscape Areas Special Development Order should be extended; the proposal for national heritage areas was rejected (comments received by the department on this were 'almost universally opposed to it'); on the question of a review of the administrative system in 1979 it was hoped that the new system would prove satisfactory, but if experience revealed 'possibilities for improvement' a review could be undertaken (in 1981). Finally, on finance, two telling points were made. First, since the Sandford Committee had been appointed in 1971, the approved level of expenditure by National Park Authorities had almost trebled – with an increase in the central government's share from about 33 per cent to some 75 per cent. (Actual 'countryside expenditure' figures are given in Table 8.6.) Secondly, given the severe economic difficulties of the time (1975–6), the national parks could not be exempted from painful expenditure cuts.

THE EXPENDITURE COMMITTEE REPORT 1976

If the Sandford review of 1971–4 was comprehensive, the Expenditure Committee's inquiry of 1975–6 was gargantuan. The report[95] and evidence total some 800 pages and constitute a mine of information (though the signposting is sadly deficient – which is perhaps inevitable in an inquiry to which all are invited to subscribe and to which a surprisingly large number in fact do so). It is with some amusement that one notes as a lead-up to their first recommendation a plea by the

Committee for a reduction in the number of public and statutory bodies involved in the field:

> We noted early in our inquiry the number of public and statutory bodies with responsibility for one aspect or another of policy in the countryside. A recent article on the subject[96] identified fourteen such bodies. Our own enquiries have revealed others and there are in addition a considerable number of voluntary organisations with interests in the countryside. Ten regional water authorities in England and Wales make provision for water recreation in addition to their other responsibilities. The National Water Council co-ordinates them and considers 'any matter relating to the national policy for water'. The Water Space Amenity Commission advises on 'the recreational and amenity aspect of the national water policy'. Inland waterways are managed by the British Waterways Board, but their amenity and recreational use is the responsibility of the Inland Waterways Amenity Advisory Council. This particular example of a luxuriant growth of official bodies should be rationalised in the forthcoming reorganisation of the water industry, and appropriate streamlining would be welcome in other countryside responsibilities. Bodies such as the Countryside Recreation Research Advisory Group and the Chairmen's Policy Group, established and serviced by the Countryside Commission, which co-ordinate fifteen public bodies, and the Committee on Environmental Conservation (CoEnCo) and the Council for the Protection of Rural England (CPRE) in the voluntary field, do a useful job in bringing organisations together, but we consider nevertheless that the position would be more satisfactory if there were fewer statutory organisations, as this might lead to staff economies and a more effective use of public funds. While appreciating the wider responsibilities of the 60 staff of the Planning Sport and Countryside Directorate in the Department of the Environment we wonder to what extent they duplicate some of the work of the 105 staff of the Countryside Commission.

This plethora of institutions must have been a source of some confusion for the Committee: it certainly led them to recommend 'that the Government give early consideration to the need for the streamlining of the statutory machinery as it affects the countryside'. Related to this was the recommendation 'that the Government should attempt to formulate an overall strategy for land use in the countryside'. References to similarly encyclopaedic inquiries – the Select Committees on Scottish Affairs[97] and on Sport and Leisure[98] – suggest that the Committee were undaunted by the enormous breadth of the issues they were touching upon. They certainly did not take great heed of the very first sentence of the evidence presented to them: 'The countryside is neither an easily defined nor a self-contained subject – whether in terms of legislation, policy, finance, or organisation.'[99]

Actually the Expenditure Committee made remarkably few recommendations. In addition to the two impossibly wide recommendations already quoted, and a number of small issues, they recommended that the review of the administration of the national parks be brought forward from 1981 to 1979 (the date originally recommended by the Sandford Committee); that the review should include forestry; and that the existing levels of expenditure on national parks should be maintained.

The government's response[100] partly parried the first recommendations by reference to the labours of the Countryside Review Committee, but also boldly stated that the existence of a large number of bodies concerned with the countryside did not necessarily mean that there were too many:

> Countryside policy . . . covers a very wide spectrum, and the number of individual aspects which have to be taken into account in the making of it can be very large. Government may need expert advice on each of these aspects and can obtain it from the agency or agencies with the appropriate knowledge and experience. It is then the job of Government to weigh and balance the advice they receive before reaching final decisions. If there were fewer agencies, they would inevitably have to cover a wider range of interests and would have to balance their advice to take account of them. This could lead to a dilution of the advice given and to the involvement of the agencies in processes which are more appropriately those of Government itself.

Table 8.6   *Countryside Expenditure 1968–9 to 1979–80*[101]

	£
1968–9	462,000
1969–70	505,000
1970–1	691,000
1971–2	1,040,000
1972–3	1,493,000
1973–4	2,644,000
1974–5	5,661,000
1975–6	6,619,000
1976–7	6,865,000
1977–8	7,981,000
1978–9	10,872,000
1979–80 (est.)	10,492,000

In a wider context this can be viewed as a stage in the elementary learning process which must be advanced, if not completed, before parliamentary committees can adequately fulfil their roles as watchdogs of the departments.

More narrowly, the government's observations included a statement that they were unconvinced of the need for an early review of national park administration, and that no definite commitments on future expenditure could be given.

NEW LEGISLATION 1981

At the time of writing (early 1981), the Wildlife and Countryside Bill is being hotly debated in the Lords. The reaction to the Bill was unexpectedly controversial. (There were 560 amendments debated in the Lords.) Much of the controversy was over the wildlife provisions which form Part I of the Bill.

Since the Bill is still subject to amendment it is appropriate merely to summarise its main objectives.

In addition to the Wildlife sections, it contains provisions 'with respect to the making of grants and loans by the Nature Conservancy Council, and the making of management agreements for the purpose of conserving or enhancing the natural beauty of land in the countryside or promoting its enjoyment by the public. It amends the powers of the Countryside Commission with respect to experimental schemes. In relation to national parks the Bill provides for the protection of moor and heath in such parks, for the giving of financial assistance for the purpose of the conservation and enhancement of their natural beauty and for the promotion of their enjoyment by the public. The Bill enables the Countryside Commission to vary national park boundaries, subject to the Secretary of State's confirmation. It also contains provisions relating to the status, constitution and finances of the Countryside Commission. In addition, the Bill amends the law relating to certain public rights of way. Among other things, the Bill makes fresh provision for the review of definitive rights of way maps and statements prepared under Part IV of the National Parks and Access to the Countryside Act 1949 and makes provision for the prohibition of bulls on land crossed by footpaths or bridleways.'[102]

RECREATION AND COUNTRYSIDE PLANNING

Despite the length of this chapter, many issues of recreation and countryside planning have been omitted. Little or no mention has been made of the Sports Councils and the whole field of planning for sport,[103] of the mammoth inquiry on *Land Resource Use in Scotland*,[104] of green belts and the Countryside Commission's urban fringe experiment,[105] of the acute problems of (and inquiry into) Exmoor,[106] of the problems (and benefits) of second homes in the countryside,[107] of planned control over the itensity of recreational use,[108] of rural decline and deprivation,[109] and a host of other issues.[110]

REFERENCES AND FURTHER READING: CHAPTER 8

1   For the earlier history, see Lord Eversley, *Commons, Forests and Footpaths: The Story of the Battle during the last Forty-Five Years for Public Rights over the Commons, Forests and Footpaths of England and Wales* (Cassell, 1910).

2   *Report of the Committee on Land Utilisation in Rural Areas* (Scott Report), Cmd 6378 (HMSO, 1942), para. 178.

3   The terms of reference were: 'to consider the conditions which should govern building and other constructional development in country areas consistent with the maintenance of agriculture, and in particular the factors affecting the location of industry, having regard to economic operation, part-time and seasonal employment, the well-being of rural communities and the preservation of rural amenities'. The Committee maintained that in order to see the problems of the countryside in perspective it was necessary to interpret these terms widely. Thus rural amenities were 'a *national* heritage' and hence 'there must be facility of access for all'. This line of reasoning led them to recommend national parks, nature reservations, and so on.

4   White Paper, *The Control of Land Use*, Cmd 6537 (HMSO, 1944).

5   *National Parks in England and Wales* (Dower Report), Cmd 6628 (HMSO, 1945); and National Parks Committee (England and Wales), *Report* (Hobhouse Report), Cmd 7121 (HMSO, 1947).

6   These figures included expenditure on the proposed 'conservation areas' (which became translated into areas of outstanding natural beauty). It took many years before expenditure rose to the levels envisaged. Total annual expenditure in England and Wales did not reach £500,000 until 1969-70 (in money terms, that is, not discounting for inflation). However, as is discussed later, expenditure rose significantly in the 1970s - to £10,872,000 in 1978-9. (Figures are from the Financial Tables given in an Appendix to the Commission's annual reports.)

7   W. S. Morrison in the Second Reading Debates, *HC Debates*, Vol. 463, col. 1491. Argument by analogy always carries the risk that the opposite party will turn it to its own advantage. So it was in this case: the minister replied that a comforter is not used to comfort the baby - 'it is used to preserve the amenities of the neighbourhood; so is the National Parks Commission!' (op. cit., col. 1657).

8   Speech by Lord Strang to the Ramblers' Association Conference on National Parks 1962. See *Thirteenth Report of the National Parks Commission 1962*, HC 34 (HMSO, 1962), pp. 70-4. The Commission has kept a vigilant watch on development proposals - from conversion of open moorland (see *Tenth Report of the Countryside Commission 1976-77*, HC 273 (HMSO, 1978), pp. 7-9, and *Eleventh Report 1977-78*, HC 111 (HMSO, 1978), p. 7) to potash mining (*Eleventh Report*, p. 9), and military uses (see particularly *Twelfth Report*, p. 8). These are only a few of the issues discussed in the Commission's annual reports.

9   *Report of the National Park Policies Review Committee* (Sandford Report) (HMSO, 1974), paras 5.24-5.25.

10 E. Haythornthwaite, 'National parks: hopes and disappointments', *Town and Country Planning*, December 1960, pp. 391-6. The phrase is still used although attitudes have changed significantly since 1960 - as has expenditure.

11 During the passage of the National Parks Bill, the government resisted several amendments designed to provide compensation for extra expenditure resulting from higher planning standards or in connection with, for example, the placing of cables underground. The justification was twofold. First, compensation for 'loss of value' resulting from conditional planning approval was already provided for. Secondly, 'the whole principle of the 1947 Act is that a planning authority can

impose high standards of conditions on development, and is not subject to compensation demands other than the £300 million which we have set aside for the purpose. That sum has bought out development rights. Against that, we impose development charges when development rights are restored, and these development charges are assessed on the value of those rights. That means that if an onerous condition is imposed on a person who wishes to develop, the size of a development charge should be by so much the less.' *HC Standing Committee Debates*, col. 592, 1 June 1949. The first point has not proved applicable and the second is no longer relevant. (For further discussion see Chapter 7 above.)

12 *Report of the Scottish National Parks Survey Committee* (Ramsay Report), Cmd 6631 (HMSO, 1945). See also *National Parks and the Conservation of Nature in Scotland*, Cmd 7235 (HMSO, 1947). This report was produced by a further committee chaired by Sir Douglas Ramsay.

13 See G. E. Cherry, *Environmental Planning, Vol. II, National Parks and Recreation in the Countryside* (HMSO, 1975), chs 4 and 8.

14 See J. Foster, 'A park system and scenic conservation in Scotland', *Parks Magazine* (US Parks Service), September 1979, on which this account leans heavily.

15 Scottish Development Department, *Report for 1978*, Cmnd 7556 (HMSO, 1979), p. 15.

16 Countryside Commission for Scotland, *A Park System for Scotland* (The Commission, 1974).

17 J. Foster, loc. cit.

18 Countryside Commission for Scotland, *Scotland's Scenic Heritage* (The Commission, 1978).

19 J. Foster, loc. cit.

20 Scottish Development Department, *Report for 1979*, Cmnd 7924 (HMSO, 1980), p. 15.

21 Countryside Commission, *Areas of Outstanding Natural Beauty: A Discussion Paper* (Countryside Commission, 1978), Annex I, 'Historical review', p. 15.

22 Countryside Commission, *Areas of Outstanding Natural Beauty: A Policy Statement* (Countryside Commission, 1980), p. 8.

23 See the publications referred to in the previous two notes (from which the quotations are taken).

24 Countryside Commission, *Areas of Outstanding Natural Beauty: Report of a One Day Conference* (Countryside Commission, 1978).

25 Countryside Commission, *A Review of Areas of Outstanding Natural Beauty* (Countryside Commission, 1980).

26 MHLG Circular 56/63, *Coastline Preservation and Development* (HMSO, 1963).

27 MHLG Circular 7/66, *The Coast* (HMSO, 1966).

28 The full list of reports is as follows (all produced by the Countryside Commission and published by HMSO):
Regional Coastal Reports:
  1 *The Coasts of Kent and Sussex* (1967)
  2 *The Coasts of Hampshire and the Isle of Wight* (1967)
  3 *The Coasts of South-West England* (1967)
  4 *The Coasts of South Wales and the Severn Estuary* (1967)
  5 *The Coasts of North Wales* (1968)
  6 *The Coasts of North-West England* (1968)
  7 *The Coasts of North-East England* (1968)
  8 *The Coasts of Yorkshire and Lincolnshire* (1968)
  9 *The Coasts of East Anglia* (1968)
The Coasts of England and Wales: Measurements of Use, Protection and Development (1968)
Coastal Recreation and Holidays (1969)
Nature Conservation at the Coast (1970)

The Planning of the Coastline (1970)
The Coastal Heritage (1970)
29 DoE Circular 12/72, *The Planning of the Undeveloped Coast* (HMSO, 1972).
30 See Countryside Commission, *Annual Reports* for 1976–7, pp. 11–12; 1977–8, pp. 3 and 15–16; and 1978–9, p. 15.
31 This was a subcommittee of the Hobhouse Committee. It published a separate report in 1948 (Cmd 7207, HMSO).
32 *Report of the Footpaths Committee* (Gosling Report) (HMSO, 1968).
33 *Report of the National Park Policies Review Committee* (Sandford Report) (HMSO, 1974), ch. 16.
34 See Countryside Commission for Scotland Leaflet, *West Highland Way: Long Distance Route* (The Commission, 1980).
35 See the Annual Reports of the Countryside Commission.
36 See also 'Nature conservation in urban areas', in *Nature Conservancy Council, Fifth Report 1978–79*, HC 451 (HMSO, 1980), pp. 15–19.
37 White Paper, *Leisure in the Countryside*, Cmnd 2928 (HMSO, 1966).
38 op. cit.
39 British Waterways Board, *The Facts about the Waterways* (HMSO, 1966). See also two other publications of the Board: *The Future of the Waterways* (HMSO, 1964); and *Leisure and the Waterways* (HMSO, 1967).
40 There is also a Water Space Amenity Commission, established under the provisions of the Water Act 1973, 'to advise . . . on the formulation, promotion and execution of the national policy for water so far as relating to recreation and amenity in England'. In the Commission's less formal words, it has 'a brief to take an interest in the recreational use of all water, and land associated with water in England and the conservation of natural, archaeological and historic features. This interest embraces active water sports, pursuits such as ornithology and nature study, and the general enjoyment of the waterside environment.' *Water Space Amenity Commission Annual Report 1979–80*, p. 7. The Board's annual reports can be obtained from its office at 1 Queen Anne's Gate, London SW1H 9BT.
41 Memorandum by the Department of the Environment to the Expenditure Committee, *Sixth Report from the Expenditure Committee, Session 1975–76, National Parks and the Countryside*, HC 433 (HMSO, 1976), pp. 3–4.
42 *Conservation of Nature in England and Wales* (Huxley Report), Cmd 7122 (HMSO, 1947).
43 Huxley Report, op. cit.; *Report of the National Parks Committee* (Hobhouse Report), Cmd 7121 (HMSO, 1947), ch. X; and *National Parks in England and Wales* (Dower Report), Cmd 6628 (HMSO, 1945), pp. 39–43.
44 *Nature Conservancy Council, Fifth Report 1978–79*, HC 451 (HMSO, 1980), p. 95.
45 DoE Circular 108/77, *Nature Conservation and Planning* (HMSO, 1977).
46 *A Nature Conservation Review: The Selection of Biological Sites of National Importance for Nature Conservation in Great Britain*, 2 vols (Cambridge University Press, 1977) (price £60).
47 *Convention on Wetlands of International Importance*, Cmnd 6465 (HMSO, 1976).
48 In England and Wales, the designated sites are Bridgwater Bay (Somerset), the Bure Marshes (Norfolk), Hickling Broad and Horsey Mere (Norfolk), Lindisfarne (Northumberland), Minsmere-Walberwick (Suffolk), the North Norfolk Coast, the Ouse Washes (Cambridgeshire), and Cors Fochno and Dyfi (Dyfed).
49 *Annual Abstract of Statistics*, 1981 edn, Table 9.10. The area of Great Britain (including inland water) is 22,999,000 hectares (or 229,990 square kilometres). (See op. cit., Table 1.1.)
50 See the *Annual Reports* of the Forestry Commissioners and the report by them on *Post-War Forest Policy*, Cmd 6447 (HMSO, 1943); also the review of *Forestry Policy*, published in June 1972.

51 *Forestry Commission 60th Annual Report 1979-80*, HC 14 (HMSO, 1980), pp. 17-18.

52 op. cit., p. 70.

53 The Ramblers Association, *Afforestation: The Case Against Expansion*, Brief for the Countryside No. 7 (Ramblers Association, 1980).

54 M. Shoard, *The Theft of the Countryside* (Temple Smith, 1980), pp. 9-10. See also the evocative and thoughtful earlier book by Nan Fairbrother, *New Lives, New Landscapes* (Architectural Press, 1970; Penguin Books, 1972).

55 A convenient, if bulky, assembly is to be found in the evidence to the Expenditure Committee on *National Parks and the Countryside*, HC 433, Session 1975-6 (HMSO, 1976). A useful updating is provided by A. W. Gilg, *Countryside Planning Yearbook 1980* (Geo Books, Norwich, 1980). This is the first of an intended annual series.

56 Generally on this, see the Annual Reports of the Countryside Commission, for example, *Tenth Report 1976-77*, HC 273 (HMSO, 1978), pp. 31-4; *Eleventh Report 1977-78*, HC 111 (HMSO, 1979), pp. 33-6; and *Twelfth Report 1978-79*, HC 615 (HMSO, 1980), pp. 32-5.

57 Countryside Commission, *New Agricultural Landscapes: Issues, Objectives and Action*, CCP 102 (The Commission, 1977; rev. edn, 1979).

58 Countryside Commission, *New Agricultural Landscapes*, CCP 76 (The Commission, 1974).

59 Countryside Commission, *New Agricultural Landscapes: A Discussion Paper*, CCP 76A (The Commission, 1974).

60 See the *Annual Reports* of the Commission listed above.

61 National Farmers' Union and the Country Landowners' Association, *Caring for the Countryside* (1978); Nature Conservancy Council, *Nature Conservation and the Countryside* (1977); Advisory Council for Agriculture and Horticulture in England and Wales, *Agriculture and the Countryside* (1978).

62 Countryside Review Committee, *Conservation and the Countryside Heritage*, Topic Paper No. 4 (HMSO, 1979). The Countryside Review Committee was a group of officials which produced five reports during its existence from 1974 to 1979. The other four reports were:
The Countryside - Problems and Policies (1974)
Rural Communities (1977)
Leisure and the Countryside (1977)
Food Production in the Countryside (1978)

63 The Commission's initial response was somewhat dead-pan: 'it is too early to see whether the balance of argument will be in favour of a radical restructuring of our protective system rather than a more gradual evolution from present designation and management arrangements'. *Twelfth Report of the Countryside Commission 1978-79*, op. cit., p. 35.

64 M. Shoard, op. cit., p. 148.

65 *Annual Abstract of Statistics 1981*, Table 7.12.

66 *Report of the Defence Lands Committee* (Nugent Report) (HMSO, 1973).

67 op. cit., p. 2.

68 *Dartmoor: A Report by Lady Sharp* (HMSO, 1977).

69 Sharp Report, op. cit., paras 29-30.

70 In paragraph 82 of the Sharp Report Lady Sayer is described as 'a member of the Standing Joint Committee on National Parks, a Vice-President of the Ramblers Association, a member of the Executive Committee of the Commons, Open Spaces and Footpaths Preservation Society. From 1951 to 1973 she was Chairman of the Dartmoor Preservation Association, of which her grandfather and great-grandfather had been founder members. She has lived on Dartmoor for most of her life and has taken a leading part in the struggle to put an end to its use for military training.'

71 Sharp Report, op. cit., para. 85.

72 op. cit., para. 58.

73 op. cit., para. 262.
74 op. cit., para. 132.
75 op. cit., para. 136.
76 op. cit., para. 271.
77 Lord Foot represented the Dartmoor Preservation Association.
78 op. cit., paras 272-3.
79 *Statement on the Non-Statutory Inquiry by the Baroness Sharp into the Continued Use of Dartmoor for Military Training*, Cmnd 6837 (HMSO, 1977), para. 9.
80 On the Nugent Committee's recommendations see *Statement on the Report of the Defence Lands Committee 1971-73*, Cmnd 5714 (HMSO, 1974). On the Sharp Report, see the reference in the previous note. See also *Twelfth Report of the Countryside Commission 1978-79*, op. cit., p. 8.
81 For a detailed study of the administration of the national parks, see the study commissioned by the Association of County Councils and carried out by C. W. Hurley, former chief executive of Northumberland County Council, *A Study into the Administration of National Parks* (Association of County Councils, January 1979).
82 A list of the plans is given in Appendix 4 (p. 81) of the *Eleventh Report of the Countryside Commission, 1977-78*, HC 111 (HMSO, 1979). A discussion of the plans is to be found in D. A. Dennier, 'National park plans: a review article', *Town Planning Review*, 1978, pp. 175-83. See also R. Hookway, 'National park plans: a milestone in the development of planning', *The Planner*, January 1978, pp. 20-2,
83 See DoE Circular 63/73, *Local Government Act 1972: Administration of National Parks* (HMSO, 1973); and DoE Circular 65/74, *Local Government Act 1972: National Parks* (HMSO, 1974).
84 *Report of the National Park Policies Review Committee* (Sandford Report) (HMSO, 1974).
85 Sandford Report, op. cit., para. 2.15.
86 It may be useful to the reader to have a list of the chapter headings of the Report:
    Part 1: Retrospect and Prospect
    1   The Origins of National Parks
    2   The Purposes Examined
    3   Looking Forward
    Part 2: The National Parks 1951 to 1972
    4   The Existing Parks and the Park Authorities
    5   The Record of the National Parks
    6   The Changing Scene: Farming and Forestry
    7   The Changing Scene: Visitors to the Parks and New Residents
    8   The Parks Appraised
    Part 3: Future Policies
    9   Farming
    10 Forestry
    11 Common Land
    12 Development, Employment and Housing
    13 Compensation Issues
    14 Recreational Uses
    15 Roads and Traffic
    16 Public Rights of Way: Footpaths and Bridleways
    17 Visitor and Local Interests
    18 Implementation of Policies
    19 Staff
    20 National Heritage Areas
    21 The Case Against Heritage Areas
    22 The Boundaries of the National Parks and New National Parks
    23 Financial Implications

87   SI 1950 No. 729.
88   Sandford Report, op. cit., para. 5.13. The Committee also discussed road improvements in paras 5.27-5.28, and at length in Chapter 15.
89   In favour were Mr Bousey, Mr Cousins, Mr Hookway and Sir Jack Longland. Opposed were Dr Davies, Mr Heaton, Mr Sibery and Mr Watson. Lord Sandford and Mr Gibson-Watt reserved their position. The arguments for and against the proposal are·outlined in paras 3.8-3.11, and developed in Chapters 20 and 21.
90   Compare Shoard's criticism of the (later) proposal of the Countryside Review Committee given in a previous section of this chapter. See also that Committee's anticipatory refutation of the criticism: Countryside Review Committee, *Conservation and the Countryside*, op. cit., para. 63.
91   Sandford Report, op. cit., paras 8.14-8.21.
92   Sandford Report, op. cit., para. 23.1.
93   DoE Circular 4/76, *Report of the National Park Policies Review Committee* (HMSO, 1976).
94   Mention should also be made of DoE Circular 125/77, *Roads and Traffic - National Parks*, which dealt in some detail with one of the issues discussed in the Sandford Report but omitted from the present account. This applies the policy of Circular 4/76 to the particular issue of roads and traffic.
95   *Sixth Report from the Expenditure Committee, Session 1975-76, National Parks and Access to the Countryside*, HC 433 (HMSO, 1976).
96   *The Architects' Journal*, 28 January 1976, pp. 201-3.
97   Select Committee on Scottish Affairs, *Land Resource Use in Scotland*, 5 vols, HC 511 (HMSO, 1972). See also *Government Observations on the Report of the Select Committee on Scottish Affairs*, Cmnd 5428 (HMSO, 1973).
98   Select Committee of the House of Lords, Second Report 1972-3, *Sport and Leisure*, HL 193 (HMSO, 1973).
99   Memorandum by the Department of the Environment to the Expenditure Committee, op. cit., p. 1.
100 Observations by the Secretaries of State . . . on the Sixth Report of the Committee in Session 1975-6, published as *First Special Report from the Expenditure Committee, Session 1976-77, National Parks and Access to the Countryside*, HC 256 (HMSO, 1977).
101 The figures are from Appendix 6 (p. 97) of *Twelfth Report of the Countryside Commission 1978-79*, HC 615 (HMSO, 1980). They include direct expenditure by the Commission, grants to local authorities and the National Parks Supplementary Grant. (Supplementary Grant was introduced by section 7 of the Local Government Act 1974 and is paid to county councils towards their national park expenditure. 'The amount of the grant is related to the level of expenditure which government, after consultation with the Commission, consider appropriate. By convention the grant is intended to cover 75 per cent of national park expenditure.' op. cit., p. 5.)
102 *Wildlife and Countryside Bill (HL), Explanatory and Financial Memorandum*, 1980.
103 Sports Council, *Annual Reports* (The Council); DoE Circular 1/73, *Provision for Sport and Physical Recreation* (HMSO, 1972); DoE Circular 47/76, *Establishment of Regional Councils for Sport and Recreation* (HMSO, 1976); DoE Circular 73/77, *Guidelines for Regional Recreational Strategies* (HMSO, 1977); *Second Report from the Select Committee of the House of Lords on Sport and Leisure*, 3 vols, HL 193 (HMSO, 1973); White Paper, *Sport and Recreation*, Cmnd 6200 (HMSO, 1975); and *Towards a Wider Use* ('Report of an inter-association working party on joint provision and dual or multiple use of facilities for recreational use by the community'), published by the Local Authority Associations in 1976.
104 Select Committee on Scottish Affairs, *Land Resource Use in Scotland*, 5 vols, HC 511 (HMSO, 1972); and *Government Observations on the Report of the Select Committee on Scottish Affairs*, Cmnd 5428 (HMSO, 1973).

105 See, for example, London County Council, *Green Belts Around London* (LCC, 1956); P. Self, *Cities in Flood* (Faber, rev. edn, 1961); D. R. Mandelker, *Green Belts and Urban Growth* (University of Wisconsin Press, 1962); D. L. Foley, *Controlling London's Growth* (University of California Press, 1963); D. Gregory, *Green Belts and Development Control* (University of Birmingham, Centre for Urban and Regional Studies, 1970); D. Thomas, *London's Green Belt* (Faber, 1970); P. Hall *et al.*, *The Containment of Urban England* (Allen & Unwin, 1973); Standing Conference on London and South East Regional Planning, *The Improvement of London's Green Belt* (1977), *The Improvement of London's Green Belt: A Second Report - Views of Member Authorities* (1979) and *Policy Towards Provision of Recreation Facilities in London's Green Belt* (1979). For details of the urban fringe experiment see the annual reports of the Countryside Commission.

106 *A Study of Exmoor: Report by Lord Porchester* (HMSO, 1977). See also the annual reports of the Countryside Commission.

107 C. L. Bielkus, A. W. Rodgers and G. P. Wibberley, *Second Homes in England and Wales* (Wye College, 1972); C. B. Pyne, *Second Homes in Caernarvonshire* (Caernarvonshire County Planning Department, 1973); C. A. Jacobs, *Second Homes in Denbighshire* (Denbighshire County Planning Department, 1972); R. Tuck, *Second Homes in Merionethshire* (Merionethshire County Planning Department, 1973); DART, *Second Homes in England and Wales* (Dartington Amenity Research Group, 1973); P. Ashby, G. Birch and M. Haslett, 'Second homes in North Wales', *Town Planning Review*, vol. 46 (1975), pp. 323-33; J. T. Coppock, *Second Homes: Curse or Blessing?* (Pergamon, 1977); and A. L. Ray, *Second Homes in Norfolk* (Royal Geographical Society, 1979).

108 S. Bainbridge, *Restrictions at Stonehenge: The Reactions of Visitors to Limitations in Access*, Office of Population Censuses and Surveys, Social Survey Division (HMSO, 1979).

109 Association of District Councils, *Rural Recovery: Strategy for Survival* (The Association, 1978); Standing Conference of Rural Community Councils, *The Decline of Rural Services* (National Council of Social Service, 1978); Association of County Councils, *Rural Deprivation* (The Association, 1979); National Associations of Local Councils, *Rural Life: Change or Decay?* (The Association, 1979); J. M. Shaw, *Rural Deprivation and Planning* (Geo Books, 1979); Standing Conference of Rural County Councils, *Whose Countryside?* (National Council of Social Service, 1979); P. Commins and P. J. Drudy, *Problem Rural Regions* (Regional Studies Association, 1980); M. Dower, *Jobs in the Countryside: Prospects for Rural Employment* (National Council of Voluntary Organisations, 1980); E. J. Woods (ed.), *Rural Decline in the UK - A Third World View* (Arkleton Trust, 1980); and the comprehensive annotated bibliography of economic and social problems in rural Britain by S. Neate, *Rural Deprivation*, Geo Abstracts, Bibliography No. 8 (Geo Books, 1981).

110 For general discussions see, for example, V. Bonham Carter, *The Survival of the English Countryside* (Hodder & Stoughton, 1971); G. E. Cherry (ed.), *Rural Planning Problems* (Leonard Hill, 1976); J. Davidson and G. Wibberley, *Planning and the Rural Environment* (Pergamon, 1977); A. W. Gilg, *Countryside Planning: The First Three Decades 1945-76* (Methuen, 1978); and *Countryside Planning Yearbook 1980* (Geo Books, 1980).

Chapter 9

NEW AND EXPANDED TOWNS

THE CASE FOR NEW TOWNS

In the context of postwar planning, the arguments in favour of new towns[1] were simple and overwhelming. The large cities – above all London – had grown too large: improved housing conditions had been obtained at unwarranted social and economic cost. Yet the need for more houses had not abated: on the contrary, it had been increased by the cessation of building during the war, by population growth and (at the time only dimly understood) household growth, and by the recognition and acceptance of the need for major reconstruction and thinning out of congested urban areas. Further large-scale peripheral expansion could not be countenanced: the only alternative was long-distance dispersal. Some of this could go to expanded small towns, but the scale of the problem was too great to be dealt with solely by this means. Further, it was obvious that the local government machinery was not suited to undertake building on the scale required, even if local housing situations made it politically viable that local authorities could contemplate a major building programme for non-local people. The basic solution, therefore, was the building of new towns by new *ad hoc* agencies.

The main alternatives were private enterprise and government-sponsored corporations. Private enterprise was rejected by the Reith Committee.[2] They stated:

> While it is desirable to provide every opportunity for private development, we have come to the conclusion that in an undertaking of so far reaching and special a character as the creation of a new town, ordinary commercial enterprise would be inappropriate. Apart from the risks involved, both in matters of finance and in execution, such a policy would of necessity result in the creation of a private monopoly.[3]

Three essential features thus characterised early post-war new town policy:

(i)   Their basic function was to relieve the housing pressures of London and other big cities.
(ii) This was to be achieved by 'the antithesis of the dormitory

suburb' – by 'self-contained and balanced communities for work and living'.

(iii) New town development was to be carried out by government-sponsored corporations.

But a fourth feature needs stressing: new towns were only part of a wider policy for the distribution of population and employment. Other parts of this policy were green belts, industrial location control and expanded towns. No proper assessment of the achievements of the British new towns can be made without a parallel assessment of these other parts of the wider policy.

THE EARLIER POSTWAR NEW TOWNS

The new towns policy was thus conceived largely as a means of dealing with urban congestion. The eight London new towns have had this as their prime objective. The policy has, however, been applied to other problems. Even in the London ring of new towns, there is one – Basildon – where a primary object has been rural slum clearance. (The area was one of extensive unplanned and largely unserviced shack development.)

Of the six original provincial new towns, five were in areas of regional decline – Peterlee, Aycliffe, East Kilbride, Glenrothes and Cwmbran. *Corby* was a special case, with the predominant objective of providing housing for the growing work-force of the Stewart and Lloyd's steel works. Yet, in a real sense, all of these six new towns were special cases. *Peterlee*, the miners' town (built on a coalfield), aimed at concentrating, in one urban area, development which would otherwise have been scattered throughout a number of small mining villages, none of which could provide town facilities and amenities. *Aycliffe*, adjacent to a major trading estate, developed from a wartime Royal Ordnance Factory. It aimed at capitalising on this investment, but (because of intense local opposition in an area where the local MP happened to be Hugh Dalton, the Chancellor of the Exchequer) was restricted initially to a target population of a mere 10,000. *Cwmbran*, 8 km from the centre of the 100,000 population county borough of Newport, but attractively placed for industry, had 8,000 existing jobs and a growing problem of journeys to work. Here the objective, as in Corby, was to serve industrial growth, but in a location which was agreed to be far from ideal, yet (to use the laconic words of the official report *Town and Country Planning 1943–51*) one to which 'there was no alternative available which would not be open to still worse objections'. (The cynics were more pointed: if England and Scotland had new towns then Wales had to have one: a badly located new town was better than none at all.) *East Kilbride*, 6½ km 'over the hill' from the edge of Glasgow, was proposed in the Abercrombie-Matthew Clyde

Valley Regional Plan: its twin aims were to take overspill from Glasgow and to act as a growth point in a favourable area of central Scotland. *Glenrothes*, again the product of a regional plan (the Mears Plan for Central and South-East Scotland), was conceived as a major plank in the policy of developing the East Fife coalfield to offset the decline of the Lanarkshire coalfields, but the disastrous failure of the Rothes Colliery led to a change in aim: Glenrothes became a centre for regional development loosely linked with Glasgow overspill.

CUMBERNAULD

Cumbernauld stands on its own – in several senses. It was the only new town designated in the 1950s. Like East Kilbride it was proposed in the Clyde Valley Regional Plan, it is close to Glasgow and has a high level of commuting. Architecturally it is unique, and for this reason (rather than its location on the top of an exposed hill in central Scotland) it has proved most popular with architects: the seal of professional approval was provided when the town became the first winner of the R. S. Reynolds Memorial Award for Community Architecture. It also claims to be the safest town in Britain: road accidents are only 22 per cent of the national average, allegedly because of the advanced road design and segregation of traffic and pedestrians.

THE NEW TOWNS OF 1961-6

Cumbernauld was the one new town designated during the ten years from 1951 to 1960. Between 1961 and 1966 seven more were designated: five in England and two in Scotland. Four of the English towns are intended for overspill from two conurbations: *Skelmersdale* and *Runcorn* for Merseyside, and *Redditch* and *Dawley* for the West Midlands. They are, therefore, essentially the same in concept as the London new towns, though Dawley differs in three ways. First, whereas the other three towns have clear locational advantages, Dawley is relatively inaccessible and outside the main line of development in the Midlands. Secondly, its terrain is, to put it mildly, inhospitable. Or, to use the more romantic words of Arnold Whittick, the site is 'rich in the relics of the iron industry and can justly claim to be the cradle of the industrial revolution'.[4] Be that as it may, it is an expensive town to develop. Thirdly, its designated area was more than doubled in 1968 when its name was changed to *Telford* and its target population increased from 90,000 to 220,000. This brings it into the 'new city' class of the later 1960s.

The fifth new town of the 1961-6 period is *Washington* – some 14 km from Newcastle upon Tyne. This was the first provincial English new town to be explicitly proposed as part of a comprehensive regional programme.[5] Also of significance is the fact that it was the first new town intentionally sited as an extension of a conurbation. Other new towns (East Kilbride, for example) may well eventually become extensions of conurbations but this was far from the intention. Washington is the prime example of a marked change in planning policy. Previously, new towns were conceived as a means of preventing urban growth: Washington is conceived as a means of accommodating it.

The two Scottish new towns of this period were both conceived as growth points in a comprehensive regional programme for central Scotland, though starting from very different bases: *Livingston*, some 24 km from Edinburgh, had a base population of 2,000 while *Irvine*, on the Ayrshire coast, had 27,000.

Newtown (Montgomeryshire) is an unusual case of the adoption of the new machinery for promoting regional development. It is situated in the largest area of rural depopulation in the country (England and Wales). Consultants reported that the case for a 'new town Newtown' was a weak one, if conceived solely in terms of a focal point for economic and social development in mid-Wales.[6] They concluded that designation could be justified only if overspill from the West Midlands were incorporated into the plan. Nevertheless, optimists strongly support the view of the previous Secretary of State for Wales that the new town will stem and, ultimately, reverse the exodus of population from mid-Wales. Whether this can be achieved with an expansion of the scale envisaged – from 5,000 to 13,000 – remains to be seen.

THE NEW TOWNS OF 1967-71

Apart from Newtown, five new towns were designated between 1967 and 1971. One of the most striking features of these latest new towns (like the enlargement of Dawley into Telford which was determined during the same period) is their huge size. In comparison with the Reith Committee's 'optimum' of 30,000–50,000, Telford's 220,000 and Central Lancashire's 500,000 appear massive. But size is not the only striking feature. Another is the fact that four of them are based on substantial existing towns. At the date of designation, *Peterborough* had 81,000 population, *Northampton* 131,000, *Warrington* 122,000 and *Central Lancashire* 236,000. Of course, town building had been going on for a long time in Britain and all the best sites have already been taken by what are now old towns. The time was bound to come when the only places left for new towns were the sites of existing towns.

In this situation, and given the scale of expansion, traditional terms such as 'new towns' and 'expanding towns' become inappropriate. Like the term 'overspill' they are now out of date. As with so many other aspects of town and country planning, new concepts are being embodied in old terms. Just as 'overspill' has been misleadingly applied to the accommodating of a major population increase, so the term 'new towns' came to be applied to major regional developments based on old towns.

Of course, few of the earlier new towns were built on virgin sites (and those that were – Aycliffe and Peterlee – have had the most difficult time). Basildon had a scattered population of 25,000, while Hemel Hempstead was a substantial township of 21,000. But none of these earlier new towns was in the same population class as the latest. Indeed, the original population of all the thirteen new towns designated between 1946 and 1951 was only fractionally greater (at 130,000) than that of the single 'new town' of Warrington (at 122,000).

It would, however, be a mistake to infer that these relatively mammoth new towns were designated because the supply of alternative locations had run out. The reasoning had a number of strands. First, older towns were in need of rejuvenation and a share in the limited capital investment programme. It was not self-evident that economic sense or social justice was to be achieved by another round of traditional-type new towns. Related to this was the old economic argument that nothing succeeds like success; or, to be more precise, a major development with a population base of 80,000 to 130,000 or more has a flying start over one which has a mere 5,000–10,000. A wide range of facilities is already available, and (hopefully) can be expanded at the margin. There are numerous other advantages such as the much more varied housing market. On the other hand, the disadvantages are yet to be assessed.

It is also noteworthy that every one of these five newest towns is on excellent communications routes for both road and rail – four of them on the electrified rail line to Euston. This is 'linear planning' on a grand scale.

But perhaps too much should not be made of common features. These newer new towns are as varied as the old ones. Probably the only strictly valid common denominator is that they were all intended to assist in the accommodation of population increase. Three – Milton Keynes, Peterborough and Northampton – are linked with London overspill, while Warrington and Central Lancashire are linked with Merseyside and South-East Lancashire, though the links are somewhat tenuous.

STONEHOUSE

Stonehouse had the distinction of being the latest, the most precarious and possibly the last of the new towns. The case for Stonehouse was set out in a *Memorandum* by the Secretary of State for Scotland in 1972.[7] Its main *raison d'être* was to meet the overspill requirements of Glasgow, while at the same time 'acting as a springboard for industrial expansion and renewal'. There is little doubt about the inherent attractiveness of the site – close to the junction of the M74 and A71 roads; but (at least with hindsight) there were serious doubts about its relevance to the rapidly declining economy of Clydeside. Indeed, the Strathclyde Regional Council pressed for the town to be abandoned on the grounds not only that it was not needed, but that it would accelerate the decline of urban Clydeside and divert resources which were urgently needed to rejuvenate this old area.

An announcement that the town was to be abandoned was made in May 1976 – with a diversion of resources to urban renewal in Glasgow. (Staff and funds were rechannelled to 'GEAR' – the Glasgow Eastern Area Renewal project.)[8]

In an extreme form, the position of Stonehouse mirrors doubts which have increasingly grown about the purpose and future of the new towns programme. This is an issue which is discussed further at the end of this chapter.

THE SELECTION OF SITES

The selection of sites for 'new' towns is very difficult in a small country such as Britain.[9] The requirements are numerous: an adequate supply of water (but avoiding the sterilisation of a material part of the catchment area for the water supplies of the region); good drainage; a reasonably flat site – not too hilly (which would be expensive) nor too flat (which would detract from the interest and potentialities of the site); near main roads and a through railway line (but not too close since this might involve extra costs for bridging, underpasses, relief roads, and so on); a reasonable distance from existing large urban developments; not forgetting the avoidance of areas of 'outstanding natural beauty', of great historical interest, of mining subsidence, or large surface workings, and of first-class agricultural land. Clearly these ideal requirements can rarely be met: the problem then becomes one of balancing costs and benefits.

Of the ten sites proposed in Abercrombie's Greater London Plan, only two – Stevenage and Harlow – were actually designated. Four were rejected on the grounds that they were too close to existing towns and therefore unlikely to survive as separate entities: Redbourn (near Hemel Hempstead, St Albans and Harpenden); Stapleford (near Hertford); Margaretting (near Chelmsford); and Holmwood (near Dorking – and in a particularly beautiful piece of countryside). Ongar was rejected partly because of its inadequate rail service (and the high cost of making it adequate) – a difficulty which applied also to Redbourn. White Waltham was situated in an area of valuable agricultural land, and, furthermore, would have put a nearby airfield out of use. Crowhurst was considered unattractive to industry and too near Crawley, which had been proposed to take the place of Holmwood.

In the provinces, the problem of the risk of subsidence has been acute. A proposed new town at Mobberley in Cheshire, though near to Manchester, was seriously considered but rejected because of liability to subsidence due to salt mining. In South Wales attempts to find a suitable site for a new town which could serve workers on the trading estate at Treforest, near Pontypridd, proved abortive.

There is, additionally, the political context within which decisions on new sites are made: this may exacerbate the physical problems or, alternatively, reduce the importance which is attached to them.[10]

DESIGNATION

Once a site has been chosen the first formal step is designation. This is accomplished by means of a draft order, following which there are consultations with interested parties – particularly the local authorities concerned. If any objections cannot be settled administratively, a public local inquiry must be held. 'The inquiry is not a judicial or quasi-judicial one; it is a step in the administrative process by means of which objections are publicly stated and the minister is made aware of the extent to which his proposals are opposed . . . Before any case comes to inquiry, the proposed site and possible alternatives will have been exhaustively investigated, so that it is unlikely that the inquiry will disclose any major factor of which the minister is not aware.'[11] Unfortunately, though such an attitude may be realistic, it is not one likely to be welcomed by local opponents: at the very least there is a clear need for an enlightened public relations policy. This was notably lacking in the early days of the new towns programme and considerable opposition – and litigation – resulted.

Objections to earlier new towns generally resulted at most in the exclusion of certain areas of agricultural land from the designated area: 128 hectares at Crawley, 159 at Harlow, 309 at Bracknell, 425 at Corby and 817 at Hemel Hempstead. The designated area can, however, be extended at a later date, in which case – unless there are no objections – a further public inquiry is held.

NEW TOWN DEVELOPMENT CORPORATIONS

The New Towns Act (now consolidated for England and Wales in the Act of 1965, and for Scotland in the Act of 1968) provides for the setting up of development corporations to plan and create new towns wherever the secretary of state is satisfied 'that it is expedient in the national interest' to do so. The corporations have powers 'to acquire, hold, manage and dispose of land and other property, to carry out building and other operations, to provide water, electricity, gas, sewerage and other services, to carry on any business or undertaking in or for the purpose of the new town, and generally to do anything

necessary or expedient for the purposes of the new town or for the
purposes incidental thereto'.

This followed the recommendations of the Reith Committee that a
new and separate agency (with no other responsibilities) should be
created for each new town. The justification for this was that the
creation of a new town was not simply a matter of erecting buildings:
it also involved 'the development of a balanced community enjoying a
full social, industrial and commercial life'.[12]

The corporations are not, however, the sole agency in new town
development. Despite the apparently all-embracing character of their
powers, they are not local authorities: education and local health
services, for example, remain the responsibility of the normal local
government machinery. Water, sewage disposal, gas and electricity,
and hospitals are likewise the responsibility of the normal local or
public authority. Nevertheless, where the necessary provision is
beyond the technical or financial resources of the local authority, the
development corporations can assist by undertaking the work themselves or by making a financial contribution: this applies particularly
to water, sewerage and sewage disposal facilities. This provides a
useful degree of flexibility, though it has often been a source of
friction between the development corporations and the local
authorities. Much time and effort has had to be spent on determining
the allocation of expenditure between these two types of authority.
The problem is aggravated by their very different characters. As a
former General Manager of Stevenage (A. C. Duff) has put it:

> relations between the New Town Corporations and the Urban
> District (or Borough) Council are likely to require careful handling,
> even granted that there is goodwill on both sides, and unfortunately
> goodwill has been the exception rather than the rule. The council-
> lors are aware that the members of the Corporation devote less of
> their time to the business of the new town than do the councillors:
> that the members are paid but the councillors are not; that the
> members are for the most part 'strangers from London', while the
> councillors are all local residents; and that the members are
> nominated by a minister while the councillors are elected by the
> ratepayers. The councillors would be rather more than human if
> they did not on occasion feel some measure of both envy and
> resentment.[13]

With the later 'partnership' towns, the relationships were, of course,
different, though not necessarily easier.

Little study has been undertaken of the actual working of new town
development corporations and, for the most part, the only insights
available are those provided by the corporations' annual reports

(which are often used as a vehicle of complaint – in the hope that the ministry or the Treasury would make life easier). Hebbert,[14] however, makes some particularly interesting observations in his review of the Building Research Establishment reports on Bracknell, East Kilbride and Washington.[15] The composite portrait presented by these three reports, he suggests,

> confirms the wisdom with which the Reith Committee specified the agency arrangements for new towns, especially the recommendation that the development corporation should not employ a single 'planner' or even a planning consultant, but instead should work through a team of senior executive staff – a business manager, a chief architect, a chief engineer, an estate manager and a public relations officer, each with subordinate officers and staff – headed by a general manager possessing 'initiative, business acumen, and proved organising ability'. 'It would be an advantage', the Committee added, 'if he knew enough of the work of the technical experts to talk their language and appreciate their point of view, but he need not himself be a specialist in any of their fields'.[16] This organisational model proved extremely robust, especially when a strong chief executive was complemented by an energetic corporation chairman, such a pair being General B. E. C. Dixon, previously chief engineer with the War Office in Palestine, Transjordan, Egypt and Italy, and Sir Patrick Dollan, a previous Labour Lord Provost of Glasgow and the first chairman of East Kilbride Development Corporation, whose partnership is described by Roger Smith. The effect was to create a structure deliberately comparable to that of a business enterprise, with the advantages of land purchase powers and Treasury financing over a sixty-year term, but without encumbering public policy controls except the general supervision of the public interest by the Minister of Town and Country Planning and Secretary of State for Scotland.[17] At a time when much utopian thinking was in the air about the prospects for social engineering, and geographers, sociologists and architects were all lending an air of spurious expertise to the concept of the optimally designed human environment,[18] the Reith Committee took a deliberately sober and management-orientated view, emphasising throughout its reports the need for an effective agency rather than a perfected blueprint. It ensured that the initiative would lie in the hands of retired military men, estate managers and general administrators, rather than with the drawing-board missionaries then so prominent in the planning movement, and that the building up of the new towns would not be paralysed, as it might so well have been, by ideological arguments over the problems of compromise between ideal and real.

FINANCE

Development corporations also differ from a local authority in that they are wholly financed from the Exchequer: advances are made from the Consolidated Fund.[19] The New Towns Act of 1946 authorised issues up to £50 million to cover the needs of the first few years, but this total has been successively increased by later Acts. (The present total, under the 1980 New Towns Act, is £3,625 million, with further provision for an increase to £4,000 million.)

Exchequer advances are payable over sixty years, with interest at the rate prevailing at the date on which the advance is made. There is no concealed subsidy in the form of a concessionary rate of interest: the loans are made at a rate which reflects the current rate for government credit. The Reith Committee had recommended that all finance should be found by the state by way of loan but, in fact, the administration of these loans has proved to be very different from the Reith conception. The Reith Committee argued that it was 'most important that the financial autonomy and responsibility of the corporations shall be assured, and that development shall not be delayed or restricted by discussions of policy arising over applications for public advances'. This posited a degree of freedom for the corporations which it would be difficult to reconcile with public accountability. The balance is not easy to achieve, particularly where expenditure is proposed on risky ventures or developments for which there is no financial return. Since it is public money which is being invested, the Treasury have to ensure that each proposal is reasonable. But the Act goes further: it specifically requires that before approval is given to any proposal the secretary of state must be satisfied that 'having regard to all the circumstances' a reasonable financial return can be expected. This gives the central departments a very large degree of control over the operations of the development corporations. In fact, new towns policy – both generally and in relation to individual towns – is framed by the Department of the Environment, not by the development corporations. Since it is the central government which is providing the capital it is difficult to see how this can be otherwise.[20]

ASSESSING NEW TOWN ACHIEVEMENTS

Twenty-eight new towns with a current population of over 2 million; ranging in original size from less than 100 to 250,000 and in ultimate size from a possible 13,000 (Newtown) to 200,000 (Milton Keynes) or more (Central Lancashire); differing in density, character, location and economic potential; and with various, and sometimes changing, objectives – what criteria can be used for assessing their achievements? And is the assessment to be in terms of the adequacy of provision (however that is interpreted) or in terms of alternatives forgone? If the

former, what is more significant: reduction in commuting, architectural merit, range of amenities, 'balance', impact on conurbation
housing problems, financial profit and loss, reduction in road
accidents, satisfaction of residents . . . ? If the latter (alternatives
forgone), would it have been a better economic investment (or a better
social policy) to facilitate a larger amount of development on the
periphery of the conurbations or, at the other extreme, to plan major
developments in Central Wales, the Borders, or the Highlands? And
how far should the new towns be judged by reference to their original
objectives – as distinct from those which now seem to be more
relevant?

Unfortunately, even a summary of physical achievements is difficult
to provide since there is no comprehensive statistical return of the
progress of development in the new towns (though the 1975 Report
from the Expenditure Committee now provides a relative feast of
information). More generally (to the bewilderment and astonishment
of foreign visitors) incredibly little attempt has been made to learn
from the experience gained in the new towns: successive governments
have taken an attitude which can only be described as nonchalant.[21]
Further, few serious academic studies have been undertaken.[22]

The Reith Committee recommended the establishment of a Central
Advisory Commission – both for 'harmonising policy and practice'
and for 'pooling information and experience'. This recommendation
was never implemented, and such research, monitoring and statistical
work which has been done within government has been on an
extremely limited scale.

The figures given in the accompanying tables (Tables 9.1 and 9.2)
are taken from the summaries provided annually in *Town and
Country Planning*: the journal of the Town and Country Planning
Association. They are subject to a number of difficulties which are
increasing as the new towns programme (as outlined below) is
radically changing in scale and character.

It would take us far afield here to examine how far the new towns
have achieved the objectives of 'balance' and 'self-containment'; (or,
indeed, how far they were – or have remained – explicit objectives);
what the concepts really mean; and how they might be measured.
There is a considerable literature on some aspects of these questions to
which the interested reader is referred.[23]

The 'balance' issue in fact was largely translated into one of getting
lower income households to move to the new towns (particularly in the
London ring), and complicated (and cumbersome) efforts were made
to achieve this by way of an 'industrial selection scheme' (later termed
the new and expanded towns scheme: NETS).[26]

However, as the towns developed it became more rather than less
difficult to control the 'factors' of balance, since it was employment
needs which determined who would be attracted. Moreover, as it grew

Table 9.1   *The New Towns 1980*[24]

London ring	Date of designation	Designated area (hectares)	Population	
			Original	At 31.3.80
Basildon	1949	3,165	25,000	98,000
Bracknell	1949	1,337	5,100	46,000
Crawley	1947	2,396	9,100	76,000
Harlow	1947	2,588	4,500	79,200
Hatfield	1948	947	8,500	26,000
Hemel Hempstead	1947	2,391	21,000	80,000
Stevenage	1946	2,532	6,700	73,500*
Welwyn Garden City	1948	1,747	18,500	41,000
Total: London ring		17,103	98,400	519,700
Others in England				
Aycliffe	1947	1,254	100	26,000
Central Lancs	1970	14,267	235,600	253,500
Corby	1950	1,791	15,700	51,000
Milton Keynes	1967	8,900	40,000	90,000
Northampton	1968	8,080	131,100	156,000
Peterborough	1967	6,451	81,000	120,000
Peterlee	1948	1,205	200	25,500
Redditch	1964	2,906	32,000	61,800
Runcorn	1964	2,930	28,500	64,200
Skelmersdale	1961	1,670	10,000	39,300
Telford	1963	7,790	70,000	103,800
Warrington	1968	7,535	122,300	137,500
Washington	1964	2,271	20,000	53,200
Total: Others in England		67,050	786,500	1,181,800
Wales				
Cwmbran	1949	1,420	12,000	45,300
Mid-Wales (Newtown)	1967	606	5,000	9,000
Total: Wales		2,026	17,000	54,000
Total: England and Wales		86,179	901,900	1,755,800
Scotland				
Cumbernauld	1955	3,152	3,000	50,400
East Kilbride	1947	4,150	2,400	75,800
Glenrothes	1948	2,333	1,100	37,000
Irvine	1966	5,022	34,600	59,000
Livingston	1962	2,780	2,000	37,000
Total: Scotland		17,437	43,100	259,200
Total: Great Britain		103,616	945,100	2,015,000

*The Stevenage figure relates to 31.12.78.

Table 9.2   *Economic Structure of the New Towns 1978/80*[25]

	Square metres of:			No. of
London ring	*Industry*	*Offices*	*Shops*	*employees*
Basildon	723,300	63,100	136,800	46,915
Bracknell	319,733	119,148	59,041	26,200
Crawley	448,040	73,986	83,845	54,400
Harlow	670,991	70,358	67,853	36,280
Hatfield	41,620	4,645	26,458	26,100
Hemel Hempstead	437,750	66,855	53,936	40,800
Stevenage	478,400	43,106	84,688	36,000
Welwyn Garden City	331,699	25,845	39,145	27,200
Total: London ring	3,451,533	467,043	551,766	293,895
Others in England				
Aycliffe	450,523	5,946	17,937	13,049
Central Lancs	105,726	340	7,638	127,000
Corby	207,921	22,284	52,055	22,758
Milton Keynes	433,828	93,548	120,349	46,700
Northampton	1,458,370	286,416	286,665	87,000
Peterborough	925,000	154,000	196,000	65,450
Peterlee	214,177	8,495	24,270	8,241
Redditch	621,090	42,100	52,500	27,140
Runcorn	330,773	32,813	67,819	22,800
Skelmersdale	499,406	20,900	40,535	14,179
Telford	858,799	47,863	80,700	44,120
Warrington	262,464	33,063	4,169	69,174
Washington	400,586	68,496	46,381	22,611
Total: Others in England	6,768,663	816,264	997,018	570,222
Wales				
Cwmbran	119,005	18,885	63,320	17,742
Mid-Wales (Newtown)	85,275	13,492	17,002	6,149
Total: Wales	204,280	32,377	80,322	23,891
Total: England and Wales	10,424,476	1,315,684	1,629,106	888,008
Scotland				
Cumbernauld	363,825	39,208	28,141	15,156
East Kilbride	627,718	64,135	77,215	30,055
Glenrothes	473,828	23,472	28,230	15,979
Irvine	495,100	27,000	56,470	19,500
Livingston	298,049	29,617	32,216	12,224
Total: Scotland	2,258,520	183,432	222,272	92,914
Total: Great Britain	12,682,996	1,499,116	1,851,378	980,922

clear that the new towns were likely to become profitable, the more important political question became that of the future ownership of the new town assets.

THE COMMISSION FOR THE NEW TOWNS

The New Towns Act of 1946 envisaged that the new towns would eventually be transferred from the development corporations to local authorities. This was in line with Howard's principle that there should be local control, and that profits (particularly those resulting from increases in land values) should accrue to the benefit of the towns themselves. It did, however, depart from the Reith Committee's majority view that it was unwise for the functions of (virtually monopoly) land ownership and local government to be combined in a single body.

In fact, as the time for the transfer approached, the Conservative government of the day became increasingly opposed to this idea and proposed, as an alternative, that ownership and management should remain in the hands of a body which was independent of the local authority. The New Towns Act of 1959 set up an *ad hoc* public body for this purpose – the Commission for the New Towns.[27]

Two new towns were transferred to the Commission in 1962 (Crawley and Hemel Hempstead) and a further two in 1966 (Hatfield and Welwyn Garden City).

The Commission was established as a permanent (or at least semi-permanent) body, charged with the duty 'to maintain and enhance the value of the land held by them and the return obtained by them from it' while, at the same time, having 'regard to the purpose for which the town was developed and to the convenience and welfare of the persons residing, working or carrying on business there'.

With the change in government in 1964, the future of the Commission came under review but, despite an election commitment to provide for 'real democratic self-government' in the new towns and – at the least – a transfer of public authority housing to local authorities, no action was taken before a further change in government (in 1970) apart from the commissioning of a study on future ownership and management of housing.[28]

Labour was returned to power again in 1974 and quickly produced 'consultation documents'.[29] Emphasis was laid on 'partnership' between the development corporations and their respective local authorities. Though it was envisaged that arrangements would vary, it was also proposed that 'agreements might, *inter alia*, provide the basis for eventual transfer on appropriate terms of housing and other assets closely associated with housing'.

More tangible and less equivocal was the *Report of the Working Party on the Transfer of Rented Housing in New Towns*,[30] following which the New Towns (Amendment) Act 1976 was passed. This provided for the transfer of housing and related assets from development corporations or the Commission for the New Towns to local authorities. The financial basis was simple: all outstanding debts and balances were simply to be passed over to the local authorities.

The Act applied only to England and Wales, and the Commission retained its responsibilities in relation to commercial and industrial assets.

In April 1978 all the Commission's housing and related assets were transferred to local authorities.[31] A similar transfer took place in six development corporation towns. (No further transfers to the Commission were made after 1966.)

The review of new towns policy started by the Labour government was continued under the Thatcher administration,[32] and target dates for the winding up of most of the new towns, as well as the Commission, have been announced. On current indications, it appears that the new towns programme will officially come to an end in the late 1980s; but whether this will be the case remains to be seen.

EXPANDED TOWNS

The New Towns Act was the first instalment of the 'overspill' plan: the second was to be an Act to facilitate town expansion by local authorities. This, however, was deferred until the immediate postwar housing shortage had been met. It was contrary to the political facts of life to expect local authorities to build houses for families from other areas while they still had severe housing problems of their own. It was, therefore, not until 1952 that the Town Development Act was passed.

The essential difference between the New Towns Act and the Town Development Act is apparent from their full titles. The New Towns Act is 'an Act to provide for the creation of new towns by means of development corporations'; the Town Development Act is 'an Act to encourage town development in county districts for the relief of congestion or overpopulation elsewhere'. The former set up special agencies to deal with a problem which was, by implication, beyond the competence of local authorities. The latter did precisely the opposite: it provided 'encouragement' to local authorities to meet the overspill problem themselves 'by agreement and co-operation'. As Macmillan (then Minister of Housing) stressed (during the Second Reading debates), 'the purpose of the Bill is that large cities wishing to provide for their surplus population shall do so by orderly and friendly arrangements with neighbouring authorities . . . it is our purpose that all these arrangements should be reached by friendly negotiation and not imposed by arbitrary power'. Such financial help was to be provided as would be 'necessary to get the job going'.

Actual development can be undertaken by the receiving authority themselves; or by the exporting authority acting either as an agent for the receiving authority or on their own account; or by the county council in whose area the receiving authority are situated. Tenants can be selected either from the housing list of the exporting authority or by means of an industrial selection scheme. In the latter case only families who secure employment in the receiving area are eligible for rehousing there.

Town development is very widely defined, as:

> Development in a district (or partly in one district and partly in another) which will have the effect, and is undertaken primarily for the purpose, of providing accommodation for residential purposes (with or without accommodation for the carrying on of industrial or other activities, and with all appropriate public services, facilities for public worship, recreation and amenity, and other requirements) the provision of which will relieve congestion or overpopulation outside the county comprising the district or districts in which the development is carried out.

This description of the Act serves to show how flexible its provisions are. Since town development is undertaken by local authorities with widely different problems and of varying size and wealth, this flexibility is essential.

A town expansion scheme can operate successfully only if all the local authorities concerned – the 'exporting' authority, the 'reception' authority and the county council – are able and willing to co-operate, and if the Department of Industry are likewise able and willing to assist in persuading industry to move into the expanding town. There are big difficulties – technical, administrative, financial, social and political – to be overcome. These constitute a severe strain on the local government machine. However, given a fortuitous combination of circumstances, experience has shown that town expansion schemes can operate to the great benefit of small towns.

Achievements have been the most significant when the 'exporting' authority has provided large-scale financial and technical assistance as was the case with the Greater London Council. Even so, the contribution made by expanded towns has, with a few exceptions, been small.

In all there were some seventy town expansion schemes, of which about a half had been completed by 1980. Over thirty of these related to London (and included major schemes such as Swindon[33] and Basingstoke). The others related to Birmingham, Bristol, Glasgow, Liverpool, Manchester, Newcastle upon Tyne, Salford, Walsall and Wolverhampton. About a third of a million people have been accommodated in these schemes.[34]

Following a review started by the Labour government,[35] but completed by the Conservatives in December 1979, the programme is now in process of being wound up.[36]

THE END OF DISPERSAL?

The heading for this final section is taken from an article by Maurice Ash in the February 1975 issue of *Town and Country Planning*. Major changes in the economy and in population growth, together with a belated but growing concern for inner city problems, have brought about some major doubts (a prelude to some radical rethinking?) about overspill policies.

Clearly, a new and expanding towns programme conceived when population forecasts envisaged over 70 million people in Britain by the turn of the century is hardly likely to be appropriate for a situation in which the outcome is projected at 58 million. This remarkable change in population projections has focused attention on the rapidly increasing problems of the inner cities. As Ash has pointed out (in the article referred to above):

> We have failed to grasp 'Ebenezer's other half': the problem of re-ordering the cities whose populations were thinning out and whose relief has been the ultimate, but forgotten, purpose of Ebenezer Howard's garden city policy. We took it for granted that lower densities were enough: that cities could virtually re-order themselves. Ebenezer never heard of the ghetto.

Planning policies for inner cities are inherently much more difficult to forge and operate than those which have been established for new towns. (And it should not be forgotten that the majority of the overspill from the urban areas has gone to developments other than those designated as new and expanded towns.) New and expanded towns cannot legitimately be blamed for 'creating' the inner city problem: what is at fault is the inadequacy of policies aimed at dealing directly with the problems of the inner city.

It is unfortunate that the development of new towns is sometimes seen as an alternative to action in the inner cities. Though the London new towns have housed fewer of the 'needy' than they might have done, they did house *some* (and the expanded towns proportionately more). The ending of the new town programme involves closing one opportunity which inner city areas require if, to borrow the subtitle of the Lambeth Inner Area Study, there are to be the needed 'policies for dispersal and balance'.[37]

REFERENCES AND FURTHER READING: CHAPTER 9

1 Generally on new towns, see M. Aldridge, *The British New Towns* (Routledge & Kegan Paul, 1979); J. B. Cullingworth, *Environmental Planning, Vol. III, New Towns Policy* (HMSO, 1979); F. J. Osborn and A. Whittick, *The New Towns: The Answer to Megalopolis* (Leonard Hill, 3rd edn, 1977); and F. Schaffer, *The New Town Story* (MacGibbon & Kee, 1970; Paladin Books, 1972). An increasing

number of books are now appearing on the history and development of individual new towns: see, for example, F. Gibberd *et al.*, *Harlow: The Story of a New Town* (Publications for Companies, 1980).

2   The Reith Committee issued three reports: *Interim Report of the New Towns Committee*, Cmd 6759; *Second Interim Report*, Cmd 6794; and *Final Report*, Cmd 6876, all published by HMSO in 1946.

3   *Interim Report*, op. cit. For further discussion, see J. B. Cullingworth, op. cit., pp. 6–18.

4   A. Whittick, 'Dawley: preservation and planned change', *Town and Country Planning*, vol. 36 (January–February 1968), p. 115.

5   See *The North-East: A Programme for Regional Development and Growth*, Cmnd 2206 (HMSO, 1963).

6   See *A New Town for Mid-Wales – Consultants' Proposals* (HMSO, 1966).

7   Scottish Development Department, *Draft New Towns (Stonehouse) Designation Order 1972: Memorandum by the Secretary of State* (HMSO, 1972).

8   See Scottish Development Agency, *GEAR Strategy and Programme* (SDA, 1980).

9   For a fascinating study of 'an analysis and appraisal of government decision-making processes with special reference to the launching of new towns and town development schemes', see P. H. Levin, *Government and the Planning Process* (Allen & Unwin, 1976). An account of the Cabinet discussion on the location of many of the new towns is to be found in J. B. Cullingworth, *New Towns Policy*, op. cit.

10   See, for example, Rodwin's comments on Cwmbran and Newton Aycliffe: L. Rodwin, *The British New Towns Policy* (Harvard University Press, 1956), pp. 122–4.

11   *Town and Country Planning 1943–51, Progress Report*, Cmd 8204 (HMSO, 1951), p. 129.

12   Reith Committee, *Interim Report*, op. cit., p. 9.

13   A. C. Duff, *Britain's New Towns* (Pall Mall, 1961), p. 45. See also M. Aldridge, op. cit., pp. 47–50 and 69–75.

14   M. Hebbert, 'The British new towns: a review article', *Town Planning Review*, vol. 51 (1980), pp. 414–20.

15   A. A. Ogilvy, *Bracknell and Its Migrants: 21 Years of a New Town* (HMSO, 1975); R. Smith, *East Kilbride: The Biography of a New Town 1947–1973* (HMSO, 1979); and W. V. Hole, I. M. Adderson and M. T. Pountney, *Washington New Town: The Early Years* (HMSO, 1979).

16   Reith Committee, *Final Report*, op. cit., paras 258–64. Hebbert also points out that the Reith Committee's 'conception of the new town general manager as an administrator *par excellence* corresponds closely with the Schuster Committee's conception of a town planning officer'. See *Report of the Committee on the Qualifications of Planners* (Schuster Report), Cmd 8059 (HMSO, 1950).

17   Reith Committee, *Interim Report*, op. cit., para. 9.

18   Hebbert instances C. B. Fawcett, *A Residential Unit for Town and Country Planning* (University of London Press, 1944); L. Wolfe, *The Reilly Plan: A New Way of Life* (Nicholson, 1945); and C. Madge, 'Reflections from Aston Park', *Architectural Review*, vol. 104 (1948), pp. 107–10.

19   As Ray Thomas has pointed out, there has been very little study of the financial performance of the new towns. R. Thomas, 'Financial performance of the development corporations', *Town and Country Planning*, vol. 49, no. 10 (November 1980), pp. 341–4.

20   The position is more complex in the 'partnership' towns where the local authorities play a major, not a subordinate, role.

21   For an account of early research by the ministry on new towns and 'The Welwyn research saga', see J. B. Cullingworth, *New Towns Policy*, op. cit., pp. 348–66.

22   Particular mention needs to be made of the work of the Open University's New Town Study Unit and earlier work by Ray Thomas at Political and Economic

Planning (*London's New Towns: A Study of Self Contained and Balanced Communities* and *Aycliffe to Cumbernauld: A Study of Seven New Towns in Their Regions*, both published in 1969).

23 M. Aldridge, *The British New Towns*, op. cit., ch. 6, 'Balance and self-containment'; A. G. Champion, 'Are the new towns likely to face population decline in the next decade?', *Town and Country Planning*, vol. 46 (1978), pp. 64–8; N. Deakin and C. Ungerson, *Leaving London: Planned Mobility and the Inner City* (Heinemann, 1977); B. J. Heraud, 'The new towns and London's housing problem', *Urban Studies*, vol. 3 (1966), pp. 8–21, and 'Social class and the new towns', *Urban Studies*, vol. 5 (1968), pp. 33–58; W. V. Hole, I. M. Adderson and M. T. Pountney, *Washington New Town: The Early Years* (HMSO, 1979); A. A. Ogilvy, 'The self-contained new town', *Town Planning Review*, vol. 39 (1968), pp. 38–54, 'Employment expansion and the development of new town hinterlands 1961–1966', *Town Planning Review*, vol. 42 (1971), pp. 113–29, and *Bracknell and Its Migrants: 21 Years of a New Town* (HMSO, 1975); R. Smith, *East Kilbride: The Biography of a Scottish New Town 1947–1973* (HMSO, 1979); R. Thomas, op. cit., and *Memorandum* to the Expenditure Committee on New Towns, *Second Report from the Expenditure Committee, Session 1974, Vol. III*, HC 305-III (HMSO, 1974), Appendix 6, pp. 408–44. (This is followed by a further memorandum by P. Cresswell, op. cit., pp. 444–73.)

24 *Town and Country Planning*, vol. 49, no. 10 (November 1980), pp. 370–1, Table 1.

25 *Town and Country Planning*, vol. 49, no. 10 (November 1980), pp. 370–2, Tables 1 and 2. The employment figures relate to March 1980, except for Stevenage (December 1978), Corby (October 1979), and Redditch and Runcorn (September 1979). In some cases (Central Lancashire, Crawley, Hatfield and Hemel Hempstead) major employment exists outside the designated area. There are many qualifications of this nature which relate to the other columns. For details, see the source.

26 See M. Aldridge, op. cit., ch. 6; and also J. B. Cullingworth, 'Some administrative problems of planned overspill', *Public Administration*, vol. 37 (1959), and *New Towns Policy*, op. cit., ch. VII; F. Gee, *Homes and Jobs for Londoners in New and Expanded Towns* (HMSO, 1972); and S. Ruddy, *Industrial Selection Schemes*, University of Birmingham, Centre for Urban and Regional Studies, Occasional Paper 5 (University of Birmingham, 1969).

27 See, generally, M. Aldridge, op. cit., ch. 5; and J. B. Cullingworth, *New Towns Policy*, op. cit., ch. VI.

28 J. B. Cullingworth and V. A. Karn, *The Ownership and Management of Housing in the New Towns* (HMSO, 1968).

29 *New Towns in England and Wales: A Consultation Document* (Department of the Environment, 1974); and *The Scottish New Towns: A Consultative Document* (Scottish Office, 1974). Both of these are reprinted in Volume IV of the *Thirteenth Report from the Expenditure Committee, Session 1974–75: New Towns*, HC 616-IV (HMSO, 1975), pp. 1007–18 and 931–5.

30 *Report of the Working Party on the Transfer of Rented Housing in New Towns* (Department of the Environment, 1975).

31 *Report of the Commission for the New Towns for the Period ended 31st March 1979*, HC 298 (HMSO, 1980), p. 1.

32 There was, additionally, the review of the Quangos (of which the development corporations and the Commission are excellent examples). See *Report on Non-Departmental Public Bodies*, Cmnd 7797 (HMSO, 1980), pp. 29–30.

33 See M. Harloe, *Swindon: A Town in Transition* (Heinemann, 1975).

34 Central Office of Information, *Environmental Planning in Britain*, Reference Pamphlet 9 (HMSO, 1979), p. 21.

35 See *HC Debates*, cols 1110–27, 5 April 1977; and *The Future of Town Development Schemes Associated with the Greater London Council: A Consultation Document* (Department of the Environment, September 1978).

36 See *HC Debates*, Vol. 975, col. 814, 14 December 1979.
37 Department of the Environment, *Inner London: Policies for Dispersal and Balance: Final Report of the Lambeth Inner Area Study* (HMSO, 1977).

Chapter 10

URBAN RENEWAL

The term 'urban renewal' has been out of fashion for some time, possibly because of its particular use in relation to public sector slum clearance and redevelopment in the United States.[1] It is, however, a useful term in that it can be taken to imply (in Britain at least) a comprehensive approach to the revitalisation of areas of urban decline. It encompasses long-established slum clearance and housing improvement programmes, the deprived area policies conceived in the 1960s and the more recent *Policy for the Inner Cities* (to quote the title of the 1977 White Paper).

Clearly, with a field as vast as this (and the literature is becoming increasingly voluminous) the discussion has to be highly selective. A logical starting point is the oldest (and now the least favoured) policy: that of slum clearance.[2]

INADEQUATE HOUSING

Britain has a very large legacy of old housing which is inadequate by modern standards. This results from the relatively early start of the industrial revolution in this country and the rapid, unplanned and speculative urban development which took place in the nineteenth century. (The contrast with, for example, the Scandinavian countries, whose industrial revolutions came later when wealth was greater and standards higher, is marked.) As a result, British policies in relation to clearance and redevelopment are of long standing, though it was the Greenwood Housing Act of 1930 which heralded the start of the modern slum clearance programme. Over a third of a million houses were demolished before the Second World War brought the programme to an abrupt halt.

By 1938 demolitions were running at the rate of 90,000 a year: had it not been for the war, over a million older houses would (at this rate) have been demolished by 1951. The war, however, not only delayed clearance programmes: it resulted in enforced neglect and deterioration. War damage, shortage of building resources and (of increasing importance in the period of postwar inflation) crude rent restriction policies increased the problem of old and inadequate housing.

It was not until the mid-1950s that clearance could generally be resumed, and some 2 million slum houses (in Great Britain) have been demolished since then. But the problem is still one of large dimensions. The 1976 House Condition Survey (England and Wales) showed that, though the number of unfit houses had fallen by over a half since the 1967 survey, the total was still 894,000. An additional 984,000 *fit* dwellings lacked one or more of such basic amenities as an internal w.c. or a bath (Table 10.1).

Table 10.1   *Number of Unfit and Deficient Houses, England and Wales*[3]

	Unfit	Fit but lacking one or more basic amenities	Total
1967	1,836,000	2,371,000	4,207,000
1971	1,244,000	1,872,000	3,116,000
1976	894,000	984,000	1,878,000

These figures (and similar ones for Scotland) are, of course, a product of the standards employed. This is only partly a matter of definition: it is also a matter of interpretation. A striking illustration of this is provided by a comparison of the 1968 and the 1973 Welsh House Condition Surveys.[4] Though the number of dwellings lacking amenities decreased, the number of unfit dwellings *rose* from 92,000 to 147,000: from 10·4 per cent of the stock to 15 per cent. The reason why such a result is possible can be seen from an examination of the statutory standard of unfitness.

STANDARDS

The size of the slum housing problem is, of course, essentially related to the standards adopted. A 'slum' is more easily recognised than defined. The quality of housing has a number of different dimensions. The Denington[5] Committee drew attention to five.

  (i)   the structure and condition of housing (stability, damp, natural lighting, etc.);
 (ii)   the equipment and services built into housing (w.c., water supply, drainage, artificial lighting, etc.);
(iii)   the quality of the surrounding environment (air pollution, noise, open space, traffic conditions, etc.);
 (iv)   the space available to individual households (persons per room, bedroom requirements, etc.);
  (v)   the privacy available in dwellings occupied by more than one household (sharing accommodation and facilities, sound insulation, etc.).

The assessment and quantification of these is no easy matter, and there is considerable scope for area variation and personal judgement. This is particularly clear when an overall assessment is required of the need for slum clearance or improvement.

Statutory definitions relate predominantly to structure, physical condition and plumbing. In England and Wales, the legislation lists a number of matters which have to be taken into consideration, but a house is deemed 'unfit for human habitation' only 'if it is so far defective in one or more of the said matters that it is not reasonably suitable for occupation in that condition'. There is thus considerable scope for judgement.

The 'said matters' are: repairs; stability; freedom from damp; internal arrangement; natural lighting; ventilation; water supply; drainage and sanitary conveniences; facilities for preparation and cooking of food and for the disposal of waste water.

In Scotland, following the Scottish Housing Advisory Committee's 1967 report,[6] new legislation – the Housing (Scotland) Act 1969 – attempted a greater degree of objectivity. Dispensing with the concept of 'unfitness', it introduced a 'tolerable' standard: a house is held to meet this standard if it:

(a) is structurally stable;
(b) is substantially free from rising or penetrating damp;
(c) has satisfactory provision for natural and artificial lighting, for ventilation and for heating;
(d) has an adequate piped supply of wholesome water available within the house;
(e) has a sink provided with a satisfactory supply of both hot and cold water within the house;
(f) has a water closet available for the exclusive use of the occupants of the house and suitably located within the house;
(g) has an effective system for the drainage and disposal of foul and surface water;
(h) has satisfactory facilities for the cooking of food within the house;
(i) has satisfactory access to all external doors and outbuildings.

Despite the greater clarity and objectivity of the Scottish standard, it is apparent that the subjective element cannot be completely eliminated. The SHAC Report suggested that it could, however, be further reduced by the use of a 'housing defects index'. Considerable work has been undertaken on this both north and south of the Border.[7]

SLUM CLEARANCE IN ENGLAND AND WALES

Local authorities in England and Wales have a duty under the

Housing Acts 'to cause an inspection of their districts to be made from time to time' with a view to dealing with a wide range of unsatisfactory housing conditions. So far as unfit housing is concerned, they can require individual owners to repair, close, or demolish. For *areas* of unfit housing, however, a 'clearance area' procedure is used. An area can be declared a clearance area if the houses are unfit or badly arranged, and if the local authority are satisfied 'that the most satisfactory method of dealing with the conditions in the area is the demolition of all the buildings in the area'. Before declaring a clearance area, the local authority must also satisfy themselves that the persons to be displaced from residential accommodation can be adequately rehoused. Usually this is interpreted as meaning that the local authorities are able to rehouse the displaced families: indeed it is often referred to as an 'obligation to rehouse'. In fact, however, local authorities are statutorily required to provide accommodation only in so far as suitable dwellings do not already exist. There are parts of the country where there is no great shortage of housing and where a significant number of displaced families do rehouse themselves: this applies particularly in the case of those owner-occupiers who receive full market value compensation for their houses.

To be included in a clearance area a house must be unfit or dangerous or injurious to health, but it need not be incapable of being made fit at reasonable cost. Other buildings – factories, schools, shops: indeed, *any* building – can also be included so long as they are so badly arranged as to be 'dangerous or injurious to health'.

Having declared a clearance area the local authority proceeds to purchase the properties (either by agreement or by compulsory purchase order).

It is useful to know the jargon which is used in relation to clearance areas. Maps have to be prepared as part of the formal procedure for submitting compulsory purchase orders to the secretary of state. On these, different categories of property have to be identified either by hatching and stippling or by colour. The names of the colours are frequently used as a shorthand description of the different categories of property. Thus, *pink* houses are those which are unfit for human habitation; *pink hatched yellow* are buildings included because of their bad arrangement; and *grey* properties are those which, though not in either of the other categories, are needed for the satisfactory redevelopment of the cleared area.

This categorisation is important for two reasons. First, the compensation which an owner receives for his property will depend upon whether or not it is 'pink'.[8] If it is, he normally receives only cleared site value (though there is provision for 'well maintained' payments); if it is not, he will receive market value for the site with the house on it. Secondly, the matters about which the local authority have to be satisfied vary. With a 'pink' house they must be satisfied that the house is unfit according to the criteria set out in the Housing Acts. These in fact make no reference to the effect of the conditions on the health of the occupants – though objectors commonly use the argument that there is no evidence that their houses cause ill-health. With 'pink hatched yellow' properties it is legally necessary to prove that there is danger to health. This is difficult to do, at least in a manner which would be acceptable to a logician. The cynic might legitimately comment that all this is a legal fiction which – though relevant to nineteenth-century conditions – is now quite archaic. Nevertheless, it is accepted that severe lack of light and air space; narrow, cramped courts, yards and alleys; and similar overshadowed and congested buildings do fall within the legal definition. In practice, these conditions are commonly found in conjunction with internal inadequacies which render the house unfit. So far as 'grey' properties are concerned, the only matter at issue is whether their acquisition is reasonably necessary for the satisfactory redevelopment of the area. It is not necessary to prove that it is *impossible* to achieve a layout without them. It is sufficient to show that acquisition is 'reasonable'.

In 1979 some 30,000 houses were demolished or closed in England and Wales (34,000 in Great Britain). (Table 10.2.) By comparison, the figure for 1969 was nearly 73,000 (over 90,000 in Great Britain). This large fall reflects a major shift in policy from demolition to improvement.

HOUSE IMPROVEMENT POLICIES

Though an improvement grants policy was introduced in 1949, it was not until the mid-1950s that it got under way. Since then, the emphasis has gradually shifted from individual house improvements, first to the improvement of streets or areas of sub-standard housing, and later to the improvement of the total environment.

Initially it was assumed that houses could be neatly divided into two groups: according to the 1953 White Paper *Houses: The Next Step*, there were those which were unfit for human habitation and those which were 'essentially sound'. As experience was gained, the 'improvement philosophy' broadened and it came to be realised that there was a very wide range of housing situations related not only to the presence or otherwise of plumbing facilities and the state of repair of individual houses, but also to location, the varying socio-economic character of different neighbourhoods and the nature of the local housing market. A house 'lacking amenities' in Chelsea was, in important ways, different from an identical house in Rochdale: the 'appropriate action' was similarly different. Later, it was better understood that 'appropriate action' defined in housing market terms was not necessarily equally appropriate in social terms. A middle-class 'invasion' might restore the physical fabric and raise the quality (and 'tone') of a neighbourhood, but the social costs of this were borne largely by displaced low-income families. The problem thus became redefined.

Growing concern for the environment also led to an increased awareness of the importance of the factors *causing* deterioration. It is clear that these are more numerous and complex than housing legislation has recognised. Through traffic and inadequate parking provision was quickly recognised as being of physical importance. The answer – in appropriately physical terms – was the re-routing of traffic, the closure of streets and the provision of parking spaces (together with cobbled areas and the planting of trees). More serious causes of physical blight such as obnoxious industries were obviously less easy to deal with. But most difficult of all is to assess the social function of an area, the needs it meets and the ways in which conditions can be improved for (and in accordance with the wishes of) the people living in an area.

Table 10.2   *Slum Clearance and Improvement*[9]

	Houses demolished or closed			Improvement grants		
	England and Wales	Scotland	Great Britain	England and Wales	Scotland	Great Britain
1955–9	231,402	61,545	292,947	219,068	16,051	235,119
1960–9	643,040	150,455	793,495	1,177,787	71,828	1,249,615
1970	71,118	17,345	88,463	156,557	23,400	179,957
1971	74,721	20,554	95,275	197,481	35,042	232,523
1972	70,234	18,518	88,752	319,169	48,899	368,068
1973	66,786	16,479	83,265	360,954	92,667	453,621
1974	43,513	11,615	55,128	231,918	68,447	300,365
1975	51,127	10,658	61,785	126,888	33,203	160,091
1976	48,964	6,881	55,845	125,631	43,318	168,949
1977	43,465	5,763	49,228	125,823	64,154	189,977
1978	34,835	4,307	39,142	127,805	54,827	182,632
1979	30,426	3,727	34,153	135,914	33,215	169,129
Total	1,409,631	327,847	1,737,478	3,304,995	585,051	3,890,046

'RENEWAL STRATEGIES'

For a considerable time this issue of the social function of areas was dealt with largely by ignoring it. The 1974 Housing Act, however, which represented a major reorientation of policy, brought it to the fore. To quote from DoE Circular 13/75 *Renewal Strategies*:

The housing activity of many urban local authorities was, for many years, dominated by the need to clear and redevelop areas of old housing for which no other solution was available, a process which often enabled extra homes to be built for families on the waiting list. Not unnaturally, run-down areas not already in the clearance programme were often assumed to be suitable only for demolition and redevelopment in due course. Residents of privately rented dwellings were usually believed to be content to change their tenancy for that of a council house or flat; adverse blighting effects of clearance and the dispersal of communities was seen as being more than outweighed by the benefits conferred by the improvement in housing standards. Within the last few years, however, the position has altered significantly. Except in a few cities the programme of large-scale slum clearance should now be drawing to a close. Where authorities have been seeking to clear housing, especially dwellings which are fit or owner-occupied, it has proved much less easy to demonstrate that redevelopment is the best course, and resistance to such action has been increasing from residents of all kinds.[10]

Emphasis is laid on a comprehensive strategy on an area basis implementing a policy of 'gradual renewal'. A further quotation from this most important circular is appropriate:

Gradual renewal is a continuous process of minor rebuilding and renovation which sustains and reinforces the vitality of a neighbourhood in ways responsive to social and physical needs as they develop and change. Rehabilitation should take place to varying standards to match the effective demand of individual occupiers. Successful management of rehabilitation, in particular, will call for a more flexible attitude by local authorities towards the rate at which desirable standards of renovation are adopted. It must be accepted – and willingly – that some houses of low quality meet a real need for cheap accommodation, a need which might not otherwise be satisfied. It would not always be sensible to press for the immediate rehabilitation of all dwellings in an area to the full ('ten-point') standard or more, or to clear them, until they cease to fulfill their present social function. For example, sub-standard dwellings occupied by elderly persons could, *if this were the residents' wish*, remain largely undisturbed for the time being, except for the carrying out of basic repairs and elementary improvements (e.g. hot water supply, better heating) with the help of the new grants where appropriate. Authorities should also consider the possibility of selective acquisition of dwellings, or rehousing of certain residents, to prevent the undue deterioration of a neighbourhood or enable better use to be made of the housing stock.[11]

The powers (and duties) conferred by the 1974 Housing Act centre upon areas of particular housing stress. Local housing authorities are required to consider the need for dealing with these as Housing Action Areas. (Confusingly this is the term used in Scotland for the different purposes described later.)

Housing Action Areas in England and Wales are areas where 'the living conditions are unsatisfactory and can most effectively be dealt with within a period of five years so as to secure – (*a*) the improvement of the housing accommodation in the area as a whole, and (*b*) the well-being of the persons for the time being residing in the area, and (*c*) the proper and effective management and use of that accommodation'. Physical conditions are to be measured by traditional indices, but particular importance is to be attached to social conditions, including not only the proportion of households lacking amenities or living in overcrowded conditions, but also the proportion living in privately rented accommodation, and 'the concentration in the area of households likely to have special housing problems – for instance old-age pensioners, large families, single-parent families, or families whose head is unemployed or in a low income group'.[12]

It should be noted that, in a Housing Action Area, *action* is of the essence – 'within a period of five years'. To achieve this goal, there is a range of powers: for acquisition, rehabilitation, protection from eviction, environmental improvement – indeed, for any action which is required to remove the underlying causes of housing stress in the area, to arrest and reverse deterioration, and to effect real improvements in the living conditions of those living in the area. But 'a basic – and novel – feature of HAAs is the statutory provision which makes the well-being of the people living in them one of the requirements for, and objects of, declaration. This means involving people and groups, in the scale, nature, and timing of proposed action programmes.' There is thus an explicit role for neighbourhood groups and such organisations as tenants' co-operatives and housing associations. Local authorities have extensive powers to compel private landlords to repair or improve properties in an HAA, and a miscellany of grants is available, for improvement, repairs and 'environmental works'.

Prior to the 1980 Housing Act, local authorities could declare Priority Neighbourhoods in area adjacent to HAAs. Here the objective was 'to prevent the housing position in or around stress areas from deteriorating further and to stop stress from rippling out from areas which were the subject of concentrated action, normally by use of HAA powers'. They could also 'serve to pave the way for later, more intensive, action by HAA treatment if still needed, or by GIA action of a kind which cannot be undertaken immediately'. (GIAs – General Improvement Areas – are discussed below.) Despite its title, a Priority Neighbourhood was essentially one which was suitable for HAA (or GIA) treatment, but where this was, for the time being, impracticable.

In fact, very few Priority Neighbourhoods were declared: the concept proved to be a singularly meaningless one, 'amounting to little more than a declaration of intent to treat an area as an HAA or GIA in due course – which due course was rarely reached'.[13]

General Improvement Areas (which were originally provided for by the 1969 Housing Act) were envisaged as being areas 'of fundamentally sound houses capable of providing good living conditions for many years to come and unlikely to be affected by known redevelopment or major planning proposals'.

The Housing Policy Review, in discussing progress with improvement policies, concluded that the tendency has been for 'a growing proportion of the resources devoted to renovation to go into the relatively high quality improvements . . . rather than into an attack on the most serious problems – the large numbers of houses, mainly in the private sector, which are unfit or without basic amenities'.[14] A change in emphasis was proposed: 'work on the renovation of older houses should be directed more at bringing larger numbers of houses up to a decent basic standard rather than on higher standard improvements of a smaller number of houses'.[15]

EMPHASIS ON NEED

The 1980 Housing Act provided the legislative framework for this new emphasis. The important features of this are described in DoE Circular 21/80 (*Housing Acts 1974 and 1980: Improvement of Older Housing*) – from which the quotations in this section are taken. The major objective is 'to secure a more flexible system that will get resources more effectively to the properties that most need improving and to those persons who have most need of financial help to undertake improvements and essential repairs'. The grant system has been overhauled and made more flexible. The standards which must be attained after improvement have been reduced, the scope of repairs grants have been widened, tenants generally have been given 'the right to improve' and to obtain the various types of grants which are available. The three main grants are *improvement grants* (given at the discretion of the local authority), *intermediate grants* for standard amenities (which can be claimed as of right) and *repairs grants* for pre-1919 dwellings. (Improvement and intermediate grants can cover repairs, but 'repairs only' grants are restricted to pre-1919 dwellings 'in order to concentrate the available resources on tackling structural disrepair in those houses shown by surveys to be most at risk of falling into unfitness'.)

The rates of grant vary but, except for intermediate grants where fixed limits apply to each of the standard amenities (for example, for a fixed bath or shower £375 in Greater London and £285 elsewhere), are generally a percentage of 'eligible expenses'. These rates have been made more flexible by the 1980 Act in order to give local authorities more freedom to pay an amount of grant which they consider to be 'appropriate to the circumstances of the dwelling and the applicant'. Furthermore, 'the new rates of grant distinguish between priority and non-priority cases, in order to enable local authorities to direct resources towards those properties which are most in need of renovation and most likely to be occupied by those who are elderly or on low incomes, and therefore least able to improve them'.

The considerably larger role of income-related criteria in these new provisions is in striking contrast to the original policy in relation to improvement grants where no account was taken of income: the whole emphasis was on the suitability of dwellings for improvement.[16]

Some changes have also been made for area improvement. Most of these have the effect of reducing central controls, but of particular significance is the increase in grant aid for 'environmental works'. 'For GIAs, the new limit equals the number of dwellings in the area at declaration multiplied by £400; for HAAs, it equals the number of dwellings, together with houses in multiple occupation and hostels, at declaration, multiplied by £400. This is a significant increase over the previous levels, particularly in housing action areas where the multiplying factor was previously £50. The combination of these wider powers and increased eligible expenditure limits is intended to give a significant new impetus to environmental works in improvement areas, particularly in HAAs.'[17]

Despite the major numerical achievements in slum clearance and in improvements, the fact remains that Britain has an 'elderly' housing stock which requires continual repair and maintenance. One of the disturbing facts revealed by a comparison of the 1971 and 1976 English house condition surveys was that the number of dwellings which were neither unfit nor lacking amenities but which required 'substantial repairs' (over £1,000 in 1976 prices) more than doubled, from 485,000 to 1 million.[18] The problems of bad housing are likely to change rather than be solved, and the changes (whether in 'objective' conditions or in perceptions) may well require shifts of direction in policy. In this connection DoE Circular 20/80 is of particular interest: this describes and commends to local authorities two additional ways in which substandard housing can be improved. The first, known as the Local Authority Improvement for Sale Scheme, 'is based on the premise that authorities improve or repair houses themselves and then sell them'. The second is 'homesteading': the sale of unimproved houses subject to the condition that they are improved by the purchaser. The circular comments: 'For the individual who is prepared to put the time and effort into improving a property, this is often the lowest cost route to home-ownership. Local authorities can support such enterprise and enthusiasm by making improvement grants available, offering improvement loans and granting mortgages or mortgage guarantees to building societies.' Discounts in price and waiver of interest payments for up to five years are available under certain conditions by virtue of the provisions of the Housing Act 1980.[19]

SCOTTISH POLICIES

Scottish housing is different from that south of the Border in significant ways. There is a high proportion of tenemental properties; dwellings tend to be smaller; rents are lower; and over a half of the housing stock is owned by public authorities. Building costs and building standards – but not space standards – are also higher. These and other differences reflect history, economic growth and decline, local building materials and climate.

Scottish housing legislation and policies are similarly different, and are becoming more so as the quantitative housing shortage is falling to small proportions. Above all, Scotland faces a major problem of tenemental slums. Though a third of a million dwellings have been demolished since the war, there still remain very large numbers of slums. A 1973 Scottish White Paper estimated the figure to be in the range 180,000–190,000: some 10 per cent of the stock.[20] The 1970 Green Paper put the figure at around 160,000.[21] The clearance or improvement of these slums still constitutes a major housing problem in Scotland.

As in England and Wales, increasing emphasis is being placed on improvement as distinct from clearance as the generally preferred policy. But with much of the older tenemental properties, particularly in central urban areas, the scope for improvement is severely restricted by the decayed fabric of the buildings, the internal physical layout of the tenements and the high cost of alterations – not to mention the severe practical problems created by multiple ownership. The tenemental problem in Scotland is of a markedly different physical and financial nature from that of terraced houses in England and Wales.[22]

Nevertheless, the social issues are very similar, and the Housing (Scotland) Act 1974 is aimed at providing procedures and subsidies which will 'enable authorities to ensure that as much as possible of their sub-standard housing stock is improved to an acceptable standard, while houses which cannot effectively be improved are demolished'.[23]

All area policies are dealt with under Housing Action Area procedures. (Though the term is the same as in England and Wales the meaning is quite different.) There are three types of HAA: for demolition, for improvement, or for a combination of the two. For an area to be declared a 'housing action area for demolition', more than half of the houses* must be below the tolerable standard. A 'housing

*The English reader should note that the Scots use the term 'house' to mean the same as the English 'dwelling', that is, it embraces a flat or tenement.

action area for improvement' or 'for demolition and improvement' can be declared where more than half the houses are either below the tolerable standard or lack one or more of the standard amenities.

It is not possible here to detail all the provisions relating to Scottish HAAs: the following is merely a brief summary.

The most striking feature of the new system is the power given to local authorities for the *compulsory improvement* of houses in areas where most of the houses lack one or more of the standard amenities. The need for this (certainly in tenemental property – where the biggest problem lies) stems from the fact that the improvement of *some* of the houses in a tenement cannot normally be carried out without affecting the other houses. To put the matter simply: it frequently is a case of 'all or nothing'. The declaration of an improvement HAA is, however, in essence a declaration of intent: it is a clear and definite proclamation by the local authority that the future of an area is to be safeguarded and that marked improvements are to be made – to the environment as well as to the houses.

Given the peculiar characteristics of tenemental property, it is typically necessary to ensure that improvements are planned *as one operation* to all the houses (at least in a close or stair, if not in the block as a whole). Concerted action of this kind can sometimes be done by the landlords or, more frequently, their factors (agents), but in any case some 'external organisation' is necessary. One method of doing this is by the establishment of *ad hoc* housing associations. Experiments in this direction are under way (particularly in Glasgow) with the assistance of the Housing Corporation.

Higher rates of improvement grant are available – and mandatory – in these areas: 75 per cent of approved costs instead of the normal 50 per cent (rising to 90 per cent where this is justified by the financial circumstances of the owner). Discretionary grants are also available, on a similar basis, for repairs. Expenditure to be met by owners can be financed by loans from the local authority.

These provisions also include a requirement that the local authority must allow two months 'for representations from the people affected and must take account of these before making a final resolution declaring a housing action area'. This is a legalistic formulation of an obligation on local authorities to act sensitively in accordance with the wishes of the people living in HAAs.

The Secretary of State attaches particular importance to this requirement, and he would urge local authorities to make the fullest use of this period to consult those affected, explaining and discussing the proposals with them. He considers that full consultation with the residents and a sensitive and sympathetic response to their wishes for the future of the area will go far to obviate opposition or resistance to what is proposed, and to ensure that once a final resolution is made the work it entails will proceed as quickly as possible.[24]

By contrast with the elaborate statutory provisions for improvement in England and Wales, the Scottish system appears remarkably simple. This is not the place to speculate on the reasons for this difference (which can equally be seen in the planning field): suffice it to say that while the English try to attain flexibility by a complex range of powers to be *adopted* by local authorities according to their various circumstances, the Scots prefer broad powers within which flexibility can be attained by local *adaptation*.

But both approaches are characterised by more sensitivity. It would be an exaggeration to say that the 'bulldozer' has been banished: given the foul conditions in some areas no alternative is possible. But clearly the relevance of this approach now has to be much more carefully established before it is employed.

THINKING ON AREA POLICIES

Several major elements can be identified in the development of thinking on deprived areas in Britain:[25] inadequate physical conditions, the presence of a 'large' number of coloured people (usually referred to as 'immigrants'), educational 'disadvantage' and a multiplicity of less easily measurable 'social problems'.

For a very long time there was a preoccupation with inadequate physical conditions (particularly in relation to plumbing). Indeed, British housing policy developed from sanitary policy,[26] and it still remains a significant feature of it. Area policy in relation to housing was almost entirely restricted to slum clearance until the late 1960s when concepts of housing improvement widened – first to the improvement of areas of housing and then to environmental improvement. Despite a number of social surveys[27] the policy was unashamedly physical: so much so that increasing powers were provided to *compel* reluctant owners and tenants to have improvements carried out. Only recently has attention been focused on the social character and function of areas of old housing.[28]

A further area of policy in the field of housing came as a response to the problems of controlling multi-occupation and overcrowding in areas of 'housing stress'. The Milner Holland Committee looked favourably on the idea of designating the worst areas as *areas of special control* in which 'some authority might be set up, with responsibility for the whole area and armed with wide powers to control sales and lettings, to acquire property by agreement or compulsorily over the whole area or part of it, to demolish and rebuild as necessary, to require improvements to be carried out or undertake such improvements themselves, and to make grants on a more generous and flexible basis than under the present law'.[29]

Similarly, the National Committee for Commonwealth Immigrants, starting from a concern for the socio-economic problems facing local authorities with substantial numbers of immigrant families, argued for the designation of *areas of special housing need*.[30] Again, the crucial issue was the control over overcrowding, exorbitant rents, insanitary conditions, disrepair and the risk of fire. The NCCI, however, noted that it was not possible to consider areas such as these 'without considering the deficiencies in all other social services that exist within such an area, and the need to rehabilitate these services at the same time as examining housing problems'.

These proposals were not accepted by the government, though increased powers to control multi-occupation and abuses were provided. Part of the reason for this was that there was considerable doubt as to the efficacy of measures designed to *control*. The NCCI Report had referred to the need for treating the problems of the stress areas 'patiently and tactfully', for giving the public 'every opportunity to understand the steps which are being undertaken' and for seeking the 'active and willing co-operation' of voluntary organisations and community groups. Indeed, without this they saw the likelihood of their proposed solution creating 'problems almost as serious as those which are being alleviated'.

It was left to the Seebohm, Skeffington and Plowden Reports to probe more deeply into this area. Before discussing this, it is interesting to note how opinion changed by the turn of the decade. Reviewing the problems of the stress areas, the Francis Report (published in March 1971) flatly stated that 'there is no short term solution to this terrible problem'.[31] Large-scale public acquisition was not even discussed: instead they proposed the designation of areas of housing stress where local authorities should be under a statutory duty 'to give information and advice to landlords and tenants', to check rents, to act in cases of harassment and unlawful eviction, and in extreme cases to temporarily take over the management of individual houses. The value of housing aid centres and legal advice and assistance was underlined.

It is unfortunate that the Committee did not spell out the philosophy underlying their recommendations, but it appears that they were impressed by the limits of public action, the need for preserving a stock of privately rented accommodation and, above all, the need for flexibility, persuasion and negotiation. But no reference was made to non-housing issues: the Committee faithfully restricted their attention to their narrow terms of reference.

Not so the Plowden Committee: appointed in August 1963, 'to consider primary education *in all its aspects*', they reported four years later in very broad terms.[32] They appreciated and underlined the complex of factors which produced seriously disadvantaged areas. Researchers are faced with attempting to abstract and measure the importance of individual factors when 'all other things are equal'. Policy-makers and administrators, on the other hand, 'must act in a world where other things are never equal; this, too, is the world in which the children grow up, where everything influences everything else, where nothing succeeds like success and nothing fails like failure. The outlook and aspirations of their own parents; the opportunities and handicaps of the neighbourhood in which they live; the skill of their teachers and the resources of the schools they go to; their genetic inheritance; and other factors still unmeasured or unknown surround the children with a seamless web of circumstances.'[33]

This web of circumstances is neatly illustrated in the following further quotation:

> In a neighbourhood where the jobs people do and the status they hold owe little to their education, it is natural for children as they grow older to regard school as a brief prelude to work rather than an avenue to future opportunities . . . Not surprisingly, many teachers are unwilling to work in a neighbourhood where the schools are old, where housing of the sort they want is unobtainable, and where education does not attain the standards they expect for their own children. From some neighbourhoods, urban and rural, there has been a continuing flow of the more successful young people. The loss of enterprise and skill makes things worse for those left behind. Thus, the vicious circle may turn from generation to generation and the schools play a central part in the process, both causing and suffering cumulative deprivation.

The Plowden Committee recommended a national policy of 'positive discrimination', the aim of which would be to make schools in the most deprived areas as good as the best in the country. Additional resources were necessary to achieve this: extra teachers and special salary increases; teachers' aides; priority for replacement and improvement in the school building programme; extra books and equipment; and expanded provision for nursery education.

The Seebohm Committee had wider terms of reference than the Plowden Committee: 'To review the organization and responsibilities of the local authority personal social services in England and Wales, and to consider what changes are desirable to secure an effective family service.' Of relevance to the present discussion is the Committee's concern for 'social planning' (which is dealt with largely in terms of administrative organisation) and their recommendations in relation to *areas of special need*. Unfortunately, the Committee did not suggest how these should be identified in spite of a recommendation that the areas should be accorded priority in the allocation of resources: 'We are convinced that designated areas of special need should receive extra resources comprehensively planned in co-operation with services both central and local, concerned with health, education, housing and other social needs.'[34]

The Committee ventured a view that areas of special need 'have a profusion of pressing social problems, offer only a dismal and squalid physical environment, are inadequately served by social services and are considered to justify special attention and a generous allocation of resources'. But, beyond a reference to the Plowden Report and *The Needs of New Communities*,[35] the only other comment was that 'recognized *problem* areas appear to lack a sense of community'.

More helpful and perspicacious was their reference to citizen participation, which underlined a point hardly recognised by the Skeffington Committee[36] even though they were specifically concerned with it. It was Seebohm, not Skeffington, who clearly saw that, if area action was to be based on the wishes of the inhabitants and carried out with their participation, 'the participants may wish to pursue policies directly at variance with the ideas of the local authorities . . . Participation provides a means by which further consumer control may be exercised over professional and bureaucratic power.'[37]

This is an issue which will be discussed in a broader context in the final chapter. Here we need to briefly survey some of the ways in which the development of thinking on 'deprived areas' was translated into policy.

THE URBAN PROGRAMME

Area policies in relation to housing improvement, however inadequate they may have been, were based on long experience of dealing with slum clearance and redevelopment. With other area policies there was no such base to work upon, and both legislation and practice was hesitant and experimental.

Legislatively, the important landmarks (modest though they were) were the Local Government Act 1966 (section 11) and the Local Government (Social Need) Act of 1969. These constituted the statutory basis for the Educational Priority Areas Programme and the Urban Aid Programme. The 1966 Act provided for grants in aid of staff costs involved in 'dealing with some of the transitional [*sic*] problems caused by the presence of Commonwealth immigrants'. The Urban Programme was broader in concept, 'designed to raise the level of social services in areas of acute social need, and thus help to provide an equal opportunity for all citizens'.[38]

'Areas of special social need' were not defined in the legislation, but government circulars referred to 'localised districts, within the boundaries of an urban authority, which bear the marks of multiple deprivation, such as old, overcrowded, decrepit houses without plumbing and sanitation; persistent unemployment; family sizes above the average, a high proportion of children in trouble or in need of care; or a combination of some or all of these'.[39]

This 'Traditional Urban Programme' (as it is termed in the DoE consultation paper of March 1980)[40] was progressively widened in scope,
extended to embrace voluntary organisations and (as announced in the
1977 White Paper *Policy for the Inner Cities*) extended to cover
industrial, environmental and recreational provision. Its expenditure
was increased and (in 1977) the major co-ordinative responsibility for
the programme was transferred from the Home Office to the Department of the Environment.

It is difficult to give a coherent account of this Programme (and its
'near relations' – referred to below) since its objectives were never
clearly spelled out and its extreme flexibility gave rise to a great deal of
confusion. Indeed it was even suggested at one time that it was 'simply
an extremely versatile ministerial weapon whose very flexibility allows
its use to be extended into any social field in which at any particular
time the government is accused of being insufficiently involved'.[41]

As the Royal Town Planning Institute noted in its response to the
Consultation Document, 'Trad Up' (to use the jargon abbreviation)
had become 'somewhat confusing in conception and procedure'.[42]
With the development (discussed below) of inner city partnerships and
'programme authorities' (which are not eligible for urban programme
funds) the position has become even more confused. However, in an
attempt to provide a reasonably clear account, the situation regarding
'Trad Up' is described up to the end of 1980.

Following the review of the traditional programme, it was decided
'notwithstanding the necessity to reduce public expenditure overall' to
continue the programme 'to help reduce urban deprivation at the local
level' in those authorities which were not 'inner city partnerships' and
'programme authorities'.[43] Local authorities with areas of 'special
need' were invited (in September 1980) to submit proposals which had
the aim 'to alleviate directly or indirectly the urban deprivation
identified in that area'. The policy guidance continued:

The Government wishes a high priority to be given to schemes run
by the voluntary sector which enable community and other groups
to devise and put into action cost effective and imaginative ways to
improve local conditions, or to enable local people to become more
self-reliant. Local authorities are asked to consider a balanced
package in relation to the projects put forward:
- involving the local community in the area to be served by the
  project;
- encouraging self help schemes;
- involving local firms and businesses in providing advice, financial
  backing, or other assistance towards the operation of a project;
- meeting the particular needs of ethnic minorities;
- having regard to the needs of the disabled (1981 has been

designated by the United Nations as the International Year of Disabled People);
– meeting the needs of the under-fives.

In addition to this wide-ranging miscellany, it is specifically stated that 'projects to promote the economic regeneration of urban areas' are to be encouraged and a proportion of the available funds set aside for this purpose.

OTHER COMMUNITY PROGRAMMES

The Urban Aid Programme was the major plank of the 'deprived area policy' stage. Additionally there were the Community Development Projects (which produced a veritable spate of publications ranging from carefully researched analysis to neo-marxist denunciations of the basic 'structural' weaknesses of capitalist society – though the original aim had been 'to overcome the sense of disintegration and depersonalisation felt by residents of deprived areas'.[44] There were twelve CDPs in all: in Birmingham (Saltley), Coventry (Hillfields), Cumbria (Cleator Moor), Glamorgan (Glyncorrwg), Liverpool (Vauxhall), Newham (Canning Town), Newcastle (Benwell), Oldham (Clarksfield), Paisley (Ferguslie Park), Southwark (Newington), Tynemouth (Percy and Trinity), and West Yorkshire (Batley).

Additionally, 1974 saw the introduction of a small number of Comprehensive Community Programmes (CCPs) in areas of 'intense urban deprivation'.

This is not the place to set out a complete list of the initiatives in this field – which, in any case, is still in a state of flux.[45] The subtleties have to be ignored in favour of more tangible events such as the publication of a White Paper or the passage of legislation. One preliminary point, however, needs to be made: as experience in deprived areas grew (and as unemployment increased) there was an increasing emphasis on economic as distinct from social policies. Given the vagueness of the articulated policy goals this is not as apparent as it might have been; indeed, to state the matter as baldly as this may be to exaggerate the situation. Moreover, as we shall see, it was not only the marxists who were (or increasingly became) critical of the very concept of area-based policies.

SETTING UP SIX TOWNS

The subheading (with a *double entendre*?) is the title of a review by Des McConaghy[46] of the 'Urban Guidelines' and 'Inner Area' studies.[47] The former have been overshadowed by the latter, partly because they had an 'action' element and partly because they had a higher political profile. Moreover, coming somewhat later, they were more clearly identified with the development of policy in relation to the inner areas.

(The White Paper makes specific reference to the inner area studies but ignores the urban guidelines studies.) There were, however, many other studies:[48] indeed, there is a bewildering number of them, and it is not easy to trace the impacts (if any) which each had on policy. The now almost-forgotten SNAP (the Shelter Neighbourhood Action Project) was probably particularly influential.[49]

No attempt is made here to summarise this mass of material but, for the inner area studies, the reader is referred to the useful volume of summaries.[50]

THE INNER CITIES 'POLICY'

The White Paper *Policy for the Inner Cities* was published in June 1977.[51] It was followed by the Inner Urban Areas Act (which received Royal Assent on 31 July 1978). This in turn was followed by a major departmental circular.[52]

Briefly, 'the policy' is 'to give additional powers to local authorities with severe inner area problems so that they may participate more effectively in the economic development of their areas'.[53] The provisions apply only to designated districts of which there are three types. The original designations were as follows.

Districts containing 'Special Areas' (Partnership Areas)

Birmingham	Islington
Greenwich	Lambeth
Lewisham	Liverpool
Newham	Manchester
Southwark	Salford
Tower Hamlets	Newcastle upon Tyne
Hackney	Gateshead

Districts containing Inner Area Programmes (Programme Authority Areas)

Bolton	Nottingham
Bradford	Oldham
Hammersmith	Sheffield
Kingston upon Hull	South Tyneside
Leeds	Sunderland
Leicester	Wirral
Middlesbrough	Wolverhampton
North Tyneside	

Other Districts

ENGLAND

Barnsley	Rochdale
Blackburn	Rotherham

Brent	St Helens
Doncaster	Sandwell
Ealing	Sefton
Haringey	Wandsworth
Hartlepool	Wigan

WALES

Blaenau Gwent	Rhondda
Cardiff	Swansea
Newport	

All the forty-eight designated areas have powers to make loans and grants for industrial building and to declare Improvement Areas (not to be confused with the General Improvement Areas for housing). The circular notes the latter as 'the most novel power in the Act'. It continues:

> It is expected that these will usually be areas of run-down industrial buildings, but the power could also be applied to older commercial areas or to areas of mixed industrial and commercial use. The declaration of an Improvement Area can be an effective means of stabilising the economic life of an older industrial or commercial area but indiscriminate use of the new power will reduce its effectiveness.

The powers are somewhat more extensive in relation to 'special areas': these are the so-called partnership areas where special administrative arrangements exist. The second category of designated districts have no formal partnership arrangements but are 'invited to draw up inner area programmes'. The remainder are simply designated districts which can make use of the powers provided by the Inner Urban Areas Act.

URBAN REGENERATION

Economic regeneration has now taken pride of place over public participation and the distributional effects of planning. The transition has been gradual and, of course, is one of degree; but there is no doubt (certainly at the time of writing in early 1981) that economic development has become of predominant importance.

Writing in 1980, Hambleton, Stewart and Underwood noted that:

> whilst not being explicitly spelt out, the present government seems to be shifting the content of inner city policy away from an emphasis on social measures to help deprived groups towards measures designed to generate wealth creation and stimulate private

sector activity in inner areas. This emphasis has never been fully articulated.[54]

The emphasis has, however, increasingly moved. The 1977 White Paper spoke of local authorities needing 'to stimulate investment by the private sector, by firms and by individuals, in industry, in commerce, and in housing'.[55] The 1981 review of inner city policy concluded (in the words of the Secretary of State for the Environment) that 'the private sector should be encouraged to play the fullest possible part. I therefore intend to make effective consultation with local industry and commerce a prior condition of providing urban programme grant.'[56]

ENTERPRISE ZONES

More tangible is the establishment of enterprise zones.[57] The announcement on these was made with a strong side swipe at main-stream traditional 'town and country planning'.[58]

> Introducing his proposals, the Chancellor said that there were some parts of the economy, particularly in the older urban areas, where more and more public authority involvement had apparently led to less and less fruitful activity. The planning process had all too often allowed, or even encouraged, whole areas, at the heart of some of the most populous cities, to be laid waste for years. Even when development plans were finally made, the public purse was often unable to provide the funds or the enterprise to match the planners' aspirations. And when private initiative might have been ready to act, it had generally been stifled by rules and regulations.[59]

Enterprise zones (for which provision is made in the 1980 Local Government, Planning and Land Act) benefit from exemption from development land tax, 100 per cent capital allowances, exemption from general rates on industrial and commercial property, and so forth. Additionally they are subject to 'simplified' planning procedures:

> It is proposed that there should be a plan for each enterprise zone prepared by the relevant local authority or development corporation and approved, prior to designation, by the Secretary of State. The plan would show which classes of development were permitted in each part of the enterprise zone; it would set out any conditions governing development e.g. those needed for health or safety or for the control of pollution; and it would specify any 'reserved matters'. Following designation, developers would not need to apply for planning permission for development that conformed to the zoning and conditions in the plan. They might need approval from the local

authority, or development corporation for the 'reserved matters', but these would relate to details such as access to the highway. Approval for developments that did not conform to the plan would require individual application in the normal way.[60]

How these provisions will work out remains to be seen. Patrick O'Leary has warned that 'dismantling planning machinery takes longer than setting it up'.[61] The local authority concerned (or local authorities where a zone straddles boundaries) has to negotiate with a range of statutory bodies, publish proposals, assess local reaction and make any appropriate changes, sit through the statutory six weeks during which legal challenge can be made, and finally make a formal submission to the Secretary of State for the Environment. If the proposals are to his liking (and also to the Chancellor of the Exchequer's) a designation order is laid before the House. Assuming that no MP prays against it, the enterprise zone officially comes into existence.

Enterprise zones cover around 200 hectares and total (in March 1981) eleven: eight in England, and one each in Scotland, Wales and Northern Ireland.

The 1981 Budget Speech referred with enthusiasm to the eleven enterprise zones which 'have stimulated intense interest among investors and the private sector has begun to respond even before the zones are formally established'.[62] Nevertheless, more was needed to assist the development of 'the small business sector'. Among the measures announced in the 1981 Budget Speech was the introduction of 'the business start-up scheme' (providing for a personal annual tax allowance of up to £10,000 for investment in newly started businesses); a strengthening of the advisory services of the Council for Small Industries in Rural Areas (COSIRA) and parallel services in urban areas; and a pilot loan guarantee scheme (involving up to £50m. annually of public funds) which will provide for 80 per cent guarantees on loans of up to £75,000, with maturities of between two and seven years. The latter is of particular interest: it is a well-developed feature in the policies of European countries, and simply aims at providing loan finance for businesses which, though viable, do not meet the normal criteria of the traditional lending institutions.

URBAN DEVELOPMENT CORPORATIONS

Yet a further economic innovation is the establishment of urban development corporations 'to secure . . . regeneration'.[63] At the time of writing (in early 1981) only two were proposed – for the London Docklands and for Merseyside. Though based on the experience of the new town development corporations, the urban development corporations have far wider powers. Indeed some of the provisions of the legislation are staggering. No public inquiry into designation is required, and powers over land are breathtaking. The secretary of state can make an order authorising that land held by local authorities, statutory undertakers, or other public bodies, both inside and outside the Urban Development Area, be vested in the UDC. Land held by Mersey Docks and Harbour Board, the Port of London Authority and the Gas Board will thus be automatically transferred to the UDC without any right of appeal. This will apply whether or not the land is in use or is included in plans for redevelopment.

The powers certainly appear to be sufficient to facilitate the government's strategy to speed up the planning process and release public land for private commercial and residential developers.[64]

Particular emphasis is placed on the role of private enterprise in development and in planning. Heavy reliance is to be placed on consultants and, in the words of Basil Bean, Chief Executive-Designate of the Merseyside Urban Development Corporation: 'We want a much greater partnership with the private sector, including joint companies and investment partnerships with banks. And this will be extending to the running of the organisation. We won't be hiring an army of architects and planners, but we shall be using private sector consultants wherever possible.'[65]

THE 'CAMPAIGN FOR URBAN RENAISSANCE'

Following European Heritage Year which, according to official sources, 'proved such a success in stimulating public awareness in the conservation of historically and architecturally important places and buildings',[66] the Council of Europe launched the 'European Campaign for Urban Renaissance' which is intended 'to embrace the much wider theme of urban renewal and the improvement of urban living, and is aimed principally at exchanging experience between the countries of the Council of Europe'.[67] The campaign is focusing on five issues:

- improving urban environmental quality;
- rehabilitating areas of older buildings;
- providing social, cultural and economic opportunities;
- achieving community development and participation; and
- illustrating the role of local authorities.

The UK is the host country for the launching of the campaign, and the DoE and the Central Office of Information have produced a 'glossy' report on 'post-war experience of urban change'. The coverage of the report – and the campaign – however, is so wide as to make separate discussion inappropriate. (Indeed it makes a useful pictorial supplement to many of the issues discussed in the present volume.) Nevertheless, there is one point of particular importance which tends to be ignored in international comparisons of this nature, namely, the very different histories of the different countries.[68] The industrial revolution largely bypassed the ancient cities such as Canterbury, Winchester and York. It grew in the great new towns of Birmingham, Manchester, Sheffield, and so forth. By contrast, the typical situation on the continent was for industry to develop in existing historic centres such as Bordeaux and Hamburg. As the post-industrial revolution developed, the new industrial towns of Britain (as of the US) were in a position of having outlived their usefulness, and they began a long and dramatic decline. Their outdated physical infrastructure (and frequently their unloveliness and their relatively unattractive climate), in addition to their lack of employment opportunities, led to massive migration to more attractive areas (selected as locations for the newer firms precisely because of their environmental attractiveness).

In John Young's words,[69] 'there is almost certainly no way in which [the older industrial cities] can be restored to their former pre-eminence. Britain is in the process of a new industrial revolution which, if successful, will replace much of its old manufacturing sector with new industries based on advanced technology. Developments in communications are likely to mean that even the white collar commuters, who have sustained the economic life of cities in recent years will either be reduced in numbers or will find it cheaper and more convenient to work elsewhere. But that does not mean, or ought to mean, that our cities will simply wither away.'

It is worth exploring this issue further in a broader context – that of the economic change in the conurbations.

THE TRANSFORMATION OF THE CONURBATIONS

Underlying the transition from a physical policy concerned with deteriorated housing to a social policy in aid of deprived areas and then to an economic policy for strengthening the base for local growth, is the dramatic change which has taken place in the character of inner cities. In the words of the Cambridge Economic Policy Group:

> The conurbations grew as industrial centres, but since the mid-1950s have progressively been converted into service centres. People have moved out of the conurbations, but increasingly commute in both for employment and for access to services. It cannot necessarily be assumed that these trends will continue in the same form in the future. For example, new technology may undermine the centralisation of services, making inward commuting less necessary and leaving the inner areas of conurbations without any clear function. In spite of the difficulties stronger policies are urgently needed, even though such policies are bound to involve some change in the advantages of different groups, notably among those working

outside the cities, the commuters and the residents of inner cities themselves.[70]

Currently, explicit inner city policies are restricted to selected areas. It is not clear whether this is for 'experimental' reasons (we are not sure *how* to go about solving the problem) or, more simply, for financial reasons (there is not enough money to go round). But it is clear that to attempt to explain – or even to describe – 'the inner city problem' is to fall into a major trap. There is no such thing as *the* 'inner city', still less a conceivable set of plans for it. The historian has the luxury of looking backwards and attempting to explain what happened why, when and where,[71] but those concerned with current issues have no such privilege. They have to wrestle with the pressing, and perhaps misleadingly articulated, problems of today. Their immediate focus is on the 'inadequacy' of government grant aid, on the 'decline' in their populations (a severe blow to civic pride) and on the apparently inexorable economic trends of which they bear the brunt. They may be told – and may accept in their hearts – that 'a city must draw upon the interests and energies of its people if it is truly to flourish',[72] yet they see only continued decline in their population and tax base. The natural reaction is to 'stop overspill', but this may do more harm than good since it is not the exodus of people that is unusual: it is the lack of newcomers. By reducing the opportunities for outward movement, an inner city area may well exacerbate the very problems it is attempting to solve.[73]

Cities (and still less 'inner cities') are not islands: they are part of the wider dynamic of change. Traditionally urban populations have improved their conditions by moving out to suburban locations and, in the process, have made room for newcomers, who have chosen the central cities because of the opportunities which they have provided. The situation is now more complex. There have been changes in the economic structure of cities (and the regions of which they form a part), in the ease of mobility (which greatly increases the area of job markets), in the difficulties of access to good-quality housing (considerably exacerbated by housing policies which have strangled the private provision of rental housing and made inner city owner-occupation prohibitively expensive for the majority), in new laws of settlement (operated through the council housing system and through bureaucratic and political stances in relation to 'homelessness') and, more generally, in the character of the post-industrial city.

These are but some of the changes which have transformed the functions of the inner cities. When other factors such as education, urban roads (and parking), the impact of public and private forces on 'community', the spread of urban blight and dereliction, the concentration of families with children in high flats (thereby raising 'child densities' to unmanageable levels), teenage unemployment, and so forth, are added, the list becomes frightening to contemplate. And overshadowing such features are fears of racial (or sectarian) violence, of a general run-down in the quality of life and in the concentration of self-exacerbating social problems.

At the same time, the Balkanisation of the government of municipal housing in metropolitan areas has created barriers to outward movement, and before there was sufficient political agreement and will to surmount these, inner cities began to face the paradox of 'difficult to let' estates (the British public sector equivalent to the 'abandonment' problem facing some American cities).

Additionally, inner city local authorities have viewed their population declines as a sign of loss of masculinity (and more tangibly of political power); and in the face of recitals of problems such as those listed above have called upon central government for 'massive financial resources' to arrest their 'decay'.

Such an analysis of the problems is, of course, superficial and exaggerated,[74] but it has a familiar ring in the arena of political debate. The White Paper was more cautious, and noted that some of the changes which have taken place in inner cities 'are due to social and economic forces which could be reversed only with great difficulty or at unprecedented cost'. Certainly the experience of Glasgow (not to mention that of some American cities) urges caution: the massive financial resources which have been poured into that city have had little apparent effect (and annual outward migration has continued – at a rate of more than 20,000 people a year). If there is one lesson to be learned from the diversity and costliness of American approaches to urban problems, it is that money is no solution. The fact that there is little public money available might therefore be a hidden blessing in that it could concentrate attention on other approaches.

Current policies lay a heavy emphasis on institutional innovations, particularly in the area of central–local relationships – or 'partnerships' as they are diplomatically called. This faith in the relevance and efficacy of administrative organisation stems from a realisation that urban problems interlock and that advance on one front may have undesirable impacts on others. The rationale is spelled out in the White Paper thus:

> The urban studies of recent years have shown that urban problems cannot be tackled effectively on a piecemeal basis. The problems interlock: education, for example, is affected by social conditions which in turn are affected by housing and employment. The best results are likely to be achieved through a unified approach in which the different activities and services of government are brought together. Concerted action should have a greater impact. It should lead to a more efficient use of resources by avoiding duplication or conflicts of effort, and it ought to be more sensitive to the needs of

the public who do not see problems in departmental or agency terms.[75]

Though the White Paper goes on to stress that the difficulties of co-ordinating functionally organised units of government 'should not be underestimated', the underlying belief is clearly that better results can be achieved by trying harder. The 'unified approach' will, by dint of effort and goodwill, achieve what the Central Policy Review Staff have described as 'a rare achievement': 'an interdepartmental view'.[76]

The logic, however, is flawed. It does not follow that because problems 'interlock', some administrative device can provide a magic key. The vision of corporate management overcoming the multiplicity of problems of inner cities is sheer delusion born of the same thinking which gave rise to the massive (and now discredited) comprehensive redevelopment approach to urban decay. The effect is more likely to be an administrative nightmare rather than effective action. (Experience with the urban programme points up the dangers of administrative machinery dwarfing the product.)

Moreover, the 'interlocks' are easily exaggerated. Of course, all the individual problems impinge on each other – economic decline, physical decay, social disadvantage, race relations, education, local government finance, and a host of others. It is delusion, however, to think that innovations in machinery can provide a new 'coherence'. Indeed, by adding to the administrative complexities it can add to the difficulties. (It would be useful to have an analysis of the experience of the Glasgow Eastern Area Renewal project – GEAR – which is a 'concerted programme for the comprehensive regeneration' of 1,600 hectares of the city. The concert embraces not only the departments of central and (two tiers of) local government but also the Scottish Special Housing Association and the Scottish Development Agency. The GEAR *Strategy and Programme*, published in 1980, significantly bore the imprint of City of Glasgow District Council, Strathclyde Regional Council, Scottish Special Housing Association, Scottish Development Agency, Greater Glasgow Health Board, The Housing Corporation, and Manpower Services Commission.)[77]

Some of the 'interlocks' are due to conflicts in objectives, for example, between housing and anti-inflation policies; some are due to the growth of separatist programmes aimed at similar targets such as housing allowances and income maintenance; some are due to dilemmas of a single policy as with employment and 'the proper distribution of industry'.

There is no easy solution (and sometimes no practicable solution at all) to some of these issues of public policy – to which eloquent testimony is provided by the abortive Housing Policy Review.

Adapting a passage from Marc Fried (who was commenting upon the concept of poverty), 'the inner city' is 'an empirical category, not a conceptual entity, and it represents congeries of unrelated problems'. The problems posed in the inner city 'are not readily accessible for study or resolution in the name' of the inner city.⁷⁸

Progress will be made, not by 'comprehensive action' but by identifying priority fields in which effort should be concentrated. For most of the problems identified as existing in inner cities these are matters of national policy relating to all areas. (Thus, though 'poverty' is undoubtedly a problem which arises in inner cities, most of the residents are not in poverty: and most poverty is not in inner areas.) Moreover, inner cities are only parts of cities, and cities are parts of city regions.

The arguments *against* inner city (or indeed any area-based) policy are strong.⁷⁹ To the extent that the problems relate to the deprived it makes more sense to channel assistance to them directly, irrespective of where they live. Only to the extent that the problems are locationally concentrated, should remedies focus on specific locations.

None of this is to deny the importance of directly tackling those problems of decay and disadvantage which are all too apparent in many inner areas. (Nor is there any argument against the desirability of attempting better organisation of services at local levels, or improved co-ordination both within and between agencies.) What is crucial is to identify the forces which have created the problems and to establish means of stemming or redirecting them.

The danger besetting the 'inner city policy' (*sic*) is that it will attempt too much, that it will dissipate public sector energies in 'co-ordination', committee meetings, 'designation' procedures and the like, and that it will divert attention from the basic social and economic problems which are primarily not spatial in character.⁸⁰

REFERENCES AND FURTHER READING: CHAPTER 10

1 See J. Q. Wilson (ed.), *Urban Renewal: The Record and the Controversy* (MIT Press, 1966).
2 For a fuller discussion of slum clearance and improvement, see ch. 5 of the author's *Essays on Housing Policy* (Allen & Unwin, 1979).
3 Department of the Environment, *Housing Policy: Technical Volume, Part I* (HMSO, 1977), p. 159.
4 Welsh Office, *Welsh House Condition Survey 1973* (HMSO, 1975).
5 Central Housing Advisory Committee, *Our Older Homes: A Call for Action* (HMSO, 1966).
6 Scottish Housing Advisory Committee, *Scotland's Older Houses* (HMSO, 1967).
7 See, for example, Scottish Development Department, *Assessing Housing Needs: A Manual of Guidance* (HMSO, 1977), Appendix I, 'House condition surveys'.
8 For further discussion on compensation as provided for by the Land Compensation Act 1973, see Chapter 4.
9 The figures are taken from various issues of the *Annual Abstract of Statistics*.
10 DoE Circular 13/75, *Housing Act 1974: Renewal Strategies* (HMSO, 1975), para. 4.
11 op. cit., para. 23.
12 Further details are given in DoE Circular 14/75, *Housing Act 1974: Parts IV, V, VI*

- *Housing Action Areas, Priority Neighbourhoods, and General Improvement Areas* (HMSO, 1975). See also DoE Improvement Note 10, *The Use of Indicators for Area Action* (HMSO, 1975). For changes - summarised below - brought about by the Housing Act 1980, see DoE Circular 21/80, *Housing Acts 1974 and 1980: Improvement of Older Housing* (HMSO, 1980).

13 A. Arden, *Encyclopedia of Housing* (Sweet & Maxwell), Vol. 2, Release No. 75, 24 February 1981, para. 2-2943.

14 Green Paper, *Housing Policy: A Consultative Document*, Cmnd 6851 (HMSO, 1977), p. 94, para. 10.19.

15 op. cit., p. 129, para. 39.

16 In similar vein the Homes Insulation Scheme 1980 provides for a rate of grant higher (than under the original Homes Insulation Act provisions of 1978) for 'applicants in special need'. See DoE Circular 12/80, *Homes Insulation Act 1978: Homes Insulation Scheme 1980* (HMSO, 1980).

17 DoE Circular 21/80, op. cit., Appendix F, para. 10.

18 See 'The changing face of bad housing', *New Society*, vol. 55 (26 February 1981), p. 376.

19 DoE Circular 20/80, *(1) Local Authority Improvement for Sale Scheme; (2) Sale of Unimproved Homes for Improvement by Purchase - 'Homesteading'* (HMSO, 1980). See also DoE Circular Letter, *Sales of Council Houses and Flats and Disposal of Housing Land* (Department of the Environment, 2 September 1980).

20 White Paper, *Towards Better Homes: Proposals for Dealing with Scotland's Older Housing*, Cmnd 5338 (HMSO, 1973).

21 *Scottish Housing: A Consultative Document*, Cmnd 6852 (HMSO, 1977).

22 A detailed account is given in the 1967 Report of the Scottish Housing Advisory Committee on *Scotland's Older Houses*, op. cit.

23 SDD Circular 67/1975, *Housing (Scotland) Act 1974: Houses Below the Tolerable Standard: Housing Action Areas* (Scottish Development Department, 1975).

24 SDD Circular 67/1975, op. cit.

25 This section is based in part on the author's *The Social Content of Planning* (Vol. 2 of *Problems of an Urban Society*) (Allen & Unwin, 1973), pp. 137ff.

26 See M. Bowley, *Housing and the State* (Allen & Unwin, 1944), and J. B. Cullingworth, *Housing and Local Government* (Allen & Unwin, 1966), ch. 1.

27 See, for example, *The Deeplish Study: Improvement Possibilities in a District of Rochdale* (HMSO, 1966), and MHLG, *Barnsbury Environmental Study* (Ministry of Housing and Local Government, 1968).

28 See particularly Department of the Environment, *New Life in Old Towns* (HMSO, 1972).

29 *Report of the Committee on Housing in Greater London* (Milner Holland Report), Cmnd 2605 (HMSO, 1965), pp. 122-3.

30 National Committee for Commonwealth Immigrants, *Areas of Special Housing Need* (NCCI, 1967).

31 *Report of the Committee on the Rent Acts* (Francis Report), Cmnd 4609 (HMSO, 1971), p. 212.

32 Department of Education and Science, Central Advisory Council for Education (England), *Children and their Primary Schools* (HMSO, 1967) (Vol. 1: *The Report*; Vol. 2: *Research and Surveys*).

33 op. cit., Vol. 1, para. 131. This must not be interpreted as a lack of concern for research. On the contrary, it reinforces the need for research, to which Volume 2 of the Report is eloquent testimony.

34 *Report of the Committee on Local Authority and Allied Personal Social Services*, Cmnd 3703 (HMSO, 1968), p. 150.

35 Central Housing Advisory Committee, *The Needs of New Communities* (HMSO, 1967).

36 Committee on Public Participation in Planning, *People and Planning* (Skeffington Report) (HMSO, 1969).

37 Seebohm Report, op. cit., pp. 151-6.
38 Home Office, *Urban Needs in Britain*, mimeo., Home Office, 23 June 1970.
39 loc. cit. Educational Priority Areas were defined in similar terms. See A. H. Halsey (ed.), *Educational Priority: Vol. 1: EPA Problems and Policies* (HMSO, 1972), especially ch. 4, 'The definition of EPA'.
40 Department of the Environment, *Review of the Traditional Urban Programme: Consultative Document* (DoE, March 1980).
41 J. McBride, 'The Urban Aid Programme: is it running out of cash?', *Quest*, 16 March 1973, quoted in R. Holman and L. Hamilton, 'The British Urban Programme', *Policy and Politics*, vol. 2 (1973-4), p. 104.
42 Royal Town Planning Institute, *Memorandum of Observations of the Royal Town Planning Institute to the Department of the Environment on 'Review of the Traditional Urban Programme' Consultative Document, April 1980*.
43 Department of the Environment, *Urban Programme Circular No. 21: Capital and Non-Capital Projects Starting in 1981/82 (England)*, DoE Circular 15/80 (HMSO, 1980).
44 Among the last of the Community Development reports (all published in 1980) were *Adamsez: The Story of a Factory Closure*, Benwell Community Project Final Report Series No. 8; *From Failure to Facelift*, Birmingham Community Development Project Final Report No. 6: Urban Renewal; and *From Rags to Ruins: Batley*.
     A review of these three reports, by Laurence Howes, is to be found in *The Planner*, vol. 67, no. 1 (January–February 1981), pp. 24-8.
45 A neat and helpful table of the 'evolution of neighbourhood policies in Britain (1964-77)' is to be found in R. Hambleton, *Policy Planning and Local Government* (Hutchinson, 1978). Hambleton's book contains much useful discussion of area-based policies.
46 D. McConaghy, 'Setting up six towns: an urban strategy gap', *Town Planning Review*, vol. 46 (1978), pp. 184-94.
47 The Urban Guidelines Studies were published by HMSO in 1973 under the general heading *Making Towns Better*. Their full titles were:
     The Oldham Study: Environmental Planning and Management
     The Rotherham Study, Vol. 1: Improving the Physical Environment; Vol. 2: Technical Appendices
     The Sunderland Study, Vol. 1: Tackling Urban Problems: A Basic Handbook; Vol. 2: Tackling Urban Problems: A Working Guide

     The Inner Area Studies were published by HMSO in 1977:
     Birmingham: *Unequal City*
     Lambeth: *Inner London: Policies for Dispersal and Balance*
     Liverpool: *Change or Decay*
     Additionally a summary was published earlier in 1977: *Inner Area Studies: Liverpool, Birmingham and Lambeth – Summaries of Consultants' Final Reports* (HMSO).
48 Including, for example, McKinsey's *A New Management System for the City of Liverpool* (1969) and their *A New Approach to the Problems of Cities* (1972); also the Shelter Neighbourhood Action Project: *Another Chance for the Cities* (1972). Reference can also be usefully made to the broader paper by J. D. Stewart, K. Spencer and B. Webster, *Local Government: Approaches to Urban Deprivation*, Home Office Urban Deprivation Unit, Occasional Paper No. 1 (Home Office, 1976).
49 As suggested in the Liverpool Inner Area Study, *Change or Decay*, p. 5. See also D. McConaghy, op. cit., p. 190.
50 *Inner Area Studies . . . Summaries*, op. cit. See also the reviews of these three studies by F. J. C. Amos, B. M. D. Smith and G. M. Lomas, 'The inner area studies: a review', *Town Planning Review*, 1978, pp. 195-208.
51 *Policy for the Inner Cities*, Cmnd 6845 (HMSO, 1977).

52 Department of the Environment, *Inner Urban Areas Act 1978*, Circular 67/78 (HMSO, 1978).
53 DoE Circular 68/78, op. cit., para. 1.
54 R. Hambleton, M. Stewart and J. Underwood, *Inner Cities: Management and Resources*, University of Bristol, School for Advanced Urban Studies, Working Paper 13 (University of Bristol, 1980), p. 8.
55 *Policy for the Inner Cities*, op. cit., para. 39.
56 *HC Debates*, 9 February 1981.
57 Any question as to whether this section would be more appropriate placed in the chapter on regional planning is clearly settled by the following statement: 'The establishment of Enterprise Zones will not be part of regional policy.' However, the statement continues: 'Nor will it have any direct connection with the application of other existing policies such as inner city policy, rural development or derelict land policy.' *Consultation Paper on Enterprise Zones*. (This is reproduced in the *Journal of Planning and Environment Law*, 1980, pp. 294–6.)
58 Perhaps this was a response to the Royal Town Planning Institute's policy statement, *Planning Free Zones*, which was issued in November 1979 before any official announcement had been made on enterprise zones!
59 *Economic Progress Report*, No. 121 (HM Treasury, May 1980).
60 *Economic Progress Report*, op. cit.
61 *The Times*, 20 March 1981.
62 *HC Debates*, 10 March 1981.
63 The relevant provisions are to be found in Part XVI of the Local Government, Planning and Land Act 1980.
64 B. Colenutt, 'Development corporations rule OK', *Roof*, July–August 1980, p. 104.
65 'Inner city – private enterprise' by Stephen Marks, in *New Society*, vol. 56, no. 961 (16 April 1981), p. 101.
66 Alan Sylvester-Evans, *Urban Renaissance: A Better Life in Towns* (HMSO, 1980).
67 The Campaign was launched amid the appropriate splendour of Lancaster House in October 1980. According to John Young, *The Times* planning reporter, 'it was a spectacularly boring occasion at which ministers took it in turns to deliver interminable accounts of the laws and regulations that their respective governments had passed and, for the most part, how well they were working. Instead of appeals for help and cooperation, there was little more than smug satisfaction.' *The Times*, 10 March 1971, p. 11.
68 This highly abbreviated account is based on John Young, 'The inner city', *The Times*, 10 March 1981, pp. 11–12.
69 loc. cit.
70 *Cambridge Economic Policy Review*, vol. 6, no. 2 (July 1980) ('Urban and regional policy, with provisional regional accounts 1966–78'), p. 41.
71 From the growing literature on urban history, particular mention should be made of S. Checkland, *The Upas Tree: Glasgow 1875–1975* (University of Glasgow Press, 1976).
72 op. cit., p. 100. Glasgow's civic motto is 'Let Glasgow Flourish'; but when formulated 'let' was an imperative, not a plea.
73 On this, see the Lambeth Inner Area Study which, significantly and appropriately, is subtitled 'Policies for dispersal and balance'.
74 For an excellent review, see A. Evans and D. Eversley (eds), *The Inner City. Employment and Industry* (Heinemann, 1980).
75 White Paper, *Policy for the Inner Cities*, Cmnd 6845 (HMSO, 1977), para. 59.
76 Central Policy Review Staff, *Relations between Central Government and Local Authorities* (HMSO, 1977), para. 5.1.
77 See *Policy for the Inner Cities*, op. cit., para. 88, and Scottish Development Agency, *GEAR Strategy and Programme*, May 1980.
78 M. Fried, 'Social differences in mental health', in J. Kosa, A. Antonovsky and

1. K. Zola, *Poverty and Health: A Sociological Analysis* (Harvard University Press, 1969), p. 149.

79   See P. Townsend, 'Area deprivation policies', *New Statesman*, 6 August 1976, pp. 168–171; C. Paris, 'Housing action areas', *Roof*, vol. 2, no. 1 (January 1977), pp. 9–14; G. Gad, 'Crowding and pathologies: some critical remarks', *Canadian Geographer*, vol. 17 (1973), pp. 373–90; J. Eyles, 'Area-based policies for the inner city: context, problems and prospects' and C. Hammett, 'Area-based explanations: a critical appraisal', both in D. T. Herbert and D. M. Smith, *Social Problems and the City: Geographical Perspectives* (Oxford University Press, 1979); and, of course, D. Harvey, *Social Justice and the City* (Arnold, 1973).

80   For a short discussion of the limitations of the area approach in relation to housing improvement, see C. Paris, op. cit. and the author's *Essays on Housing Policy*, op. cit., pp. 95–6.

Chapter 11

REGIONAL PLANNING

The term 'regional planning' is used in several different senses, thus abetting the confusion which surrounds governmental policy in relation to the 'regions'. In terms of physical planning, the regional dimension implies, for example, an extension of the planning area beyond a tightly defined urban area: the 'city region' is a logical area within which analysis and land use planning can effectively take place. Here the archetype is Abercrombie's *Greater London Plan*[1] though, of course, London is unique in its size and influence.

Beyond this essentially land use conception, there are two main other concepts of regional planning. For both, the physical area may be the same (for example, the economic planning regions): the difference lies in the approach. On one the focus is on the planning of land use, economic investment and such like *within* the region. On the other the focus is on the allocation of resources *between* the regions. The former is a regional responsibility (if there is an effective regional organisation – which there is not); the latter is a central government responsibility which is carried out in the light of regional needs (and political pressures).

The neatness of this threefold classification fails to square with the realities of planning and politics, if only because major locational decisions cut right through it. A Stansted, Belvoir or Windscale involve central decisions (and local–regional–central relationships) of a different order.

These are, however, exceptions. For the most part, the important distinction is that between the differing perspectives of regional planning held by central and local government. As Senior has put it:

What *central* government means by 'regional planning' is primarily the correction of economic imbalance *between* one 'region' and another; and it is only with reluctance that central government is reconciling itself to the fact that this purpose – crucial to its central function in the economic field – necessarily involves the making of investment decisions *within* 'regions' on a territorial as well as a functional basis. What *local* government means by 'regional planning', on the other hand, is primarily the expression of national policies in terms of a comprehensive long-term strategy for economic and physical development *within* each provincial-scale 'region', in the context of which local planning authorities can work out meaningful structure plans for their own areas.[2]

There exists no bridge between these two types of regional planning in England and Wales since there are no regional governments. (The position in Scotland, which has been discussed earlier – and is summarised below – is markedly different.) At present central government can channel (or block) resources to regions, but there is no machinery for rationally distributing resources *within* regions on the basis of a comprehensive strategy. The Department of the Environment has a role and powers which are quite inadequate for this task; and in any case, it is not a proper task for central government – it is essentially a regional matter. Any plan involves the submerging of some interests in favour of others. At the national level, the priority given to development areas is a clear case in point. But at the regional level there is no system for determining policies. Each local authority have the interests of their ratepayers at heart and, since there is no effective agency of regional government, development needed for a wider benefit is jeopardised. Thus (for instance), if a conurbation authority sees industrial overspill as having undesirable effects on its rateable value and a potentially good overspill authority sees development as an intolerable local burden, an overspill policy is killed at birth, even if it is in the wider interests of the region as a whole. To quote Senior again:

Any plan which seeks to guide development in the interests of the region as a whole must call for the concentration of investment in particular parts of it and the prevention of development in others. But so long as the region is divided between different implementing authorities, one of them is bound to find that it is being called upon to bear more than its share of the cost and get less than its share of the benefit of giving effect to particular provisions of the overall plan: if this were not so there would be no need for such a plan. And it would be not only altruistic, but positively undemocratic, for that authority thus to subordinate its own ratepayers' interests to that of its neighbour's ratepayers. It is quite unreasonable to expect a wrongly organized local government structure to behave as it would automatically tend to do if it were rightly organized, when the wrong organization automatically produces a different incidence of the costs and benefits of acting in the interest of the region as a whole.[3]

AGENCIES OF REGIONAL PLANNING

The missing 'middle tier' in the administration of physical planning (noted at the end of Chapter 1 above) is a marked feature of the British planning system – with some important exceptions in Scotland. Here the position has been transformed by the establishment of multipurpose regional authorities which are now responsible for producing regional reports and, significantly, have taken over responsibility for water services which, south of the Border, have been transferred to new *ad hoc* authorities.

Separate from local government, however, there is a multiplicity of regional planning machines some of which are purely advisory (such as the 'standing conferences'[4] and the former regional economic planning councils) while others are important executive agencies (such as the Scottish and Welsh Development Agencies, the Land Authority for Wales, the Highlands and Islands Development Board, the Council for Small Industries in Rural Areas, and so forth). Additionally there are the nationalised industries, and bodies ranging from the Nature Conservancy Council to the Tourist Boards which have their own regional organisations, and, of course, the regional offices of government departments. Indeed, it would be easy to make this chapter a directory of agencies. Rather than attempting to be comprehensive, however, attention is focused on a selection of regional physical and economic problems and the development of machinery to deal with them.

REGIONAL THINKING

A number of strands can be identified in the evolution of thinking on regions. Two are of particular relevance in this book – the physical planning and the economic planning strands. Some account of the former from the local end has already been given. It is now necessary to supplement this with an outline of the situation as it has developed at the centre.

At the end of Chapter 1 some stress was laid on the lack of a regional tier of planning between local authorities and the central departments. This lack did not seem as important in the mid-1940s as it appeared to be when population growth, economic development, increased personal mobility, a rising standard of living and a host of other related factors conspired in the 1950s to increase pressures on land and the machinery of land planning control. In any case, it was not possible to go further at the time. For a period, the framework of regional advisory plans (particularly in the London and Glasgow regions) had to suffice. They had some impact: they enabled some broad planning objectives to be communicated to and, more important, to be acknowledged by local planning authorities. Informal arrangements, professional contacts and a generally shared planning philosophy also helped.

By the end of the 1950s it became clear that something more was needed. Development plans had become hopelessly out of date due to cumbersome procedures and the great change in the underlying forces with which they were supposed to cope. Furthermore, in England the disbandment of the regional organisation of the Ministry of Housing in 1954–6 had (according to the department's former Permanent Secretary)[5] the opposite effect to that intended. 'There was a strong feeling at headquarters that the divisions did not know their regions or their authorities as well as they should; and that it would be better if headquarters staff could be enabled to devote more time to travelling out. It was thought that the abolition of the regional organization would improve Whitehall's knowledge of, and contacts with, the North, the Midlands, the East and the South West to the benefit of all; and that officers and representatives of local authorities might be encouraged to come more frequently to Whitehall, as they had done in pre-war years. It did not come off.' And so the problems changed in character and increased in complexity at the very time when the central department was in insufficient touch with local government.

REGIONAL STUDIES

The turn of the tide came in the early 1960s in three areas for three different reasons. In 1962 a Northern Housing Office of the ministry was opened in Manchester to assist the large programme of slum clearance and redevelopment in the North and North-West. In 1963 another regional office, with both housing and planning functions, was set up in Newcastle in connection with the 'Hailsham Plan' for the North-East, to which there was a clear political commitment.[6] Probably of greater importance was the beginning, in 1961, of a series of regional studies.* These resulted from the awareness within the department of the inadequacy of the development plans and land allocations to meet the rising pressures for development. These studies started, in traditional manner, as 'regional conferences' and 'land studies' undertaken jointly by officers of local authorities and the department. In the South-East and the West Midlands they developed into new-style regional studies covering unprecedentedly large areas.

The *South East Study* was published in March 1964 and included regionally based proposals of a kind and on a scale which had not been seen since the wartime and immediate postwar period of optimistic planning. New cities (*sic*) were suggested in the Southampton-Portsmouth area, the Bletchley area (later to become Milton Keynes) and the Newbury area. New towns were considered for Ashford and Stansted. Large-scale expansions were proposed for Ipswich, Northampton, Peterborough and Swindon. Consultants

---

*A list of regional studies and plans is given in the Bibliography.

were appointed to consider, with the local authorities concerned, many of these proposals.

The next clearly identifiable step in this period of intense examination and thinking came with the decision of the Labour government in 1964 to set up regional economic planning machinery. The trend towards this was already in evidence. Early in 1964 the President of the Board of Trade was made responsible for 'trade, industry and regional development'. The White Paper *South East England*, outlining the government's reaction to the *Study*, was published jointly by the department and the Board.[7] Indeed, *The South East Study* was the only one to bear the imprint of the Ministry of Housing and Local Government. Before the next studies were completed (on the West Midlands and the North-West) the Department of Economic Affairs had been set up (taking over the regional development division of the Board of Trade). During its lifetime (1964-9) the DEA had responsibility for the direction and publication of regional studies. (This now rests with the Department of the Environment.)

REGIONAL ECONOMIC PLANNING COUNCILS 1964-79

The regional economic planning councils were in operation for some fifteen years. There were ten of them – eight in England and one each in Wales and Scotland. The councils were advisory bodies and consisted of a chairman and about twenty-five members all appointed by the appropriate secretary of state. The members were appointed as 'individuals having a wide range of knowledge and experience in their regions': they were not delegates or representatives of particular interests. The councils' main functions were 'to study and advise on the needs and potentialities of their regions and on the development of a long-term planning strategy for their regions, and to advise central government on aspects of national policy which have a bearing on regional development'.

Alongside each council was a board consisting of senior civil servants from the main government departments concerned with regional planning. In the English regions, the chairman of the boards were all senior officials of the DoE. The functions of the boards were 'to co-ordinate the regional economic planning work of Departments, and to co-operate with the Economic Planning Councils in developing the long-term planning strategies for the regions'.

The functions of this regional advisory machinery were officially stated in 1965 as being:

(i) to work out broad objectives for each region and so provide a comprehensive framework within which decisions in particular sectors can be taken;

(ii)   to advise on the formulation of national policies where these can significantly affect the regions;

(iii) to advise on the application in the regions of national policy;

(iv)   to stimulate interest within each region and build up a common approach within each region to its problems.

Initially the work was of a kind which might be described as being 'regional stocktaking'. The primary objective was to assemble the facts and figures relating to the regions which could form the basis for an overall assessment and for a broad regional strategy. Attention was concentrated on preparing 'studies' on the lines of *The South East Study*. The first two were published in 1965 for the North-West and the West Midlands.[8] Both of these were undertaken by 'a group of officials from government departments concerned with regional planning', and were 'referred' to the planning councils for the respective regions (without any commitment on the part of government to the studies' findings or to the proposals which might be made by the councils). Following the establishment of the regional councils, further studies were undertaken and published. Unlike the earlier two, these were reports by the councils themselves. But they were not 'regional plans'; indeed they both specifically disclaimed any pretension to be. As the foreword to *The East Midlands Study* put it, the objective was 'to present to the public an account of the region as it is, and as it is changing; it draws attention to problems and opportunities, with an indication of what is involved in them. It is hoped that the study will form an adequate basis for the public discussion out of which the main lines of the region's planning will emerge; until adequate opportunity for that discussion has been provided it would be presumptuous to go further.'

This approach stemmed from two important factors. First, the essential information and research needed for an adequately based system of regional planning was lacking. Secondly, the regional councils had no executive powers and no authority over either the central government or local authorities. They 'represented' the regions only in a very indirect way. They had to tread warily between the cautiousness of Whitehall and the sensitivities of the county and town halls. It could hardly be expected that they would rapidly resolve the conflicts between the constituent local authorities (and particularly between town and county) which had for so long frustrated attempts to plan on any scale other than that circumscribed by local authority boundaries. Essentially the regional councils constituted an experiment in forging new and wider loyalties – loyalties to a region rather than to a locality.

The studies and reports were thus not sets of policies agreed by the regions and submitted to the central government for consideration and action; rather were they the interim findings and thoughts of a group of individuals with experience of and interests in the regions, submitted to all concerned (government at all levels, and public and private bodies) as a first exercise in regional thinking.

The abolition of the councils in 'the slaughter of the Quangos' by the Conservative government in 1979[9] was neither unexpected nor lamented. Murray Stewart has suggested as a fitting obituary:

> Set up in a vacuum between central and local government, with no powers, no funds and little staff; dragged towards strategic land-use planning concerns rather than to the economic; discredited in the eyes of local government because of the failure to influence national policies; overproductive in the preparation of strategies and plans which had no implementation bite; and above all, divorced from the political process at both central and local levels. In retrospect, much of this was predictable and indeed was recognised by many of the EPCs themselves over the period. Equally, the EPCs have been victims of the change from the growth euphoria of the mid 1960s to the standstill somnolence of the 1970s; in a period when industrial (sector) policies and inner city policies have become popular with Government at the expense of regional planning.[10]

PLANNING STRATEGIES

The councils have gone, but their strategies linger on. Indeed most of the country is covered by some kind of regional strategy. Though their legal status may be dubious, local authorities are required, in the preparation of structure plans, 'to have regard' to any approved regional strategies.[11] Powell, in reviewing a decade of regional planning, stresses the importance of this. His general conclusions are worth spelling out:

– Emerging structure plans are related to the regional strategy with commendable enthusiasm where county policy coincides with strategic aims and proposals . . . and with something less than enthusiasm where it does not. Even in the latter case the structure plans recognise the significance of approved strategies and are at pains to develop their counter arguments in depth. This accords with government intentions that the strategies should be thoroughly tested in structure plan preparation;
– The same factor is emphasised again in the time devoted in public examination of structure plans to the relationship of plan to strategy and the strength of reasoning for deviation from the strategy. This process is repeated in the final stages of modification and approval of structure plans;
– Arguments on appeal, whether from planning authority or appellant, also lean heavily on the strategy. The significance of approved

strategies is not lost in such cases, notably in the context of development in growth areas and elsewhere;

- Production of an approved strategy in which both central and local government have co-operated creates a large measure of common ground on existing situations from which new issues can be approached on a basis which is acceptable to both sides – with substantial savings on discussion of facts;
- Finally, the strategies and supporting documents have created a wealth of factual data and analysis which is relevant to many issues (for example, devolution and local authority finance) related to regional administration in fields other than planning and which is used in the public debates which help determine future policy.[12]

PHYSICAL PLANNING AND ECONOMIC PLANNING

A further extract from Powell's article brings us to the question of the relationship between physical and economic planning – or, to be more precise, the lack of it in Britain:

Physical planning still suffers from an inability to recognise fully that the best land-use pattern for any part of the country is the resultant of the interplay of constantly changing economic and social forces which have their own inate and powerful strengths and momentums. Unless land-use is seen as the physical expression of the economic and social forces which underlie the life of country, region or city, plans will either fail or succeed only in impeding the achievement of economic and social ends. The limits of physical plans are defined by economic and social realities and the scope for the art and design of the planner is flexible only within the tolerances of economic and social needs. The fundamental requirement for the planner is the deepest possible understanding of the strength, momentum, changes and consequences of the economic and social forces at work in the community concerned. The limits within which such forces can be manoeuvred must be recognised or they will react to constrain the freedom of the planner to implement his plans. Analysis and examination of economic and social conditions, understanding of the power which they develop and the limits within which trends can be steered, culminating in a designed response in the optimal pattern of development reflecting the forces and the powers to control them, are the main strands from which the fabric of regional strategies is woven. The regional strategies developed during the 1970s have recognised this truth and, although much effort is still required before they can be regarded as satisfactory, the evolving sequence of strategies has at least begun to break down the false dichotomy between the economy and physical life of the regions.[13]

This raises some major issues concerning the nature of physical planning, economic planning, regional economics and, indeed, a host of related areas. Here it must suffice to note that, whatever economic analysis or policy has underpinned regional physical planning, for the most part the 'economics' has been concerned with unemployment.

ECONOMIC PLANNING POLICIES

Employment and economic change lie at the heart of regional planning. This, indeed, was the starting-point for the Barlow inquiry over forty years ago. Postwar industrial location policies have been directed towards reducing unemployment in the development areas and restraining new industrial building in 'congested' areas. This has been the interpretation given to the statutory phrase 'a proper distribution of industry'. For most of the postwar period, however, this has been regarded, in the main, as a *social* policy running alongside, but not supporting, *economic* policies. A classic exposition of this view was given by the President of the Board of Trade (R. Maudling) in the Second Reading debates on the Local Employment Bill:

> We should start from the assumption that the economic and industrial expansion of the country should proceed freely in response to growing and changing consumer demand, and that it should proceed on the principle of the most effective use of our national resources . . . This principle of the most effective use of our resources must clearly be mitigated in some cases by Government action to deal with certain social consequences which the nation does not regard as acceptable.[14]

During the 1960s, however, there was an increasing awareness that a maldistribution of employment had serious economic effects on the national economy. The 1963 Report of the National Economic Development Council on *Conditions Favourable to Faster Growth* provided a good illustration of this thinking:

> The level of employment in different regions of the country varies widely, and high unemployment associated with the lack of employment opportunities in the less prosperous regions is usually thought of as a social problem. Policies aim, therefore, to prevent unemployment rising to politically intolerable levels, and expenditure to this end is often considered a necessary burden to the nation, unrelated to any economic gain that might accrue from it. But the relatively low activity rates in these regions also indicates considerable labour reserves. To draw these reserves into employment would make a substantial contribution to national employment and national growth.[15]

This argument, it should be noted, was put forward not by physical planners but by economists. It differed markedly from the traditional type of economic argument; and it rejected the idea that the long-term solution to regional economic decline lay in migration to the prosperous areas. Apart from the social cost of large-scale migration that this would involve, there were two other significant objections. First it would add to the problems of congestion in the South-East and the Midlands – problems which were already straining to the utmost the British machinery of town and country planning. Secondly, it was thought to be quite impracticable for these prosperous areas to absorb the required number of migrants. Furthermore, if the less prosperous regions were allowed to run down, their future problems could become even more difficult to solve. (The opposite argument was seldom heard.) It followed that the objective should be the formulation of a regional development policy which aimed at achieving self-sustaining regional growth.

It is here that the relationship between economic planning and town and country planning was most explicitly articulated: potential industrial developers (so it was argued) were concerned not only with labour supply and good sites, but also with adequate services, educational provision, and so on. In short, if industrialists were to be attracted to the less prosperous regions then these regions had to have both economic and social advantages on a significant scale. In the words of the White Paper on *The North East*: 'even generous assistance to enterprise may not be fully effective unless it is backed by faster progress in making towns and villages more pleasant, in improving communications, and in removing scars on the industrial countryside'.

The problems thus began to be seen as a compound of the economic and the social. The promotion of industrial activity had to be accompanied by a modernisation of the general environment. This was not merely a question of providing a 'bait' to industrialists: it was also a matter of economic efficiency – 'to ensure that the scale of the public services and facilities match the needs of a modern society'.

Allied to this line of thinking were arguments on historic legacies: the regions where economic growth was comparatively slow were the regions where there was a concentration of physical obsolescence. Indeed, some observers spoke of a geographical division of the country into two nations – separated roughly by the River Trent. The 'fortunate regions' of the South had a high level of employment, a large amount of private enterprise, a high standard of health, a relatively high standard of social service and social amenity. On the other hand, the 'unfortunate regions' of the North, of Wales and of Scotland – the boom areas of the coal age – had an enormous legacy of obsolete social capital, a slower rate of economic growth, an accompanying higher rate of unemployment, a poorer standard of

health and social service, and a not unrelated migration of population.
The image of the two nations was clearly overdrawn even in the
1960s. (As is argued later it is much more so now.) Nevertheless, it had
some truth in fact and became increasingly compelling politically. It
was partly for this reason that so much emphasis was laid on improving infrastructure.

Nevertheless, it did not follow that all existing towns and settle-
ments should be modernised. Some areas had lost their economic
raison d'être and had little or no potentiality for growth. In any case, a
policy of promoting growth was now thought to be most effective
when applied to carefully selected areas with high development potentialities. During the 1960s industrial location policy became aimed at
relieving high unemployment in development districts. This was a
major departure from the previous policy of promoting growth more
generally in regions. The 'selection' of development districts was
made, however, on the basis of unemployment rates. Yet unemployment in itself is neither an adequate measure of the regional problem
nor an indicator of what needs to be done. It is inadequate as a
regional indicator because of the large numbers of potential workers
who would figure among the employed if jobs were available. It is also
inadequate in that it obviously cannot take account of those workers
who have already migrated from the region to areas where jobs are
available. Indeed, it is a measure of only one aspect of a regional
economy, and ignores a whole range of other factors such as incomes,
demand, locational attributes, and so forth.

Given this narrow approach, the appropriate – equally narrow –
policy was predetermined. (Just as the definition of the problem of
inadequate housing in terms of 'slums' determined that the policy
response should be 'slum clearance', so the definition of the regional
problem in terms of insufficient employment determined a policy of
stimulating employment.)

REGIONAL UNEMPLOYMENT

As a result, 'policies' have waxed and waned in line with regional
unemployment rates. More fundamentally, the policy response has
always been too small in relation to the real size of the problem, as
well as misdirected. As Cairncross has put it, by concentrating on
unemployment rates, and ignoring other more significant economic
indicators (particularly the level of earnings), governments underestimated the scale of action required:

Calculations were made implying that x more jobs would bring
down unemployment by x. It was assumed that the provision of
additional jobs would offer no check to outward migration and
produce little or no overflow of demand to goods and services

furnished by workers in other regions. The post-war tendency to treat regional growth exclusively in terms of unemployment percentages persisted. Yet it should have required little demonstration that the hierarchy of unemployment percentages reflected a corresponding hierarchy in locational preferences. If the aim was to overturn the one hierarchy, it presupposed a capacity to overturn the other. To achieve a higher pressure of demand in the assisted areas required an actual *preference* for these locations over locations elsewhere. If such a preference manifested itself, it would not only bring down the level of unemployment in the assisted areas but would stem the outflow of labour from them and raise the level of earnings in comparison with other regions.

It is doubtful whether any government in post-war Britain would ever have been prepared to go quite so far as to aim at reversing the existing hierarchy. Aid is one thing; but turning preferences upside-down is another matter altogether.[16]

GROWTH POINTS

The 1963 Report on *Conditions Favourable to Faster Growth* took a mid course, and proposed 'growth points' selected on the basis of potentialities:

> Better results might be secured for the slowly expanding regions as a whole by identifying their natural growth points and seeking to attract industry to them. Within the bigger areas a wider choice of location than at present would be available to incoming firms. This would increase the likelihood of attracting a larger number and a greater variety of firms, and of stimulating the development of industrial complexes. Firms would then benefit from the presence of kindred industry. These complexes and other places especially attractive to industry could be developed into growth points within the less prosperous regions. It could be expected that the benefit of new growth in any part would repercuss fairly quickly throughout the region.[17]

The two regional programmes for Scotland and North-East England represented the first essays in comprehensive regional planning by central government. Their importance lay not so much in the actual proposals made, but in the advance in thought and policy which they represented. They (like the Welsh report, *Wales: The Way Ahead*),[18] however, did differ from succeeding reports – or 'studies' as they are typically called. They involved a degree of commitment which was notably absent from their successors, even when they had been prepared by central government. (The 'official' preface to *The South East Study* underlined that its main purpose was 'to provide a basis for discussion': the point was rubbed home even more clearly in the preface to *The West Midlands* regional study where it was stated that the government 'are not in any way committed by the Study Group's findings'.)

The point is, of course, that regional planning is not simply a matter of planning *within* a region. It has to take place within a framework of national policies which can be translated into decisions about the allocation of resources *between* regions. The White Papers on Scotland and the North-East proposed increases in public service investment which would have involved (for 1964–5) Scotland receiving 11 per cent of the Great Britain total (for a country with less than 10 per cent of the population) and the North-East receiving 7 per cent (with 5½ per cent of the population). These proposals were drawn up on the basis of a political assessment of the needs of these regions, but clearly there were problems in continuing with this approach for all regions.

THE 'INTERMEDIATE AREAS'

Indeed, as aid to the development areas increased during the 1960s, there was mounting political pressure from 'intermediate areas' (or 'grey areas', to use the more popular term). It was this pressure which led to the setting up of the Hunt Committee, whose report *The Intermediate Areas* was published in April 1969.[19] The terms of reference of this Committee were 'to examine in relation to the economic welfare of the country as a whole and the needs of the development areas, the situation in other areas where the rate of economic growth gives cause (or may give cause) for concern, and to suggest whether revised policies to influence economic growth in such areas are desirable and, if so, what measures should be adopted'.

The Committee quickly found that it was no easy matter to judge the presence and severity of 'causes for concern'. In the existing state of regional knowledge and analysis, political judgement had a very large role to play. Nevertheless, a brave and useful attempt was made. The major 'cause for concern' was 'slow economic growth . . . where it is associated with unused or under-used labour resources, low earnings, a concentration of industries with a declining labour force, poor communications and a run-down physical environment making areas unattractive for new economic growth, and net outward migration'. The chosen criteria were:

(*a*) Sluggish or falling employment ⎰ as the major indicators of
(*b*) A slow growth in personal incomes ⎱ slow growth.
(*c*) A slow rate of addition to industrial and commercial premises – as indicating a low level of industrial and commercial investment and a slow rate of economic growth.

(d)   Significant unemployment – as the most obvious measure of wasted human resources.
(e)   Low or declining proportions of women at work – as indicating a particular under-use of resources, especially in areas with a tradition of female employment.
(f)   Low earnings – as throwing some light on the efficiency of the use of labour and as one of the factors relevant to the economic opportunity of individuals.
(g)   Heavy reliance on industry whose demand for labour was growing slowly or falling and was likely to continue to do so – as an indication of vulnerability to economic change resulting in possible under-utilisation of labour resources.
(h)   Poor communications as material to slow growth in the recent past and to the potential for growth.
(i)   Decayed or inadequate environment, including dereliction as material to slow growth in the recent past and to the potential for growth.
(j)   Serious net outward migration – as a pointer to the danger of accelerating decline, and as a summing up of the reactions of individuals to a complex of social and economic factors such as the local range of employment opportunities, educational and social activities and the state of the social and physical environment.

They concluded that the severest problems were undoubtedly in the development areas and that there was not a clear-cut and well-defined category of 'intermediate area'. Rather there were 'symptoms of concern' present to a varying extent and a varying degree in different parts of the country. Nevertheless, they felt that the North-West and Yorkshire & Humberside stood in the greatest need of a new impetus and recommended special assistance for these regions, together with more limited assistance to the Notts-Derbyshire coalfield and to North Staffordshire.

In recommending assistance to such a large area of the country (containing a fifth of the population of Great Britain) there was no suggestion that the 'growth-area' policy should be abandoned. On the contrary, the Committee were simply following the logic which underlay the setting up in 1966 of broad development areas in place of the former narrower and relatively scattered development districts, chosen on the basis of high unemployment: 'as a result of inducements being made available to industry throughout these wider areas, industrialists are not tied to locations of greatest need, which may not be the most viable long-term locations for industry'. It followed that the recommended aid might go to relatively prosperous parts of an intermediate area, but this was in principle no different from the position in the development areas.

This, however, ignored the political difficulties. Any aid to intermediate areas which was effective in increasing new industrial development must (at least in the short run) affect the development areas. As the Hunt Committee ruefully pointed out at the beginning of their report, 'the supply of mobile industry available to stimulate economic growth is, taken as a whole, insufficient at present to match the needs of the development areas and overspill towns, let alone areas of slow growth. We recognize that remedial measures for areas of slow growth may hold back progress elsewhere.'

The reaction of the government of the day was that assistance should be concentrated in more narrowly defined localities within the regions concerned. The selection of these intermediate areas was to be governed strictly by 'criteria of need', in particular the level and character of unemployment, the rate of outward migration and the scope for industrial growth. On this basis, seven intermediate areas were designated: the Yorkshire Coalfield, North-East Lancashire, the Nottingham/Derbyshire Coalfield, North Humberside, Plymouth, part of South-East Wales, and Leith. Other areas were added in the early 1970s.

POLICIES IN THE 1970s

With the return of the Conservative government in 1970, the stage seemed set for significant changes in regional policy;[20] and these were announced with appropriate flourish early in the new parliamentary session.[21] Controls over industrial and office building were relaxed and assistance for regional development made more 'selective'. More tangible was the institutional change brought about by the amalgamation of the Board of Trade with the Ministry of Technology in a mammoth new Department of Trade and Industry.

Any hope of a disengagement from active regional policy, however, was quickly shattered by the recession of 1970–1 and the failure of budgetary and grant provisions to ameliorate it. A 1972 White Paper, *Industrial and Regional Development*,[22] set out 'a programme to stimulate industrial and regional regeneration', and the 1972 Industry Act reversed some of the financial aid systems introduced in 1970 (and introduced what were now known as Regional Development Grants). It also provided a host of measures for selective financial assistance in assisted areas. Intermediate Area status was extended over the North and Wales (as had been recommended by the Hunt Committee): the result was that almost a half of the country's population lived in designated assisted areas (development areas, special development areas and intermediate areas).

Expenditure on regional aid increased but its effectiveness came under sharp critical attack from the Expenditure Committee in 1973: 'Much has been spent and much may well have been wasted. Regional policy has been empiricism run mad, a game of hit-and-miss, played with more enthusiasm than success . . . Everything in this inquiry pointed to the need for government to create a more rational and systematic basis for the formulation and execution of national policy.'[23]

Undaunted by these harsh words, the Labour government which was returned in 1974 reaffirmed its strong commitment to active regional policies.[24] Controls over industrial building were tightened, a major programme to disperse government offices from London was announced, a Job Creation Programme was initiated, the Department of Industry was re-established as a separate ministry, a National Enterprise Board was set up, followed by the Scottish and Welsh Development Agencies. Responsibilities for financial assistance in Scotland and Wales were transferred to their respective secretaries of state.

This initial unequivocal commitment to regional policy was dramatically affected towards the end of the 1970s by such factors as the severe recession, by the national 'industrial strategy'[25] which involved support for industry outside the 'assisted areas', by the dramatic rise of unemployment in the South and West, and by the rise of the 'inner city problem'. Indeed, the context for regional policies in May 1979, when the Conservative government was elected, was markedly different from that which had faced it at the beginning of the decade. The Thatcher government, however, lost no time in announcing its reshaped regional policy – which might be described largely as 'the same but less so'. The stated intention was 'to concentrate on those parts of the country with the most intractable problems of unemployment'. Total assistance was to be reduced but would be rendered more selectively with an emphasis on projects which demonstrated enterprise 'in making businesses competitive and profitable'.[26]

Policies may, of course, change and, rather than attempt a description of what happen to be the details of these at the time of writing, it is more useful to examine further the major change in context within which regional policies must now operate.

'SOLVING' THE REGIONAL PROBLEM

Whatever the achievements of regional policy (and these are difficult to measure),[27] it is now clear that earlier confidence that 'the regional problem' could be solved was misplaced. It would no longer be possible, even with qualification, to suggest – as did the 1969 Hunt Report – that 'it may be reasonable to hope that by the mid 1970s the major problems in many parts of the development areas will have been largely overcome, at least so far as unemployment is concerned'.[28]

Such approaches are now generally regarded as quite unrealistic.[29] As Randall has argued:

The more realistic assessment of the long time-scale needed to solve regional problems stems from an improved understanding of the dynamic nature of the processes that create and sustain high rates of unemployment in some regions. At the time of the National Plan there was a tendency to think in terms of a 'once-and-for-all' effort to bring unused labour reserves into use and to transform the industrial structure of the problem regions. More recent work emphasises the strength of the forces that perpetuate regional disparities and hinder adjustments: (*a*) the need for regions with an unfavourable industrial structure to sustain a higher level of investment than nationally even though the main influence on investment in the region is the macro-economic climate of the country as a whole;[30] (*b*) a positive association between rapid growth in output and productivity and the institutional factors that prevent wage levels in regions of low productivity adjusting to allow greater regional competitiveness;[31] and (*c*) the various kinds of short-run and long-run regional multiplier mechanisms that make regional economic growth or decline to some extent self-reinforcing.[32] The regional problem and regional policy are now seen as long term and continuous in nature; in this respect we can conclude that it is our understanding of, rather than the fundamental nature of, the problem that has changed.[33]

Of particular importance is the stress now laid on factors indigenous to the regions – their own capabilities and potentialities for development. Institutionally this is reflected in the establishment of such bodies as the Highlands and Islands Development Board, the Scottish and Welsh Development Agencies and, most recently, enterprise zones and the provision in the 1980 Local Government, Planning and Land Act for urban development corporations. The Conservative government's regional policy lays emphasis (at least in words) on local enterprise: to quote the secretary of state: 'regional differences will not be reduced simply by redistributing money from taxpayers; there need also to be local enterprise and plenty of cooperation in making businesses competitive and profitable'.[34]

Such an emphasis on local potentialities is not new. Thompson produced eloquent evidence of the importance of human skills and entrepreneurship:

If the rich always did get richer (and the poor poorer) in interregional competition, long-range urban forecasting would be much easier than it actually is. But victories can bring complacency and defeats can be challenges . . . On careful quantification, we might find that the challenge of an employment crisis elicits its response in a resurgence of local economic leadership with a lag of fairly predictable length.[35]

THE WIDER CONTEXT

Experience with assisted local initiatives may well prove positive – as has been the case to a limited extent with some expanding town schemes. However, the contrary experience of much of the community development programme underlines the importance of wider issues of a 'structural' nature and of forces well beyond the control, or even the influence of a single locality. One such factor, of course, is the rise of the very large firms which are international in character and ownership. In Manners's words:

> Compared with the single plant or single office of the relatively small firm that they have replaced, these multi-facility, multi-process, multi-product, multi-service corporations not only have quite different decision-making styles, but also a contrasting set of locational perceptions and options. They can switch their processes between plants; they can import (at transfer prices) components or information from overseas; they can measure the productivity of comparable facilities in different countries; and they can invest and expand accordingly. Less responsive to controls, they more readily react to incentives and political persuasion.[36]

The last point has been eloquently demonstrated in recent years with automobiles, oil and steel to mention but a few. At the extreme the result can be 'a Government's regional heart overruling the commercial heads'[37] as was the case with the Rootes development at Linwood near Glasgow. The fact that it was a Conservative government which took the decision indicates the strength of political and social factors. A later Labour government abetted the policy when it rescued the Chrysler Corporation (which took over Rootes in the mid-1960s). Finally, the Thatcher government acquiesced in the closure of the plant by the successor Peugot-Citroën.

At the time of writing (early 1981) consideration is being given to 'selective assistance' for a bid to persuade Nissan, the Japanese car manufacturer, to build its proposed new plant in an assisted area.

As these examples show, growth and decline can now take place in larger 'lumps' with consequentially dramatic changes for local and regional economies. The international dimension is also extended further by the growing relationship with the European mainland (following Britain's joining the Common Market in 1973). In addition to economic linkages, access to the European Economic Community investment and social funds, a more surprising element appeared with the 're-ranking' of the affluent South East of England. Manners notes (and comments):

> Whereas the South East of England . . . for long has stood as the wealthiest region in Britain, set in an EEC context it ranked only

seventeenth in income per head in 1970, with a Gross Domestic Product only 40 per cent of the richest E.E.C. region (Hamburg). Such comparisons raise all manner of questions about the validity of exchange rate conversions, about the role of different regions in the various national economies of Western Europe, and about the implications to be drawn for inter-regional policies. Nevertheless, the low rankings of all the British regions, and the relatively poor status of its most successful, at the very least challenges traditional notions about the ways to restrain development in southern England – and raise some doubts about the wisdom of restraint at all.[38]

Other features of the changed context for regional planning include the dramatic change in population growth and forecasts (and the accompanying abandonment of major growth philosophies such as were epitomised by the Humberside, Severnside and Tayside Studies).[39] These studies are now largely irrelevant: all that remains are the reports and the three bridges which themselves contribute to yet a further relevant change: the new transport 'map' of Britain. This is now crisscrossed with motorways, and served by extremely fast inter-city rail services and a still growing network of air services. The 'accessibility map' of Britain has been transformed beyond recognition and, as a result, so has the distribution of locational advantages. It was against this background that increased emphasis was placed on retraining (for example, the Training Opportunities Scheme) and on assisted geographical mobility (the Employment Transfer Scheme).[40] Unfortunately, overshadowing these eminently sensible schemes was an increasing rate of unemployment for which they were quite ill-fitted.

RECESSION AND REGIONAL POLICY

A major economic argument for regional policy is that by moving jobs it reduces labour shortages in the prosperous areas and increases employment not merely in the depressed areas but also in total. This argument is less relevant when no area has a labour shortage. Indeed, it can be argued that 'the case for regional policy must now be a social one, resting mainly on the desirability or otherwise of reducing involuntary migration'.[41] Certainly it is clear (in the words of Maclennan and Parr) that there is a 'mutual relationship between regional policy and national economic performance . . . A sound regional policy can contribute much to well-being throughout the nation, but at the same time the pursuit of an effective regional policy is largely conditional upon the existence of a thriving national economy.'[42]

The issues clearly extend beyond the confines of the present discussion, and views on what line of regional policy should be followed will depend on ideas concerning overall economic policy. Given a national policy of retrenchment and restraint of public expenditure, the main line must be a highly selective one. An alternative (as argued by Wynne Godley and the Cambridge Economic Policy Group) 'would require an entirely different overall economic strategy allowing a different attitude to total public spending'. Ths in turn would point towards a strong regional policy.[43]

Curiously, given the new conditions, the question of the relationship between economic and physical planning is resurrected, with a major emphasis on the inner city problem. Indeed, 'the emerging economic problem of urban areas has become a dominant source of spatial imbalance and inequality; but it has tended to fall into a policy "gap" caused by the separation of "industrial" (economic) and "physical planning" policies'.[44] This 'inner city problem' was discussed in the last chapter.

REGIONAL PLANNING IN THE DOLDRUMS

The spate of regional plans of the late 1960s and early 1970s has abated (south of the Border). New reports are relatively rare,[45] as indeed are revisions and updating of earlier regional plans.[46]

The reasons for this provide food for thought. In Scotland, the regional reports and the SDD national planning guidelines[47] provide an adequate framework for structure planning. South of the Border, there is a noticeable lack of enthusiasm (and visible machinery) for regional plan-making. Government responses to earlier plans (for example, for the North-West in 1975 and for Yorkshire & Humberside in 1977, and most notably, to the Greater London Development Plan) have hardly been encouraging to the erstwhile regional planner. On a cynical view, therefore, the impetus has gone out of regional planning.

But there are other factors which point to a less pessimistic verdict. First, most of Britain is now covered by strategic plans, and some effort (though uneven) is being applied to keeping these up to date. Secondly, the intense pressures (of anticipated growth) have now evaporated. As a result the regions are equipped with strategies which, in line with pragmatic planning practice, can now be amended and rephased to cover a much longer time-horizon. Even the less fortunate areas are now in a relatively improved position, with the worsening of the position elsewhere! (As a 1977 OECD report notes, this is not a uniquely British situation.)[48] In short, the perceived problems of the fundamental economic basis for regional planning have shifted more to the national level. And at the local level, effort is being concentrated on structure and local planning. When the cutback in the inter-urban road programme is added to the picture, there seems little left for regional planners to do except to 'monitor' the changing scene.

The position might have been different had there been strong and effective regional planning agencies; but in their absence, regional planning has moved into the doldrums. Given the restraints on public expenditure this situation can be expected to continue; and it is hardly likely to change unless there is a major transformation of the demographic or economic scene. In the meantime specific regional planning problems are being dealt with by such bodies as the Scottish and Welsh Development Agencies, the regional water authorities, the regional health authorities, the regional tourist boards, the regional sports councils and the regional arts associations.

The question remains as to whether this is adequate: there are some who forcefully argue that it is not. Foremost among these is the Town and Country Planning Association with whose 1981 Policy Statement we conclude this chapter.

A REGIONAL DIMENSION FOR LOCAL GOVERNMENT?

With the state of the economy, the abolition of the regional economic planning machinery, the ageing of the published regional economic strategies, the weakness of the few Standing Conferences of Local Authorities and the marked centralist stance of recent governments (of which the apotheosis is the 1980 Local Government, Planning and Land Act) there is a clear need for 'a regional dimension for local government in England and Wales'. A policy statement with this title was prepared by the Town and Country Planning Association in October 1980 and published in January 1981.[49] It makes a convincing case.

The TCPA believes this trend towards centralised government is both unnecessary and undesirable. In the Association's view it is essential to retain a regional dimension in government for the following reasons:
(a) To establish a voice in Europe; substantial EEC funds are now allocated on a regional basis and the regions need to be able to press their claims forcefully if they are to receive a fair allocation in competitive circumstances.
(b) To provide an effective means of communication with Westminster and Whitehall, particularly in respect of issues of overall regional concern, such as employment and economic development.
(c) To monitor and, where appropriate, to co-ordinate the expenditure programme of public agencies so as to prevent unnecessary overlaps or duplications.
(d) To offer a convenient forum for liaison with other regional bodies (e.g. the water authorities) and statutory undertakers (e.g. British Rail, Coal Board, Gas and Electricity Boards

etc.), whose decisions so often affect or interact with the activities of the county and district councils.

(*e*)   To provide a wider context for the consideration of structure plan reviews, the proposed regional statements, and issues of regional significance – e.g. airports, green belts, mineral workings, nuclear power stations etc.

The machinery proposed is a resuscitation and reform of the old Standing Conferences, and their extension to cover the whole country. In the longer run, the TCPA remains convinced that 'regional authorities should and will [*sic*] be created as a part of a further reorganisation of local government' though 'when and how . . . remains to be seen'. But as a temporary measure, *faute de mieux*, local authorities should review and improve their own regional institutions.

If the opportunity is grasped, the regions will be in a much better position not only to respond to the many pressures which will be placed upon them over the next few years, but also to counter the current trend towards centralisation and to influence the form and shape of any longer-term changes in the structure of government.

REFERENCES AND FURTHER READING: CHAPTER 11

1   P. Abercrombie, *Greater London Plan 1944* (HMSO, 1945).
2   Report of the Royal Commission on Local Government in England, Vol. 2: *Memorandum of Dissent by Mr D. Senior*, Cmnd 4040-I (HMSO, 1969).
3   op. cit.
4   See Standing Conference on London and South East Regional Planning, *A History of the Conference and Its Work 1962–1974*, published by the Standing Conference (28 Old Queen Street, London SW1H 9HP). Periodic reports on specific issues are published by the Conference, for example, *Policy Guidelines to Meet the South East Region's Need for Aggregates in the 1980s* (July 1979); and *Monitoring Housing Development* (July 1980).
    The West Midlands Planning Authorities Conference appears to be a looser body which has concentrated on contributing to the succession of West Midlands Plans, Studies and Strategies. The most recent of these (1979) was *A Developing Strategy for the West Midlands: Updating and Rolling Forward of the Regional Strategy to 1991 – The Regional Economy: Problems and Proposals*. It will be interesting to see what happens to this Conference now that the resources (and stimulus?) of the Economic Planning Council have gone.
5   E. Sharp, *The Ministry of Housing and Local Government* (Allen & Unwin, 1969).
6   See particularly *The North East: A Programme for Development and Growth*, Cmnd 2206 (HMSO, 1963).
7   White Paper, *South East England*, Cmnd 2308 (HMSO, 1964).
8   *The North-West: A Regional Study* (HMSO, 1965); and *The West Midlands: A Regional Study* (HMSO, 1965).
9   See *Report of Non-Departmental Public Bodies*, Cmnd 7797 (HMSO, 1980). A 'Quango' is a quasi-autonomous non-governmental organisation.
10 *RTPI News*, September 1979.
11 See DoE Circular 4/79, *Memorandum on Structure and Local Plans* (HMSO, 1979), paras 2.39–2.40.

12 A. G. Powell, 'Strategies for the English regions: ten years of evolution', *Town Planning Review*, vol. 49, no. 1 (January 1978), p. 11.
13 op. cit., p. 6.
14 *HC Debates*, 9 November 1959.
15 National Economic Development Council, *Conditions Favourable to Faster Growth* (HMSO, 1963), p. 14.
16 A. Cairncross, Foreword to D. Maclennan and J. B. Parr, *Regional Policy: Past Experiences and New Directions* (Martin Robertson, 1979), p. xii.
17 National Economic Development Council, op. cit., p. 26.
18 *Wales: The Way Ahead*, Cmnd 3334 (HMSO, 1969).
19 *The Intermediate Areas: Report of a Committee under the Chairmanship of Sir Joseph Hunt*, Cmnd 3998 (HMSO, 1969).
20 See J. D. McCallum, 'The development of British regional policy', in D. Maclennan and J. B. Parr, op. cit., particularly pp. 19–38.
21 See particularly, the White Paper of October 1970, *Investment Incentives*, Cmnd 4516 (HMSO).
22 White Paper, *Industrial and Regional Development*, Cmnd 4942 (HMSO, 1972).
23 House of Commons Expenditure Committee (Trade and Industry Sub-Committee), Session 1973–4, *Regional Development Incentives: Report*, HC Paper 85 (HMSO, 1973), pp. 72–3. (Quoted in J. D. McCallum, op. cit., p. 24.)
24 See White Paper, *Public Expenditure to 1979–80*, Cmnd 6393 (HMSO, 1976).
25 Department of Industry, *An Approach to Industrial Strategy*, Cmnd 6315 (HMSO, 1975). For a discussion of this, see G. C. Cameron, 'The national industrial strategy and regional policy', in D. Maclennan and J. B. Parr, op. cit.
26 Department of Industry, 'Government announces "more selective" regional policy', *Trade and Industry*, 20 July 1979, pp. 99–102. An indication of the immediate attenuation of regional policy is provided by the following table, taken from p. 1 of the *Cambridge Economic Policy Review*, vol. 6, no. 2 (July 1980):

The Changing Force of Regional Policy

Financial year	Total government spending on regional policy in real terms (£ million, 1975/6 prices)	IDC refusals (in the Midlands and South) %
1960/1	34	17
1964/5	75	26
1969/70	612	16
1972/3	493	10
1975/6	611	12
1979/80	322	2

27 See, for example, J. A. Schofield, 'Macro evaluations of the impact of regional policy in Britain: a review of recent research', *Urban Studies*, vol. 16 (1979), pp. 251–71; and J. Marquand, *Measuring the Effects and Costs of Regional Incentives* (Department of Industry, 1980).
28 *Hunt Report*, op. cit., p. 39, para. 109.
29 The same lack of optimism can be seen in many fields of policy. Gorham and Glazer neatly sum up the common situation as one in which 'confidence in our ability to frame solutions [to urban problems] has declined as understanding of problems has grown'. W. Gorham and N. Glazer, *The Urban Predicament* (Urban Institute, 1976), p. 2.
30 G. McCrone, 'The determinants of regional growth rates', in J. Vaizey (ed.), *Economic Sovereignty and Regional Policy* (Gill & Macmillan, Dublin, 1975).
31 N. Kaldor, 'The case for regional policies', *Scottish Journal of Political Economy*,

vol. 17 (1970), pp. 337–48; and G. C. Cameron, 'Economic analysis for a declining urban economy', *Scottish Journal of Political Economy*, vol. 18 (1971), pp. 315–45.

32   A. J. Brown, *The Framework of Regional Economics in the United Kingdom* (Cambridge University Press, 1972).

33   J. N. Randall, 'The changing nature of the regional economic problem since 1965', in D. Maclennan and J. B. Parr, *Regional Policy*, op. cit., p. 123.

34   Department of Industry, 'Government announces "more selective" regional policy', *Trade and Industry*, 20 July 1979, pp. 99–102.

35   W. R. Thompson, *A Preface to Urban Economics* (Resources for the Future, 1963), pp. 6–8. See also N. S. Segal, 'The limits and means of "self reliant" regional economic growth', in D. Maclennan and J. B. Parr, op. cit., pp. 211ff.

36   G. Manners *et al.*, *Regional Development in Britain*, 2nd edn (Wiley, 1980), p. 17.

37   Peter Hill, 'Linwood: the muddled optimism that turned a "real winner" into a lame duck', *The Times*, 20 February 1981. The accompanying saga of the strip mills is told in J. Vaizey, *The History of British Steel* (Weidenfeld & Nicolson, 1974).

38   G. Manners *et al.*, op. cit., p. 57.

39   *Humberside: A Feasibility Study* (HMSO, 1969); *Severnside: A Feasibility Study* (HMSO, 1971); and *Tayside: Potential For Development* (HMSO, 1970).

40   And, much less effectively, on easier access to public authority housing. See, for instance, Central Housing Advisory Committee, *Council Housing: Purposes, Procedures and Priorities* (HMSO, 1969), ch. 9, 'Housing and labour mobility'; and Housing Services Advisory Group, *Allocation of Council Housing* (Department of the Environment, 1978), ch. 9, 'Mobility'. On retraining, see the publications of the Manpower Services Commission. On the ETS see P. B. Beaumont, 'Assessing the performance of assisted labour mobility policy in Britain', *Scottish Journal of Political Economy*, vol. 24 (1977), pp. 55–65; P. B. Beaumont, 'An examination of assisted labour mobility policy', in D. Maclennan and J. B. Parr, op. cit.; and J. H. Johnson and J. Salt, 'Employment transfer policies in Great Britain', *Three Banks Review*, no. 126 (June 1980), pp. 18–39.

41   *Cambridge Economic Policy Review*, vol. 6, no. 2 (July 1980) ('Urban and regional policy, with provisional regional accounts 1966–78'), p. 37.

42   D. Maclennan and J. B. Parr, op. cit., p. 2.

43   *Cambridge Economic Policy Review*, op. cit., p. 38.

44   J. T. Hughes, 'An urban approach to regional problems', in D. Maclennan and J. B. Parr, op. cit., p. 173.

45   Among the last of these was that of the Northern Region Strategy Team, *Strategic Plan for the Northern Region* (Department of the Environment, 1977).

46   An exception is the 1979 updating of the West Midlands Regional Strategy, *A Developing Strategy for the West Midlands*.

47   Scottish Development Department, *National Planning Guidelines*. The first batch of these was issued with SDD Circular 19/1977. Further Guidelines were published subsequently. A list is given in the Bibliography.

48   Organisation for Economic Cooperation and Development, *Regional Policies: The Current Outlook* (OECD, 1977).

49   'TCPA policy statement: a regional dimension for local government in England and Wales', *Town and Country Planning*, vol. 50, no. 1 (January 1981), p. 27.

Chapter 12

PLANNING AND THE PUBLIC

PUBLIC OPINION

Public opinion – your opinion – is of the utmost importance in the making of planning decisions. Elected members and officers go to considerable lengths to find out what you think about the issues and problems facing us in planning and to discover your reaction to the proposed solutions. The City does not belong to the Council much less the Planning Committee. It is your City and your views matter.

This passage comes from the foreword to *Planning for Leicester*, a publication of the Leicester City Council, which is aimed at explaining the planning process and seeking the participation of the Leicester citizens in it.[1] Such publications, though once rare, are now a common means of enlisting public support for, and involvement in, the making of planning policies. This stems from an increased realisation of the essentially political nature of the planning process and the crucial importance of public acceptability. It was this lack of public acceptability which (arguably) was one of the main reasons for the failure of the compensation-betterment provisions of the 1947 Act and the short-lived Land Commission. It is a major purpose of the current planning system to achieve a greater flexibility and sensitivity than had proved possible under the earlier system.

Part of the difficulty lies in the fact that much planning is regulative, and there is a natural tendency to forget or fail to see the real gains that have been made, for instance, in protecting the countryside from unsightly advertising hoardings; but the issue goes much deeper. Throughout the 1950s and 1960s planning proposals were generally presented to the public as a *fait accompli*, and only rarely were they given a thorough public discussion.[2] Though there was (and still is) machinery for objections and appeals, this quasi-judicial process was devised for use by a restricted range of interested parties. As will be shown later in this chapter, it was modified in its operation in response to increasing public pressures, but the general attitude to this system was (and remains) less favourable than to the normal judicial system with which it is frequently – though inappropriately – compared. However, the important issue is not that of the scope for registering 'objections', but that of the extent to which planning involves active public participation. This in turn demands a high degree of political sophistication and understanding on the part of the public.[3]

This is more than a matter of jolly public relations. People need to understand the problems with which planning is concerned and the constraints under which planners work. To quote again from *Planning for Leicester*: 'planners work within the tight limits of the law and they are not the all-powerful gods that they are sometimes thought to be'. Moreover, the effect of planning decisions on land values must not be forgotten. Advance knowledge of planning proposals can markedly affect the value of the land concerned. This may lead to speculation or to premature objections on the part of owners who expect to be adversely affected. As a result, a planning department often have to operate under a veil of secrecy. This can only serve to increase public suspicion. Strangely, this situation is itself in part the result of previous lack of public support. As already suggested, though it is by no means the full explanation, there can be no doubt that the divorce between planners and the public is one of the factors which has led to the curious half-dismantled planning legislation which we now have – what Lord Holford once called 'a set of spare parts'. It must be axiomatic that compensation for acquisition of land or restriction on its use must be at a level which is publicly acceptable. This is not so merely on grounds of equity but also because 'inadequate' compensation will arouse such opposition as to inhibit public authorities from using their powers. This was the position under the 1947 Act. Each amendment of this Act has been designed to remove further injustices. But injustices still remain and will continue to do so until a scheme is devised which will at one and the same time be adequate for achieving planning objectives and prove publicly acceptable.

The point is basically a simple one: planners cannot effectively move too far ahead of public opinion. This applies not only to town and country planning: it applies equally to the social services, to the nationalised industries and indeed to any form of public or private monopoly or near-monopoly. It goes to the root of democratic government in modern industrial society; and it thus leads far from the central questions which form the subject matter of this book. All that can be attempted here is a discussion of a selection of relevant topics.

PLANNING APPLICATIONS

Around a half of a million applications for planning permission are made each year to local planning authorities in Britain, of which over four-fifths are granted.[4] This enormous spate of applications involves great strains on the local planning machinery which, generally speaking, is not adequately staffed to deal with them and at the same time undertake the necessary work involved in preparing and reviewing development plans. Yet full consideration by local planning staffs is needed if planning committees – the elected members who have the responsibility for granting or refusing applications – are to have the requisite information on which to base their decisions.

The importance of this is underlined by the fact that planning committees often have remarkably little time during a meeting in which to come to a decision. Agendas for meetings tend to be long: an average of five to six minutes for consideration of each application is nothing unusual, and in some cases the time may be as little as two minutes. It cannot, therefore, be surprising that in a large proportion of cases (in the bigger authorities at least) the recommendations of the planning officer are approved *pro forma*. This may, of course, result in part from the harmonious relationship which commonly exists between local authority representatives and their officers; and, in any case, lay members tend to accept the technical expertise of their officials, while, on the other hand, the officials well know the minds of their political masters. Yet the point remains that both the elected representatives and the planning officials are hard pressed to cope with the constant flood of applications.

Several important implications follow from this. First, and most obvious, is the danger that decisions will be given which are 'wrong' – that is, which do not accord with planning objectives. Secondly, good relationships with the public in general and unsuccessful applicants in particular are difficult to attain: there is simply not sufficient time. Thirdly, this lack of time corroborates the view of many (unsuccessful) applicants that their case has never had adequate consideration: a view which is further supported by the manner in which refusals are commonly worded. Phrases such as 'detrimental to amenity' or 'not in accordance with the development plan', and so on, mean little or nothing to the individual applicant. He suspects that his case has been considered in general terms rather than in the particular detail which he naturally thinks is important in his case. And he may be right: understaffed and overworked planning departments cannot give each case the individual attention which is desirable.

This, of course, is not the whole picture. For instance, individuals who may wholly agree with a general planning principle will tend to see it in a different light when it is applied to their own applications. As Grove has pointed out:[5] 'the man who has his home in one part of a green belt and owns what an estate agent would call "fully ripe building land" in another part, is as vociferous in relying on green belt principles to oppose building near his home as he is in denouncing the extreme and ridiculous lengths to which those principles have been carried when he is refused planning permission on his other land, and frequently seems to achieve this without any conscious hypocrisy'.

This normal human failing is encouraged by the curious compromise situation which currently exists in relation to the control of land. On the one hand, it seems to be generally accepted in principle (as it definitely is in law) that no one has a right to develop his land as he wishes unless the development is publicly desirable (as determined by a political instead of a financial decision). On the other hand, though the allocation of land to particular uses is determined by a public decision, the motives for private development are financial – and the financial profits which result from the development constitute private gain (though subject to capital gains tax). This unhappy circumstance (which is discussed at length in Chapter 7) involves a clash of principles which the unsuccessful applicant for planning permission experiences in a particularly sharp manner. It follows that local planning officials may have a peculiarly difficult task in explaining to a landowner why, for example, the field which he owns needs to be 'protected from development'.

Nevertheless, the success which attends this unenviable task does differ markedly between different local authorities. (The Dobry Report, summarised in Chapter 4, illustrates the range of current practices.) The question is not simply one of the great variations in potential land values in different parts of the country or in the relative adequacy of planning staffs. Though these are important factors, there remains the less easily documented question of attitudes towards the public. All that can be said is that in some local authorities a great effort is made to assist and explain matters to an applicant, whereas in others the impression one gains is that of a bureaucratic machine which displays little patience and no kindness towards the individual applicant who does not understand 'planning procedures'.

DELEGATION OF PLANNING DECISIONS TO OFFICERS

The 1968 Planning Act (now consolidated in the 1971 Act)[6] made provision for the delegation to officers of planning decisions. This is in line with the recommendations of the Maud Report on *Management of Local Government*,[7] the Mallaby Report on *Staffing of Local Government*[8] and the report of the *Management Study on Development Control*.[9]

The background to this is that 70 per cent of all planning applications are of 'a simple nature'. The *Management Study on Development Control* found that a large proportion of these 'simple' applications were determined by a committee or by the council without presentation of details, without discussion, and in accordance with the recommendations of the officers. They concluded that very many development control applications were already effectively delegated to officers for decision but were required to go through a formal procedure for ratification by a body of members. This created unnecessary work for the local authority and unnecessary delay for the applicant. Consideration was given to the possibility of a system which allowed for *approvals only* to be issued by a planning officer on certain clearly defined classes of application:

(*a*)   construction of one house in a residential area;
(*b*)   construction of a block of private garages;
(*c*)   changes of use not conflicting with the development plan and not requiring advertising;
(*d*)   erection of temporary buildings and extension of existing temporary permissions;
(*e*)   construction of vehicular access on other than trunk roads;
(*f*)   construction of extensions to existing residential properties.

It was estimated that this would reduce by up to 50 per cent the number of cases needing to go to committee, 'would save committee time for more important work, would save a considerable amount of administrative work and time, and would speed up the issue of decision notices to applicants'. The Mallaby Committee added that greater delegation would provide more attractive and challenging official careers, and thus stimulate recruitment. In this way a better service would be rendered to the public.

The statutory provisions go further than the proposals of the *Management Study*. They enable local authorities to delegate decisions on all kinds of planning application except those for listed building consent. The power is entirely discretionary: it is for local authorities to decide which officers, if any, should be given delegated powers and for which kinds of application. A decision of an officer exercising delegated powers has the same standing as one given by the council itself.

This streamlining at the local level reflects the principle underlying the current legislation – that the planning system should be so organised that decisions are taken at the appropriate level. Thus the department are responsible for broad policy issues, the local authority for local plans, and officials for detailed administrative issues which do not warrant committee involvement. In this way, a real attempt is being made to reduce the bureaucratic, cumbersome and unwieldy system which has been paralysing the machinery. The relationships with, and service to, the public should improve considerably; but much will depend on the more subtle factors than formal rearrangements of power: an issue to which we return shortly.

MALADMINISTRATION AND THE 'OMBUDSMAN'

Most legislation is based on the assumption that the organs of government will operate efficiently and fairly. This is not always the case, but, even if it were, provision has to be made for the citizen who feels aggrieved by some action (or inaction) to complain, have his complaint investigated and be satisfied that the investigation is impartial. As modern industrial society becomes more complex, the pressures for a machinery of protest, appeal and restitution grow – as is evidenced in such widely differing fields as social security, race relations and press publicity.

At the parliamentary level, the case for an 'ombudsman' was reluctantly conceded by the government, and a Parliamentary Commissioner for Administration was appointed in 1967. He is an independent statutory official whose function is to investigate complaints of maladministration referred to him through Members of Parliament. His powers of investigation extend over all central government departments and he has the right of access to all departmental papers.

Only a small fraction of the Parliamentary Commissioner's cases relate to planning matters and, of course, his concern is with administrative procedures, not with the merits of planning decisions. His reports give full but anonymised texts of reports of selected cases which he has investigated. In a 1975 report, for instance,[10] he reports on cases involving a complaint that the Secretary of State for the Environment failed to understand the grounds on which he had been requested to intervene in (that is, to use his default powers in relation to) a redevelopment scheme; a complaint by a Motorways Action Committee that, following a motorway inquiry, the inspector called for further evidence from the DoE (much of which, the committee submitted, was 'highly dubious and contentious, and contained a number of misleading assumptions') on which they were not given the opportunity to cross-examine the department's witness; a complaint by a group of local residents that an appeal decision to allow a gypsy caravan site paid little heed to local residents' objections, ignored important relevant facts and was taken on the basis of inconsistent attitudes; and a complaint that an appeal refusal to allow the replacement of a coach house was unfair and improper in that the reasons given in the decision letter were not in accordance with the facts and that the decision could not be reconciled with the policies followed by the local planning authority or with planning permissions they had given for other development in their area. In all these cases the Parliamentary Commissioner concluded that the complaint could not be upheld. This was not always the case, however; the Commissioner has had occasion to criticise some aspects of the department's handling of particular cases and this has led to changes in internal administrative procedures.

The cases in which the Commissioner does find 'maladministration' are often of extraordinary complexity, if not actual confusion. Indeed, complexity and confusion can be major factors in the failures in communication and the misunderstandings which result in 'maladministration'. These very features make it difficult to summarise an illustrative case: the reader is referred to what the Commissioner termed the 'sorry tale' of the demolition of buildings in a conservation area – a case in which there was 'a deplorable failure by a Government

Department [the Department of the Environment] to attend properly to the legitimate interests of the private citizen'.[11]

The Parliamentary Commissioner has, in a number of cases, noted that part of a complaint is against the actions of a local authority. He has no jurisdiction in this area, and any reference made to local authorities is simply 'to provide background, and place in context the actions of the Department'. The position is now, of course, changed by the establishment of the 'local government ombudsman' – or, to be more precise, the Commissioner for Local Administration. Separate Commissions have been set up (under the provisions of the Local Government Act 1974 and the Local Government (Scotland) Act 1975) for England, for Wales and for Scotland.[12]

A high proportion of complaints concern planning matters (one-third in 1979–80):[13] only 'housing' vies in importance. As with the Parliamentary Commissioner, complaints have to be referred via an elected member – a procedure on which there is considerable controversy. There is also concern about the situation which arises when a local authority refuses to 'remedy' a case in which maladministration or injustice is found by a Commissioner. To date, however, the general attitude of government, with one exception, is that there has been insufficient experience to warrant legislative change. The exception (enacted by the Local Government Act 1978) enables a local authority to incur expenditure to remedy injustice without specific authorisation by the secretary of state. However, further changes can be expected in the light of greater experience.[14]

It is less clear, however, whether the impact of the ombudsmen might not be to increase the bureaucracy of local planning – by creating greater caution and record-keeping in order to be able to counter charges of maladministration.

A further impact is the widened opportunity which the ombudsmen provide for third parties to object to planning proposals. In a review of cases reported in the *Journal of Planning and Environment Law* up to December 1976, Williams found that of nineteen complaints only three came from applicants themselves.[15] Thirteen came from near neighbours and three from residents' associations and an amenity society.

The statutory provisions relating to publicity and to third parties (which are outlined later) are limited, and local authorities have considerable freedom to devise their procedures according to their own views of what is appropriate. Not all have taken kindly to the 'interference' of the local ombudsman. Indeed, a concerted effort was made in 1979 by one local authority association to restrict the ombudsman's scope for action.[16] Following a 'consideration of cases where a local ombudsman had found maladministration because of failure to consult neighbours on planning applications where the authority had a policy to consult, but no statutory obligation to do so', the Association of District Councils circularised member authorities advising them:

(a) to avoid making formal resolutions committing the authority to undertake specified neighbour or general public consultations in connection with planning applications in their area;

(b) formally to authorise their planning officers to undertake such informal consultations entirely at their own discretion but having due regard to the advice contained in Circular 71/73 issued jointly by the Department of the Environment and the Welsh Office on June 5, 1973;[17]

(c) formally to delegate to their chief planning officer the power to accept and agree amendments to submitted applications at his discretion; and

(d) to suggest that their planning staff never make firm commitments to consult neighbours in respect of future possible applications not yet received.

The advice concluded: 'District councils who have already adopted the above suggestions have successfully avoided investigation and it is hoped that other member authorities will be able to benefit from the experience which they have gained.'

Not surprisingly, the Commission were 'disturbed' at this. (The *Journal of Planning and Environment Law* were more forthright and sarcastically suggested that 'a certain way for any public authority to avoid a finding of maladministration is to cease to administer altogether, and we believe the Association's advice goes a long way down that particular road'.)[18] Discussions between the Commission and the Association followed, though, from the evidence of the Commission's annual report, they were not very fruitful.[19] (The Association 'claimed that whilst the advice issued was aimed at reducing time-consuming investigations and findings of maladministration, it was likely to lead to more consultation about planning applications rather than less'.)

At the time of writing the matter of publicity for planning applications is being considered by the newly created National Development Control Forum.

LOCAL GOVERNMENT AND THE ELECTORATE

The innovation of a local ombudsman is of interest in a wider context. By comparison with the position of Parliament (and through Parliament, the taxpayer) *vis-à-vis* central government, the ratepayer is badly placed *vis-à-vis* local government. There is little at the local level to compare with such institutions as those of the Parliamentary Question, the Public Accounts Committee, the Expenditure Committee and the Comptroller and Auditor General. There are, of course, the provisions for district audit in England and Wales, and in Scotland, the Commission for Local Authority Accounts (the first chairman of which – Tom Fraser, a former Labour Minister of Transport – is on record as saying that they are interested 'in more than balancing the books': they would 'ensure that the ratepayers get value for money; that there was no unnecessary duplication of services between region and district; that rents and charges for local authority services were regularly reviewed').

In such ways local government is beginning to come under unprecedented scrutiny, though still on a modest scale. This trend is a most healthy one and promises to make local government more sensitive and responsive to its electorate.

A sharp statutory 'push' in this general direction has now been provided by the Local Government, Planning and Land Act 1980 which imposes a duty on local authorities 'to publish information . . . about the discharge of their functions and other matters'. It is, as yet, too early to assess what impact this will have, or even what is involved.

There is, however, a certain irony (if that is not too weak a term) in the fact that the central government is imposing a duty of this nature on local government at precisely the same time as it is cutting down on the publication of departmental annual reports and following a pricing policy for new publications which puts them beyond reasonable reach. The 1980 Act is priced at £9.30, while the five-page – three-sheet – GDO Amendment of 1981 is £1.10. On the latter basis, local authorities charging the going HMSO rate of 70 pence a sheet may find few buyers (or, alternatively, if they have a real sales drive they may be able to make a good profit and reduce the rates).

PLANNING APPEALS

An unsuccessful applicant for planning permission can, of course, appeal to the secretary of state and, as noted in Chapter 2, a large number do so. Each case is considered by the department on its merits. This allows a great deal of flexibility, and permits cases of individual hardship to be sympathetically treated. At the same time, however, it can make the planning system seem arbitrary – at least to the unsuccessful appellant. Although broad policies are set out in such publications as the *Development Control Policy Notes*, the general view in the department is that a reliance on precedent could easily give rise to undesirable rigidities. As Mandelker has pointed out:

> Conditions vary so fundamentally from case to case and from one part of the country to another that it would be impossible, if not wrong, to draft rules that would hold good uniformly. The basic problem is that a variety of factors operate in a planning case; the

art of making a decision lies in the striking of a proper balance. Under the circumstances, there is little that the Department can do beyond listing those factors which it considers crucial, and expressing rules of thumb which will help select those which should preponderate.[20]

Other issues relevant to this view are the traditional local-central government relationship (in which local authorities are considered as equal partners in the processes of government) and the particular character of town and country planning in this country. The flexibility of the development plan, the wide area of discretion legally allowed to the planners in the operation of planning controls, and the very restricted jurisdiction of the courts, necessitate a judicial function for the department. However, this function is only quasi-judicial: decisions are taken, not on the basis of legal rules as in a court of law or in accordance with case-law, but on a judgement as to what course of action is, in the particular circumstances and in the context of ministerial policy, desirable, reasonable and equitable. By its very nature this must be elusive, and the unsuccessful appellant may well feel justified in believing that the dice are loaded against him. The very fact that public inquiries on planning appeals are heard by ministerial 'inspectors' (and probably in the town hall of the authority against whose decision he is appealing) does not make for confidence in a fair and objective hearing. The contrast with the courts is striking; to quote Grove again:

> The usual complaint of the civil litigant is not that his case is not fairly and impartially heard and determined, but that, owing to the complexity of the system, the delay and expense are excessive. The views of the planning applicant, except where he is successful, are quite different. He rarely complains of the cost (though quite often of the delay) but frequently takes the view that the inquiry or hearing was nothing more than an opportunity for him to 'let off steam'.

Of course, part of the expressed dissatisfaction comes from those who are compelled to forgo private gain for the sake of communal benefit: the criticisms are not really of procedures, and they are not likely to be assuaged by administrative reforms or good 'public relations'. They are fundamentally criticisms of the public control of land use – in particular, if not in principle.

Nevertheless, the appeals procedure has had shortcomings which have attracted strong and relevant protest. For example, the department used not to publish the reports prepared by their inspectors on appeal inquiries. Their main argument against publication was that this would cause misunderstanding and embarrassment. In their evidence to the Franks Committee on *Administrative Tribunals and Inquiries*, they stated:

> The objection in principle that we should see to publication is that our inspectors really act in a dual capacity. They act first of all as the inspector who goes down to see the site and who, being a technical man, can give us an appreciation of the soundness of the authority's proposals; they hear the arguments and report to the minister what took place, what impression is made upon them, what view they take of the site and so on. Then they make a recommendation and in that capacity they are acting as officers of the department because their recommendation is essentially what should be the application of policy to the facts they found. That is why you can have identical facts but different decisions. They have got to be *au fait* with current policy and say what they think that the minister, his policy being what it is, would wish to do in the particular case as they found it. We think that publication of the recommendation would cause embarrassment.[21]

This passage clearly illustrates how a public inquiry is different from a judicial review. It is usual to apply the term 'quasi-judicial', but this is not very satisfactory, as the Franks Committee implied. They saw the problem essentially as one of finding a reasonable balance between conflicting interests:

> On the one hand there are ministers enjoined by legislation to carry out certain duties. On the other hand there are the rights and feelings of individual citizens who find their possessions or plans interfered with by the administration. There is also the public interest, which requires both that ministers and other administrative bodies should not be frustrated in carrying out their duties and also that their decisions should be subject to effective checks or controls.[22]

The Franks Committee argued that inspectors' reports should be published, and this view was accepted by the government. It is interesting to note that in the great majority of cases (on planning appeals), the minister's decision has been 'broadly in line' with the recommendations of the inspector.

This is not the place to discuss all the issues relevant to these procedures: the interested reader is referred to the report of the Franks Committee. The immediate point is simply that neither the statutory provisions, nor the arguments on administrative inquiries, are concerned primarily with the encouragement of public participation in the planning process. To achieve this a local authority have to forge their own procedures.

Nevertheless, significant changes have been made in recent years to broaden the scope and to change the character of public inquiries on planning appeals, particularly in the case of proposals of major importance. Before outlining these, however, it is necessary to consider the statutory position of 'third parties'.

'THIRD PARTY' INTERESTS

The rights of 'third parties' – those affected by planning decisions but having no legal 'interest' in the land subject to the decision – were highlighted in the so-called Chalk Pit case.[23] This, in brief, concerned an application to 'develop' certain land in Essex by digging chalk. On being refused planning permission the applicants appealed to the Minister of Housing, and a local inquiry was held. Among those who appeared as objectors at the inquiry some were substantial land-owners, including a Major Buxton, whose land was adjacent to the appeal site and was being used for agricultural and residential purposes. The inspector's recommendation was that the appeal should be dismissed, mainly because there was a serious danger of chalk dust being deposited on the land of Major Buxton and others in quantities which would be 'detrimental to the user of the land'; and that there was no present shortage of chalk in the locality. The minister disagreed with the inspector's recommendations and allowed the appeal.

Major Buxton then appealed to the High Court, partly on the ground that in rejecting his inspector's findings of fact, the minister had relied on certain subsequent advice and information given to him by the Minister of Agriculture without giving the objectors any opportunity of correcting or commenting upon this advice and information. But Major Buxton now found that he had no legal right of appeal to the courts: indeed he apparently had had no legal right to appear at the inquiry. (He only had what the judge thought to be a 'very sensible' administrative privilege.) In short, Major Buxton was a 'third party': he was in no legal sense a 'person aggrieved'. Yet clearly in the wider sense of the phrase Major Buxton was very much aggrieved, and at first sight he had a moral right to object and to have his objection carefully weighed. But should the machinery of town and country planning be used for this purpose by an individual? Before the town and country planning legislation, any landowner could develop his land as he liked, provided he did not infringe the common law which was designed more to protect the right to develop rather than to restrain it. The law of nuisance and trespass was not a particularly strong constraint on the freedom to use land. But, as the judge stressed, the planning legislation was designed 'to restrict development for the benefit of the public at large and not to confer new rights on any individual member of the public'.

This, of course, is the essential point. It is the job of the local planning authority to assess the public advantage or disadvantage of a proposed development – subject to a review by the secretary of state if those having a legal interest in the land in question object. Third parties cannot usurp these government functions. Nevertheless, it might be generally agreed that those affected by planning decisions should have the right to make representations for consideration by a planning committee. The present position is that third parties have an 'administrative privilege' to appear at a public inquiry, but generally no similar privilege in relation to a planning application.

There is one group of exceptions to this. The Town and Country Planning Act of 1959 introduced a provision designed to give an opportunity for the public ventilation of objections to certain planning proposals of an 'unneighbourly' character. Such developments are advertised, and objectors allowed to make written 'representations' to the local planning authority. If the planning application is granted, there is no further opportunity for objections – however much the objectors may be affected. But, if the application is refused and the applicant appeals, the objectors have the normal privilege of appearing and being heard at the public inquiry. In short, the only new provision here is the requirement for publicity and the formal right to make representations.

The types of development covered by these provisions are very limited – public conveniences, refuse disposal and sewerage works, slaughterhouses and theatres, dance halls, skating rinks, and so on. It might be possible to extend this list somewhat (to include, for example, fish and chip shops and petrol stations), but to extend it to cover all applications would, quite apart from any objections on principle, lead to the danger of a breakdown in planning procedures. The machinery of planning is already burdened with development applications and appeals. An extension of the opportunities for representations, objections and appeals would slow down procedures and make them dangerously cumbersome.

This is a practical issue of importance, but the fundamental point is that it is the job of local planning authorities to assess what is publicly desirable. Measures designed to make the system fair are all to the good. Openness and fairness were two of the principles which the Franks Committee sought to apply to administrative tribunals and inquiries. Their third principle – impartiality – cannot be applied without qualification to planning procedures (as the Committee pointed out). If a local planning authority were merely a judicial body seeking to achieve a fair balance between conflicting interests, many of the arguments for extending the rights of individuals to be heard and to object could be accepted. But the local planning authority are not an impartial body: they are an agency of government attempting to secure what they believe to be the best development for its area. In short, they have a fundamentally political responsibility.

As already indicated (in the earlier discussion on the local ombudsman), the whole issue of publicity for planning applications is under review by the National Development Control Forum.

THE CHANGING NATURE OF PUBLIC INQUIRIES

This fundamental political responsibility, however, has to be soundly based, and an increasingly articulate and 'environmentally aware' public has forced changes even within the narrow confines of an inquiry on a planning appeal, particularly where major development proposals are at issue (and even more so in the case of called-in applications and motorway proposals, where the inquiry is concerned with whether planning permission should be given, rather than with whether the decision of a planning authority should be upheld or reversed).

The purpose of a public inquiry is to enable the secretary of state to decide whether a planning authority have been correct in refusing permission for a particular development.[24] Originally, the main emphasis in the inquiry procedure was on the strength (or otherwise) of the objections made by the appellant, though even here the secretary of state was concerned with the intrinsic merits of the case. But increasingly, public inquiries on major issues have become more searching, a larger number of third parties have been involved and the department have been at pains to ensure that all the relevant issues have been covered. The most explicit statement of this development of the public inquiry system is to be found in a memorandum issued by the Scottish Development Department in 1975.[25] This was issued as a code of guidance for reporters (as 'inspectors' are called in Scotland) *and for all parties to inquiries.* Though it was envisaged that the recommended procedures would be adopted as a whole, the covering circular drew particular attention to five points:

(i) The importance on the one hand of applicants giving full, public explanations of their proposals and their effect and, on the other hand, of planning authorities discussing the proposals thoroughly with applicants and with objectors to improve public understanding, open the way to compromise and perhaps even to avoid the need for an inquiry at all.

(ii) The need to circulate in advance of the inquiry as much written evidence as possible and to discourage the use, for tactical advantage, of surprise evidence, with reserve sanction to treat such action as unreasonable behaviour to be taken into account for the purpose of award of expenses.

(iii) The avoidance of repetitious cross-examination.

(iv) The importance of the role of the reporter in directing the proceedings. He should not necessarily be a silent listener to the proceedings: he should be free to seek any clarification he deems necessary or to direct questions to issues which he thinks will be important to the secretary of state's decision, but which may not have been adequately covered in the evidence.

(v) The desirability of the maximum informality of procedure, so that the ordinary interested person does not feel inhibited from making a contribution without professional representation.

DISSATISFACTION WITH ROAD INQUIRIES

In striking contrast with this positive approach has been the disarray in connection with road inquiries. Some of the problems here (such as the forced postponement of the inquiry into the Airedale Trunk Road and the disruption at the inquiries on road proposals in Epping Forest and in Cornwall) are the result of pressure groups who are opposed to the building of any road anywhere, irrespective of the merits (or otherwise) of particular projects. The arena for much of this debate should be Parliament: it is nonsensical at every local inquiry. On the other hand, national transport policy has, for some time, been in a confused state – to say the least. Objectors have made the most of this, and no solution is possible until some clear guidelines are laid down (after appropriate national debate).

This in turn means that policy should be clear and broadly acceptable. So far as roads are concerned, this is certainly not the case at present. As a result, public confidence in the inquiry process has been seriously weakened, and this problem has been exacerbated by the sheer volume of inquiries. A paper by Frank Layfield[26] neatly sets out the relevant considerations in a broader context, but until road policies in general are settled and generally accepted, there is a real danger that the public inquiry process will be thrown into widespread disrepute.

However, it is not only roads and road inquiries which are at issue.*

---

*It was not until after this book was complete that I obtained Patrick McAuslan's *The Ideologies of Planning Law* (Pergamon, 1980). This presents a fascinating, penetrating study of a range of issues dealt with in this volume. On the particular point of road inquiries, he writes: 'the disenchantment with public inquiries into road proposals is only the most public and publicised manifestation of a general disenchantment with the system of land use planning, to which the conflict of ideologies within and over the use of the law is an important contributor. This conflict is heightened in public inquiries into road proposals because the issues of substance give rise to such sharp divisions of opinion, and because participators are making such explicit use of the inquiry for the promotion of alternative policies and versions of the public interest. What this use of the inquiry has shown is that the reforms introduced as a result of the Franks Report twenty years ago based on the principle of openness, fairness and impartiality, and concentrating on procedures did not change (perhaps were not designed to change) the overriding purpose of the public local inquiry which was and is to advance the administration's version of the public interest.' Using McAuslan's terminology, this is a triumph of 'the public interest ideology' over 'the ideology of public participation' (pp. 72-3). McAuslan later has some important things to say about the Windscale Inquiry.

Indeed public disquiet goes far wider (and deeper). This is particularly the case with major planning inquiries. Tom Hancock is only one among many who have referred to 'the scepticism, which is surprisingly widespread in our society, about the inquiry system':

> The major reason is that the statutory local inquiry is being asked to do things which are well beyond its capacity. The Windscale Inquiry was a particularly vivid example. That forum in timing, in briefing, in scope, in method and in reportage proved, in my view, to be incapable of properly informing Parliament and the Secretary of State for the Environment of the immensely important issues at stake. As an example of information provided it was appalling in that the Parker Report was generally and misleadingly accepted as the official record of proceedings, by Parliament, prior to debate and the subsequent acceptance of the recommendations for the granting of planning permissions 'without delay' for the proposed Thermal Oxide Reprocessing Plant.[27]

The Windscale Inquiry has aroused particularly fierce passions, no doubt because of concern with nuclear power and its implications (whether real or feared). Following Hancock's line of argument, was not Windscale precisely the type of proposal for which the provisions relating to a Planning Inquiry Commission were designed?

PLANNING INQUIRY COMMISSIONS

In the 1967 White Paper[28] which preceded the 1968 reforms of the planning system it was stated that the government was reviewing planning cases which raised 'wide or novel issues of more than local significance'. For such cases, 'the ordinary public local inquiry is not satisfactory either as a method of permitting the full issues to be thrashed out or as a basis for a decision which can take into account the whole range of practicable alternatives'.

What emerged were provisions for a Planning Inquiry Commission, consisting of three to five members, which would be appointed by the secretary of state to examine major proposals. The types of proposal envisaged were those to which there had previously been fierce public opposition, 'such as those for processing natural gas at Bacton, Norfolk; a new London airport at Stansted, Essex; a hovercraft terminal at Pegwell Bay, Kent; and a gasholder at Abingdon, Berkshire'.[29] In terms of the statute, the proposals are those which raise 'considerations of national or regional importance' or where there are unfamiliar 'technical and scientific aspects'.[30]

Of particular interest is the fact that a Planning Inquiry Commission can consider alternative sites for the proposed development. The way in which a Planning Inquiry Commission would operate was explained during the second reading debate on the 1968 Act in the following words:

> The Commission's work will be in two stages. It will start by considering the broad background of the proposal on the basis of evidence provided by the promoters of the scheme, the local planning authority, government departments and interested individuals and organisations including the amenity societies. At this stage its procedure will be similar to that of a Royal Commission or Public Committee . . . The second stage of the investigation will be a local inquiry, following the usual pattern, into the scheme and the objections to it. At this stage the promoters or their representatives will be expected to deploy their case and will be subject to cross examination. Anybody or any organisation with something relevant to say may attend or be represented, and will be heard.
>
> The Commission will prepare its report after it has completed both stages of its work.[31]

The obvious question arises as to why a PIC was not established in connection with the Windscale proposal – or, indeed, why a PIC has never been used.[32] It has been suggested that one reason is that experience with the Roskill Commission on the Third London Airport was regarded by the government as being an unhappy indication of what difficulties a PIC might raise – 'a case of the sins of the father being visited on the son'.[33] These difficulties were of time (Roskill took about two years), of cost (the Roskill Commission's costs alone amounted to well over £1 million) and of fear of challenge to government policy.

It is probably the last which is of most importance.[34] A thoroughgoing inquiry will inevitably touch upon and perhaps even question government policy. This was certainly a major issue in the furore at several motorway inquiries: the objectors wanted to question the *need* for the road (not simply its alignment). A temporary victory for this position was won in 1979 when Lord Denning quashed the building of proposed sections of the M40 and M42. He did so on the grounds that the inspector was wrong to disallow examination of traffic flows and forecasts. These were not 'government policy' but 'predictions by experts about the future'. The Lords reversed Denning's finding and thus 'government policy' (even if based on dubious statistics) is safeguarded from investigation at a public inquiry.

The matter will not remain there: proposals for new forms of inquiry are currently being canvassed – a revised investigatory process is proposed by the TCPA,[35] and a new form of 'project inquiry' by the (alas now defunct) Outer Circle Policy Unit.[36] Nevertheless, continued governmental reluctance can be expected since 'impartial' inquiries tend to open up too many questions. These are difficult enough when the matter is a *general* one, such as one-parent families or prostitution, but with matters such as those there is rarely any urgency for action. Planning proposals constitute a very different matter: decisions have to be taken; and the greater the degree of understanding of the problems involved the more difficult are the decisions likely to be![37] It is perhaps significant that while an inquiry for the development of Stansted had still to be completed, the Secretary of State for Trade noted that 'Stansted had really chosen itself'.[38]

STATUTORY PROVISION FOR PUBLIC PARTICIPATION

Despite the difficulties with public inquiries (and the reluctance of government to make significant changes in the system), there are contrary forces at work at the local and county level. It is here, of course, that the focus of the participating public lies. (Few are interested in the location of motorways in general: all are interested in a motorway which passes through their back garden.)

A major landmark was the 1968 Planning Act (and its Scottish equivalent of 1969) which makes public participation a statutory requirement in the preparation of structure plans.

The main stimulus for this came, not from the grass-roots (still less from local government), but from central government themselves. Under the old development plan system, the department were becoming crippled by what a former Permanent Secretary called 'a crushing burden of casework'. The concept of ministerial responsibility was clearly shown to be inapplicable over the total field of development plan approval and planning appeals. Not only was much of this work inappropriate to a central government department: its sheet weight prevented central government from fulfilling their essential function of establishing major planning policies. A new system was therefore required which would remove much of the detailed work of planning – including approval of local plans – from central to local government. But this necessitates public confidence in local government: hence the importance of public participation. This now becomes, not a desirable adjunct to the planning process, but a fundamental basis. If public participation does not work, the system will collapse.

The legislation provides only the barest sketch of the new system: public participation is much more than adherence to formal procedures. It is merely provided that, in drawing up a structure plan, a local authority must:

(i)   give 'adequate' publicity to the report of the survey on which the plan is based, and to the policy which they propose to include in the plan;

(ii) provide publicity for their proposals and 'adequate opportunity'

to enable representations to be made by the public;
(iii) take into account these representations in drawing up the structure plan;
(iv) place the plan on deposit for public inspection, together with a statement of the time within which objections may be made to the secretary of state;
(v) submit the plan to the secretary of state, together with a statement of the steps which have been taken to comply with the above requirements, and of consultations which have been carried out with 'other persons'.

A local plan is drawn up within the policy framework of an approved structure plan and does not normally have to be submitted to the secretary of state for approval (though a copy has to be sent to him and, exceptionally, he can direct that it 'shall not have effect unless approved by him'). It follows the same procedure as a structure plan, but if there are any objections these are sent to the local authority (not the secretary of state) and are heard at a public inquiry which is held by an independent inspector who reports to the authority. The secretary of state is not normally concerned with local plans (though he will presumably check that they do properly reflect the policy approved in the structure plans).

At first sight it might appear that local authorities are to be judges in their own case, particularly since there is provision for inspectors to be appointed by local authorities. Indeed, much has been made of this 'unfair judicial process'. But the fact is that the process is not a judicial one: it is essentially administrative and political. This is why citizen-participation is so crucial. If local authorities do not succeed in carrying their citizenry with them the new system will fail: public opposition will necessitate a move back to the previous system.

THE SKEFFINGTON REPORT

Concern with - and even interest in - public participation has not been a particularly obvious strength of British local government, and it will be even more difficult to achieve with the now larger local authorities. With little experience to build on, it was perhaps inevitable that a Committee should be appointed 'to consult and report on the best methods, including publicity, of securing the participation of the public at the formative stage in the making of development plans for their area'. The Committee were set up under the chairmanship of the late Arthur Skeffington (then Joint Parliamentary Secretary to the Minister of Housing and Local Government) in March 1968 and their report was published in July 1969.[39]

The Skeffington Report made a number of rather obvious recommendations which did not carry the issues much further, for example:

people should be kept informed throughout the preparation of a structure or local plan for their area;

local planning authorities should seek to publicize proposals in a way that informs people living in the area to which the plan relates;

the public should be told what their representations have achieved or why they have not been accepted;

people should be encouraged to participate in the preparation of plans by helping with surveys and other activities as well as by making comments.

The mundane nature of many of the recommendations is testimony to the distance which British local government had to go in making citizen-participation a reality.

Unfortunately, the report did not discuss many of the really crucial issues, though passing references suggest that the Committee were aware of some of them. For instance, it is rightly stated that 'planning' is only one service 'and it would be unreasonable to expect the public to see it as an entity in itself'. The report continues: 'public participation would be little more than an artificial abstraction if it becomes identified solely with planning procedures rather than with the broadest interests of people'. This has major implications for the internal reorganisation and management of local authorities. So have the proposals for the appointment of 'community development officers . . . to secure the involvement of those people who do not join organizations' and for 'community forums' which would 'provide local organizations with the opportunity to discuss collectively planning and other issues of importance to the area', and which 'might also have administrative functions, such as receiving and distributing information on planning matters and promoting the formation of neighbourhood groups'.

What is conspicuously lacking in this debate on public participation is an awareness of its political implications. The Skeffington Report noted that it was feared that a community forum might become the centre of political opposition: but the only comment made was: 'we hope that that would not happen; it seems unlikely that it would, as most local groups are not party political in their membership'. The issue is not, however, one of *party politics*: it is one of local politics, pressures and interest. Public participation implies a transfer of some power from local councils to groups of electors. It is power which is the crucial issue – not in any sinister sense, but simply in terms of who is to decide local issues. The department do not want to be concerned with these (except where they have ramifications over a larger front: hence central approval of structure plans). This will be a matter of intimate concern for local councillors – and officials as well.

The transfer of considerable statutory power from central to local government will show only too clearly that planning is essentially a

political process – a fact which has been confused by the semi-judicial
procedures with which the department have been so preoccupied.

None of this is to argue that the philosophy underlying the new
legislation is misplaced: far from it. The intention is to demonstrate
that the real problems of citizen-participation and local democratic
control go far deeper than issues of formal procedures, of social
surveys and public exhibitions. If the new system works it will have a
major impact on British political processes; and it will not be confined
to 'town and country planning'.

Curiously, it was not the Skeffington Committee but the Seebohm
Committee[40] which highlighted another related issue (and one which
the proposed community development officer would particularly face):

> the participants may wish to pursue policies directly at variance with
> the ideas of the local authorities, and there is certainly a difficult
> link to be forged between the concepts of popular participation and
> traditional representative democracy. The role of the social worker
> in this context is likely to give rise to problems of conflicting
> loyalties. The Council for Training in Social Work suggest in
> evidence that if community work is to be developed by the local
> authority, then the authority 'will need to recognize the fact that
> some of its staff may be involved in situations which lead to
> criticism of their services or with pressure groups about new needs.
> The workers themselves will need to be clear about their pro-
> fessional role and this will depend upon their training and the
> organizational structure within which they work' . . . Participation
> provides a means by which further consumer control can be
> exercised over professional and bureaucratic power.

A further problem in public participation is that of determining
how representative are the views expressed by participating citizens.
As the Skeffington Report implies, the views of 'the non-joiners and
inarticulate' are as important as those of 'the actively interested and
organized'. And as American experience shows, public participation
can lead to strong demands to keep an area 'white', to exclude public
authority housing and to safeguard local amenities at a high cost to
the larger community. It is not every community which is best placed
to assess its needs in relation to a wider area.

Finally, reference needs to be made to the tricky problem of
planning blight. The best way of avoiding this is to maintain the
utmost secrecy until definite plans can be presented to the public as a
fait accompli. Obviously this is not easy to reconcile with a greater
degree of public participation. There is no easy answer to this. Indeed,
the Skeffington Committee were probably right in saying that 'some
increase in planning blight may have to be accepted if there is to be
increased participation by the public'. Whether the compensation provisions for planning blight are adequate is another matter.

The essential ingredient of effective public participation is a concern on the part of elected members and professional staffs to make participation a reality. But it cannot be effective unless it is organised. This, of course, is one of the fundamental difficulties. Though a large number of people may feel vaguely disturbed in general about the operation of the planning machine (and particularly upset when they are individually affected), it is only a minority who are prepared to do anything other than grumble. The minority may be growing, and with the general rise in educational levels it can be expected to continue to do so. It has to be recognised, however, that public participation will, as far as can be seen, always be restricted. In the words of Maurice Broady: 'the activity of responsible social criticism is not congenial to more than a minority. Most of us for most of the time are content to remain complacently acquiescent in our social niche . . . The activist, the social critic, the reformer, will always be a small section of any society. Their activities require not only an extra effort which few are willing to expend, but also the ability to criticise and organize which comparatively few possess.'[41]

PLANNING AID

The minority is, nevertheless, an important one and, as the success of the Consumers' Association and similar bodies has shown, it can be instrumental in activating widespread interest and support (even if this stops short of actual participation). A little official encouragement might have surprisingly widespread effects. At the local level this could be on the lines suggested by the Coventry experiment (summarised in an Appendix to the Skeffington Report). It is early days yet to assess the potentialities of the community and neighbourhood councils, but there is one model which is of proven worth, namely, the Planning Aid Service of the Town and Country Planning Association. In the words of the Association:

> The function of the planning aid unit is to develop means of providing planning support for community self-help initiatives and to help groups and individuals become involved in planning and improving their environment. It provides advice and information for individuals who are getting involved in planning and it promotes and coordinates the national planning aid network. The latter involves:
> – contacting and maintaining contact with individual volunteer planning aid helpers;
> – encouraging, helping, promoting and maintaining contact with planning aid groups;
> – gathering and disseminating planning aid experience;
> – making contact between users and providers of planning aid in response to inquiries; and

– monitoring progress of planning aid cases referred to other groups and organisations.[42]

The Unit has a growing range of publications, particularly leaflets, explaining such matters as 'how to make representations on an application for planning permission' and 'your right to attend planning committee meetings'.[43]

It is fortunate that there is now available an independent assessment of the Planning Aid Service by Curtis and Edwards.[44] Their conclusions are worth reproducing in full:

(*a*) There is conclusive evidence that those members of the public with the least power to influence decision making in planning have been unable to participate in the planning process often because of a lack of awareness of the procedures involved and an insufficient access to independent planning expertise.

(*b*) The invitation to participate for these groups is inadequate without the corresponding access to some form of independent advice.

(*c*) The evidence points clearly to the need for an independent and free source of information, advice and assistance on planning matters which is accessible to these groups who are at present inadequately represented politically, and lack access to sources of assistance.

(*d*) The TCPA's experimental Planning Aid Service in attempting to meet this need has certainly given 'value for money' in terms of the Department of the Environment's grant.

(*e*) The TCPA's scheme has been, and continues to be, the most significant planning aid service available.

(*f*) Our work has identified shortcomings in the current provision of planning aid, and suggests possible improvements.

(*g*) The main deficiency is the inability of those groups most in need to obtain access to planning aid services.

(*h*) The provision of planning aid could be made more effective by the concentration of resources at the local level possibly in the form of a centre offering multi-disciplinary expertise and assistance.

(*i*) The effectiveness of this local level of provision could be greatly increased through the support services of a co-ordinating body.

(*j*) These suggestions, and indeed the concept of planning aid, need to be examined in more detail than has been possible in this research.

ENVIRONMENTAL EDUCATION

The matter of planning aid brings us back to a point made at the beginning of this chapter: the need for high degrees of political sophistication and understanding on the part of the public. In this connection the Environmental Board's report on *Environmental Education in Urban Areas* is of special relevance.[45] This particular report was concerned 'to examine in detail what is already being done by the various agencies concerned in the field of environmental education, and, in so doing, to identify gaps and elicit what the public expects of the environment, all with a view to determining if a new initiative in this area is required'.

Immediately striking is the number of 'bodies concerned with urban environmental education' – Civic Trust (founded in 1957), Council for Environmental Education (1968), Council for Urban Studies Centres (1973), Environmental Education Advisers Association (1978), Heritage Education Group (1976), Institution of Environmental Sciences (1972), National Association for Environmental Education (1963) and the Town and Country Planning Association Education Unit (1971). In fact these are only the main organisations: there are many others involved (whether centrally or peripherally) with 'environmental education'.[46]

Fortunately there was no proposal for 'co-ordination' of all these activities: indeed, there was a clear awareness of the need for a wide variety of endeavours spread across the country. The conclusions reached were:

Firstly, that environmental education in this country today is very uneven. Good things are being done, perhaps as good as anywhere in the world; there are many individual programmes and projects involving both schoolchildren and adults; there is a certain amount of dissemination and exchange of ideas through a network of central organisations. Yet overall, the picture is patchy: islands of light exist in a general sea of darkness. The aim should be to extend what is now being done well, to reach more places and more people.

Secondly, that the critical aims of urban environmental education are twofold: to develop (both in children and adults) a sense of feeling for the built environment and a capacity to judge its quality; and to learn how to act, individually and collectively, to help influence the ways this environment is changed.

Thirdly, that these aims can best be realised through local education programmes which focus on people's actual experience of their own built environment, and which work outwards from there. Of course, liaison between local groups as well as centrally produced material may have a great value in feeding in to and communicating between these local programmes; but the main task must be for local people to develop materials and projects appropriate to the special circumstances of their own towns and cities.

Particular emphasis was laid on the development of urban studies centres:

> The role they were designed to play was a multiple one; it has not been fulfilled due to inadequate funding, but we believe it is important to provide the resources to allow centres to discharge this multiple brief properly. Thus they should develop locally relevant educational material, using resources already existing in the Department of the Environment, in local planning departments, in libraries and in other places. They should answer queries from schools, thus taking a heavy load off over-worked local planning departments and small voluntary organisations. They should provide short informal adult courses with a variety of participants including professional architects and planners and engineers, councillors, the general public, perhaps students and sixth formers. They should provide planning aid through local surgeries for people who are uncertain or aggrieved about plans for their neighbourhood. They should offer advice to local groups – amenity, resident, tenant, community and the like – which often lack time and resources to discover technical information; they can provide a meeting place together with secretarial and other facilities, and perhaps a chance of contact with other groups, and they may also provide links between these groups and schools. They could also provide a setting for architecture and planning workshops where professionals could critically examine their own contributions to environmental education. Assistance to teachers in looking at and critically appraising local buildings, especially modern ones, would also be a valuable contribution.

IN CONCLUSION

During the first half of the 1970s the planning scene was dominated by a veritable orgy of institutional change. Not surprisingly, this had a restraining influence on the adaptation of policies to changing conditions and perceptions. Indeed, it could be argued that it added to the confusion over the role of 'town and country planning' in relation to regional and national economic planning, to the management of the economy, to the increasingly strident demands for environmental protection, to the place of public participation in the planning process, and to even more intractable issues such as 'the energy question', the distribution of incomes and 'access to opportunity'. It is, however, a nice question as to whether a more stable institutional structure would have facilitated the formulation of more appropriate and effective policies in the context of the baffling economic and social problems of the time. Certainly the outcome of the huge effort expended on the attempt to come to grips with housing policy does not suggest that the answer is a straightforward one.[47]

What does seem clear is that the faith in the efficacy of institutional change was misplaced. The reorganisation of local government (the term 'reform' has significantly fallen out of use) seems to have created as many problems as it solved. Some of the difficulties can be ascribed to the form of the reorganisation (which was essentially different from that which was envisaged by the new-style development plan system); but the problems go deeper. A further reorganisation of local government by way of 'organic change' or whatever, may divert attention from these problems, as would the further reviews which could follow from the establishment of the Scottish and Welsh Assemblies. In Matthew Arnold's words, 'faith in machinery is our besetting danger'.

The deeper problems relate to the function, scope and practicability of 'town and country planning'. The Greater London Development Plan Inquiry was perhaps the most dramatic illustration of the fact that many of the crucial issues with which 'planning' is concerned do not fall within the responsibility or competence of the planning authority, or even within that of local government – jobs and incomes being the two most obvious ones. Hence central government wrestles with the political pressures to which problems in such areas give rise, though typically with disappointing results.

From a cynical viewpoint, much effort is wasted at both local and central levels in preparing plans for controlling the uncontrollable. This is to give a meaning to the proclamations of politicians which is unwarranted, but the illusion that problems can be 'solved' turns easily into a delusion,[48] and constant failure debases the political process and breeds cynicism.

However, while the main focus of attention in recent years has been on these matters, wider discussion of the limits, role and purpose of planning has developed. A greater understanding of the operations of governments has been provided by writings ranging from the Crossman Diaries to academic studies and reflections such as those of Heclo and Wildavsky, King, Solesbury and Gellner (to mention but a few).[49] More remarkable are the signs of some fundamental rethinking within the planning profession itself, of which the most striking is a 1976 'discussion paper', *Planning and the Future*, published by the Royal Town Institute.[50] Hopefully this can be interpreted as a burgeoning of intellectual analysis of planning which, though of long (and perhaps exhausting) standing in the United States, has been almost completely absent from the British scene.

It would be interesting to speculate why this untypically deep questioning came when it did. Perhaps it is a sign of 'the coming of age of planning'. Certainly there is a new humility in the face of current problems which may well have been fostered in part by the perceived irrelevance of policies designed to control or channel perpetual growth to the unaccustomed problems of stagnation – at the same time that sections of the public who articulate their views through pressure groups have become increasingly vocal in opposing developments. The perceived 'failures' of 'planning' – high rise development, 'difficult to let' council housing schemes, urban motorways, inner city decline, and the like – have added to the mounting concern about the role and character of planning. (Whether – or to what extent – these have been 'failures' and, if so, the degree to which 'planning' is to blame are questions which are seldom raised, let alone answered in their historical context: it is sufficient here to note that such 'failures' are perceived as symbols of the inadequacy of planning.)

An alternative explanation would lay emphasis on the growth of public participation which has received increasing encouragement by both central and local government – even to the extent of making it a statutory requirement. DoE Circular 52/72 stressed that 'publicity and public participation are essential factors in the new development plan system'. Public participation is not a subsidiary process which can be held in check: once it begins to work effectively it transforms the nature of the planning process. On occasion it can get 'completely out of control', as in some well-publicised highway inquiries. Though 'disruptive', these led to a major reappraisal of both highway inquiry procedures and highway planning – an issue which has been discussed above. Here the point is that the lesson was learned: it had become apparent that 'participation' could be effective.

The professional acceptance of public participation (though by no means unanimous) is a remarkable feature of the 1970s. That it came in planning but not in other fields such as education or health may be related to the transformed nature of planning education and the changed character of the 'intake' to the profession.[51] Indeed, it may be that it is this which above all explains the new humility, the introspective questioning and the new intellectualism which is so marked a feature of current planning. In this respect, planners have departed from the norms of professionalism (though not without internal strife).[52] Professionalism generally is currently under challenge: this stems from a variety of current changes, including an unprecedented (and increasing) demand for greater information ('more open government') and for meaningful participation in the making of decisions by those who are affected by them. In essence this amounts to the demotion of professionalism in the public esteem. However, there are also less apparent factors: given the tempo of change, professionals of one generation face problems of understanding (and even of communication) with those of another generation; and all – after a relatively short time practising their professional skills – find themselves having to deal with problems for which their training does not adequately prepare them.

These are general problems. (The newly trained dentist of the 1980s hardly speaks the same language as his colleague who was trained a decade earlier; lawyers are increasingly having to enter quite new areas such as racial and sexual discrimination.) But planning faces even more intractable problems. Not only has it developed from a basic concern with physical, land use activities; and not only has it led the vanguard in public participation; it also constantly finds itself engaged in major debates on its distinctive function. This is more than a boundary dispute. By its very nature, planning is a co-ordinative activity. It seeks to resolve conflicts: originally of competing claims on the use of land, but increasingly of conflicting social and economic objectives. This raises major questions of the nature of 'planning' undertaken by professional planners (RTPI), by economic planners, by corporate planners and a host of other types of planners. (A very specific illustration of the issue is formulated in the question as to whether, in the Scottish situation, regional reports should be prepared by professional planners or by 'corporate planners'.)

The debate on the nature of planning is not, of course, a new one: it has proceeded, with varying degrees of intensity, at least since the war years when the foundations of the prewar planning machine were being laid by a group of virtually unknown (and almost completely forgotten) officials in the Reconstruction Secretariat and the Ministry of Town and Country Planning.[53] What characterises the current debate is its intensity, its breadth and the diversity of its participants. Though there is an uncanny resemblance, so far as the first two features are concerned, between the early 1940s and the late 1970s,[54] the last constitutes a new (and healthy) feature. Moreover, it is not simply a matter of planning being too important to be left to planners: more significantly, this is agreed by many planners. Most professions see this question (if they see it at all) in terms of their public image. The planning profession, however, raises it with the serious objective of establishing and improving their role in society. (It has to be established, of course, whether the authors of the RTPI *Planning and the Future* are representative of their profession.)

The debate will continue but the subject is now clearly placed where it properly belongs: centrally in the political arena.[55]

REFERENCES AND FURTHER READING: CHAPTER 12

1 Leicester City Planning Department, *Planning for Leicester* (Leicester City Council, 1975).
2 There is a large number of studies on this, for example, D. M. Muchnick, *Urban Renewal in Liverpool*, Occasional Papers on Social Administration No. 33 (Bell, 1970); C. Ungerson, *Moving Home*, Occasional Papers on Social Administration No. 44 (Bell, 1971); Southwark Council of Social Service, *From Rumour to Removal* (The Council, 1971); J. G. Davies, *The Evangelistic Bureaucrat: A Study of a Planning Exercise in Newcastle-upon-Tyne* (Tavistock, 1972); N. Dennis, *Public Participation and Planners' Blight* (Faber, 1972); J. English, R. Madigan and P. Norman, *Slum Clearance: The Social and Administrative Context in England and Wales* (Croom Helm, 1976); S. Jacobs, *The Right to a Decent House*

(Routledge & Kegan Paul, 1976); N. Wates, *The Battle for Tolmers Square* (Routledge & Kegan Paul, 1977); and B. Anson, *I'll Fight For You: Behind the Struggle for Covent Garden* (Cape, 1981).
More generally, see J. Simmie, *Citizens in Conflict* (Hutchinson, 1974); A. R. Long, *Participation and the Community* (Pergamon, 1976); M. Fagence, *Citizen Participation in Planning* (Pergamon, 1977); W. R. D. Sewell and J. T. Coppock, *Public Participation in Planning* (Wiley, 1977); and in a rather different style, A. Jay, *The Householder's Guide to Community Defence Against Bureaucratic Aggression* (Cape, 1972).

3 Ways in which public understanding can be improved (and public involvement increased) are discussed in the report by the Environmental Board, *Environmental Education in Urban Areas* (HMSO, 1979). Further reference to this is made later in the chapter.

4 See Table 4.1 in Chapter 4.

5 G. A. Grove, 'Planning and the applicant', *Journal of the Town Planning Institute*, vol. 49 (1963), p. 130.

6 In Scotland the 1969 and 1972 Acts respectively.

7 *Management of Local Government* (Maud Report) (HMSO, 1967).

8 *Staffing of Local Government* (Mallaby Report) (HMSO, 1967).

9 *Management Study on Development Control* (HMSO, 1967).

10 *Fourth Report of the Parliamentary Commissioner for Administration 1974-75*, HC 405 (HMSO, 1975).

11 Parliamentary Commissioner for Administration, *Selected Cases 1980 - Volume 4*, HC 799 (HMSO, 1980), pp. 15-23.

12 Each of the three Commissions issue an annual report but, presumably to emphasise their independence, these are not published by HMSO, but by the individual Commissions.

13 *Commission for Local Administration in England: Report for the Year Ended 31 March 1980*, para. 37.

14 There have been two studies of the experience of the 'local ombudsman': N. Lewis and B. Gateshill, *The Commission for Local Administration: A Preliminary Appraisal* (Royal Institute of Public Administration, 1978); and V. Moore and H. Sales, *The Local Ombudsmen: A Review of the First Five Years* (Justice - British Section of the International Commission of Jurists, 1980).

15 R. Williams, 'Local planning and the ombudsman', *The Planner*, vol. 63 (1977), pp. 78-80.

16 *Commission for Local Administration in England: Report for the Year Ended 31 March 1980*, paras 39ff.

17 DoE Circular 71/73, *Publicity for Planning Applications, Appeals and Other Proposals for Development* (HMSO, 1973).

18 *Journal of Planning and Environment Law*, 1980, p. 557.

19 Commission for Local Administration in England, loc. cit.

20 D. R. Mandelker, *Green Belts and Urban Growth* (University of Wisconsin Press, 1962), p. 117.

21 *Committee on Administrative Tribunals and Enquiries: Evidence* (HMSO, 1956), pp. 71-2.

22 *Committee on Administrative Tribunals and Enquiries: Report* (Franks Report), Cmnd 218 (HMSO, 1957).

23 *Buxton and Others* v. *Minister of Housing and Local Government* (1960) 3 WLR 866. The account given here of the case is based on a summary contained in *Public Law*, Summer 1961, pp. 121-8. See also, 'The Chalkpit case' in J. A. G. Griffith and H. Street, *A Casebook on Administrative Law* (Pitman, 1964), pp. 142-74.

24 The discussion is focused on inquiries on an appeal against a decision of a local planning authority to refuse planning permission for a particular development. It applies also to other inquiries, for example, on an appeal against conditions imposed by a local authority in granting planning permission. Inquiries on

structure plans have now been replaced by 'examinations in public': these are discussed in Chapter 3.

25 Scottish Development Department, *Memorandum of Guidance on the Procedure in Connection with Statutory Inquiries*, and Circular 14/1975, *Public Inquiry Procedures* (Scottish Development Department, 1975).

26 F. Layfield, 'The role of inquiries in land planning', Royal Town Planning Institute, *Town and Country Planning Summer School 1974: Report of Proceedings*.

27 T. Hancock, 'The big decisions: who decides?', *Town and Country Planning Summer School 1980: Report of Proceedings* (RTPI, 1980), p. 28. The Windscale Report was published in 1978: *The Windscale Inquiry: Report by the Hon Mr Justice Parker* (HMSO).

28 White Paper, *Town and Country Planning*, Cmnd 3333 (HMSO, 1967).

29 D. Heap (ed.), *Encyclopedia of the Law of Town and Country Planning* (Sweet & Maxwell), Vol. 2, para. 2–2711.

30 See Town and Country Planning Act, sections 47 to 49. (The Scottish provisions are in sections 44 to 47 of the Town and Country Planning (Scotland) Act 1972.)

31 *HC Debates*, Vol. 757, col. 1372, 31 January 1968. See also *Standing Committee G Debates*, cols 903ff., 2 April 1968 (quoted in D. Heap, op. cit., Vol. I, paras 1–277/8.

32 L. Edwards and J. Rowan-Robinson, 'Whatever happened to the Planning Inquiry Commission?', *Journal of Planning and Environment Law*, 1980, pp. 307–15; and D. Pearce, L. Edwards and G. Beuret, *Decision-Making for Energy Futures: A Case Study of the Windscale Inquiry* (Macmillan, 1979).

33 L. Edwards and J. Rowan-Robinson, op. cit., p. 310.

34 See L. Edwards and J. Rowan-Robinson, op. cit.; T. Hancock, op. cit., and speech by Mr Peter Shore (then Secretary of State for the Environment) in Manchester on 13 September 1978 (quoted by Hancock, op. cit., p. 29).

35 Town and Country Planning Association, *Energy Policy and Public Inquiries: Policy Statement*, May 1978. See also D. Hall, 'Progress with major planning inquiries', *Town and Country Planning*, November 1978.

36 *The Big Public Inquiry: A Proposed New Procedure for the Impartial Investigation of Projects with Major National Implications*, published by the Outer Circle Policy Unit with the Council for Science and Society and the Council of Justice, 1979.

37 In this connection it is relevant to read A. King, 'Overload: problems of governing in the 1970s', *Political Studies*, vol. 23 (1975), pp. 284–96.

38 See R. Cowan, 'The public inquiries fraud', *Town and Country Planning*, April 1980, p. 109. For a very different stance, see R. Klein, 'The case for elitism: public opinion and public policy', *Political Quarterly*, vol. 45 (1974), pp. 406–17. Other references include P. H. Levin, 'Highway inquiries: a study in governmental responsiveness', *Public Administration*, vol. 57 (1979), pp. 21–49, and 'Public inquiries: the need for national justice', *New Society*, 15 November 1979, pp. 371–2; *Windscale: A Summary of the Evidence and the Argument* (Guardian Newspapers, 1977); I. Breach, *Windscale Fallout* (Penguin, 1978); M. Stott and P. Taylor, *The Nuclear Controversy: A Guide to the Issues of the Windscale Inquiry* (Town and Country Planning Association and Political Ecology Research Group, TCPA, 1980); and R. E. Wraith and G. B. Lamb, *Public Inquiries as an Instrument of Government* (Allen & Unwin, 1971).

39 *Report of the Committee on Public Participation in Planning: People and Planning* (Skeffington Report) (HMSO, 1969).

40 *Report of the Committee on Local Authority and Allied Personal Social Services*, Cmnd 3703 (HMSO, 1968).

41 M. Broady, *Social Change and Town Development*, paper given to the Town and Country Planning Association National Conference (mimeo.), 1963. See also his *Planning for People* (Bedford Square Press, 1968).

42 *Eighty-Second Annual Report, Town and Country Planning Association, 1981*, p. 16.

43 In addition to the *Planning Aid Leaflet* series, there is also a *Planning Aid Paper* series which includes such titles as *Planning Aid: The Legal Aid Model* (1976) and *Planning Inquiries: Paying for Participation* (1977). See also D. Lock, 'Legal aid funds for planning aid', *The Planner*, vol. 64 (1978), pp. 14–15. Since 1980 a monthly supplement, *Planning Aid*, has been issued with the Association's weekly news digest *Planning Bulletin*.

44 B. Curtis and D. Edwards, *Planning Aid: An Analysis Based on the Planning Aid Service of the Town and Country Planning Association*, University of Reading, School of Planning Studies, Occasional Papers 1 (University of Reading, 1980).

45 Environmental Board (Department of the Environment), *Environmental Education in Urban Areas* (HMSO, 1979).

46 The author may be excused for making particular reference to the Scottish Planning Exchange: see J. B. Cullingworth, *The Planning Exchange: A Personal Account of Its Establishment and Early Experience* (Centre for Environmental Studies, 1977), and *The Planning Exchange Scotland: A Guide to its Organisation and Activities* (1978), The Planning Exchange, 186 Bath Street, Glasgow G2 4HG. There is, of course, a huge variety of local organisations. One type which is of particular relevance in the present context is the Town Development Trust, defined as 'a people's entrepreneurial organisation (probably taking the form of a charity owning a trading company), created by a local community – whether that be a street, part of a town, a village or part of a region – to revitalise, by rebuilding or renovating, that community's physical surroundings and, in so doing, the community spirit itself'. See D. Rock, *The Grassroots Developers: A Handbook for Town Development Trusts* (Royal Institute of British Architects Conference Fund, 1980).

47 See J. B. Cullingworth, *Essays on Housing Policy* (Allen & Unwin, 1979).

48 cf. Illich's contention that the mid-twentieth century is 'The age of the disabling professions': an age when people had 'problems', experts had 'solutions' and scientists measured imponderables such as 'abilities' and 'needs' – an age which, he asserts, is now at an end. I. Illich *et al.*, *Disabling Professions* (Boyars, 1977), p. 11.

49 R. Crossman, *The Diaries of a Cabinet Minister* (Hamilton/Cape, 3 vols, 1975, 1976 and 1977); H. Heclo and A. Wildavsky, *The Private Government of Public Money: Community and Policy Inside British Politics* (Macmillan, 1974); A. King, 'Overload: problems of governing in the 1970s', *Political Studies*, Vol. 23 (1975), pp. 284–96; W. Solesbury, 'The environmental agenda: an illustration of how situations may become political issues, and issues may demand responses from government: or how they may not', *Public Administration*, vol. 54 (1976), pp. 379–97; E. Gellner, 'A social contract in search of an idiom: the demise of the danegeld state?', *Political Quarterly*, vol. 46 (1975), pp. 127–52. The list could easily be greatly lengthened. Of particular relevance to students of British planning are the four volumes in the Peacetime History series, *Environmental Planning 1939–1969*. (The first two volumes were published in 1975, the third in 1979 and the fourth in 1981, by HMSO.)

50 *Planning for the Future* (RTPI, 1976). See also D. Eversley, *The Planner in Society* (Faber, 1973) (and an American counterpart, J. Friedman, *Retracking America: A Theory of Transactive Planning*, Anchor/Doubleday, 1973).

51 See G. E. Cherry, *The Evolution of British Town Planning* (Leonard Hill, 1974), p. 210; and Centre for Environmental Studies, *Education for Planning*, Progress in Planning, Vol. 1, Part 1 (Pergamon, 1973).

52 See references quoted in the previous note. For a striking illustration of the two extreme ('physical' and 'social') planning philosophies, compare Eversley's *The Planner in Society* with Keeble's standard textbook, *Principles and Practice of Town and Country Planning*.

53 J. B. Cullingworth, *Environmental Planning 1939–1969, Vol. I: Reconstruction and Land Use Planning 1939–1947* (HMSO, 1975).

54   op. cit., ch. IX.
55   As noted earlier in this chapter, Patrick McAuslan's *The Ideologies of Planning Law* arrived too late to enable me to incorporate his thinking in my discussion. Those who read McAuslan will readily appreciate that this was most unfortunate.

BIBLIOGRAPHY OF OFFICIAL PUBLICATIONS

OFFICIAL REGIONAL STUDIES AND PLANS
(HMSO unless otherwise indicated)

Surveys by Central Government Officials

The South East Study 1961–1981 (1964)
The West Midlands: A Regional Study (1965)
The North-West: A Regional Study (1965)
The Problems of Merseyside: An Appendix to the North-West Study (1965)

Reports by Economic Planning Councils

Challenge of the Changing North (1966)
A Review of Yorkshire and Humberside (1966)
The East Midlands Study (1966)
A Strategy for the South-East (1967)
A Region with a Future: A Draft Strategy for the South-West (1967)
The West Midlands: Patterns of Growth (1967)
The North-West of the 1970s (1968)
Halifax and the Calder Valley (1968)
Huddersfield and the Colne Valley (1969)
Opportunity in the East Midlands (1969)
Doncaster: An Area Study (1969)
The Plymouth Area Study (1969)
South-East Kent Study (1969)
Yorkshire and Humberside: Regional Strategy (1970)
The West Midlands: An Economic Appraisal (1971)
Strategic Settlement Pattern for the South West (1974)

Command Papers

Central Scotland: A Programme for Development and Growth, Cmnd 2188 (1963)
The North-East: A Programme for Development and Growth, Cmnd 2206 (1963)
The Scottish Economy 1965–70, Cmnd 2864 (1966)
Wales: The Way Ahead, Cmnd 3334 (1969)

Reports of the Central Unit for Environmental Planning

Humberside: A Feasibility Study (1969)
Severnside: A Feasibility Study (1971)

Reports of the South-East Joint Planning Team

> *Strategic Plan for the South-East* (1970)
> *Studies: Vol. 1: Population and Employment*
>   *Vol. 2: Social and Environmental Aspects*
>   *Vol. 3: Transportation*
>   *Vol. 4: Strategies and Evaluation*
>   *Vol. 5: Report of Economic Consultants Ltd*
> *Strategy for the South-East: 1976 Review*
> *Strategic Plan for the South-East: Review: Government Statement*
>   (1978)

Regional Strategy Team Reports

> *Strategic Plan for the North West* (1974)
> *Strategic Choice for East Anglia* (1974)
> *Strategic Plan for the Northern Region* (1977)
> *A Developing Strategy for the West Midlands: Report of the Joint*
>   *Monitoring Steering Group;* and *Report of the West Midlands*
>   *Economic Planning Council and the West Midlands Planning*
>   *Authorities Conference* (1979)

Scottish Reports

> *Lothians Regional Survey and Plan* (1966)
> *Grangemouth-Falkirk Regional Survey and Plan* (1968)
> *The Central Borders: A Plan for Expansion* (1968)
> *Tayside: Potential for Development* (1970)
> *A Strategy for South-West Scotland* (1970)
> *West Central Scotland Plan* (1974) (published by the West Central
>   Scotland Plan Team)

Consultants' Reports

> *Northampton, Bedford and North Bucks Study: An Assessment of*
>   *Inter-Related Growth*, 1965
> *A New City: A Study of Urban Development in an area including*
>   *Newbury, Swindon and Didcot*, 1966
> *A New Town for Mid-Wales – Consultants' Proposals*, 1966
> *Dawley: Wellington: Oakengates – Consultants' Proposals for*
>   *Development*, 1966
> *Expansion of Ipswich Designation Proposals: Consultants' Study of*
>   *the Town and its Sub-Region*, 1966
> *Expansion of Northampton – Consultants' Proposals for Designa-*
>   *tion*, 1966
> *Expansion of Peterborough – Consultants' Proposals for Designa-*
>   *tion*, 1966

Expansion of Warrington – Consultants' Proposals for Designation, 1966

South Hampshire Study: Report of the Feasibility of Major Urban Growth, 3 vols, 1966

Ashford Study: Consultants' Proposals for Designation, 1967

Central Lancashire: Study for a City – Consultants' Proposals for Designation, 1967

Central Lancashire New Town Proposal: Impact on North East Lancashire, 1968

Expansion of Ipswich: Comparative Costs – A Supplementary Report, 1968

Llantrisant – Prospects for Urban Growth, 1969

New Life in Old Towns – Two Pilot Studies on Urban Renewal in Nelson and Rawtenstall, 1971

Study of the Cambridge Sub-Region, 1974

DEPARTMENTAL CIRCULARS

Ministry of Town and Country Planning (HMSO)

40 (1948), *Survey for Development Plans*
100 (1950), *Development by Government Departments*

Ministry of Housing and Local Government (HMSO)

49/59, *Purchase Notices*
58/59, *Delegation of Planning Functions*
30/60, *Local Employment Act, 1960: Rehabilitation of Derelict, Neglected or Unsightly Land*
42/60, *Caravan Sites and Control of Development Act, 1960*
47/63, *Town and Country Planning Act, 1963*
51/63, *Development near Buildings of Special Architectural or Historical Interest*
64/65, *Control of Office and Industrial Development Act, 1965*
17/67, *Rehabilitation of Derelict, Neglected or Unsightly Land: Industrial Development Act, 1966 and Local Government Act, 1966*
53/67, *Civic Amenities Act, 1967*
5/68,   *The Use Conditions in Planning Permissions*
44/68, *Countryside Act, 1968*
49/68, *Caravan Sites Act, 1968*
61/68, *Town and Country Planning Act, 1968 – Part V: Historic Buildings and Conservation*
1/69,   *Town and Country Planning (Tree Preservation Order) Regulations, 1969*

15/69, *Town and Country Planning Act, 1968 - Part IV: Acquisition and Disposal of Land*

26/69, *Purchase Notices*

63/69, *Housing Act 1969*

64/69, *Housing Act 1969: House Improvement and Repair*

65/69, *Housing Act 1969: Area Improvement*

68/69, *Housing Act 1969: Slum Clearance*

96/69, *Control of Advertisement Regulations*

16/70, *Mines and Quarries (Tips) Act 1969: Grants to Local Authorities*

17/70, *Derelict Land*

46/70, *Town and Country Planning Acts 1962 to 1968: Planning Blight*

82/70, *Town and Country Planning Act 1968 - Part I: The New Development Plan System of Structure and Local Plans*

Department of the Environment (HMSO)

3/71, *Industrial Development - Exemption Limits for Industrial Development Certificates and Time Limits on Planning Permissions*

42/71, *The Dangerous Litter Act 1971*

44/71, *Town and Country Planning Act 1968 - Part I: The Town and Country Planning (Structure and Local Plans) Regulations 1971*

60/71, *Town and Country Planning (Minerals) Regulations 1971*

80/71, *Development by Government Departments*

12/72, *The Planning of the Undeveloped Coast*

52/72, *Town and Country Planning Act 1971: Part II Development Plan Proposals: Publicity and Public Participation*

102/72, *Land Availability for Housing*

1/73, *Provision for Sport and Physical Recreation*

10/73, *Planning and Noise*

12/73, *Town and Country Planning: General Development Order 1973*

63/73, *Local Government Act 1972: Administration of National Parks*

71/73, *Publicity for Planning Applications, Appeals and Other Proposals for Development*

73/73, *Land Compensation Act 1973*

74/73, *Local Government Act 1972 - Town and Country Planning: Co-operation Between Authorities*

104/73, *Local Transport Grants*

122/73, *Land Availability for Housing*

138/73,	*Nature Conservancy Council*

138/73,   *Nature Conservancy Council*
142/73,   *Streamlining the Planning Machine*
6/74,   *Tree Preservation and Planting*
27/74,   *Transport Supplementary Grant: More Details of the New System*
43/74,   *Town and Country Planning, General Development (Amendment) Order 1974*
60/74,   *Transport Supplementary Grant: Submissions for 1975/6*
65/74,   *Local Government Act 1972: National Parks*
76/74,   *Local Government Act 1974 – Part III: Local Complaints*
147/74,   *Town and Country Amenities Act 1974*
13/75,   *Housing Act 1974: Renewal Strategies*
14/75,   *Housing Act 1974: Housing Action Areas, Priority Neighbourhoods and General Improvement Areas*
17/75,   *Town and Country Amenities Act 1974*
77/75,   *Clearance of Unfit Houses – Procedural Requirements*
86/75,   *Conservation of Wild Creatures and Wild Plants Act 1975*
96/75,   *The Town and Country Planning (Development Plans) Direction 1975*
113/75,   *Review of the Development Control System*
121/75,   *Community Land – Circular I: General Introduction and Priorities*
4/76,   *Report of the National Park Policies Committee*
9/76,   *The Dobry Report: Action by Local Planning Authorities*
16/76,   *National Land Use Classification*
20/76,   *Petroleum and Submarine Pipe-Lines Act 1975*
47/76,   *Regional Councils for Sport and Recreation*
71/76,   *Large New Stores*
75/76,   *Development Involving Agricultural Land*
7/77,   *Town and Country Planning Act 1971: Development by Government Departments*
17/77,   *Derelict Land*
23/77,   *Historic Buildings and Conservation Areas – Policy and Procedure*
28/77,   *Caravan Sites Act 1968 – Part II: Gypsy Caravan Sites*
43/77,   *(New Towns) Special Development Order 1977*
49/77,   *Redevelopment of Contaminated Land*
55/77,   *Memorandum on Structure and Local Plans*
68/77,   *Town and Country Planning Act 1971: Section 13, Local Plans: Public Local Inquiries*
73/77,   *Guidelines for Regional Recreational Strategies*
79/77,   *Control of Pollution Act 1974, Part I (Waste of Land): Licensing of Waste Disposal (Amendment) Regulations*

82/77,   *Town and Country Planning (Amendment) Act 1977*
91/77,   *Control of Office Development*
96/77,   *Large New Stores*
108/77,   *Nature Conservation and Planning*
109/77,   *Enforcement of Planning Control: Established Use Certificates*
125/77,   *Roads and Traffic – National Parks*
1/78,   *Report of the Committee on Planning Control over Mineral Working*
12/78,   *Report of the Mobile Home Review*
29/78,   *The Control of Pollution Act 1974, Part I – Waste on Land*
36/78,   (and Memorandum), *Trees and Forestry*
39/78,   *Amendments to the Booklet Entitled 'Structure Plans: The Examination in Public'*
43/78,   *Index of Planning Circulars*
44/78,   *Private Sector Land: Requirements and Supply*
47/78,   *Control of Pollution Act 1974, Part I – Waste on Land*
50/78,   *Report of the Advisory Committee on Aggregates*
57/78,   *Accommodation for Gypsies: Report by Sir John Cripps*
58/78,   *Report of the Committee on Planning Control Over Mineral Workings*
63/78,   *Report of a Study on General Improvement Areas 1969–1976*
4/79,   *Memorandum on Structure and Local Plans*
14/79,   *Town and Country Planning (Minerals) Regulations 1971: Time-Limited Planning Permissions*
26/79,   *Index to Circulars and Publications*
9/80,   *Land for Private Housebuilding*
22/80,   *Development Control – Policy and Practice*
2/81,   *Local Government, Planning and Land Act 1980; Health Services Act 1980: Town and Country Planning – Development Control Functions*

Scottish Development Department (issued by SDD)

13/1961, *Town and Country Planning (Control of Advertisements) (Scotland) Regulations 1961*
28/1965, *Advertisement Appeals Procedure*
49/1971, *Publicity for Planning Proposals*
52/1971, *The New Development Plan System*
47/1974, *Regional Transport Planning: Policies and Programmes*
48/1974, *Public Passenger Transport – The Role of Local Authorities*
79/1974, *Housing (Scotland) Act, 1974*
83/1974, *Town and Country Amenities Act, 1974*

4/1975,   Town and Country Planning – Regional Reports
5/1975,   Regional Transport Planning: Form and Content of Transport Policies and Programmes
13/1975, Regional Roads and Passenger Transport Expenditure: Financial Support
14/1975, Public Inquiry Procedures
67/1975, Housing (Scotland) Act, 1974: Houses Below the Tolerable Standard: Housing Action Areas
96/1975, Commission for Local Administration in Scotland
100/1975, Housing Needs and Strategies
126/1975, Town and Country Planning (Listed Buildings and Buildings in Conservation Areas) (Scotland) Regulations, 1975
28/1976, Development Plans
16/1977, Town and Country Planning (Scotland) Act, 1977
19/1977, National Planning Guidelines
30/1977, Development Planning and Development Control
49/1977, Development by Government Departments
56/1978, Transport Act, 1978
46/1978, Report of the Advisory Committee on Aggregates: Government Response
65/1978, National Planning Guidelines on the Location of Major Shopping Developments
68/1978, Rescue Archeology in Scotland
77/1978, Environmental Improvement in Housing Action and Housing Treatment Areas
10/1979, Inner Urban Areas Act 1978
18/1979, Transport Act 1978: Control of Off-Street Parking
19/1979, Environmental Improvement: Housing (Scotland) Act 1969
39/1980, (A) Developments in the Vicinity of British Gas Installations – Notification Procedures; (B) Commercial Pipelines: Planning Advice and Notification Procedures
47/1980, The Town and Country Planning . . . Regulations and Rules (Appeals, Inquiries etc.)

Department of Transport (HMSO)

8/78   Transport Act 1978: Public Transport Planning in Non-Metropolitan Counties
11/78   Guide to Community Transport
1/79   Ways of Helping Cyclists in Built Up Areas
3/79   Transport Act 1979: Control of Off-Street Parking
4/79   Transport Policies and Programme Submissions for the 1980/81 TSG Settlement

OTHER DEPARTMENTAL PAPERS

Scottish National Planning Guidelines (issued by SDD)
  Large Industrial Sites and Rural Conservation
  Petrochemical Developments
  Agriculture
  Forestry
  Nature Conservation
  Recreation and Landscape Conservation
  Land for Industry
  Oil, Gas and Petrochemicals
  Electricity
  (The above were packaged with SDD Circular 19/1977)

  Aggregates (SDD Circular 51/1977)
  Location of Major Shopping Developments (SDD Circular 65/1978)

Scottish Planning Advice Notes (issued by SDD 1975-6)

  1 *Agriculture in Scotland*
  2 *Forestry Guidelines*
  3 *The Countryside*
  4 *Forecasting Employment for Regional Reports and Structure Plans*
  5 *Planning for Sport, Outdoor Recreation and Tourism*
  6 *National Coal Board (Scottish Area) Trends and Developments 1975/80*
  7 *Planning and Electricity*
  8 *Demographic Analysis for Planning Purposes*
  9 *Nature Conservation Guidelines*
  10 *British Rail in the Scottish Local Government Regions 1976-1985*
  11 *Economic Monograph*
  12 *Scottish Fishing Industry*
  13 *Planning and Geology*
  14 *The Approach to Development Planning*
  15 *Structure Plans: Form and Content*
  16 *Local Plans: Form and Content*

DoE Development Control Policy Notes (HMSO, 1969-75)

  1 *General Principles*
  2 *Development in Residential Areas*
  3 *Industrial and Commercial Development*
  4 *Development in Rural Areas*

5 *Development in Town Centres*
6 *Road Safety and Traffic Requirements*
7 *Preservation of Historic Buildings and Areas*
8 *Caravan Sites*
9 *Petrol Filling Stations and Motels*
10 *Design*
11 *Amusement Centres*
12 *Hotels*
13 *Out of Town Shops and Shopping Centres* (replaced in 1977 by *Large New Stores*)
14 *Warehouses*
15 *Hostels and Homes*

DoE Development Advice Notes (HMSO)

1 *The Development Brief: Private Residential Development*, 1976
2 *Residential Density in Development Briefs*, 1976
3 *Provision of Land for Private Residential Development*, 1977
4 *Land Acquisition and Disposal Procedures: Management Network*, 1978

DoE Area Improvement Notes (HMSO)

1 *Sample House Condition Survey*, 1971
2 *House Condition Survey within a Potential General Improvement Area*, 1971
3 *Improving the Environment*, 1971
4 *House Improvement and Conversion*, 1972
5 *Environmental Design in Four General Improvement Areas*, 1972
6 *The Design of Street and Other Spaces in General Improvement Areas*, 1972
7 *Parking and Garaging in General Improvement Areas*, 1972
8 *Public Participation in General Improvement Areas*, 1973
9 *Traffic in General Improvement Areas*, 1974
10 *The Use of Indicators for Area Action*, 1975

DoE Pollution Papers (HMSO)

1 *The Monitoring of the Environment in the United Kingdom* (1974)
2 *Lead in the Environment and its Significance to Man* (1974)
3 *The Non-Agricultural Use of Pesticides in Great Britain* (1974)
4 *Controlling Pollution* (1975)
5 *Chlorofluorocarbons and their Effect on Stratospheric Ozone* (1976)

6 *The Separation of Oil from Water for North Sea Oil Operations* (1976)
7 *Effects of Airborne Sulphur Compounds on Forests and Freshwaters* (1976)
8 *Accidental Oil Pollution of the Sea* (1976)
9 *Pollution Control in Great Britain: How it Works* (2nd edn) (1978)
10 *Environmental Mercury and Man* (1976)
11 *Environmental Standards* (1977)
12 *Lead in Drinking Water* (1977)
13 *Tripartite Agreement on Stratospheric Monitoring between France, the United Kingdom and the United States of America: Joint Annual Report 1976-77* (1977)
14 *Lead Pollution in Birmingham* (1978)
15 *Chlorofluorocarbons and their Effect on Stratospheric Ozone. Second Report* (1979)
16 *The United Kingdom Environment 1979: Progress of Pollution Control* (1979)

This series is complemented by a series of Pollution Reports which provide information on pollution matters which may be of more limited public interest or which is not yet in a form which would merit publication as a Pollution Paper. The titles already published in the Pollution Report series are:

1 *The Monitoring of Environmental Pollution: Report of the first UK/USSR Monitoring Symposium* (DoE, 1977)
2 *Monitoring the Marine Environment of the United Kingdom: The First Report of the Marine Pollution Monitoring Management Group 1975-1976* (DoE, 1977)
3 *Elaboration of the scientific bases for monitoring the quality of surface water by hydrobiological indicators: Report of the First UK/USSR Seminar held at Valdai, USSR, 12-14 July 1976* (DoE, 1978)
4 *Digest of Environmental Pollution Statistics No. 1 1978* (HMSO, 1978)
5 *Glossary of Air Pollution Terms: Air Pollution Monitoring Management Group* (HMSO, 1979)
6 *Monitoring the Marine Environment; the Way Ahead: The Second Report of the Marine Pollution Monitoring Management Group 1977-1978* (DoE, 1979)
7 *Digest of Environmental Pollution Statistics No. 2 1979* (HMSO, 1980)

ROYAL COMMISSION ON ENVIRONMENTAL POLLUTION (HMSO)

First Report, Cmnd 4585, 1972

Second Report: Three Issues in Industrial Pollution, Cmnd 4894, 1972
Third Report: Pollution in Some British Estuaries and Coastal Waters, Cmnd 5054, 1972
Fourth Report: Pollution Control - Progress and Problems, Cmd 5780, 1974
Fifth Report: Air Pollution Control - An Integrated Approach, Cmnd 6371, 1976
Sixth Report: Nuclear Power and the Environment, Cmnd 6618, 1976
Seventh Report: Agriculture and Pollution, Cmnd 7644, 1979

WHITE PAPERS (HMSO)

Employment Policy, Cmd 6527, 1944
The Control of Land Use, Cmd 6537, 1944
Town and Country Planning Bill 1947: Explanatory Memorandum, Cmd 7006, 1947
Town and Country Planning Act, 1947: Amendment of Financial Provisions, Cmd 8699, 1952
London - Employment: Housing: Land, Cmnd 1952, 1963
The Land Commission, Cmnd 2771, 1965
Leisure in the Countryside, Cmnd 2928, 1966
Transport Policy, Cmnd 3057, 1966
Town and Country Planning, Cmnd 3333, 1967
Public Transport and Traffic, Cmnd 3481, 1967
The Older Houses in Scotland: A Plan for Action, Cmnd 3598, 1968
Old Houses into New Homes, Cmnd 3602, 1968
Transport in London, Cmnd 3686, 1968
Information and the Public Interest, Cmnd 4089, 1969
The Protection of the Environment: The Fight Against Pollution, Cmnd 4373, 1970
The Reorganisation of Central Government, Cmnd 4506, 1970
Investment Incentives, Cmnd 4516, 1970
Industrial and Regional Development, Cmnd 4942, 1972
Development and Compensation: Putting People First, Cmnd 5124, 1972
Homes for People: Scottish Housing Policy in the 1970s, Cmnd 5272, 1973
Widening the Choice: The Next Steps in Housing, Cmnd 5280, 1973
Towards Better Homes: Proposals for Dealing with Scotland's Older Housing, Cmnd 5338, 1973
Better Homes: The Next Priorities, Cmnd 5339, 1973
Land, Cmnd 5730, 1974
Development Land Tax, Cmnd 6195, 1975
Sport and Recreation, Cmnd 6200, 1975
An Approach to Industrial Strategy, Cmnd 6315, 1975

Nuclear Power and the Environment, Cmnd 6820, 1977
Transport Policy, Cmnd 6836, 1977
Policy for the Inner Cities, Cmnd 6845, 1977
The Water Industry in England and Wales: The Next Steps, Cmnd 6876, 1977
Planning Procedures: The Government's Response to the Eighth Report from the Expenditure Committee Session 1976-77, Cmnd 7056, 1978
Airports Policy, Cmnd 7084, 1978
Policy for Roads: England, Cmnd 7132, 1978
Report on the Review of Highway Inquiry Procedures, Cmnd 7133, 1978
The Challenge of North Sea Oil, Cmnd 7143, 1978
Organic Change in Local Government, Cmnd 7457, 1979
Central Government Controls over Local Authorities, Cmnd 7634, 1979
Policy for Roads: England 1980, Cmnd 7908, 1980

APPENDIX 1980–1984

This appendix is in three parts. The first is an introductory essay which attempts to comment in a useful (and somewhat provocative) way on some salient features of the planning scene in the first half of the nineteen-eighties. The second is a summary of some of the significant changes in planning which have taken place since 1980. The third part is a bibliography of official publications issued between 1980 and mid-1984.

PART 1 INTRODUCTION

Planning has continued its troubled path through the beginning of the eighties, but a new and clear political philosophy has emerged: the objective of planning now is to facilitate private development with the minimum of constraints. Public enterprise is to aim at promoting private enterprise (as with the introduction of urban development corporations and enterprise zones). Planning controls have been reduced, most of the new town development corporations abolished, and a White Paper, *Streamlining the Cities*, proposes the abolition of the Greater London Council and the Metropolitan Counties.

Much of this dramatic change stems from the explicit political stance of the Thatcher government, but there are also some deeper undercurrents. Above all, the poor state of the economy has raised the importance of the *promotion* of development (as compared with *control*), while virtually zero population growth has reduced the urgency (and perhaps the need) for long-term developments of new-town character. Successive public expenditure crises have also taken their toll (for example on housing and roads). The problems of urban decay are seemingly of a growing intractability. More widely, there is increasing confusion about the role of planning. The transfer of most county development control functions to districts has further severed the link between the making of planning policy and its implementation which first cracked in 1974 when structure planning and local planning were separated.

The promises held out by the 'new' structure planning system have largely failed to materialise. It appears to be no more effective, speedy, flexible, or satisfying than the system it was designed to replace. More deeply, there is real doubt about its validity in times of economic stagnation. More subtly, the fact that local planning powers can now be exercised (and to some extent defined) by local authorities without ministerial supervision widens the questions relevant to 'what is planning?'; and these questions are underlined by the range of new initiatives promoted by the Thatcher administration in relation to regeneration and the harnessing of market forces. (See M. Loughlin, 'Planning control and the property market', *Urban Law and Policy*, vol. 3, 1980.) The amount of space devoted in this appendix to issues which fall on the edge or beyond the boundaries of the Planning Acts illustrates the point. So in a very different way does the growth in litigation on discretionary aspects of development control. (See M. Grant, *Urban Planning Law* (Sweet and Maxwell, 1982), chapter 7; and M. Loughlin, 'The scope and importance of "Material Considerations"', *Urban Law and Policy*, vol. 30, 1980, pp. 171–92.)

The increasing attention being paid to adapting (and extending) the planning machine within a framework of private-sector involvement will be discussed in this appendix. Before doing so, however, it is interesting to note a number of other features of the contemporary planning scene. Some of these may be causally related; others may simply be accidental accompaniments. The result, however, is that the 'landscape' of planning operations in 1984 looks very different from that of a decade earlier. One is the growth of interest in Britain (long established in the United States) in 'planning theory'. Another is a burgeoning of studies of the actual operations of the planning machine. Very different is the marked shift in the centre of gravity of local–central relationships.

The latter is, of course, taking place in a very different arena from the academic and research centres which are swelling the shelves of planning libraries. But it is not too great a strain on the imagination to see some interconnections.

PLANNING THEORIES

As noted, there is a long (and continuing) tradition of theorising about planning in the United States. (The cynic who remarked that this is because there is so little actual planning in practice may be painfully near the truth, but the remark is not wholly valid.) The pages of the *Journal of the American Planning Association* (and its predecessor the *Journal of the American Institute of Planners*) are replete with theoretical articles, a good sample of which found their way into A. Faludi, *A Reader in Planning Theory* (Pergamon, 1973). It is noteworthy that a later collection by the same editor, *Essays on Planning Theory and Education* (Pergamon, 1978) is largely of British authorship. Chris Paris's *Critical Readings in Planning Theory* (Pergamon, 1982) suggests that a British 'tradition' is now established.

There are, of course, many earlier books, but the 1980s saw a veritable flood:

P. Cooke, *Theories of Planning and Spatial Development* (Hutchinson, 1983); P. Dunleavy, *Urban Political Analysis* (Macmillan, 1980); M. Goldsmith, *Politics, Planning and the City* (Hutchinson, 1980); P. Healey *et al, Planning Theory: Prospects for the 1980s* (Pergamon, 1982); I. Masser, *Evaluating Urban Planning Efforts* (Gower, 1983); S. McConnell, *Theories for Planning* (Heinemann, 1981); N. Moor, *The Planner and the Market* (Godwin, 1983); P. Saunders, *Social Theory and the Urban Question* (Hutchinson, 1981); M. P. Smith, *The City and Social Theory* (Basil Blackwell, 1980).

The list could be lengthened with ease, but it shows some of the range of approaches being adopted. Perhaps never before have so many questions been asked about 'planning'. One particularly amusing (if not entirely conclusive) transatlantic exchange was sparked off by Wildavsky's paper, "If planning is everything, maybe it's nothing', (A. B. Wildavsky, *Policy Sciences*, vol. 4, 1973, pp. 127–53), which was followed by Alexander's "If planning isn't everything, maybe it's something' (E. R. Alexander, *Town Planning Review*, vol. 52, 1981, pp. 131–42). This in turn stimulated Reade's 'If planning isn't everything . . .' (E. Reade, *Town Planning Review*, vol. 53, 1982, pp. 65–78) and 'If planning is anything, maybe it can be identified' (E. Reade, *Urban Studies*, vol. 20, 1983, pp. 159–71).

The play on words in the titles should not lead one to conclude that all this is a piece of academic irrelevance. Nevertheless, it is not always easy in the welter of words (dealing with everything from neo-Marxism to corporatism and from equity to power politics) to see the relevance of much of the writing in the 'theoretical' field. A notable exception is P. McAuslan's *The Ideologies of Planning Law* (Pergamon, 1980), referred to in the footnote on page 331.

Some of the most relevant and interesting of the writing on planning theory is concerned with the limits of planning in practice. The 'limits' are variously seen as being set by economics, administrative feasibility, the class structure, intragovernmental relationships, public support, and a host of other factors, including, of course, the more embracing *Limits of Power*, to use the title of Anthony Blower's study (Pergamon, 1980).

PLANNING PRACTICE

The question of 'limits' arises particularly in the debates on the 'reform of planning'. As with local government reforms to date, the record has not been encouraging. Here there is a welcome stream of studies of how the planning machine actually operates. Again McAuslan is useful here (neatly bridging 'theory' and 'practice'), and note should also be taken of another legal writer who has profitably strayed from the course of the traditional legal text – Malcolm Grant, *Urban Planning Law* (Sweet & Maxwell, 1982). Among the other studies are the following.

On local plans and development control
M. Breakell and M. Elson, *Development Control and Industry* (Oxford Polytechnic, 1983).
M. J. Bruton, 'Local plans, local planning and development plan schemes in England 1974–1982', *Town Planning Review*, vol. 54, no. 1 (January 1983), pp. 4–23.
Department of the Environment, *Audit Inspectorate*, *Local Planning: The Development Control Function* (HMSO, 1983).

M. Elson, 'Structure plan policies for pressured urban areas', in A. L. Gilg (ed.), *Countryside Planning Yearbook 1981* (Geo Books, 1981), pp. 49–70.
R. Farnell, *Local Planning in Four English Cities* (Gower, 1983).
B. G. Field, 'Local plans and local planning in Greater London', *Town Planning Review*, vol. 54, no. 1 (January 1983), pp. 24–40.
C. Fudge, *Approaches to Local Planning* (University of Bristol, School for Advanced Urban Studies, 1979).
C. Fudge *et al*, *Speed, Economy and Effectiveness in Local Plan Preparation and Adoption* (University of Bristol, School for Advanced Urban Studies, 1983).
A. Glyn-Jones, *Planning in Action* (Devon County Council and University of Exeter, 1983).
P. Healey, *Implementation of Development Plans* (Oxford Polytechnic, 1982).
P. Healey, *Local Plans in British Land Use Planning* (Pergamon, 1983).
M. T. Pountney and P. W. Kingsbury, 'Aspects of development control', *Town Planning Review*, vol. 54 (1983), pp. 139–54 and 285–303.
J. Underwood, 'Development control: a case study of discretion in action', in S. Barrett and C. Fudge (eds), *Policy in Action* (Methuen, 1981).
J. Underwood, *Development Control: A Review of Research and Current Issues*, Progress in Planning, vol. 16, Part 3 (Pergamon, 1981).

On structure plans
I. Bracken and D. Hume, *An Analysis of Welsh Structure Plans* (University of Wales Institute of Science and Technology, Department of Town Planning, 1980).
P. Cloke and D. Shaw, 'Rural settlement policies in structure plans', *Town Planning Review*, vol. 54, no. 3 (July 1983), pp. 338–54.
D. T. Cross and M. R. Bristow (eds), *English Structure Planning: A Commentary on Procedure and Practice in the Seventies* (Pion, 1983).
Journal of Planning and Environment Law, Occasional Papers, *Structure Plans and Local Plans – Planning in Crisis* (Sweet & Maxwell, 1983).
J. Jowell and D. Noble, 'Planning as social engineering: notes on the first English structure plans', *Urban Law and Policy*, vol. 3 (1980), pp. 293–317.
Planning Advice Note, *Structure Planning* (Scottish Development Department, 1981).
U. Wannop, 'The future for development planning', *The Planner*, vol. 67, no. 1 (January–February 1981), pp. 14–18.

This by no means exhaustive list illustrates the amount of examination which the British planning machinery has had in recent years. Further references to other aspects of planning will be given later at appropriate places in the text. Here two other references are worth highlighting. The first is a highly critical analysis, by an American lawyer, of planning delays which arise in the British planning system: D. McBride, 'Planning delays and development control – a proposal for reform', *Urban Law and Policy*, vol. 2 (1979), pp. 47–64. The essence of the argument is the (typically American) concern with the range of administrative discretion which the system allows, but the discussion goes beyond a mere expression of alarm that the rule of law imposes so few limits on administrative discretion. Indeed, we are brought up against the choice between a discretionary system of planning control and a system of zoning. How far current governmental attitudes may be favouring something nearer the latter than the former is an issue worthy of more serious discussion than it has so far received.

The RTPI inquiry was particularly disappointing in that it circumvented the issues arising here. To quote: '. . . the development plan system does not need to be radically changed at present. . . . It is appreciated that other methods of control are sometimes advocated, such as, for example, a zoning system as operated in the United States; and whilst these must obviously be kept under review . . . [the British system is a] much more effective system than such fundamental alternatives' (*Development Control into the 1980s: Final Report of the Development Control Working Party*, Royal Town Planning Institute, 1979, p. 4). One wonders what review has been or is being undertaken of the extremely varied and sometimes highly sophisticated systems of zoning currently operated in the United States.

The second reference to be noted is, at the time of writing, still a promise: this is the Nuffield Foundation inquiry 'into the assumptions and purposes of the town and country planning system, its past and present performance and proper role in the future'. (See *Cities*, vol. 1, no. 1, pp. 93–4 for details.) This is even more wide-ranging than the Expenditure Committee's inquiry into *Planning Procedures* (HMSO, 1977–8). It is to be hoped that its report will be both shorter and more effective.

LOCAL–CENTRAL GOVERNMENT RELATIONSHIPS

Chapter 2 of this book refers (on p. 31) to the 'partnership' of local and central government. It is doubtful whether such a term could be considered appropriate today, twenty years later. Central government, though abolishing or relaxing certain outdated controls, has moved into the dominant position. For both political parties the motive was financial control; but for the Conservative government there was also a determination to impose on Labour councils philosophies and approaches to which they were (and remain) opposed. The final (?) blow came with the 1983 proposals for the abolition ('streamlining') of the Greater London and Metropolitan Counties (outlined below). The extent of the changes in the control of local authority finance, the prohibition of supplementary rating, 'rate-capping', expenditure controls, huge cutbacks in local authority housing programmes, a major recasting of housing finance, enforced sales of council houses ('the right to buy'), and so forth add up to a dramatic shift in the relationships between central and local government. There is little here that bears any affinity to the proposals for 'organic change' (see p. 51). (For an account of these changes, See P. McAuslan, 'Local government and resource allocation in England: changing ideology, unchanging law', *Urban Law and Policy*, vol. 4, 1981, pp. 215–68. The following section on planning draws upon this paper.)

In planning, however, there have been some differences. These stem from two factors. First, it was generally agreed that some change was needed in the allocation of functions between counties and districts to reduce planning delays. Second, while the Conservative Party was in favour of finance and housing 'reforms', it was much more ambivalent to the reduction of county planning controls. The point at issue is the effect of the removal of county controls over district permissions for large-scale housing development. The same point arose in late 1983 when fears of demands from builders for green-belt development sites 'pushed Tory shires into support for the threatened metropolitan counties and the GLC. . . . What emerges is a widespread fear that the disappearance of the authorities will result in the breakdown of a cohesive policy for the cities, and for rural counties into a showdown with builders anxious to convert prime greenbelt sites into lucrative developments' (*Architects' Journal*, 18 January 1984).

What will transpire from this political wrangle will be known to the reader by the time this book is published. So far as the 1980 Act is concerned the result was a number of amendments which appear to give the counties some vestigial role in 'protecting' their areas. In McAuslan's words:

> District planning authorities are obliged to take into account any representations received from the counties, and are furthermore placed under the high sounding but relatively meaningless duty when determining planning applications, 'to seek the achievement of the general objectives of the structure plan, for the time being in force for their area'. Since there is no appeal from a decision to grant planning permission, a determined district planning authority can now flout the wishes of the county planning authority, and put its own interpretation on the county's structure plan without the county being able to do very much about it. (P. McAuslan, op. cit., p. 245)

How significant the problem of planning delays was by 1980 is arguable. More important is the impact of the 1980 Act on structure planning and the relative roles of central and local government.

The umbilical cord between structure plans and local plans has been gradually cut, first by the reorganisation of local government (which allocated the former to counties and the latter to districts), later by the provision allowing the adoption of local plans in advance of the approval of structure plans (Scotland, 1977; 'inner areas', 1978), and finally by the transfer of virtually all planning decisions to the districts.

THE RESTRUCTURING OF BRITAIN

Central government has not had an easy time with some of its planning changes, for political reasons of the type already mentioned. Nevertheless, significant changes have been effected. The more important of these are referred to later. Here only one point is raised, but it is perhaps the most important underlying reason for the change in British planning. It is, of course, the economic transformation of Britain. This is more than just a matter of 'regional problems', or 'stagflation', or any other temporary difficulty. The basic structure of the British economy is changing, and from this follow major locational and organisational implications. One small but eloquent indicator of the change is provided by a statistic of unemployment: in 1960 'regional aid' was given to all districts with more than 4½ per cent unemployment. By the end of 1983 there was only one district (Alton in Hampshire) which did better than 4½ per cent (D. Thomas, 'Should we still help the regions?', *New Society*, 1 December 1983, p. 358).

Equally if not more eloquent of the dramatic change is the transformation of the West Midlands from an area which was viewed as a blood bank transfusing new life into the depressed regions to an area which itself is in deep depression.

As Doreen Massey has pithily expressed the situation, 'the geographical pattern, and the nature, of British regional and subregional geography have been substantially restructured' (D. Massey, 'Industrial location', *Economic and Social Research Council Newsletter*, No. 5, Supplement (1984), p. xv). An excellent analysis of the changes is given in J. B. Goddard and A. G. Champion, *The Urban and Regional Transformation of Britain* (Methuen, 1983).

In the second part of this appendix, a summary is given of the current (1983) policies espoused by the Thatcher administration, but it is obvious that the issues are far too complex (and serious) to be adequately dealt with in a summary fashion. The reader is referred to a range of recent publications, a sample of which is given at the end of the section on regional planning. A broader perspective is provided by A. Norton, *The Government and Administration of Metropolitan Areas in Western Democracies* (University of Birmingham, Institute of Local Government Studies, 1983).

PART 2 1984 UPDATE

'MINIS 4'

1982 saw the publication of the fourth edition of the *Management Information System for Ministers* (MINIS) of the Department of the Environment. This is divided into eight parts (and eleven volumes) as follows:

(1) Private Offices, Central Policy and Organisation, and Establishments,
(2) Planning,
(3) Directorate of Ancient Monuments and Historic Buildings,
(4) Environmental Services,
(5) Housing and Construction (2 vols),
(6) Departmental Support Services and Water,
(7) Finance and Local Government,
(8) Regional Offices and Merseyside Task Force (3 vols).

The purpose of MINIS is to provide comprehensive statements detailing the Department's activities and probable costs. 'They are used by Ministers and senior officials to review the Department's performance and take decisions in accordance with Ministerial priorities and objectives.'

The volumes provide a huge, virtually indigestible amount of information (pity the new minister who has to master his area rapidly); but they give a new insight into the operation of Whitehall which justifies persuading a university library to pay £64·50 for the set (from the DOE, not HMSO).

The *Planning* volume deals with five areas: inner cities; regional policy and development; planning land use policy; planning policy, minerals and new towns; and the planning inspectorate.

By the nature of the material it is not easy to either summarise or illustrate. However, the recent innovation of a DOE annual report, *Department of the Environment Report for the Year 1 April to 31 March 1983* (available direct from DOE at £4), gives the flavour – though one must cavil at the secretary of state's statement that 'this is the first time the Department of the Environment has produced an Annual Report'. This is technically true, since no annual report has been issued since the DOE was established in 1970: an outrageous situation for one of the major departments of state. But it also ignores the fine set of annual reports issued by its predecessor, the Ministry of Housing and Local Government. These constituted an invaluable source of public information (not merely for academic book-writers).

The new DOE report is very different from that of its predecessors – in coverage, depth, glossiness and price. It certainly represents a different 'generation' of reports. Under 'Planning', for example, it first sets out the 'key objective':

> To develop and maintain policies for land-use management promoting efficiency, economy, and amenity in the use and development of land, including the reclamation or recycling of derelict, neglected and under-used land, in ways that serve the needs of development and the interests of conservation.

Several pages summarise the main achievements, various costs, and a description of machinery. The latter figures more significantly in the section on inner cities (including enterprise zones, ethnic issues, research, and urban development corporations).

The summary is neatly done, with some excellent photographs, including one showing the preparations for Liverpool's International Garden Festival being developed on the site of its famous docks.

The report provides a fair overview of the enormous range of activities of the (largely) English activities of the DOE. (Scotland and Wales have similar activities, though their 'publication of activities' reports are much more modest.) The question arises, however, whether the central departments are providing sufficient information on their range of responsibilities. This is not merely a matter of interest to academic writers: it is important for a wider understanding of the difficult problems of policy which arise; the clash of objectives; the problem of allocating resources. British central government is inadequately served with basic information and the electorate even more so.

(A useful discussion of Minis is to be found in A. Likierman, 'Management information for ministers: the minis system in the Department of the Environment', *Public Administration*, vol. 60, summer 1982, pp. 127–42.)

'STREAMLINING THE CITIES'

The phrase 'streamlining the cities' means the abolition of the Greater London Council and the Metropolitan County Councils (listed on p. 46 above). The White Paper bearing this title (Cmnd 9063, 1983) refers disparagingly to the time (the 1960s and early 1970s) 'when it was assumed that growth would automatically provide the funds for ever-increasing expenditure'. It continues:

> It was also the heyday of a certain fashion for strategic planning,

the confidence in which now appears exaggerated. It is perhaps not surprising that, in this climate, structural reform was approached with too little regard for economy, and that the structures created in that era tend sometimes to give inadequate weight to the need to obtain value for money.

But 'times have changed' and 'priorities now are more practical and less theoretical'. Efficiency is the objective, and this means 'a determined attack on the *national overhead*' – by which is meant the public service. A major reorganisation of the National Health Service has completely removed one tier of organisation, all governmental organisations have been subjected to 'rigorous discipline'. The number of civil servants has been cut. Now it is the turn of local government or, to be precise, the GLC and the six metropolitan counties.

These areas are differentiated from the shire counties in that whereas the latter are the major providers of services in their areas this is not the case with the former. Thus 'on average shire county councils have budgets 50 times the size of those of the shire district councils and are responsible for 87 per cent of the total expenditure on local services in their areas. In metropolitan areas the position is reversed: the London borough councils and the metropolitan district councils are the major providers, and the GLC and the MCCs are responsible for 16 per cent and 26 per cent respectively of the total expenditure on local services in their areas.'

On the basis of this political arithmetic, and the fact that the GLC and the MCCs have sole responsibility for very few services, the conclusion is reached that these upper-tier authorities 'have found it difficult to establish a role for themselves'.

Given the predispositions of government, no argument about 'strategic planning' is persuasive: indeed, since strategy in the two-tier system requires the agreement of both tiers, it is 'a recipe for conflict and uncertainty'. Moreover, their 'search for a role' brings the GLC and the MCCs into conflict not only with the district councils but also with central government, both in terms of expenditure and policy.

The conclusion is clear: the structure is 'fundamentally unsound' and 'has imposed heavy and unnecessary burdens on ratepayers'. The 'reorganisation' is expected to take place on 1 April 1986, with as many services as possible being transferred to the districts; others will need to be transferred to joint authorities or other statutory bodies. Transport in London is dealt with separately (see below).

Functions proposed to be transferred to the districts include highways and traffic management; minerals and derelict land reclamation; waste regulation and disposal (where the government 'will wish to be satisfied that the authorities concerned have made

effective cooperative arrangements'); sport; historic buildings; recreation, parks and green-belt land; and gypsy sites. Additionally,
and of prime importance, is the planning function. Here the major
difficulty is that of the relationship between the structure plans for the
individual districts.

The void created by the abolition of the counties is to be filled by
central government. The secretary of state, following local consultation, proposes to issue 'guidelines for the review and preparation of
individual structure plans by each of the borough or district councils'.
These are envisaged as being 'short policy statements' which will
provide 'the general context for local plans'.

Little more than 'conferences' of local authorities is thought to be
necessary in the MCC areas, but in the case of London an advisory
London Planning Commission is proposed. A consultation paper,
*The Reallocation of Planning Functions in the Greater London
Council and Metropolitan County Council Areas* (DOE, 1983) notes:

> Although the Commission would have no formal powers in relation
> to the borough councils, it would be expected to consult the local
> authorities in London, other planning authorities in the South
> East, and other interested bodies before making its recommenda-
> tions to the Secretary of State. The Secretary of State would
> consider these recommendations, and issue guidelines set in the
> regional context.

Of particular note in this new scheme of things is the reduced role
for structure planning. Indeed, it has now been so downgraded as to
appear to be of little significance. Under the subheading 'Resource
Implications', the consultation paper states:

> Devolving structure plan making to borough and district councils
> will increase the total number of structure plan authorities from 49
> to 111. Giving powers to the authorities in London and the
> metropolitan areas to adopt the plans themselves and ensuring that
> the plans will be short policy documents will avoid a significant
> increase in central and local government workload. The borough
> and district councils will want to make economical arrangements
> for discharging their additional responsibilities.

Reactions to these proposals have been mixed, but largely
predictable. The (Conservative-controlled) London Boroughs Association supports the abolition of the GLC but rejects the proposal for
a planning commission: in their view its role could be undertaken by
the Standing Conference on London and South East Regional
Planning (SCLSERP) (*Streamlining The Cities: The Association's
Response to the Government's White Paper*, January 1984). That

body, without referring to itself, argues the case for 'a properly-constituted strategic planning authority for London as a whole' (SCLSERP, *The Abolition of the Greater London Council*, February 1984).

Professional organisations such as the RTPI have decried the break-up of the strategic planning system and/or (like the TCPA) have expressed dismay at the shallow and inadequate arguments of the White Paper.

The GLC, of course, is wholly opposed, and has set out its objectives at length in a document neatly entitled *From Order to Chaos* (GLC, November 1983). In the provinces, the six metropolitan counties have commissioned an independent study from Coopers and Lybrand. But the major political focus is on London.

PUBLIC TRANSPORT IN LONDON

In *Streamlining the Cities*, the government proposes that in the metropolitan counties the former system of passenger transport authorities (PTAs) should be resuscitated. The PTAs will in effect be joint boards of elected representatives from the relevant district councils. Their responsibility will be for major policy, including decisions on revenue support, and hence on fares and service levels – subject to the new financial controls established by the Transport Act 1983 (see White Paper, *Public Transport in Cities*, Cmnd 8735 (HMSO, 1982) and Department of Transport Circular 1/83, *Transport Act 1983* (HMSO, 1983)). The proposals for London, however, were issued in a separate White Paper (*Public Transport in London*, Cmnd 9004, HMSO, 1983). The fact that this paper was issued separately – and in advance of *Streamlining the Cities* – suggests that it was looked upon as a separate issue. (However much the Conservative government disliked the GLC generally, they disliked London Transport even more.)

A justification can presumably be found in the report of the House of Commons Transport Committee (*Transport in London*, HC 127, HMSO, 1982). This report was highly critical of the organisation of public transport in London, and recommended the establishment of a metropolitan transport authority with responsibility for all modes of transport and all operators (including British Rail).

The White Paper proposals are different. In a crisp thirty-five paragraphs it surveys the field, berates the GLC for its inadequacies, and (with no in-depth analysis) concludes that a new body should be set up with responsibility solely for public transport – excluding British Rail:

> The Government has decided that control of the London Transport Executive should be transferred as soon as possible from the GLC to the Secretary of State for Transport. It will then be reconstituted

on the pattern of a small holding company, with its bus and Underground operations established as separate subsidiaries.

As the RTPI were quick to point out, this implies the divorce of land use planning and transport planning, 'by removing the control of the major public transport operator from the strategic planning authority for London'. But, since the government are also abolishing the strategic planning authority, this argument is hardly likely to carry much weight. The real responsibility will shift to the central government.

STRUCTURE PLANS AND LOCAL PLANS

Comment has already been made on the downgrading of structure plans (which is discussed in more detail in P. McAuslan, 'Local government and resource allocation in England: changing ideology, unchanging law', *Urban Law and Policy*, vol. 4, 1981, particularly p. 243). However, there is (at least in England and Wales) some lack of clarity in what the current situation is. Certainly there has been a good deal of unease over the last few years, perhaps epitomised by the conference report *Structure Plans and Local Plans – Planning in Crisis* (Sweet & Maxwell, 1983). In June 1982, the DOE issued a lengthy draft *Memorandum on Structure Plans and Local Plans*, but this contained 'guidance' on green belts and such delicate matters to which strong and vociferous opposition was made. It was therefore withdrawn and a decision was taken to publish a separate circular on green-belt policy and a new version of the memorandum which, it was hoped, would prove to be uncontroversial. A later draft on green belts (in the words of the RTPI) replaced 'certainty with ambiguity' (*Planner News*, December 1983). Later drafts (e.g., *Land for Housing*, DOE, April 1984) apparently did not settle the arguments (*Planning*, no. 565, 20 April 1984), and the debate becomes increasingly clouded.

It would be tedious (and, of course, inconclusive) to examine the issues – and the precise words – in detail, but the draft circular provides an appropriate quotation:

The essential characteristic of green belts is their permanence and their protection should be long-term. It follows from this that:
(a) Once a green belt has been approved as part of the structure plan for an area it should be altered only in exceptional circumstances. If such an alteration is proposed the Secretary of State will wish to be satisfied that the authority has considered opportunities for development within the urban area contained by and beyond the green belt. Similarly, detailed green belt boundaries defined in adopted local plans or earlier development plans should be altered only excep-

tionally. It is particularly important that full use is made of opportunities for bringing back into use areas of neglected or derelict land and for recycling urban land, including obsolete industrial sites and buildings unlikely to be required in future for their original purpose. The development of such sites can make a valuable contribution to inner city renewal and reduce the pressures on undeveloped land. The maintenance of effective green belt policy will assist in this.

(b) Where detailed boundaries have yet to be defined in local plans – for example, where approved structure plans have extended the area of the green belt to include areas previously referred to as 'interim' green belt – it is necessary to establish boundaries that can be maintained in the long-term.

What is really at issue here is the clash between the short-term need to safeguard the green belt and the long-term need to allocate sufficient land for house building. Generosity on the latter may lead to short-term pressures which defeat the original plans. The matter is, of course, greatly complicated by a widespread lack of trust and confidence between the various agencies involved. (An examination of practice (in the form of planning decisions) makes the issue no easier: see K. Smith, 'Planning decisions: the application of green belt policy', *Journal of Planning and Property Law*, 1983, pp. 777–89.)

In the meantime, the DOE has made it clear that structure plans should deal not with broad social objectives but with specific *land use* problems. (See D. T. Cross and M. Bristow, *English Structure Planning*; and J. Jowell and D. Noble, 'Structure plans as instruments of social and economic policy', *Journal of Planning and Environment Law*, 1981, p. 480; and the same authors' 'Planning as social engineering: notes on the first English structure plans', *Urban Law and Planning*, vol. 3, 1980.) There has also been increasing emphasis on *shortening* structure plans. (How short is short?) Indeed, even with the growth in the concern for economic issues, not much seems to be required. In the words of a DOE under-secretary:

The Government's present position on regional planning is that, in broad terms, enough is enough, and far better than too much. (J. Barber, in *Structure Plans and Local Plans – Planning in Crisis*, Sweet & Maxwell, 1983, p. 95)

One wonders how far planning (be it 'structural' or 'local') is being changed into a reactive process, guided by the broadest of informal, non-statutory plans – arguably not necessarily a bad thing. (See M. J. Bruton and D. J. Nicholson, 'Non-statutory local plans and supplementary planning guidance', *Journal of Planning and Environmental Law*, 1983, pp. 432–43.) Further speculation on this beguiling theme must await another time and place. Here we conclude with a summary of some of the more interesting points of the 1982 statutory instrument on the structure and local plan regulations (SI 1982, No. 555). The summary is taken from the *Journal of Planning and Environment Law*, 1982, p. 434. The principal changes made by these regulations are:

1 Local authorities are allowed to advertise certain stages in the local plan process in local newspapers only, and not in the *London Gazette*
2 The period for the making of representations is fixed at six weeks, rather than not less than six weeks
3 The matters prescribed to be contained in structure plans are changed so as to take account of the new system under the 1980 Act. This Act provides for the plan to consist only of the policy and general proposals and key diagram. The reasoned justification for the policy and proposals, which formerly formed part of the plan, will appear separately in an explanatory memorandum
4 The 1980 Act allows a local authority to dispense with a local inquiry into a local plan if objectors indicate that they do not wish to appear and the regulations prescribe the procedure to be followed in such cases
5 Modifications to local plans which do not materially affect the plans' contents need not now be advertised
6 The 1980 Act allows for the repeal and replacement of structure plans in addition to their simple alteration and the regulations provide for the new procedure
7 In the case of local plans there is now no requirement in the regulations that local authorities should consult each other.

STRUCTURE AND LOCAL PLANS IN SCOTLAND

Following the inevitably confused account of the situation in England and Wales (which hopefully will be clarified by the time this book is published), we can now turn with some relief to Scotland, where life seems less complicated. (In fact the problems are more difficult to deal with, but policy-making, institutional co-ordination, and implementation are easier because of the smaller population of the country, and the fact that anyone who is of significance in the administrative and political arenas is well known to all others of significance.)

The recent changes in Scottish planning provisions are embodied in the Local Government (Miscellaneous Provisions) (Scotland) Act 1981; the Local Government and Planning (Scotland) Act 1982; SDD Circular 29/1982; and SDD Circular 32/1983.

The provisions (and the philosophy) closely follow those being introduced south of the Border. Alterations to structure plans and local plans have been made simpler (without the requirement for 'unnecessary wide-ranging publicity and consultation'). Local plans do not require 'unwarranted' public local inquiries.

Certain adjustments have been made to the division of planning responsibilities between regions and districts. This had been a matter of considerable discussion by the Stodard Committee (*Report of the Committee of Inquiry into Local Government in Scotland*, Cmnd 8115, 1981), who concluded that 'the existing distribution of planning functions at the strategic and the local level should remain'. Most of the changes are of a minor or technical nature. The more important have the objective, in the words of Circular 29/1982, 'to clarify the division between regions and districts, and in particular to ensure that regions have all the powers necessary to them to fulfil their structure planning responsibilities, without introducing any element of concurrency'.

Some significant changes in listed building procedures are noted later in this appendix.

The Town and Country Planning (Structure and Local Plans) (Scotland) Regulations 1983 (SI 1590) are discussed in an annex to SDD Circular 32/1983.

OFFICE AND INDUSTRIAL LOCATION CONTROLS

As noted on p. 41 above, office development permits were abolished in 1979. As the economy worsened it became increasingly clear that industrial development certificates were of little relevance. Between 1975 and 1981 only 28 out of 7,000 applications for IDCs were refused. Moreover, refusals had proved to be ineffective in achieving their objective: firms modified their projects to avoid the need for an IDC, or purchased a building already designated for industrial use, or simply abandoned the project. (See *Fifth Report from the Committee of Public Accounts 1980–81*, HC 206, HMSO, 1981.) In December 1981 it was announced that the government had concluded that the procedure had outlived its usefulness and it would no longer be operated (*Journal of Planning and Environment Law*, 1982, p. 73). To avoid 'pressures on parliamentary time', this was given effect by regulations which suspended all IDC controls until further notice (SI 1981, No. 1826).

PLANNING AGREEMENTS AND PLANNING GAIN

The debate on planning agreements, "bargaining", and planning gain (see pages 83–5 above) has continued. A slim report by the Property Advisory Group (*Planning Gain*, HMSO, 1981) added fuel to the controversy by concluding that with minor exceptions 'the practice of bargaining for planning gain is unacceptable and should be firmly discouraged'. A spate of articles followed, of which the following constitute a good cross-section:

M. Grant, 'False diagnosis, wrong prescription', *Town and Country Planning*, vol. 51, no. 3 (March 1982), pp. 59–61.
D. Heap *et al.*, 'Planning Gain', *Journal of Planning and Environment Law* (1982), pp. 1–6.
D. Henry, *Planning by Agreement in a Berkshire District* (Oxford Polytechnic, Department of Town Planning, 1982).
Law Society, 'Planning gain: the Law Society's observations', *Journal of Planning and Environment Law*, 1982, pp. 346–51.
M. Loughlin, 'Planning gain – another viewpoint', *Journal of Planning and Environment Law*, 1982, pp. 352–8.
J. Jowell and M. Grant, 'Guidelines for planning gain?', *Journal of Planning and Environment Law*, 1983, pp. 427–31
M. T. Pountney and P. W. Kingsbury, 'Aspects of development control, Part 2: the applicant's view', *Town Planning Review*, vol. 54, no. 3 (July 1983), particularly pp. 291–2.
E. J. Reade, 'Section 52 and corporatism in planning', *Journal of Planning and Environment Law*, 1982, pp. 8–16.
J. Rowan-Robinson and E. Young, *Planning by Agreement in Scotland: The Law and Practice* (The Planning Exchange, Glasgow, 1982).
I. Simpson, *Planning Gain: The Implications for Planning in the UK*, (University of Strathclyde, Department of Urban and Regional Planning, 1984).
A. J. Ward, 'Planning bargaining: Where do we stand?', *Journal of Planning and Environment Law*, 1982, pp. 74–84.
D. G. Wiltshaw, 'Planning gain: a theoretical note', *Urban Studies*, vol. 21 (1984), pp. 183–7.
E. Young and J. Rowan-Robinson, 'Section 52 agreements and the filtering of power', *Journal of Planning and Environment Law*, 1982, pp. 673–85.

After considerable debate a DOE circular finally emerged, bearing the lengthy title *Town and Country Planning Act 1971: Planning Gain – Obligations and Benefits Which Extend Beyond the Development for Which Planning Permission Has Been Sought* (DOE Circular 22/83, HMSO, 1983). The leitmotiv of this circular is 'reasonableness' – which is dealt with at some length though without a clear conclusion. One quotation will have to suffice:

The test of the reasonableness of imposing obligations on developers depends substantially on whether what is required:

(1) is needed to enable the development to go ahead, e.g. provision of adequate access, water supply and sewerage and sewage disposal facilities; or

(2) in the case of financial payments, will contribute to meeting the cost of providing such facilities in the near future: or

(3) is otherwise so directly related to the proposed development and to the use of the land after its completion, that the development ought not to be permitted without it, e.g. the provision, whether by the developer or by the authority at the developer's expense, of car-parking in or near the development or of reasonable amounts of open space related to the development; or

(4) is designed in the case of mixed development to secure an acceptable balance of uses.

There is more in similar vein, but the matter is inherently troublesome, and no easy resolution is likely.

ENFORCEMENT OF PLANNING CONTROL

Substantial changes have been made to the provisions relating to the enforcement of planning control and the control over listed buildings by the Local Government and Planning (Amendment) Act 1981. The Act also changes the maximum amount of fines on conviction for certain offences involving a breach of control, and amends provisions for enforcement of tree-planting requirements and waste-land notices ('Local Government and Planning (Amendment) Act 1981: A Guide', issued by the DOE and reprinted in *Journal of Planning and Environment Law 1981*, pp. 740–4).

Details are given in DOE Circular 26/81 (*Local Government and Planning (Amendment) Act 1981*, HMSO, 1981). See also DOE Circular 38/81, *Planning and Enforcement Appeals* (HMSO, 1981); 'Enforcement notices', *Journal of Planning and Environment Law*, 1982, pp. 141–2; M. Grant, *Urban Planning Law*, (Sweet & Maxwell, 1982), pp. 400–13; and *Enforcement Notice Appeals: A Guide to Procedure* (DOE, 1983)

MOBILE HOMES

Following a spate of inquiries and studies, 1983 saw the passing of the Mobile Homes Act. This statute is outside the boundaries of 'town and country planning', and is nearer in spirit to landlord and tenant legislation. It provides some solid basis for 'mobile home agreements' between mobile-home occupiers and site owners. (See P. H. Kenny, 'The Mobile Homes Act 1983', *Journal of Planning and Environment Law*, 1983, pp. 524–9,)

This legislation is quite separate from that relating to caravan sites (see pp. 94–7 above) on which a new circular has been issued by the DOE, Circular 23/83, *Caravan Sites and Control of Development Act 1960*. The problems of gypsy sites seems to have dropped off the agenda of debate. See R. K. Home, 'Planning problems of self-help gypsy sites', *Journal of Planning and Environment Law*, 1982, pp. 217–24; and R. K. Home, 'The Caravan Sites Act 1982: progress and problems with designation, *Journal of Planning and Environment Law*, 1984, pp. 226–34. But see also DOE, *The Accommodation Needs of Long-Distance and Regional Travellers: A Consultation Paper* (DOE, 1982); and *The Management of Local Authority Gypsy Sites* (DOE, 1982).

PURCHASE NOTICES

A revised and up-dated circular on *Purchase Notices* was issued by the DOE in April 1983 (DOE Circular 13/83, HMSO, 1983). This incorporates amendments introduced by the Local Government, Planning and Land Act 1980. The changes are not of major significance. (For a useful discussion of purchase notices, see M. Grant, *Urban Planning Law*, Sweet & Maxwell, 1982, pp. 653–61.)

SEX SHOPS

Sex has been firmly cast beyond the pale of town and country planning, and sex shops (see p. 116 above) are now subject to a totally separate licensing scheme, under the provisions of the Local Government (Miscellaneous Provisions) Act 1982. (See also C. Manchester, 'Much ado about the location of sex shops', *Journal of Planning and Environment Law*, 1982, pp. 89–95.)

REGIONAL REPORTS

The unique Scottish provision for regional reports remains on the statute book, and all the regions have produced their reports. It seems unlikely, however, that a second round will be called for. (See E. Gillett, *Investment in the Environment: Recent Housing, Planning and Transport Policies in Scotland* (Aberdeen University Press, 1983), pp. 61–4.) At first sight this may seem strange, particularly in view of the increased concern of government at all levels with economic and social issues. It was precisely this type of issue that the regional reports were supposed to cover (see SDD Circular 4/1975, *Town and Country Planning* – Regional Reports, SDD, 1975).

   Though there has been a good deal of support for the preparation of revised regional reports (and, indeed, one council – the Central Region – actually produced one on its own initiative in 1979), there are some serious difficulties involved. Gillett explains that the Local Government Act 'required reports to be based on planning surveys, and the clear implication was that they were to be preliminary to the structure plans required under the Town and Country Planning Acts.

By 1979 most structure plans were either recently completed, or at an advanced stage, and it did not seem possible to insist on regional authorities submitting a report on their policies when most of those policies had been, or were about to be, formally set out in the structure plan. It also seemed unlikely that in these circumstances the Scottish Office could once again insist on an interpretation of the regional report idea which went beyond the terms of statute, where it was an adjunct of the planning of land use. Furthermore, the earliest date for the completion of the new regional reports would have been late 1981, six months before the next regional elections. A report by an outgoing council would lack credibility, and would in any case have to be re-examined by the new council. So the Scottish Office decided to put off a decision on a further round until after the 1982 elections.'

In 1982 the Secretary of State for Scotland announced that he would not be calling for a further round of regional reports 'in the foreseeable future'. In a letter to the regional and islands councils, he gave four reasons for this decision:

1) The problems associated with local government reorganisation had been largely overcome;
2) Other policy plans and programmes had been developed, for example, in relation to housing, transport and finance;
3) Substantial progress had been made on the preparation of structure and local plans;
4) Financial and manpower restraints had become severe.

(A. W. Gilg, *Countryside Yearbook* vol. 4, 1983, p. 23)

DEVELOPMENT CONTROL POLICY FOR SHOPPING AREAS

In recent years, rapid growth in the service sector of the economy has led to increased demand for outlets for personal services both in high street locations and in neighbourhood shopping centres. This has produced difficulties for planning control policy and also some legal doubts – when is a shop not a shop? New guidelines (also covering amusement centres, building society offices, estate and employment agencies, hot food take-away shops, laundrettes and dry cleaners) are currently under discussion (*Draft Development Control Policy Note – Service Uses in Shopping Areas*, DOE, 1984.)

FEES FOR PLANNING APPLICATIONS

After a great deal of initial bitter argument, fees for planning applications appear to have settled down as a normal part of the machinery of planning control. However, as also normally seems to happen, they have become complicated, subject to numerous exemptions, and under frequent revision. Their immediate effect is unclear (except for their bothersome nature). In the longer term – which is even more unclear – it may be, as Malcolm Grant suggests, that they are 'likely to lead to some significant changes . . . in the relationship between applicants and local planning authorities' (M. Grant, *Urban Planning Law*, Sweet & Maxwell, 1982, p. 212).

The relevant circulars are DOE 14/82, *The Town and Country Planning (Fees for Applications and Deemed Applications) (Amendment) Regulations 1982*, (HMSO, 1982), and SDD 33/1983, *Town and Country Planning (Fees for Applications and Deemed Applications) (Scotland) Regulations 1983*, (SDD, 1983). Draft regulations to amend and consolidate the English provisions were introduced at the end of 1983 (see *Journal of Planning and Environment Law*, 1983, pp. 578–9).

OUTDOOR ADVERTISING CONTROL

Amending regulations were laid before Parliament in 1984 (The Town and Country Planning (Control of Advertisements) Regulations 1984). These contain new and modified provisions in the present regime for control by local planning authorities over outdoor advertising.

The regulations make two main changes. First, a new 'deemed consent' is introduced for *temporary* poster hoardings around certain construction sites (but *not* sites in conservation areas or other designated areas), for a maximum period of two years, while construction work is taking place, so that this type of advertisement will not need the planning authority's specific consent before it can be displayed.

Secondly, captive balloon advertisements are brought formally within the system of outdoor advertisement control and are given the benefit of a limited 'exemption' from control (but *not* on sites in conservation areas or other designated areas) for a maximum period of ten days in any calendar year.

The regulations also contain a number of other minor modifications and improvements; and they consolidate the existing provisions.

LISTED BUILDINGS

Control over listed buildings and conservation areas has been strengthened both north and south of the Border. Details are to be found in SDD Circular 29/1982, *Local Government and Planning (Scotland) Act 1982: Planning Provisions* (SDD, 1982), especially paragraphs 12 to 16; and in DOE Circulars 12/81, *Historic Buildings and Conservation Areas* (HMSO, 1981) and 26/81, *Local Government and Planning (Amendment) Act 1981* (HMSO, 1981). See also C. Mynors, 'Conservation areas', *Journal of Planning and Environment*

Law, 1984, pp. 144–57 and 235–47; DOE, *Organisation of Ancient Monuments and Historic Buildings in England: A Consultation Paper* (HMSO, 1981); and DOE, *Organisation of Ancient Monuments and Historic Buildings in England: The Way Forward*, (HMSO, 1982); and SDD, *New Uses For Older Buildings in Scotland* (HMSO, 1981).

The National Heritage Act 1983 (see page 130 above) is now in operation, and an early 'progress report' on 'The Work of the National Heritage Memorial Fund' by the Fund's chairman, Lord Charteris, is to be found in the *Journal of the Royal Society of Arts*, April 1984, pp. 325–38. (The National Heritage Fund should not be confused with the Architectural Heritage Fund, whose annual report can be obtained from its offices at 17 Carlton House Terrace, London SW1Y 5AW.)

The National Heritage Act also provides for the replacement of the Historic Buildings Council for England and the Ancient Monuments Board for England by the Historic Buildings and Monuments Commission for England. (See DOE, *Organisation of Ancient Monuments and Historic Buildings in England: A Consultation Paper*, HMSO, 1981; and F. A. Sharman, 'The new law on ancient monuments', *Journal of Planning and Environment Law*, 1981, pp. 785–91.) No similar change is proposed for Scotland, where, in the words of the secretary of state, 'the present arrangements worked well and provided the best framework for developing the successful preservation, management and presentation of the heritage in Scotland' (A. Gilg, *Countryside Planning Yearbook 1983*, p. 25). The new Commission for England has the duty 'so far as practicable', to:

- secure the preservation of ancient monuments and historic buildings situated in England;
- promote the preservation and enhancement of the character and appearance of conservation areas situated in England; and
- promote the public's enjoyment of, and advance their knowledge of, ancient monuments and historic buildings in England, and their preservation.

The change-over has not proceeded without criticism. For example, the Royal Town Planning Institute has pointed to the need for the appointment of professional staff on a significantly larger scale than under the previous arrangements – 'under which the organisation tended to become hidebound with career administrators who did not always have a flair for dealing with historic buildings and artefacts'. In no uncertain terms, the Institute has stressed that 'the idea of a new commission was to get the right professional expertise on to problems quickly and to cut out unnecessary bureaucracy' (*Planning*, 6 January 1984). It is, however, early days yet, and it is unlikely that the character of the new body will be established at any great speed, particularly in view of the continuing public expenditure cuts.

GOOD DESIGN

Good design continues to be as problematic as ever. A somewhat dismal conclusion emerged from the studies of Philip Booth and Anne R. Beer (see 'Development control and design quality', *Town Planning Review*, vol. 54, pp. 265–84 and 383–404, together with the references cited; and the same authors' five volumes bearing the same title, published by the Sheffield Centre for Environmental Research, University of Sheffield, 1981).

A leisurely review is currently under way at the DOE following the distribution of a draft circular on *Good Design and Development Control* (DOE, October 1983). The covering letter to this notes that the secretary of state is not committed to publishing the circular in its present form: 'At this stage, we are anxious to stimulate public debate, both in the profession and amongst the wider public concerned with design and the environment. . . . No time limit is set for your response at this stage.'

What will finally emerge from Marsham Street remains to be seen, but the draft circular has been warmly welcomed by the Royal Institute of British Architects and the Royal Town Planning Institute, who set up a joint committee in 1983 to examine problems of development control, and 'to improve the collaboration of the two professions in the planning process' (*The Planner*, April 1984, p. 7). However, reservations remain, and particular stress is laid on the necessity of employing skilled professional staff.

POLLUTION

It is not clear whether the problems of pollution are becoming more complex and difficult, or whether public concern is growing. It seems likely, however, that both are true: the public is getting increasingly concerned about pollution at the same time as the problems are growing. This is an international phenomenon, ranging from dying forests in Germany to acid rain in Canada and the USA, to a baffling array of issues in Britain. (A glance at the titles of the reports of the Royal Commission on Environmental Pollution and of the DOE Central Directorate of Environmental Pollution clearly illustrates the range of problems involved.)

Pollution knows no boundaries, and to the Scandinavian countries Britain is the 'dirty old man' of Europe (*New Society*, 22 September 1983). See also G. Wetstone and A. Rosencranz, 'Transboundary air pollution in Europe: a survey of national responses', *Columbia Journal of Environmental Law*, vol. 9, 1983, pp. 1–62; and G. S.

Wetstone and A. Rosencranz, *Acid Rain in Europe and North America* (Environmental Law Institute, 1983). British-created acid rain falls across the North Sea. These international disputes do not appear likely to be easy of solution. (Even basic facts are at dispute: Britain argues that the link between sulphur dioxide and acid rain has yet to be proved; the USA argues similarly. But Scandinavia on the one hand and Canada on the other have no doubts.)

The tenth Report of the Royal Commission on Environmental Pollution (*Tackling Pollution – Experience and Prospects*, HMSO, 1984) is a disturbing statement (often implicitly rather than explicitly) of the seriousness of the situation, but more alarming is the governmental reaction to the work of the Commission. In a July 1981 statement, it was announced that existing and future reports (that is, the tenth) 'will provide the Government with comprehensive and authoritative surveys covering the major areas of interaction between energy policy and the environment. . . . The Secretaries of State for the Environment, Energy, Scotland and Wales, have therefore decided to allow the commission to fall into abeyance for the time being. The body will, of course, be reconstituted should it prove necessary' (*HC Debates*, vol. 8, col. 215, 9 July 1981).

In the meantime, the stream of academic studies is increasing. See, for instance, G. Richardson *et al.*, *Policing Pollution* (Clarendon Press, 1982); and C. Miller and C. Wood, *Planning and Pollution* (Clarendon Press, 1983).

This is one of the areas in which governments are reluctant and slow to react. Radioactive waste management is another (see annual reports of the Radioactive Waste Management Advisory Committee, 1980f.; and White Paper, *Radioactive Waste Management*, Cmnd 8607, HMSO, 1982). To deal more effectively with this matter, a new organisation has been established within central government: the Hazardous Waste Inspectorate. This has the following terms of reference:

> To examine the management of hazardous waste at all its stages from the point of arising to that of final disposal by visiting facilities being used to handle, store, treat, process and dispose of such waste either separately, or in conjunction with other controlled waste; to advise waste disposal authorities on the execution of their duties under Part I of the Control of Pollution Act 1974; to make recommendations with the object of ensuring that standards of operation, site licensing and enforcement are both adequate to protect health and the environment, and also equitable and consistent across the country; and periodically to publish a report. (DOE Circular 20/83, *Hazardous Waste Inspectorate*, HMSO, 1983)

NOISE

Under the Control of Pollution Act, the secretary of state is empowered to issue codes of practice for minimising noise. Three such codes were published in 1981. These provided guidance on methods of limiting noise from loudspeakers fixed to vehicles used for the conveyance and the sale to the public of a perishable commodity for human consumption (ice-cream van chimes); from audible intruder alarms (burglar alarms); and from model aircraft (SI (1981) 1828, 1829 and 1830).

The codes of practice do not in themselves create offences and are not legally enforceable but it is considered that 'non-compliance with their terms is something which a court may wish to take into account in any proceedings for noise nuisance' (*Journal of Planning and Environment Law*, 1982, p. 239).

A particularly interesting project on noise abatement was the Darlington Quiet Town Experiment. A report bearing this title was published by the Noise Advisory Council (HMSO, 1981). The report contains much of value and concludes that 'the experiment overall was successful in conveying the message that noise is a problem worth tackling to the great majority of people in Darlington; providing lessons for further work in the field of cooperation between local authorities and industry in noise abatement; and in indicating particular areas of public education and exhortation which might be developed for use elsewhere'.

The term 'elsewhere' quickly came to have a double meaning when, following the abolition of the Clean Air Council and the Clean Air Council for Scotland, the Thatcher administration disbanded the Noise Advisory Council in 1981 as part of its 'continuing review of the role of advisory bodies' (*HC Debates*, vol. 998, col. 423, 12 February 1981). At the same time it was announced that, under the enforcement provisions of the Control of Pollution Act, local authorities have been increasingly active in dealing with noise complaints from the public either informally or through the courts. A new power provided by the Local Government, Planning and Land Act enables local authorities to act on their own to designate noise abatement zones (*Journal of Planning and Environment Law*, 1981, p. 267).

COAL, MINERALS AND DERELICT LAND

A new Derelict Land Survey was carried out in England in 1982. This showed that 'between 1 April 1974 and 31 March 1982 in England 17,000 hectares of derelict land were restored to beneficial use, the majority of it with the aid of central Government derelict land grants. This represents the equivalent of 50 per cent of the derelict land identified in 1974 as worth reclamation, an overall reclamation rate of over 2,000 hectares a year.

'Nearly 45,700 hectares are now recorded as derelict, of which 34,300 hectares are considered to justify reclamation. The northern region has shown a significant decrease in derelict land, reflecting the progress made in coal-tip reclamation, but there have been increases in most other regions, mainly through the pattern of individual change in the north-west, the West Midlands and docklands.

'For the first time the survey includes information about the distribution of derelict land between urban and rural locations and its ownership. Forty-six per cent is in urban areas but 92 per cent of this land is considered to justify reclamation compared with only 62 per cent of rural land. Sixteen per cent of derelict land is owned by local authorities, 25 per cent by other public bodies and the remainder is in private ownership' (DOE press notice, 28 February 1984).

Less sanguine views are expressed in reports from the West Midlands (*Derelict Land in the West Midlands County*, West Midlands County Council, 1983) and South Yorkshire (M. Thompson, 'Reclaiming our dirty little country', *Town and Country Planning*, January 1984, pp. 18–19); and also in M. J. Thompson and D. A. Edmondson, 'Whither derelict land grant?', *The Planner*, vol. 70, 1984, pp. 16–18).

More to the forefront has been the Report of the Commission on Energy and Environment on *Coal and the Environment* (HMSO, 1981, price £23) and the government's response (Cmnd 8877, HMSO, 1983). Sadly the Commission will not report again since it has been disbanded. The issues at stake are wide-ranging and, though there is little new in either the Commission's report or the government's response, the two documents form a useful synthesis of the relevant issues.

A different type of synthesis has been effected by the Derelict Land Act 1982, which is largely a consolidating measure (incorporating provisions spread over four separate Acts).

Most dramatic, however, is the new legislation relating to minerals: the Town and Country Planning (Minerals) Act 1981. This implements many of the recommendations of the Stevens Committee on *Planning Control over Mineral Working* (see above, pp. 142–3). The Stevens Committee argued that conditions, standards and attitudes have changed so greatly since the early days of minerals planning that a major recasting of the legislative framework was needed. Indeed, they went so far as to propose that there should be a separate planning code for minerals. Though this was unacceptable to the government, the new Act establishes a range of new powers within the existing planning system and a totally new system for compensation. The main purposes of the Act are as follows.

First, to improve the conditions that can be imposed on a planning consent for the restoration of mineral working. In particular to ensure that land that is to be restored to agriculture, forestry or amenity uses can be managed in a suitable way for a period after the restoration itself is complete to ensure that it returns to a proper level of productivity by an 'after-care' condition.

Second, to provide that existing conditions on a mineral planning permission can be changed with reduced or no compensation payable provided the changes do not affect certain fundamental elements of the permission.

Third, to deal with mineral workings where the working itself has ceased but the planning consent still remains outstanding. Two new orders can be promoted: a suspension order, where the minerals are being held for future working, and a prohibition order where, the operator has no intention of working any minerals that remain. Both orders allow a certain number of new conditions to be imposed, again with reduced compensation being payable.

Fourth, to put mineral planning authorities (county councils except within the GLC area) under a duty to review the planning situation in respect of every mineral operation within their area. This review is to be repeated as frequently as the county council determines. The carrying out of the review, however, is not a prerequisite to the use of the new powers contained elsewhere in the Act (J. R. Trustram Eve, 'The Town and Country Planning (Minerals) Act 1981', *Journal of Planning and Environment Law*, 1981, p. 857.)

The Act applies to Scotland as well as to England and Wales. Circulars have been issued by the DOE (1/82) and the SDD (5/1982).

COAL, MINERALS AND DERELICT LAND: REFERENCES

P. Arnold and I. Cole, *The Development of the Selby Coalfield: A Study in Planning* (University of York, Department of Social Administration and Social Work, 1981).
Business Statistics Office, *Business Monitor PA 1007: Minerals* (HMSO, 1983).
M. J. Chadwick, *Restoration of Land* (Blackwell, 1980).
Commission on Energy and the Environment, *Coal and the Environment* (HMSO, 1981).
Council for Environmental Conservation, *Scar on the Landscape* (The Council, 1979).
DOE, *Vale of Belvoir Coalfield Inquiry Report* (HMSO, 1981).
DOE, *Town and Country Planning (Minerals) Act 1981*, Circular 1/82 (HMSO, 1982).
DOE, *Guidelines for Aggregates Provision in England and Wales*, Circular 21/82 (HMSO, 1982).
M. Grant, 'Planning act solves the long-life problem of mineral working', *Local Government Chronicle*, 2 October 1981, pp. 1012–14.
M. Harrison and S. Machin, *Mineral Planning Appeals in Great Britain 1981*, (Mineral Planning Publications, Northallerton, 1982).

K. Hawkins, *Environment and Enforcement: Regulation and the Social Definition of Pollution* (Oxford University Press, 1984).

A. D. Jelley, 'The control of mineral working', *Journal of Planning and Environment Law*, 1982, pp. 287–94.

A. and M. MacEwen, *National Parks: Conservation or Cosmetics?* (Allen & Unwin, 1982), Chapter 11.

G. Manners, *Coal in Britain: An Uncertain Future* (Allen & Unwin, 1981).

C. Miller and C. Wood, *Planning and Pollution* (Oxford University Press, 1983).

G. Richardson *et al.*, *Policing Pollution: A Study of Regulation and Enforcement* (Oxford University Press, 1984).

P. W. Roberts and T. Shaw, *Mineral Resources in Regional and Strategic Planning* (Gower, 1982).

SDD, *Town and Country Planning (Minerals) Act 1981*, Circular 5/1982 (SDD, 1982).

J. Sheail, '"Deserts of the Moon": the Mineral Workings Act and the restoration of ironstone workings in Northamptonshire, England, 1936–1951', *Town Planning Review*, vol. 54 (1983), pp. 405–24.

D. Spooner, *Mining and Regional Development* (Oxford University Press, 1981).

Standing Conference on London and South East Regional Planning, *Aggregates Monitoring 1974–1980* (The Conference, 1981).

J. R. Trustram Eve, 'The Town and Country Planning (Minerals) Act 1981', *Journal of Planning and Environment Law*, 1981, pp. 857–63.

PLANNING FOR TRAFFIC

The latest English roads White Paper (*Policy for Roads in England: 1983*, Cmnd 9059, HMSO, 1983) opens enthusiastically: 'The growing importance of road transport to the economy has been evident for many years. Travel by car is now some 7½ times the level of thirty years ago; freight moved by road is three times as high. Today about nine-tenths of all mechanised passenger travel and four-fifths of all inland freight go by road.'

The enthusiasm is later tempered by reference to 'tight financial constraints', but these were ameliorated by the government's privatisation policies – including the phasing out of the road construction units (employing 1,600 staff): major design and supervisory work is now done in the private sector. Additionally, leaseholds on 38 motorway service areas were sold for £48 million. 'This has expanded competition and led to very marked improvements in services for motorway travellers.' More generally, the basic policy has been to concentrate resources 'on making progress with urgently-needed schemes and those with a genuine prospect of early construction'.

Viewing road-building over a longer time period, some 1,400 miles of motorways have been built in the last twenty years, resulting in a totally new 'map of accessibility'. Currently the major priority is the completion of the M25 around London (which is briefly discussed later in the section on regional planning).

But, while new roads are still being built, existing roads are deteriorating. Though the problem may not be as acute as in the USA, 'spending in the 1970s did not keep up with the need for repairs: a backlog built up'. (For a thorough analysis of the American situation – extending far beyond roads – see M. Barker (ed.), *Rebuilding America's Infrastructure: An Agenda for the 1980s*, Duke University Press, 1984.) The 1983 White Paper asserts that priority will be given to the continuing repair programme: '. . . it does not make sense to let the assets deteriorate, and we need to make the best use of what we have.'

In Scotland, a slim report summarises progress with the long-standing objectives of 'designing a road programme which will promote industrial development and environmental improvement' (*Roads in Scotland: Report for 1982*, Cmnd 9010, HMSO, 1983).

Not all are agreed that the current road programme is adequate. The British Road Federation in a 1984 report, *Room to Move*, presents a case for a £7 billion programme. This has not had a sympathetic reception.

Three other 'transport' issues are selected for discussion here: lorries, public transport subsidy, and cycling. (Reference to the reorganisation of transport in London has been made earlier, and a subsequent section refers to the NEDO report on *Pre-construction Procedures for Motorway and Trunk Road Schemes*.)

A reference to the Armitage Report on *Lorries, People and the Environment* is made in note 53 on page 169 above. Its terms of reference were 'to consider the causes and consequences of the growth in the movement of freight by road and, in particular, of the impact of the lorry on people and their environment; and to report on how best to ensure that future development serves the public interest'. The report deals with a wide range of issues to which there are no easy solutions: every aspect studied proved to bristle with troublesome issues. It was debated in the House of Commons on 27 January 1981; and a White Paper was issued at the end of 1981. The White Paper gives emphasis to the major contentious issue:

> The central conclusion in the Armitage Report is that the public interest would be best served by maintaining and developing the economic benefits from heavy lorries and at the same time reducing their adverse effects. The Government agrees with this approach. We have the technical skills and resources over time to make heavy lorries as quiet as cars. We must aim to provide modern roads for all substantial flows of heavy traffic. We must frame our regulations so that operators can make the most efficient use of their vehicles. In this way we shall get on top of the problem. There will be fewer

lorries, and they will be quieter, cleaner, safer and more efficient. New bypasses will be built to keep them away from where people live. This White Paper sets out the measures with which the Government now proposes to initiate this change for the better.

These measures include the trunk road programme 'to give high priority to bypasses and to motorways which take lorries out of historic towns and villages', but there was disagreement on the Armitage conclusion that 'it seems to us beyond question that heavier lorries offer large and continuing economic benefits particularly in the form of reduced transport costs [and] of reduced road damage'.

This particular argument is not resolved, and it seems likely to continue both within the confines of British politics and, more broadly, in relation to EEC proposals.

Public Transport Subsidy in Cities (White Paper, Cmnd 8735, 1982), on the other hand, is very much a domestic issue. Matters came to boiling point with the Greater London Council's low-fares policy (described in the White Paper as 'a political decision to plunge ahead with artificially low fares'). This (and subsequent events) gave the government the basis for submitting that there were uncertainties about the lawfulness of subsidies and a clear revelation that subsidy decisions had been made on an 'inadequate basis'.

The case could be argued at length, but the 1982 White Paper concluded, in succinct terms, that 'legislation is needed which will provide for a reasonable, stable and lawful subsidy regime'. What this meant was that central government would take unto itself greater powers to control local government in its public transport policies. Legislative effect to the proposals was provided by the Transport Act 1983 (see Department of Transport, Circular 1/83).

To turn to a much slower tempo, the Department of Transport issued a consultation paper on cycling in 1981. This raised a host of difficult (if not unanswerable) questions, but was followed by a Traffic Advisory Unit leaflet on *Policy on Provision of Facilities for Cyclists* (Department of Transport, 1982), and a statement by the Secretary of State for Transport on *Cycling Policy* (Department of Transport, 1982). In the latter, the bottom line reads: 'the Government remains committed to the encouragement of cycling, and will continue to support these efforts, without attempting to impose central direction upon the variety of local circumstances.'

It will be noted that this is a very different stance from that taken on public transport studies.

(A useful account of Scottish transport policies from the 1970s up to 1982 is now to be found in E. Gillett, *Investment in the Environment: Recent Housing, Planning and Transport Policies in Scotland*, Aberdeen University Press, 1983, pp. 90–114.)

TRANSPORT: REFERENCES

Armitage Report: *Report of the Inquiry into Lorries, People and the Environment* (HMSO, 1980).

G. Bell, D. A. Blackledge and P. Bowen, *The Economics of Transport* (Heinemann, 1983).

British Road Federation, *Annual Report 1983* (The Federation, 1983).

British Road Federation, *Local Authority Roads and Their Financing: A New Approach* (The Federation, 1983).

British Road Federation, *Road Maintenance: The Decline of Britain's Roads* (The Federation, 1983).

British Road Federation, *To Keep London Moving* (The Federation, 1983).

British Road Federation, *Basic Road Statistics*, 1984 (The Federation, 1984).

British Road Federation, *Room to Move* (The Federation, 1984).

Bus and Coach Council, *The Future of the Bus* (The Council, 1982).

Bus and Coach Council, *We All Need the Bus* (The Council, 1983).

Central Transport Consultative Committee, *The Missing Link: A Report on Bus-Rail Interchange Facilities* (The Committee, 1981).

Civic Trust, *Bypasses and the Juggernaut: Fact and Fiction* (Civic Trust, 1983).

Confederation of British Road Passenger Transport, *Urban Planning and Design for Road Public Transport* (The Confederation, 1981).

Department of Transport, *Cycling: A Consultation Paper* (1981).

Department of Transport, *Policy for Roads: England 1981*, Cmnd 8496 (HMSO, 1982).

Department of Transport, *Policy on Provision of Facilities for Cyclists*, (1982).

Department of Transport, *Roads in England 1982* (The Department, 1982).

Department of Transport, *Cycling: A Consultation Paper* (1981).

Department of Transport, *Policy for Roads in England 1983*, Cmnd 9059 (HMSO, 1983).

Department of Transport, *Circular 1/83: Transport Act 1983* (HMSO, 1983).

Department of Transport and Home Office, *Report of the Inter-Departmental Working Party on Road Traffic Law* (HMSO, 1981).

Freight Transport Association, *Designing for Deliveries* (The Association, 1983).

House of Commons, *Second Report from the Transport Committee, Session 1980–81: The Inquiry into Lorries, People and the Environment*, HC (1980–1) 192 (HMSO, 1981).

House of Commons, *Fifth Report from the Transport Committee, Session 1981–82: Transport in London, Vol. I: Report*, HC (1981–2) 127–1, (HMSO, 1982).

House of Commons, *Transport Committee, Road Maintenance, Vol. I*, HC (1982–3) 28-I (HMSO, 1983).

A. M. Mackie and C. H. Davies, *Environmental Effects of Traffic Changes* (DOE Transport and Road Research Laboratory, 1981).

N. MacLeod, 'Major road inquiries: a change of direction?', in Journal of Planning and Environment Law, Occasional Papers, *Planning Inquiries: A New Dimension*, 1983, pp. 34–48.

T. M. Pharoah, *Improving the Safety of Local Streets* (Polytechnic of the South Bank, 1983).

S. Plowden and M. Hillman, *Danger on the Road: The Needless Scourge* (Policy Studies Institute, 1984).

G. Roth and E. Butler, *Private Road Ahead: Ways of Providing Better Roads Sooner* (Adam Smith Institute, 1982).

Royal Town Planning Institute, *Public Transport in London: Report by the Transport Working Party* (RTPI, 1983).

A. Samuels, 'New roads: the assessment of need, usefulness and desirability', *Journal of Planning and Environment Law*, 1981, pp. 15–25.

Scottish Development Department, *Roads in Scotland: Report for 1981*, Cmnd 8644 (HMSO, 1982).

Scottish Development Department, *Roads in Scotland for 1982*, Cmnd 9010 (HMSO, 1983).

P. A. Stanley, *Planning for Public Transport Needs*, Oxford Polytechnic, Department of Town Planning, Working Paper no. 68, 1982.

D. Starkie, *The Motorway Age: Road and Traffic Policies in Post-War Britain* (Pergamon, 1982).

Welsh Office, *Roads in Wales 1983* (WO, 1983).

White Paper, *Lorries, People and the Environment*, Cmnd 8439 (HMSO, 1981).

White Paper, *Public Transport in London*, Cmnd 9004 (HMSO, 1983).

LAND POLICIES

Though the Community Land Act was repealed by the Local Government, Planning and Land Act 1980, local authorities still retain considerable powers of compulsory acquisition of land. Under the new Act a local authority may, with the consent of the secretary of state, compulsorily acquire:

> any land which is in their area and which is suitable for and is required in order to secure the carrying out of one or more of the following activities, namely, development, redevelopment and improvement [and] any land which is in their area and which is required for a purpose which it is necessary to achieve in the interests of the proper planning of an area in which the land is situated.

The Act also settles a doubt concerning the legality of compulsory land acquisition for the purpose of disposal to a private developer. Indeed, the government has made it clear that these 'planning purposes' powers (which are of particular importance in bringing land on to the market) are generally to be used to assist the private sector. Circular 8/81 notes that 'although the Community Land Act is repealed, authorities still have a valuable, though limited, role to play in ensuring that land is brought forward for private development. Their compulsory purchase powers may be useful in circumstances where the private market is not operating smoothly (e.g. in land assembly exercises, where a monopoly of land ownership is retarding development, or where access to land ripe for development is blocked by an owner who is unwilling to sell).'

Additionally, the secretary of state has some formidable powers himself. First he has the reserve power to direct a local authority to make an assessment of land available and suitable for residential development (see page 190 above). Second, his powers to acquire any land 'necessary for the public service' have been extended by the 1980 Act to authorise acquisitions '(a) to meet the interests of proper planning of the area, or (b) to secure the best, or most economic, development or use of land'. (Ironically these provisions are a modified re-enactment of a section of the repealed Community Land Act.)

Considerable debate has taken place since 1980 (as well as before) on the adequacy of land availability. Given the powers available, the problem is clearly not a legal one. It is, in fact, partly a financial one (providing the necessary infrastructure), but mainly a political one. This is particularly the case for a Conservative government aiming at privatisation and the reduction in controls, an ample supply of land for private development, and the retention of land-use planning at the local level.

Patsy Healey has analysed this situation in *Local Plans in British Land Use Planning* (Pergamon, 1983), and submits that the crux of the political dilemma lies in the traditional Conservative support in the shire counties:

> This support combines a concern to preserve the attractive environments in which they live and a commitment to local democracy at the smallest scale. The 1972 Local Government Act ensured continuing Conservative control of suburban and rural areas. Conservative governments thus face a dilemma. At national level they may be concerned to shift land policies more towards production than consumption purposes. Yet they must not lose the support of the environmental lobby or local Conservative councillors. In other words, the ideology of limited intervention which the current Conservative administration espouses sits uneasily with its need to respond to the demands of industrial and property production and to those for environmental conservation and local control over land policy. (p. 269)

Of course, the debate is not carried on in these terms. Instead there are numerous surveys and a barrage of figures. (See, for example, A. Hooper, 'Land availability in south-east England'.) A recent illustration is the Standing Conference on London and South East Regional Planning 1983 study of *Housing Land Supply in the South East (Outside London)* which concluded that 'not only is there sufficient land for building another 252,000 dwellings [in the study area] over the next five years, but already capacity has been identified for building an additional 117,000 dwellings after five years'. This compares with structure plan estimates of need totalling 231,000 to 233,000 over the five-year period.

All such exercises, of course, rest on assumptions concerning 'need'. This involves estimating such factors as new household formation (which itself can be affected by housing supply and prices), the rate of slum clearance, the role of improvements and major repairs to existing houses, and the geographic shift of jobs, retirement migration, second homes, and improved housing standards. All these are dealt with in the latest report of the Joint Land Requirements Committee, *Housing and Land 1984–1991: 1992–2000*. (This committee consists of members nominated by the Royal Town Planning Institute, the House-Builders Federation and the Housing Research Foundation.) The figures which are used in this report could be juggled in varying ways. (Indeed, in one section – concerned with the effects of improvement and major repairs on the number of houses to be replaced – the report comments that 'Solomon himself would not have known the correct answer'.)

Among the many points raised by this report is the 'appropriate' rate of demolition of old houses. A figure of 40,000 a year is used (though 'we have formed no final view about whether this number of demolitions will actually take place'). In fact, in England and Wales demolitions fell from 49,000 in 1976 to 30,000 in 1979 and to 16,400 in 1982–3.

Their total estimate is for 220,000 dwellings annually until 1991 (and rather less in the last decade). The 220,000 is made up of 60,000–80,000 for replacement of 'demolitions, geographic shift of industry', and other factors; plus 145,000+ for new household formation.

The report is coy on major policy implications. Indeed, the committee submit that 'throughout our aim has not been to advance any particular viewpoint, but simply to identify the relevant facts. Where opinions are offered, we have tried to separate these from the facts.' This may well have been the intention, but in fact the implications are clear: 'demolition rates are too low, compulsory purchase of homes for redevelopment is inevitable in the future; owner-occupiers cannot be trusted to be the final arbiters of whether their homes are unfit; and some existing environments "may be so drab as to be not worth preserving". The report believes that "there is scope for both demolition and rehabilitation", but implies that the latter need not be an increased preoccupation of the building industry' (A. Fyson, 'Still *No* to the bulldozers', *The Planner*, April 1984, p. 3).

The overall figures and the implications for land rest heavily on the role to be played by slum clearance, the need for which must be greater than current rates (an issue which is discussed in a later section on housing). Thus for the last decade the report envisages that 25 per cent of new building should be for replacement: at such a rate the demand for green-field sites might fall. The report is certain about this:

> . . . patently the demand for new land would fall as these sites are recycled, and new houses are built on cleared sites. Moreover, some of the new units will be designed for one or two persons, so that it may be possible to come closer to a one for one replacement on cleared sites than would be expected by past experience.

This is clearly debatable, but the major point is important: the amount of demand for new land will be determined in part by the amount of available land in existing urbanised areas, and this in turn will be determined in part by slum clearance.

A rough estimate of the current amount of house-building in towns of over 50,000 population is around 15 per cent. The report comments that 'with vigorous efforts it may be possible to raise this proportion this decade to say 20 per cent, but even this is not certain'.

Thus, some four-fifths of new building is (on the arguments presented) to be in rural areas. However, given government commitments on green belts (which increased from 1,475,000 hectares in the old development plans to 1,800,000 hectares in 1983 structure plans), and the very small amount of land needed (estimated at 1 per cent of the total land area in England), no national problem exists. Nevertheless, 'those areas where pressure to build is greatest are precisely those where pressure not to build is also greatest'; but, ending on an optimistic note, 'the encouraging fact is that in most areas there is capacity to allow both for the protection of the countryside and to build the number of houses we need. Wise use of our planning system should make it possible to achieve both objectives.'

The report is a challenging one, open to much debate which, it is to be hoped, will be continued in the current inquiry of the House of Commons Environment Committee.

One issue which constantly arises in this area is that of the 'loss' of agricultural land. The Joint Land Requirements Committee carried out an interesting public survey which showed that very few people (8 per cent) have even a broadly correct impression of the actual proportion – and a third perceived the proportion to be ten times greater than it is. Robin Best's work has failed to dispel popular images, yet his latest figures show that the annual average transfer of agricultural land to urban use in England and Wales was only 9,300 hectares between 1975 and 1980 (compared with 17,500 between 1945 and 1950, and 25,100 between 1931 and 1939). The total urban area is about 1,640,000 hectares: about 11 per cent of the total. For a full discussion see R. Best, *Land Use and Living Space* (Methuen, 1981). (A short article is to be found in the January 1984 issue of *Town and Country Planning*.)

LAND REGISTERS

In addition to exhortation and land availability studies, the government has taken a number of other steps. One is the preparation and publication of land registers of unused and underused land owned by public authorities (see pages 190–1 above). These provisions relate to England (where all districts have now published registers) and to Wales (where the secretary of state has announced that registers are to be published for six areas). There is no provision for registers in Scotland.

The secretary of state has stressed that:

The publication of land registers for the greater part of the country represents a major opportunity to secure the better use of massive acreages of underused land. Given the resources also available for dealing with dereliction, it is important that action should be taken to dispose of the land to the best advantage as soon as possible . . . It is up to builders and developers to examine registers and seek out the owners to make an offer for any sale in which they are interested. (*HC Debates*, vol. 21, col. 40, 29 March 1982)

The latest available figures (for 1 July 1983) are given below. In an accompanying note, the DOE comments that 'the registers have been scrutinised to pick out sites which merit particular attention. Nearly half the land appears to have moderate to high potential for development. The Department is in contact with the owners of selected sites about their intentions. As yet no disposal directions have been issued.'

Land Registers: Ownership of Land on 1 July 1983 (acres), England

	Owned	Disposed of	Brought into use
Local government	63,304	3,222	2,743
Nationalised industries and statutory undertakers	30,587	2,054	287
New towns and other non-Crown public bodies	9,421	196	82
Government Departments and other Crown bodies	7,231	1,094	85
Total	110,543	6,566	3,197

It is probably too early to judge whether this exercise is worthwhile. Previous research, though on a small scale, suggests that land vacancy is typically a transient feature of the environment (see M. J. Bruton and A. Gore, 'Vacant urban land', and D. J. Nicholson, 'The public ownership of vacant urban land').

JOINT VENTURE SCHEMES

One other plank of current land policy is the promotion of 'Joint Venture Schemes' involving private housing development on local-authority-owned land. The issue is dealt with in the Property Advisory Group's 1981 report on *The Climate for Public and Private Partnerships in Property Development*, and in SDD Circular 21/1983.

LAND AUTHORITY FOR WALES

A surprising anomaly in the institutional arrangements for land policy is the survival of the Land Authority for Wales (LAW), an *ad hoc* body originally established under the Community Land Act. This provides precisely what is missing from the English scene: a body with a long-term and wide-ranging view of the land situation complete with powers to act positively in order to solve land availability problems.

Its legal function is that of 'acquiring land in Wales which in its opinion needs to be made available for development, and of disposing of it to other persons (for development by them) at a time which is in the Authority's opinion appropriate to meet the need'.

Grant has commented that this represents 'the clearest and least restrictive legislative authorisation for positive planning that now exists'. (M. Grant, *Urban Planning Law*, p. 521.) He also explains why LAW exists:

Two factors in particular contributed to the Authority's success under the 1975 Act, and prevented their abolition. First, they are a single purpose authority, and, unlike the local planning authorities of England and Scotland, were able, and indeed required, to pursue positive planning as their first priority. Second, the Authority are not themselves a planning authority. They operate within the confines of the planning policies administered by the Welsh local planning authorities, and, where their planning applications are refused they have the usual right of appeal to the Secretary of State for Wales. They have managed therefore to avoid the suspicion of conflict of interest which has often attached to the positive planning efforts of local planning authorities. In practice they have also assisted Welsh local authorities in land availability studies and with advice on land disposal for development.

A useful description of the work of the Authority is to be found in a paper by the Chief Executive (E. W. G. C. Howell, 'A working model for land supply'). The Authority has a rolling programme (e.g., *Strategy and Programme 1983–1988*), and operates on a self-financing basis.

LAND POLICIES: REFERENCES

M. Ball, 'Planners and builders agree on land', *Roof*, vol. 9, no. 3 (May–June 1984), p. 5.

S. Barrett and G. Whitting, *Local Authorities and Land Supply: Final Report of Research on the Role of Local Authorities in the Supply of Development Land to the Private Sector* (University of Bristol, School of Advanced Urban Studies, 1983).

R. H. Best, *Land Use and Living Space* (Mcthuen, 1981).

R. H. Best, 'Are we really losing land?', *Town and Country Planning*, vol. 53, no. 1 (January 1984).

M. Bruton and A. Gore, 'Vacant urban land: South Wales survey questions some basic assumptions', *The Planner*, vol. 67 (1981), pp. 34–5.

V. N. Dennington and M. J. Chadwick, 'Derelict land and waste land: Britain's neglected land resource', *Journal of Environmental Management*, vol. 16, no. 3 (April 1983), pp. 229–39.

DOE, *Derelict Land Scheme – General Note* (DOE, 1983).

DOE, *Grants for the Reclamation of Derelict Land in England – Local Authorities: Guidance Note* (DOE, 1983).

DOE, *Grants for the Reclamation of Derelict Land in England – Persons and Public Bodies other than Local Authorities* (DOE, 1983).

DOE, *Land Registers* (note and statistics), February 1984.

DOE, *Survey of Derelict Land in England 1982* (DOE, 1984) and *Summary Tables* (DOE, 1984).

A. Fyson, 'Still *No* to bulldozers', *The Planner*, April 1984, p. 3.

M. Grant, *Urban Planning Law* (Sweet & Maxwell, 1982), Chapter 12.

F. Harrison, 'UK land policies and the political parties', *Land Use Policy*, vol. 1, no. 1 (January 1984), pp. 25–33.

P. Healey, *Local Plans in British Land Use Planning* (Pergamon, 1983).

A. Hooper, 'Land availability in south-east England', *Journal of Planning and Environment Law*, 1982, pp. 555–60.

E. W. G. C. Howell, 'The Land Authority for Wales', in Regional Studies Association, *New Agencies for Wales* (RSA, 1980).

E. W. G. C. Howell, 'A working model for land supply', *Estates Gazette*, vol. 266 (16 April 1983), pp. 193–4.

Joint Land Requirements Committee, *Is There Sufficient Housing Land for the 1980s? Paper I: How Many Houses Should We Plan For?*

Joint Land Requirements Committee, *Is There Sufficient Housing Land for the 1980s? Paper II: How Many Houses Have We Planned For: Is There a Problem?* (Housing Research Foundation, 1983).

Joint Land Requirements Committee, *Housing and Land 1984–1991: 1992–2000: How Many Houses Will We Build? What Will Be The Effect On Our Countryside?* (Housing Research Foundation, 1984).

Land Authority for Wales, *South Wales Housing Land Availability Study* (The Authority, 1980).
Land Authority for Wales, *Accounts for the Year Ended 31 March 1983* (The Authority, 1983).
Land Authority for Wales, *Strategy and Programme 1983–1988* (The Authority, 1983).
G. Moss, *Britain's Wasting Acres* (Architectural Press, 1981).
D. J. Nicholson, 'The public ownership of vacant urban land', *The Planner*, vol. 70 (1984), pp. 18–20.
Property Advisory Group, *Structure and Activity of the Development Industry* (HMSO, 1980).
Property Advisory Group, *The Climate for Public and Private Partnerships in Property Development* (DOE, 1983).
SDD, *Circular 21/1983, Private House Building Land Supply: Joint Venture Schemes* (SDD, 1983).
Standing Conference on London and South East Regional Planning (SCLSERP), *Housing Land Supply in the South East* (The Standing Conference, 1983).

THE COUNTRYSIDE

Legislative and institutional change has characterised the last few years of countryside policies – the passing of the Wildlife and Countryside Act 1981, and the Countryside (Scotland) Act 1981; the abolition of the five Scottish 'national park direction areas' in 1980 and the designation of 40 'national scenic areas'; and the granting of independent status to the Countryside Commission, and full executive powers to the Development Commission. At the same time there has been a flood of reports and studies, some stimulated by widespread concern at the inadequacies of the Wildlife and Countryside Act and some by the new lease of life which independence has bestowed on the Countryside Commission.

The Wildlife and Countryside Act had a stormy passage through Parliament and was considerably amended during the process. Its purpose (to quote the preamble) is (in Part 1) to repeal and re-enact with amendments the Protection of Birds Acts 1954 to 1967 and the Conservation of Wild Creatures and Wild Plants Act 1975; to prohibit certain methods of killing or taking wild animals; to amend the law relating to protection of certain animals and plants; to amend the Endangered Species (Import and Export) Act 1976; (in Part 2) to amend the law relating to nature conservation, the countryside and national parks and to make provision with respect to the Countryside Commission; and (in Part 3) to amend the law relating to public rights of way.

A detailed account of the passage of the Act is given in G. Cox and P. Lowe in 'A battle not the war: the politics of the Wildlife and Countryside Bill' (in A. W. Gilg (ed.), *Countryside Planning*

Yearbook 1983 (Geo Books, 1983), pp. 48–76). The military terminology of the title serves to underline the fact that 'countryside issues have now become thoroughly political'; and though the legislation is now in operation the basic controversies rage on.

The major focus of argument (with the strong National Farmers' Union and the Country Landowners' Association holding the line against a large but diffuse environmental lobby) was the extent to which voluntary management agreements can be sufficient to resolve conflicts of interest in the countryside. The government steadfastly maintained that neither positive inducements nor negative controls were necessary. Indeed it was held that controls would be counter-productive in that they would arouse intense opposition from country landowners.

Three issues aroused particular concern: "the rate at which Sites of Special Scientific Interest (SSSIs) were being seriously damaged . . ., the rate at which moorland in national parks was being converted to agricultural use or afforestation . . ., and the adverse impact of agricultural capital grants schemes both on landscape and on the social and economic wellbeing of upland communities' (A. and M. MacEwan, 'An unprincipled Act?', *The Planner*, vol. 68, 1982, pp. 69–71).

On the first issue the government finally made a concession and provided (Section 28 of the Act) for a system of 'reciprocal notification'. This requires the Nature Conservancy Council (NCC) to notify all landowners, the local planning authority and the secretary of state of any land which, in their opinion, 'is of special interest by reason of any of its flora, fauna, or geological or physiological featues', and 'any operations appearing to the [NCC] to be likely to damage the flora or fauna or those features'. For the landowner, there is a requirement that he gives three months' notice of his intentions to carry out any operation listed in the SSSI notification. This three months provides the NCC with an opportunity 'to discuss modifications or the possibility of entering into a management agreement'. (The quotation is from a slender booklet entitled *Code of Guidance for Sites of Special Scientific Interest*, HMSO, 1982.)

On the issue of moorland loss, the Act (Section 43) requires county planning authorities in national park areas to publish maps identifying 'any areas of moor or heath the natural beauty of which it is, in the opinion of the authority, particularly important to preserve'.

The third issue, that of agricultural grants, is a complex one on which the government only narrowly scraped a sufficient majority. Attempts to extend grants from 'agricultural business' to countryside conservation were defeated and a host of amendments divided the Opposition and confused the issues. The amendments did little (or nothing?) more than exhort the Minister of Agriculture, when considering grants in areas of special scientific interest, to provide advice on 'the conservation and enhancement of natural beauty and amenities of the countryside' and suchlike – 'free of charge'. There is, however, power to refuse an application for an agricultural grant on various 'countryside' grounds but – and this is perhaps the most startling provision of the Act – such a refusal renders the objecting authority (the county planning authority in national parks and the NCC in SSSIs) liable to pay compensation. This is a return to the pre-1947 planning system (even though it applies to only a small part of the country), and it has – not surprisingly – given rise to a considerable amount of debate. Nevertheless, the legal provisions are not clear (see A. and M. MacEwen, op. cit.), and it seems unlikely that the situation will remain as it is for long.

A more optimistic note in relation to planning for the countryside is provided by an interesting set of reports, including M. MacEwen and G. Sinclair, *New Life for the Hills: Policies for Farming and Conservation in the Uplands* (Councils for National Parks, 1983); the Labour Party's *Out of Town, Out of Mind* (1981); the Friends of the Earth, *Proposals for a Natural Heritage Bill* (1983); the latest reports of the Development Commission (HMSO, 1982 and 1983); and an impressive series of publications of the (now independent) Country-side Commission, including *Our Programme for the Countryside 1983–88: A Five-Year Programme of Action to Conserve the Countryside and Provide for Public Enjoyment and Recreation* (1983); *Areas of Outstanding Natural Beauty: A Policy Statement* (1983); *The Broads: A Review* (1984); and *A Better Future for the Uplands* (1984).

On national parks, an important study by Ann and Malcolm MacEwen was published in 1982, *National Parks: Conservation or Cosmetics?* (Allen & Unwin). The title suggests the tone: this is more than a 'study'; it is a heartfelt, eloquent plea for a more appropriate, effective and sensitive range of policies in relation to national parks than the present weak, cheap, and 'cosmetic' subservience to 'agricultural business'. The authors' strong commitment, however, does not detract from the value of the detailed study. This surpasses, by far, all the official reports on national parks (etc.) which have littered the path of policy-makers for the last forty years. The coverage is wide, and no summary is attempted here, but a few illustrative extracts are appropriate.

In addition to the widespread criticism of the administrative apparatus for national park policy (if such a term might be admitted), the MacEwans point to the basic economic weakness of (most of) the national parks:

The national parks are by and large the more economically handicapped parts of the least prosperous regions of England and

Wales . . . [They rely heavily] on the primary industries, in which employment has been falling sharply. They have benefited little from the measures taken within the depressed regions to promote economic growth. . . . Mineral extraction illustrates the way in which highly capitalised enterprises lower unit costs but shed jobs. . . . The small mines and quarries that used to provide part-time jobs for hill farmers have gone. Control has shifted from local or regional firms to international companies. . . . Large-scale investment and technological change directed at purely economic or financial objectives have been the cause of dramatic, even catastrophic, losses in jobs. (pp. 96–104)

Additionally, the analysis stretches (in more terms than one) the debate on the nature of national parks, 'the landscape', 'agribusiness', the ambiguous roles of forestry, conservation, and the rights, privileges and responsibilities of land ownership. This is a most important and timely book.

THE COUNTRYSIDE: REFERENCES

M. A. Anderson, 'Planning policies and development control in the Sussex Downs AONB', *Town Planning Review*, vol. 52 (1981).

M. J. Appleby, *Suffolk New Agricultural Landscapes Project, 1978–1983* (Suffolk County Council, 1983).

M. Blacksell, 'Government policy and the uplands in the late twentieth century: a review article', *Town Planning Review*, vol. 55 (1984), pp. 102–9.

M. Blacksell and A. W. Gilg, *The Countryside: Planning and Change* (Allen & Unwin, 1981).

J. K. Bowers and P. Cheshire, *Agriculture, the Countryside and Land Use* (Methuen, 1983).

British Waterways Board, Annual Report and Accounts 1982 (The Board, 1983).

British Waterways Board, Annual Report and Accounts 1983 (The Board, 1984).

I. Brotherton, *Conflict, Consensus, Concern, and the Administration of Britain's National Parks* (University of Sheffield, Department of Landscape Architecture, 1981).

J. T. Coppock, 'Conflict in the Cairngorms: price of progress', *Geographical Magazine*, 1980, pp. 417–25.

Council for the Protection of Rural England, *Planning: Friend or Foe?* (The Council, 1981).

Countryside Commission, *Countryside Issues and Action* (CCP 151) (The Commission, 1982).

Countryside Commission, *Our Programme for the Countryside 1983–88*, (The Commission, 1983).

Countryside Commission, *Fifteenth Report of the Countryside Commission 1981–82* (HMSO, 1983).

Countryside Commission, *Sixteenth Report of the Countryside Commission* (The Commission, 1983).
Countryside Commission, *A Better Future for the Uplands* (CCP 162) (The Commission, 1984).
Countryside Commission, The Broads: A Review – Conclusions and Recommendations (CCP 163) (The Commission, 1984).
Countryside Commission for Scotland: Fifteenth Report 1982 (HMSO, 1983).
Countryside Commission for Scotland: Sixteenth Report 1983 (HMSO, 1984).
A. B. Cruickshank (ed.), *Where Town Meets Country: Problems of Peri-Urban Areas in Scotland* (Aberdeen University Press, 1982).
DOE, *Code of Guidance for Sites of Special Scientific Interest* (HMSO, 1982).

Exmoor National Park Committee, *Management Agreements in Exmoor National Park and Moorland Conservation on Exmoor: The Porchester Maps: Their Construction and Policies*, 2 vols (The Committee, 1981 and 1982).
Friends of the Earth, *Proposals for a National Heritage Bill* (1983).
J. F. Garner, *Rights of Way and Access to the Countryside*, 4th edn (Oyez, 1982).
Labour Party, *Out of Town, Out of Mind* (1981).
A. W. Gilg (ed.), *Countryside Planning Yearbooks*, Vol. 1, 1980; Vol. 2, 1981; Vol. 3, 1982; and Vol. 4, 1983 (Geo Books).
D. Goode, 'The threat to wildlife', *New Scientist*, vol. 89, no. 2347.
D. Grigg, *The Dynamics of Agricultural Change* (Hutchinson, 1982).
A. and M. MacEwen, 'An unprincipled Act', *The Planner*, vol. 68 (1982), pp. 69–71.
A. and M. MacEwen, *National Parks: Conservation or Cosmetics?* (Allen & Unwin, 1982). (This contains an excellent pre-1982 bibliography.)
M. MacEwen and G. Sinclair, *New Life for the Hills* (Council for National Parks, 1983).
J. McEwen, *Who Owns Scotland? A Study in Land Ownership*, 2nd edn (Edinburgh University, 1980).
Martin and Voorhees Associates, *Review of Rural Settlement Policies 1945–80* (DOE, 1981).
R. Mabey, *The Common Ground* (Hutchinson, 1980).
K. Mellanby, *Farming and Wildlife* (Collins, 1981).
R. Moore, *The Social Impact of Oil: The Case of Peterhead* (Routledge & Kegan Paul, 1982).
G. Moss, *Britain's Wasting Acres* (Architectural Press, 1980).
Nature Conservancy Council, Eighth Report, 1 April 1981–31 March 1982 (The Council, 1983).
Nature Conservancy Council, Ninth Report, 1 April 1982–31 March 1983 (The Council, 1984).
H. Newby, *Green and Pleasant Land?* (Penguin, 1980).
T. O'Riordan, *Putting Trust in the Countryside: Earth's Survival – A Conservation and Development Programme for the UK: World Conservation Strategy* (Nature Conservancy Council, 1982).
M. Parry and T. R. Slater, *The Making of the Scottish Countryside* (Croom Helm, 1980).
University of Edinburgh, *The Economy of Rural Communities in the National Parks of England and Wales* (Tourism and Recreation Research Unit, 1982).

G. Wibberley, *Countryside Evaluation: A Personal Evaluation* (Wye College, University of London, 1982).

NEW TOWNS

Chapter 9 ended an account of new and expanded towns policy with a brief discussion headed 'The End of Dispersal?'. Given the economic and demographic changes that have taken place in the last four years, the issues involved here (implicitly as well as explicitly) have become much more problematic. Yet it is difficult to believe that the main thrust of the Lambeth Inner Area Study (p. 257 above) is not still valid.

Be that as it may, the Conservative government had no truck with such subtleties: the new-towns programme had 'completed' its purpose at vast public expense; the time had arrived to wind it up and to realise assets. Surprisingly little opposition has been aroused by this, probably in part because the winding-up process is being handled smoothly and efficiently, partly because development activity is continuing in propitious places, partly because senior staff of the new towns are at retirement age, but mainly because there is no body which can effectively challenge the government policy. It really is a case of an ending 'not with a bang but a whimper'.

The exception is Scotland, where a 1981 policy statement (*New Towns in Scotland*) unequivocally sets out 'a defined future as an expression of confidence in their further operation'. The stated justification is the strong role being played by the five Scottish new towns in the economic development of Scotland.

NEW TOWNS: REFERENCES

J. Balchin, *First New Town – An Autobiography of the Stevenage Development Corporation 1946–1980* (The Corporation, 1980).

B. Butler (ed.), *The Dream Fulfilled: Basingstoke Town Development 1961–1978* (Hampshire County Council, 1983).

S. G. Checkland, 'The British new towns as politics: a review article', *Town Planning Review*, vol. 52, no. 2 (April 1981), pp. 223–7.

Commission for the New Towns, *Report 31 March 1983*, HC (1983–4) 82 (HMSO, 1983).

DOE, *Planning and Building New Towns – Britain's Experience* (DOE, 1983).

DOE, *Review of the Target Wind-up Dates for New Town Development Corporations in the North East of England* (DOE, 1984).

S. Fothergill *et al.*, 'The impact of the new and expanded town programmes on industrial location in Britain, 1960–78', *Regional Studies*, vol. 17 (1983), pp. 251–60.

F. Gibberd *et al.*, *Harlow: The Story of a New Town* (Publications for Companies, 1980).

M. Hebbert, 'The British new towns: a review article', *Town Planning Review*, vol. 51, no. 4 (October 1980), pp. 414–20.

S. Holley, *Washington: Quicker by Quango: The History of Washington New Town 1964–1983* (Publications for Companies, 1983).

New Town Development Corporations [England], *Report 31 March 1983*, HC (1983–4) 81 (HMSO, 1983).

New Town Development Corporations [Wales], *Report 31 March 1983*, HC (1983–4) 70 (HMSO, 1983).

Scottish Development Department, *New Towns in Scotland: A Policy Statement* (SDD, 1981).

R. Thomas, 'New town obituaries', *Urban Law and Policy*, vol. 4, 1981, pp. 285–96.

R. Thomas, 'The 1972 Housing Finance Act and the demise of the new towns and local authority housing programmes', *Urban Law and Policy*, vol. 5 (1982), pp. 107–27.

Town and Country Planning, special issue on new towns, vol. 52, no. 11 (November 1983).

URBAN RENEWAL: THE INNER CITY

With the dismal state of the British economy and the widespread (if not almost ubiquitous) problems of urban areas (and, of course, their increasingly vociferous rural neighbours), 'urban renewal' has lost both focus and definition. Problems are increasingly a matter of degree rather than of specific location.

Reports on 'the inner city' nevertheless proliferate. At the turn of the decade, the Social Science Research Council issued eleven reports, followed in 1981 by a 'final report', *The Inner City in Context*, edited by Peter Hall and published by Heinemann. The eleven specialist reports, published by the SSRC were:

1   *Understanding Urban Land Values: A Review*, M. Edwards and D. Lovatt,
2   *Changes in the Resident Populations of Inner Areas*, D. Eversley and L. Bonnerjea,
3   *Transport and the Inner City*, A. E. Gillespie,
4   *Technological Change and the Inner City*, J. B. Goddard and A. T. Thwaites,
5   *The Inner City Problem in Historical Context*, M. Hebbert,
6   *Local Government Fiscal Problems: A Context for Inner Areas*, S. Kennet,
7   *The Inner City in the Context of the Urban System*, S. Kennet,
8   *The Inner City in the United States*, R. Kirwan,
9   *Rural Development and its Relevance to the Inner City Debate*, M. J. Moseley,
10 *Housing Market Processes and the Inner City*, A. Murie and R. Forrest,
11 *Urban Governments and Economic Change*, K. Young, C. Mason and E. Mills.

See the series of reviews, 'Review Symposium: the inner city in context', *Town Planning Review*, vol. 52, no. 1, January 1981, pp. 89–105. It is interesting to compare these with the reviews of the earlier 'Inner area studies', *Town Planning Review*, 1978, pp. 195–208.

A selection of other publications is given at the end of this section. They range from Urlan Wannop's report on the future management of GEAR – the Glasgow Eastern Area Renewal project – to David Donnison's plea for a major rethinking on approaches to urban policy, *Urban Policies: A New Approach* (Fabian Society, 1983). Drawing upon experience such as that of GEAR, Donnison deals with an issue which goes far wider than 'inner area' problems: he analyses the inadequacies of the traditional functional professional and centralised services, and argues for a new approach 'based on the solution of problems rather than delivery of a service: an approach economically oriented, area focused and community based, to tackle the problems unresolved by traditional organisation and themselves the cause of alienation to the very (remote and professionalised) services provided'.

The possible role of the 'voluntary' sector in this is, nevertheless, problematic. Gwyndaf Williams in *Inner City Policy: A Partnership with the Voluntary Sector?* (Bedford Square Press, 1983) concludes that the inner city partnerships, 'whilst undoubtedly facilitating opportunities for enhancing contact between the voluntary and statutory sectors, [have] provided little evidence of any significant increase in voluntary sector influence either over programme content or implementation'. Similarly, Murray Stewart in 'The inner area planning system' (*Policy and Politics*, vol. 11, no. 2, 1983, pp. 203–14) stresses the dependency and vulnerability of this sector.

Stewart's paper is of considerable interest for its insightful analysis of the increasingly complex inner area planning system – which now includes the continuation of the 'traditional' urban programme, the Inner Urban Areas Act, urban development corporations and enterprise zones, urban development grants and 'the extensive involvement of the private sector'. Focusing on the 'partnership' and 'programme' schemes (see p. 279 above), he notes highly significant features such as absence of a unified approach, an extraordinarily wide range of projects, departmentalism at the local level, and in general a 'lapsing of potentially innovatory partnerships in relation to inner city programme management into a more traditional form of central/local relationship'. To quote from his conclusions:

The direction of the programme has shifted towards economic development with an emphasis on private sector involvement, capital investment, and a concern for the area as much as for the residents being the key feature of policy. The strategic framework for inner city programmes is one which emphasises infra-structural and environmental improvement as a basis for private investment, wealth creation and employment generation. . . .

The evolution of Inner Cities policy towards the joint administration of a largely economic development programme has led to a situation where partnership and the planning system has been largely by-passed as a forum for significant debate between central and local government. . . .

This feature of the programme has been increased by the growth of additional institutional schemes which, though serving the same or similar objectives, have been conceived and operated separately – enterprise zones, urban development corporations, urban development grants, the Financial Institutions Group, and the Merseyside Task Force.

In short, there is little that can really be called an 'inner-city planning system'. Instead there is a wide variety of programmes. Some of these are outlined in Chapter 10, typically in a brief form since at the time of writing the new provisions were not clear. Now (in 1984) it is the effects of these innovations which are not clear.

URBAN RENEWAL AND THE INNER CITY: REFERENCES

B. J. Berry, 'Inner city futures: an American dilemma revisited', *Transactions of the Institute of British Geographers*, vol. 5 (1980), pp. 1–28.
Commission for Racial Equality, *Local Government and Racial Equality* (The Commission, 1982).
P. Coppin, *Small Firms in the Inner City: A Review of the Literature* (London Borough of Hammersmith and Fulham, Research Report 48, 1981).
P. Damestick and C. Howick, 'Economic regeneration of the inner city: manufacturing industry and office development in Inner London', *Progress in Planning*, vol. 18, no. 3 (1982).
R. L. Davies and A. G. Champion, *The Future for the City Centre* (Academic Press, 1983).
Department of the Environment, *The Urban Programme: The Partnerships at Work* (DOE, 1981).
Department of the Environment, *Local Enterprise Agencies: A Guide*, 2nd edn (DOE, 1982).
Department of the Environment, *Local Authorities and Racial Disadvantage: Report of a Joint Government/Local Authority Working Party* (Inner Cities Directorate, 1983).
Department of the Environment, *The Urban Programme: Tackling Racial Disadvantage* (DOE, 1983).
Department of the Environment, *Community Project Review* (DOE, 1984).
D. V. Donnison, *Urban Policies: A New Approach* (Fabian Society, 1983).
D. Gosling, 'The Isle of Dogs, London Docklands: discrepancy in approaches to urban design', *Cities*, vol. 1, no. 2 (November 1983), pp. 150–66.

P. Harrison, *Inside the Inner City: Life Under the Cutting Edge* (Penguin, 1983).

D. A. Hart, *Urban Economic Development: Lessons for British Cities from Germany and America* (University of Reading, School of Planning Studies, 1980).

R. H. Home, *Inner City Regeneration* (Spon, 1982).

House of Commons Environment Committee, Session 1982–3, *The Problems of Management of Urban Renewal (Appraisal of the Recent Initiatives in Merseyside)*, HC (1982–3) 18, 3 vols (HMSO, 1983).

R. J. Johnston and J. C. Doornkamp, *The Changing Geography of the United Kingdom* (Methuen, 1982).

D. Latham, 'Inner city renewal: a new approach', *The Planner*, May 1984.

P. Lawless, *Britain's Inner Cities: Problems and Policies* (Harper & Row, 1981).

London Borough of Tower Hamlets, *Isle of Dogs: A Plan for the 1980s* (The Borough, 1981).

M. Loney, *Community Against Government: The British Community Development Project 1968–1978: A Study of Government Incompetence* (Heinemann, 1983).

C. Madge and P. Willmott, *Inner City Poverty in Paris and London* (Routledge, 1981).

P. Marris, *Community Planning and Conceptions of Change* (Routledge, 1982).

J. Mawson and D. Miller, *Agencies in Regional and Local Development* (University of Birmingham, Centre for Urban and Regional Studies, 1983).

J. McCarthy and M. Buckley, *Birmingham Enveloping Schemes Survey* (prepared for DOE by Research Bureau Ltd, 1982).

R. Nabarro, 'Inner city partnerships: an assessment of the first programmes', *Town Planning Review*, vol. 51 (1980), pp. 25–38.

National Council for Voluntary Organisations, *Inner Cities Report 1980–82* (NCVO, 1982).

Lord Scarman, *The Brixton Disorders*, Cmnd 8427 (HMSO, 1981).

D. Sim, *Change in the City Centre* (Glasgow) (Gower, 1982).

K. Spencer, 'Comprehensive community programmes', in S. Leach and J. Stewart, *Approaches in Public Policy* (Allen & Unwin, 1982).

M. Stewart, 'The inner area planning system', *Policy and Politics*, vol. 11 (1983), pp. 203–14.

U. Wannop, *Report on the Future Management of Gear* (Governing Committee Glasgow Eastern Area Renewal Project) (University of Strathclyde, 1982).

K. Young and C. Mason, *Urban Economic Development: New Roles and Relationships* (Macmillan, 1983).

J. A. Webman, *Reviving the Industrial City: The Politics of Urban Renewal in Lyon and Birmingham* (Croom Helm, 1982).

G. Williams, *Inner City Policy: A Partnership with the Voluntary Sector?* (Bedford Square Press, 1983).

K. Young and C. Mason, *Urban Economic Development: New Roles and Relationships* (Macmillan, 1983).

M. Young et al., *Report from Hackney: A Study of an Inner City Area* (Policy Studies Institute, 1981).

See also list of DOE inner cities research programme reports in Bibliography, Part 3 of the Appendix.

ENTERPRISE ZONES

Enterprise zones have changed considerably in concept since Peter Hall first espoused the idea in 1977 or since it was taken up by Sir Geoffrey Howe (Sir Geoffrey's statement is reproduced in *Journal of Planning and Environment Law*, 1980, pp. 294–6) and other Conservative politicians (then in opposition). A popular version was neatly, amusingly and misleadingly summed by Sir Keith Joseph, who envisaged these bright new stars of Conservative freedom being zones within which 'the Queen's writ shall not run' (see S. M. Butler, *Enterprise Zones: Greenlining the Inner Cities*, Heinemann, 1981). The position in 1982 is set out in P. J. Purton and C. Douglas, 'Enterprise zones in the United Kingdom: a successful experiment?', *Journal of Planning and Environment Law*, 1982, pp. 412–22. Though fanciful, there was an important administrative issue here which Sir Geoffrey's more considered statement spelled out:

> The establishment of enterprise zones will not be part of regional policy. Nor will it have any direct connection with the application of other existing policies such as inner city policy, rural development or derelict land policy. The sites chosen will continue to benefit from whatever aid is available under these policies.

Their independence (in principle if not so much in practice – as we shall see) from the mainstream is underlined by the benefits which (in 1984) apply in enterprise zones for a period of ten years following designation:

1 Exemption from rates on industrial and commercial property.
2 Exemption from Development Land Tax.
3 100 per cent allowances for corporation and income tax purposes for capital expenditure on industrial and commercial buildings.
4 Employers are exempt from industrial training levies and from the requirement to supply information to industrial training boards.
5 A greatly simplified planning regime; developments that conform with the published scheme for each zone will not require individual planning permission.
6 Those controls remaining in force will be administered more speedily.
7 Applications from firms in enterprise zones for certain customs facilities will be processed as a matter of priority and certain criteria relaxed.
8 Government requests for statistical information will be reduced.

These benefits apply to both new and existing industrial and commercial businesses in an enterprise zone. As at February 1984, the enterprise zones were as follows:

Zone	Area (ha)	Date of Designation
Belfast	207	October 1981
Clydebank	230	August 1981
Corby	113	June 1981
Delyn	118	July 1983
Dudley	253	July 1981
Glanford	50	(Anticipated 1984)
Hartlepool	109	October 1981
Invergordon	60	October 1983
Isle of Dogs	147	April 1982
Londonderry	109	September 1983
Lower Swánsea Valley	314	June 1981
Middlesbrough	79	November 1983
Milford Haven Waterway	146	(Anticipated 1984)
NE Lancashire	114	December 1983
NW Kent	125	October 1983
Rotherham	105	August 1983
Salford/Trafford	352	August 1981
Scunthorpe	105	September 1983
Speke	138	August 1981
Tayside	120	January 1984
Telford	113	January 1984
Tyneside	454	August 1981
Wakefield	89	July 1981
Wellingborough	54	July 1983
Workington	87	October 1983

This is a considerably larger number (25) than originally envisaged and the total list of specially aided areas seems likely to increase with the announcement of six freeports and the prospect of 'simplified planning zones'. Information on the latter is still scanty and it is unclear whether it represents a simplified planning *system* or a second category of enterprise zones. (Over 50 local authorities were unsuccessful in their bids for enterprise zones.)

Freeports (which have worldwide popularity – from Colombia to Taiwan) are areas to which goods can be imported free of customs duties and other levies provided they are sent abroad after processing; alternatively, no duties are levied until they enter the home market from the freeport. There are six UK freeports: Belfast, Birmingham, Cardiff, Liverpool, Prestwick and Southampton (*Planning Bulletin*, 10 February 1984).

In this rapid escalation of initiatives, little account seems to have been taken of the monitored experience of the first generation of enterprise zones. Three annual reports, *Monitoring Enterprise*

Zones, have been written (and published) by Roger Tym and Partners. As might be expected, some of the relevant questions are extremely difficult to deal with, for example on the *net* effects of the zones. Do they merely attract firms from other locations? The answer in fact seems clear:

> Probably three-quarters of the incoming firms would be operating in the same county and at least 85% in the same region if there were no EZ. The rest will have considered other locations beyond these areas and may have chosen to locate there. In terms of net effects attributable to the level of output of firms, the surveys indicate that between 4% and 12% of the wholly new firms might not have been started but for the EZ. Changes in the levels of output and employment in existing firms are much harder to identify: perhaps 10% of firms have achieved higher levels than they would have done in the absence of the EZ, this being attributable mainly to the relief from rates and to a limited extent to non-EZ incentives. (*Monitoring Enterprise Zones: Year Three Report*, Roger Tym and Partners, *et al.*, January 1984, pp. 144–5).

This is only a short extract from a lengthy analysis. A full summary cannot be attempted here, but a number of salient points are well worth reproducing.

First, very heavy 'up-front' expenditure has been required to enable the enterprise zones to generate employment. The total public cost for the period 1981–3 (for the original eleven zones) was £132·9 million, made up as follows:

	£ Million
Rates relief	16·8
Capital allowances	38·0
Public sector development	39·8
Other public investment	38·3

The report comments:

> The most important lessons from the experience of implementing EZs is the importance of support measures to ensure that development takes place in the zones. There are two main aspects to these measures:
>
> (a) public expenditure to finance the assembly, reclamation and servicing of land where physical and economic conditions are such that land will not be brought forward for development under the stimulus of the EZ measures alone;
>
> (b) the public professional and management resources required

to plan and implement land development programmes, whether the land be in public or private ownership.

The EZs are powerful marketing tools and in most cases have provided the Zone Authorities with their best opportunity for attracting activity and investment. The authorities have therefore mostly been willing to give priority to facilitating development in the zones and to coordinating public expenditure for that purpose.

The public investment has been particularly useful in facilitating planning agreements (under Section 52 of the Planning Act), and it is clear that the zones have been effectively organised and administered because of the special efforts made. 'The essence of the arrangements is that the EZs get *priority*.' There is, of course, a limit to the number of areas which can get priority and this throws some doubt on whether the increase in zones and similar priority areas can lead to even the same modest successes achieved in the zones.

Particularly perplexing is the emphasis laid on the popularity of the eased planning restrictions (*Municipal Journal*, 2 March 1984). The Tym reports certainly do not suggest that a bonfire of controls has released time-saving dynamic efficiency. Case studies showed that a very considerable amount of negotiation (whether it be termed 'planning' or not) still had to take place, both between the developers and local authorities and also between developers and other agencies:

It is clear that the EZ planning schemes have, for the most part, worked well. There have been few operational problems, and fears that EZs would entail lower environmental standards have not been realised.

The scheme *can* help a developer to get on site more quickly, but as the case studies clearly show, it does not always do so. Developers have their own problems to sort out (with regard to finance, design, relationships with contractors and so on). Moreover, there are other statutory controls and these still remain. Nevertheless, planning *is* seen as an important obstacle by developers partly because the outcome is never quite certain. What the scheme offers is the advantage of certainty. The conditions are set out and known from the beginning.

As we have seen, however, the schemes do not seem to have emancipated developers completely. The amount of continuing interchange between developers and Zone Authorities seems, on the contrary, to have been considerable. (*Year Three Report*, 1984, p. 138).

ENTERPRISE ZONES: REFERENCES

P. J. Burton and C. Douglas: 'Enterprise zones in the United Kingdom: a successful experiment?', *Journal of Planning and Environment Law*, 1982, pp. 412–22.

S. M. Butler, *Enterprise Zones: Greenlining the Inner Cities* (Heinemann, 1981).

Department of the Environment, *Advice on the Enterprise Zone Planning System in England and Wales* (1983).

Department of the Environment, *Enterprise Zones* (information package) (1984).

Department of the Environment, *Simplified Planning Zones: A Consultation Paper* (1984).

P. Hall, 'Green fields and grey areas', *Proceedings of the Royal Town Planning Institute Annual Conference* (1977).

P. Hall, 'Enterprise zones: a justification', *International Journal of Urban and Regional Research*, vol. 6 (1982), pp. 416–21.

P. Hall, *Investing in Innovation*, Tawney Pamphlet 1 (The Tawney Society, 1982).

E. Humberger, 'The Enterprise Zone Fallacy', *Journal of Community Action*, vol. 24 (1981).

S. Taylor, 'The politics of enterprise zones', *Public Administration*, vol. 59 (1981), pp. 421–39.

Roger Tym and Partners *et al.*, *Monitoring Enterprise Zones: Year One Report* (March 1982); *Year Two Report* (April 1983); and *Year Three Report* (January 1984).

S. E. Unger, 'Enterprise zones: some perspectives on Anglo-American developments', *Urban Law and Policy*, vol. 5 (1982), pp. 129–47.

OTHER INNER-CITY PROGRAMMES

The proliferation of programmes in, or related to, or affecting inner cities is becoming baffling. At the time of writing, new programmes include the UDG (Urban Development Grant) in England and Wales, and LEGUP (Local Enterprise Grant for Urban Projects) in Scotland – both modelled on the American UDAG (Urban Development Action Grant) – and the SGP (Special Grants Programme), which has taken the place of the Small Grants Programme (see R. Boyle, *The Urban Development Action Grant*, University of Strathclyde, Department of Urban and Regional Planning, 1983). The two Urban Development Corporations for the Merseyside and the London Docklands are in operation – the latter only after considerable parliamentary debate. (See *Report from the Select Committee of the House of Lords on the London Docklands Development Corporation (Area and Constitution) Order 1980*, HL 198 (HMSO, 1981). A succinct summary is to be found in M. Grant, *Urban Planning Law* (Sweet & Maxwell, 1982), pp. 540–2.) As I have stated (pp. 282–3 above), no public inquiry into the designation of an urban development corporation is necessary. This is true, but the point was omitted that an order establishing an urban development corporation requires parliamentary approval.

Progress by the two urban development corporations cannot yet be described as dramatic but, of course, the same was true of the early history of their godparents, the new town development corporations. (See *Town and Country Planning*, vol. 51, no. 5, May 1982, which has several articles on dockland redevelopment. See also Nigel Broackes (Chairman of the London Docklands Development Corporation), 'The regeneration of London's docklands', *Journal of the Royal Society of Arts*, January 1984, pp. 105–17.)

The 'traditional' inner areas programme continues, as is exemplified by *Fifth Inner Areas Programme for South Tyneside 1983/84 – 1985/86* (published by the Borough of South Tyneside Planning Department, 1982). Economic regeneration has now become a major concern of a very large number of local authorities. Reports and studies are being produced at an impressive – if not overwhelming – rate. (Achievement unfortunately typically does not match input.) A good example is provided by the London Borough of Hammersmith and Fulham, which has a well thought out programme of local employment strategies. (See *Strategy for Employment and Economic Development: 1982/83 Review and Programme for 1982/83–1983/84*, London Borough of Hammersmith and Fulham, Directorate of Development Planning, 1983. See also M. Allan, 'Local employment strategies', *The Planner*, vol. 69, no. 5, September/October 1983, pp. 151–2.) There will remain, however, those who argue that area-based policies are inherently flawed:

> Families living in the shadow of . . . industrial decline can only be helped by area based schemes if they form part of an overall strategy aimed at eradicating low pay and restoring full employment. (C. Playford, *In the Shadow of Decline*, Low Pay Unit, 1981).

The message is as eloquent and valid as it ever was.

OLD HOUSING

The problem of old and inadequate housing has worsened in the last decade and is seemingly continuing to do so. (Unfortunately, up-to-date figures are available only for England.) The character of the inadequacy, however, is changing. The 1981 English House Condition Survey (which includes revised estimates for earlier years) shows that there was a significant fall in the number of dwellings lacking basic amenities from 2·8 million in 1971 to 1·5 million in 1976, and to 0·9 million in 1981. The reduction of 1·9 million was due to 20 per cent demolition and 80 per cent improvement. The impact of the improvement grants policy is apparent.

Though there has been this marked improvement in 'amenity standards', the number of unfit dwellings had remained fairly constant at around 1·1 and 1·2 million. It thus seems that dwellings are falling into a state of unfitness at about the same rate that unfit dwellings are being removed from the stock. More alarming, however, is the major increase in dwellings in serious disrepair (i.e., needing repairs costing £7,000 or more at 1981 prices): the number increased from 859,000 in 1976 to 1,049,000 in 1981.

Changes in English Housing Conditions 1971, 1976 and 1981

	1971 No.	1971 %	1976 No.	1976 %	1981 No.	1981 %
Dwellings lacking one or more amenities	2,815,000	17·4	1,531,000	8·9	910,000	5·0
Unfit dwellings (revised estimates)	1,216,000	7·5	1,162,000	6·8	1,116,000	6·2
Dwellings in serious disrepair	864,000	5	859,000	5	1,049,000	6
Unfit dwellings by tenure						
Owner-occupied	356,000	29	396,000	34	483,000	43
Public authority	65,000	5	60,000	5	67,000	6
Private rented	629,000	52	506,000	44	370,000	33
Vacant	166,000	14	200,000	17	196,000	18
Total	1,216,000	100	1,162,000	100	1,116,000	100
Dwellings in serious disrepair by tenure						
Owner-occupied	314,000	36	371,000	43	539,000	51
Public authority	37,000	4	47,000	6	50,000	5
Private rented	463,000	54	384,000	45	343,000	33
Vacant	50,000	6	57,000	7	117,000	11
Total	864,000	100	859,000	100	1,049,000	100

Some of the main figures from the survey are reproduced in the accompanying table, but there is a great deal more information in the report. One final illustration is the tenure pattern: whereas in 1971 only 29 per cent of unfit dwellings were owner-occupied, by 1981 the proportion had risen to 43 per cent. Similarly, the proportion of dwellings in serious disrepair which were owner-occupied rose from 36 per cent to 51 per cent.

This gives point to the discussion on slum clearance in the Joint Land Requirements Committee report on *Housing and Land*:

We do not state these figures as targets, and it is wholly unrealistic to expect demolitions to reach this scale in the foreseeable future. An underlying problem is that many of the unfit houses are owner occupied and that, although there is a mechanism which could encourage the demolition of owner occupied properties, there are social and financial difficulties associated with this. Moreover, it has been shown that houses may be 'unfit' by the judgement of technical experts but nevertheless seem adequate to their owners. Other unfit houses can economically be put in good repair. Compulsory purchase in such circumstances is a difficult nettle for politicians to grasp. Incentives to owners to sell are a better approach but, as was found in the slum clearance programmes of the sixties and seventies, need to be backed by compulsory purchase as the last resort. Otherwise, redevelopment of entire areas can become impossible because of the wishes of a single small plot owner, and 'pepper potting' becomes the only solution. There are no easy answers to these problems.

The 1980 Housing Act streamlined the renovation grant system, removed a range of controls, liberalised grants, and provided new powers for 'improvement for sale' and shared ownership schemes (see DOE Circulars 21/80, 5/81, 18/81, 11/82 and 29/82). The result was a boom in private sector repair and renovation grants – from 158,500 in 1979 to 308,000 in 1983 (figures are for England only and are taken from DOE press notices). Progress in the public sector, which has suffered from financial constraints, was poor. The figures were 93,200 in 1979, falling to 64,200 in 1981, and then rising to 94,000 in 1983. Experiments with the DOE sponsored 'Priority Estates Programme' and the Birmingham-led 'Enveloping' scheme have had little impact.

Enveloping is dealt with in DOE Circular 29/82 and a paper by T. Brunt *et al.* Essentially it is (to quote the circular) 'the renovation of the external fabric and curtilage of the dwellings which have deteriorated beyond the scope of routine maintenance. . . . Experimental work financed under the Urban Programme has shown that enveloping can in some circumstances be more effective than previous methods used in Housing Action Areas in improving living conditions in the worst part of the older housing stock. . . . Whole blocks may be repaired where blight is widespread and a single dramatic action is needed.' Obviously enveloping is only a first step in a rehabilitation process: it has to be followed up by improvements to the insides of dwellings. Its major feature, however, is that (if successful) it so enhances the quality of the exterior environment that owners are stimulated to improve their individual houses, with the secure knowledge that decay of the area has been reversed. (See also DOE, *Good Practice in Area Improvement*, HMSO, 1984.)

The major problem in the public sector is a financial one (including the staffing shortages to which this leads). The Association of Municipal Authorities in a 1981 report, *Ruin or Renewal: Choices for Our Ageing Housing*, have recommended a major consolidation and revision of housing legislation and a 'sufficient' level of resources to deal with older housing. More recently, problems of 'non-traditional' dwellings have come to the fore, and at the time of writing a Housing Defects Bill is before Parliament. This provides grants for rectifying the defects of the non-traditional housing of the 1940s and 1950s. But the problems seem to be growing more rapidly than the solutions. The latest (1984) report by the AMA suggests that there is a massive problem with dwellings built by 'industrialised' methods in the 1960s and 1970s.

At the same time, the Scottish Affairs Committee has produced an alarming report on the incidence of *Dampness in Housing*, while the Paintmakers Association has issued an eloquent report on the inadequacy of building maintenance, particularly painting: *Blight on Britain's Buildings* (1984).

Attention is usually focused on urban housing conditions: a useful corrective (with bibliography) is to be found in the paper by Phillips and Williams on 'The social implications of rural housing policy: a review of developments in the past decade'.

The overall picture is a depressing one, particularly since there are currently no indications of policy innovations which would significantly affect Britain's increasing problems of old housing.

OLD HOUSING: REFERENCES

Association of Metropolitan Authorities, *Ruin or Renewal: Choices for Our Ageing Housing* (The Association, 1981).
Association of Metropolitan Authorities, *Defects in Housing: Part 1: 'Non Traditional' Dwellings of the 1940s and 1950s* (The Association, 1983).
Association of Metropolitan Authorities, *Defects in Housing: Part 2: Industrialised and System-Built Dwellings of the Late 1960s and 1970s* (The Association, 1984).
Association of Metropolitan Authorities, *The Redevelopment Process: An Interim Working Paper* (published jointly by the Association and the House Builders Federation, 1984).
M. Bone and V. Mason, *Empty Housing in England*, Office of Population Censuses and Surveys (HMSO, 1980).
T. Brunt et al., 'The Birmingham Envelope Scheme', *Housing Review*, July–August 1982, pp. 130–3.
DOE, *Priority Estates Project: Upgrading Problem Council Estates* (DOE, 1980).
DOE, *Priority Estates Project 1981: Improving Problem Council Estates* (HMSO, 1981).
DOE, *Circular 29/82: Improvement of Older Housing – Enveloping* (HMSO, 1982).

DOE, *English House Condition Survey 1981: Part 1: Report of the Physical Condition Survey* (Housing Survey Report No. 12) (HMSO, 1982).

DOE, *Priority Estates Project 1982: Improving Problem Council Estates: A Summary of Aims and Progress* (DOE, 1982).

DOE, *English House Condition Survey 1981: Part 2: Report of the Interview and Local Authority Survey* (Housing Survey Report No. 13) (HMSO, 1983).

DOE, *Good Practice in Area Improvement* (HMSO, 1984).

M. S. Gibson and M. J. Langstaff, *An Introduction to Urban Renewal* (Hutchinson, 1982).

House of Commons, Environment Committee, Session 1981–2, First Report, *The Privately Rented Housing Sector*, HC (1981–2) 40, 3 vols (HMSO, 1982).

Joint Land Requirements Committee, *Housing and Land 1984–1991: 1992–2000* (Housing Research Foundation, 1984).

A. Kirkham, *Improvement for Sale by Local Authorities* (HMSO, 1983).

Paintmakers Association, *Blight on Britain's Buildings: A Survey of Paint and Maintenance Practice* (The Association, 1984).

D. Phillips and A. Williams, 'The social implications of rural housing policy: a review of developments in the past decade', in A. W. Gilg (ed.), *Countryside Planning 1983* (Geo Books, 1983).

Scottish Affairs Committee, House of Commons, Session 1983–4, *Dampness in Housing*, HC (1983–4) 206, 1984.

REGIONAL PLANNING

If, as is clearly the case, the current economic climate has shaken the basis for local and structure planning, the plight of regional planning is even worse. Indeed, it is difficult to provide a clear picture, since the reality is confused. Over most of the country, regional planning is dormant if not dead; but there are areas of activity, analysis or simply thinking on the regional scale which hold some promise for the future. Most obvious are bodies such as the Scottish and Welsh Development Agencies, the Highlands and Islands Development Board, the Countryside Commission, the Land Authority for Wales, and so forth, which are enabled (and sometimes able) to operate on a level and at a scale greater than that of the areas bounded by local authority limits. Additionally there are the various land availability studies which, though not functioning as a permanent tier of land use planning, do take an occasional snapshot picture of one issue.

The demise of the Greater London Council and the metropolitan counties, on the other hand, takes away major instruments of regional policy-making (though it is debatable how successful they were). One interesting response has been the change in attitude (leading to a stronger commitment to regional planning) in the south-east and in the west midlands. In the south-east, a press notice of the Standing Conference on London and South East Regional Planning declares that the constituent authorities 'have strengthened their commitment to regional planning' and are agreed to improve their 'effectiveness'. The notice continues:

> The South East needs to speak with a powerful and united voice on the major planning problems confronting the region today. A firm regional strategy is required to defend the Green Belts and to provide land for essential housebuilding. Only with policies agreed by all authorities can we locate all industry and commerce where they are most needed and take advantage of the M25 motorway without allowing urban sprawl. (SCLSERP press notice, 'Councils united on regional planning', 12 December 1983).

In a Humpty-Dumpty way such regional planning as is currently being done is essentially in response to specific major developments, of which the M25 is a good example (which also illustrates the type of work undertaken by SCLSERP – the Standing Conference on London and South East Regional Planning).

THE M25

The M25 was conceived purely as a traffic facility: a huge ring road round London. In the 1980 White Paper (*Policy for Roads: England 1980*, Cmnd 7908, 1980), the M25 was cited 'as an outstanding example of a road which would aid economic recovery and development, by providing a quick, safe and convenient route around Greater London and enabling traffic to find its way in and out of London by the most appropriate route'. A further quotation underlines the point:

> The M25 has been seen by the Government strictly as a transport planning issue. It has not up to now been regarded as a general strategic planning issue. . . . However: will the M25 have an impact on locational pressures and choices, particularly those generated by industry and commerce; and are there any consequences for the current strategy of regenerating inner London and the long-established strategy of concentrating growth at specific locations in the rest of the South East and restraining it elsewhere? (Standing Conference on London and South East Regional Planning, *The Impact of the M25*, 1982, p. 1).

In short, the M25 is more than a traffic route: it is 'a ring around the periphery of the metropolis [which] will significantly alter the pattern of accessibility in the south-east region in a way which will change locational perceptions and decisions. This could result in a significant increase in development pressures in certain parts of the region, including the Metropolitan Green Belt where strict restraint policies apply.'

This is a simple, eloquent example of how narrowly conceived policies (in this case relieving the pressure of through traffic in London) turn into major regional planning issues. Whether or not 'regional planning' is applauded, rejected, espoused, demanded, or whatever, it *happens* – by design, by default, or by accident. Perhaps it would be more accurate to say that planning decisions having major regional impacts are taken, whether or not they are conceived in terms of 'regional planning'.

The possible impacts of the M25 are highly significant (as is highlighted in the SCLSERP report), but much depends on how the pressures generated are dealt with. Government statements to date have been firm and clear: the M25 is a 'relief' to London; it is not a new magnet for growth. Yet the potentiality (to put it no more strongly) is clearly there, and the M25 may prove to be a testing ground for the operation of regional policies in the south-east. (Given the absence of a regional level for decision-making, the 'test' will not be conclusive since, though major decisions may be taken by central government, numerous, cumulative, minor decisions will be taken by local government.)

What happens as a result of the M25 is of significance far wider than the south-easten region; It has implications for all regions. As the Committee of Welsh District Councils have commented:

> The problems of the regions, to which UK regional policy should be addressed have to do with the destructive overcentralisation of wealth and power in London and the southeast. (*Municipal Journal*, 11 May 1984).

This comment was made in relation to the 1983 White Paper *Regional Industrial Development*, of which a brief summary follows.

THE 1983 WHITE PAPER

The White Paper is a curious document in that although major policy changes are proposed most are accompanied by a request for comment upon them. The paper is more 'green' than 'white' but, despite much vagueness, several points emerge clearly. Most important is the underlying philosophy which is illustrated in this quotation:

> Although an economic case for regional industrial policy may still be made, it is not self-evident. The Government believe that the case for continuing the policy is now principally a social one with the aim of reducing, on a stable long term basis, regional

imbalances in employment opportunities. . . . The argument that regional industrial policy produces a net national economic benefit is open to debate. . . . The Government believe that regional industrial incentives still have an important role to play in influencing the location of new economic development . . . but the incentives must be made much more cost-effective than at present, with greater emphasis on job creation and selectivity, and less discrimination against service industries. They also need to focus on encouraging new and indigenous development in the Assisted Areas, rather than simply transferring jobs from one part of the country to another. The Government welcome views on these aspects of regional industrial incentives.

The review is continuing and decisions are promised for the autumn of 1984.

REGIONAL PLANNING AND THE M25: REFERENCES

M. Boddy, *Local Government and Industrial Development* (University of Bristol, School of Advanced Urban Studies, 1982).

A. G. Champion, *Counterurbanisation and Rural Rejuvenation in Rural Britain* (University of Newcastle upon Tyne, Geography Department, 1981).

Development Commission, *Reports on the Work of the Development Commission and its Main Agency, the Council for Small Industries in Rural Areas 1983*, HC (1983–4) 87 (HMSO, 1983).

D. R. Diamond, 'The uses of strategic planning: the example of the National Planning Guidelines in Scotland'. *Town Planning Review*, vol. 50 (1979), pp. 18–35.

D. R. Diamond and N. A. Spence, *Regional Policy Evaluation: A Methodological Review and the Scottish Example* (Gower, 1983).

P. Elias, 'The regional impact of national economic policies: a multi-regional simulation approach for the UK', *Regional Studies*, vol. 16, pp. 335–44.

S. Fothergill *et al., Industrial Location Research Project Working Papers* (University of Cambridge, Department of Land Economy, 1982–4).

S. Fothergill and G. Gudgin, *Unequal Growth: Urban and Regional Change in the UK* (Heinemann, 1982).

F. Gaffkin and A. Nickson, *Jobs Crisis and the Multinationals* (Third World Publications, 1984).

A. Gillespie (ed.), *Technological Change and Regional Development* (Pion, 1983).

A. Glyn-Jones, *Planning in Action: Visions and Realities in a Country Town* (Devon County Council and the University of Exeter, 1983).

J. B. Goddard and A. G. Champion, *The Urban and Regional Transformation of Britain* (Methuen, 1983).

G. Gudgin, B. Moore and J. Rhodes, 'Employment problems in the cities and regions of the UK: prospects for the 1980s', *Cambridge Economic Policy Review*, vol. 8, no. 2 (1982).

P. Hall, *Great Planning Disasters* (Weidenfeld & Nicolson, 1980).

G. Hallett, *Second Thoughts on Regional Policy* (Centre for Policy Studies, 1981).

B. W. Hogwood and M. Keating (eds), *Regional Government in England* (Clarendon Press, 1982).

R. Hudson and J. Lewis, *Regional Planning in Europe* (Pion, 1982).

Industrial Development Act 1982, *Annual Report 31 March 1983*, HC (1982–3) 72 (HMSO, 1983).

A. Johnston, 'Metropolitan housing policy and strategic planning in the West Midlands', *Town Planning Review*, vol. 53, no. 2 (April 1982), pp. 179–99.

R. J. Johnston and J. C. Doornkamp, *The Changing Geography of the United Kingdom* (Methuen, 1982).

C. M. Law, *British Regional Development Since World War I* (Methuen, 1982).

D. Massey and R. Meegan, *The Autonomy of Job Loss* (Methuen, 1982).

J. Mawson and C. Skelcher, 'Updating the West Midlands regional strategy: a review of inter-authority relationships', *Town Planning Review*, vol. 51, no. 2 (April 1980), pp. 152–70.

J. Mawson and D. Miller, *Agencies in Regional and Local Development* (University of Birmingham, Centre for Urban and Regional Studies, 1983).

R. Moore, *The Social Impact of Oil: The Case of Peterhead* (Routledge & Kegan Paul, 1982).

Regional Studies Association, *Report of an Inquiry into Regional Problems in the United Kingdom* (Geo Books, 1983).

R. Rothwell, 'The role of technology in industrial change: implications for regional policy', *Regional Studies*, vol. 16 (1982), pp. 361–70.

P. Self, *Planning the Urban Region: A Comparative Study of Policies and Organisations* (Allen & Unwin, 1982).

J. Short, *Public Expenditure and Taxation in the UK Regions* (Gower, 1981).

D. M. Sucksmith and M. G. Lloyd, 'The Highlands and Islands Development Board, regional policy and the Invergordon closure', *National Westminster Quarterly Review*, May 1982, pp. 14–24.

Standing Conference on London and South East Regional Planning (SCLSERP), *A Region in Transition* (The Standing Conference, 1980).

SCLSERP, *Emerging Issues in the South East Region* (1982).

SCLSERP, *Infrastructure and the Regional Strategy* (1982).

SCLSERP, *The Impact of the M25* (1982).

SCLSERP, *1981 Census: South East Regional Monitor* (1982).

SCLSERP, *Councils United on Regional Planning* (press notice) 12 December 1983.

D. Storey, *Entrepreneurship and the New Firm* (Croom Helm, 1983).

A. R. Townsend, *The Impact of Recession* (Croom Helm, 1983).

White Paper, *Regional Industrial Development*, Cmnd 9111 (HMSO, 1983).

G. Williams, 'Rural advance factories: a programme in search of a policy', *The Planner*, March 1984, pp. 11–13.

G. K. Wilson, 'Planning: lessons from the ports', *Public Administration*, vol. 61, no. 3 (Autumn 1983), pp. 265–81.

K. Young and C. Mason, *Urban Economic Development: New Roles and Relationships* (Macmillan, 1983).

D. Yuill, *Regional Development Agencies in Europe* (Gower, 1983).

D. Yuill, K. Allen, and C. Hull, *Regional Policies in the European Community* (Croom Helm, 1980).

PLANNING AND THE PUBLIC

The hey-day of public participation has passed. In the words of the RTPI's 1982 report on *The Public and Planning*, 'A divergence between the desire of the public for more participation and that of the Government for less is becoming ever more apparent; too often public participation is being equated in local and central government circles with delay, excessive cost and inefficiency.' This trend is continuing. Recent legislation (noted earlier) on, for example, structure plans and local plans has reduced the duties of local authorities in relation to public participation. The RTPI report, thoughtful and convincing as it may be, has fallen on stony ground. There is very little likelihood of any of its recommendations being implemented.

Its proposals are wide-ranging: they include extending participation in plan-preparation, easing access to information, widening the scope for the publicising of planning applications, opening the examination in public to all comers, introducing a system of regular public review of all planning policy on a district basis, providing financial aid for objectors, and establishing community planning councils.

At the same time the problems demanding major public inquiries (see page 332 above) are increasing; or, to be more precise, there are major issues for which the public inquiry procedure is inappropriate. The third London airport was the first case of this kind and a special commission (the Roskill Commission) was set up to investigate thoroughly the best viable location – which it did over a period of two and a half years and at a cost of over £1 million. Its 1971 report was to no avail and the complex political process of planning the airport continues to this day. (Peter Hall gives a neat analysis of the background to and the conclusions and consequences of the Roskill report in his *Great Planning Disasters*, Weidenfeld & Nicolson, 1980, Penguin, 1981.) The Greater London Development Plan (and its motorways component) is perhaps even more dramatic. This vies with Roskill as the 'biggest ever', with a specially appointed panel sitting for 237 days to deal with 28,000 objections, of which 20,000 related to the transport proposals. The direct result of this was the replacement of the traditional public inquiry by the examination in public (see pages 72–4 above). A pungent analysis of this is given in W. G. Le-Las, 'The major public inquiry: politics and the rational verdict', *Urban Law and Policy*, vol. 6 (1983), pp. 39–51; see also P. Hall, op. cit. The Windscale inquiry followed (see p. 332 above), as did inquiries on mining in the Vale of Belvoir and a host of others.

Currently, a lengthy inquiry is proceeding into a proposal for a US-designed pressurised-water reactor at Sizewell, Suffolk. (Progress on this is being monitored by Jennifer Armstrong, and reported in the pages of the monthly *Town and Country Planning*.)

The RTPI report, noting the great diversity in the character of these schemes, points to certain common features:

> They call for a balanced judgement between national, regional and local issues, informed by technical argument. They usually have major environmental implications and are likely to be unpopular locally. They are promoted by large organisations commanding expertise and resources far in excess of those of most of the potential objectors to them. It is scarcely surprising that the traditional inquiry has been creaking under the strain of dealing with projects of this sort, particularly against the background of an increasingly well informed and articulate public, less prepared to leave unchallenged the views of ministers, civil servants and technical experts.

There is, however, another aspect to this which needs stressing – as is done in the RTPI report: 'The situation tends to be particularly serious where government appears both to promote and judge a proposal, and the public wish to question whether the project is needed at all.'

The outcome of the strains and stresses on this system (well considered in the RTPI report) is unclear, though for an indication of the current state of play the reader is referred to Jennifer Armstrong's note 'Procedures at the Sizewell Inquiry' (*Journal of Planning and Environment Law*, 1983, pp. 508–10). The overall picture is confused and looks like remaining so for the foreseeable future.

It should not be thought, however, that public participation is becoming defunct. In March 1984, the fourth inspector at the Archway Road inquiry resigned. Around the same time, the National Economic Development Office in a report blandly entitled *Pre-construction Procedures for Motorways and Trunk Road Schemes* raised the ire of bodies like Friends of the Earth (see *Planning*, no. 558, 2 March 1984) for proposing a drastic diminution in the role of objectors at public inquiries on new road schemes.

More positive – and curiously ignored – is the major change in one aspect of public participation in Scotland. This is to be unearthed in Section 41 of the Local Government and Planning (Scotland) Act 1982, which greatly extends the scope of publication of planning applications. This, in part, stems from distinctive features of Scottish administration. In Eric Gillett's words:

> Under the building regulations it had always been necessary to

notify neighbours and allow them to put in their objections, but since the granting or refusal of building warrant depended on whether the building met the requirements of the building regulations, and not on planning or other environmental considerations such as neighbours are likely to be interested in, the majority of objections had to be ruled out of order. By that time planning permission had probably already been given. In 1981, the Scottish Office took the logical step of making it necessary to notify neighbours of a planning application rather than of an application for a building warrant. This meant that planning committees would see objections in time to take them into account.

Such are the paths of bureaucratic evolution.

At the same time, relatively new institutions are continuing to stir up muddy waters in the machinery of government and generally to make life more difficult for politicians and administrators who (genuinely) feel that they could do a better job if they were left alone. (On this crucially important issue, see P. McAuslan's *The Ideologies of Planning Law*, Pergamon, 1980.) Much of the work of the Commissioners for Local Administration (the ombudsmen) for England, Scotland and Wales is concerned with housing and planning. One quotation will have to suffice; it is from the 1981 report of the Welsh Ombudsman and refers to the operation of the circular on development control (WO 40/80; DOE 22/80). The laudable objective of this circular is to secure a general speeding up of the development control system and to ensure that development is prevented or restricted only when this serves a wider community benefit. But speed has its problems, and the Welsh Ombudsman expresses concern at the legitimate feelings of aggrieved parties who were unaware of proposed developments. He continues:

It would be highly regrettable if planning authorities were to view this Joint Circular, with its emphasis on the speedy determination of planning applications, its discouragement of the control by planning authorities of external appearance of new buildings, and its silence in relation to the reasonable protection of the amenities of neighbours to new development, as an indication that less consideration than hitherto need be given to the rights and feelings of individuals whose lives and homes are likely to be affected. Whilst the protection of a neighbour's interests may not be a primary function of planning authorities, the recognition of those interests, whenever they are significant, will redound to the credit of those enlightened and considerate authorities which bear them in mind when dealing with development control. In furtherance of this principle, I would urge local authorities in Wales to ensure, through public advertisement or specific consultations, that no individual or group of individuals likely to be affected adversely by development proposals should be allowed to remain ignorant of those proposals until it is too late for them to make meaningful representations in relation to the relevant planning applications. The reluctance of certain local planning authorities and of some planning officers to exercise their discretion in favour of publicising planning applications or notifying individuals of their existence has, in my opinion, contributed largely towards a feeling of cynicism in relation to the planning function and a bitterness against the planning authorities concerned among complainants who have written to me.

THE PLANNING INSPECTORATE

Finally, mention should be made of the work of the Planning Inspectorate, which now publishes annual reports (formally presented to the Secretaries of State for the Environment, Transport and Wales). These reports are replete with interesting information and statistics of the Inspectorate, which how deals with the great majority of appeals.

This constitutes a remarkable change from the position in the mid-seventies. Central government (the DOE, the Scottish Office and the Welsh Office) retain powers to 'call in', but these are sparingly used.

It is interesting to note that (slowly) the appeal machinery is being separated from the mainstream of central planning administration. As with so much in the field of town and country planning, major issues appear to be in a state of flux, doubt, and inquiry.

PLANNING AND THE PUBLIC: REFERENCES

J. ARMSTRONG, 'PROCEDURES AT THE SIZEWELL INQUIRY', *Journal of Planning and Environment Law*, 1983, pp. 508–10.

N. Boaden *et al.*, *Planning and Participation in Practice: A Study of Public Participation in Structure Planning* (Pergamon, 1980).

N. Boaden *et al.*, *Public Participation in Local Services* (Longman, 1982).

M. Bruton, 'The cost of public participation in local planning', *Town and Country Planning*, vol. 50, no. 6 (June 1981), pp. 164–7.

Commission for Local Administration in England, *Annual Reports* (The Commission, 21 Queen Anne's Gate, London SW1H 9BU).

Commission for Local Administration in Scotland, *Annual Reports* (The Commission, 5 Shandwick Place, Edinburgh EH2 4RG).

Commission for Local Administration in Wales, *Annual Reports* (The Commission, Derwen House, Court Road, Bridgend, Mid-Glamorgan CF31 1BN).

Council on Tribunals, *Annual Reports*, (HMSO).

DOE, *Structure Plans: The Examination in Public: A Guide to Procedure 1984* (DOE, 1984).

E. Gillett, *Investment in the Environment: Recent Housing, Planning and Transport Policies in Scotland* (Aberdeen University Press, 1983).

K. G. Gundry and T. A. Heberlein, 'Do public meetings represent the public?', *Journal of the American Planning Association*, vol. 50 (1984), pp. 175–82.

W. B. Gwyn, 'The Ombudsman in Britain: a qualified success in government reform', *Public Administration*, vol. 60 (Summer 1982), pp. 177–95.

P. Hain, *Neighbourhood Participation* (Temple Smith, 1980).

P. Hain, 'The nationalisation of public participation', *Community Development Journal*, vol. 17 (1982), pp. 36–40.

P. Hall, *Great Planning Disasters* (Weidenfeld & Nicholson, 1980; Penguin, 1981).

J. D. Hutcheson, 'Citizen representation in neighbourhood planning', *Journal of the American Planning Association*, vol. 50 (1984), pp. 183–93.

Journal of Planning and Environment Law, Occasional Papers, *Planning Inquiries – The New Dimension* (Sweet & Maxwell, 1983).
Includes the following papers:
    Rt Hon. Tom King, 'Opening address';
    Mr Justice Parker, 'The major inquiry – evolution of the present system';
    D. Widdicombe QC, 'A new approach';
    J. R. Trustram Eve, 'The big inquiry: where stands the individual?';
    N. Macleod, 'Major road inquiries – a change of direction';
    P. R. Everett, 'The role of the lawyer';
    R. Mercer, 'The role of the expert Witness'.

W. G. Le-Las, 'The major public inquiry: politics and the rational verdict', *Urban Law and policy*, vol. 6 (1983), pp. 39–51.

P. McAuslan, *The Ideologies of Planning Law* (Pergamon, 1980).

R. Macrory and M. Lafontaine, *Public Inquiry and Enquête Publique: Forms of Public Participation in England and France* (Institute for European Environmental Policy and International Institute for Environment and Development, 1982).

National Economic Development Office, *Pre-construction Procedures for Motorway and Trunk Road Schemes*, Civil Engineering EDC, Discussion Paper 1 (NEDO, 1983).

C. Pateman, *Participation and Democratic Theory* (Cambridge University Press, 1970).

Planning Inspectorate, *The Chief Planning Inspector's Report*, annually from the Inspectorate, Tollgate House, Houlton Street, Bristol BS2 9DJ.

A. Richardson, *Participation* (Routledge & Kegan Paul, 1983).

J. Rowan-Robinson, 'The big public inquiry', *Urban Law and Policy*, vol. 4 (1981), pp. 373–90.

J. Rowan-Robinson and L. Edwards, 'The special inquiry', *Town and Country Planning*, vol. 50, no. 3) March 1981), pp. 79–80.

Royal Town Planning Institute, *The Public and Planning: Means to Better Participation* (Final Report of the Public Participation Working Party) (RTPI, 1982).

Scottish Development Department, Circular 47/1980, *Determination of Appeals . . .* (SDD, 1980).

W. Sewell and J. Coppock (eds), *Public Participation in Planning* (Wiley, 1977).

J. Smith, *Urban Renewal: Securing Community Involvement* (Community Projects Foundation, 1983).

L. Susskind and M. Elliott, *Paternalism, Conflict and Coproduction: Learning from Citizen Action and Citizen Participation in Europe*, (Plenum, 1983). See also their paper with the same title in *Planning and Administration*, vol. 9 (1981), pp. 12–27.

A. Thornley, *Theoretical Perspectives on Planning Participation* (Pergamon, 1977).

Town and Country Planning Association, *Planning and Plutonium* (TCPA, 1978).

Town and Country Planning Association, *The Nuclear Controversy* (TCPA, 1980).

Town and Country Planning Association, *Annual Reports* (TCPA).

B. Wynne, *Rationality and Ritual: The Windscale Inquiry and Nuclear Decisions in Britain*, British Society for the History of Science, Monograph No. 3 (1983).

PART 3   BIBLIOGRAPHY OF OFFICIAL PUBLICATIONS
1980–1984

DEPARTMENTAL CIRCULARS

Department of the Environment (HMSO)

21/80	*Housing Acts 1974 and 1980: Improvement of Older Housing*
2/81	*Local Government, Planning and Land Act 1980; Health Services Act 1980 – Town and Country Planning: Development Control Functions*
5/81	*Housing Act 1980 . . . House Renovation Grants*
8/81	*Local Government, Planning and Land Act 1980 – Various Provisions*
9/81	*Town and Country Planning General Development (Amendment) Order 1981; Town and Country Planning (National Parks, Areas of Outstanding Natural Beauty and Conservation Areas) Special Development Order 1981; Town and Country Planning (Fees for Applications and Deemed Applications) Regulations*
12/81	*Historic Buildings and Conservation Areas*
18/81	*Local Authority Improvement for Sale Scheme*

Ministerial Letter, 2 June 1981, *Sales of Council Houses and Flats and Disposal of Housing Land*

23/81	*Local Government, Planning and Land Act 1980 – Town and Country Planning: Development Plans*
26/81	*Local Government and Planning (Amendment) Act 1981*
32/81	*Wildlife and Countryside Act 1981*
38/81	*Planning and Enforcement Appeals*
39/81	*Safeguarding of Aerodromes, Technical Sites and Explosives Storage Areas; Town and Country Planning (Aerodromes) Direction 1981*
1/82	*Town and Country Planning (Minerals) Act 1981*
11/82	*Homes Insulation Act 1978: Homes Insulation Scheme 1982; Housing Acts 1974 and 1980: House Renovation Grants and Compulsory Improvement*
13/82	*Town and Country Planning (Structure and Local Plans) Regulations 1982*
14/82	*Town and Country Planning (Fees for Applications and Deemed Applications) (Amendment) Regulations*
17/82	*Development in Flood Risk Areas – Liaison Between Planning Authorities and Water Authorities*
21/82	*Guidelines for Aggregates Provision in England and Wales*
22/82	*Lead in the Environment*
29/82	*Improvement of Older Housing: Enveloping*
1/83	*Public Rights of Way*

4/83   *Wildlife and Countryside Act; Financial Guidelines for Management Agreements*
6/83   *(1) Airey Houses; (2) Improvement to Older Housing: Housing Acts 1974 and 1980*
13/83   *Purchase Notices*
22/83   *Town and Country Planning Act 1971: Planning Gain – Obligations and Benefits which Extend Beyond the Development for which Planning Permission has been Sought*
23/83   *Caravan Sites and Control of Development Act 1960*

Scottish Development Department Circulars (SDD)

38/1981   *Countryside (Scotland) Act 1981*
5/1982   *Town and Country Planning (Minerals) Act 1981*
29/1982   *Local Government and Planning (Scotland) Act 1982: Planning Provisions*
21/1983   *Private House Building Land Supply: Joint Venture Schemes*
32/1983   *Structure and Local Plans*
33/1983   *Town and Country Planning (Fees for Applications and Deemed Applications) (Scotland) Regulations 1983*

SCOTTISH PLANNING ADVICE NOTES (Issued by SDD)

17 *High Pressure Methane Gas Pipelines*, 1977
18 *Survey*, 1977
19 *Publicity and Consultation*, 1977
20 *The Local Plan Proposals Map*, 1977
21 *The Structure Plan Key Diagram*, 1977
22 *Social Surveys*, 1978
23 *Scottish Economic Monograph*, 1978
24 *Design Guidance*, 1980
25 *Commercial Pipelines*, 1980
26 *Disposal of Land and the Use of the Developer's Brief*, 1981
27 *Structure Planning*, 1981
28 *Local Planning*, 1981

POLLUTION PAPERS (HMSO or DOE)

17 *Cadmium in the Environment and its Significance to Man* (1980)
18 *Air Pollution Control* (1982)
19 *Lead in the Environment* (1983)

POLLUTION REPORTS (HMSO or DOE)

8 *Elaboration of the scientific bases for monitoring the quality of surface water by hydrobiological indicators: Report of the Second UK/USSR Seminar held at Windermere, UK, 24–26 April 1979* (DOE, 1980)
9 *Digest of Environmental Pollution and Water Statistics No. 3* (HMSO, 1980)
10 *European Community Screening Programme for Lead: United Kingdom Results for 1979–1980* (DOE, 1981)

11 *The Glasgow Duplicate Diet Study, 1979/80. A joint survey for the Department of the Environment and the Ministry of Agriculture, Fisheries and Food* (DOE, 1981)
12 *Department of the Environment Sponsored Research on Radioactive Waste: Progress Report* (DOE, 1981)
13 *Digest of Environmental Pollution and Water Statistics No. 4* (HMSO, 1982)
14 *Monitoring the Marine Environment: Into the Eighties: The Third Report of the Marine Pollution Monitoring Management Group 1979–1981* (DOE, 1982)
15 *Blood-lead Concentrations in Pre-School Children in Birmingham: A report of the Steering Committee on Environmental Lead in Birmingham* (DOE, 1982)
16 *Digest of Environmental Pollution and Water Statistics No. 5* (HMSO, 1982)
17 *State of the Art Review of Radioactivity Monitoring Programmes in the United Kingdom* (DOE, 1983)
18 *European Screening Programme for Lead: United Kingdom Results for 1981* (DOE, 1983)
20 *Oil Pollution of the Sea: The Government Response to the Eighth Report of the Royal Commission on Environmental Pollution* (1984)
22 *Agricultural Pollution: The Government Response to the Seventh Report of the Royal Commission on Environmental Pollution* (1984)

ROYAL COMMISSION ON ENVIRONMENTAL POLLUTION (HMSO)

Eighth Report: Oil Pollution of the Sea, Cmnd 8358 (1981)
Ninth Report: Lead in the Environment, Cmnd 8852 (1983)
Tenth Report: Tackling Pollution – Experience and Prospects, Cmnd 9149 (1984)

NOISE ADVISORY COUNCIL REPORTS 1971–1981

The Noise Advisory Council was disbanded in 1981. The following is a complete list of its publications:

Aircraft Noise: Flight Routeing near Airports (HMSO, 1971)
Neighbourhood Noise (HMSO, 1971)
Aircraft Noise: Should the Noise and Number Index be Revised? (HMSO, 1972)
Traffic Noise: the Vehicle Regulations and their Enforcement (HMSO, 1972)
Aircraft Noise: Selection of Runway Sites for Maplin (HMSO, 1972)
A Guide to Noise Units (Noise Advisory Council, 1974)
Noise in the Next Ten Years (HMSO, 1974)
Aircraft Engine Noise Research (HMSO, 1974)
Aircraft Noise: Review of Aircraft Departure Routeing Policy (HMSO, 1974)
Noise in Public Places (HMSO, 1974)

Bothered by Noise? How the Law can help you (Noise Advisory Council, 1975)

Noise Un. . (HMSO, 1975)
Helicopter Noise in the London Area (HMSO, 1977)
Concorde Noise Levels (HMSO, 1977)
Hearing Hazards and Recreation (Noise Advisory Council, 1977)
Noise Implications of the Transfer of Freight from Road to Rail (HMSO, 1978)
The Third London Airport (HMSO, 1980)
Hovercraft Noise (HMSO, 1980)
A Guide to the Measurement and Prediction of the Equivalent Continuous Sound Level Leq (HMSO, 1980)
A Study of Government Noise Insulation Policies (HMSO, 1981)
The Darlington Quiet Town Experiment (HMSO, 1981)

DOE INNER CITIES RESEARCH PROGRAMME REPORTS

1 A. M. McIntosh and V. Keddie, *Industry and Employment in the Inner City*, 1979
2 H. Williams *et al.*, *Industrial Renewal in the Inner City: An Assessment of Potential and Problems*, 1980
3 D. Bishop *et al.*, *Underground Services in the Inner City*, 1980
4 D. C. Nicholls *et al.*, *Private Housing Development Process: A Case Study*, 1981
5 G. Markall and D. Finn, *Young People and the Labour Market: A Case Study*, 1982
6 P. Lloyd and P. Dicken, *Industrial Change: Local Manufacturing Firms in Manchester and Merseyside*, 1982
7 S. J. Cameron *et al.*, *Local Authority Aid to Industry: An Evaluation of Tyne and Wear*, 1982
8 J. Cousins *et al.*, *Working in the Inner City: A Case Study*, 1982
9 B. Hedges and P. Prescott-Clarke, *Migration and the Inner City*, 1983
10 R. Richardson, *Unemployment and the Inner City: A Study of School Leavers in London*, 1984.

All obtainable from the Inner Cities Directorate, Department of the Environment, 2 Marsham Street, London SW1P 3EB.

WHITE PAPERS (HMSO)

Proposals for a Code of Civic Government in Scotland: A Consultation Paper, Cmnd 7958 (1980)
Committee of Inquiry into Local Government in Scotland (Stodart Report), Cmnd 8115 (1981)
Lorries, People and the Environment, Cmnd 8439 (1981)
Policy for Roads: England 1981, Cmnd 8496 (1982)
Radioactive Waste Management, Cmnd 8607 (1982)
Public Transport Subsidy in Cities, Cmnd 8735 (1982)
Coal and the Environment: The Government's Response to the Commission on Energy and the Environment's Report, Cmnd 8877 (1983)
Public Transport in London, Cmnd 9004 (1983)

Rates, Cmnd 9008 (1983)

Roads in Scotland: Report for 1982, Cmnd 9010 (1983)

Policy for Roads in England: 1983, Cmnd 9059 (1983)

Streamlining the Cities: Government Proposals for Reorganising Local Government in Greater London and the Metropolitan Counties, Cmnd 9063 (1983)

Regional Industrial Development, Cmnd 9111 (1983)

INDEX TO MAIN TEXT

INDEX